# PATHWAYS TO THE PRESENT

PATHWAYS TO THE PRESENT
A New History of the United States

Bernard A. Weisberger
Vassar College
HARPER & ROW, PUBLISHERS
New York, Hagerstown, San Francisco, London

Sponsoring Editor: John Greenman
Special Projects Editor: Mary Lou Mosher
Project Editor: Karla B. Philip
Designer: Gayle Jaeger
Production Supervisor: Francis X. Giordano
Photo Researcher: Myra Schachne
Compositor: University Graphics, Inc.
Printer and Binder: The Murray Printing Company
Cartographer: Andrew Mudryk



Library of Congress Cataloging in Publication Data
Weisberger, Bernard A Date-
Pathways to the present.
Includes bibliographies and index.
1. United States—History. I. Title.
E178.1.W414 973 75-30561
ISBN 0-06-046994-3

# Acknowledgments

W. J. Cash. From *The Mind of the South* by W. J. Cash. Reprinted by permission of Alfred A. Knopf, Inc.

A. E. Housman. From *The Collected Poems of A. E. Housman.* Copyright 1922 by Holt, Rinehart and Winston, Inc. Copyright 1950 by Barclays Bank Ltd. Reprinted by permission of Holt, Rinehart and Winston, Publishers.

F. Scott Fitzgerald. From *The Great Gatsby* by F. Scott Fitzgerald. Copyright 1925 by Charles Scribner's Sons, renewed 1953 by Frances Scott Fitzgerald Lanahan. Reprinted by permission of Charles Scribner's Sons, publisher.

Vachel Lindsay. "Bryan, Bryan, Bryan, Bryan" from *The Collected Poems of Vachel Lindsay.* Copyright 1920 by Macmillan Publishing Co., Inc., renewed 1948 by Elizabeth C. Lindsay. Reprinted by permission of the publisher.

# Credits

Below are listed the pages on which illustrations appear by special permission. We appreciate the right to reproduce the following illustrations:

*PART ONE: 2–3, Library of Congress;* 7, *Mexican National Tourist Council; 13, Museum of the American Indian, Heye Foundation; 20, Library of Congress;*

*32, Motyka, Monkmeyer; 37, Courtesy of The Henry Francis du Pont Winterthur Museum; 39, Library of Congress; 46, Portrait by John Singleton Copley. Courtesy of the North Carolina Museum of Art; 57, Pennsylvania Evening Herald.*

PART TWO: *70, Library of Congress; 90, Library of Congress; 91, Library of Congress; 99, Library of Congress; 112, American Philosophical Society; 117, Library of Congress; 128, Library of Congress; 131, Abby Aldrich Rockefeller Folk Art Collection, Williamsburg, Virginia; 136, Library of Congress.*

PART THREE: *142–143, Library of Congress; 156, Library of Congress; 166, Library of Congress; 184, Bettman Archive; 187, Library of Congress; 191, Library of Congress; 206, Library of Congress; 207, Granger Collection; 209, Library of Congress.*

PART FOUR: *216–217, Union Pacific Railroad, Library of Congress, New York Public Library Picture Collection, The Anaconda Company; 229, Library of Congress; 246, Library of Congress; 251, Library of Congress; 264, Library of Congress; 269, Library of Congress; 271, Courtesy of The Anaconda Company.*

PART FIVE: *280–281, New York Public Library Picture Collection, UPI, Library of Congress; 292, Courtesy of The Eastman Kodak Company; 295, Culver; 297, Wide World; 308, Culver; 313, Library of Congress; 315, Library of Congress; 322, Culver; 329, Library of Congress; 334, Library of Congress; 334, Library of Congress; 342, Library of Congress; 350, Wide World.*

PART SIX: *356–357, UPI, Library of Congress, New York Public Library Picture Collection; 371, Library of Congress; 377, Eastfoto; 385, Granger Collection; 394, Wide World; 406, Wide World; 408, Library of Congress; 414, The National Archives.*

PART SEVEN: *420–421, Shelton, Monkmeyer, Library of Congress, Beckwith Studios, UPI; 434, Wide World; 438, Wide World; 449, Wide World; 452, Library of Congress; 458, Wide World; 465, Georg Gerster, Rapho/Photo Researchers; 474 (top), Wide World; 474 (bottom), UPI; 483, Boeing; 488, Bell Laboratories; 495, Air Pollution Control District, Los Angeles; 499, Wide World.*

PART EIGHT: *504–505, Wide World; 515, Wide World; 528, Singer Corporation; 550 (clockwise), Wide World, UPI, Wide World, Wide World; 551, UPI; 557, Library of Congress; 558, Library of Congress; 560, Wide World; 560, Courtesy of The Anaconda Company; 562, Culver; 563, Wide World; 564, Library of Congress; 565, Wide World; 566, Motyka, Monkmeyer.*

Contents

## *part two: Making a Nation 62*

## PART THREE: TESTING A NATION 142

# part four: Division and Reunion 216



# part five: The Machine Age 280

# Preface to the Teacher

*Pathways to the Present* aims at being a new and different kind of textbook that maintains conventional strengths but breaks away from past limitations. It is shorter than many traditional "surveys" and less academic in tone. It is, above all, *selective*. Its focus is on good narrative and on raising questions that students will find valuable in an immediate and personal way.

The American history textbooks of an earlier time assumed a continuous and orderly flow of interconnected events, all moving toward predetermined results. The theme was "how the United States grew larger and more powerful and how American democracy, through various trials, was improved." Almost all the writers, whatever their social or political outlooks, assumed logical sequences among a welter of campaigns, acts, explorations, treaties, scandals, wars, and movements. They laid on detail generously, believing that through it all the clear outlines of a master blueprint of development would be visible.

Such expectations do not underlie this book. It assumes that there are many pathways to the present and that it is not necessary to travel all of them. It also assumes that there are various ways of weaving connections among events and that not all must be used. It is, therefore, nonlinear. Its chapters are in chronological order and cover the entire span of U.S. history. But each may deal with a broad or a narrow time period and may take up one or several topics. The text covers them largely through stories that invite speculation about some basic questions that open each chapter.

As a rather broad generalization, these questions fall mainly in the realm of inquiry about societies and how they work. Most of today's struggles over values—over priorities in the use of resources, national goals, population control, environmental management, ethnic and sexual equality, traditional roles—arise out of attempts to adjust tribal values to the shock of swift, stunning, overwhelming change. The questions posed, therefore, attempt to do two things:

1. They raise for the student the issues of how we got to where we are now: What roads were taken and not taken? How much free choice was there? What values were implicit in the decisions made? How are they holding up now? How are we strengthened and limited by the tug of the past?

2. They raise for the student general "behavioral" questions such as: How do societies hold together? What are their goals? Who chooses the goals and how? What instruments are used to attain them? How are roles defined in accordance with the goals? How are such roles taught to the young? How do they change, and with what results?

The second battery of questions, in particular, is heavily "social scientific." Social scientists ask questions and try to answer them with hypotheses tested by rigorously controlled and analyzed data. Historians do not have the same precise mastery of their information. They cannot submit questionnaires to the past or easily pick significant samples from an incomplete record. But they can certainly ask the social scientists' questions and then explore historical materials with them in mind. Historians can only "answer" for a limited area. But even tentative and partial answers are useful. And, when placed in a context of inquiry about values and feelings, they can be of greater interest than "scientifically correct" propositions derived from the scrutiny of graphs and symbols.

*Pathways to the Present* sometimes chooses meaningful comparisons over comprehensiveness to zero in on issues that have contemporary importance. This approach gives extra flexibility to the teacher, who may decide to supplement it with whatever background information seems desirable for a particular discussion. Appendixes, illustrations, maps, and subsidiary material are included in the book. But the important goal is not to fill the student's memory bank with information for retrieval on exams. It is, rather, to give students a basic grasp of broad themes, main currents, and unanswered riddles in American history and in human life as a whole. This is how the book is "humanistic" as well as "behavioral," if there is such a distinction. Its key rules, which teachers may well (and willingly) bear in mind, are these: (1) Teachers do not have to tell *everything;* (2) grand, overall designs do *not* have to emerge; and (3) the cardinal sin is to be uninteresting. Historians may be dull. History should never be.

# *PATHWAYS TO THE PRESENT*

# part one:

# Colonial Foundations

*Without always being aware of it, each of us lives a life that is shaped by institutions. We are born into a family, enrolled in schools, and possibly attend church. We may study for a profession or work for a corporation. At a certain stage in life we will go through courtship and enter marriage. We will pay taxes to our local and national governments or else face trouble in the courts. We will follow the wars and other calamities of the world through the mass media. And we will hope to reach old age without too many trips to the hospital and with a bit of retirement money in the bank.*

*Each underlined word represents an institution. Each describes a thing, a place, a system, or a habitual pattern or practice that sets standards for our behavior. There is a wide array of human societies on the globe and each one has its own institutions, which, taken all together, add up to a distinctive group way of life called a culture. (A culture that has reached a high state of complexity and technology is called a civilization.)*

*It is a human peculiarity that members of almost every culture think of their institutions as natural and eternal, like the physical landscape around them. But the fact is that institutions are always changing, sometimes slowly and sometimes with almost blinding swiftness. History deals with those changes.*

*In the first portion of this book the subject matter will be the planting of certain European institutions in the Americas between 300 and 500 years ago. The region was then unknown to European peoples—a New World, as they called it. There was, of course, nothing "new" about it to the various peoples already living there. But with the kind of conceit that all cultures apparently share, the Europeans tended to dismiss these American tribes (whom they casually misnamed "Indians") as not worthy of perpetuating their life-styles on their own lands. Instead, the Americas became, in European eyes, a place in which to establish their own ways. How that work of transplantation proceeded is the book's opening theme.*

*The first chapter observes how one European nation, Spain, moved in on several of the Indian peoples inhabiting Mexico and the present-day southwestern United States. The general questions it proposes concern the interplay among cultures and how when one life style sinks roots in soil plowed by another, the resulting growth is new and special. As you read, ask yourself these general questions (to be followed by more sharply detailed inquiries at the end of the part): How did the Spanish view what they were doing in the New World? What ambitions and sense of mission drove Hispanic conquerors to their tremendous exertions? How did the Indians fit into the Spanish picture of life, in which there was a place for God, king, nobles and commoners, each having a special role? And what of the Indians? How did they make sense out of life, and what happened to their views when they underwent the shock of invasion? How did their notions of the gods, of human fate, and of obedient and lawful behavior change, if at all? Finally, what happened to both Indian and Hispanic institutions as years of daily contact fused them together? How did each set subtly adapt to common needs and to the presence of the other?*

*The second chapter narrows the focus and*

*closes in on a single institution (or concept)—community—a group of people bound together in sundry ways. It shows that inside the broad frame of a single culture, there are many different threads in the pattern. The chapter turns to seventeenth-century England, which was beginning to plant New World colonies. Each of these would become home to a body of men and women sharing common tasks, hopes, dangers. How would they be held together? Who would rule them? How would they divide lands, jobs, responsibilities? How would they settle quarrels? To what common purposes would they appeal?*

*The answer might seem obvious—to do as they did in England. But in England there was no uniformity. Many ideas about such matters were under discussion, in a time of political, religious, and social upheaval. Moreover, London had no overall plan of colonial settlement. It made land grants to different groups and individuals and, within general guidelines of royal authority, left it to these "planters" to work out local problems. So many of the colonies became laboratories of community organization. The chapter scrutinizes several plans that were tested against the realities of strange surroundings and unexpected challenges. It illustrates not only how ideas on one subject, such as the proper framework of community, can vary within a single culture but also how such ideas are modified in the flame of experience.*

*Lastly, the final chapter of Part One studies the connections between the European "mother culture" and the colonial offshoots. The English colonies are the model here, following a century of growth. How had their societies developed as they prospered? Were their lawyers, merchants, tinkers, tailors, landowners, preachers, fishermen and servants, males and females, the spit and image of the same groups in England? Or had the wilderness life and distance from home made English seeds bear strange fruit? And what of the connections with Europe that continued? The colonists traded with England and with European nations—and they fought in wars that European kings undertook and European generals led. Colonies were both pawns and battlegrounds in the game of diplomacy and war. How did contact with Europeans as suppliers and customers or as enemies and allies in war affect the colonists' views of themselves and other peoples?*

*And what of the reverse influences? How did Europe react to the development of the New World? How were its rulers tempted by the prospects of snatching already developed colonies from rival powers? How was its economic life affected by the inflow of "American" gold, furs, fish? How did the wealth of the Americas change the balance of power among nations and classes? And how did the existence of a new world remodel the thinking of philosophers and scholars? What changes in European life drove or lured men and women to become settlers in that brave but strange new world?*

*It might be said, in conclusion, that the two continents acted on each other culturally. Changes in European life brought about the settlement of the Americas and kept on spurring changes in American ways. And the existence of the Americas sped the transition of Europe into the modern age. That process of interaction still goes on, at jet speed. What can be learned by looking at it as it developed at the pace of oxcarts and square-riggers?*

# chapter I

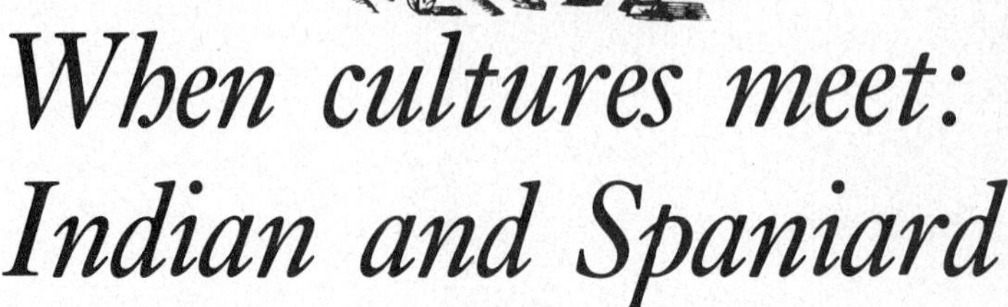

# When cultures meet: Indian and Spaniard

Moctezuma,[1] emperor of the Aztecs, was troubled. True, his reign seemed secure. He was the ninth ruler in his line, and his people had dominated Mexico for over two full sacred cycles of fifty-two years each. Aztec priests kept faith with the gods by frequent mass human sacrifices. Piles of skulls scattered throughout the realm were evidence of them. The capital city of Tenochtitlán, now Mexico City, showed Moctezuma encouraging scenes of prosperity. Human traffic surged over its fine roads through marketplaces, public gardens, and gleaming temples.

But when he first became emperor, there had been unlucky omens. They reminded him of an ancient legend of the Toltecs, an earlier people of Mexico. According to the legend, a god had once walked the land, teaching men "by word and deed the way of virtue." But the people cast him out. One day, however, he would return, and his arrival would signal calamities and destruction for the empire. He and his sons would come from the East. Like him, they would be light skinned and bearded. His name was Quetzalcoatl.

Now, in the sixteenth year of his rule, word came to Moctezuma that on the shore of the Great Sea (which we know as the Gulf of Mexico) watchers had seen "towers" moving on the water. From these towers men had descended and

[1]The form "Montezuma," commonly used in English, is not accepted Mexican usage.

*Solid, inescapable, mysterious and powerful, Quetzalcoatl, the Aztec god of life and death—here represented in an undated Mexican statue—reminds the onlooker of eternal riddles. (The rumor of his return filled Moctezuma with a sense that a great upheaval was in the making.)*

come to land in small canoes. And these men had very white skin, "whiter than ours, but most of them have long beards, and their hair comes down to the ears." Moctezuma knew at once that the worst had happened. Quetzalcoatl was back.

"Quetzalcoatl" was, in fact, a thirty-four-year-old Spaniard, Hernán Cortes. He brought ashore with him in 1519 500 soldiers, 16 horses, and 14 pieces of artillery. After a brief pause to get organized, he marched inland, toward Tenochtitlán. He met little resistance. In part, his success lay in the terrified reaction of the Indians to wonders new to them—horses, muskets, and cannons. Part of it was due to Moctezuma's reluctance to fight "Quetzalcoatl," who was the divinely chosen agent of fate. Another factor—probably the most important—was in the Aztec past. Moctezuma's tribe had tightly ruled the other Indian peoples whom they had only recently subdued. Thousands of these subjects at first joined with Cortes, hoping to shatter Aztec rule. They added irresistible power to Spanish superiority in weapons. As one historian has written, Moctezuma's doom was due to "intrinsic social and political weaknesses [in] Aztec culture itself."

After a time, Moctezuma's people realized that the Spaniards were neither gods nor godlike. They rose against them, but the rebellion was too late. Temporarily driven from Tenochtitlán, Cortes returned with reinforcements in 1521. The city was battered into submission. By then Moctezuma was dead, probably murdered by his own angry people.

What did the conqueror Cortes believe about *his* destiny? First, he believed that it would be greatly to his honor to acquire much of the gold that was so freely displayed in the ornaments of Moctezuma and his courtiers. The yellow metal was a decoration to the Indian. To the European it meant power, dignity, and wealth. "The Spaniards," Cortes told Moctezuma through an Indian interpreter "are troubled with a disease of the heart for which gold is the specific remedy." The Spaniards, moreover, were entitled to seize the gold of these people who had only spears and arrows to fight with. They were heathen. Cortes explained to the Aztec potentate that he and his men "were the vassals and servants of a great Prince called the Emperor Don Carlos [Charles V of Spain], who held beneath his sway many and great princes." Don Carlos wanted Moctezuma and his people "to become Christians so that his soul and those of all his vassals might be saved." And Christians, it was explained, were those who "worshipped one true and only God," whereas those of other people were not gods but "devils, which are evil things, and if their looks are bad their deeds are worse."

### *A Fresh Look at "The American Nation"*

In blood, greed, fear, pride, and faith European and Indian cultures met in North America four and one-half centuries ago. But why begin a history of the United States with this tale? Why bother with the Spanish empire in the Americas? After all, it was England that planted the northern colonies that

---

*CHRONOLOGY*

| | |
|---|---|
| 1492 | *Columbus sights land in New World* |
| 1519 | *Cortes invades Mexico* |
| 1539–1542 | *De Soto explores southeastern North America* |
| 1610 | *Santa Fe made capital of New Mexico, province of New Spain* |
| 1718 | *Franciscan mission (the Alamo) established at site of San Antonio, Texas* |
| 1776 | *Spanish garrison set up in San Francisco; United States declares independence from Britain* |
| 1848 | *United States acquires Mexican territory north of the Rio Grande after the Mexican War* |
| 1898 | *Cuba and Puerto Rico lost as last Spanish colonies in western hemisphere* |

became part of the country that U.S. citizens proudly, if arrogantly, call "*the* American nation."

One good reason for telling the Spanish story is to gain a fresh perspective. England's settlements in the New World were part of a general expansion of Europe that brought the cultures of that continent into contact with those developed by the peoples of the Americas, Africa, and Asia. (The word *culture* as used here means the sum of a group's skills, tools, beliefs, and rules of conduct—the instruments by which it carries on its collective life.) The interaction of these cultures, dramatically illustrated by the story of Cortes-Quetzalcoatl and Moctezuma, is a basic moving force in the history of humanity.

Historians of the United States have said little about Indians and Spaniards because of two assumptions. One is that the "backward" Indians had little to teach the bringers of Western "civilization." The other is that the great nations of the 1500s and 1600s, Spain, France, the Netherlands, and England, were in competition to control North America. Because England was the eventual "winner," she deserves the most attention.

Such ideas show how bound we are by our own culture. The very words *civilization*, meaning a state of social development, *nation*, meaning a political unit, *competition*, meaning a relationship between two parties, only have those particular meanings to someone educated, like an American, in the Western European tradition.

Moreover, when historians of the United States talk of how the Spaniards overcame the Indians, and the British proved better North American empire builders than the Spaniards, they leave a dangling, unspoken hint. Since the Americans later overthrew British rule in the Revolution, they were the final winners in a set of contests, like a play-off series. History written in that way is flattering to national feelings. It also helps the historians to pick and judge among topics. Those that explain automatic progess toward national greatness are valuable and important.

But that kind of history can be dull. The end of the story is known in advance. And the verdicts on heroes and villains are cut and dried.

In this book we will try to look at some familiar events in U.S. history in ways that should open new perspectives and raise new questions. We will not assume that things had to happen as they did or that they were necessarily good or bad. The traditional survey of U.S. history has shown a line of march from crude beginnings to a complicated present. Each event was a trail marker, blazing the way to where we now are. But this book assumes that where we are, as Americans, and even *who* we are, are questions to be asked and answered again in every generation. Past events then become clues to our national identity and guideposts to understanding human behavior in general.

So we begin with the story of Spain and the Aztecs, not because of its place in "the American story," but because it lets us raise some questions about different styles of human existence and what happens when they mingle through conquest and migration.

### *The Spanish Empire: Success or Failure?*

Was Spain really a failure in colonizing? How does anyone judge the success of an overseas empire? By the simple extent of land conquered? In that case, it is difficult to cast Spain as a "loser" in the New World. In 1800 her flag flew from California's Golden Gate to the Strait of Magellan, a stretch of some 8000 miles, and from ocean to ocean in much of North and South America. Moreover, these lands—"innumerable provinces, kingdoms and nations" as one proud Spaniard called them—were held by only handfuls of troops. The bulk of the empire was swiftly seized. Havana became a Spanish city in 1515, Panama in 1519, Mexico City in 1521, Lima in 1535, and Santiago in 1541. Spanish soldiers, sailors, and explorers were constantly on the move in the first fifty years after the New World was discovered.

But the empire continued to grow, though more slowly, long afterward, even when Spain was weakening as a European power. Santa Fe was established as the capital of New Mexico in 1610, two years after the French just began their Canadian conquests by founding Quebec and three years after the first successful English North American colony was started in Jamestown. Nor was that the end of Spanish energy. Several short-lived missions were established in Arizona in the early 1700s. In 1718 a mission, known as the Alamo, was set up in San Antonio, Texas. And in 1776, the year the Continental Congress proclaimed the independence of the United States, a mission and a *presidio*, or garrison, was set up by the Spanish in San Francisco.

If durability is a yardstick of imperial success, the Spanish also rank high. The first colony they planted was Hispaniola (an island now comprising Haiti and the Dominican Republic). It dates from the second voyage of Columbus in 1493–1494. The Spanish did not lose effective control of their New World empire until Latin American revolutions between 1810 and 1825 drove them out. They held on to Cuba and Puerto Rico until 1898, so that the life span of Spain's western hemisphere empire is roughly between 300 and 400 years—no mean span.

If the test of a colonizing power is how well it passed on its institutions to native peoples, the Spanish rate even more highly. In Spanish America as a whole a blending of Indian, Hispanic, and African races, styles, and cultures was achieved, resulting in a distinctive, separate civilization. The depth of Spanish influence is rarely realized in the United States because our histories deal only with Spanish settlements that later became U.S. territory: California, Texas, New Mexico, Arizona, and Florida. But these were frontier areas for

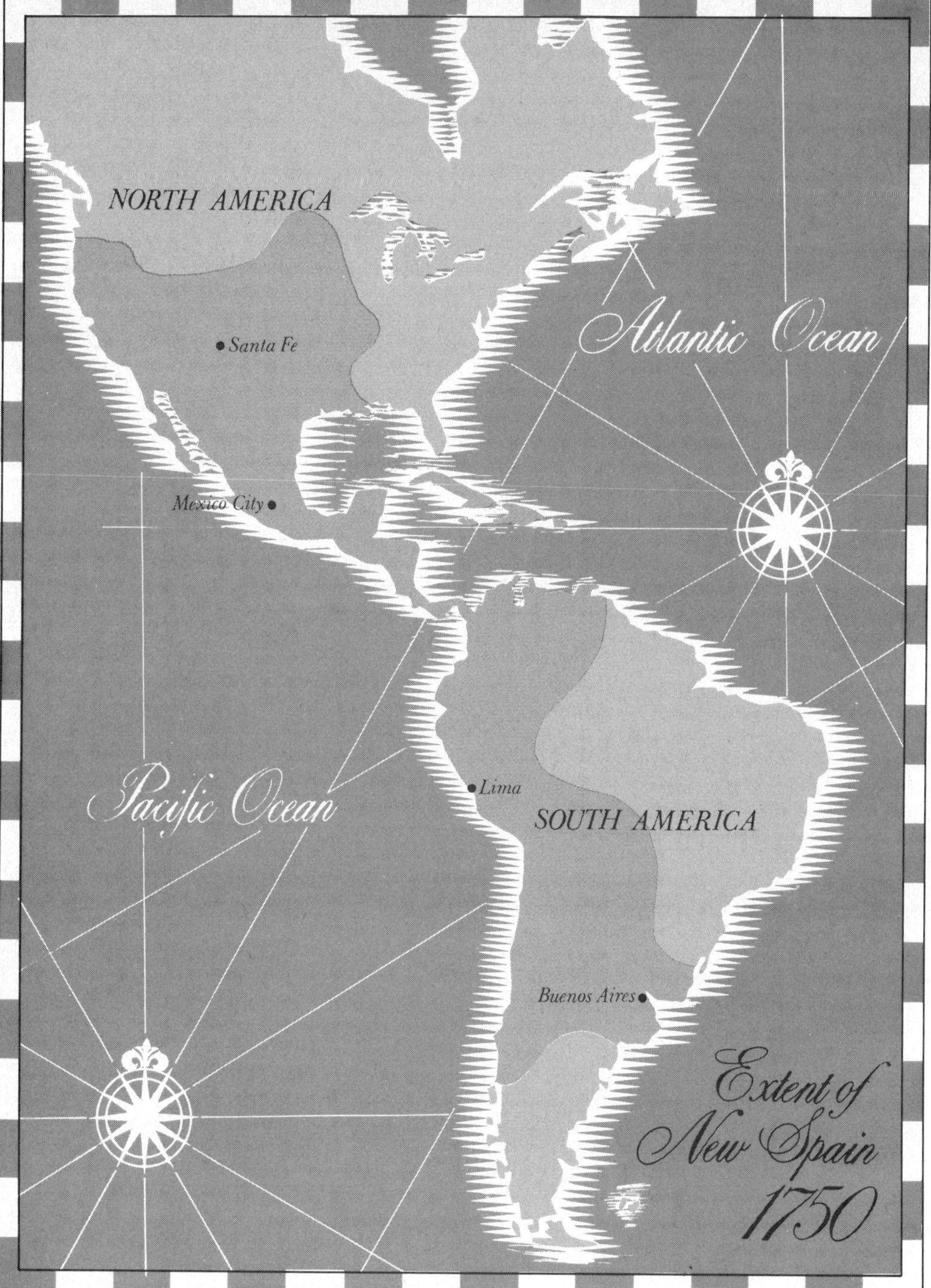

NORTH AMERICA
Santa Fe
Atlantic Ocean
Mexico City
Lima
Pacific Ocean
SOUTH AMERICA
Buenos Aires
Extent of
New Spain
1750

Spanish America. They did not contain the many great cities and universities of Hispanic America. Their institutions were the unsophisticated ones suitable to borderlands. One historian of those areas has written that Anglo-Americans have "concluded that Spain did not really colonize, and that, after all, she failed. The fallacy came . . . from mistaking the tail for the dog."

But even the "tail" was important. Today there are 10 million Spanish-speaking residents of the United States—Mexican, Puerto Rican, Cuban, and West Indian. They are living evidence of the survival strength of Spanish culture. Some of them are now challenging the long-asserted supremacy of Anglo ways. A glimpse at the fringe of the Spanish colonial empire north of the Rio Grande and in Florida teaches valuable lessons in cultural clash and accommodations.

*Spain and the Indians of North America*

It would be tempting but misleading to begin by comparing Spanish values with those of the Aztecs. Aztec civilization was fairly complicated and advanced by modern standards. Moctezuma's people had the engineering know-how to build temples and causeways, the agricultural skills to raise corn, beans, squash, cotton, tobacco, and other New World crops adopted by the Europeans, and the mathematical and astronomical ability to devise a complicated calendar. But they had borrowed or seized most of these social resources from the older peoples whom they had conquered, just as the ancient Romans did when they overran Greece and the Near East. And Aztec ways have little direct relationship to U.S. history.

The Indians of Florida and the modern Southwest, however, are another story. Their tribes had not yet been gathered into political structures like the modern state. In fact, the variety among all Indian tribes makes it difficult to speak in catchall terms about "Indian behavior." We use the word *Indian* to describe peoples divided into hundreds of language and culture groups and spread over two continents, as if they were one body. But we can make some useful statements about the Indians of the later American Southwest, at the "upper margin" of Spain's New World empire.

The most strikingly visible southwestern tribe was that of the Pueblo Indians of present-day New Mexico. They were farmers leading a strongly communal life. They dwelt in villages whose distinctive architecture to this day is the flat-roofed, communal dwelling of adobe (brick made of sun-dried clay or earth). These dwellings contained numerous "apartments," which reminded one Spanish chronicler of "a little crowded village, looking as if it had been crumpled together."

The Pueblo people included two language groups, the Hopis and the Zunis. Both had similar patterns of existence. The members were subdivided

*This gorgeously painted and plumed modern Kachina doll shows the vitality that Pueblo culture expressed in giving shape and form to imagined creatures of the spirit world.*

into clans, each with a special totem (a plant or animal that was the clan symbol), rituals, costumes, and sacred objects. Their religion was a powerful force in their lives. It was carried on by various priesthoods and cults. Each of these had its special house of worship, or *kiva*. In the kiva, fasts, dances, and ceremonies of purification took place. They might include the use of drugs to encourage visions and the infliction of wounds upon one's own body to triumph over pain. Among the Zuni cults there were those that worshiped the sun, various beasts, and a group of spirits called *kachinas*. The kachinas "visited" the villages annually, impersonated by tribal males wearing masks. Each mask wearer would perform dances to act out those things that he hoped the god would do—make rain, bring a good harvest, provide the tribe with healthy children. The idea was that this imitation, reinforced by the dancer-actor's sacrifices, zeal, and purity of spirit, would influence the god to perform as he wished.

The Pueblo peoples are only isolated examples of a southwestern Indian tribal organization and pattern of worship. But it is easy to see that their life stressed certain themes that were also visible in other Indian cultures. There was a strong sense of community. Each individual man or woman was a member of several "families"—clan, cult, brotherhood—whose history he or she shared. All fates were bound together. Feats of individual strength won admiration, but the idea of any one person having a life independent of the whole tribe was unthinkable. Member was inseparably bonded to member.

And human animals were bonded to Nature, too. All the Indians whom the Spaniards met—whether the fierce Comanches and Apaches; their peaceful and hivelike New Mexico neighbors, the Zunis; the scattered and small California tribes; or, tribes with a complicated social order, like the Natchez of Mississippi—shared the faith that birds, beasts, trees, and crops did not "belong" to man but were part of his world on an equal footing. All derived life from the same mysterious sources; all had spirit and soul. Indians hunted and trapped but they believed (depending on the tribe) that gods might inhabit or protect bears, wolves, coyotes, or tortoises; therefore, they killed none of these animals without rituals to appease the gods. Indians grew beans and tobacco, but they believed that the soil's fertility was not due to their management, planning, and effort, but rather that it was a gift from the mysterious beyond.

The entire Western idea of man as the master of Nature, of scientific "laws" that could be discovered by "reason" and applied to make the earth produce more for its "owners," was alien to most Indians. So was any idea of "progress" or "freedom." Life was harsh and painful and meant to be so. It did not improve from generation to generation. And although each Indian might be strongly set in his own ways, those ways had to match the traditions, legends, and needs of his people.

Such Indian beliefs contrasted sharply with the dominant ideas of Protestant Europe in the seventeenth and eighteenth centuries but not necessarily with the Spanish outlook on life. The underlying view of the world held by Catholic Spaniards had elements of mystery and tragedy that could find echoes in Indian life and made "conversion" of the Indians easy. This is more evident when we look closely at the Spanish.

## *Conquistadores and Friars*

When Spain founded her New World empire in 1493, she had just emerged from nearly 800 years of occupation by Islam and from a savage battle for independence. As a result, Spanish Christianity in the 1500s was fiercely orthodox. Spaniards had rescued the holy faith from the Muslims and purified it by driving the Jews out of the country in 1492. So when Martin Luther arose in Germany in 1517 to reform the Catholic church, Spain was in no mood to listen. As one historian of New Mexico notes, Spanish religion was not "a compartment where they kept their worship and faith, but . . . a condition of their very being, like the touch by which they felt the solid world." The flame of Spanish Christianity produced two very different types of people who came to the outposts of Spain's empire. One was the *conquistador*. He enacted a drama of obedience and dedication to God's word, but his position was a worldly one with advantages to himself. The other was the friar, who embodied the monastic ideal of retreating from the world's temptations to give it an example of purity and sacrifice.

The Spanish "captain" in the New World was full of pride and dignity. He might come from a family whose worn-out estates no longer yielded any revenue, so that his cloak was ragged and his belly empty. No matter. He drew himself taller, expected more courtesy, and continued to disdain occupations unworthy of him. These included manual labor—not because he was lazy but because work, as one Spanish writer has noted, was "dishonourable only for the gentlemen in that it implied a lack of courage to make a living and even a fortune by more dangerous ways."

Even 300 years after the age of Spanish conquest, in 1840, a young New Englander, Richard H. Dana, described the Hispanic gentleman's style as he observed it in California. "I have often seen a man with a fine figure and courteous manners—dressed in broadcloth and velvet, . . . without a *real* in his pockets, and absolutely suffering for something to eat." Yet such a man would never have sold his velvet jacket to buy a meal. This disdain for work, which was shocking to an American like Dana raised to believe in honest toil, might have made sense, however, to an Indian male who would rather do nothing if he could not be a hunter or warrior.

It is true that the conquistador sought gold with a kind of greedy excitement. But the gold was a means to style, not an end in itself or the key to an easy life. A Spaniard like Cortes would not have multiplied his gold by prudently investing it, like a Dutch or English capitalist, in a trade in wine, oil, figs, or cheese. It was the struggle and then the spending that counted. Spain as a nation, in fact, did not invest the gold of the New World in factories or merchant ships. Instead, her kings squandered it in magnificent displays and European wars until it was gone and Spain had declined. This attitude toward wealth, too, an Indian might have understood better than an Englishman.

Actually, the proud Spaniards endured incredible hardships, often for little gain. No Spanish conqueror found golden cities in any part of the later United States. But they were driven by "impossible dreams," often based on flimsy evidence. They kept going when more reasonable leaders might have decided that becoming lords of New World acres, complete with golden plate and Indian slaves, was not worth it.

Take the case of Pánfilo de Narváez. In 1527 he was commissioned to become *adelantado* (overlord) of Florida. The following year, he set out northward from a point near present-day Tampa to find a fabled kingdom called Appalachen, which supposedly teemed with gold. Before long his 300 men, 40 officers, and 8 priests had run through their supplies and were living on cooked shoots of the wild palms that they found along the way. When they finally reached Appalachen (about where Tallahassee is now) it was only a collection of clay huts. Narváez finally reached the Gulf of Mexico and decided to build ships and sail along its coast to the Spanish settlements in Mexico. His men lacked everything but ingenuity. They killed their horses, ate the meat, and built boats by stretching the horses' hides over improvised wooden frames. They made nails and tools by melting and reworking armor. They fashioned sails from clothing. In these frail craft they struggled along the coast as far as Galveston, Texas. There a storm shipwrecked them and Narváez drowned. Four of the survivors, including a black (a "Christianized Moor") named Estevanico, spent five incredible years wandering through the Southwest. Sometimes they were slaves of the Indians; sometimes, after escaping, they were taken for medicine men and gods and were handsomely treated. Finally, they reached Mexico and safety.

Or consider Hernando De Soto. The king authorized him, in 1538, to search for golden realms in "Florida." He sailed from Cuba with 600 soldiers, 150 horses, and, among other things, implements for the Mass, and iron collars and chains to use on any natives he might enslave en route. For three years he led his men through the future states of Georgia, Tennessee, Alabama, Mississippi, Arkansas, Louisiana, Texas, and Oklahoma in search of elusive kingdoms. Frequent pitched battles with the Indians cost them many casualties and most of their equipment. De Soto, himself sickened, died and was buried by night in the Mississippi River, which he was the first white man to explore. Eventually, the survivors, now ragged skeletons, straggled back to Spanish outposts to babble of strange beasts, "savages," dark forests, mighty rivers—and no gold! Time after time other explorers set out to duplicate the feats of Cortes, but found only heartbreak instead of gold. They discovered other things, too—the Mississippi, the Great Plains, the Grand Canyon—that would some day yield fortunes in fish, timber, minerals, grain, and cattle to other men. But Spanish adventurers' eyes were not set on those goals.

Yet they remained convinced that their labors were acceptable offerings to God. The pain they endured was not fruitless just because they found no gold. Pain was to be suffered when life demanded it. After all, the king of Spain himself, Charles V and his son, Philip II, who between them ruled Spain from

1516 to 1598, lived lives of hard self-discipline. Charles occasionally beat himself with a flail. Philip drove himself to exhaustion with the routine administrative work of the empire.

The founders of England's colonies also toiled and suffered, they believed, in doing God's work. But the goal of most of them was to create steadily growing communities that honored God through productive works. The conquistadores, on the other hand, were acting out dramas of sacrifice. There was possible glory at the end of the road, but the sacrifice was as important as the glory.

These values of the conquistadores were similar to those of some Indians. The Spaniards had faith in the existence of cities of gold, fountains of youth, and magic kingdoms, because their belief in the supernatural, in the wonders of an "unseen world," was still alive. Such wonders were part of medieval Christianity, and they had not quite disappeared from the European mind in the sixteenth century. The Indian, too, believed in such a world. And the Indian, too, prided himself on courage and physical endurance under hardship. He also felt that the body must sometimes suffer to fulfill the demands of the spirit.

But the Indians and the early Spanish conquerors never discovered their common ground. At first, each side tried to fit the other into the mold of its own culture. The Spaniards began by referring to Indian chieftains as "kings" and spoke of their "nobles" and "priests." Eventually, though, they discovered that these European terms did not fit. Too many "kings" had no power over their subjects, it seemed. Too many "commoners" were indistinguishable in dress and manner from the "priests" and "nobles." The Spanish soldiers and governors then began to treat the Indians as enemies blocking the way to the golden cities or as conquered servants without class distinctions.

The Indians, in turn, believed at first that fair-skinned men with such awesome "magic" as cannons, metal armor, and horses could only be more-than-human creatures. In time, though, they rid themselves of this belief, partly through experiences like that of some Puerto Rican Indians who deliberately drowned several Spaniards they were carrying across a stream to prove that they were mortal. But by then it was too late to stave off defeat. The Spanish had the edge in military technology and organization. The Indians—even the Aztecs—had neither guns nor a political structure that allowed the tribes to combine against their enemies.

Indians were not inferior peoples because they were so quickly beaten. Their various cultures simply had not prepared them for the particular kinds of battles they had to fight after 1500. They were capable of learning about and adopting elements of European culture such as metal tools and utensils, horses, and the irresistible firearms. And cultural exchange was a two-way street. The

Spanish were swift to learn from Indian captives and allies things such as the use of poultices of herbs and barks for curing wounds or the value of the animal skins, bones, and sinews in making clothes and tools in the wilderness.

But the real interchange between Indian and Hispanic ways did not take place under the warrior captains. It came later, when Spanish priests replaced Spanish soldiers as the dominant figures in the empire. It was when the conquistador gave way to the friar and the mission became the basic institution of the borderland that contact with the Spaniard meant something other than annihilation for the Indian.

### *Spanish Catholicism in the New World*

The Roman Catholic church took a quick and keen interest in the missionary possibilities of New Spain. Spain's pious kings demanded no less. In addition, by showing energy and zeal in winning new souls for Christ, Spanish Catholics wanted to offset criticism by Protestants that the Church of Rome had grown corrupt and fat. Finally, the Spanish religious world felt the stirrings of new learning about the ancient world, the wonders of science, and the many varieties of mankind. Though they held tightly to traditional religious rules, educated Spanish clergymen were eager to learn about the strange lands beyond the horizons and to compile dictionaries, atlases, and guides to their natural wonders. They hoped to improve the earth, which explorers were revealing, by sowing the Christian gospel, like seed, in its waste places. In the words of one historian, the non-Christian peoples of the Americas were to be "civilized, taught, humanized, purified, and reformed."

In other words, just as Indian culture was not ready for invasion, Spanish culture was exactly at the right point to encourage an aggressive effort to convert the "heathen" in the new lands. But first it was necessary to establish the simple fact that the Indians were indeed human, had souls, and were potential Christians. The first reaction of many Europeans on encountering clearly human creatures so different from themselves was to deny the basic identity between European and non-European. Doubts were expressed that the Indians were "people" in the ordinary sense. The same disbelief was expressed about Africans, whom the Portuguese, Dutch, Spanish, and English were enslaving throughout the fifteenth and sixteenth centuries. The conquistadores tended to think of the Indians merely as occupying some level between wild beasts and mankind, and they killed or enslaved them, too, without remorse. But before quickly condemning the Spanish, ask yourself if you are genuinely ready to admit that a naked New Guinea tribesman, who lives on insects and roots, has the same human potential as an astronaut or a Nobel Prize-winning novelist.

The Spanish government, however, did not automatically assume the worst about the native populations of the Americas. Though some clergymen and scholars, when asked officially for their views, believed the Indians to have few "vestiges of humanity," others, like Bartolomé de Las Casas, insisted otherwise. It was this less brutal view that gradually gained support.

In 1550, after various laws to protect the Indians from exploitation had been declared, Charles V actually ordered a halt to future wars of conquest while the issue was thrashed out. In the long run, official Spanish policy was to protect the Indians, but its actual application, thousands of miles from Madrid, was often spotty. From 1550 onward, the missionary spirit carried hundreds of Spanish clergymen to America. They planted Hispanic influence in the Southwest. Early attempts to establish extensive missions failed in Florida, Texas, and Arizona but took hold in New Mexico. Early in the 1600s the Franciscan fathers, who were in charge of religious work in that province, had built no fewer than 25 missions and had converted over 60,000 Indians. A fierce Indian revolt in 1680 set their efforts back for a long time, but by 1744 the number of missions was restored to 25, and Christianized Indians numbered about 17,500. In 1769 the Franciscans moved into California. By 1795 some 45 friars were at work there, and before California became American in 1848, 21 missions had been created.

The missionaries began in New Mexico by going among the Indians in simplicity. "They go about poor and barefoot as we do," one Indian is supposed to have related; "they eat what we eat, sit down among us, and speak to us gently." But after they had baptized enough Indians, the fathers became the superintendents of a complex society. The job of conversion was followed by heavy tasks of organization and building. They taught the Indians to put up churches in what became a distinctive southwestern style. The walls were not of hewn stone but of sun-baked clay bricks. There were no scarce stained-glass windows, but the insides were given color by scenes painted on whitewash by the converted Indians. In these drawings Christian legends were illustrated in the tan and earth-colored tones of Indian pottery and in the angular lines of traditional Indian drawings of birds, beasts, and wonders. The European sounds of the Latin mass came from Indian throats. Robes and vestments bore Christian symbols, but were of native wool, and Indian faces rose over their collars. The churches were neither Indian pueblos nor Spanish cathedrals; they were both. Earth colored and simple, they were part of the stark land around them. Yet they kept the crosses and domes and floor and window plans of the Spanish ecclesiastical style.

The mission was more, however, than just a church. Its walls enclosed warehouses, barns, living quarters, classrooms, hospitals, and other buildings of a functioning community. In one traditional sense the Spanish priests "civilized" their Indian charges. They taught them how to use iron tools, breed

*This fresco from the Mission San Xavier del Bac, near Tucson, Arizona (date unknown), gives a distinctly Mexican look to a Christian angel conceived in the European tradition.*

stock, make wine, store and preserve foods. They instructed some Indians who became acolytes (assistants to the priests) in the mysteries of reading and writing and in some elementary rules of applied science, medicine, and architecture. They passed on to apprentices historic crafts: carpentry, blacksmithing, working in precious metals, tanning, plastering. They felt that they were leading their flocks along the paths of civilization.

But the Indians were not wholly passive pupils. They taught the priests and other Spaniards a few things in return. They showed them how to cultivate the corn that was their traditional staple grain. They introduced into the diet of their conquerors other New World crops, too—chili peppers, many varieties of beans and squashes, tobacco, and (counting North and South America together) chocolate, quinine, chicle, vanilla, potatoes, tomatoes, guava, avocados, and peanuts. When Indian workmen created religious objects in silver, under Spanish instruction, the end product might be a cup or a cross or a tray that was Christian in concept but very Indian in design and feeling. And the Indians needed no instruction in weaving or in extracting colorful dyes from locally available plants or in using many of those plants in folk medicines, which the Spanish adopted.

What was created in the Southwest, and especially in Mexico, was a mixed culture of Indian and Hispanic, Christian and "pagan" elements. Indian Christianity was not like that of northern Europeans', which focused on fulfilling God's commandments to subdue and fill the earth. It was full of reverence for Nature and astonishment at the mysteries of the universe, like fertility and death. It had room for faith healers, fasts, and rituals of self-punishment for purification. It expected life to go on mostly unchanged for time eternal.

Southwestern Indian faith was something like that of the Spaniard, but not quite. It was something like the religion of pre-Christian America, but not quite. It was part of a cultural blending that took place over the hundreds of years of Hispanic occupation of a particular Indian world.

In 1848 the United States took over most of northern Mexico. Within a few decades there was a new kind of blending going on. Now the "Hispano" way of life had to cope with "Anglo" ideas of speed and progress brought by a new kind of conquistador, the American promoter of mines, railroads, and cow towns. What would the resulting mixture be? The answer, even late in the twentieth century, was uncertain. The story was still in progress.

## *FOR FURTHER READING*

Before digging into the question of cultures in conflict, it is a good idea to get an anthropologist's general definitions of culture; a helpful book for this purpose is Ralph Linton, *The Tree of Culture* (1955).

Looking at the Indian cultures that the Spaniards encountered is easier with the assistance of two works: John Collier, *Indians of the Americas*, (1947) and Alvin Josephy, *Indian Heritage of America* (1968). Moving from there into the general story of the Spanish conquest, a rewarding book is Miguel Covarrubias, *The Eagle, the Jaguar, and the Serpent* (1954) which deals with Cortes and his adventures. Some readable general and biographical studies of particular conquistadores and the world they made are *Great River* by Paul Horgan (1960), a history of the valley of the Rio Grande; Herbert E. Bolton, *Coronado: Knight of Pueblos and Plains* (1949); and Timothy Severin, *Explorers of the Mississippi* (1968), whose early chapters relate the incredible story of Hernando De Soto and his men.

What about firsthand accounts of what it was like? One is Bernal Diaz del Castillo,

*The Discovery and Conquest of Mexico* (paper, 1956), the memoirs of one of Cortes' troopers. There is also a work by a Spanish-educated Indian, Garcilaso De La Vega, *The Florida of the Inca* (1951), an eyewitness account of De Soto's campaigns by "the Inca," as the author calls himself.

An example of how lively the history of ideas can be is Lewis Hanke, *Aristotle and the American Indians* (1970), the complete story of the great debate over the future of Spain's Indian subjects.

Finally, how did the Southwest look three centuries after the Spanish conquest? What evidence was there of the mingling of cultures? Two books help to give an answer. One is a novel by Willa Cather, *Death Comes for the Archbishop* (1927), all about a Catholic church leader in nineteenth-century New Mexico; the other, Susan B. Magoffin, *Down The Santa Fe Trail* (1952), is a diary by an eighteen-year-old bride, moving to Santa Fe with her trader husband in 1846—full of likeable innocence and sharp observations.

# chapter 2

# The evolution of community: four colonies

> Historians are like doctors. They are always telling you what a country died of. But I'd like to know what it lived of. When I see the Greeks and Romans fighting with the neighbors and worrying about paying the coal bill, then I'll believe there was a Greece and Rome, but not before.

These are the remarks (purged here of their thick Irish brogue) of "Mr. Dooley," a fictitious Irish-American bartender invented in the 1890s by newspaper columnist Finley Peter Dunne. His words dealt with the then common practice of historians to concern themselves mainly with war, revolution, and statecraft and rarely with who paid the coal bill. Only in fairly modern times has there been a great deal of emphasis on social history—the bread-and-butter details of ordinary people's existence. Such history often tries to use the materials of daily life to answer the basic questions of human existence.

One such question, especially urgent in contemporary life, is that of bringing people together. Community planners, politicians, sponsors of new movements or mini-utopias—all are looking for a way to firm up human connections in a machine age. Can we learn anything from history about how such networks of feeling and habit grow? We can, perhaps, by looking at England's North American colonies. They were especially interesting laboratories of human development. All of them were "errands into the wilderness."

Their founders could, or thought they could, build as they chose. There were no set patterns to be followed. The local Indian populations were easily broken or pushed aside. Control "from the top" was relatively light because London was far away. What was more, for almost the duration of the seventeenth century there was friction between the king and Parliament, flaring into civil war from 1642 to 1660. One king was beheaded in 1649 and another was forced to abdicate and flee in 1689. Among the results of the strife were (1) an enlarged stream of English emigrants to the colonies, (2) the spread among the settlers of the popular idea that as Englishmen they had certain God-given rights to a degree of self-rule, and (3) the heavy involvement of the English government in home problems, leaving little time for colonial management.

The colonies, therefore, enjoyed a certain freedom. Their various promoters had leeway to work out their own ideas of how to run things. Their liberty was not total, of course. Often they made plans that were changed by economic necessity or by the special conditions of life in the New World or by the stubbornness of their human material, the settlers. They proposed, and events disposed. But they did have a certain freedom to be the architects of new societies. Out of the interplay of deliberate blueprints and accidental changes and necessities, "American" patterns of community living emerged.

Four colonies stand as case studies of how communities were forged. Two were founded twenty-three years apart: Virginia in 1607, and Massachusetts Bay, as it was first called, in 1630. They rose out of the commercial, scientific, and religious revolutions that were hammering the modern world into shape. The other two came later. Pennsylvania was founded in 1682, and Georgia a half-century later in 1732. Both had some roots in humanitarian impulses, efforts to soften some of the harshness of the expanding world. The earlier two had to struggle for survival against plague, starvation, and the terrors of an undeveloped wilderness. The latter two had to square their hopes against certain already established colonial practices. In all four, nothing went quite as planned.

*CHRONOLOGY*

| | |
|---|---|
| 1607 | *Jamestown, Virginia, founded* |
| 1619 | *First Africans brought to Virginia* |
| 1630 | *Massachusetts Bay Colony founded* |
| 1634 | *Connecticut Valley settlements begun* |
| 1642–1660 | *Civil war in England* |
| 1682 | *Pennsylvania founded* |
| 1732 | *Georgia founded* |

## *Virginia: A Company Town*

The magnet that drew people to Virginia was profit. All through the 1500s, English merchants listened, wide-eyed, to the reports of rare and rich merchandise to be brought home from new parts of the earth—pepper and other spices, silks, jewels, furs, precious metals, ivory, and slaves. New Spain, the Indies, and Africa were waiting treasure houses. Various "companies of adventurers" were formed to exploit these opportunities. "Adventure," with its implications of risk, was the right word because merchant members put up large sums to purchase shares of stock in the enterprise. The joint-stock company thus created sent out ships loaded with trade goods. The returns (which might take two years or more to come in) might be fabulous, but the risks of total loss by storm, war, or piracy were always present. Overseas investment required boldness.

By the 1580s, "hungry" English capitalists were looking to the Americas. The Spaniards already controlled the rich mines of Mexico and lands southward. But early voyages of exploration under the English flag, like those of John Cabot in 1489 and 1497, had given England a claim to parts of North America. Such claims might be vague and overlap some established by the French and Dutch (whose vessels had also touched those shores of mystery)—but what matter! If colonies (plantations, as they were called) of Englishmen could be set ashore, they would discover mines of their own. They might find mysterious routes to fabled Indian kingdoms rolling in jewels, or they might discover soils and climates where silks and spices grew. And the promoters would reap the profits. Such ambitious imaginings led to attempts to found English fishing stations in Newfoundland in 1578 and in present-day North Carolina in 1585. Both failed.

Then, in 1606, a group of London investors secured a charter as the Virginia Company of London. There was another Virginia Company, headquartered in Plymouth. The charter gave them both royal authorization to settle subjects in a part of "Virginia" (the name of England's fuzzily defined claim on the North American shoreline). Virginia extended roughly from the modern Carolinas to Maine and westward to the South Sea, as the Pacific was then called. The Virginia Company of London began to plan a settlement. Its plan was revealed in a provision of the charter stating that the king should have a share in any mines discovered, and that there would be a search for a passage through North America to the trade routes of the Orient.

The plantation was to be ruled by a council, chosen by the company, which could elect its own president. The company's rule would be reviewed by another body chosen by the king. No thought was given to the wishes of those who would go to Virginia. They would have whatever (few) seventeenth-century rights Englishmen had, but they were going out as employees, not settlers. Virginia would be, in modern terms, a company town. There would be no local authority other than the company.

In December, 1606, three small ships weighed anchor from London and five months later deposited some 105 souls on a low spot of ground at the mouth of the James River. The names of about 67 people are known, and of those 67, 29 were listed as simply "gentlemen" of no occupation in particular. Only 12 were identified as "laborers." Captain Christopher Newport promptly turned his ships around, went back to England, and brought back a "first supply" of new colonists, tools, and food in January, 1608. Seventy-three of 120 persons in that second contingent are identifiable. Gentlemen outnumbered laborers 28 to 21, and among the other colonists were jewelers, refiners, goldsmiths, and a perfumer. Obviously the company was not yet aware that the settlers' first jobs were to build cabins, storehouses, and fortifications and to plant the crops that would mean food in the next year.

Quarreling among themselves, the settlers neglected these priorities. Within a year, starvation and sickness, most likely malaria, had killed most of the colonists. Between 1607 and 1609, the company in London recruited and "supplied" about 300 persons. Only about 80 survived. These owed their lives, in part, to the exertions of Captain John Smith, who was president of the council—that is, ruler of the colony—from the autumn of 1608 to the summer of 1609. Smith, a remarkable twenty-eight-year-old soldier of fortune, saw that the real wealth of Virginia was in the products of its soil rather than in mythical mines. He drove the settlers to cut lumber, make glass, tar, and other building materials, and raise poultry and livestock so as to become independent of new supplies from home. He snarled in his memoirs that "in Virginia, a plaine souldier that can use a pickaxe and spade is better than five knights."

Such views (and compulsory work programs to enforce them) made Smith unpopular and were among the reasons why his fellow councillors ousted him in 1609. By then the company stirred itself to fresh efforts. It raised more money and 500 new settlers and appointed Lord Thomas De La Warr, a veteran soldier, as virtual dictator of the settlement. De La Warr arrived in the spring of 1610, just in time to find the ragged, half-starved, feverish remnant of the settlers about to give up altogether. He drove them back, and there began a period of nearly nine years during which the colony, planned as a business enterprise in which skilled artisans and gentlemen would direct laborers in profitable doings, became a midget totalitarian state. Various governors after De La Warr put the settlers to work building and planting. They were marched to their tasks by drumbeats and hustled to compulsory church services. Under De La Warr's penal code, called "Laws Divine, Moral and Martiall," they were jailed, whipped, or executed for such offenses as slacking, unauthorized trading with the Indians, theft, and slander against the company. They groaned and complained, as did one Richard Ffrethorne, who wrote home to condemn the bad food, hard work, and to say: "I . . . rue and curse the time of my birth with holy Job. I thought no head had been able to hold so much water as hath and doth daily flow from mine eyes."

But during this period important changes took place that put the colony on a firm footing and finally led to the end of martial law. In 1614 a crop of tobacco, which the Indians taught the English to grow and use, was sent home and commanded top prices. Soon after—about 1616—a kind of tobacco boom started. Suddenly, the most desirable commodity in Virginia became land. A Virginia aristocracy rose on the so-called Indian weed, and the colony's pressing need became hands, willing or unwilling, to grow callused in clearing, planting, and harvesting the crop.

The company tried to attract willing hands. Various charter reforms and amendments, some dating back before 1612, began to distribute lands as bait to both shareholders and actual settlers. Stockholders received grants. Actual colonists were encouraged to settle by deals in which the company paid their passage in return for several years of work from them; then after completing their work agreement, the company gave them some land. Shareholders who brought over "servants" (actually other settlers) were given, in addition to what they received for buying stocks, 50 acres for each person so transported. Whole associations of investors were encouraged by land grants to outfit and send shiploads of workers.

The company, without quite realizing it, was preparing to phase itself out of existence. Its grants of 50, 100 or hundreds and thousands of acres were creating a class of independent landholders. They would soon develop ideas of their own about what was best for the colony. If the company wished to attract more emigrants to Virginia, it could not easily ignore landholders' complaints of one kind or another. In 1619 the company had to authorize a historic convocation of landholders to discuss common problems. This gathering of "burgesses" later became regularized into a representative assembly, the basis for colonial self-rule.

In 1619 another fateful development took place. A Dutch ship dropped off "20 Negars" at Jamestown. At first, the status of these Africans was unclear. It was theoretically possible that, like white laborers, they would work for a fixed term of years, and then be freed. But, in fact, even then prejudice against darker skins was powerful. By 1661 a series of laws and court decisions had established the pattern of the Africans' servitude. It would be for life. Seventeenth-century English and European race feelings had transplanted black slavery to still another part of the New World. It already existed in Spanish possessions, and would also flourish under Portuguese, Dutch, and French flags.

From 1619 to 1625 the curve of emigration rose. More than 4800 settlers came to Virginia, including tradesmen, artisans, and marriageable women (sent by the company "to make the men more settled"). There were also apprentices and even a few vagrants and convicts, whom the settlers resented as "desperate villains." Hundreds died of disease during the "seasoning" process—the period of adjustment to the new climate and living conditions. Moreover, an Indian uprising in 1622 devastated some plantations on the edges of the settlement. These losses bowed the company with debts it could not easily pay, since thousands of Virginians now spent more time in pursuit of their own fortunes than in working on company projects. In 1624 the company went bankrupt, and the crown took over.

So Virginia was "planted." From a company outpost run like a garrison, it was becoming a society of large landholders and small, indentured servants and slaves, skilled craftsmen and merchants, lawyers and clergymen—a complex order of rank, possession, and political influence. By the 1670s it was becoming a little nation, more sophisticated than its planters had dreamed.

## *Massachusetts Bay: "As a City upon a Hill"*

The lure of trade begot Virginia. The fires of Christian zeal forged Massachusetts. The term "Puritan" presents to many of us a mental picture of a dried-up hater of life and its pleasures. The facts are quite the contrary. It is true that seventeenth-century Puritans were wary of whatever pleased the senses. They did believe that sensual indulgence weakened the will in the mighty struggle to live righteously, but they were also full of vitality. Their battles to give life proper shape, as they saw it, not only threw Old England into turmoil, but helped to settle New England and stamp their ideas on American life for three and one-half centuries.

In brief, who were the Puritans? They were originally members of the Church of England who had become religious radicals. They believed that God showed His excellence and His power over Satan by choosing a handful of men and women to whom He would grant eternal life after death. This company of the "elect" or "saints" was chosen, not through any merit of its own, but simply by God's will; it was "predestined" to salvation rather than to the hellfire that wicked mankind justly deserved.

No one knew for certain if he was among the elect. But members of the group could almost surely be recognized by earnestness in the study of God's revelations in Scripture, by their zealous prayers, and by diligence and effort in their "callings" in the world, that is, by hard work at their crafts and trades. They would show God's might and love by the excellence of their lives and by making His earth fruitful.

Life for the Puritan, then, called for tireless work, steady soul searching, and devout attention to happenings that might show God's will. An earthquake, a storm, the sudden death of a neighbor or a child—all had meanings. They were "revelations," punishments or warnings to sinners. They were clues to the behavior God was demanding. Life was very serious, but it was not necessarily dull. The Puritan was like a modern revolutionary, willing to sacrifice his own pleasures and purposes to change the world for the better. To be used by Almighty God as evidence of His goodness and power was what gave humdrum existence its meaning and bite. Puritans did not ask themselves the troubling modern question: What is the point of living?

But their zeal made the Puritans intolerant of outsiders. They disliked their own Church of England or in fact any other church that (in their view) substituted rituals and priestly authority for the zealous search for salvation in deeds and study. No robes, no chants, no candles, no statues. A true church on earth ought to consist only of the "visible saints," led by ministers whose authority came from holy lives and biblical and other studies, not from Pope or king. They wanted their religion "pure," hence their name.

In government they believed that a community's purpose was to execute God's will. Even those Puritans who obeyed all laws but lacked the emotional conviction that they were saved, should accept the rule of those who had it. And the Puritans were entirely intolerant of all non-Puritan faiths. What else could they be? They thought they were soldiers in the Lord's wars. How could they smile on mutineers and deserters who questioned orders from the high command?

These beliefs were in the background of the founding of Massachusetts. A good number of well-off Puritan gentlemen combined in the Massachusetts Bay Company in 1629. They received a grant from the authorities to occupy the land between the Merrimack and the Charles rivers, "from sea to sea." King Charles I had little use for Puritans but was quite willing to have their money develop his North American territories. The Massachusetts Bay charter was seemingly like those issued to other groups to trade, plant, and fish in the New World. But it had a clause that the directors of the corporation (the governor and his assistants) should be considered a "body politique and corporate." What this meant was soon made clear enough. The incorporators voted to transfer the company headquarters to their overseas plantation, taking with them as many of the stockholders as wished to go. So, unlike Virginia, the company and the colony became one. The business directors became the government on the scene. The founders wanted it so. Now they could actually build a community of their own, a safe ocean's distance away from English control and "corruption."

It was a serious, planned movement. It took heavy outlays of money that would someday have to be repaid out of the earnings of farm and fishery. In the first year alone perhaps 1000 people came over, as compared with the handful that first entered Virginia. And for months before the first fleet of 16 ships left England, the company leaders were busy buying ammunition, soap, candles, spades, hoes, nails, furnishings, pigs and chickens and goats, dried grain and hay—the items necessary to get through a year of building before a crop could be harvested. The idea was to create an orderly, functioning society from the start.

The men who drafted these schemes were religious zealots, but not unworldly fanatics. Most were talented and successful individuals, often with a generous share of the world's goods, natural leaders in any community. Yet their vision of a good life drove them to abandon their comfortable homes, to risk dangerous ocean voyages of many weeks in crowded little sailing ships, and to begin life anew in a wild setting where storms, hunger, and "savages" and other enemies constantly threatened. That is one measure of how strong their drive was. How they planned to use their opportunities is best shown by looking at their leader, John Winthrop.

Winthrop's father was a lawyer and landholder. His mother was the daughter of a wealthy tradesman. He attended Cambridge University, studied law, and soon had a successful practice in London. Still young, he enjoyed a full measure of success: a country estate, a local judgeship, and plenty of money. He even had enough to invest something in trade and to send one of his sons to establish a plantation in Barbados, in the West Indies.

Yet he left it all to join the migration, because he was convinced that the sinful ways of non-Puritan England would soon bring her into deep trouble. But there was hope. He wrote:

> Who knows but that God . . . provided [New England] to be a refuge for many whom he means to save out of the general calamity, and seeing the Church hath no place left to fly into but the wilderness, what better work can there be than to go and provide tabernacles and food for her.

The faithful few would keep the light alive. Winthrop's energy, skill, persuasiveness, and commitment soon made him one of the company's leaders. He would become Massachusetts' first governor at the age of forty-one and hold the office nine times in the colony's first nineteen years of existence.

Winthrop spelled out the kind of community he foresaw in a sermon that he delivered aboard the *Arbella*, the little ship of 350 tons burden, on which he and several hundred others made the transatlantic passage of nine and one-half weeks in the spring of 1630. (Once a Mediterranean privateer, the vessel was leased to the Puritans for holy purposes.) Winthrop told his fellows that their job was to improve their lives in order to be preserved from the common corruptions of this evil world. "We must be knit together in this work as one man," said Winthrop.

> . . . We must entertain each other in brotherly affection . . . must delight in each other, make others' conditions our own, rejoice together, mourn together, labor and suffer together . . . for we must consider that we shall be as a city upon a hill; the eyes of all people are upon us; so that if we shall deal falsely with our God in this work . . . we shall shame the faces of many of God's worthy servants, and cause their prayers to be turned into curses.

How would this model community work? As Winthrop and others like him hoped, the overall government of the plantation would rest with the governor and his assistants, the "magistrates." They would frame sound codes of behavior, pleasing to God. To find what was acceptable to Him would require close consultation with the ministers, though they had no formal power of rule. (It is a popular misconception that Massachusetts was a "theocracy," that is, officially church governed.) The magistrates were to be chosen by the "freemen" (property holders and churchmen) of the colony. Originally, that meant only stockholders. Later, newcomers were admitted as "freemen," but only if they were full members of the church—that is, if they could publicly testify to a deep religious experience ending in the conviction that they were saved.

As population increased, groups of families would petition the colony's leaders to form new congregations and to settle in towns. Towns were little models of the colony, with the freemen electing their officials. The officials would lay out the town boundaries, assign each head of a family a house lot (its size depending on the number of persons in the family), and a field for growing his crops. Meadowlands and wooded lots would be held in common, with each settler entitled to share in their use.

So within each town the freemen and church members would live in fellowship. They would choose their leaders, who would make decisions by consulting with church elders to "inform us of the mind of God." The whole community would be bound by a covenant, a contract with God to uphold His law, as well as a covenant among themselves to help each other in that work.

Of course, the model was not democratic. Many settlers were not admitted to church membership and were not stockholders. They remained without a vote. And as poor people and propertyless workers joined the population, they would in no way be regarded as the social equals of their betters or have a share in decision making.

But if the elect were properly guided, God would smile on the entire community. All would prosper in their fashion. All would have the "freedom" to do what was *right*, which was not always the same as what they wanted or thought they needed. As Winthrop said in a 1645 sermon (which shows the Puritan idea of a woman's role), the true freedom of a citizen was his freedom to accept proper authority, just as a woman was free to choose a husband, "yet being so chosen, he is her lord and she is to be subject to him, yet . . . a true wife accounts her subjection her honor and freedom, and would not think her condition safe and free, but in her subjection to her husband's authority."

Under this blueprint Massachusetts began its civil life. In one sense, the pattern seemed to work, for the colony grew as planned. Under "the singular Providence of God," migrants continued to come. By 1645, 23 churches had been formed; two years later there were some 33 towns, embracing perhaps 15,000 people.

Great foundations were being laid. A "colledge" named Harvard was

*The white, steepled Congregational or Presbyterian meeting house, hard by the village green, was a significant center of New England town life.*

created in 1636; a printing press was established in 1639, and the towns were filling up with tradesmen: glovers, candlemakers, butchers, tailors, millers, blacksmiths. In 1631 Massachusetts launched its first home-built ship, the *Blessing of the Bay*. Winthrop owned the 30-ton vessel. But eleven years later, ships of 200 tons were being constructed in Boston. There are records showing their travels. The first voyage of a typical ship, the *Trial*, which was blessed with a well-wishing sermon from John Cotton, was to the Canary Islands and the West Indies. There she undoubtedly picked up wine and sugar. Later she went to Malaga and Bilbao, Spain, returning with iron, fruit, wine, and wool. Still later she voyaged to Canada, where the cargo loaded was probably fish and lumber, and to London and Holland to bring back manufactured goods such as cloth, glass, paper, and ironware. With dozens of such ships at sea, the "city upon a hill" was thriving.

Yet the very things that caused Massachusetts to prosper tended to disrupt that ideal Puritan community. To begin with, the growing number of nonsaints chafed under the authority of the magistrates. As early as 1632, the inhabitants of Watertown, both freemen and nonfreemen, objected to the levying of a tax upon them, by the governor and assistants at Boston, without their consent. They said that it was not safe to pay such money "for fear of bringing themselves and posterity into bondage." Rising complaints of this kind led to a gradual change in the company charter. The assistants came to be elected by the freemen instead of being named by the original leaders of the migration. By 1642 they were sitting regularly in a General Court, that is, a scheduled annual meeting, instead of a special "court" convened at the pleasure of the rulers. By 1644 a two-house legislature had emerged. The upper house consisted of the governor's chosen advisers, his council. The lower house was made up of elected representatives of the towns. Naturally, this led to a weakening of the tight hold of the original planters, as various discontented groups put spokesmen in the assembly.

Secondly, the lure of new lands pulled many congregations away from the influence of the Boston elite. The nature of this process is illustrated by the petition of one congregation, in 1634, to move to the Connecticut River valley because of "the excellent fruitfulness and fertility therof" and "the strong bent of their spirits thither." Distance broke up the closeness that resulted in most early decisions being unanimous.

Thirdly, the Puritan insistence on constant religious self-analysis and discussion inevitably bred rebellions and heresies. A community of mere individuals will accept imperfections in government. A community of saints breeds men and women who must fight for their interpretations of divine commandments. Such a man was Roger Williams. A brilliant and formidably well-educated Puritan minister, he fell into dispute with the Boston leaders in 1635 over the question of the union between church and state. He believed in their absolute separation. Actually, Williams did not arrive at that position like a modern liberal, who is afraid that ministers will force their views on the public. On the contrary, he feared that politicians would dictate religious attitudes—possibly the wrong ones—to believers. But even that position was too much for Massachusetts' leaders, who could not conceive of a community and a church without each other. In October 1635 they banished Williams from the colony.

Two years later, Anne Hutchinson, called by Winthrop "the American Jezebel," disturbed the peace. She was an outspoken and learned woman in an age that distrusted both qualities in females. She argued that God sometimes reached a believer by lighting up his soul with powerful feelings. Those emotions were surer guides to right action than scriptural texts strained through the meshes of ministers' interpretations. She began to preach these doctrines at small meetings in her home.

This doctrine was a threat to the whole Puritan concept of social order. If anyone could impose mere feelings over the dictates of proper, learned authority and could choose which divine commandments to obey on his own, what would become of cooperation, common purpose, law and order? Like Williams' "liberty of conscience," Hutchinson's religion of the heart was unacceptable. So she, too, was banished. She moved to "Aquidneck," later Rhode Island, a colony created when Williams, some other emigrants from Boston, and their followers combined their settlements. Massachusetts had now rid itself of the dangerous disease of private revelations from God. But these rips in the "body politique" were not part of the original dream of a pious, tight community.

Finally, the worldly success of the colony cooled the zeal of the founders. The number of men and women who could publicly testify to the intense experience of becoming saints declined so much that the churches were in danger of having no members at all. The original requirements for membership had to be modified and softened. Moreover, as society grew more complex, the sins of the world—the alehouse, the love of finery, the lust for displaying wealth in splendid houses and coaches—crept in to weaken the old Puritan spirit.

The transition from commune to colony, by 1700, had been made. The Virginia Company of London had seen private landholding weaken loyalty to the company and change the original idea. So, too, the Puritan founders of Massachusetts Bay watched the world overtake their model society of small bands of saints. However, the Puritans' basic ideas about work, worth, and community responsibility would long outlast Winthrop's generation.

## *Pennsylvania: The Holy Commonwealth*

Massachusetts at first tolerated no challenges to its religious views. Among those whom it whipped, fined, pilloried, and even hung during its first sixty years were visiting spokesmen for another religious outlook, Quakerism. But though driven from the Bay Colony, Quakers were to have their special home in English America.

The year 1644 saw the birth, in England, of a young man named William Penn. Penn's father was a wealthy landholder and an admiral. He must often have despaired of his scapegrace youngster, who seemed to take a long time in finding himself. Young William was expelled from Oxford University after two years, finding university life dull and mechanical. Instead, he traveled in

Europe for a while, reading and thinking on his own. Then he returned to England and studied law, but he had no interest in practicing. Finally, his father sent him to Ireland to manage the family estates. There he seemed to be settled when his father died.

The truth was that Penn did not lack purpose. He simply was not thinking in his father's terms of success, meaning wealth, power, and family honor. As a young man, Penn had been drawn to a group called the Society of Friends, better known then and now as Quakers. Like the Puritans, they believed that the purpose of life was to walk justly and in holy ways. But unlike them, they felt that the key to Christian behavior was individual conscience and following the "inner light" that God planted in the seeking heart.

They did not have priests or ministers. They believed that each man was potentially the equal of any other in God's sight; so they had little use for ranks, ceremonies, finery in dress that bespoke class privileges, even though some of them were comfortably rich. They even used the informal second-person singular of seventeenth-century English—"thee" and "thou"—and used it as readily when speaking to kings as to chambermaids. They were pacifists who believed that power must be resisted (peaceably, with suffering if need be, even to the point of death) when it interfered with the dictates of conscience.

Ideas such as those kept the Quakers in trouble, both in England and the colonies, throughout the early and middle 1600s. People who refused military service, would pay no taxes to support official churches, and kept their hats on when talking to authorities were regarded as troublemakers. Penn, in joining them, was exchanging an easy life for one of risks and rebuffs.

In 1681 Penn had a unique chance to do something for his hard-driven brethren. King Charles II owed Penn's father a debt of 16,000 pounds, for money which the admiral had spent out of his own pocket equipping ships during one of the country's wars. To pay the debt the king offered Penn an enormous tract of land lying between the colonies of New York on the north and Maryland on the south. Charles simply wanted another colony there to tighten England's hold in America and bring in revenues. Penn saw opportunities for profit, too, in renting lands to settlers. He was not completely unlike his father in this respect. But he would also have a chance to build a "holy commonwealth" on Quaker principles. His fellow Quakers could rule there, be tolerated, and tolerate others.

In 1682 Penn arrived in his colony with several shiploads of settlers. The name of his New World property was Pennsylvania, or Penn's woods. The king insisted on the name (over William's objections) in recognition of Admiral Penn. A utopian planning was evident from the beginning. On land between the Delaware and Schuylkill rivers, a city was carefully laid out and named Philadelphia (meaning "brotherly love"). English and Welsh Quakers who had come with the founder built houses and gardens and set to work. Some quickly prospered in trade with the mother country. Docks and warehouses rose along the Delaware to mark their industry. Others practiced their crafts and trades in newly built mills, bakeries, and printing shops. In the rich soils around Philadelphia farms flourished, for Pennsylvania was planned from the start to be a food-growing colony. Its first comers brought over abundant seed, livestock, tools, and building materials, as well as the servants and large families needed to provide the hands to plant and plow.

Penn was a careful as well as an idealistic promoter. He wanted Pennsylvania to grow by voluntary immigration. He offered settlers a large degree of self-government. There would be an elected assembly, and almost all taxpayers—not merely landowners, but those who possessed only a house or shop—could vote for its members. (But its powers were limited, and Penn, plus a council of advisers, kept a great deal of control.) The newcomers were guaranteed "the rights and freedoms of England," including some, such as religious toleration, that were by no means common in England. Penn even took the unusual step of dealing fairly with the Indians and bought lands from them. Though the Indians operated on the assumption that the earth could not be "owned" by any individuals, once they learned that Europeans would pay them to give up their hunting lands, they became willing to bargain, not realizing that the process would never stop.

Land was offered on generous terms. It was sold in large blocks of several thousand acres for 100 pounds, a sum within the reach of upper middle-class English farmers. It could also be rented for as little as a penny per acre. It was given away in 50-acre lots to "indentured" servants, who worked out a fixed term of years, or to settlers who would pay to bring over a relative, a servant, an apprentice, or a bride.

Penn built an unusual future for Pennsylvania, moreover, by recruiting vigorously in Europe as well as in England. He made several missionary trips for the Quakers to Holland and the scattered little states of Germany in the 1670s. He also wrote three long accounts of his province, touting its attractions like a busy real-estate salesman. Pennsylvania, he said, had good soil, abundant game, 40- and 50-pound wild turkeys and other birds, plenty of fish, fresh air, and sunny skies. Translated into German, these words sounded sweet to Germans who disagreed with their rulers' religious ideas, high taxes, and military drafts. One such dissenter was Francis Pastorius, a German university graduate who said that Penn's words "begat a desire in my soul . . . to lead a quiet, godly and honest life in a howling wilderness." Pastorius joined with other Germans to form a company that bought 15,000 acres of Penn's lands. In 1683 he led a large party to a location just outside Philadelphia, which came to be called Germantown. By the century's end it was a thriving, neat community. "All sorts of very good Paper are made in the German-Town," said one traveler

*Though it dates from the 1830s, the intricate and loving craftsmanship in this Pennsylvania Dutch desk illustrates the invisible imports that settlers brought with them to the colonies, namely, sophisticated skills to transform the raw settlements.*

in 1697, "as also very fine German Linen, such as no Person of Quality need be asham'd to wear." Philadelphia itself was using that paper and linen and giving work to shoemakers, carpenters, bricklayers, tailors, weavers, and potters. It also had "several good Schools of Learning for Youth, in order to the Attainments of Arts and Sciences." The city's prosperity rested on its sale of the pork, beef, butter, cheese, fruit, corn meal, and other provisions that came in wagons from the thriving nearby farms.

The fame of Pennsylvania spread. In less than fifty years it became a magnet for immigrants. More Englishmen came, as did great numbers of Scotch-Irish Presbyterians. And more Germans, including members of small and little-known sects such as the Mennonites, the Dunkards, the Moravians, and the Schwenkfelders. There were so many of these that the "Pennsylvania Dutch" (a corruption of the German word for a German, *Deutsch*) became a fixture of American folk life. What Penn, Pastorius, and others had created was a cosmopolitan little society, functioning as a colonial breadbasket.

Penn watched the success of his enterprise, mostly from England. (He only lived in Pennsylvania for two-year stretches.) Curiously enough, its very prosperity, like that of other colonies, changed its original design. As the 1700s wore on, Pennsylvania's merchants, manufacturers, farmers, and frontiersmen, representing many different faiths, nationalities, and viewpoints, fell into the kinds of political conflict to be expected in a many-layered society. Pennsylvania, meant to be a showcase of social harmony, remained peaceable, but it lost some of the intensity and unified idealistic leadership of its earliest days. A "holy commonwealth," like a "city on a hill," was difficult to sustain.

### *Georgia: A Philanthropic Failure*

Like Pennsylvania, Georgia began as the idea of an upper-class young man with a social conscience. It, too, did not hold to its original outline. The father of Georgia was James Oglethorpe, who had begun life with the usual expectations for a noble youth. By the age of twenty-three he had an Oxford degree, a good estate, the right contacts in London, and a fine record as a veteran army officer. But he also had, according to one friend, "uncommon vivacity of mind and variety of knowledge." More to the point, he had a "strong benevolence of soul." That benevolence became apparent when Oglethorpe was a member of a parliamentary committee investigating conditions in English prisons. Seeing the wretchedness of London's outcast poor and how miserably they were treated by society, Oglethorpe was struck by an idea. It was to form a group of "trustees" who would plant a colony in North America where such unfortunates could have a new start in life.

The plan was heartily received, for the time was right; 1730 saw the beginning of a general movement in the direction of humanizing English religion and law and making them concern themselves with the oppressed. The Church of England, therefore, had many powerful officials who supported Oglethorpe's idea. The merchant classes liked the idea of a new colony that would buy English manufactured goods and send cargoes of New World staples

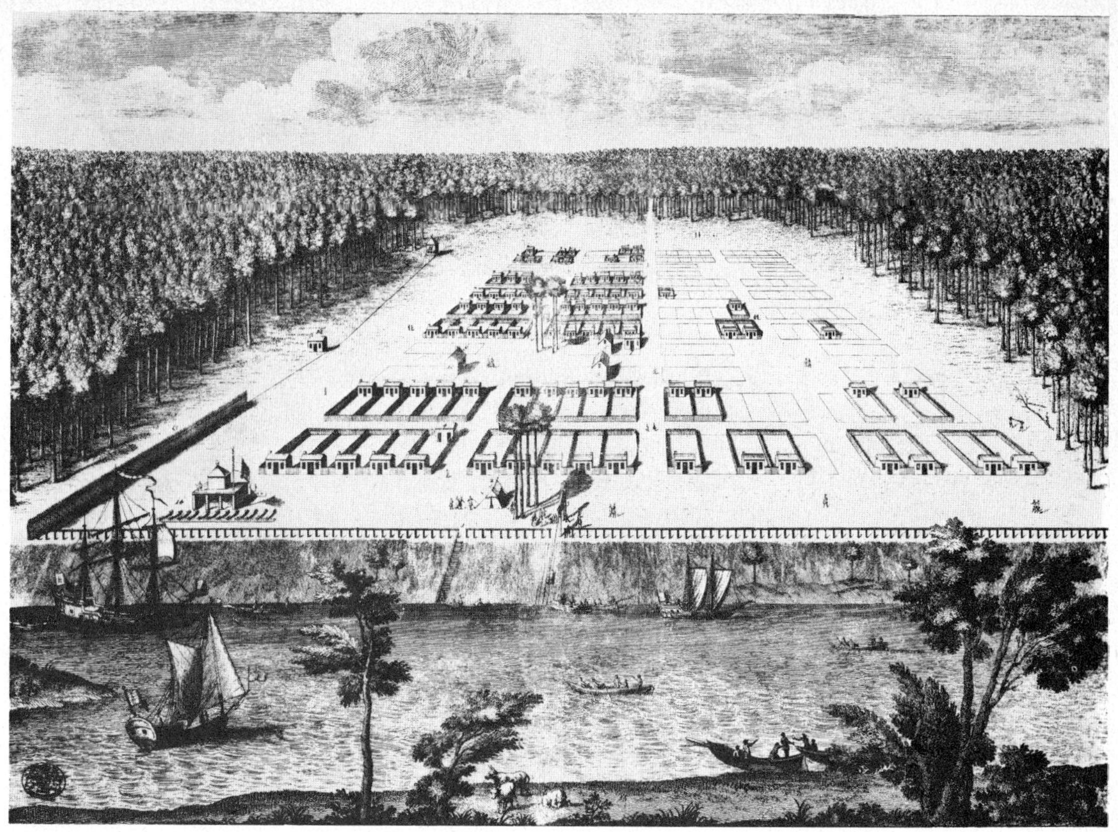

*Over this geometrically neat and fanciful plan of Savannah, Georgia (as it was supposed to be), hovers the orderly spirit of eighteenth-century humanitarian planning for a reasonable and good society. Reality turned out to be more complex.*

back for resale. Finally, the proposed site of the colony—south of the Carolinas and north of Florida—struck the royal ministers as particularly good. It would raise a barrier against possible Spanish plans to expand northward.

Subscriptions to finance Georgia were quickly raised. Parliament alone gave 10,000 pounds. The trustees' plans were high minded. Various agricultural and scientific societies, for example, were to contribute the seeds of new plants that might prosper in the climate of the colony. One cherished idea was to send cuttings from mulberry trees to nourish silkworms that would spin a shining web of prosperity for the province (named Georgia in honor of King George II). The church was active, too. The 35 families who left in the *Ann* in November 1732 were amply supplied not only with farm tools but also with religious books.

The trustees also intended to avoid the "sins" of other colonies. Slavery was to be forbidden, for although Oglethorpe was a director of the Royal Africa Company, which traded in "black ivory," he wanted his settlers to do their own labor. The maximum size of a landholding was to be 500 acres. Rum, so often used to debauch and cheat the Indians and breed crime and strife in the cities, was forbidden. When the first settlement, Savannah, was laid out, it was a splendid planned community, with squares reserved for marketplaces; each family would get a spacious home and garden area.

These philanthropic dreams of liberal London soon fell afoul of New World reality. Although many of the early settlers were not ex-convicts, they were the same substantial fortune seekers that filled all the colonies. They set to work with a will. But they were not immune to the ambitions of their colonial neighbors, namely, to get rich by owning large quantities of slave-worked land. Within twenty years, under pressure from the settlers, slaves had been introduced into the growing colony. By 1749 there were 1000 known to be in the colony. At that point the trustees gave in and abandoned the no-slavery rule. Likewise, the Georgians persistently ignored the ban on making or importing rum, and in 1742 the rule was abandoned. (The motive was not merely lust for drink. Rum was indispensable in trade with the West Indies and Africa.) The law limiting the size of a landholding to 500 acres was discarded by 1750. Finally, in 1752 the trustees, confronted with the stubborn reality of human nature, gave in and abandoned the project. Georgia was taken over by the crown and became a typical colony, not a place whose chief goal was social redemption.

Although Georgia was a philanthropic failure, it was an economic success. The silkworms venture had not worked out, but the colony had proved to be a bountiful producer of rice and indigo. The rice found ready markets in Europe and the Carribean, and the indigo, the basis of a dye, was prized by textile makers. Savannah was a prosperous port. New villages were springing up in the river valleys. A Spanish attack had been beaten back. Wealthy Georgians were building stately mansions, and lawyers (whom Oglethorpe had wanted to bar from the colony as encouragers of arguments and suits) were doing a splendid business in land claims, wills, taxes, and contracts. They were becoming numerous in the assembly and formed part of an emerging middle class that was the surest sign of the colony's ripening sophistication.

Thus the four commonwealths—the Virginia one of profit, the Massachusetts one of saintliness, the Pennsylvania one of toleration, and the Georgia one of philanthropy—had all gone their historic ways. Each was a part of a different kind of effort to create society anew across the Atlantic and each had taken a different shape dictated by the various opportunities and resistances it met. The making of communities had turned out to be a process in which rigid rules and final forms were—perhaps fortunately—impossible.

## FOR FURTHER READING

For the English background, a lively work is A. L. Rowse, *The Elizabethans and America* (1959). An adventurous summation of English exploration in North America by a master is in Samuel Eliot Morison, *The European Discovery of America: The Northern Voyages* (1971).

Also by S. E. Morison is *Builders of the Bay Colony* (1963), a basic history of Massachusetts. The feelings of the Puritan settlers themselves cannot be better expressed than in the *Journal of John Winthrop* (1908), but if the original journal is rough going, there is a good, short life history of Winthrop by Edmund Morgan entitled *The Puritan Dilemma: The Story of John Winthrop* (1958). If you want to know how Puritan mothers and fathers got along with their children, you can look at Morgan's *The Puritan Family* (1965).

There is a great abundance of material on Virginia. A popular and useful summary is *Virginia: A New Look at the Old Dominion* (1959) by Marshall Fishwick. An interesting set of documents on early Virginia history is contained in Sigmund Diamond, ed., *The Creation of Society in the New World* (1963). There are many biographies of John Smith, and an old but readable example is by a namesake, Bradford Smith's *Captain John Smith, His Life and Legend* (1953). You might even enjoy a short dip into *The Travels of Captain John Smith*, his own biased account of things. You will also be amused, if you like modern novels, by John Barth's *The Sot-Weed Factor* (1967), in which Smith figures prominently.

For Pennsylvania, the standby biography of Penn is C. O. Peare, *William Penn* (1957). An excellent account of Georgia's development is a general colonial textbook, Curtis P. Nettels, *The Roots of American Civilization* (1963). For a look at the religious enthusiasm that helped found Georgia, read Edwin S. Gaustad, *Religious History of America* (1966).

# *chapter 3*
# *Success in the world: the colonies and the Atlantic powers*

By the middle of the 1700s England's North American plantations were flourishing. Wilderness was yielding to farms; crude settlements were changing into villages. Expansion had created new colonies, which made up an English world both linked to and separated from the mother country by the Atlantic. The colonial populace, as it grew, deliberately imitated many English patterns. Yet, at the same time, the colonies were shedding some of their dependence on England. They were taking, even before they were to announce it in 1776, a separate (though not yet equal) station among the nations of the earth. They were rising in the world by dealing with its kingdoms.

Nowhere was this more evident than in colonial commercial growth. Englishmen and Europeans in the days of cocked hats and knee breeches smoked Virginia and Maryland tobacco. West Indian slaves wearily wolfed down salted New England cod and Carolina or Georgia rice. New York, Philadelphia, Boston, and Salem ships chased whales off Greenland, loaded wine in Mediterranean ports, or swapped Yankee-made rum for slaves on Africa's west coast.

In return, these same ships brought European goods, both indispensable and frivolous: spades, shovels, plows, knives, saws, nails, grindstones for farmer and artisan; pots, pans, dishes, tankards, buttons, needles, thimbles, and thread for the housewife; arms and traps for the frontier hunter; navigational instruments for the sailor; beer taps, lanterns, tinderboxes, calendars, combs, washbasins, inkwells, and cloth for stockings and petticoats and jackets for everybody. For the wealthy they carried silks and laces, handcrafted furniture, silver tea sets, fine brandies, creamy parchment paper, leather-bound books, gilded carriages, hand-painted fans, and other evidence of how far colonists had come from the starving and freezing days of the first plantings.

The colonists had a place in the world at large. They supplied vital provisions that made possible the functioning of French, Dutch, and English plantations in the Caribbean. The plantations, in turn, made fortunes for those who dealt in flax, cotton, cocoa, sugar, tobacco, indigo, and coffee. North American raw materials and food crops had a steady market in Europe. And European and English makers and merchants prospered on American purchases of manufactures.

The virgin forests of the colonial back country not only held potential wealth in furs but also in military assets—the wood and raw material for naval stores (pitch, tar, and turpentine) which were to sailing navies then what oil and steel are to modern ones. Being so valuable to the English throne, the colonies attracted the jealous eye of England's rivals. They became elements of national power and therefore pieces in the chess game of European war and diplomacy.

In turn, the world made itself felt in the raw colonial settlements. When European nations warred with England, colonial frontiers resounded with shots and war whoops, colonial ports were threatened with blockade, and the costs and responsibilities of colonial defense became subjects of hot internal debate. Social upheavals in Europe shook loose thousands of men and women who emigrated to the colonies, carrying with them their different religious patterns and various life styles, to be worked into the new, "American" fabric. Finally, key developments in European thought, embodied in books that crossed the Atlantic along with more prosaic cargoes, were pondered and absorbed by colonial clergymen, teachers, lawyers, and administrators.

In short, Europe and the Americas were closely related. Despite the difficulties of communication, there was an Atlantic civilization. (Include the slave trade, and Africa becomes part of the network of European colonial contacts.) The connections between societies on both shores of that great ocean were always strong. They were invisible wires, alive with messages. In this chapter we will try to trace some of the "wires" and analyze the communications.

### *The Mercantile Leaders*

First, there were the links provided by trade and traders. Those colonists who succeeded as merchants deeply influenced the lives of their communities. In Boston, New York, Philadelphia, Charleston, and Savannah, they bought and stored the crops, furs, fish, and other products of the countryside before sending them abroad. And they received and unloaded European goods before sending them inland. These dealings were not as extensive as they later became. Over 90 percent of all colonials, north and south, lived on farms and bought very little. They made most of what they needed, from shoes and soap to medicines and children's toys. Moreover, southern planters tended not to sell their harvests through colonial merchants but dealt directly with London firms and agents.

All the same, the mercantile classes grew, particularly in the northern colonies. And they grew in their natural habitat, the city. So the colonists began to sense a connection between their own prosperity or hard times and decisions made in the seaport towns. It was there that prices were set, both for what was sold and what was bought. It was there that moneyed people lived, governors and judges issued orders, assemblies met, and laws were passed that seemed very often to be designed to help the moneyed people. Colonial businessmen might argue that they did not control world monetary supplies, freight and insurance rates, or the ups and downs of peace and war—all of which had more to do with prices than they did. In spite of such claims, the infant urban leadership was exerting a heavy impact on inland settlements.

The merchant leaders set a particular life style that was strictly urban. It was their patronage, for instance, that brought colonial newspapers into being. The first one to last more than a day appeared in Boston in 1704. By 1770, there were some two or three dozen in the colonies. They were tiny, four-page affairs, crudely printed in a few hundred copies on hand presses. But they were full of advertisements of goods for sale, and they were eagerly scanned, not only for gossip and legal and political information, but for news of events that would affect prices.

The urban aristocrats, too, provided a market for the services of a variety of craftsmen. Planters could train their servants or slaves to keep their homes in running order and themselves presentable. But rich families in town houses needed chimney sweeps, barbers, perfumers, bakers, potmenders, wigmakers, boot makers and a variety of other specialists who kept their own shops.

---

*CHRONOLOGY*

| | |
|---|---|
| 1672 | *Joliet and Marquette reach Mississippi River* |
| 1704 | *First colonial newspaper of note, Boston* |
| 1701–1713 | *Queen Anne's War* |
| 1740–1748 | *King George's War* |
| 1754 | *Albany plan for all-colony council proposed* |
| 1756-1763 | *French and Indian War* |

Urbanites did not, like the planters, import private tutors for their children. Instead, they formed private academies or patronized dancing or drawing "masters" who had studios of their own. The mercantile outlook—practical, sober, geared to useful skills—underlay the founding of two colonial schools that later became universities. The Philadelphia College was opened in 1755 to teach subjects such as the natural sciences and mathematics. That was a departure from the classical curriculum, which emphasized philosophy and the ancient languages. The new school found these subjects of little use in keeping the world running. Later it became the University of Pennsylvania. One of its major sponsors was Benjamin Franklin, a successful Philadelphia publisher.

In 1767 a well-off merchant family of Providence, the Browns, took the lead in establishing the Rhode Island College, later Brown University. The Browns were evidence of the vitality that flourished even in the second-line mercantile towns. In them, as in Boston, Philadelphia, New York, and Charleston, the spirit of public improvement was strong. Property owners and tradesmen led in setting up municipal hospitals, streetlighting and fire-fighting services, as well as charitable and fraternal organizations. They were tackling jobs left to church, charity, or government in the Old World.

The mercantile families also had interests and connections everywhere in the Atlantic world. The early merchant aristocrats of New England were of English stock. But in the eighteenth century, commanding positions in the world of business were also won by Huguenots—descendants of French families expelled from their motherland for the "crime" of Protestantism in 1685—and Jews and Scots. All of them, the English included, took advantage of their European backgrounds and connections. In a day of slow communications and strong family loyalties, having a trusted relative on the spot in some foreign port to make a business deal was worth a fortune. So a bright young member of one of the trading clans was often sent to sea as a supercargo (in charge of the goods on board) at an early age. Later he would put in some time at an office in Tobago, St. Kitts, Barbados, London, Amsterdam, or Hamburg. Finally, seasoned, he might return home, having acquired along the way a wife who was likely to be the daughter of another mercantile family. His sons would continue the process; his daughters would marry other traders.

They were similar in style, whether they were the Pepperells (English) of Maine, the Faneuils (Huguenot) of Boston and New York, the Lopezes (Jewish) of Newport, the Shippens and Logans (English and Scottish) of Philadelphia. They gave scrupulous attention to their far-reaching correspondence, to local political issues, and to their prayer books, piously asking God's blessing to fall with equal grace on cargoes of salt and grain and of rum and slaves. Among their neighbors, they carried weight through their investments in local banking and real estate and the number of their relatives who held official jobs. Gener-

*John Singleton Copley was a Tory, an expatriate, and one of Revolutionary America's rare and distinguished artists. Much of his work consisted of portraits of wealthy New England mercantile families, like the Pepperells shown here. Their children would grow up to follow the paternal footsteps in keeping eighteenth- and early nineteenth-century commerce a family affair.*

ally, they were political conservatives, supporting royal authority against popular discontent.

But they took the lead in demanding strong diplomatic action to guarantee their rights to trade where they chose. And they vigorously opposed English laws designed to restrict colonial trade and were willing to evade those they could not change. They were especially likely to smuggle in forbidden goods from the non-British West Indies. So they were both militant and peaceful, pillars of the empire and "radical" lawbreakers, depending on where their interests lay. The merchant families embodied qualities of foresight, energy, and prudence, which would come to be thought of as particularly American qualities from the time of *Poor Richard's Almanack* to the day in the 1920s when an American president would say that "the business of America is business."

War, like trade, was a powerful force in shaping colonial self-consciousness. Friction with the Indians dated from the first settlements. Most English colonial promoters, with honorable exceptions like Penn and Williams, found Indian rejection of private land ownership and cultivation barbaric. Had not God commanded Adam to fill the earth and make it fruitful? And was it not, therefore, His work to do so, driving out the "pagans" in the process?

*War and Colonial Progress*

Virginia had an Indian war when it was fifteen years old. The Puritans of Massachusetts, six years after their settlement, slaughtered several hundred Pequots. Several New England tribes united under a leader known as "King Philip" and tried to thrust the invaders back in 1675, only to be defeated and virtually wiped out. These clashes, by 1689, gave the colonists some experience in raising, supplying, and using small bodies of troops and ships. Then came a long series of imperial struggles for power involving, among others, France, Spain, and England, the major North American colonial powers. Lasting, with brief intermissions, from the 1690s to 1763, these wars kept the colonial frontiers in a state of intermittent siege. Small European regular forces, swelled by colonial militiamen and Indian allies, battled each other in the forests for control of forts and portages. There was none of the starched formality of combat in Europe, with orderly ranks and well-planned assaults. There was only fire and the scalping knife. In the Americas the wars even had different names: Queen Anne's War (1701–1713) instead of the War of the Spanish Succession; King George's War (1740–1748) instead of the War of the Austrian Succession; and the bluntly titled French and Indian War (1756–1763) instead of the imprecise Seven Years' War.

These clashes planted the first seeds of intercolonial cooperation. In 1643 Massachusetts, Connecticut, Plymouth, and New Haven established a New England Confederation to present a united front against the Indians, the French to the north, and the Dutch in the south. It more or less fell apart by the 1660s, however. In 1690, during King William's War, Massachusetts, Plymouth, Connecticut, New York, and Maryland agreed to furnish nearly 855 troops for an expedition into Canada. Only Connecticut and New York furnished troops, however, and the attack failed. In 1709 and 1711 several northern colonies planned to furnish men jointly for a grab at Montreal. They were frustrated by lack of British support, the senior American commander helplessly tearing off his wig and stamping on it in vain rage. In 1745 a truly impressive intercolonial expedition was mustered to move against the great French fortress of Louisbourg, in Canada, a constant threat to New England's fishing fleets. Four thousand troops, plus ships and guns furnished and supplied by Massachusetts, Connecticut, New Hampshire, New York, Pennsylvania, and New Jersey, captured the citadel only to have the British negotiators return it to France at the peace conference.

The best-known attempt at intercolonial cooperation was a conference held in Albany in 1754 to coordinate strategies for the French and Indian War, which was just beginning. Out of it a plan was evolved—much of it the work of Benjamin Franklin—for a formal council of all the colonies, with a president general to be appointed by the king. The scheme, which might have created the "United States" as a British dominion, was never acted upon by the colonial assemblies. Nor did the British government approve it. But it was clearly born of military experience and need, and it painted a pathway to possible future unity.

The colonial wars loosened up provincial societies. They exalted some individuals and set down others, as some made reputations while in command of successful forays against the enemy. There was Benjamin Church of Plymouth, for example, a carpenter's son, who led a company in King Philip's War. He was so devastatingly successful that he eventually became a colonel and headed no fewer than five expeditions into Maine and Canada. And there was William Phips, a Boston ship carpenter who married well and graduated to building and owning his own vessels. In the 1680s he added to his wealth by salvaging a sunken Spanish treasure ship, the feat that caused him to be named to head an expedition against Nova Scotia. When the expedition achieved its objectives, Phips, now Sir William Phips, was chosen governor of Massachusetts. Another example is William Pepperell, a successful Maine merchant and landowner. When he captured Louisbourg in 1745, London was so delighted that Pepperell was made a baronet, a then unheard-of honor for a colonial subject.

Some merchants who did not become soldiers made money in supplying the armies. Some colonies rewarded their veterans with land grants, especially in unsettled new areas. So the wars kept people on the move, both physically and socially. At the same time they sowed seeds of political strife. Frontier towns, always the first to feel the shock of war, wanted heavy expenditures on defense. Seacoast merchants and planters resisted military budgets. The conflicts sometimes clashed into near violence, as in Pennsylvania in 1763, when a group of western settlers calling themselves the "Paxton Boys" actually marched on Philadelphia to wring more money out of the lawmakers there. They carried with them the scalps of their fallen neighbors for convincing evidence.

The wars had long-range psychological results, too. They probably strengthened colonial self-awareness and pride, as provincial soldiers and skippers now and then defeated French regular troops and showed British soldiers (who were not always willing to learn) the tricks of wilderness fighting. On the other hand, the occasional colonial defeats and intercolonial quarrels led the British to underestimate the difficulties of controlling the "Americans"—a fatal misjudgment when the Revolution came. Finally, for the colonists, the wars lent further respectability to the never-ending campaigns to dispossess the Indians.



Involvement in European wars, in short, shook up colonial society, forced the colonies to think about submerging their jealousies in common efforts, and increased both their dependence on and potential enmity to the mother country.

## *The Americas and the European Mind*

Meanwhile, the mere existence of the Americas was having a heavy impact on Europe. What the Renaissance was all about, in one sense, was a rediscovery of the tremendous potential of man to grow and to transform the world in which he lived. Whatever kindled his imagination, fed his mind, or stirred his appetites became important as a modernizing force. The discovery of a New World did all three. That world appeared in the European mind in several settings.

First, it was the place where "savage" societies were to be found unlike any in Europe or where brand new ones could be created. Reports from America encouraged some writers to describe utopias, fictional model societies free of all the vices and pains of existing ones. The book that gave the name to the whole category of such works, Sir Thomas More's *Utopia* (1515–1516), was set in an imaginary new world land. One hundred and fourteen years later, Francis Bacon's *The New Atlantis* also sketched a paradise located somewhere in the sea west of Peru. Books like these were actually devices for criticizing European society as it was. So were those that examined the customs of the Indians without automatically condemning them as "un-Christian." Both kinds of works nourished the spirit of challenge to tradition that, in the late eighteenth century, moved societies to revolution.

Secondly, America was also the land of wealth, Golconda (a city in India famed for both its real and imaginary treasures), as well as a utopia. The accounts of the gold and silver acquired by the conquistadores first awakened the hunger of adventurers, kings, and colonizers. When it became clear that the mines were not inexhaustible, the hope of fortune continued to blaze among merchants. They buoyed themselves up with expectations of the Northwest Passage, the short route to the glittering trade with the Orient. Later, when that passage proved to be a fantasy, others foresaw the fortunes in furs from the American wilderness or in sugar, cocoa, and coffee from islands in warm American seas.

Both of these ideas—America as the seat of possible perfection in human society and America as the site of the big boom, the get-rich-quick paradise—were to become part of the thinking of the people of the United States. In the earliest colonial days they helped to change the old order in Europe.

A third way that the Americas molded the mind of Europe was in furnishing data that encouraged the growth of science. The natural wonders of the New World harbored an enormous amount of information. New animals and birds (the turkey, the raccoon, the opossum, the bison, the passenger pigeon), new plants and drugs (corn, squash, pumpkins, tomatoes, cocoa, quinine, chicle—all found or cultivated by the Indians) stretched the minds of those who were laying the foundations of modern botany and zoology, geology and paleontology.

Americans were quick to record the natural history of their unfolding country, describing scenic panoramas like Niagara Falls and the Cumberland Gap, mapping mountains and rivers or setting down minute variations in climate and vegetation and animal life. The Puritan preacher Cotton Mather was an early corresponding member of London's prestigious Royal Society, for investigating Nature. The Quaker farmer John Bartram traveled extensively in the colonies and filled books with important botanical information that reached the universities in Europe's capital cities. Thomas Jefferson was known to Europeans as the author of not only the Declaration of Independence but also the widely quoted *Notes on the State of Virginia.* That book is full of well-informed speculation on what accounted for the differences between the plants and creatures of the New World and the Old. The wealth of subject matter in the undeveloped continent fed scientific curiosity in the way that America's plentiful wildlife fed hungry pioneers.

## *War and Trade: The Colonies and the European Power System*

European thinkers, then, had the Americas very much on their minds as the eighteenth century unrolled its tapestry of events. And so did European diplomats and power brokers. The age of exploration gave way to the age of settlement, and the American possessions of Europe's kings became valuable cards in royalty's never-ending poker game of war making and treaty making.

Just how it worked is illustrated in the story of the ending of the Seven Years' War. The background to that conflict in North America (where, as you will recall, it was called the French and Indian War) was a century of rivalry between London and Paris in the New World. While the English settlements were slowly filling, France had extended her theoretical control over a gigantic Canadian-American heartland. Her explorers followed the watery routes into the interior—up the St. Lawrence, across the Great Lakes, then down the Mississippi. By 1673 two Jesuit priests, Louis Joliet and Father Jacques Marquette had reached that great river, and a few years later Robert de la Salle descended it as far as the Gulf of Mexico and claimed all the land drained by its tributaries for his monarch. Louisiana, as he named the region, contained virtually all of the United States-to-be from the Rockies to the Appalachians, with incredible riches in grazing lands, forests, and mines.

But the French did little to exploit these potential resources. To them the "gold" of New France was in the fur trade. They collected their furs by alliances and barter with the Indian tribes, whom they left generally undisturbed except for the efforts of hard-working missionaries. They held their hundreds of thousands of square miles of wilderness with only a few troops and a tiny handful of Quebec- and Montreal-based administrators who were given little authority.

Eventually, French outposts in the St. Lawrence and Ohio valleys were seen as threats to the westward and northward expansion of the English colonies, particularly Maine (then a part of Massachusetts), New York, and Pennsylvania. English and French interests also clashed around Hudson's Bay to the north and in offshore fisheries. And, of course, in Europe itself in the 1600s and 1700s, France and England were constant rivals: one Protestant and the other Catholic; each wanting naval superiority and trade advantages, both in the waters around Europe and in parts of the globe other than North America, particularly India.

As we saw earlier, Anglo-French conflict flared around the margins of their American colonies from the 1690s onward. The climactic Seven Years' War saw the British victorious. Not only was France beaten, but so was her ally in that war, Spain. And British triumphs had taken place on many battlefields other than in Canada. The British had seized French trading posts in India; they had taken Manila, in the Philippines, and Havana from Spain; and they had also taken the French West Indian islands of Guadeloupe and Martinique.

The war had been worldwide, a sign of Europe's continuing expansion. And the peace was a game of swapping that illustrated eighteenth-century notions of the balance of power. The idea was not to crush a defeated enemy nation but to keep it strong enough to maintain peace and order within its boundaries and to help keep European supremacy over other peoples. A rival kingdom was part of a system of organizing humanity; it could lose a game, but it must not be eliminated entirely. When diplomats sat down at the peace table in Paris in 1763, everyone on all sides understood and played by the rules.

The French wanted—and got—Guadeloupe back. Its sugar plantations seemed much more valuable to them than the "acres of snow" (even fur-rich snow) represented by Canada. Canada went to Britain. The British also pacified the southern frontier of Georgia by taking Florida from Spain. But they then "compensated" Spain for the loss by forcing France to give her Louisiana, which was far away from English territory and less threatening.

In short, North American lands and resources were items that added to the power of Europe's great nations. Haggled and fought over, their very existence made the emerging great-power system work, just as the appetites of those powers were partly responsible for the original colonial settlements.

But war and diplomacy were also tightly linked to trade. And the colonies of England especially were woven into a system, called mercantilism, that used trade as an element of power. There were a number of sides to mercantile thought, but the principal points, so far as the American colonists were concerned, were these: (1) to provide raw materials, which Britain, the mother country, would then not have to buy from other powers; and (2) to be a steady market for British manufactured goods. Their economic health was tied to that of Britain: the more they produced and consumed, the better for London. Therefore, London had a stake in their growth. But in any conflict London's interests would come first.

The English enacted these principles into a series of laws, called the Navigation Acts, passed in the 1650s and 1660s, with a late addition in 1696. In essence, they ordered that trade among the colonies and between them and the world must be carried on only in English and colonial ships. Then, certain "enumerated articles" (staples such as tobacco, rice, and indigo) could be sold only to English dealers, not directly to European customers. Finally, most manufactured articles could be imported only from England. The colonists were to buy and sell strictly on terms set by English manufacturers and merchants.

There were other restrictions, too, which were part of the system, though not of the Navigation Acts. Americans could not export foodstuffs to England, because the English market was reserved for English farmers. And not only could Americans not import non-British manufactures, but they could not set up home industries. Specifically banned was the large-scale production of woolens (1699), hats (1732), and iron (1750). The iron-production ban brought forth the comment from Benjamin Franklin that a colonist could not so much as make a nail without some sooty ironmonger in Britain screaming that he was injured.

The system seemed to be exploitative. A tobacco planter, for example, could not advertise his year's crop and wait to see what the highest bid was from Dutch, English, and French skippers waiting to load cargo at the riverside wharves. A New York dry goods merchant could not compare the prices of English and French calicos or muslins and make the best deal for himself and his customers. And the system was hardest on the provisions-producing colonies. Southerners could at least trade their tobacco or indigo for English-made goods, even at English prices. But the northern and middle colonies had to turn their flour, fish, salted beef, and hay into something else—into silver coin, sugar, slaves, fruit, wine, and other goods acceptable in England. That was what drove more Yankee vessels to the West Indies, Africa, and the Mediterranean each year.

Yet, oddly enough, the mercantilist system was tolerated with only occasional conflict for almost a century. There was a double reason. First, as British defenders of the acts pointed out, the system also benefited the colonies. For

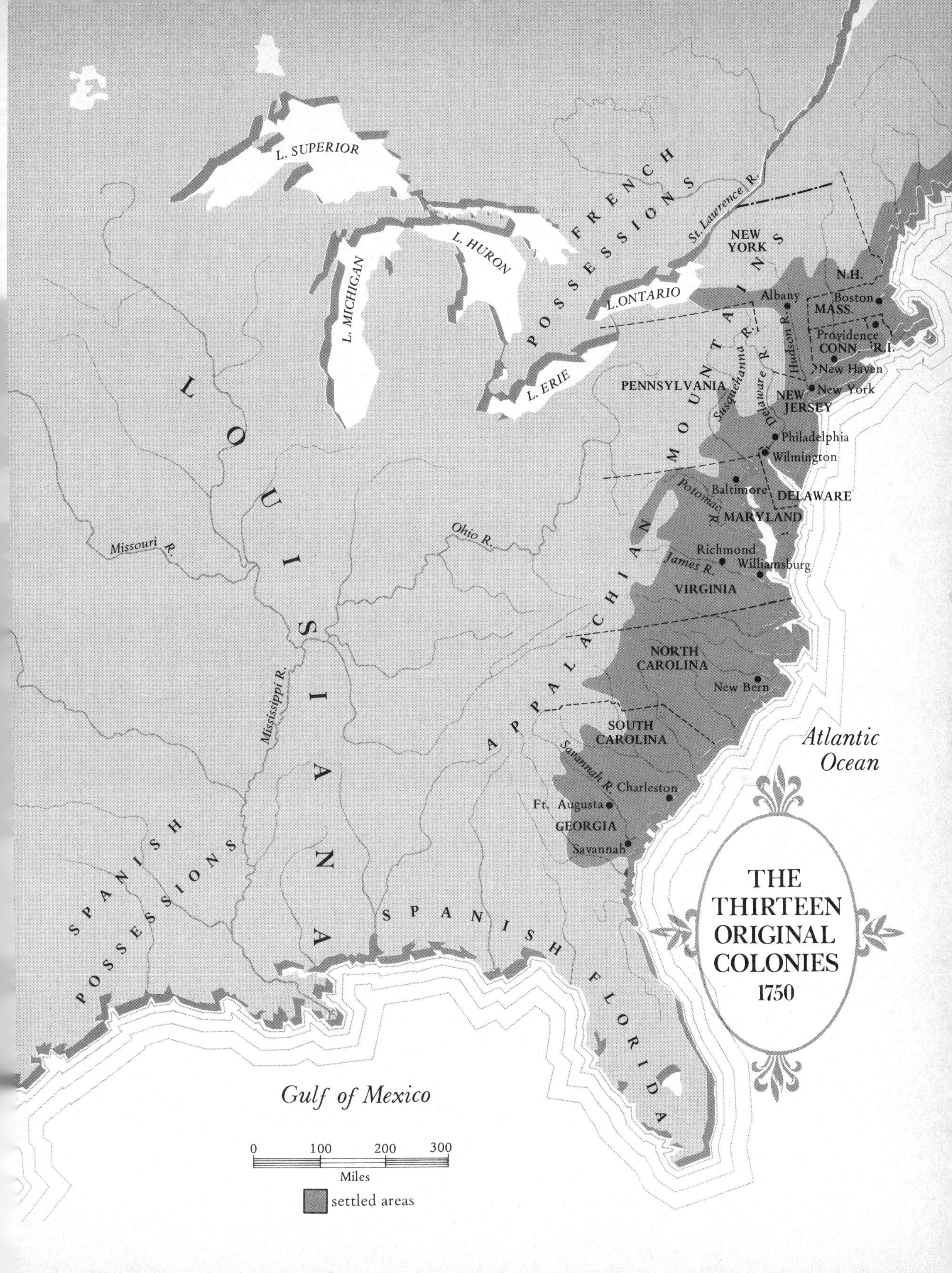

L. SUPERIOR
FRENCH POSSESSIONS
St. Lawrence R.
NEW YORK
L. HURON
L. MICHIGAN
L. ONTARIO
L. ERIE
N.H.
Albany
Boston
MASS.
Providence
CONN.
R.I.
New Haven
New York
Hudson R.
Susquehanna R.
Delaware R.
PENNSYLVANIA
NEW JERSEY
Philadelphia
Wilmington
Baltimore
DELAWARE
Potomac R.
MARYLAND
LOUISIANA
Missouri R.
Ohio R.
Richmond
Williamsburg
James R.
VIRGINIA
APPALACHIAN MOUNTAINS
NORTH CAROLINA
New Bern
Mississippi R.
SOUTH CAROLINA
Savannah R.
Charleston
Ft. Augusta
GEORGIA
Savannah
Atlantic Ocean
THE THIRTEEN ORIGINAL COLONIES 1750
SPANISH POSSESSIONS
SPANISH FLORIDA
Gulf of Mexico
0
100
200
300
Miles
settled areas

example, reserving colonial trade routes for "English" vessels (which included colonial-built windjammers) freed American shippers from tough foreign competition. And holding colonial purchases of manufactured wares to those produced by Great Britain did not work major harm. By the 1700s Britain was moving rapidly toward industrial supremacy. Even in a free market she could have undersold most potential European rivals. And even where the great staples were concerned, the Navigation Acts gave tobacco, rice, and indigo planters a protected market in Britain. The British themselves were not allowed to buy these goods from the colonies of other nations. In addition, the British government actually gave bounties, or payments, to grow some products like indigo or hemp, which was used in making the rope that fleets needed. Mercantilism actually helped nurse the colonial economy to maturity.

Secondly, the potential damage of the Navigation Acts was reduced by their ineffective application. It was vital, for example, that the northern colonies ship foodstuffs to the French and Dutch West Indies in exchange for sugar, which was decidedly cheaper than that grown in the English islands. And because this trade was vital, the colonists simply went ahead with it. The British customs service, archaic, corruptible, undermanned, and run from the top by political appointees was unequal to the task of stopping smuggling. So Yankee merchants peddled their "illegal" wares, and Yankee distillers made rum from "unlawfully" imported sugar and somehow managed to face God with a good conscience on Sundays.

The shoe of mercantilism really pinched only when two fateful developments followed 1763. First, the French were thrown out of North America. Until then the colonists, no matter how they resented British policies, had keenly sensed how much they needed British power to protect their weak and divided settlements.. So they had put up with many London-sponsored vexations, which they were now free to denounce. Secondly, Britain herself began to upgrade and modernize the administrative machinery of her empire. This process included plans to put teeth into the customs service, so that the Navigation Acts would really work—and really hurt.

By the 1760s, too, the growing colonial economy could survive without mercantilist benefits such as monopolies and bounties, so serious objection and conflict followed. Until then, however, the story of British economic regulation provided still another example of the interlocked destinies of America and Europe.

### *America as Asylum for Quarreling Europe*

One final significant story is that of the changing pattern of eighteenth-century migration to the colonies. The newcomers of the 1600s had been almost exclusively English. Yet by 1782, in a famous quotation, a French-born migrant to America named Michel-Guillaume Jean de Crevecoeur could ask:

> What then is the American, this new man? He is either a European or the descendant of a European. . . . I could point out to you a man whose grandfather was an Englishman, whose wife was Dutch, whose son married a French woman, and whose present four sons now have four wives of different nations. . . . Here individuals of all nations are melted into a new race of men.

Crevecoeur would most probably have ignored the contribution of black Africa's kidnapped slaves to the "new race of men," but it was nevertheless there.

War and persecution furnished new streams of non-English migration. Mention has already been made of colonial Jewry: the first members of that religious community to reach America landed in New Amsterdam in 1654. Over the next hundred years, several thousand fellow worshipers joined them. Most were of Spanish origin. In 1685 there was an influx of French Protestants, or Huguenots, expelled by Louis XIV as he tightened his control over France and rejected non-Catholics as being untrustworthy.

From the 1680s through the 1750s, the many small states that made up Germany seethed with social unrest. Part of it was caused by battles among various rulers. In these vest-pocket wars, peasants were drafted and taxed, and contending armies swept over villages, looting and raping as they went. In the states of southern Germany, neither Protestantism nor Catholicism had clearly triumphed. Each prince adopted his own religion and tormented those of his subjects who dissented. Under the pressure of hard times, religion tended to splinter, and prophets and seers multiplied. Numerous small sects sprang up—Moravians, Schwenkfelders, Dunkards, Mennonites—and their followers, with visions of perfection on earth flaming before them, boarded ships for America. They were joined by thousands of other Germans seeking bread and peace. Many came as "redemptioners," selling themselves to a ship's captain for passage money. He, in turn, sold them to American farmers as indentured servants for a fixed term. These Germans constituted the second biggest single eighteenth-century migration.

The largest consisted of the so-called Scotch-Irish. Germans in the white population of some 3 to 3.5 million numbered about 176,000 on the eve of the Revolution. The Scotch-Irish were probably 220,000 strong, though no accurate figures of colonial immigration are available. These Ulster Scots had been settled in the now troubled six northern counties of Ireland early in the seventeenth century. They were supposed to be the seedbed of a Protestant population that would hold the wild, rebellious Catholic Irish in line. This they were willing to do, being staunch and dogged Presbyterian Calvinists. (They shared the Puritans' beliefs but used a different form of church organization.) But after 1700 they were ruined by British laws that forbade them to sell the butter and cheese and meat and grain they grew and the excellent woolen cloth they wove, in Britain herself—the same laws that forbade American food sales to the British.

So economic need drove thousands of Ulster Scots across the water after 1700. Most of them, after indentured service, moved to untaken lands on the Pennsylvania, Virginia, and Carolina frontiers. Known there as the Scotch-Irish, they became devastating Indian fighters, great consumers of corn whiskey, fiery participants in shouting, enthusiastic attenders of religious meetings, diligent farmers, hunters and trappers—and ancestors of some of America's most distinguished statesmen, including Andrew Jackson, John C. Calhoun, James K. Polk, and Woodrow Wilson, to name but a few.

Migration on such a scale had a deep meaning for the colonists. Though the basic colonial stock remained English, the institutions of the mother country had to be adjusted to new languages, faiths, and styles. The process of gathering in Europe's exiles started to stamp American political and social life with a diversity not yet lost. Immigration was a strong stimulus to political ingenuity (the art of reconciling many diverse group wills) in the host country. It also fostered educational and cultural diversity.

But it affected the contributing countries as well as the Americas. Emigration from the Old World came about when the modern state tightened its rules and procedures and expelled heretics and rebels. It was also stimulated by economic change, as, for example, by landowners' shifting to new crops (like wool) or to new and more efficient ways of growing old ones and by their throwing out tenants who could no longer be "used" efficiently on tiny plots that were left over from feudal times.

The existence of America as an asylum made it possible for many members of these uprooted classes to be drawn off without plunging into rebellion or crime. It is difficult to know what the course of European history would have been had America not existed as a refuge and a magnet for surplus labor. Her very presence kept alive the possibility of a new start in life and checked despair and rage. At the same time, the existence of a new land encouraged dreamers, as we saw, to sketch new human possibilities.

So the mere idea of America fed change and ferment in the world but perhaps slowed it down, too. The two-way relationship between the New

---

*Nothing better suggests the colorful variety and richness of colonial societies than contemporary newspapers. This issue of a Pennsylvania paper, just after the Revolution, bursts with information on what citizens of the new America bought and sold, what they expected of their government, how they traveled, and for whom they worked and under what conditions. See how much you can find out for yourself.*

PENNSYLVANIA EVENING HERALD, AND THE AMERICAN MONITOR:

Price, Five-pence.] SATURDAY, SEPTEMBER 24, 178- [No. 18.

Total No. 70.] BE JUST, AND FEAR NOT.

WHERE LIBERTY DWELLS, THERE IS MY COUNTRY. Franklin.

RAN-AWAY last night from the subscriber, living in Front-street, between Market and Arch-streets, an Irish servant lad named Hugh Morgan, by trade a taylor, is about nineteen years of age, pale complexion, short dark brown hair, in which he wears a crooked comb, is well made, and about five feet six inches high; had on when he went off—a green coat and breeches, spotted waistcoat, round hat, thread stockings, light shoes, and common plated buckles,—has likewise a light coloured coat, white dimity waistcoat fringed, a pair of black silk breeches, and two pair of thread stockings; the cloaths are all half worn. Whoever apprehends and secures said servant so that his master gets him, shall be entitled to four dollars reward, and all reasonable expences paid.

All masters of vessels are forbid taking said servant off at their peril.—He is supposed to have gone off with one John Hosses, who worked in the shop with him.

Philadelphia, Sept. 17, SAMUEL HARVEY.

TO BE SOLD,

THE FAST SAILING SLOOP

RAMBLER,

HENRY DAVIS, Master;

Now lying at Mr. Warder's Wharf. This vessel is new---well-built, and well fitted, will carry about 1000 bushels of grain, draws little water when loaded, and is well calculated for the bay trade. Any person inclined to purchase may see the vessel, and know the terms by applying to Messrs. Jeremiah Warder, Parker and Co. or the Master on board.

September 12.

LOST, about eight o'clock, on Sunday evening, in South-street, the corner of Third-street, a RED MOROCCO POCKET BOOK, containing a ten dollar bank note, and sundry other papers, which are of no value but to the owner. Whoever will deliver said pocket-book with its contents to the printers of this paper, or to the subscriber, shall be rewarded with the above-mentioned bank-note, and ten dollars besides. *** No questions shall be asked.

September 10. JOHN BEALE living in Water-street, below South-street.

Imported in the last vessels from Europe, and for sale by

JAMES SMITH, Junior,

At his store in Second-street, the corner of Carter's-alley.

BLANKETS & ruggs by the bale
Striped and blue duffils
Low-priced yard wide coatings
Hunter's cloths and plains
Kersey's and half thicks
Scarlet, red, yellow and white flannels
Ribb'd and plain worsted hose
Several trunks of cottons and callicoes
Bales of Scotch and German oznabrigs, and some of the best ticklenburghs
Boxes of glass ware assorted
Pipes and salt-petre in small casks
Also a good assortment of most of the articles in the dry goods line, with cutlery, &c. which will be disposed of at moderate prices.

September 20th.

NEW NOVELS.

The Casket, two vols.
Vale of Glendor, two vol.
History of Sir Henry Clarendon, two vols.
Imogen, a pastoral romance, two vols.
Matilda, or the effects of love, three vols.
Original love letters, two vols.
Edward and Anne
The Nabob, two vols.
Conquests of the heart, two vols.
Rencontre, two vols.
History of Christiana princess of Swabia, two vols.
The Myrtle, or effects of love, two vols.
Belford and Woodley, three vols.

LAW BOOKS.

Jacob's law dictionary
Blackstone's commentaries, four vols.
Ruffhead's statutes, fourteen vols. quarto
Every man his own lawyer
Groon's bankrupt laws
Sheridan's practice of the court of king's bench
Every landlord or tenant his own lawyer
Wood's institutes
Digest of adjudged cases in the king's bench

World and the Old always had many angles and possible meanings. These would shift and change as the connection endured into modern times, when the colonies would become a nation and when the power center of the transatlantic civilization would shift from Europe to America.

## *FOR FURTHER READING*

A broad overview of American colonial life is Max Savelle, *Seeds of Liberty* (1948). A kind of "portrait" by a gifted historian, Richard Hofstadter, can be found in *America at 1750* (1971).

Zeroing in on particular areas, regions, and classes we find a wide variety of reading material. For example, Louis B. Wright's *The Cultural Life of the American Colonies* (1957) has interesting things to say about how Americans sang, played, read, and thought. Carl Bridenbaugh, *Cities in the Wilderness* (1938) touches on urban life, while Dale Van Every, *Forth to the Wilderness* (1961) looks at the other side of the coin, the strife-torn colonial frontier.

Scholars and literary artists provide different perspectives that reinforce each other interestingly. Bernard Bailyn, *The New England Merchants of the Seventeenth Century* (1955), for example, shows how Boston family fortunes were founded. Then one can move to a fine book by Esther Forbes, *Paul Revere and the World He Lived In* (1943), that describes what happened to Boston society in the next century. Frederick Tolles, *Meeting House and Counting House: The Quakers of Colonial Philadelphia* (1948) shows how Quaker merchants prospered in the new world, while early chapters of Oscar Handlin, *Adventure in Freedom* (1954) recount the "connections" of Jewish merchants in the colonies.

For the diplomatic and military story, the classic works are those of Francis Parkman, *A Half Century of Conflict* and *Montcalm and Wolfe*, still readable though rather ornate by modern standards.

Nothing tops firsthand accounts, so for life in New England, see the *Diary of Samuel Sewall;* for the middle colonies, the incomparable *Autobiography of Benjamin Franklin;* and for the south, *The Secret Diary of William Byrd* (a Virginia planter). There are various editions in any good library.

# Thought provokers

Two hundred years after Cortes' "towers" on the water had startled Moctezuma, three European powers held on firmly to North America. In Mexico and the future American states of Texas, New Mexico, Arizona, and California, Spanish priests, soldiers, and officials ruled thousands of dependent Indians, who had learned to adapt themselves to Hispanic imperial styles. The French were implanted in the upper part of the continent, Canada-to-be. From a handful of outposts in the St. Lawrence valley, they sent fur traders and missionaries into the deepest and wildest reaches of western America. They were the overlords of many acres and had alliances with Indian tribes, but they did not actually occupy Indian hunting grounds nor create a very noticeable Franco-Indian culture. Finally, nestled on the Atlantic slope of the Appalachian Mountains that slashed down the eastern flank of the continent, English settlements were growing steadily. They all had an increasing population from many different backgrounds and pursued a wide range of economic activities. Their compact settlements had driven the Indians from the coastal areas. And on the frontier the relations between English settlers and the tribal people could be summed up in one word: hostile.

Now that you have examined some of the details of that colonizing process, some of its broad implications can be pinpointed by a second look at the historical evidence, armed with specific questions.

In the first chapter, for example, how important was the fact that the Aztecs deeply believed their legends and folktales? Did the Spaniards have myths of their own that they trusted? How did Spanish Christianity prepare the conquistadores for the role they played?

Why do you think that the Indian peoples whom the Spaniards encountered in the 1500s had not yet developed the kind of scientific curiosity that was then important in Europe? Was it because of attitude toward Nature? Or their understanding of the meaning of life? What beliefs are necessary in order to investigate, control, and change the way Nature works?

Here is an interesting set of facts to contemplate. The conquistadores did not believe that work was an honorable undertaking. Yet they underwent tremendous exertions to gain their ends. So work did not simply mean effort. The friars generally thought of themselves as being withdrawn from the world. Yet they were enormously busy putting up churches, growing food, and preaching to the Indians. So being withdrawn from the world did not prevent them *from performing a great deal of sweaty labor to improve that world. Exactly what did friars and conquistadores mean by work? What was "proper" work? What were its goals? Who should do it? Contrast these views with those of the Puritans and other English settlers described in the second chapter. Contrast them with your own views today. Do the different attitudes of the English and the Spaniards toward work account for the different forms their colonies took? Or for the "success" of the English ones?*

*In studying English settlements, you may find some interesting questions to ponder. For example, if the Virginia Company's original plans for the colony had gone through, would a large population have been necessary? In other words, what does the economic goal of a community have to do with its size and organization? Would it have been possible to keep the semimilitaristic organization that first prevailed at Jamestown if the colony had remained small and wrapped up in doing the company's bidding? What broke down that pattern? What did the boom in tobacco do to society and government?*

*If the manner of making profits affects a community's life, so does the way of facing God. For the Puritans of Massachusetts what was the whole point of a community? Once that point was granted, was it natural to make church membership essential to good citizenship? And follow the lead of ministers? From a Puritan's point of view what was the answer to Williams' idea that church and state should be separated? Is it possible to take both community participation and religion seriously and to separate them?*

*Pennsylvania and Georgia were set up to benefit humanity in general. Does that goal differ from the Spanish idea, as applied to the Indians, of saving souls? How? How does it compare to the Puritan idea of building God's kingdom in the wilderness? Which idea is closest to the twentieth-century idea of government responsibility for human welfare? Did Pennsylvania follow Penn's original blueprint more successfully than Georgia followed Oglethorpe's? Why? If there were differences in the patterns of development of the two colonies, were they traceable to Penn's being a Quaker? Or to the kinds of settlers who came to both colonies? Or to the characteristic economic activities that each pursued? In a nutshell, then, what forces made Pennsylvania different from Georgia: religion, leadership, population base, or economic life? When you ask yourself these questions, you are tackling a large, general problem—what makes communities differ?—by asking sharper, more manageable questions: Who came? What did they work at? How were they led? Thus you are getting an introduction to the "method" of the social sciences.*

*Try using it to form general questions of your own about the third chapter, and then subdivide them into specific questions. Here are two examples to get you started. The broad question might be: How do the major activities of a leadership group encourage different kinds of cultural activity? To make the question specific, would the conquistadores and friars ever have needed newspapers in the way that the mercantile classes of the English eighteenth-century colonies did? Were such papers part of a commercial, instead of a martial or pious, culture? Would the original Puritan settlers have needed newspapers as much as schools?*

*And here, as a second example, is a general question about migration: What forces bring about large-scale movements of populations from one area to another? Are they primarily social, economic, or otherwise? To answer the question you might find it useful to look at the people who populated the colonies in the eighteenth century—the English, the Huguenots, the Scotch-Irish, the*

*Germans. Did they have common problems from which they were fleeing? Were there common opportunities that they sought? After you have arrived at what you consider a general explanatory statement, test it by asking yourself if the rule applies to the African immigrants who came here.*

*You may try your hand at this process in other wide areas such as the effect of worldwide expansion on the power balance among existing nations; the impact of economic growth on social classes; the challenge of new ideas and how they affect the life-styles of individual leaders and heroes.*

D Y-k
M-q-s R-m
Q C
K GIII[d]
O thou whom next to Heav'n we most revere
Fair LIBERTY! thou lovely Goddess hear!
Have we not woo'd thee, won thee, held thee long
Lain in thy Lap, & melted on thy Tongue
Thro Deaths & Dangers rugged paths pursu'd
And led thee smiling to this SOLITUDE
Hid thee within our Hearts most golden Cell
And brav'd the Powers of Earth & Powers of Hell
GODDESS! we cannot part, thou must not fly;
Be SLAVES! we dare to scorn it – dare to die
FRESH TEAS.
FRESH TEAS.
FRESH TEAS.

# part two: Making a Nation

*The explosions of terrorist bombs in Tel Aviv, Belfast, Saigon, and Quebec —blasts that have made headlines since the* 1960s,*—emphasize the enormous power that* nationalism *possesses, even today, to drive some men and women to deeds of unthinking fury. The idea that separate peoples of the earth should each be organized into a political state that they control has been gaining ground since the seventeenth century, when the major countries of western Europe emerged from feudalism. Acceleration has been steady. Only in the past hundred years did peoples of eastern and southern Europe break away from the Turkish, Russian, and Austrian empires to achieve nationhood. And only in the past thirty years have the new nations of Africa and Asia risen on the ruins of colonialism. The rage that inflames groups still fighting, in their own view, to reach independent status or to liberate their brothers and sisters under alien flags, is the rage of those who see history cheating them out of what others are getting.*

*But what, exactly, is a "nation"? What is a "people"? Is it a body of human beings linked by a common tongue? Common culture? Common boundaries? Common history? The answer to all these questions is at least a partial yes. But there is no single always accurate response. Nationalism can only be defined by studying its workings in different places and at different times. And the United States offers one of the best opportunities for such a close-up look. It came into existence at the beginning of the great modern spurt of nation building (the title of a recent book calls it "the first new nation"). It had no past to speak of, great stretches of unpopulated territory, and a very diversified population. How did these blend into a national identity?*

*This second portion of the book deals with precisely these problems. First it looks at the actual process by which Americans separated themselves from British political control and took a "separate and equal station," in the words of the Declaration of Independence, "among the powers of the earth. . . ." In the opening chapter of this part, Chapter* 4, *we will trace the steps leading to the breach and introduce some problems of how historians explain events. The major questions to bear in mind are general ones such as: How do little streams of grievance become united into a river of protest? What is the role of communication in inspiring a revolt? How do the leaders reach their positions? We will also see a rather swift change in loyalties among "British North Americans," who went from deep respect for the symbols of royal authority to rejection of them inside of fifteen years. (At least, some of them changed, and they turned out to be the winners in the contest to control the direction of affairs.) What does this tell us about the meaning of loyalty and respect? What conditions must be fulfilled by a government in order to earn them? And can government be effective without them? Still another question to weigh is whether or not conflicts between rulers and ruled are inevitable in certain circumstances. Could Britain, an island, govern America forever, a continent* 3000 *miles away? Especially when British and American societies were growing in different directions? If the answer is no, at what point did that impossibility become clear? And if it is yes, then what could Britain have done to avoid the break? How do historians weigh and assign individual responsibility for the developments they record?*

*Chapter* 5 *raises the general question of how a new nation, born out of revolution, establishes itself solidly without betraying its revolutionary past. This is done through a careful look at the problems of the infant United States, the contradictory solutions offered, and the compromise answers embodied in the Constitution. The general question that provides the framework of this chapter arises out of a strange contradiction. A revolution is an overturning of authority, a cry to the oppressed to resist. But, after the storm has passed, order must replace the chaos of war. In order to rebuild for the future, new authority must be established. The same people who have been urged to resist must now be coaxed to compromise and to conciliate and to give up part of their liberty to safeguard the rest. What arguments were made to gain this end in the United States? What new symbols were appealed to? And what were the results in spelling out the details of the plan of government actually adopted? If all government of free people is a compromise between liberty and safety, what were the particular limits of the compromise of 1787? What lessons might the story hold for other new nations?*

*Nations do not live in vacuums. Their interests often bring them into conflict with powerful neighbors, and their success in providing economic stability for their populations almost always requires at least some trade with other parts of the world. International life is, in some ways, a state of constant war or imminent war. The problems of each nation, therefore, are compounded by its need to function in such a threatening atmosphere. Chapter 6 examines the fate of the United States in its first twenty-five years under the Constitution. Almost all of them were spent during a major European war, and the period ended with the youthful republic itself once more at war with Britain. What we examine here is another dimension of national life, the interplay between foreign relations and domestic politics. How did the emerging political and cultural life of Americans become affected by the perils and the gains of being neutrals in a strife-torn world? How did the issues of that world war divide Americans? How did the need for presenting a united front to the world unite them? And how, once the United States itself got into battle, did the feelings and stresses of combat weaken or reinforce the connections among the sections and classes making up the American people? Since "diplomatic" history is often taught in a vacuum, separately from "straight" history, it may be difficult for you to think in this new fashion. But you will find it rewarding to try to escape from the effects of your earlier miseducation.*

*Finally, passing on to the years following 1815, we will examine the cultural forces that create a sense of nationality. Here what you should bear in mind is that nationhood is not simply a matter of paying taxes into a common treasury and saluting the same flag. It involves a web of connection among millions of peoples separated by distance, and often by education, class, and tradition. Nationality becomes something felt and experienced in the texture of daily living and feeling. Just how does that happen? What are the shared attitudes of the early American people? How were they expressed in ordinary activities? How were they communicated from group to group? To answer these questions we study three particular institutions. You may then find it useful to apply the answers you derive to still others.*

# *chapter* 4

# *When is a revolution?*

Paris was long a city known for charm, good wine, and pleasant company. It was, therefore, a popular place for diplomatic conferences. There British envoys sat down in 1763 to conclude a peace treaty that, as we saw, swept France from North America and ended a long agony of colonial warfare. The inhabitants of British America greeted the event with the joy of people in a garrison just relieved of a long siege. Throughout the towns from Massachusetts to Georgia, there were numerous public declarations of gratitude to His Majesty, George III. Along with them went vows of undying loyalty.

Just twenty years and seven months later, in September 1783, another peace of Paris was concluded. In this one the same king recognized his 13 former colonies, now titled "the United States of America," to be "free, sovereign and independent States." And, "for himself, his heirs and successors," he relinquished "all claims to the Government, proprietary and territorial rights of the same, and every part thereof."

In one short stretch—in the years it would take one modern child to go from kindergarten through medical school—a great change had taken place. The American Revolution shifted the balance of world history. It brought a future superpower into being, and it gave tremendous impetus to a philosophy of government, democracy, and a doctrine of political organization, nationalism, both of which have almost totally transformed the world in the nearly two centuries since 1783. The first shot of the Revolution may not literally have been heard around the world, but its echoes are not yet dead.

### *How Historians Work*

How did this take place so quickly? How, in fact, did it come to take place at all? The answer is somewhat complicated and provides an interesting lesson in what is called historical relativism. A historian can approach a subject like this in several ways. He can ask himself and his readers large, philosophical questions of definition. Just *what* is a revolution? If the answer is "a swift, historical change," on what scale does he measure "swift" and "change"?

Or he can ask what led Britons and colonists from debate and contention within the imperial "family" to polarization and armed confrontation. He may deal with whether confrontation was avoidable and throw in a question of value: Was it "better," in the long run, for all parties? Or he can broaden the question of avoidability and ask whether the entire American Revolution was "inevitable." If so, at what stage of the quarrel was the point of no return reached?

These are only a few examples. To answer his questions, the historian will select certain facts and episodes from the information available to him. His choice of characters and events to study will be influenced by what he wants to learn. He will be giving his story a certain shape, depending on how he intends it to be used.

Some historians object to this procedure. They see their job as one of telling the story as it happened. It is their claim that simply setting down the facts, in order, leads to a more objective, more impersonal, and, in the long run, more honest kind of history.

But this approach has a built-in flaw. For a story is *always* an arranged selection of facts from a huge available number of them. We know that George Washington was a Virginia landholder. We also know he was unusually tall. Both are facts. Yet the first is significant in a discussion of Washington's role in the American Revolution, and the second is trivial (although it might matter to a biographer who believed that a man's character was formed by his being tall or short). So the most objective historian in the world cannot and will not present all the facts. He will choose. And he will probably arrange facts in an order that is set by a predetermined question (as, for example: What did the British do that stirred American anger?). But even if he simply sets facts down in the time order in which they happened, with no guiding inquiries, he is still going to leave a record that can be interpreted in many different ways. The barest chronological outline is the raw material of many stories, not of a single truth.

If we imagine all the events between 1763 and 1783 strung out on a time line, we will find that in order to make any sense of them, we must look at them closely, piece by piece. And we will then find that where one looks—the particular segment of the time line we choose—will actually affect our judgment of what is happening.

Every seasoned reporter knows that a good story must have an angle, a viewpoint or a framework that pulls the parts together, identifies the characters, and gives meaning and interest to the facts. He must find a possible way in which the story "adds up" if it is not to be a dull, routine piece. Telling a story does not mean changing or distorting facts. It means, rather, justifying the facts included by showing how they fit together to make a point.

Let us illustrate by looking at the various periods of prerevolutionary crises, one after another. What we should find is that each suggests a different and defensible interpretation of what happened and why, with a different set of leading characters and principal happenings. When we are through, we may not have a final answer to why the Revolution happened or what it actually meant or even whether it *was* a revolution. But we will have a clear notion of the fascinating intellectual challenge of history as a set of open propositions (instead of a closed book of "lessons" from a frozen past) and of why a good historian is somewhat like a good reporter.

## *A Question of Modernization?*

Suppose we begin by simply restating some of the best-known events of 1763 to 1767, the opening phase of the conflict between London and the colonies. The end of the Seven Years' War left Britain saddled with an enormous debt. Since the war had been fought in part to protect the colonists from French attack, it seemed only just to George III and his officials that His Majesty's American subjects should bear a fair share of war costs. So two measures were taken to increase the amount of imperial revenue flowing in from the colonies.

The first was the Sugar Act of 1764, providing for a revision of the duties

*CHRONOLOGY*

| | |
|---|---|
| 1763 | *Treaty of Paris settles French and Indian War* |
| 1763 | *Proclamation Line bars settlement west of the Allegheny Mountains* |
| 1765 | *Stamp Act; repealed* 1766 |
| 1770 | *Boston "Massacre"* |
| 1773 | *Boston Tea Party* |
| 1775 | *Battles of Lexington and Concord* |
| 1776 | *Tom Paine publishes* Common Sense |
| 1776 | *Declaration of Independence* |

on imported foreign sugar. The new law actually set lower rates than the statute it replaced, the Molasses Act, dating from 1733. But that act had been continually and blithely ignored by New England merchants, who habitually smuggled in French and Dutch sugars to sweeten their tea and produce their rum. The new act, however, called for an increase in the number of royal customs officials and for better and tighter antismuggling procedures. These, it was calculated, would substantially increase the actual "take" from the duties by up to 100,000 pounds annually. The calculations did not count on a storm of objection that blew up at once among influential colonists who, in one way or another, were affected by the prosperity of the foreign sugar trade. The act drove a wedge between the colonial mercantile classes and the throne; later measures would hammer it in deeper.

One of those was enacted in 1765, when Lord George Grenville, the new chancellor of the exchequer, put a stamp tax through Parliament. It provided that almost every legal document, for example, contracts, warrants, commissions, deeds, and the like, as well as various other printed items, such as books, newspapers, pamphlets, and even playing cards, would have to bear an official stamp. These would be purchased from agents in the colonies appointed by the king. This kind of tax was nothing new. (In fact, even today, certain legal papers, such as property deeds carry stamps to show that taxes on them have been paid.) In Grenville's view, the act was a simple and well-tested device to harvest more tax money out of the provincials for whom so much had been done.

But the colonists, from one end of the Atlantic seaboard to the other, saw it quite differently. They were accustomed to being taxed only by their own, elected provincial assemblies. They felt that they had borne their share of fighting and paying for the wars. There was hardly a professional or businessman in the colonies who did not see himself as being burdened with unwanted and unfair additional costs through the Stamp Act. Landowners, merchants, lawyers, editors, shopkeepers, craftsmen—all raised a roar. The feeble voices of those who spoke up for the king and Parliament were drowned out. Not only were special angry town meetings called, not only did legislatures pass resolutions of protest, and not only did denunciations thunder from the colonial newspapers, but violence first made its appearance on the scene. In every port men who accepted appointment as stamp agents ran into illegal punishment. Mobs broke windows in their homes with showers of stones and tarred and feathered the unlucky ones. In some places they took the hated stamps out of storage places and made bonfires of them. A flash fire of rebellion seared the world of ordinarily loyal "North American Britons." The uproar was so great, in fact, and so uniformly spread through all segments of colonial society that Parliament, in 1766, agreed to repeal the law. But to please those who did not

*Stormy passions, mob violence, and resistance like that pictured here made the Stamp Act unenforceable in the colonies, and spelled out a warning of crisis that England ignored.*

believe in backing down before "mob law," a declaratory act was simultaneously passed, asserting Parliament's flat right to "bind the colonies in all cases whatsoever." There matters stood, temporarily, in 1766.

Meanwhile, in 1763 another important step in imperial reorganization had been taken—the promulgation of the Proclamation Line. Soon after the conclusion of hostilities with the French in the Ohio valley, British planners were jolted by new fighting in the colonial West. The agent of this shock was an Indian chief, Pontiac. He briefly united the western tribes, laid siege to Detroit, and was finally overcome only after a bitter struggle. Pontiac's rebellion speeded up a policy already in formation in London—to stabilize the western frontier, calm the Indians, and work out an intelligent future policy for the fur trade. This would temporarily, at least, mean keeping frontiersmen away from Indian lands. So a royal proclamation barred any settlement west of a line drawn down the spine of the Alleghenies until further notice.

The trouble with this policy was that the West had already become, for the people living in British North America, the future. To cut them off from the future was to cut them off from hope, and they had already learned to live through today's troubles by drinking deep from the cup of tomorrow's expectations. Every small farmer in the colonial back country dreamed of striking out for new, rich, productive lands. And large landowners, too, especially in the south, had already formed organizations to buy huge new tracts beyond the mountains. Some day, they expected, they would reap the profits of selling these acres, on which towns and homes would rise, to a tidal wave of settlers. In that way they would wipe out debts to London merchants, which money from tobacco sales never seemed to cover.

So the Proclamation Line, like the Sugar and Stamp Acts, tended to unite various classes and groups in the colonies in hostility to mother England, not merely for what it did but for the threat it contained. The future seemed at stake. The purpose of both bills was to make money, to raise revenues in the colonies. But this was something that had been done, for years, strictly by the colonial assemblies. They alone had set taxes. The colonists had come to think that they alone had the right to do so. Now Britain was denying that claim.

Where would it end? Was Britain ready to overthrow America's town meetings and colonial assemblies and substitute control from the top? There were alarming signs this might be so. The Currency Act of 1764 strictly forbade the assemblies to meet financial emergencies by issuing paper money. Plans were afoot for a standing army of British regulars in the colonies. There was talk of sending a bishop of the Church of England to exert royal authority in godly matters, a horrifying idea to the non-Anglicans who so far had been left alone and not hedged in by legal restrictions, fines, and penalties (or forced to pay for Anglicanism) like dissenters in the home country.

In short, were the British about to abandon their live-and-let-live colonial policy? Modern historians suggest that the answer was actually yes. Great Britain was moving steadily toward the modern age. Cabinet ministers, over considerable resistance from George III, were becoming answerable to Parliament, rather than to the king. There was a growing number of bureaus and red tape. The monarch himself spent more time at a desk, reading reports and minutes, than in the saddle reviewing troops or at sport. The empire, suddenly, was no longer a collection of piecemeal scraps of territory. What ministers like Grenville vaguely had in mind for it was long-range planning and coordination from the top. Eventually, there might have been a modern setup, with various policies for taxation, defense, migration, Indian control, trade, and religion. Each would be the responsibility of a set of permanent officials, reporting to a cabinet minister, who in turn reported to a prime minister, who defended the whole scheme of things in Parliament.

But such a drift would have destroyed the self-rule that the colonists had developed under the sloppy old system of "salutary neglect," as Edmund Burke (a parliamentary friend of the colonial position) called it. The colonists were defending decentralization, the "time-tested" way, against the new trend toward bureaucratic centralism.

In this version of the revolutionary story, then, the villain—if there must be a villain—is modernity. The unwitting agents of this force are two groups: the ministers who sought to update imperial administrative machinery and the crusty conservatives in Britain who insisted that the changes be forced on the colonists to teach them to respect law and order. Both groups were challenged by a very practical group of Britons who were also modern in outlook, the businessmen involved in trade with America. They called for a soft line, because the colonists' uproarious resistance, expressed often through boycotts, was ruining that trade. The British merchants were willing to sacrifice a little efficiency or a little principle for the sake of profit.

If the focus of the story was to remain here, then, the center of study would be in London. The background would require attention to significant internal changes in the British government. The key figures would be chosen from among those closely involved with these changes. The moment of inevitability would be when there was no turning back on the road to modern bureaucracy. And the American episode would be part of a larger story of changing patterns of government.

### *An "Exploding" Colonial Society?*

But let us look at it another way, by proceeding onward in time, from 1767 through 1773. After the repeal of the Stamp Act, a new British finance minister, Charles Townshend, tried to find a less objectionable way to raise revenues from the thriving North American settlements. In the Stamp Act battle most colonial leaders had said that they would willingly continue to accept import duties. These were part of the king's right to control trade. What they did not like about the Stamp Act was its exclusive motive of fund raising. So Townshend decided to levy new taxes on imports of paint, lead, glass, paper, tea, and other goods heavily imported from Great Britain. These could be defended as a mere extension of the Navigation Acts, which the colonists had not openly challenged. Presumably, this approach would work.

It did not. The main tide of resistance kept rising for several reasons. One was that the colonists resented any additional burdens on their growing commerce. Another was anger over the core purpose of the Townshend taxes. Like the Sugar Act, they did not merely regulate trade, but they raised revenue. In the continuing colonial protest, several different elements of colonial society stood out.

The merchants struck back with boycotts. In most towns they signed agreements to refuse British-made articles until justice was done through repeal of the taxes. Backing these measures was the willingness of customers to do without imports. But there was coercion, too. Americans who tried to buy British goods in defiance of popular sentiment were themselves boycotted, beaten, or worse. By 1770 the freeze-out was hurting the British economy badly.

Politically, the main weight of protest was carried by the colonial assemblies through resolutions of censure. Among the drafters of such statements were lawyers like Virginia's Patrick Henry, Boston's James Otis, or Pennsylvania's John Dickinson. Many of them wrote pamphlets—sometimes fiery, sometimes coolly reasoned—but all adding up to a set of propositions that all colonial opponents of British measures could agree on.

They held that all Englishmen, on both sides of the Atlantic, had the right to be taxed only by representative bodies of their own choosing. Parliament might represent the people of England, but not the "Americans," whose lawful taxing bodies were their own assemblies. They sent no delegates to the House of Commons. The shorthand version of the argument was "no taxation without representation." It carried an emotional punch only eighty years after the English had finally won a long battle to curb absolute kings. Colonial subjects knew their history and took it seriously. They believed that the freedoms won for all English subjects between 1642 and 1688 were worth battling for.

Another group that carried on the work of dissent in 1768 and after was the small band of colonial newspaper owner-editors. There was only a handful of four-page weeklies, concentrated in the few major towns, but they were giants in mobilizing opinion. Almost all the editors objected to the British policies and prominently featured the pamphlets and letters of the resisters. They also printed news of debates, proceedings, and acts of resistance organized in the colonial meeting houses. They informed readers of boycotts and gave the names of those businessmen who would not go along and needed "persuasion." They printed the notices of meeting times and places of organizations such as the Sons of Liberty, the name given to clubs of opponents of the new British policy that sprang up in Boston, New York, and elsewhere. They publicized the sermons of those clergymen who told the colonists that God embraced their side of the quarrel. In short, they provided an indispensable element in the struggle. They brought various protesting groups together and gave them a propagandistic voice.

The leading figures of trade, politics, and opinion making clamored so successfully and boycotted so effectively that, in April 1770, all the Townshend taxes were repealed, except for that on tea, which was kept to assert Britain's right to tax. But before then, there was a famous and significant episode that introduced another set of characters into the story.

Riots and disturbances had made life so hectic for royal officials and sympathizers in Boston that troops were sent to maintain calm in 1768. These British regulars, especially when off duty, brawled with the nonpropertied, "ordinary" population of Boston—the sailors, wagon drivers, cooks, waiters, dock workers, and apprentices and helpers to blacksmiths, butchers, bakers, tailors, and other craftsmen—who were the nearest thing to a colonial urban working class.

On March 5, 1770, one of these affairs got out of control. A group of soldiers was surrounded by an angry crowd. (At least one of the Britons, Private Kilroy, had only recently been in a fight. He had been asking around for a spare-time job to make a little money, and one of the local wits had invited him to clean out his outhouse!) Snowballs were thrown; then rocks. The British commander feared a general attack. In the confused situation, some of his men thought they had orders to fire. Musket blasts shattered the air. When the smoke lifted, five men—one of them, Crispus Attucks, a mulatto who may have been part Indian—lay dead or dying. America had her first "martyrs," one of them nonwhite. Later, the soldiers were tried and acquitted of premeditated murder. But the Boston "Massacre" remained as an issue to be exploited by the anti-British side, who were beginning to call themselves the Patriots.

In 1773 a new British prime minister, Lord North, emerged with a fresh plan. The huge East India Company was in trouble. Its warehouses were crammed with unsold tea imported from India. A bill was passed providing that the company might export that tea to the colonies to sell directly to customers through its own agents. London would refund the import duty that the company had already paid. Thanks to this giveaway, the company could cut the price below that of any competing tea, even after adding the Townshend tea tax, still on the books, to the cost. Once more, a happy solution seemed in reach. The colonists would get cheap tea. The Townshend tax would be paid.

The East India Company would make money and be saved. No one, it seemed, would be a loser.

But by that time, even the bribe of lower tea prices did not mollifty the colonists. What was more, the plan of selling the tea through company stores was full of paralyzing implications. Suppose London chose, every time a British trading company was in trouble, to give it a monopoly of the American market by tax and other advantages? The colonial business class might be wiped out entirely and replaced by a crowd of favorites and flatterers of the ruling circles in London.

Drastic action was demanded and taken. Resistance leaders warned that the odious tea would never be allowed to land. And in Boston, on the night of December 16, 1773, a band of Sons of Liberty, only lightly disguised as "Mohock" Indians, marched boldly down to the wharves where three ship-loads of East India tea lay. They broke open the holds and dumped every chest into the harbor. The Boston Tea Party ended 1773 on a note of militant, radical lawbreaking in the name of justice.

Now let us return to the interpretation—the making of a story. If we examine these events in detail, new angles come to light. By concentrating on the story after 1766, the focus shifts from London to the colonies and the growing mood of anger there. The short-term protest over the Stamp Act was growing into a lasting feeling of dissatisfaction with the entire arrangement of the empire. Though no one was saying so, the mood had changed from that of a happy household with an occasional domestic quarrel to a sullen one in which the idea of divorce was taking root. The characters whom a historian would select as "leads" in this story would be those who sustained and developed this new feeling. They would be members of the special-interest groups that led the attack on Britain.

Which ones? That depends, of course, on what part of the record is examined. If the smuggling and boycotting activities of the merchants are in the foreground, then the chief actors become persons like John Hancock of Boston: importer, Son of Liberty, member of the Massachusetts legislature, and (eventually) signer of the Declaration of Independence and governor of Massachusetts. If the story is told through the eyes of Hancock and those like him, then a strongly economic flavor seasons it. Sometimes it may seem that the Revolution had little to do with the love of liberty and much to do with the love of lucre, with protecting the profits of land speculation and smuggling.

But if we look at the legislators, pamphleteers, editors, and lawyers, and their doings, a new configuration appears. How do we explain the motives of a Patrick Henry, a Thomas Jefferson, a Sam Adams, an Isaiah Thomas (editor of the hotly anti-British *Massachusetts Spy*), or any one of 40 or 50 men, some now well known, some forgotten, who emerged as the voices of a colonial opposition? The answer will, of course, vary from individual to individual. A firm believer in the theory that all political behavior is economic at root would simply say that they spoke for the classes they served—that a Patrick Henry was simply a voice for Virginia landowners or a Sam Adams was a mouthpiece for the likes of Hancock.

But such a theory overlooks bitter quarrels between some radical leaders and their backers. Nor does it explain why other budding colonial politicians chose to take the king's side in the contest. Individual biography seems to hold the key to some cases. A well-known study of Sam Adams, for instance, concludes that he was a failure in business, law, and politics who somehow found his element in organizing rebels and publicizing their demands. In other words, he was a great propagandist because he could infuse others with his own inborn hostility to authority. Such an emphasis on personality will be made by a historian who believes that a person's psychological make-up and inner drives, rather than cold reason, propel him to particular actions.

Another interpretive possibility is that the lawyers, pamphleteers, and politicians were a class by themselves, learning to speak for the needs of a growing society. Despite occasional depressions, the colonies were plainly booming. Towns rose, lands changed hands, population grew, and it all meant more business for everyone. Those who could raise funds, negotiate deals, control votes in the assemblies, or provide public arguments to justify growth—those were the people of the future. They pleaded the cause of the American future, even though they looked to British history to make their case. It has been pointed out that most of the Patriot leaders (with some exceptions, like Franklin) were young men. Some historians declare that the movement toward freedom was really an outburst against tradition by the up and coming and the youthful.

But that theory seems to run counter to a traditional interpretation that says the revolutionaries were essentially property-loving conservatives, fearful of social upheaval, and only using popular discontent to lever themselves loose from British control. And that view, in turn, is challenged by another group of historians who argue powerfully that ordinary, propertyless people took a strong interest in the movement for freedom. Modern researchers are looking for materials (such as popular ballads) that give them some clue to the feelings of "commoners" who did not write letters or make speeches. Their look at history "from the underside" suggests that those at the bottom of the social heap endorsed any change that might open up new opportunities for them. They might regard Hancock as a snob and a would-be aristocrat, but they sensed that the pro-Royalist governors and officials were even more hostile to social change than local citizens of wealth and standing. They also were injured when British regulations hurt business or raised the prices of sugar, tea, and calico or kept a person from heading westward for a new chance. So the Bostonian mob reacted to the redcoats as some people today react to police. They saw in them the keepers of an "order" that always seemed to work against people at the bottom.

Whichever group gets the spotlight, then, in this phase of events from 1765 to 1773, the story is one of how different classes came to feel grievances. If modernity is the key to early developments in London, then group self-interest is the unifying force that explains the rise of colonial opposition. Once more, the angle of vision is determined by the time slice studied, and that angle sets the priorities of subject matter and chooses the cast of characters.

*An Emerging American Nationality?*

The final phase was crowded and dramatic. The British responded to the Boston Tea Party with a set of measures designed to punish unruly Massachusetts. These so-called Coercive or Intolerable Acts suspended the functioning of the Massachusetts legislature and some of its courts, closed the port of Boston (until the tea was paid for), and quartered fresh troops in the city. From the British point of view, this was reasonable. If Massachusetts' authorities could not keep order, they would be removed from their jobs until they could. And since the merchants of Boston had stirred up the trouble, they could raise the funds to pay for the property destroyed.

But the scene was set in a different light for Americans. As the colonists saw it, the British had put a sister province under martial law, stripped her citizens of self-government and basic rights, and aimed to starve the people of her major town—all for objecting to a basically unjust law. The colonies were at last sparked into united action. A new and much stiffer boycott began. Other provinces and towns sent food and supplies into Boston. Committees of correspondence formed in all the colonies, coordinated these actions, and reported on their progress. They formed a live network of resistance, humming with messages of encouragement, strategy, and support. A Continental Congress of delegates from every colony was called to meet in Philadelphia. And militia units, especially in Massachusetts, drilled and readied their weapons. Debate became shrill between the Patriots and the Tories (or Loyalists, as they preferred to be called), who still supported the British viewpoint.

In the spring of 1775 events exploded. British troops in Boston marched out, in April 1775, to seize some arms being stockpiled by the local militiamen in the little neighboring village of Concord. At the town of Lexington fighting broke out when the "minutemen" exchanged shots with the redcoats, who were driven back into Boston, with heavy losses, by the locals. A second Continental Congress, meeting in May, issued a "Declaration of the Causes and Necessity of

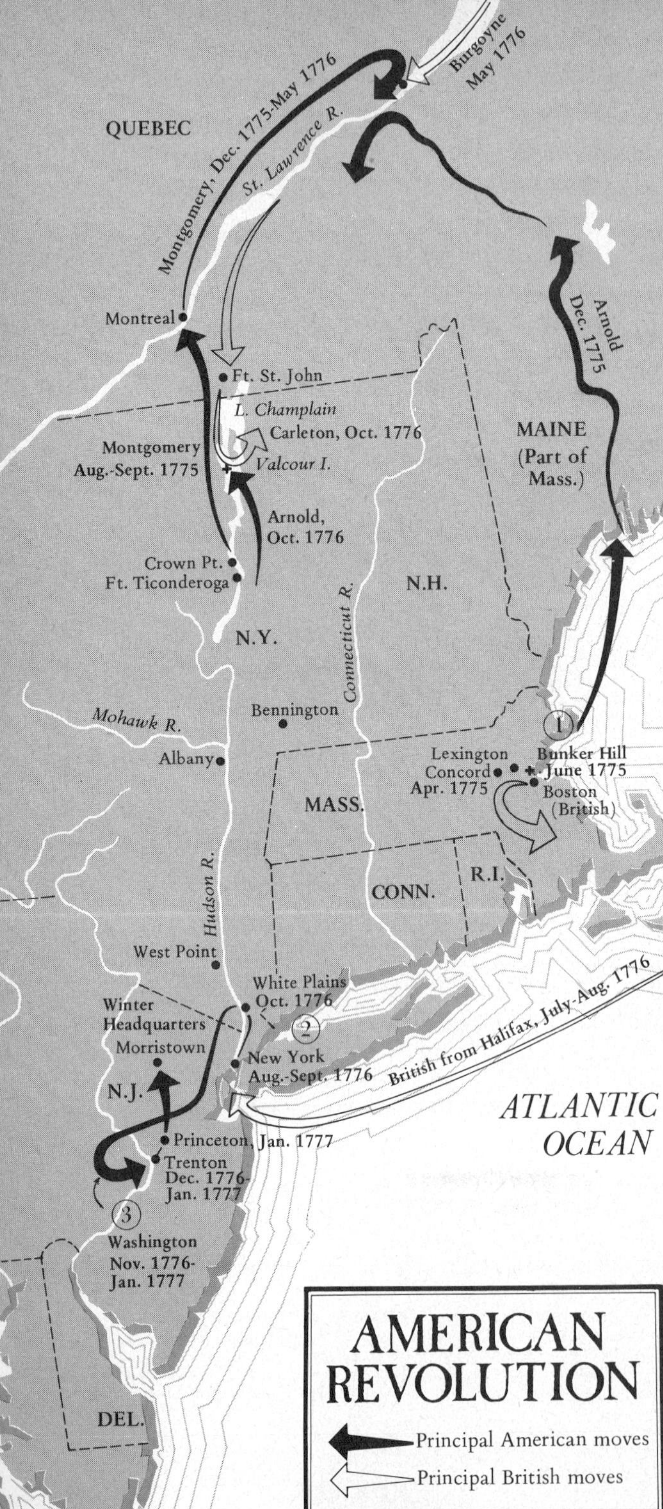


*The fighting began well for the Americans. After the opening skirmishes at Lexington and Concord in April of 1775, they captured Fort Ticonderoga which opened the road to invade Canada. In June the British assaulted the American positions next to Bunker Hill (1), and though the redcoats dislodged their enemy, they took such huge losses that the battle was in fact a Yankee victory. British General Thomas Gage's troops were bottled up in Boston and, in March of 1776, were forced to abandon the city by sea. Then the tide turned dramatically in favor of the British. Already a two-pronged American assault on Quebec, December 31, 1775, had been disastrously rebuffed. In June of 1776, General Sir William Howe sailed southward from Canada to New York. Howe drove Washington's defending army out of New York (2) between August and September, and in the next two months inflicted two more heavy defeats on him at White Plains and Fort Lee. In early December the American chief, taking heavy losses from desertion and sickness, retreated across New Jersey to defend Philadelphia. The only bright spot at this time for the Americans was provided when General Benedict Arnold turned back a British thrust southward along Lake Champlain at the battle of Valcour Island in October of 1776. This, however, was still not enough to offset pessimism about Washington's chances of survival. American troop morale was low when, between Christmas Eve, 1776 and January 3, 1777, the Virginian struck back brilliantly. At Trenton (3) he surprised and captured a force of Hessians (paid German soldiers fighting on the British side), then mauled a British force at Princeton. He then took winter quarters at Morristown while the British did the same at New York.*

*The start of 1777 found the United States having declared herself independent, but with an army outnumbered, underequipped, and facing strong British forces in control of the seas. The next two years, however, would turn the tide and prove that the British, masters of the seacoast, could not destroy the revolution in the interior.*

# AMERICAN REVOLUTION

# 1775-1777

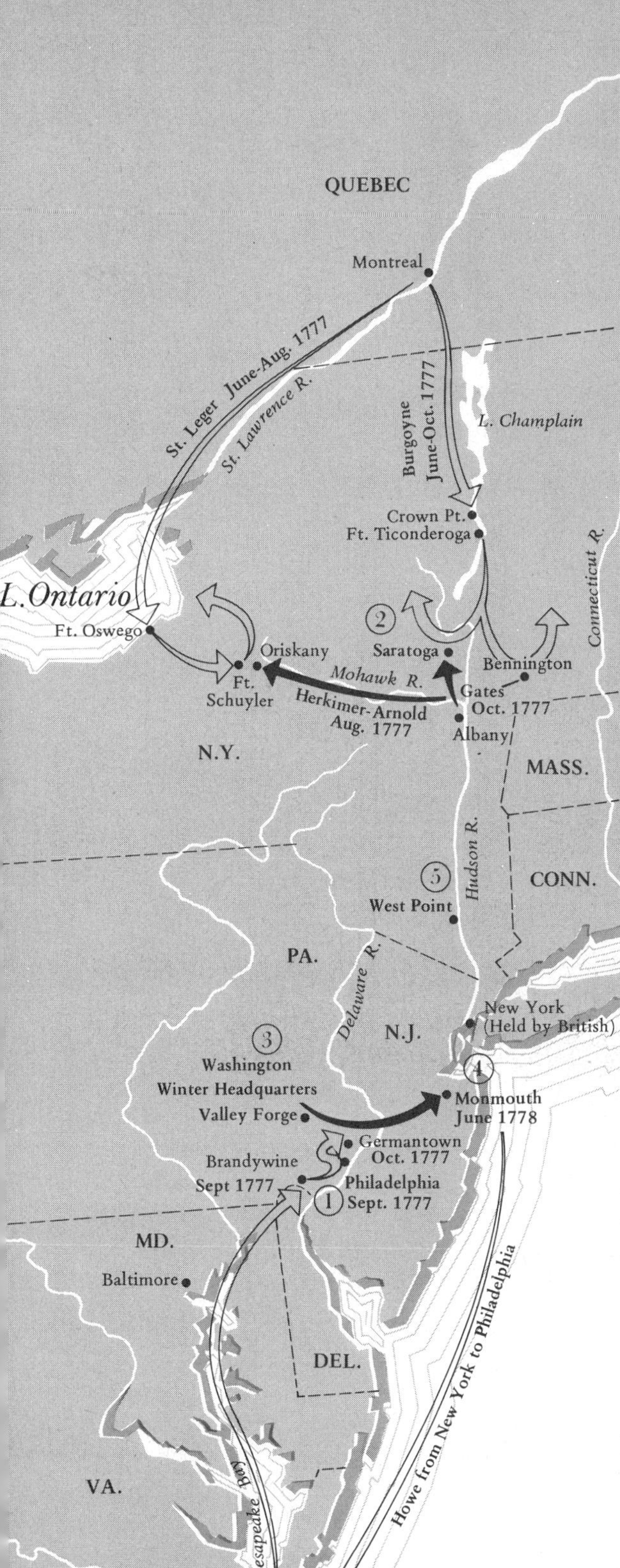


*In late spring, 1777, General Howe took his army by sea from New York to the Chesapeake Bay and began an easy march on Philadelphia (1), which fell as summer ended. But Howe's self-congratulation was misplaced. He had actually wrecked a master plan devised by the British to end the war in 1777. Under it, General John Burgoyne would lead a force from Canada to Albany. Howe would meet him in Albany, where both armies would be joined by a third force, under Colonel Barry St. Leger. Rebellious New England would be cut off and, with that amputation, the revolt would crumple. But instead, Burgoyne was left in the lurch. His troops were hit hard and constantly by New England militia, and Howe, who should have been diverting such attacks by a move on Albany, was not there. Moreover, in August St. Leger's column was turned back by General Nicholas Herkimer at Oriskany. By September 26, when Howe was triumphantly in Philadelphia, Burgoyne, alone and under murderous pressure from Arnold and Horatio Gates, was in deep trouble. On October 17 he surrendered his entire army at Saratoga (2). This feat of American arms won over the French, who recognized the United States and allied themselves with her in 1778 (later to be joined by Spain and Holland). With French expertise, money, supplies, and seapower available, the Americans faced a much brighter future, but it did not dawn immediately. During the winter of 1777–1778 Washington's army suffered bitterly from shortages at their encampment in Valley Forge (3). But their morale held and their training improved. In June of 1778 they met the British, who had come out of Philadelphia, at Monmouth (4) and held their own in a drawn battle. Washington then moved to a base at West Point (5) where he could keep an eye on the British in New York. In the summer of 1778 and spring of 1779, George Rogers Clark drove the British out of posts in Kaskaskia and Vincennes (in the future states of Illinois and Indiana) winning the "west" for the colonials. Four years into the war, the rebellion was healthier than ever, and the British still frustrated.*

# 1777-1778

*Having failed to subdue the northern ex-colonies, the British decided to try a conquest of the South. They had controlled Georgia since the end of 1778, and in the spring of 1780 the new top commander of the British, General Sir Henry Clinton, sent Lord George Cornwallis, with a force of several thousand, to conquer the Carolinas. Cornwallis easily captured Charleston in May and decisively beat the Americans under Horatio Gates at Camden in August. Gates was succeeded by General Nathaniel Greene, who described his strategy thereafter in these terms: "We fight, get beat, rise, and fight again." Even victories like that of the British at Cowpens ① in 1781 did not guarantee firm control. In March of 1781, after a drawn fight at Guilford Court House, Cornwallis withdrew to the coast at Wilmington to rest. Refit, he then swung up into Virginia. Because Greene continued to plague remaining British forces in the Carolinas, Cornwallis pushed aside American defenders under Lafayette, captured Charolottesville (almost bagging Thomas Jefferson), but then marched down to Williamsburg in July to get help by sea. This proved to be a fatal mistake. Unknown to Cornwallis, a French fleet from the West Indies had defeated a British force sent from New York in September, so for the moment, the British did not control the seas. Learning of this, Washington took his army and a French force of 6,000 under Count Rochambeau and pushed them by land and water to Yorktown ②. There, Cornwallis—his back to the ocean controlled by the French, a river on either side, and confronted by 16,000 Americans and French against his own 7,000—was caught. On October 19 he surrendered. With that, the British government gave up its efforts to win the war. A treaty was negotiated in 1782 and signed the next year. The Revolutionary War—an American victory—was over.*

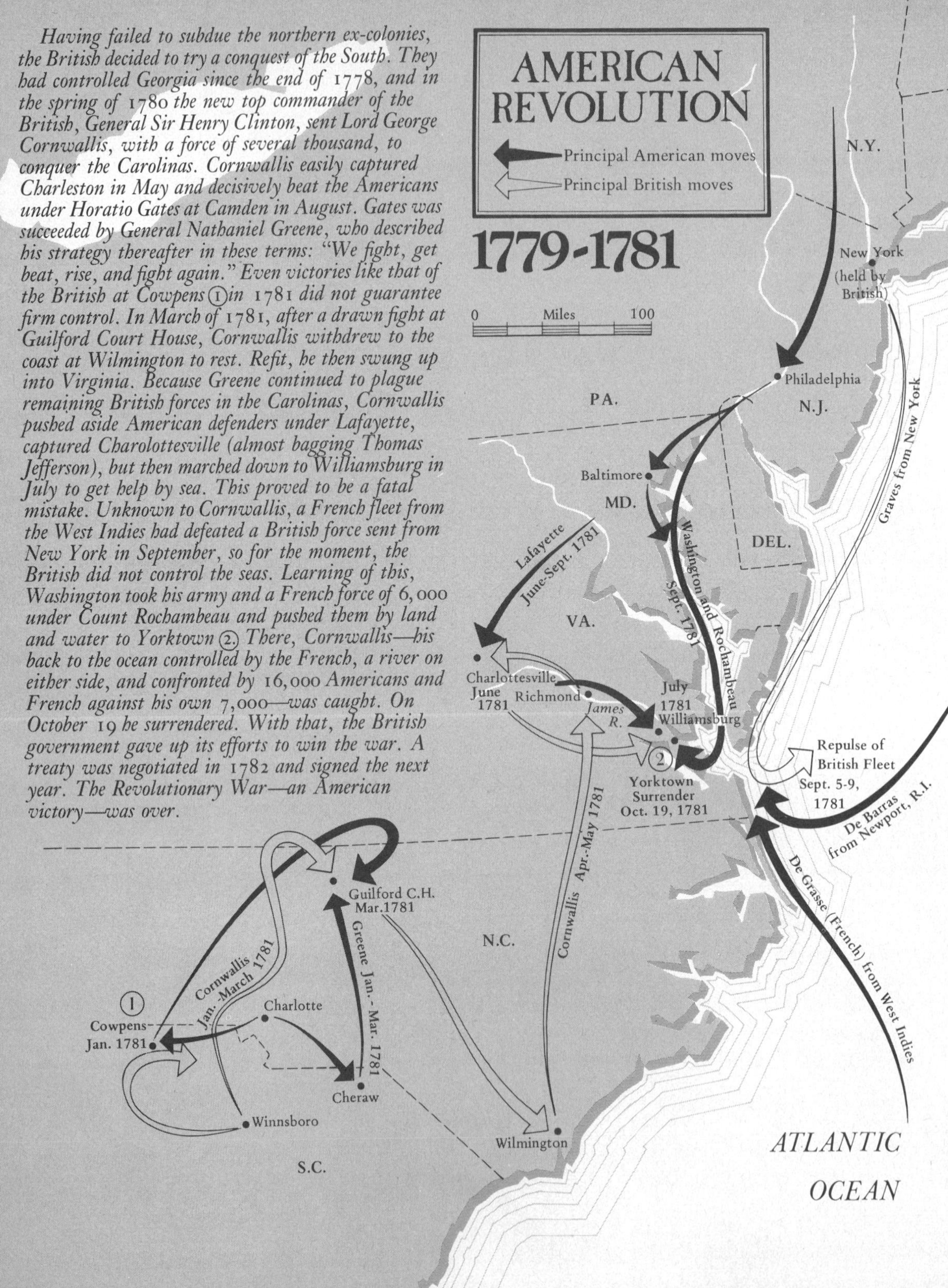

Taking up Arms" and prepared for a long war. The British prepared to send a fleet and army to subdue the American rebels. In an opening year of battle the Americans seemed to hold their ground, and by mid-1776, although the darkest days were still ahead for them, they were neither beaten nor ready to compromise.

What mattered between June 1775 and July 1776, however, was not so much how the fighting went as the mere fact of fighting itself. Each month, it became less and less possible for the Americans to pretend that they were true and faithful subjects only seeking fair treatment from a beloved monarch. They could not shift all the blame to Parliament. The king was authorizing the dispatch of troops to quell them. So the king had to become the enemy, and, as a result, the idea of monarchy itself became the enemy.

The steps down this road were slow but certain. Those Americans who simply could not face confrontation with their "lawful" sovereign dropped out of the argument early, to become Tories. Those remaining in support of what was now openly referred to as the "American" cause still debated, through early 1776, whether they wanted independence or only some special status within the British empire. The case for independence was given a boost in January 1776 by Tom Paine's potent pamphlet, *Common Sense*, which soon sold an astonishing 120,000 copies in a few months—the equivalent of a multimillion-copy best seller today. Paine, a recent immigrant from Britain, simply battered down all talk of loyalty with sentences as blunt as projectiles. The king, he said, was no loving royal parent but a "royal brute" whose title rested on the invasions and conquests of a "French bastard" (William of Normandy) five centuries earlier. Mankind had outgrown kings. And America, with a potential future as a continental nation had outgrown rule by a foreign island. The great reception given to *Common Sense* shows that Paine had said what many felt.

Those minds in the Continental Congress that were not changed by Paine were changed by military logic. If the war was to be won, it would be necessary to seek allies and loans. France stood in the wings, waiting to help—but not to help George III regain his lost empire, only to help him lose it. In June 1776 the motion to declare the colonies independent was made. On July 2 it was passed. The job of writing the Declaration of Independence was given to a committee, but it wound up being almost entirely written by Thomas Jefferson—lawyer, planter, scholar, and a man with high literary skill. The document he produced, formally approved on July 4, 1776, was more than an argument defending separation. It was a stirring assertion of the basic principles of freedom and self-government. The colonists had come around to making eternally valid arguments in defense of humanity's basic right to liberty. The local struggle of merchants and landowners against imperial policies had become important to the oppressed everywhere. It took another five years of war after 1776 to win

American independence. The job of building a society that lives up to the principles of the Declaration is still unfinished.

Clearly, the meaning of this final phase of events is best found by looking at it as the stage of final emergence of an American nationality. As the various colonies were drawn reluctantly into a joint struggle, they had no choice but to think of themselves as "Americans." And perhaps this feeling was most sensitively experienced, not by those who began their lives in the colonies with the notion that they were "Englishmen," but by the immigrants who had been flocking into the port cities and fanning out to the frontier for sixty or seventy years before 1775.

A fine central figure for the story of this last period could be Henry Muhlenberg (or Heinrich Mühlenberg). He was an immigrant preacher from Germany who founded the first Lutheran synod in the United States. The approach of war filled him with anxiety. .He had no desire to be caught up in a quarrel that would pit him against authority, any authority. But his sons, Peter and Frederick, saw things through "American" eyes. Both were clergymen, too, but deeply involved in the world of daily affairs. Peter literally threw off his clerical robes as he finished a sermon in 1775 on the moral duty of resistance, to reveal an American army uniform. He became a major general. Later, he was elected to Congress. So was his brother Frederick, who became Speaker of the House of Representatives and gave the oath of office to George Washington at his inauguration. There was actually an entire Muhlenberg political dynasty in Pennsylvania for years after the Revolution.

The key figure of an account that stresses the birth of a feeling of "Americanness," then, might be an immigrant such as Paine or the son of an immigrant like Muhlenberg. Or it might be anyone who, like Jefferson, at first thought of himself as a citizen of "British America" and then lived to see the "British" label disappear from his countrymen's minds. Or a historian might create an interesting and dramatic subject by studying someone who began as a defender of the colonists' cause but who in the end became a reluctant Tory because he or she could not go all the way to independence and chose instead tradition, habit, and loyalty to the established order. There were many such people.

So, in various ways, the story of the past can be shaped to illustrate various ideas. In this chapter we have suggested how some questions about the Revolution have been or might be answered, questions of why and how resistance was born and became rebellion. After the war new questions arose—of what had actually been changed and to whose benefit. Historians try to answer those questions in various ways, and one logical point of departure is in a study of the document that tried to sum up and make permanent the results of the Revolution: the Constitution of the United States, which forms the subject of the next chapter.

## *FOR FURTHER READING*

Overall histories of the movement towards revolution are a good starting point. A brief survey is Edmund Morgan, *The Birth of the Republic* (1956). A more detailed look can be found in John C. Miller, *Origins of the American Revolution* (1943)—old but still useful. For a military overview, John Alden, *The American Revolution* (1954) does well.

There are two fine studies, both by Arthur M. Schlesinger, of the part played by particular groups in bringing on the revolution. A very old but classic work of his is *The Colonial Merchants and the American Revolution* (1918). Forty-one years later, showing that he had not lost his literary touch, Schlesinger (now deceased) published *Prelude to Independence: The Newspaper War on Britain* (1958), which deals with the role of colonial editors.

Two "heavy," old, but very important looks at the English side of the story are Lewis H. Namier, *England in the Age of the American Revolution* (1930) and Lawrence H. Gipson, *The British Empire Before the American Revolution,* published in several volumes between 1936 and 1968. You will find it an important reference work.

Biographies, as always, are great keys to understanding a period. A random sample would include *John Adams* by Page Smith (1962), which is solid but possibly less readable than Catherine Drinker Bowen's *John Adams and the American Revolution* (1957). Robert D. Meade, *Patrick Henry* (1969) illustrates the life and times of a southern patriot. The loyalists are often overlooked; an impressive study of an American who chose allegiance to the crown is Bernard Bailyn, *The Ordeal of Thomas Hutchinson* (1974). You should not miss Esther Forbes' *Paul Revere and the World He Lived In.* The standard recent life of Washington consists of four volumes by James T. Flexner (1965, 1968, 1970, 1972) and provides deep background on the entire Revolution.

# chapter 5 Getting together: the Constitution

Suppose that, in 1787, an official of a foreign bank had been asked to draft a report on whether the brand new United States was a good credit risk. His views would likely have been mixed. True, the young nation had managed a successful war of liberation against its colonial mistress, though only with the major help of France, a great power. And in the peace treaty it had received a huge and valuable territory. It had 890,000 of acres of virgin soil, timber, and other natural resources. It was bounded by a great river, by huge inland lakes, and a long ocean coastline with plenty of commercial and fishing harbors. A population of 4 million energetic people should prove well able to make good economic use of such gifts.

But, on the other hand, the newcomer to the world community was underdeveloped to say the least. And it had potentially damaging political problems. Most of its area was still wilderness claimed by hard-fighting aboriginal tribes. It had no transportation system worth the name. Nor did it have any business leaders with industrial experience and investment capital; so it was not likely that those fine natural resources would be turned into profitable manufactures in any reasonable time. Besides, the U.S. population was poor raw material for working smoothly together. It included one-half million black slaves, mostly unskilled and potentially rebellious. Of the whites, perhaps one in six was foreign-born. The original English stock was mingled with Germans, Scots, Irish, French, and Dutch, and there were Protestants, Catholics, and Jews, groups whose ancestors had been at each other throats for generations.

Nothing held this mass of people together—no state church or established aristocracy to which all citizens looked for leadership in beliefs, manners, customs. The political system was unfocused, too. There was no true national government. There was no uniform currency system, no standard trade regulations from state to state, nothing to give businessmen a sense that they could confidently make long-range plans. There was no army or navy to speak of, to back U.S. diplomacy. It seemed clear that the chances for the new nation's falling apart were better than even.

So the report might have run. Perhaps, it might have concluded, the United States could get financial help and protection from another power. Then, of course, the country would be a puppet. The United States of America was only dubiously ready for nationhood, and it was a poor banker's risk.

### *The Problem of Conflicting Goals*

That is how a specialist in "North American affairs," looking on from Europe in the 1780s, might have seen the United States under the Articles of Confederation. Actually, the leaders of the young association of ex-colonies were facing a problem that would later challenge other successful revolutionaries: how to give an effective form to the forces of liberty and nationalism. How could they perpetuate and strengthen the machinery that had been developed, under crisis conditions, to act for a people scattered from Massachusetts to Georgia, while holding common goals and dreams of freedom from outside control?

The problem was that the basic ideas of the American Revolution were sometimes in conflict with each other. For instance, the war had been a struggle to become a new nation-state, a unified, separate political community taking its place among the powers of the earth. But the actual fighting had involved 13 separate colonies, almost 13 separate societies, each with its sense of being a special, one-of-a-kind community. The Patriot pamphleteers of the 1760s and 1770s had talked about the *assemblies* (plural!) as being the equals of Parliament; of the colonial *charters* (multiple!) as giving them special privileges. The creation of a single national American state after 1781 was bound to chip away at some of these separate rights. So there was a root question: At what point did steps taken to create a free America, one land, undercut the principles of that other revolution that had announced the rights of separate colonies to be rid of central authority?

Nor was this quite all. There was another issue. The 13 colonies had been demanding the rights of self-government. But the very idea of *government* carries with it the notion of authority, order, command, and execution. Government is the tax collector, the constable on his beat, the soldier on guard, the judge on the bench, the schoolmaster behind his desk.

Yet the Revolution had also invoked the idea of *liberty*, of individuals as well as communities. And liberty is, in many ways, a concept that thrives on the basis of an understanding about what government must *not* do: seize property without compensation, tax unfairly, muzzle dissent, coerce belief, and imprison without just cause, to name only a few. The revolutionary leaders were wary of government. Like fire, they thought it made a good servant and a bad master. Even governments chosen freely by the people had to be watched, and leashed if necessary. If not, they could be as tyrannical (in the name of the majority) as those governments that claimed to draw their power from God or any other source except the people.

The problem was to make the several meanings of the Revolution march in step—to team liberty and authority, unity and diversity comfortably together. It was not easy, because supporters for many viewpoints had strong feelings and good arguments on their sides. Supporters of states' rights, American union, popular democracy, and respect for law and property could all claim, to some extent, that their principles were the basic ones behind the "Spirit of '76."

## *The Practical Problems*

All might well have agreed on one thing in 1787. To paraphrase the poet William B. Yeats, things were falling apart. The center could not hold. The government of the United States was virtually powerless. The charter of the nation, the Articles of Confederation, had been drafted after a halting march toward collaboration that began with the Stamp Act Congress. That was only a temporary body to deal with the immediate crisis. So was the First Continental Congress, which met in 1774, to strike back at the Intolerable Acts. Its main accomplishment was to lay plans for an "association" of the colonies to boycott British goods. The delegates went home in October and set a meeting date for a

---

*CHRONOLOGY*

| | |
|---|---|
| 1781 | *Articles of Confederation* |
| 1786 | *Shays' Rebellion* |
| 1787 | *Constitutional Convention, Philadelphia* |
| 1787–1788 | *State conventions for ratifying the Constitution held* |
| 1791 | *Bill of Rights (first ten amendments to Constitution)* |

Second Continental Congress for May 1775. By then, fighting had begun, and this gathering became the Continental Congress that managed the war effort. But in May 1775 there was still no "country" to govern. Not until the following summer did the colonies declare independence. For more than five years after that, the Congress had to tackle problems concerning diplomacy, Indian policy, finance, and western lands without any clear authority to act as a government of all the states.

The "states" themselves, meanwhile were changing over from "colonies." They were electing new legislatures, drawing up constitutions in some cases, and performing such routine tasks as collecting taxes, mending roads, and naming judges and other public officials. They were also coping with war-related matters such as punishing Tories or outfitting state militiamen. They were often doing these things without the benefit of experienced proroyal officials, who had fled. All in all, they were tasting real independence and were naturally slow to give it up to any new central government.

Hence plans for a permanent union lagged. Proposals were made in 1777, but the consent of all the states was not secured until 1781. That was not entirely surprising. Each state had interests to protect. The smaller states, in particular, feared that in a new union they would be dominated by larger neighbors. A symbolic roadblock was the question of western lands. Some states claimed boundaries under old colonial charters, running all the way to the Mississippi. Others had no such claims, but argued that the western territories ought to be shared equally among the partners in the war for independence, who were sharing equal pains and risks. In the end, union was only made possible when the states with western claims gave them up. States whose prosperity rested on seagoing trade wanted no part of a government that could tax and control them as the British had done. States dominated by large landholders feared a strong government that would put most of the tax burden on them. These were natural anxieties of ex-colonists, breaking the chains of past authority.

The Articles of Confederation, adopted in 1781, therefore were clearly anticentral. Each state kept its "sovereignty, freedom and independence." The "United States" was a name only for a "firm league of friendship," not a nation. Each state got one vote. Nine votes were needed for any joint action. And responsibility for any such action was not delegated to any one executive but to a steering committee of delegates from all the states. That committee's chairman, though titled "President," had no special authority. The states alone could tax, and the confederation government could only "requisition" funds. This was also true for troops; militia would be "lent" to the confederation by the states, but each state would keep control of its own armed forces, thus ensuring that it could resist tyranny, whether imposed either from abroad or home.

That was a victory for the principle of local self-rule. But since the states hung back in supplying both funds and troops, the government under the Articles had no military power whatever. One immediate result showed itself in the West. The British kept possession of a number of forts near the Canadian border that were clearly in American territory. From there they dominated the fur trade and hurt American pride. Spain, which in the 1780s owned New Orleans, refused to let American shipments of grain, pork, or whiskey pass through. There was a sense that the American future was in the West, but that future was now being shaped, for the worse, by decisions made in London and Madrid.

There was yet another problem. The currency of the new government was worthless. Its debts to foreign powers, to its own soldiers in the form of back pay, and to those Americans who had lent it money seemed unlikely ever to be paid. American exporters were shut out of the trade with the British West Indies. British manufactured goods began to pour into the country, but Congress could not protect American home manufacturers, for it was forbidden, except by unanimous consent, to enact a tariff. In short, the new general government seemed unable to take care of its citizens in any sense that would win their loyalties. Governments are kept afloat, to some extent, by patriotism. But eventually there must be some concrete appeal to self-interest, to justify a freeman's allegiance to a flag. This was what "the United States" was not delivering.

### *The Rise of National Thinking*

In theory, the weakness of the confederation system did not matter too much. Most Americans of the revolutionary generation gave their deepest commitment to their states, anyway. The states were theoretically capable of giving the guarantees of life, liberty, and safety for which the Revolution had been fought. But if there was any lesson in the war itself, it was that the states separately could not deal with the British, the Spanish, the Indians, or the world's bankers and businessmen. Only a united front won things, on the battlefield and at the bargaining table.

Besides, even in managing their internal affairs, the states were doing poorly in economic matters. All of them had unpaid debts. They also had various groups of citizens hard-hit by a postwar slump in trade of every kind. To help the situation at least seven states tried large issues of paper currency. This led to a ruinous inflation. No one would accept the paper at face value, and prices climbed very high. Then a clamor arose either for forcing creditors to take the worthless paper or for "stay laws," which would give all debtors an automatic arbitrary grace period during which they would not have to pay. Such laws might sound charitable, but if states were going to prosper, those few who had money would have to invest it in farms, factories, ships, and business enterprises, which provide growth, jobs, sales, and tax revenues. But clearly, no investor would risk losing his shirt if he was going to be paid off in worthless paper or not at all.

Local independence seemed to be threatening economic stability and eventual growth. For that reason businessmen were loudest in criticizing the states, and the firmest defenders of states' rights were apt to be farmers and debtors instead of bondholders and merchants. This had led some historians to argue that the movement for a strengthened general government was mainly a creditors' drive to make a safer climate for the dollar. But that argument is not quite complete.

Those who wanted a business revival, sparked by a vigorous Union, were generally believers in a bigger America to be. Many were "continentalists," looking optimistically toward future growth in the West. It is not accidental that George Washington, a leading nationalist, was not merely an investor in western lands but also in canals that would improve communication with the interior wilderness. Others were excited by the promise of a United States that could be a worldwide trading power. They were thrilled by news like the voyage of the *Empress of China,* a small vessel that cleared New York, under American colors, in 1784, voyaged to far-off Canton, and returned in 1785 with a hold crammed full of precious silk and tea. Where might the American flag not go if there was a strong government to provide a diplomatic corps and a navy that could safeguard commerce?

The critics of the government under the Articles were believers in the future, and were wedded to the idea of progress through individual and group growth. They wanted a government with the reach and energy to foster that growth. Of course, their position may be debated now. In a sense they thought that what was good for business was automatically good for the future nation. And they were willing to trade some local liberty for a "promotional" government. But they believed that there would be a compensating gain in a growing economy that allowed each individual to make best use of his talents by doing well for himself in the world. Theirs was a new idea of community.

### *Energy and Unity Versus "Anarchy"*

Through the complaints of these progressives and nationalists ran a common theme. Rightly or wrongly, they deplored the lack of vitality and cohesion in the feeble United States. "I predict the worst consequences from a half-starved, limping government, always moving upon crutches and tottering at every step," Washington wrote a friend in the fall of 1786.

What upset him was an episode called Shays' Rebellion, in Massachusetts. A number of debt-ridden farmers, led by a Revolutionary War veteran, Daniel

*Alexander Hamilton was gifted, ambitious, successful, and feared. His strongly nationalistic and elitist conceptions deeply influenced the Constitution, though he took little part in the actual writing.*

Shays, forcibly prevented courts from meeting to foreclose mortgages on their properties. It was a very minor "revolution." Massachusetts militiamen chased Shays out of the state and reopened the courts. Shays himself was condemned to death in his absence, but later he was pardoned and lived peaceably for another third of a century. But the fact that Shays' Rebellion could happen at all convinced Washington that there was a dangerous lack of backbone in government everywhere in the country. "We are fast verging to anarchy and confusion," was his comment. In the general's view there could be no true liberty

*Benign-looking James Madison might well have spent his life as a teacher of political philosophy instead of a founding father to a nation born in revolution; but fate ruled otherwise. A brilliant thinker and good diplomat, he was a relatively ineffectual President, finding it easier to describe than to practice the arts of power.*

when there was no respect for lawful authority. But in the eyes of Shays' "rebels," a government that did not protect citizens against an economic squeeze was not providing true liberty. The argument remains alive today. In the 1780s it was carried on amid a sense of crisis, and nationalist-minded persons like Washington were the most disturbed by it and the most active in seeking a remedy.

Washington, James Madison, John Jay, Alexander Hamilton, and others like them took the lead, therefore, in a major effort to get Congress to strengthen its own powers. Their biggest opportunity came in 1786, when a meeting was held in Annapolis for Maryland and Virginia to discuss navigation on their common boundary, the Potomac River. This led to a recommendation for a general convention in Philadelphia the following May to "take into consideration the trade and commerce of the United States." Congress went further and authorized that gathering to consider "revising the Articles of Confederation." The 55 men sent to Philadelphia by their states went further still and wrote a totally new framework of government.

The delegates who wanted a complete replacement of the Articles can be called "youthful nationalists." Their average age was forty-three, and many were in their thirties, no more than ten or fifteen years older than today's college graduates. Yet they had packed a great deal of experience into their few years. Nearly four out of five had been in the Continental Congress; many had been state legislators as well. Seven had been state governors, and more than one in three had fought in the war. They had plenty of grounding in the practice as well as the theory of government.

Of the best-known men there, Hamilton and Madison may best illustrate the nationalist frame of mind. Hamilton, just turned thirty, was born in the West Indies to a merchant, James Hamilton, and a woman to whom his father was not legally married. Moreover, his father died, a business failure, while Hamilton was still young. The illegitimate boy was left poor and without influential connections, but he showed early signs of brilliance. Some citizens of his home island, recognizing this, sent the local prodigy to King's College (now Columbia University). The ambitious Hamilton proved a good scholarship choice. At the age of seventeen he was writing pro-Patriot pamphlets. At nineteen, with the war already on, he was a captain of artillery. At twenty he was a lieutenant colonel and an aide-de-camp to General Washington, helping the commander with an enormous correspondence and fuming with him over state jealousies that deprived the army of vital supplies. At the war's end Hamilton, now married to a socially prominent heiress, began a law practice. Much of the energy he had left over after serving rich clients went into agitation for a new government, one suitable to a nation with huge untapped resources, one that would give bold individuals the chance to lead it to economic greatness while making their own fortunes. Individuals like Hamilton.

Madison, like Hamilton, was a voracious reader of history, biography, political theory, and philosophy. The oldest of ten children of a prosperous Virginia planter, he entered Princeton at eighteen. Two years later, he had his B.A. Five years after that found him a delegate to the convention to draw up a state constitution for Virginia. He was elected to the Continental Congress in 1780, saw for himself its struggles, and even fled with it from Philadelphia briefly in 1783 to avoid being mobbed by unpaid, unhappy troops. Madison, too, took up law as his postwar calling, and he was soon chosen to the state legislature. There he worked hard to improve Virginia's communications between east and west, strengthen her finances, develop a school system, and promote trade. He was a man welcoming the future.

Scholarly but active individuals like these made up the basic membership of the convention. They did not take long to agree, according to the best available evidence, that their job was to build a stronger national government. Since they referred to their new creation as the "federal government," they were called Federalists, though Nationalists would have been more accurate. But if they concurred on nationalism, they had many diverse ideas on how the new structure should be raised. In compromising these disagreements they spent four long months in secret sessions, listening to reports, debating, writing notes to themselves and letters to friends, mopping their brows, and fighting Philadelphia's summer insects.

*Issues and Answers: The Power of Compromise*

What were some of the disagreements? They existed in almost every area. Each proposed rule of government raised knotty questions of fairness or bucked existing powerful interests. For example, there was the question of state representation in any new legislature. If large and small states alike had an equal vote (as they did under the Articles), then a few states with a minority of the population could block action beneficial to the country as a whole—clearly unfair. But if voting power was measured by a state's size or wealth or population, then a handful of the big states could dominate and manipulate all the rest—likewise unfair.

Or, to take another instance, did slaves count in counting population to decide how many votes a state got in the national lawmaking body? If the answer was yes, the South, with most of the country's half-million slaves, had an unfair edge. But if it was no, then the Southern states were unlikely to enter any new union.

Should voting and officeholding be open to all? Or confined to solid citizens who had some property or paid taxes or were well educated? Should officials be chosen for long or short terms? Short terms meant frequent, costly elections and officeholders busier courting votes than working. Long terms might mean creating a pack of arrogant bureaucrats who rarely had to answer for their deeds at the polls.

Should nationwide federal taxes require a unanimous vote of the legislature? Or just a simple majority? If unanimity was demanded, no tax might ever be levied. If only a majority was required, one section of the country with just over half the voters might slap an unfair tax on another. An export tax on tobacco, for example, would hit the South hard but not the North. Was there a magic, fair percentage between 51 and 100?

These questions were only a few of the many faced by the perspiring delegates, trying to weld 13 communities into one. (You will find it a useful exercise to see how they were actually handled by consulting the finished Constitution.) In the end they were settled by compromise and "deals," the absolute bedrock of cooperation among different thinking groups. Though "deals" sounds underhanded, not all deals are necessarily sinister. A deal is another name for a bargain. Provided that a bargain is open and that all parties to it understand the terms and freely consent to them, it is an absolutely necessary instrument for free government in a *pluralistic* society, that is, a society with many viewpoints and interests.

Every line of the Constitution reflects compromises. We can see their importance in community making when we focus on two areas as samples. We saw earlier that there were two areas where principles butted into each other in the aftermath of the Revolution. How were Americans going to reconcile local self-rule with unified, efficient government? How were they going to yoke together liberty and authority?

To illustrate the compromises between the concepts of *localism* and *centralism*, we can look at the powers of Congress and the federal courts. And to shed light on how the makers of the Constitution squared freedom and power, we can select the articles defining the presidency, and the Bill of Rights.

### *Grass-Roots Power Versus Central Control*

First there was a ringing but not-quite-clear statement of principle in the Preamble to the Constitution. "We the People of the United States," it says, " . . . do ordain and establish this Constitution for the United States of America." That was a nationalistic battle cry; there was a *single* body called "the people of the United States." But the Preamble did not create any specific governmental machinery. The body of the Constitution did that. It set up a three-branched federal government: legislative, executive, and judicial. The president and Congress would be chosen by people meeting in their states, under rules set *by* the states. Federal judges would not be named by "the people" at all but appointed. Nothing would in any way erase a state line in the process of choosing those who would govern.

Generous chunks of *exclusive* power went to the central government. It had the *sole* right to conduct wars, make treaties, coin money, and impose tariffs. The Constitution makers believed that diplomacy, warfare, and the regulation of trade could not be left to many separate managements. Both safety and commercial prosperity demanded national unity. The same logic led to exclusive federal control over interstate commerce; business on a country-wide scale could only thrive under uniform rules.

Some of the exclusive powers given to the federal government seemed simply practical. Patents were an example; an inventor was probably likelier to develop a gadget or a process if he got the exclusive right to market it throughout the land by only one application to a patent office (instead of having to prove that his idea was original in 13 or more state patent bureaus). And it was common sense to have a single rule of naturalization for foreigners and to have only one government managing the postal system.

But these new powers were carefully listed, or enumerated, and the federal government was held very strictly to them and no others. The framers seemed to take it for granted that any powers not expressly given to the central government would stay exclusively with the states. But, just to make certain, this point was spelled out in the Tenth Amendment. That amendment was, like the nine preceding it, part of the Bill of Rights, and the whole package of ten amendments was added to the Constitution immediately upon its adoption, at the insistence of those Americans who wanted to be sure that the federal government stayed under tight control.

The states, therefore, were left with the exclusive rights that they still have. They controlled education, family matters, the licensing of trades and professions, and the regulation of banking and business affairs. They were sovereign over public lands and properties and transportation within their own boundaries. In modern times the huge growth of interstate commerce has given the federal government a ruling voice in the management of the economy. But as set up in 1789, the Constitution reserved that crucial area of government almost entirely to the states, because few businessmen operated beyond state lines. What the Constitution seemed to do was to allow for 13 separate societies to grow in their possibly differing directions but to provide that when they confronted the world or had common business to transact, there would be one voice alone to speak for them.

The federal government and the states each got exclusive powers. And some powers they exercised concurrently. Each could levy its own taxes. And each had its own court system. The courts were, as it worked out, the great balancing point between the two power systems. The federal courts dealt only with violations of federal law, say, robbing a post office, to take a crude example, or violating a patent. The state courts did (and still do) the bulk of the nation's legal work, handling matters that were not within the federal government's scope. But both federal and state judges were bound by the Constitution, and that Constitution plus laws or treaties made under it were to be "the supreme Law of the Land; and the Judges in every State [should] be bound thereby, any Thing in the Constitution or Laws of any State to the Contrary notwithstanding."

What that meant in practice is this. If a citizen in a state felt that some state practice deprived him of a right under the Constitution, he had a right to test that claim in the state courts. If they ruled against him, he could appeal to the federal judiciary. If he won there, the state courts had to recognize the victory. State judges were, and are, as fully bound by the Federal Constitution as federal judges. There was no way for a state judge to say, in effect, "the Constitution reads in a special way in our state." Of course, federal judges might very well uphold a state court ruling, but that then became the authorized version on that constitutional point in all the states. The principle of uniformity was not cracked.

The states were held in constitutional line, not by federal troops, but by federal *and state* judges deliberating in their chambers. The system did not always work. It broke down totally during the Civil War. It has provoked terrific clashes, most recently in our own times over the issue of federally ordered school integration. But despite boycotts and protests and mob scenes, local judges in Alabama and Massachusetts alike have issued the same kinds of orders, forcing their own states to obey the U.S. Supreme Court. Nothing could illustrate better how the Constitution used respect for the law itself as a tool to create the necessary "togetherness" to make a nation.

### *Liberty and Authority: President and Bill of Rights*

One thing the Articles of Confederation had taught the budding nationalists of 1787 was the horror of government by committee. There were times when decisions would have to be made quickly and quietly, or, as they would have put it, with "energy, secrecy and dispatch." That spelled out the need for a single, responsible "boss"—a strong executive. But behind the scenes at Philadelphia lurked ghosts of the English and American pasts. There were autocratic Stuart kings who had ridden hard over Parliaments, and there were tough colonial governors who had tried to whipsaw colonial assemblies. The problem was to create a strong, but controlled executive.

The presidency as outlined in the Constitution was the answer. The president would have broad powers, but he would be "checked" and "balanced" against Congress and the courts. He was the commander in chief of the armed forces, but Congress alone could raise, supply, and pay the troops and fleets. He could freewheel diplomatically and conclude treaties with foreign powers, but two-thirds of the Senate (where each state had equal voting power) had to ratify such agreements. His consent was necessary for any congressional bill to become law, but a two-thirds vote in each house could enact a measure even over his opposition. He could appoint ambassadors, consuls, ministers, cabinet officials, and a wide variety of other federal officeholders. But he could not simply pass such favors out to loyal friends who would support him in dictatorial power grabs, because Congress had to approve such choices. Nor could he buy votes in Congress with jobs, because no congressman could keep his seat while holding any other federal job.

Finally, the very method of choosing the president potentially opened the door to strong congressional influence. Electors in each state (chosen however the state itself decided) were to vote for candidates for the top office. If no one got a majority, Congress (with each state, regardless of size, casting one vote) would choose from among the candidates with the highest totals. Before the party system was adopted, which put two candidates in the field, it was assumed that the electors would scatter their votes among many choices and that the failure of any one to get a majority would be fairly frequent. Congress was expected to be deeply involved with picking presidents. As it turned out, only two elections (1800 and 1824) were decided in this way, and Congress also settled one that was disputed, in 1876. But the idea of the election system itself as another "check" was clear enough.

In practice the power of the presidency, like that of the entire federal government, has grown enormously in the past two centuries. The reasons for this will form part of the story ahead. But the careful architecture of compromise in the Constitution has, on the whole, been remarkably lasting. The lines of the original blueprints are still visible in the greatly expanded modern governmental establishment.

The first ten amendments, one of the sharpest sets of curbs on governmental power in any nation's history, were also made part of the Constitution. These were added as barriers against tyranny, spelling out the things the government might *not* do. It might not create an "official," tax-supported religion; it might not muzzle the press, deny people the right to assemble and protest their grievances; it might not deprive individuals of rights such as trial by jury; it might not authorize unreasonable arrests and searches of their homes or quarter troops on them in time of peace or prevent them from having a local militia for self-protection.

Such basic safeguards against oppression were taken for granted as being indispensable in the new country by almost everyone involved in the Constitutional Convention. The framers assumed that whatever they did not empower the federal government *to* do, it was automatically banned *from* doing. But during the debates on ratification, opponents of the Constitution claimed that without specific limits on it the new government might turn into a monster. So the defenders of the document, to win votes, promised and delivered a "bill of rights" by amendment.

These examples are only a few of the dozens of political balancing acts devised in Philadelphia that summer. The framers tried to coordinate the rights of large states with small, of agricultural sections with manufacturing ones, of property owners with nonproperty owners. If they failed, as modern critics note, to give anything but short shrift to blacks, Indians, women, and "underclass" groups, they nevertheless opened doors through which such victims of prejudince might later progress. The Constitution was not a democratic document or one that stressed, like the Declaration of Independence, that "all men are created equal." But it tipped the balance slightly in that direction. It also left room for future stretching, by interpretation and amendment, to accommodate more freedom.

In any case, the Constitution's warmest advocates, the nationalists, were not so much interested in democracy as in getting the virtues of unity and energy in government, without losing the equally valuable blessings of grass-roots power and individual freedom. The preceding examples show some of their work on this problem. It seems fair to say that they did rather well in answering a dilemma expressed very well by Abraham Lincoln in 1860: how to make government strong enough for its own protection (and effectiveness) but not too strong for the liberties of its people.

### *Ratification and the Climate of Unity*

Finally, the work was done. Thirty-eight men signed the document. Fourteen of the drafters were absent; four of them opposed the final version. Three convention members present also refused to sign. But those who did made it a festive moment. Franklin gave a short graceful speech about a half-sun painted on the back of the presiding officer's chair. (The presiding officer was Virginia's delegate, Washington.) Franklin said he had long wondered if it were a setting or a rising sun, but now he knew it to be rising. Then Washington led all the members to a tavern dinner. The universally respected general was pleased with the Constitution and was a key figure in the campaign for its adoption. Everyone assumed that he would be the first president under it, and that fact alone made it acceptable to many.

The country now debated the Constitution hard and long in specially elected state ratifying conventions. Both the Federalists (defenders) and Antifederalists (opponents) mobilized plenty of biting arguments. The Federalists used all the well-known criticisms of the government under the Articles that had led to the Philadelphia convention. The Antifederalists, who included a number of distinguished revolutionary leaders, found plenty to challenge. They disliked the potentially great powers of the president, the possibility of enormous federal taxes, the scaling down of local freedom. Patrick Henry, of "give-me-liberty-or-give-me-death" fame, warned that the spirit of "consolidation" was "about to convert this country into a powerful and mighty empire." A Massachusetts farmer-opponent warned that the "lawyers and men of learning, and moneyed men . . . expect to be the managers of this Constitution, and . . . they will swallow up us little fellows . . . just as the whale swallowed up Jonah." A North Carolina Antifederalist foresaw that from the "Federal City" (that is, what would later be the District of Columbia) "an army of 50,000 or

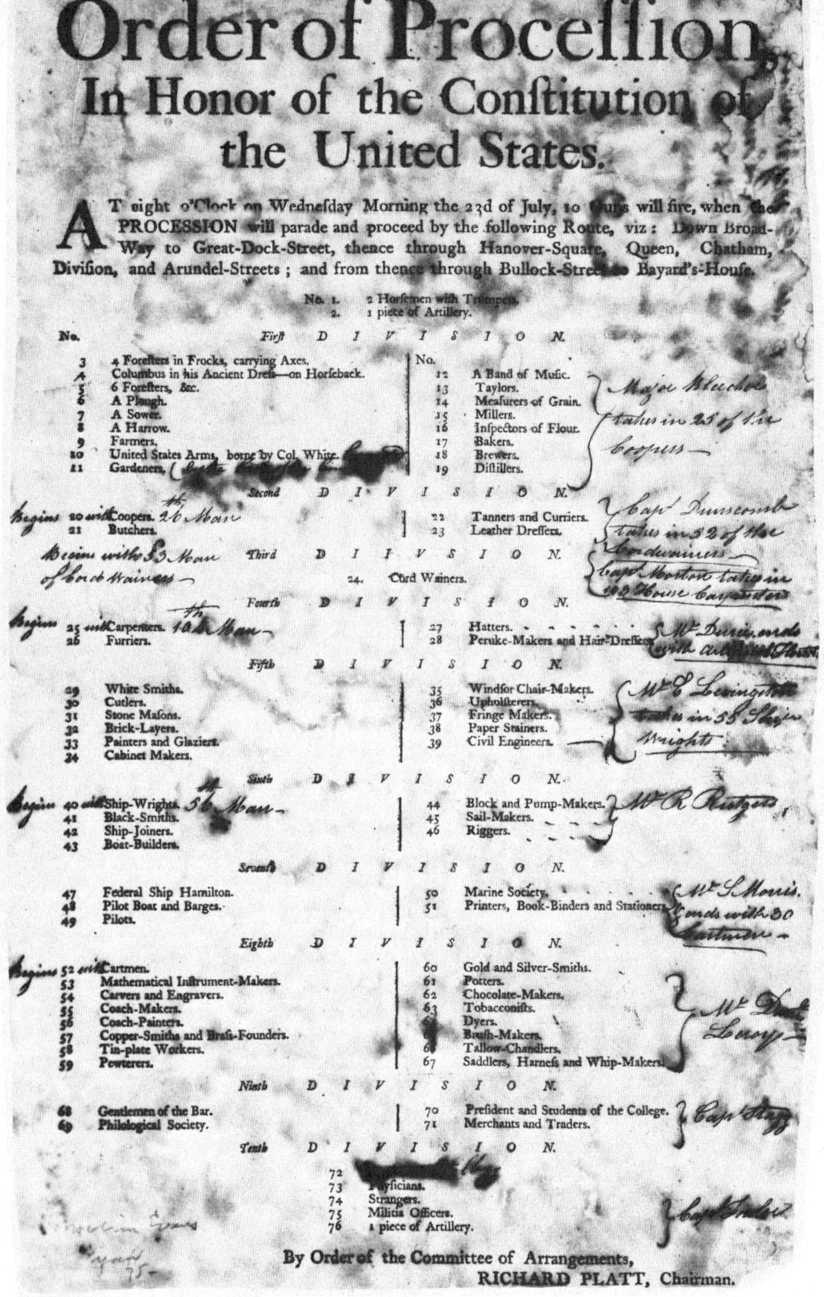

# Order of Proceſſion,
## In Honor of the Conſtitution of the United States.

AT eight o'Clock on Wedneſday Morning the 23d of July, 10 Guns will fire, when the PROCESSION will parade and proceed by the following Route, viz: Down Broad-Way to Great-Dock-Street, thence through Hanover-Square, Queen, Chatham, Diviſion, and Arundel-Streets; and from thence through Bullock-Street to Bayard's-Houſe.

No. 1. 2 Horſemen with Trumpets.
2. 1 piece of Artillery.

*First* D I V I S I O N.

No.
3 4 Foreſters in Frocks, carrying Axes.
4 Columbus in his Ancient Dreſs—on Horſeback.
5 6 Foreſters, &c.
6 A Plough.
7 A Sower.
8 A Harrow.
9 Farmers.
10 United States Arms, borne by Col. White.
11 Gardeners.

No.
12 A Band of Muſic.
13 Taylors.
14 Meaſurers of Grain.
15 Millers.
16 Inſpectors of Flour.
17 Bakers.
18 Brewers.
19 Diſtillers.

*Second* D I V I S I O N.

20 Coopers.
21 Butchers.
22 Tanners and Curriers.
23 Leather Dreſſers.

*Third* D I V I S I O N.

24. Cord Wainers.

*Fourth* D I V I S I O N.

25 Carpenters.
26 Furriers.
27 Hatters.
28 Peruke-Makers and Hair-Dreſſers.

*Fifth* D I V I S I O N.

29 White Smiths.
30 Cutlers.
31 Stone Maſons.
32 Brick-Layers.
33 Painters and Glaziers.
34 Cabinet Makers.
35 Windſor Chair-Makers.
36 Upholſterers.
37 Fringe Makers.
38 Paper Stainers.
39 Civil Engineers.

*Sixth* D I V I S I O N.

40 Ship-Wrights.
41 Black-Smiths.
42 Ship-Joiners.
43 Boat-Builders.
44 Block and Pump-Makers.
45 Sail-Makers.
46 Riggers.

*Seventh* D I V I S I O N.

47 Federal Ship Hamilton.
48 Pilot Boat and Barges.
49 Pilots.
50 Marine Society.
51 Printers, Book-Binders and Stationers.

*Eighth* D I V I S I O N.

52 Cartmen.
53 Mathematical Inſtrument-Makers.
54 Carvers and Engravers.
55 Coach-Makers.
56 Coach-Painters.
57 Copper-Smiths and Braſs-Founders.
58 Tin-plate Workers.
59 Pewterers.
60 Gold and Silver-Smiths.
61 Potters.
62 Chocolate-Makers.
63 Tobacconiſts.
64 Dyers.
65 Bruſh-Makers.
66 Tallow-Chandlers.
67 Saddlers, Harneſs and Whip-Makers.

*Ninth* D I V I S I O N.

68 Gentlemen of the Bar.
69 Philological Society.
70 Preſident and Students of the College.
71 Merchants and Traders.

*Tenth* D I V I S I O N.

72 [illegible]
73 Phyſicians.
74 Strangers.
75 Militia Officers.
76 1 piece of Artillery.

By Order of the Committee of Arrangements,
RICHARD PLATT, Chairman.

*What the Constitution created was a stable political order within which a potentially great economy could flourish. Its supporters included most of the expectant capitalists of the 1780s, as a glance at these parade marshal's instructions will show.*

perhaps 100,000 men will be finally embodied and will sally forth and enslave the people."

Historians have tried hard to divide the Federalists and the Antifederalists into neat categories: rich against poor, city folk against farmers, big landholders against owners of stocks, bonds, ships, and businesses. But there are no neat answers. People lined up on the ratification issue according to whether they held strong cards in the politics of their states and whether they expected to win or lose as the states shared power with the new government. These two pigeonholes included some people of almost every class. In general, investors, manufacturers, shippers, and sailors—all who hoped to prosper by a revival of commerce—liked the Constitution. So did western settlers, who liked the notion of a strong national army to deal with neighborhood Indians, Britons, and Spaniards.

These groups comprised a clear majority of the energetic forces in the country, and the Federalists, who were a well-organized group, successfully took the offensive. Delaware promptly ratified the Constitution unanimously (in December 1787); Pennsylvania gave a psychological lift with a 2-to-1 vote a few days later. New Jersey, Georgia, and Connecticut soon fell into line. Massachusetts gave the first close vote (187 to 168). But Maryland, South Carolina, and New Hampshire were in the fold by June 1788, making the needed nine states for ratification, and the battle was over. The remaining four states did not choose to stay out in the cold for long.

Many factors helped the Federalists. There was the promised Bill of Rights. The amending process offered a chance to change parts of the system that proved unworkable. And the lack of sharp detail on many points meant that even Antifederalists might later interpret the Constitution their way. As Jefferson wrote from Paris: "It is a good canvas, on which some strokes only want retouching." As president himself twelve years later, he retouched a good number.

But above all, the Constitution was a nationalistic document, and nationalism was on the move as the 1800s approached. Peoples united by common boundaries, histories, and languages were drawing together into political units. In America the 1780s were a decade of *national* adventure. The Northwest Territory, which belonged to the whole nation, not to any one state, was filling. American church organizations were being formed to replace authorities in England and Europe. American magazines and newspapers were springing up. The first play by an American went before the footlights. Schoolchildren thumbed Noah Webster's American spelling book of 1783 and Jedidiah Morse's *American Geography*, which appeared in 1789. Poets rhymed America's "rising glory." Every Yankee ship in foreign seas, every settler trekking into the wilderness seemed a messenger of American destiny. Local and state patriotism could not stem such a tide. The feeling of the times is best sampled in the description of a great parade, held July 4, 1788, in Philadelphia. On and on the marchers came—mounted militia and bands, a vehicle in the shape of an eagle, visiting foreign dignitaries in an elegant coach, a citizen and an Indian chief smoking the peace pipe in another, a model of the "Grand Federal Edifice" (a building with 13 columns supporting a dome), and then delegations from the local agricultural society, the manufacturing society, and various craft unions: brickmakers, clockmakers, ribbon weavers, saddlers, shoemakers, shipwrights, coopers, blacksmiths, coachmakers, skinners, glovers, goldsmiths, brewers, bakers, wigmakers, and barbers. And through the crowd moved parade officials distributing an ode composed for the occasion:

*Hail to this festival!—all hail the day!*
*Columbia's standard on her roof display!*
*And let the people's motto ever be,*
*United thus, and thus united, free!*

The community-making process begun on wild shores by starving colonists 180 years or so earlier, had reached a mighty culmination.

---

## *FOR FURTHER READING*

As a start, it is necessary to look at the Declaration of Independence, whose ideas underlie the Revolution that made the Constitution possible. Still charming and thought provoking is a small book by Carl Becker, *The Declaration of Independence* (1922). From there, you may wish to discover what was happening during the Confederation period. The conventional view that things were terrible is challenged by Merrill Jensen in *The New Nation* (1950). A close look at Shays' Rebellion, one of the episodes most responsible for alarming Nationalists and Conservatives, is Marion L. Starkey, *A Little Rebellion* (1955).

Accounts of the Constitutional convention are numerous, and you will find it worthwhile to compare two books separated by some twenty years: Carl Van Doren, *The Great Rehearsal* (1948) sees it as a model for a movement toward world government, which he hoped to see develop in his time; Catherine Drinker Bowen, *Miracle at Philadelphia* (1966) is no less admiring of the founding fathers, but keeps the story in a purely American and 1780s context.

The most outstanding man in an active role at the convention was James Madison, and Irving Brant's *James Madison, Father of the Constitution* (1950) is full of good information. Though an arch-Nationalist himself, Alexander Hamilton was not involved deeply in the convention proper; still, his biography by Nathan Shachner (1946) contains interesting material on who he wrote to and what he thought in 1787.

What about the records of the convention itself? Charles Tansill edited a volume of *Documents Illustrative of the Formation of the Union* (1927) which, though brief, contains some flavor of the debates. And then there is *The Federalist*—the essays of Hamilton, Madison, and John Jay in defense of the Constitution. They are difficult reading for a modern student, but deal beautifully with the basics of power, freedom, and government and are worth the effort.

# chapter 6
# Of war, neutrality, dissent, and freedom

One day in April in 1789, amid colorful ceremonies, George Washington was inaugurated in New York City as first president of the United States. In the very next month, with even more pomp and pageantry, King Louis XVI of France presided over the opening of the Estates-General, a gathering of representatives of various classes of the nation, called to discuss the problems of the kingdom.

Four years later, Washington took the oath for a second term. By then, poor Louis was dead, having been publicly beheaded by his subjects. The French Revolution was in full career, and France herself was at war with Britain, Austria, and Prussia. That war would widen into a world struggle and last for nearly twenty-three years. In those flaming decades Napoleon Bonaparte became emperor of France, and his troops subdued all of Europe. French and British fleets fought each other from the coasts of Egypt to the shores of the West Indies. Old feudal customs toppled, and proud kings became puppets of Napoleon, a commoner whom they regarded as a "Corsican bandit." The world was undergoing one of its bloody transitions to a new social order.

For the United States this long war was a critical period. It was a young, weak nation on the fringe of the battle. But the European struggle raised basic policy issues that sorted Americans into political parties. These turned out to be valuable agencies for holding a scattered people together, but their debates sometimes seemed to threaten to tear the nation apart. Tension blasted away, for a time, the First Amendment of the Bill of Rights. Wartime conditions gave the United States, as a neutral, a jolt of prosperity through trade with the fighting nations. But that trade was dangerous and threatened always to involve the country in the war. In 1812 war finally came. Despite a relatively happy ending, it was a near disaster. The country was invaded, the capital burned, the American merchant marine bottled up, and a serious secessionist movement was barely headed off.

In a short span of years the country went through a mini-era, a testing time of turbulence and danger. As in colonial days, what happened in America was strongly shaped by what was happening in Europe. Reaction to the world crisis drove wedges among Americans. But it also developed strong unifying forces, which won out in the end.

## *Drifting Toward Disunion?*

By 1792 domestic issues already divided the country into factions. Hamilton, as secretary of the treasury, was working to strengthen the new government by winning the support of the wealthy and powerful classes. He put successful pressure on Congress to charter a national bank, to impose a protective tariff, and to take over the debts of the states. These measures gave investing classes a stake in the financial health of the federal government. They also won the loyalty of manufacturers and merchants.

But Hamilton's maneuvers angered those who preferred strong state governments and saw agriculture, not shipping and manufacturing, as the sturdiest underpinning of a free country's economy. Chief among these opponents was Thomas Jefferson, lawyer, naturalist, philosopher, writer, inventor, and, above all, gentleman-farmer. Jefferson believed that the model free citizen was a

---

*CHRONOLOGY*

| | |
|---|---|
| 1789 | *Washington inaugurated in New York City as first president of United States* |
| 1790 | *First American textile mill, Rhode Island* |
| 1793 | *Eli Whitney invents cotton gin* |
| 1798 | *Alien and Sedition Acts* |
| 1800 | *Jefferson elected president* |
| 1803 | *France sells Louisiana territory to United States* |
| 1803–1806 | *Lewis and Clark explore Louisiana territory* |
| 1811 | *Battle of Tippecanoe, Northwest Indians defeated* |
| 1812–1814 | *War of 1812* |

landowner who could always feed himself and so depended on no other man for a living. Followers of the two men soon were on collision course. The Jeffersonians in various states organized themselves under the name of Democratic Republicans. Those who shared Hamilton's views also organized themselves, and they took the name of Federalists. This development was part of the nationalism of the day. The parties continued and tightened the network of correspondence and common action that had linked the states together since the 1770s.

But when Americans were confronted with the French Revolution, party conflict was honed to an emotional edge that cut deeper than economic issues. That revolution began as a movement to reform the monarchy and give it a constitution. Gradually, however, it became a radical tempest under leaders who beheaded the king, executed thousands of his supporters, and challenged the whole system of religious and political authority under which Europe lived. The French experience struck panic into conservatives (mostly Federalists), even in republican America. But it excited the hopes of those progress-minded Americans (mostly Jeffersonian Republicans) who believed that only on the ruins of the established order could mankind build a future of reason, good will, and liberty. The French "leftists," or Jacobins, were to Federalists what Communists were later to be to traditionalists in American life. Jeffersonians, however, tended to overlook the persecutions of the revolution in their enthusiasm for what it was trying to do, just as twentieth-century liberals would make allowances for Soviet Russia or the People's Republic of China (Communist China).

This emotional identification with the French Revolution or its enemies took a practical turn when Britain and France went to war. In the British system they had earlier fought against, Federalists now found a guarantee of order and property against mob passions. So they endorsed the British outlook on the revolution as an infection to be cured by arms. Republicans, however, were more inclined to see France as the friend of necessary changes in the political order of the world.

In fact, there was good reason for all Americans to be angry with both nations. Each showed cavalier disregard of American needs and interests. The French seized American ships bound for British-controlled ports in the Atlantic, Mediterranean, and Caribbean. The British, in turn, pounced on American vessels carrying food and supplies for the French. In both cases, international law, which allowed free neutral trade in nonmilitary goods, was flouted. The British aggravated the United States in additional ways. They refused to leave their fur-trading posts located in territory given to the Americans by the 1783 treaty. They barred American shipping from trade with their West Indian islands, which had been the lifeblood of New England. Finally, they followed the practice of "impressment." They would halt American ships and search them for Britons who had deserted from hellish conditions in British men-of-war. Often, these raiding parties simply kidnapped American sailors who could not prove their citizenship. In both Washington's second administration and John Adams's administration, war with either power was in the air. It was averted only because both presidents had the sense to realize that the shaky new nation could not afford battle. In 1794 Washington sent Chief Justice John Jay to England to negotiate a treaty on outstanding problems. Jay returned with a document in which the British conceded very little. Cries of outrage from Republicans rocked the country, though the treaty managed to win Senate consent. The passionate tone was conveyed in one such protest, which declared: "The treaty . . . hold[s] forth to the world, that. . . . like fawning spaniels we can be beaten into love and submission."

Only four years later it was Britain's friends who were outraged. French attacks on American shipping stung Congress into providing for the beginnings of a navy. But in 1797 Adams sent three American commissioners to Paris to see whether the issues could be settled peacefully. They were met by a trio of anonymous agents, referred to as X, Y, and Z, who let it be known that the French government would consider a treaty with the United States, provided that a large bribe was given to the foreign minister. When this news reached America, the Federalists' reaction was explosive. Rather than seeing the matter as a sad commentary on the morals of some of France's rulers, they focused on the insult. America had been treated like some favor seeker at a corrupt court, ordered to "shell out" to buy official attention. An outcry for war arose. Washington was to be called from retirement to lead the army, and ex-Colonel Hamilton polished up his sword, too. But Adams, a Bible reader who recalled the verse, "He that is slow to anger is better than the mighty, and he who rules his spirit than he who takes a city," held firm. Against strong pressure from his own party, he appointed a new special envoy, who worked out a compromise that averted an unprepared-for war. But the wrath of the more warlike Federalists not only destroyed Adams politically but led to an action that turned a foreign-policy issue into a constitutional crisis of civil liberties and states' rights.

The Federalist majority in Congress enabled them to pass three Alien Acts and a Sedition Act. The most drastic alien measure authorized the president to deport any noncitizen whom he deemed dangerous. It was aimed at a number of French and English supporters of Jefferson who had taken up residence in America. The Sedition Act made it a crime to "write, print, utter or publish . . . any false, scandalous and malicious writing or writings against the government of the United States." Both laws together, especially the latter, made hash of the Bill of Rights.

In response, the state legislatures of Virginia and Kentucky passed resolutions (written respectively and anonymously by Madison and Jefferson). These argued that the two laws were plainly unconstitutional. And, the key resolution went on, since the Constitution was a compact among the states, each state had a right to judge when it was violated. And if, in the state's judgment, it was, then that state and any agreeing with it had a positive duty to concur in declaring such acts "void and of no force." The issue that was to create a Civil War sixty-three years later was drawn; did the states have the right to obey only those federal laws they approved? Or was the Constitution truly the supreme law of the land, to be interpreted *only* by the central government? The European war had finally threatened to split the young Union.

### *Underlying Forces: In Tune and Jangling*

To understand the depth of the crisis it is necessary to have some perspective. There was deep-rooted distrust between the parties, starting with Jefferson and Hamilton themselves. They saw each other in the grotesque enlargements of amusement-park mirrors. Jefferson wrote late in life that when he was Washington's secretary of state, the table talk of his fellow federal officials was usually political, "and a preference of kingly over republican government was evidently the favorite sentiment." One night, at dinner, Jefferson was horrified to hear Hamilton declare that the British government, "with all its supposed defects," was "the most perfect government which ever existed." Hamilton might have meant only a practical statement that human wickedness exists in every government, even the best. But Jefferson took it to mean that Hamilton was "so bewitched and perverted by the British example" that he thought "corruption was essential to the government of a nation."

Jefferson haters, in turn, put few limits on their imagination in caricaturing the Virginian. Timothy Dwight, the Federalist president of Yale College, was appalled by Jefferson's religious skepticism. He warned, when Jefferson ran for president in 1800, that if he was elected, the country would see "the Bible cast into a bonfire . . . our sons become the disciples of Voltaire . . . our daughters the concubines of the Illuminati [the French radical intellectuals, or left-wing 'eggheads' of the day]." Timothy Pickering of Massachusetts said even more briefly: "There is no nefarious act of which we may not suppose him capable."

Such strong feelings disturbed Washington, who was above all a nationalist. He believed that taking sides with the French *or* the British only fed the fires of passion. That is the basic meaning of his famous Farewell Address, in which he warned against "permanent alliances" with European nations. He was not merely warning his fellow Americans against plunging into other peoples' battles. He was saying that strong attachments to one country or another promoted factionalism, the division of a people into battling groups, and that

America, a model of republican government to the world would be doing herself and humanity inconceivable mischief if she allowed herself to be torn apart. Hamilton put the same theme more bluntly in a letter; republican (by which he meant nonmonarchical) government was desirable enough, he said, but perhaps not consistent with that "*stability* and *order* which are essential to public strength and private security." If liberty provoked "the spirit of faction, . . . all regular and orderly minds will wish for a change." Only demagogues, those whose one wish was to please the crowd, would profit by stirring up unreasoning anger.

In short, the Federalists really feared what would now be called divisiveness. They believed that a society with no strong *consensus* (shared values) or steady leadership would begin to unravel, and then there would be a chaotic situation from which people would be glad to be saved by a strong man who took dictatorial reins.

The counterargument of Jeffersonians, then and now, could have been that a society thrives on free debate. When free debate is choked off, those who *have* get more and more; those who *lack* are unable to change matters by peaceable means. Revolt is therefore the fruit of too much oppression, not a surplus of liberty to argue. The issue still lives.

Yet despite this deep and lasting difference of philosophies, the warring Federalists and Republicans did not consume the nation in the fires of their conflict. A national community is not destroyed overnight, and, as we have seen, many streams in the 13 states had been flowing together to form a tide of common American purpose. The United States could absorb party conflict because there was actually an underlying American consensus in 1800. Both Federalists and Republicans agreed that the United States was something special to the world, with a bright future of growth in size, population, wealth, and power. They disagreed on who should lead it and according to what principles; in other words, they disagreed on the style of government but not on the certainty of national success. To show how this difference unfolded in personal terms, we look at the early careers of two sons of Connecticut and Yale, Joel Barlow and Lyman Beecher, one a Jeffersonian, the other conservative.

Barlow, born in 1754, planned to be a minister after leaving Yale. It was a learned profession, open to a young man gifted with words. But it was too narrowing mentally, and he soon left it for law and for writing on the side. In 1787 he composed an epic poem, *The Vision of Columbus*. In it a dreaming Columbus sees his New World giving birth to America, which soon furnishes the Old World a spectacle of brilliant leadership in every field of thought and action. Next, Barlow went to France as sales agent for a land company, selling acres of Ohio wilderness (described in the most gilded terms) to trusting French buyers who thought of America as a natural paradise where crops grew without work. When the French Revolution broke out, Barlow became its enthusiastic supporter. He was enchanted by an apparent European copy of our own Revolution and quickly composed a book entitled *Advice to the Privileged Orders*. It warned kings, nobles, and priests that the human race, free of superstition, was going to build a new social order and that they had better get in step. The delighted French made Barlow a citizen of their republic. But revolutions are unkind to their prophets and poets. Later, Barlow's friends in power were overthrown, and he had to flee to Britain.

Elastic to the core, however, Barlow now became a top Jeffersonian diplomat. He negotiated deals with various small "pirate" kingdoms of North Africa that were capturing American ships and sailors. Barlow got men and cargoes released, for a price, and received a percentage for himself. He invested his earnings in land, and on one of his sojourns in the United States he built a fine estate called Kalorama outside of present-day Washington, D.C. Barlow saw America as a place that could encourage a philosopher of freedom and also let him do well in the marketplace. In 1811 he was asked to go to Europe and in 1812 to talk over issues with Napoleon. He had to follow the emperor deep into Russia, from which the French were then retreating. In the harshness of a Polish winter he came down with a fatal illness and lies buried in that country, a wandering Yankee at rest.

Beecher, twenty-one years Barlow's junior, was a bright farm youth who was also packed off to Yale and a potential preacher's career in 1793. But unlike Barlow, Beecher truly believed in the faith of his Puritan ancestors. It must be revived, he thought, in young America. Beecher graduated firm in the belief that "infidels" such as Jefferson's Republicans must be fought and that as many Americans as possible must be "saved" from Satan by works of piety, for the end of the world might be near at hand and God's kingdom on earth had to be established before then in America. From pulpits in Long Island, Connecticut, and Boston, Beecher taught this mixture of old-fashioned faith and new patriotism. And he was always working. He organized societies to combat drinking and Sabbath breaking, to send off missionaries to the churchless "heathen" on the frontier, to give away Bibles, and to herd children into Sunday Schools. His amazing energies were not exhausted by constant sermons, lectures, correspondences, and meetings. He also hunted, fished, hiked, sawed wood, and even shoveled sand from one corner to the other of his cellar to work off steam. He was a stern parent with his many children, who included Harriet Beecher Stowe, the author of *Uncle Tom's Cabin*. In 1832 Beecher moved from Boston to Cincinnati to head a school for training ministers to fight infidels and Catholics, also on Beecher's enemies list. Like so many others, he wound up going West toward the future. Naturally, Beecher supported Federalists for the lifetime of that party.

On the surface, he and Barlow were poles apart. Yet a common pattern appears. Both men were doers, or activists; they were promoters and organizers. Barlow had his land speculations, and Beecher his crusades. Each believed the future was in America. For Barlow, the age of reason would triumph here, and for Beecher, the reign of Christ. Neither hesitated to take whatever came to him in the way of worldly glory as a result of his "crusade." They both represent a kind of basic American character.

Most Americans, at least until very recently, shared these feelings of optimistic patriotism. In good times the underlying unity shone clearly. But in days of crisis, disagreements on particular issues clouded over the consensus. It was at just such times that there were occasional efforts to force harmony by smothering dissent. In 1798 there was the first such crisis.

Luckily, the storm over the Alien and Sedition Acts was brief. They were not very vigorously enforced, which eased their dangerous possibilities. The mere threat of presidential deportation drove a few aliens from the country. And 25 prosecutions were brought under the Sedition Act, resulting in 10 convictions. One of the worst sufferers was a Vermont congressman named Matthew Lyon, who was heavily fined and kept in a jail cell about 16-by-12 feet, a common receptacle for horse thieves, moneymakers, runaway blacks, or any felons. It had a half-moon hole in the door through which food was passed and an open toilet in the corner, which made it stink, said Lyon, "like the Philadelphia docks in the month of August." Lyon remained unrepentant, and Vermont voters reelected him triumphantly while he was in jail.

In 1800 the nationwide vote resulted in the election of Jefferson and a Republican Congress. The offending laws, which were only to run for a few years, died and were not renewed. That was the end of them. What followed for the next few years was a shift in the tide, back toward unity and nationalism. When that happened, the temperature of debate cooled, and suppression was no longer urged. Much of the credit went to Jefferson. Conservatives had trembled for fear that the incoming administration might try to wipe out its enemies. That had been the pattern in France, which the Republicans so admired. And it might have seemed natural after the sizzling language of the 1790s. But Jefferson, though he had taken no part in writing the Constitution, now gave it an enormous boost. He proved that under it a peaceful change of leadership could take place without violent revenge upon opponents. Upon his inauguration he called for political peace. "Every difference of opinion," he said, "is not a difference of principle. We have called by different names brethren of the same principle. We are all Republicans, we are all Federalists."

These conciliatory words were followed by actions that reinforced a growing national pride. The most striking of them was made possible by the course of the European war and the impulsiveness of Napoleon.

### *Jefferson: A States' Righter Turns Nationalist*

In 1800 Napoleon forced Spain to give Louisiana, taken by the peace of 1763, back to the French. He intended to move into the territory and use it as a base from which to smash British overseas outposts. When this news, kept secret at first, finally leaked, it put Jefferson into deep alarm. It was one thing to have a weak and overage power like Spain on the U.S. western flank and in control of New Orleans, through which the growing commerce of the West had to pass. Spain had, in fact, promised in 1795 not to interfere with the vital flow of western farm exports down the Mississippi. But France, then the military mistress of Europe, was more apt to make trouble. Jefferson brooded over the problem; he even considered balancing off France by making an alliance with the nation he hated, Great Britain. Meanwhile, however, he sent emissaries to Napoleon to test the unlikely chance that Napoleon might sell New Orleans.

Luck was with him. By 1803 Napoleon had changed his mind. He had new plans for Europe that would busy all his forces. An army he had sent to Haiti to suppress a slave revolt was wiped out by yellow fever. And British naval successes made it clear that the French could easily be cut off from supplying Louisiana. So the French emperor stunned the American envoys by offering to sell not only New Orleans but the entire province. After some maneuvering the deal was completed. For $15 million the United States gained a territory of about 828,000 square miles, stretching from Canada to Mexico and from the Mississippi to the Rockies. It encompassed a future treasure house of rich soil and grass, timber, gold, silver, coal, iron, copper, and oil, the great heartland of the North American continent. Despite some Federalist grumbling that this enormous "desert" could never be populated or ruled and some uncomfortable speculation by Jefferson over whether he really had the right to act quickly and without Congress, the sale was approved—and it was popular.

It became even more so in May 1804, when Jefferson sent two army officers, Meriwether Lewis and William Clark, with about four dozen men to explore the new area and go beyond it to the Pacific. So began a classic exploration. By keelboat and dugout canoe they fought the currents of the Missouri to its source in the Rockies. By packhorse and on foot they struggled through the mountain passes, wintering in the wilderness. Finally, they reached the Columbia River and floated down to its mouth in Oregon in the late autumn of 1805.

They gaped at wonders that still exist, towering, frosted mountains and rivers that hurtled through deep, green gorges in explosions of foam. And they

*Jefferson's instructions to Lewis and Clark were to report fully on every aspect of the vast region between the Missouri River and the Pacific. The brilliance with which the orders were executed is reflected in these neat, descriptive pages from the expedition's journals.*

saw others that have since been swept aside by "progress," acres of virgin timber, prairies colorfully ablaze with meadow flowers, and herds of elk and buffalo, prairie chickens, jack rabbits, and other beasts of the untamed open spaces. They saw Indian tribes new to Americans, Mandans, Shoshones, Sioux, and Pawnee.

They never knew what their reception from these would be, greetings and food or the sudden buzz of arrows. And they suffered. Canoes overturned in rapids. Blizzards almost froze them and put them on starvation rations by killing the wild game on which they tried to live. Accidental injuries and sicknesses went untended or were crudely doctored by the medically untrained leaders.

But they pushed on, filling notebooks with notations of latitudes and longitudes, temperatures, and heights; with maps, sketches of birds, insects, animals, grasses, berries, herbs, shrubs—a true new world pouring itself into orderly jottings for later assessment.

The expedition was a national achievement. Though their reports were not widely known to the public of the early 1800s, Lewis and Clark were part of a sunburst of national enterprise that opened the new century. The new navy fought a successful war against the Barbary pirates. Ohio, first state to be carved out of the Northwest Territory, was admitted in 1803. There was a boom in cotton growing and textile making. Both stemmed from developments in 1790s, sparked by bright mechanically gifted young men. Eli Whitney invented the cotton gin, whittling out a wooden model in a day. And Samuel Slater, a brilliant English immigrant, slipped out of his homeland carrying in his memory the closely guarded plans for water-powered spinning machinery, which he introduced in Rhode Island.

Perhaps it was this glow of achievement that led to a kind of bumptiousness that now nudged the United States toward war with Britain. It was to be both unpopular and badly fought. The Federalists did not want it. And the Jeffersonians, who hated large military budgets, left the country unprepared for it. In its shocks, new strains in the American system were revealed. But it would end, ironically, by strengthening nationalism.

## *Foreign Wars and Debates at Home*

The collapse of neutrality was gradual but steady. During Jefferson's second term, France and Great Britain continued to war on each other's trade and to squeeze the neutral United States between them. Britain, through a series of so-called Orders in Council, banned nonbelligerent ships from direct trade with the ports of Europe, which Napoleon controlled. She had the ships to enforce these rules and to compel neutrals to stop in British ports for clearances and licenses. Napoleon lacked a strong navy, but his counterplay was a decree in 1807 that any neutral ships that obeyed the British rules and then put into "his" waters should be seized. In short, if an American ship tried to go straight to a European port, it could be seized by the British. If it headed for British harbors, it might be grabbed by what was left of the French sea forces. And if it went to Europe after a stop in Britain, it risked confiscation in port.

Jefferson and his successor, Madison, working with Congress, tried to fight back with economic pressure. Britain and France both wanted shipments of American grain. Britain was also beginning to use American cotton extensively in her factories. Perhaps withholding these would bring the two combatants to heel. Jefferson experimented, first with a total embargo on all American trade with the world. It lasted from December 1807 to March 1809 and almost ruined the American merchant marine as well as inland farmers who now had no place to sell their products. Moreover, it did not convince London or Paris to change their minds. The embargo was then repealed, and other moves were tried. First, trade was reopened with all parts of the world except for France and Britain. Then something like a bribe was tried, with an 1810 law known as Macon's Bill Number Two. It said that if either France or Britain repealed her odious anti-American laws, the United States would voluntarily embargo the other. Napoleon pretended to go along and repealed his decrees (but continued to seize ships). The British held firm, however, even in the face of fresh American refusal to trade with them.

Nevertheless, through 1811, pressure grew within Great Britain to repeal the Orders in Council. Most of it came from businessmen who prospered on the exchange of British manufactured goods for American raw materials. To them, letting the Yankees trade with the enemy was cheaper in the long run than losing them as customers. Finally, in June 1812, the Orders *were* repealed. But by then it was too late. The Americans had declared war.

Why was war declared on Britain instead of France? An obvious answer might be that the Republicans disliked Britain more than France. But other forces, about whose relative strength historians still argue, had made it clear by 1811 that war was going to come and that it would be with the one-time mother country, not Napoleon.

For one thing, through impressment, the British wounded the pride and dignity of the Americans in a way that the mere dollar losses through ship seizures could not. Nations do not like being overpowered, and just how weak the United States was became clear in 1807, when the British cruiser *Leopard* stopped the American naval vessel *Chesapeake*, only a few miles off American shores, to search for deserters. When the *Chesapeake* refused permission, the British fired into her, killing several seamen. The British simply were displaying the arrogance of power—and the United States was like some modern-day small nation, helpless under foreign guns and bombs.

In addition, and most important, Britain (through Canada) had a land frontier with the United States. Canada was thinly populated and weakly defended. Angry Americans could therefore dream of "punishing" Britain by seizing Canada. It looked easy to some cocky Americans. Henry Clay, Kentucky's young congressman, announced that the militia of his state were "competent" to lay the province at Congress's feet. Canada would also add hugely to the available free land of the United States, and its capture would wipe out the British bases from which the Northwest Indians were supplied. Americans were now moving briskly westward, and the Indians, sensing this tide running against them, were resisting more vigorously. In 1811 the Shawnee leader Tecumseh and his brother, the Prophet, tried to unite the tribes in a stand. They were defeated at the battle of Tippecanoe. It did little for Anglo-American relations when the victors found their dead enemies supplied with British muskets, powder, blankets, and parts of uniforms. So the clamor for war grew and was loudest in the new states of the West. "We shall drive the British from our Continent—they will no longer have an opportunity of intriguing with our Indian neighbors, and setting on the ruthless savage to tomahawk our women and children." So spoke Tennessee's Representative Felix Grundy, one of the rising "war hawks" of 1811.

The rising war fever of the West, however, was not matched in Federalist New England, which suffered most from British ship seizures. The reason was that high freight rates and prices made trade prosperous even if only some ships got through the blockade. War would cut off business altogether, and every sailor and shopkeeper in coastal towns and every farmer with goods to sell overseas would be hurt. That cooled military ardor considerably. Baby-faced John Randolph of Virginia argued on the floor of Congress that only the westerners wanted battle and that they had "but one word—like the whip-poor-will, but one eternal monotonous tone—Canada! Canada! Canada!"

Historians often refight past battles. One school of American writers long echoed Randolph and said that blockade and impressment took a back seat to Canada hunger in bringing on the war. Another school, the most recent group of scholars, prolongs the debates of 1811 by taking issue. Westerners, they note, steamed over the insult of impressment as much as over Indians in Ohio carrying British-made guns. Moreover, westerners were also pinched by wartime swings in grain prices, which they blamed on the blockade. And westerners were aggressive and bombastic by character due to their constant struggle to survive on the harsh frontier. Unlike easterners, they demanded quick action. Trigger-happiness was programmed into their style. And besides, there were many eastern prowar voices.

Nevertheless, by the summer of 1812 it seemed to the Americans that the British would not yield without force. President Madison, not a war hawk himself (but not precisely a dove either), sent a message to Congress listing the "injuries and indignities" wreaked by the British. He urged the lawmakers to decide whether to "continue passive under these. . . . accumulating wrongs" or choose force and "commit a just cause into the hands of the Almighty Disposer of Events." As always, God was to be on our side. As we have noted, the British *had* yielded. But slow transatlantic communications kept the news from the Americans. And war came, by a 79-to-49 vote in the House and a 19-to-13 vote in the Senate.

*War and a Creaky System*

The war was one calamity after another. At sea a few ships of the youthful navy—notably the U.S.S. *Constitution*, the *Wasp*, the *Hornet*, and the *Essex*—outgunned individual British warships in one-to-one battles. But long before the war's end, British blockading squadrons had completely bottled up American commerce. The gloomiest visions of the Federalists came true. As for the land war, it was, until its final hours, disastrous. Three separate expeditions to take Canada sputtered out. One was driven back to Detroit, which was captured. Another succeeded in taking Toronto (then called York) but could not press further on toward Montreal. One halted at the New York State boundary when many of the state militiamen in its ranks refused to go further. Although naval victories on Lakes Erie and Champlain prevented the British in Canada from sweeping down into New York, the crowing of the war hawks turned out to have been pure noise.

Meanwhile, a British task force sailed up the Chesapeake Bay and landed in Maryland in midsummer 1814. Easily routing Maryland militiamen, they captured Washington. President Madison and other federal officials had to flee, with wagons and buggies hastily crammed full of official papers. The First Lady, Dolly Madison, wrote later of her hasty scramble to collect White House furniture and how she insisted on rescuing a portrait of George Washington while her escorts waited impatiently to leave.

The British occupied the Capitol and held a mock session in the House chamber; as they lounged, booted, and spurred, in the congressmen's chairs, they voted to burn the "nest of Yankee democracy." They then set fire to all the government buildings and the White House. They did spare the patent office, thanks, it is said, to the impassioned speech of the commissioner of patents, Dr. William Thornton, who begged them not to be such barbarians as to destroy works of the mind. Only a heavy rain on the night of August 24 prevented the whole city from being laid in ashes. The only glimmer of light was the failure of the British to move on and take Baltimore. It was during the unsuccessful bombardment of that city's guardian Fort McHenry that Francis Scott Key wrote *The Star-Spangled Banner*. Our national anthem came from our worst-handled war.

*Though the star-spangled banner waved triumphantly over Fort McHenry in Baltimore while under British attack, the national anthem fails to reveal that the War of 1812 was generally a military disaster. This busy scene of the capture of Washington is truer to reality, but good luck, sharp diplomacy, and exuberant nationalism managed to make the conflict appear to be a successful second war for independence.*

The reason for this shabby record was the total lack of preparation of an infant, localistic democracy for war. All of the government departments were manned by a few clerks. All had operated on starvation budgets under Jefferson, who distrusted bigness in government. There were few supplies and almost no factories to make more. There was no central U.S. agency to hold the government's revenues and pay its bills. Hamilton's First Bank of the United States, which had done just that, was allowed to die in 1811. As a result, the U.S. government often could not get its IOU's accepted. The states, especially those of New England, failed to supply requested men and materiel. There was almost no high-level army staff, and West Point—then less than ten years old—furnished no professional officer corps.

In short, the country learned in the hardest possible way that war demands centralization and sweeping powers for public officials. Since these were all things that the Jeffersonians detested, they should have avoided war at all costs. The Federalists in the 1790s, who *did* approve of centralization, knew how badly it was lacking. Thanks to Washington and Adams, they had avoided conflict with major powers.

But the Federalists themselves were destroyed by the war's insanity. Their leaders in New England watched, with mounting dismay, Madison's stumbling. Some of the more extreme among them believed that the time had come for drastic moves. What they lamented especially was the apparent supremacy of the South and West in the national government. By 1812 the nation was in its twelfth year of rule by a Virginia Republican president, supported largely by votes from the nonmaritime districts, the planting South and the farming West. Federalists, looking at the continuing westward surge of population, saw eventual doom for New England under an avalanche of votes from new western states, unless they could constitutionally reverse the situation.

Late in 1814 the Massachusetts legislature called for a meeting of delegates from the New England states at Hartford, Connecticut. They gathered in secret in mid-December and deliberated until January 5, 1815. The final result was a report with a series of proposed constitutional amendments. The first of them would have changed the three-fifths rule, so that the South could no longer count 60 percent of its slave population in determining the number of its representatives. A second required a two-thirds vote from each house of Congress to admit new states, to declare war, or to ban trade with any foreign nations. A third would have limited embargoes to no more than sixty days. The fourth proposed to close membership in Congress and federal offices to all but native-born Americans. Finally, there was one proposal to limit a president to one term and to prevent the election of a president from the same state two terms in succession.

These propositions were never acted upon. Nor is there any clear evidence of what the "Hartford Feds," as they were called, planned to do if their appeal fell on deaf ears. Three days after the convention closed, a small force of Americans under Andrew Jackson ("Old Hickory") mowed down a British invading force at the Battle of New Orleans. They killed some 2000 veteran regulars. The American frontiersmen in Jackson's ranks counted only 70 casualties. The war thus concluded with a "famous victory" that made a national hero of Jackson and apparent fools of those who were grumbling that the war was a failure. Then came truly ironic news. Both the Hartford Convention *and* the

Battle of New Orleans had come after the war's end. Once more, slow-traveling news changed history's course. Early in December 1814 American and British commissioners who had been meeting at Ghent in Belgium signed a treaty of peace. For many months they had been negotiating to end the war that the British did not want and the Americans could not successfully fight. The treaty simply called for the return of captured territory by both sides and further discussion of unsettled problems.

Time had made the war obsolete. The Napoleonic Wars had ended the preceding summer, with the emperor's defeat. The matters of wartime trade and impressment now became dead letters. And the British, with home issues raised by their rapid industrialization piling up on them, were willing to work with the somewhat cooled-down Americans to settle boundary and Indian questions in North America. So a period of peace between the two nations opened, and the long struggle passed into the history books.

But the Federalists appeared to be the ultimate in villainy. Looking only at the happy ending and forgetting what went before it, young America celebrated the conflict as the Second War of Independence. They remembered only "Old Ironsides" reducing British warships to splintered hulks, "Old Hickory" mowing down the redcoats, and the flag still flying "midst the rockets' red glare" at Fort McHenry.

History, to some extent, "teaches" whatever it is that people want to learn. Before the war there had been ship seizures, impressment, and a Canadian frontier aflame. After the war these things did not exist. Therefore, the war was the cause of their disappearance. And the opponents of the war entered the history books under a cloud of infamy.

The real oddity of the Hartford Convention was overlooked. The Federalists, believers in a strong energetic national government, now demanded measures to slow down its actions and to require majorities in every section to enact foreign-policy legislation. They were betraying the ghost of Hamilton in order to punish his enemies. Their demands would one day be echoed by Southern nullifiers and secessionists. And both Hartford Feds and secessionists would be harshly handled by history. The modern world has automatically assumed that national growth is a sign of progress and that local power and traditions have no choice but to disappear in the face of modern machinery and communications. It is an idea that you may want to reevaluate for yourself.

Another problem of the Hartford Feds was that they used their enemies' means to gain their own ends. Their central-power-oriented philosophy had much to commend it in wartime. Yet they could think of no other way to get back at the Jeffersonians than to echo the Jeffersonian call for *more* local autonomy and more power to the states to block action by Washington. Their story raises the interesting general question of whether a party can ever successfully divorce its tactics from its philosophy. There have been modern dictatorships that proposed to act in the name of the people. Can such things be? There have been administrations devoted to saving free capitalistic enterprise, which have done so by nationalizing many parts of the economy in order to avert really radical change. Did that work? There have been Socialists, opponents to all middle-class government, who have entered alliances with their "bourgeois" enemies to achieve their goals by votes and not revolutions. Were these sellouts? Perhaps the Hartford Feds were only an early group to encounter this dilemma.

In any case, the pendulum of national feeling kept swaying. It had swung toward divisiveness in the late 1790s, then toward unity from 1800 to 1810, and toward fragmentation again from 1811 to 1816. Now its arc led back toward unity. New forces made it a heady and exciting feeling to be American. Old political issues changed to line up with them. Until new social questions were clearly drawn, from 1816 to about 1824, political life entered a period known as the Era of Good Feeling.

---

## *FOR FURTHER READING*

The flavor of the 1790s is best tasted in the biographies and autobiographies of leading actors on the national scene at the time. In addition to biographies of Hamilton, Madison, Washington, and John Adams, referred to at the end of Chapters 4 and 5, you might enjoy reading Merrill D. Peterson, *Thomas Jefferson and the New Nation* (1970); Raymond Walters, *Albert Gallatin* (1947), about Jefferson's secretary of the treasury; Samuel Eliot Morison's sketch of super-Federalist, *Harrison Gray Otis* (1969); Marquis James' *Andrew Jackson, The Border Captain* (1933), full of Tennessee heroics; and Nathan Shachner's *Aaron Burr* (1937), the story of Jefferson's vice president who killed Hamilton in a duel and who was either an unsung hero or an unpunished traitor, according to which historians you consult. An old, heavy, but very colorful and useful biography that repays browsing is Albert J. Beveridge, *The Life of John Marshall* (4 vols., 1916–1919).

Since special mention is made of Lyman Beecher and Joel Barlow, you may enjoy reading Beecher's own peppery *Autobiography of Lyman Beecher* (1961). There is a biography of Barlow by James Woodress (1958), but it would be rewarding to read the livelier sketch in Vernon L. Parrington's *Main Currents in American Thought* (1927–1930).

Studies on special topics mentioned in the chapter include James M. Smith, *Crisis in Freedom: The Alien and Sedition Acts* (1951) and Bradford Perkins, *Prologue to War* (1961) about the coming of the War of 1812. A fine account of the Treaty of Ghent can be found in Samuel F. Bemis, *John Quincy Adams and the Foundations of American Foreign Policy* (1949).

Firsthand writings include *The Journal of William Maclay* (1927), a Pennsylvania congressman in the First Congress; Adrienne Koch and William Peden, *The Life and Selected Writings of Thomas Jefferson* (1944); Bernard De Voto, ed., *The Journals of Lewis and Clark* (1953); and Joel Barlow, *Advice to the Privileged Orders* (1960).

# chapter 7 What made America American?

"In all the four quarters of the globe," asked the English clergyman Sydney Smith early in the nineteenth century, "who reads an American book?" And to this tart question he added further sneers: Who attended an American play? Looked at an American picture? Or heard an American piece of music? The answer was plainly "Nobody!" And the whole passage meant to rebuke the barbarous Yankees, who claimed to be setting the world an example of enlightened freedom but who were adding nothing to the civilized world's arts and letters.

It is true that, according to one dictionary definition of "culture," namely, "the enlightenment and refinement of taste acquired by intellectual and aesthetic training," the young republic lagged behind Europe. Its people, on the whole, were more familiar with axe and hoe, warehouse and quarterdeck than with galleries, concert stages, and libraries. But in the broad, anthropological framework of the word "culture," which we used in the opening chapter to discuss the meeting of the Spaniard and the Indian—that is, the sum total of the distinctive activities of a particular people—there *was* an American style of life emerging. Many foreign visitors in the early 1800s came to witness the then new spectacle of a working democracy on an untouched continent. And all of them sensed a specialness about American life that made it unforgettable.

The ingredients of that new national identity were many. They included things like the Kentucky rifle and the Mississippi steamboat, a plantation spiritual and a stump speech, a white-spired Congregational church house at a New England crossroads and a bull-whacker's melodious stream of curses as he urged his oxteam and loaded wagon through a river ford on the Santa Fe trail. Each of these elements in what we may call popular culture told its own story of the American people's expectations, attitudes, needs, and achievements.

The monuments of traditional "high culture" were formal works of disciplined art produced by trained and inspired craftsmen and paid for, usually, by an aristocratic group that took the responsibility for making the beauty and lessons of art available to all. An example would be the great buildings, statues, and paintings made for the princes and Popes of Renaissance Italy. The encouragement and preservation of such art, as well as poetry, drama, and music, seemed to be impossible in a democracy, because a sponsoring elite was needed.

Young America *had* a native elite—the ultra-Federalists of New England, the Knickerbocker landlords of New York, the long-established tobacco lords of Virginia. But they and their children were not fated to express the themes of American life in gilded monuments or epic volumes. In fact, the small native aristocracy had disappeared for the most part by 1845. American institutions were to be fashioned by people of action and newcomers to power. The influences that shaped the national mind included the principles of equality and freedom (even though they were not always lived up to), the open frontier, and the growing factories and cities. These were expressed in a variety of expressive behavior shared by multitudes. Democracy, in fact, produced in the United States a popular culture that made it impossible to mistake an American for any other national. A good question for a student to ask is just how that elusive substance, a national character, is revealed. Is it more likely to be found in items of popular culture or of high culture? Can a French folk song tell us things that a heroic poem about Charlemagne cannot? Can we learn something from the wood carving on a German peasant's barn that we do not reach through a Bach cantata? Think of the question not in terms of what is good or bad but in terms of what provides clues for history.

Perhaps the best way to illuminate these forces at work is to look at three American and democratic institutions that rose in the thirty years after the War of 1812 ended. They are the political party, the "revivalized church," and the

---

*CHRONOLOGY*

1790–1820 *Heyday of frontier revivalism in religion*

1828 *Andrew Jackson elected president*

1835 *James Gordon Bennett founds New York* Herald

newspaper. None was a purely American invention. But each rapidly took on an appearance that was almost entirely unlike that of similar institutions in Britain or Europe. In seeing how this happened, we may make precise judgments about what popular culture says and does. And you may then wish to test them by applying them to other American institutions you know.

*Politics: From Lace to Homespun*

It is a Saturday in March 1821 in Heckman County, Tennessee. A huge barbecue is in progress. It follows a two-day squirrel hunt, during which a thirty-five-year-old ex-soldier in the Creek War against the local Indians, by name Davy Crockett, has piled up an impressive heap of bloody squirrel skins. Crockett is a largely unsuccessful farmer. He is also, as it happens, a candidate for the state legislature. On the scene is his rival. Presently, the crowd urges both men to spice up the frolic with a speech. As Crockett himself is later to admit, speechmaking is "a business I was as ignorant of as an outlandish Negro." But undaunted he climbs up on a stump, and tells the people that he is like a man who was seen at the roadside, beating on an empty barrel. A passerby asked what he was doing. He answered that there had been some cider in the barrel a few days before, and he was trying to see whether there was any left, but he could not get at it. "I had a little bit of speech in me a while ago," Crockett grins at his listeners, "but I believe I can't get it out." The buckskin-clad crowd roars; Crockett is a good fellow. He is also a good judge of his neighbors' tastes. He tells a few more jokes, then suggests that he is dry as a powder horn, and it is time for a general whistle wetting. While the other candidate makes his speech, Crockett lounges by a whiskey barrel, where the better part of the crowd has followed him. There he rolls on with an easy flow of banter, now and then "taking a horn" of liquor, and making sure that his audience is encouraged to do likewise. Later, he moves on to other gatherings, always amiable, always good humored, and always making sure that when his turn comes to speak, he has a supply of jokes at hand and a nearby keg. In the final tally, he beats his competitor 2 to 1.

It is not likely that the Founding Fathers had expected this style of election politics. They saw voting as confined to the property owners and taxpayers of relatively small communities. The issues would be primarily local, and the weight of tradition and custom, together with the opinions of respected community leaders, would play a large part in swinging the result one way or another. The pattern they had in mind was partly in existence. In southern counties for example, a handful of the best-known planters were acknowledged pacesetters. They often served as local judges. They took the lead in trying new agricultural methods. They led the drive for subscriptions to set up a local school or bring in a member of the clergy or undertake some other civic improvement. And they were listened to attentively on political matters. Another example of such elitism was in New England towns, where the clergy was often consulted concerning nominations to office. Who, it was thought, had a better right to judge the moral qualities of a potential officeholder than the persons who baptized the babies, performed the weddings, buried the dead, and counseled the troubled ones of a village? Who more intimately searched the hearts and minds of the cluster of families that comprised a township?

In short, the country's leaders in the eighteenth century thought of the political process as a way of reaching community consensus through established channels of authority. They distrusted "factions," as they would have called parties, because factions tended to pit the interests of a single group against the whole. And they distrusted the nontaxpaying, nonproperty-owning "mob" (in which no individual of character could be trapped for long in a land bursting with opportunity!), because they believed its members would think of their own immediate needs and appetites before considering the long-range interests of society at large—rather like children who, given the chance, might spend a whole family budget on sweets and never lay in a supply of winter fuel.

These ideas began to run afoul of reality almost from the moment the Constitution went into effect. They were virtually destroyed in the boom times that followed the end of the War of 1812. Swift movement westward and to the growing towns stripped population from the old communities that had nursed eighteenth-century models of leadership. The political results came in three great shock waves before 1840. One was the coming of virtually universal suffrage; another was the election of Jackson as president. Finally, came the emergence of the national party and its machinery.

The push to enfranchise the unpropertied gathered headway steadily from 1790 to 1825. "Universal suffrage" was not really universal, as it was restricted to white males over twenty-one. But even at that it was a powerful novelty, for it implied that the right to vote was not tied to having a so-called stake in society. That right was given "universally" in the new western states coming steadily into the Union (Kentucky in 1792, Tennessee in 1796, Ohio in 1803, Louisiana in 1812, Indiana in 1816, Mississippi the next year, Illinois in 1818, and Alabama in 1819). It was difficult to deny suffrage there, since most settlers began almost penniless and shared alike the risks and chances of frontier life. Once voting was granted in the West without producing predicted social disasters such as confiscation of all property or abolition of taxes, it was difficult to resist pressure for writing it into revised state constitutions in the older communities. Such pressure came from the working people or "mechanics" of new factory towns as well as from the frontier line. By 1828 only three states (Rhode Island, Virginia, and Louisiana) kept property qualifications or other significant restrictions on casting the ballot.

Universal suffrage was a national demand in a society of rising expectations. It did not come about through contempt for property. Rather, Americans thought of themselves as having the ability to become propertied. Therefore, they wanted a voice in arranging public affairs so that each individual would have a chance. Privilege may be resented in a standstill society with few hopes of change. But it is fiercely hated in a swift-moving social order, where it seems to block good chances of getting ahead. Americans simply would not leave the public business to the votes of a chosen few who would bar the way for others.

Once universal suffrage was established, it set up a momentum of its own. Voters demanded more open decisions by officeholders. They insisted that more public servants be elected, not appointed. And the idea took root that there was some special wisdom in the "common people" that eluded their betters. It was argued that whatever a majority of the people wanted was somehow bound to be right. There is a Latin motto that embodies the feeling: *vox populi, vox Dei* ("the voice of the people [is] the voice of God"). A more universal and folksy version of the same idea was that God must have loved the common people, since He made so many of them. And since educated and sophisticated men and women were always in a minority, the new-style democracy carried with it an anti-intellectual bent, a distrust of experts and experience in favor of the prejudices of "plain folks."

These feelings were the power behind the rise of Jackson to the political peaks. Born in 1767 in the frontier district of the Carolinas, he worked and fought his way up from the hardscrabble existence of wringing a crop out of wilderness clearings. Jackson was tutored in law by an older attorney. That was the normal apprenticeship system of his day. It combined life and education, sometimes to the disadvantage of the latter. He made his way to Tennessee in 1788. Handling cases there, he often took his fees in land. Soon he had enough to be a successful planter. Popular with his friends, he was soon elected to a judgeship. The very idea of electing judges was itself new and somewhat radical. On the bench he made up for his lack of normal legal training by acting on the rule: "Always do what is right between parties. That is what the law *means.*" He had few doubts, if any, about the rightness of his decisions. Neither did voters, who had sent him on to the House and Senate.

He was also chosen to posts in the militia, which suited his violently combative temperament. He fought in several street brawls and duels and carried an opponent's bullet in him to the day of his death. At the time of the War of 1812 he became commander of an army in the South. Jackson smashed the Southern Indians at the battle of Horseshoe Bend, and later, as we noted, the British at New Orleans. In 1818 he was commanding the Southern military district of the United States when he learned that two British fur traders in Spanish-owned Florida were allegedly stirring up the Indians. Jackson marched troops in and seized and hung the two, boldly flouting both Spanish and British rights and sovereignty. Nothing happened, and the following year Spain prudently sold Florida to the United States.

By 1828 Jackson was *the* popular hero of the ordinary American. They all admired his energy, his self-made quality, his head-on thrusts against his enemies, and the deep gulf of difference between him and the presidents who had served since 1800. Those men—Jefferson, Madison, James Monroe, and John Quincy Adams—were cultivated, experienced diplomats, widely read in several languages. Against their seasoning in the great world, Jackson's experiences in Tennessee courts and even in tiny Washington looked provincial. Nevertheless, the populace insisted that he was their choice to lead the nation.

Popular pressure on state legislatures got his name on the presidential ballot in every state in 1824. Up to that time nominees had been chosen only by private meetings, or caucuses, of party leaders. But now King Caucus was dethroned. King Electoral College, however, was not. Jackson got the most popular votes but not an electoral majority. The election went to the House of Representatives, and there John Quincy Adams was chosen, despite outraged cries that Congress should have rubber-stamped the popular will.

Four years later, however, it was another story. Jackson was elected and memorably sworn in. A vast mob followed him from the Capitol, where he took the inaugural oath, to the White House. There a reception took place. A proper Washington lady described the scene as a "a rabble, a mob of boys, Negroes, women, children, scrambling, fighting, romping. What a pity! What a pity!" Furniture, glass and china were smashed as the crowd pressed forward to congratulate its hero. Only the expedient of opening the windows so that some of the crowd could escape prevented Jackson from being suffocated in the swarm. It was "the People's day, and the People's President."

In office Jackson was less of an idol breaker than some feared. But he was unmistakably something new. Best known was his wholesale housecleaning of previous federal appointees, whom he replaced with loyal friends. Jackson was not the first president to do this. But he was the first to defend it as a matter of principle, arguing that: "The duties of all public officers are, or at least admit of being made, so plain and simple that men of intelligence may readily qualify themselves for their performance." Hence no one, experienced or not, had a right to remain on the public payroll. Jackson called this the principle of rotation in office, but one of his associates said more bluntly: "To the victor belong the spoils," and it was under the name of the "spoils system" that the practice found its way into national life. Jackson could not foresee that some day "right-thinking" Americans would denounce the spoils system for depriving the nation of the services of experts in the increasingly complex jobs of government, or that one day the "people" would include blacks, Indians, Hispanic Americans, and women. He was a democrat for his time, but the meanings of such words change with time.

Jackson's first term in office was marked by furious conflicts. One raged over his frequent use of the veto. Another was triggered by his assault on the Second Bank of the United States. The Bank, chartered in 1816, was a public and private partnership. It transacted the financial affairs of the federal government. But is also undertook its own banking operations, and its stock was held by both the United States and private individuals. With the United States as a chief depositor, the Bank was the biggest and most powerful lender, with rural banks and many politicians in its pocket. Yet Jackson vetoed a congressional renewal of its charter, due to expire in 1836. His grounds were that private investors (some of who were foreigners) had no right to get rich as a result of the government's giving them a monopoly of its business. And, moreover, the Bank was a dangerous concentration of power in a free country. Thus the war on "privilege" was opened on another front.

Jackson's sandpapery qualities polarized opinion for and against him. This led to the re-creation of parties, which had tended to disappear between 1815 and 1825 as the old issues of the 1790s vanished. By 1832 a clear party of pro-Jackson people had appeared. They unhesitatingly called themselves the Democrats. The anti-Jackson elements had combined in the so-called Whig Party. That was the name of the British and American groups opposing royal power in the 1760s, and the American Whigs of the 1830s were trying to label themselves as valiant battlers against "King Andrew," the veto-flourishing tyrant.

These new parties were something different from the Democratic- Republicans and the Federalists. Their ancestors, for one thing, extended deep into the hearts of every community in every state. There were party clubs and party committees in each state, county, congressional district, and township. Each Whig or Democratic organization made it a mission to cultivate new voters. It urged them to go to the polls, staged meetings for them to eat, drink, and be spellbound by oratory, gave them pamphlets to read, and aspired to raise political awareness. The work of all these local organizations, from fund raising to naming new candidates, was increasingly coordinated by men who gave full time to political life. So the second change from the 1790s was the emergence of the professional party manager, someone who might hold a government job or office but whose real work was putting together winning combinations on Election Day.

From Washington outward, therefore, a network of political activity webbed the country. At its center and intersections were persons who lived for and by elections. Finally, in 1831, following the example of a short-lived splinter party known as the Anti-Masons, both Whigs and Democrats began the practice of holding a national convention every four years to nominate a

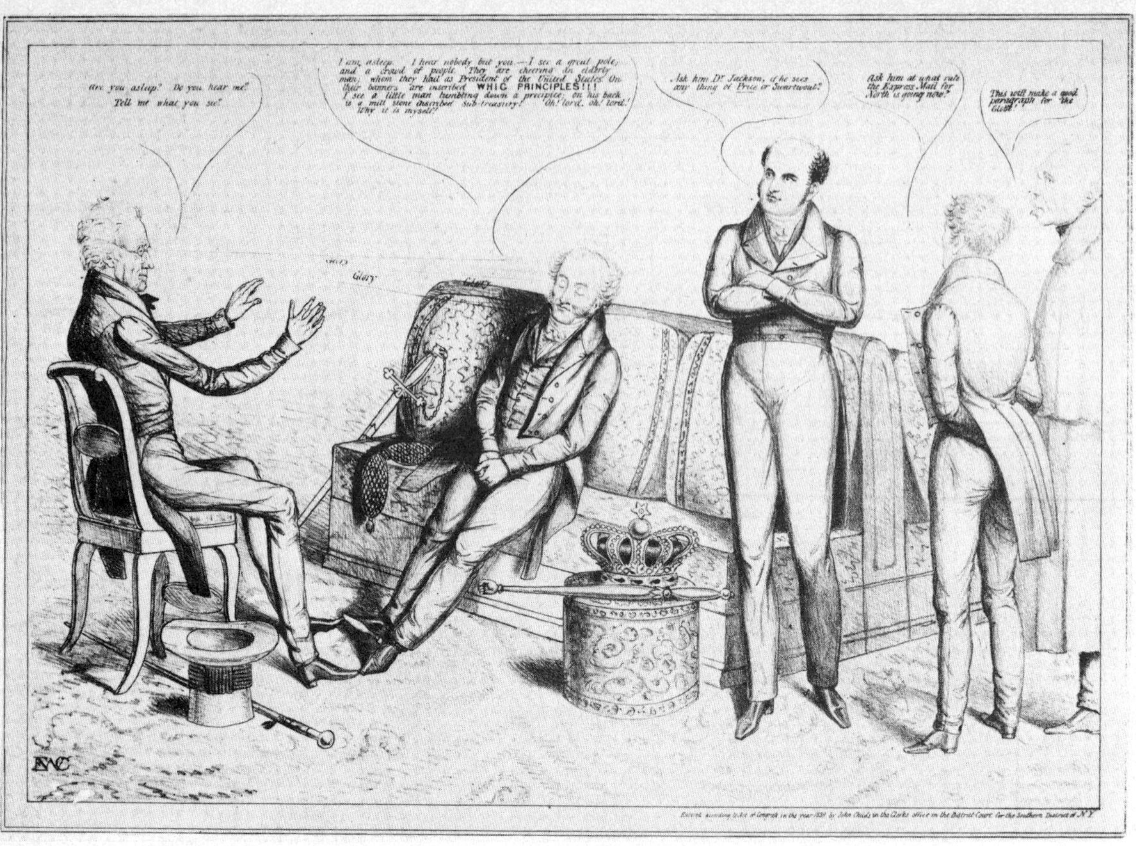


*In the 1830s as now, political cartoons made their points without much subtlety. Here "King Andrew" Jackson hypnotizes his Vice-President and successor, Van Buren. The words are less important than the evident ridicule. In the age of the common man, political argument rocked—and united—the entire nation.*

presidential candidate. These gatherings quickly took their modern form. Speeches rallied the faithful and blamed the opposition for all disasters that had befallen or might yet befall the nation. The merits of the various candidates were promoted with whoops, bands, and after the hoopla and the final choice there was a party love feast of reconciliation in preparation for the campaign ahead.

The fullest flowering of the system came in 1840. Until then the Whigs had generally appealed to the well-financed members of society. But in that year they nominated a western Indian fighter, William Henry Harrison, and brazenly imitated the Jacksonian tactics. "Old Tippecanoe" was presented as a buckskin-clad, homespun hero who lived contentedly in a log cabin and drank hard cider. Meanwhile, President Martin Van Buren, Jackson's Democratic successor, was accused of living high, sipping champagne, and dining on White House gold plates, bought with taxes wrung from the people's sweat. The fact that Harrison was a wealthy landowner was buried in the bray of thousands of torchlight parades, rallies, and barbecues. When the votes were in, Harrison had not only won, but it is now estimated that an astonishing 80 percent of the eligible electorate had taken part in the voting, compared with averages of less than 60 percent in most presidential contests.

The nation was politicized. Politics was a kind of self-realization, an entertainment in an era before media-made spectacles, and almost a passion. A brilliant young Frenchman, Alexis de Tocqueville, visited the United States in the 1830s to observe the workings of democracy first hand. Of elections he noted:

> The political activity which pervades the United States must be seen in order to be understood. No sooner do you set foot upon American ground, than you are stunned by a kind of tumult: a confused clamor is heard on every side; and a thousand simultaneous voices demand the satisfaction of their social wants. Everything is in motion around you; here, the people of one quarter of a town are met to decide upon the building of a church; there, the election of a representative is going on; a little further, the delegates of a district are posting to the town in order to consult some local improvements; in another place, the laborers of a village quit their ploughs to deliberate . . . the cares of politics engross a prominent place . . . and almost the only pleasure which an American knows is to take part in the government, and to discuss its measures. . . . Even the women frequently attend public meetings, and listen to political harangues as a recreation from their household labors. . . .

## *Religion: Democratizing Heaven*

A kind of universal suffrage was taking hold in the world of religion, too, in this period. Old patterns were twisted into new shape to meet the pressures of the theory of equality.

In the colonies, especially in New England, the Puritan vision had molded religious practice. Its core was the belief in predestination—the notion that God, in His majesty, had chosen some to be damned and others to be saved. All were to ponder their unknown fate as they awaited death, the final mystery. The path of righteousness was furnished by the Scriptures. God's shepherds, the pastors, unraveled the difficult passages, and passed the wisdom on in their sermons. The pattern was doubly authoritarian. It set up an elite of the saved, or elect, and laid awesome influence on the preacher. "Do you serve the congregation here?" one of them was once asked by a visitor. "I rule here" was the majestic reply.

But as settlers went into newly developed areas, they passed out of range of a learned clergy. Backwoods people, spread thinly over hundreds of wooded square miles, could not build neat white-steepled meeting houses or sustain a Yale- or Harvard-trained preacher. Yet, as they would have put it, God found a way to bring them the blessings of religion. From among their own ranks rose up a number of individuals who both farmed and prayed, who wore the same buckskins as their parishioners and "murdered the King's English every lick."

But what they lacked in literacy they made up in zeal. They could bellow the Lord's message to a crowd in a voice loud enough to wake the spiritually dead. Some were Presbyterians; more came from the ranks of the Baptists and Methodists, two sects that always had many followers among the uneducated.

The word of God, on the frontier, was changed. Frontier parsons did not officially abandon predestination, in fact they left it behind them as they roared to their listeners that a person who *truly* repented of his abominations was almost sure to be saved. They held great meetings in the wilderness, in which torchlights and shadows swayed and danced, and in the gloom they exhorted their packed listeners to humble themselves before God, confess their sins openly, and then to accept joyfully the promises of the Bible that salvation would be theirs. As hundreds fell under their spell, the clergy rejoiced in what they called a revival of the old-time spirit of Christ. *Revivalism* became the name that clung to these mass conversions of Americans to red-hot faith and dedication.

Backwoods revivals were a stormy new kind of religious ritual. They involved men and women who lived forever in the shadow of death on the violent frontier, people who were tough but expressive and informal in their emotions where eternity was concerned. Those "mourners" who were "convicted of sin" flung themselves to the bare earth, screamed, and tore at their clothes. Those who felt themselves finally "born anew" capered in wild joy. Believers were seen barking like dogs, jabbering in strange tongues, or quivering and twitching in a frenzy known as "the jerks." No modern-day, drug-high audience at a rock festival ever acted out wilder scenes.

From about 1790 to 1820 these revivals seared frontier communities. Then they became part of an institutional machinery designed to perpetuate their essential spirit. Some entirely new church bodies were formed around a core of revivalism like the Cumberland Presbyterian church, formed in 1810, after many quarrels with eastern Presbyterians who frowned on revival fury. The outdoor revival hardened into the camp meeting. Instead of a special event, it became a regular combination of yearly camp-out and cookout. Families came in wagons, pitched tents, and lingered three or four days to hear the preaching, to socialize, and to fortify their spirits with ham, turkey, chicken, potato salads,

*Preachers in homespun in the American West turned Christianity into a folk religion with a strong pattern of homespun about it. According to tradition, this figure is Henry Ward Beecher, son of pioneer revivalist Lyman Beecher. It was supposedly carved during the younger Beecher's early pastorate in rural Indiana.*

pickled vegetables, pies, cakes, cookies, jams, biscuits, corn bread, and other outpourings from rural kitchens.

A new breed of preachers rose in the West, especially among the Methodists. These were the circuit riders, ministers with no settled churches, who traveled a regular route among cabins in the clearings. They were the mobile troops of the Lord, and an American wonder. They "roughed it along the trails in snow and rain, taking their chances on bears, wolves, cutthroats and Indians." They grew used to bedding down on dirt floors and living on corn meal and pork. They knew dirt and bugs perpetually and intimately. And they were beyond discouragement. A folk saying had it that when the weather was at its worst, there was "nobody out but crows and Methodist preachers." All for salaries of about $64 a year and for the glory of God.

Frontier religion generated new ideas of godly life, too. The newly won holiness of a camp meeting convert did not take the form of contemplation, study, and withdrawal from the world. Mostly all it meant was observing a long list of "don'ts"—chief among them the avoidance of drunkenness, swearing, and Sabbath breaking. Outside of the Deep South a convert who owned slaves was expected to give them up, for it was not only sinful to own another soul but also to let others do one's work. Work, in fact, was a blessing, so long as part of what it earned went to support churches, schools, and charitable institutions. The American revival put its strongest focus on diligence and productiveness, exactly what a fast-developing society needed.

Revivalism was not confined to the West, though it was liveliest there. It struck the East in a somewhat different fashion. In the small towns of New England and western New York State, religious enthusiasm brimmed over in frequent prayer meetings and constant sampling of the moral temperature and pulse rate of small communities where everyone's sins and virtues were public topics. Local ministers were thrilled when dozens of converts began to appear. There were fewer outbursts of nervous hysteria, but the steady work of adding to the harvest of souls saved for the Lord (who always seemed to be close by) went on.

The lasting by-product was the organization of societies to oversee the chores of piety. Clubs blossomed to combat rum, send missionaries abroad, found Sunday schools, print Bibles. They were agencies of the churches managed by lay people but led by the clergy. Yet this was a new kind of clergy. No longer did the Yankee minister speak for a mighty Jehovah who denied heaven to all but a chosen few. Everyone wanted a chance at salvation. Nor was the clergyman the top figure in all church affairs; the local lawyer or druggist might do better at raising funds for the Bible society.

Yet the minister was not powerless. He was still the explainer, the go-between of God and the town. Beecher, whom we met in the last chapter, was appalled in 1818, when Connecticut disestablished (that is, cut off tax support to) the Congregational church. But later he came to see it differently. If the ministers were no longer social idols, their role as organizers left them with power nonetheless. "By voluntary efforts," he wrote, "societies, missions and revivals, they exert a deeper influence than ever they could be queues, and shoe-buckles, and cocked hats, and gold-headed canes." But it was work! "Nowadays," an aging Beecher grumbled to his children "they wear a man out in a few years."

From its small-town and frontier bases the revival grew urbanized. The career of Charles Grandison Finney best tells that story. Finney was a young lawyer in upstate New York, when, one night in 1821, the Lord overwhelmed him. Alone in his office, he experienced a blazing, emotional storm. During its course, he wept, fainted, and finally saw Jesus face to face. From this moment, he wrote, he knew that the Lord had appointed him to plead His cause.

Finney abandoned the law, studied for the ministry, and began an active career of traveling from town to town, holding revival meetings. His technique deftly blended reason and passion. Dressed in a plain business suit, instead of the old-fashioned ministerial gowns and collars, he addressed audiences in lawyerlike terms. The message was that God had made a covenant with humanity, and the terms were in the Bible in plain English for all to read. To obey them guaranteed salvation. To those who doubted, Finney could be a terror. His booming voice and deep, blazing eyes were skilled at branding a "sinner" before the entire gathering. (As an example, when a woman once came in dressed in a bonnet whose nodding plumes shrieked worldly vanity, Finney scalded her with: "Did you come here to make people worship *you?*") Under Finney's lash, women and men often fainted or burst into hysterical sobs. By 1831 he was known throughout the Northeast as a man who could set lukewarm churches on fire.

Now some pious merchants of New York City invited Finney to come and settle in a church, which they would build for him, where he could, in a single meeting, address more sinners than lived in an entire rural township. Finney finally accepted the offer, and revivalism moved into another phase. It would continue in small-town America. But Finney would father a kind of big-time revivalism held in huge auditoriums, a form of mass religious entertainment, rather than an outpouring of local godly enthusiasm.

Revivalism was the force that galvanized American Protestantism, then the religion of the majority, into meeting the challenge of change. In a rough way the religious structure that had emerged by 1845 bore some resemblance to the new political system. Each denomination was something like a party. Various denominational leaders engaged in dialogue with each other and competed for members, though no one often expected a person to leave either the church *or* the party he grew up with. Just as the political parties organized debate on questions of national growth, so the denominations—parties in the republic of Christ, so to speak—publicized strides toward moral improvement. The missionary and other societies matched the various Whig or Democratic clubs that did the pick-and-shovel work of organizing election rallies and turnouts.

Religion permeated social life, much as politics did. Everyone was expected to make some formal profession of religion, however he might live his life. With rare exceptions, the individual who did not belong to a Protestant denomination was at a disadvantage in any business requiring social acceptance. Churchgoing was a cement uniting society. The local benevolent, missionary, and uplift associations were all linked loosely in national bodies. Their network was another element holding a widely scattered nation together. A Bible society president in Missouri and one in Connecticut were both "Americans," sharing a faith and a mission as well a flag and a Constitution.

### *The Potent Popular Press*

Communications were another key to unification, and the flag bearer of communication was the newspaper. It, too, underwent swift evolution after 1800. Before the 1780s the few dozen colonial newspapers, which appeared weekly, were almost identical in appearance. Each consisted of a large single sheet folded over to make a small, four-page paper. In it the editor, owner, and publisher—usually all one person—put local advertisements, snippets from almanacs, letters from political debaters signed with splendid Latin names, official proclamations, bits of poetry by local bards, and interesting news items from other newspapers that came in the mail. The "press run" of these journals was about 200, squeezed off on wooden presses. The type was handset, hand-inked, and hand-pressed on the paper, one side at a time.

By the 1840s a number of inventions eased the task of printers and gave them a wider audience. The most sophisticated equipment consisted of rotary presses. In them the type was clamped to a cylinder that rolled back and forth over the paper. The biggest of them were steam driven and could produce thousands of newspapers within a few hours, plenty for big-city journalism with circulations of up to 50,000. But even humble country printers enjoyed presses that were sturdier, faster, and capable of running off enough copies for a whole county with little trouble.

The public hungered for newspapers. Almost every village had at least one. The printer-editor came along in the vanguard of civilization with the pioneer farmer, the doctor, the lawyer, and the land seller. There were almost 2000 country weeklies by 1840. What did they contain? To begin with, they carried "exchanges" from other papers. Newspapers traveled free in the mail. So country editors could clip for their readers the latest news from neighboring states, from great cities like Philadelphia, Boston, and New York and even from Europe. These exchanges kept the American people remarkably well informed about public matters. Their information was a guardian of the health of democracy and was responsible for the statement of Jefferson that, given a choice between a government without newspapers and newspapers without a government, he would prefer the latter.

In addition, the country weekly contained local gossip, news of meetings, appeals from local candidates for support, and advertisements that let everyone know where the best buys could be made. It told farmers the prices of potatoes and pork. It gave the local schoolmaster a chance to show off his learning in an occasional essay or poem. It summarized cases being heard in the local courts. It was read from cover to cover by its subscribers, and those who could not pay $4 to $8 a year (in cash or produce) could find copies in the local tavern. It was a community entertainment, a bulletin board, and a vehicle for self-expression.

There were other journalistic breakthroughs in larger towns. The newspaper mania was so great and the cost of starting one so cheap that almost any group with a special message found a journalistic voice. Every major religious denomination had a weekly. So did reform, agricultural, and professional societies. A special category included the so-called commercial newspapers, huge, blanket-sized sheets, down whose six or eight columns ran inky ladders of important information such as ship arrivals and departures, prices of goods, new transportation routes, offerings of stock, and bank interest rates. There were also party newspapers after the 1830s. Openly supported by subsidies, their job was to snipe at the opposition, boost their own candidates, and provide party loyalists with argumentative ammunition.

The greatest outburst of novelty came in the largest cities with the introduction of the cheap daily newspaper, which frankly aimed at a growing audience of workingmen and women, a group just achieving literacy through the new public schools. In 1833 a New York editor, Benjamin Day, began a tiny paper (8-by-11¼ inches for a copy that sold for a penny) named *The Sun*. It promised "ALL THE NEWS OF THE DAY" to its audience, but it interpreted that term very broadly to include jokes, humorous sketches, police reports, and other lively but lowly items. It was a success and inspired the emergence, two years later, of a spectacular competitor. This was the New York *Herald*. Its founder, James Gordon Bennett, a cross-eyed, terrible-tempered Scottish-born dynamo, was the true father of the modern mass media.

Bennett fancied himself the Napoleon, the Shakespeare, of the daily press. His exact words, in fact, convey his style better than any paraphrase, and he addressed his readers daily in highly personal terms in his lead editorials. (Besides writing these editorials, he was at first his own reporter, business manager, advertising salesman, and everything else—working out of a base-

*CAUSE . . .*
*A quote from the New York* Herald, *August 19, 1848 in a report on affairs in California: "Several mines have lately been discovered in this country . . . I am credibly informed that a quantity of gold, worth in value, $30, was picked up lately in the bed of a stream of the Sacramento."*

ment office from a desk consisting of a plank laid across two barrels.) When he married, for example, he told the world: "I must fulfill that awful destiny which the Almighty Father has written against my name in broad letters of light against the wall of heaven. I must give the world a pattern of happy married life." His journalistic ambitions not only included infusing papers with "wit, humor, sentiment and glowing taste" but were expressed thus:

> What is to prevent a daily newspaper from being made the greatest organ of social life? Books have had their day—the temple of religion has had its day. A newspaper can be made to take the lead of all these in the great movements of human thought and of human civilization. A newspaper can send more souls to Heaven, and save more from Hell, than all the churches or chapels in New York—besides making money at the same time.

*. . . AND EFFECT*
*The desolate appearance of the California mining camp at "Poverty Bar" in 1859 mirrors an important part of the frontier process. Wealth was sucked from Nature in violent haste, with little time or thought for aesthetic values or future needs.*

To this conception of his mission he was utterly faithful. He set out to make his newspaper the biggest, best, and most read in the country. He flung respectability to the winds and crammed his pages with stories of prize fights, arrests, suicides, scandals, divorces, and all of the human drama of a great city. But he did not stop there. He hired and dispatched correspondents to the gold fields of California, the battlefields of the Mexican and Civil Wars, the revolution-torn capitals of Europe, and to every place where news was made. When the telegraph was introduced in 1844, he paid liberally for wire dispatches. In the days before the Atlantic cable, he had his own swift little boat racing out to meet steamers from Europe, so that he could beat all rivals with the hottest news from foreign papers. By the time of his death in 1872, he had revolutionized journalism. And big-time journalism also bound society together.

The emerging culture of nationalism and democracy was a success story, and the parties, the churches, and the newspapers were key elements in it. Conservatives like the Federalists had distrusted democracy. They feared that without authority and tradition society would fly apart or burn out like an engine run too fast. And on the other side, Jefferson, though hospitable to democracy, feared growth. He and those like him believed that a people spread over a vast territory would lack a steadying sense of local roots. And as for cities, they would breed a working population without a center of gravity—without property, independence, or firm loyalties.

There was, in short, an uneasy feeling that swift growth would rupture old community structures and bring chaos. And, in fact, westward expansion and urban-industrial growth *did* wipe out old patterns of group life. But what forestalled chaos was the development of new controls and unifying forces. The revivalized churches spelled out proper moral behavior on which most Americans could agree. The party system tied together many scattered knots of population. The press publicized the successes, failures, and expectations of these institutions. It diffused the new culture. That culture was sometimes oppressive. It did not allow, for example, for much dissent from standard social beliefs. It was, in fact, sometimes described as "tyranny of the majority" or "rule by public opinion."

But it did permit the young republic to grow and stay united. That was its major strength. Some of its weaknesses remain to be examined—particularly the harsh fate that it dictated for natural barriers and peoples who stood in its expansive, triumphant way.

## *FOR FURTHER READING*

So far as politics is concerned a very good introduction to the Jacksonian period is George Dangerfield's beautifully written *The Era of Good Feelings* (1952). A more general survey of the period is Glyndon Van Deusen, *The Jacksonian Era* (1959). Robert V. Remini, *The Election of Andrew Jackson* (1964) zeroes in on 1828.

For a modern scholarly report read R. P. McCormick, *The Second American Party System* (1966). A good local study is in an old, but recently reprinted work, Dixon R. Fox, *The Decline of the Aristocracy in the Politics of New York* (1918). To get the taste of Crockett-style campaigning, read *A Narrative of the Life of Col. David Crockett* (1927).

There is some good general material in Bernard A. Weisberger, *They Gathered At the River* (1958). A special, useful, and colorful look at old-time religion is Charles A. Johnson, *The Frontier Camp Meeting* (1957). For a firsthand look at the revivalist's world, actual memoirs are good. The *Autobiography of Peter Cartwright* (1856) is a frontier evangelist's memoir and *The Life of Charles Grandison Finney, Written By Himself* (1966) presents the spellbinding preacher in his own style.

For accounts of the newspaper world, the most recent readable survey is Robert Rutland, *The Newsmongers* (1973). To read the life of James Gordon Bennett you will have to locate Oliver Carlson, *James Gordon Bennett: The Man Who Made News* (1942). Brief glimpses of other fathers of the penny press are in B. A. Weisberger, *The American Newspaperman* (1961). If your library has it, a taste of crusading journalism (1840s-style) can be gotten in Horace Greeley, *Recollections of a Busy Life* (1930).

# *Thought provokers*

*The long struggle to establish the United States on a firm footing was clearly won by 1815 if we think only in terms of safety from foreign invasion. Yet only five years after that date, a battle over the admission of Missouri as a free or slave state would raise the threat, eventually fulfilled, of a civil war. That only proves that national identity and unity are forces that can come under attack from many directions and thus cannot remain the same at all times. Questions about the nature of nationalism, therefore, will have different answers for different periods of a people's history. We can see this in specific questions on the chapters just studied.*

*For example, in the coming of the Revolution was the conflict between Britain and her colonies predominantly political? Or was it cultural as well? Did the issues that aroused Americans, for the most part, have anything to do with religion? Language? Family life-styles? Or would an "average" Briton and an "average" colonist have seen more or less eye to eye on matters concerning faith, respect for the past, and goals of life? Did such questions become part of the debate between mother country and provinces? Were they a necessary ingredient of revolution?*

*The term* liberal *is often used in historical writing to describe one who welcomes change and is confident about good things in the future.* Conservative *is its opposite. But were the British ministers who were trying to restructure the empire's machinery liberal by this definition? Or were they conservative? And what of the colonists who kept insisting that they only wanted to restore the good old days when Britain left them alone? Were they conservatives? If the answer to that is yes, how can we make sense of the fact that these American conservatives were such firm believers in the great future potential of the colonies if left to their natural growth? To unravel this muddle you must learn to apply terms such as "conservative" and "liberal" to specific areas of action and belief, rather than as general labels. Try to do that with any of the individual figures mentioned in all four of these chapters—Hamilton, Madison, Barlow, Beecher, Crockett, Bennett. You will find that such distinctions make it harder to deliver easy statements, but they will deepen your understanding of the complexity of human motives.*

*In looking at the Constitution, what, in your own view, was the minimum number of adjustments that would have kept the government under the Articles of Confederation workable? In other words, how much of the Constitution's machinery went directly to the critical problems of unity, and how much was additional? Do political conventions tend to go beyond their original assignments often?*

*How much democracy do you find in the Constitution's voting provisions, especially for president? Was it really set up primarily for the benefit of those already powerful? What about the objections to the office of the presidency? Was it really too strong, as some Antifederalists said? Does the history of the modern presidency bear out their fears? Or, on the other hand, could the government have really survived the first twenty years* without *a strong president? Look back to the chapter on the United States during the Napoleonic Wars, and ask yourself whether Jefferson and Madison fulfilled the expectations of the framers about the ability of the president to provide "energy" to government. How much did their personal histories have to do with their performance, as well as the powers vested in them? Is the Constitution capable of being stretched in many directions, depending on who holds office under it? Give some examples.*

*As for the Alien and Sedition Acts, to what extent was there any reason to think that "foreign-born" citizens would be less loyal than "native-born" Americans? How does one define what makes an American other than birth? Given the fact that the king of Britain at the time was the grandson of a German prince who spoke almost no English, how important do you think "native" birth is as a symbol of national character?*

*What about the rise of democracy, described in Chapter 7, as it relates to nationality? Does nationalism have a different meaning in a country with universal suffrage than in an absolute monarchy? Is it different to be a "subject" of a king and a "citizen" of a nation in terms of responsibilities and obligations? Do modern democracy and modern nationalism always go hand in hand? Did they grow together in the United States from 1787 to 1815?*

*Finally, how did the "new" politics of the Jacksonian era affect the kinds of individuals who got into government? Did it downgrade the value of education? Did Crockett-style campaigning put more emphasis on "getting along" than on independent thought? If so, why were Crockett and Jackson such "characters"? Is there a difference between personal eccentricity and political independence? And is political independence the same thing as freedom from majority pressure? Did the press and the churches work to reinforce majority power? If so, how did they change their own roles in the process? That is, would Franklin have been able to put out Bennett's New York* Herald? *And would the Puritan fathers of Massachusetts have recognized the God of Finney?*

DOWN WITH THE LIQUOR TRAFFIC
LOVE
PURITY
FIDELITY
Know all men by these
for the consideration
do Bargain
to have and to Hold
it being understood
then the above bargain
shall be void

# PART THREE:

# TESTING A NATION

*If you think back to your own adolescence, you know that sudden growth is both an exciting and a disturbing experience. The excitement comes from the daily discovery of new powers and new possibilities. The body can do more, and the mind can understand more. It is possible to try new pleasures, escape old taboos, dream new dreams.*

*But there are also frightening parts. New responsibilities must be met, new roles filled, as a part-time worker, an advanced student, a partner in love. There is always the haunting question:* "Do I measure up?" *Success depends on your own efforts, not those of your parents. That knowledge creates anxiety.*

*Gradually, however, most young men and women get both their anxieties and ambitions whittled down to realistic size and develop adult personalities that combine their childhood traits with the new styles they have learned as independent people.*

*It is possibly misleading to talk about societies and nations as if they had stages of growth comparable to those of individual humans. Group life has its differences from personal life. Yet sometimes, merely to get a point of view, such a comparison can be helpful in historical study. The great spurt of growth experienced by the United States from* 1816 *to* 1860 *has sometimes been referred to as America's "adolescence" or "awkward age." Without being too literal about it, we can possibly deepen our understanding of that period if we do consider it in that way. What were the new powers of the young nation's people as a whole? What were the new stresses upon them? And how did the coming of "maturity" change the characteristic behavior of various American institutions? How did the United States respond to the tests of growth? These are the theme questions of this part.*

*The opening chapter of this part, Chapter 8, talks about the great physical growth of the country as settlers moved into the unfarmed West. It asks what happened to neighborhoods, villages, and even whole states as young families left them by the thousands, lured by cheap land. How did American society react to this tug at a basic binding force, the sense of place and of local roots?*

*We ask, too, what the presence of a bonanza of free land did to people's expectations of what life had to offer them. For centuries human social groups had felt a sense of limits imposed by their natural environment—there was only so much food, so much water, so much building material, so much fuel. What happened when, thanks to invention, the environment suddenly seemed to be a storehouse to be ransacked at will? What did that do to attitudes toward natural resources and natural creatures?*

*And how did constant improvement in living standards affect the way men and women looked at the past and future? If the future always seemed to be promising better things, did that put less value on the hand-me-downs of the past? Did it change the way families thought about their children and their ancestors, for example? If expansion changed the sense of place, what did it do to the sense of time?*

*Chapter 9 discusses new breakthroughs in production that changed economic life by making large-scale business possible. What were the human results of mass production, a nationwide market, a work force numbering in thousands, and private fortunes of millions of dollars? How did human relationships in a joint economic effort change when the scale grew larger? After all, a farm home was a production unit for raising food, making clothes, building shelter. A small workshop, say, a carpenter's, with only a few apprentices helping to do the work, was something of a family affair. What happened when an economy basically built on family farms and shops entered the factory age? How did people view themselves and organize to replace some of the lost closeness and to gain some control of their lives? The chapter searches for answers in a study of factories, early unions, and business corporations.*

*Economic organizations alone, however, do not solve broad questions of what ideals men and women should live by. The swift changes of the era caused some people to question the most basic rules of society, those governing marriage, property, and personal moral behavior. Because the country was so vast and so new, a number of people believed that almost any kind of social invention could be tried and any longstanding custom changed. The United States seemed to open the possibilities of fundamental changes in human nature. So various reformers tried to change society from the roots upward. Sometimes they founded model communities; sometimes they agitated for political, legal, or social changes that they believed would purify all human behavior. We will look at some "patent-office" communities and also at movements to curb the abuse of liquor, win equal rights for women, and end slavery. Each one ran into basic questions of what reformers can and cannot achieve in a particular political and social setting. But they all illustrate how quick growth sent the American people on a search for the deepest meanings of their experience together.*

*But not all people were reform minded. The final chapter of this part, Chapter 10, looks at a region that resisted change, the American South. It did not grow in the same way or at the same rate as the rest of the nation. It also clung to a racial and labor system, slavery, so ardently that it came to fear any change that might affect that institution. So its answers to the big questions of existence were often different. The chapter looks not only at the social values of the masters but at the slaves themselves. How did they view American life from their bottom-of-the-heap position? What might we learn from seeing things through their eyes? What kind of behavior did they develop in their situation? What price in personal and group development did slavery exact from them? And what price did white Southerners pay, in that same coinage, for keeping the slaves down? How did black and white make out, finally, by living under a rigid, old-fashioned system, in an age of progress?*

# chapter 8 The assault on nature

In 1818 a British traveler watched hundreds of wagons lurching along the muddy trails to the newly opened state of Illinois and wrote: "All America seems to be breaking up and moving westward." Historians since then have focused on the process of moving westward and ignored the meaning of the phrase "breaking up." But perhaps the historical importance of the westward movement can be grasped better if the spotlight is turned on the unraveling of old patterns rather than the weaving of the new.

What the Briton Morris Birkbeck perhaps accidentally hit upon in his choice of words was the fact that the institutions of the pre-1815 United States were shaped for a fairly compact, cohesive society. The sudden rush westward was bound to "break up" or at least stretch those institutions out of shape. Their critical role, in providing the cement of society, would have to be handled in another way. New attitudes would have to grow within the shell of old beliefs. New meanings would have to be given to words such as "family," "religion," "progress," "state," and "nation."

We already have seen, in the preceding chapter, how the rush to new lands affected politics and religion, by encouraging stump politics and camp meetings. But how did it touch the notions of what families meant? Or ideas of whether the United States had some special purpose in the world? What did the Americans of Jackson's era as compared with those of John Adams's time think about the meaning of the future? And how did their changing views paint their images of the natural wealth and "primitive" peoples around them? To follow such trails shows us the connections between growth on a map and the more complicated "geography" inside people's minds.



*The Great Rush Westward*

The facts of expansion, to begin with, were impressive even to a nineteenth-century generation not as saturated with statistics as our own. Between 1790 and 1860, 20 states were added to the Union. Each new decade saw a fresh "West" open up, as settlers by the hundreds of thousands took up new lands or found jobs in the western cities that were opening up: Pittsburgh, Wheeling, Cincinnati, St. Louis, Louisville. Though we think of the pioneer as a farmer, there was also an "urban frontier." It offered chances for success to those who founded or worked in the West's distilleries, ropewalks, packing houses, salt furnaces, ironworks, lead mines, boatyards, sawmills, and other manufacturing establishments.

The basic causes of this surge toward new horizons was a transportation revolution. Even before 1800 there were movements afoot in various states to invest money in improving American roads. The roads needed improvement badly. They were rutted, rocky, pockmarked with holes, turned to soupy mud in wet weather, and raised clouds of dust in dry seasons. Improvements in road building, such as proper grading, ditching, and the use of broken rock or gravel packed into a tight mass to provide a hard but well-drained surface, gradually crept into American engineering practice in the first half of the nineteenth century. Often these improvements came from self-taught surveyors, builders, and designers. In 1815 the federal government started to build a national road westward from a point near Washington to Vandalia, Illinois. This effort took until 1852. A growing number of states also sank money into improving their underdeveloped road networks.

The building of canals also dated back to the earliest days of the republic. George Washington had been among those proposing to dig short canals around rocky stretches of the Potomac. In Massachusetts the Middlesex Canal, completed in 1803, was one of the first of several to connect the seacoast with the inland farm country. The canal that caught the imagination of the country, however, and had the greatest economic impact led farther westward. It was the Erie, plowed across New York State from Buffalo to the headwaters of the Hudson between 1817 and 1825. It really, therefore, linked the Atlantic and the Great Lakes and made water travel—slow but cheap—possible all the way from New York to Minnesota. It would become the major east-west water highway of the country and the inspiration for dozens of similar projects in the so-called canal boom of the 1830s and 1840s.

Early trials of applying steam power to water transportation also went back to the 1780s. John Fitch had run a crude steamboat on the Delaware in 1787 but could not find backers to develop it; so it was Robert Fulton's *Clermont*, in 1807, that won fame as the first successful steam-powered vessel in America when it chuffed its way up the Hudson from New York to Albany in thirty-two hours. In 1811 Nicholas Roosevelt successfully ran a steamboat on the Mississippi. Soon the earliest models of the well-known river side-wheeler appeared. They themselves were an American creation. They were almost flat bottomed, so that they could run on the shallow rivers of the South. Their engines and cargo were out on an open lower deck, and above that was an airy stateroom deck, railed about like a front porch, where passengers could sit or stroll. This openness was made possible by the mild climate. And the river queens burned wood, which appeared to be in endless supply along the forested shores.

In 1828 the railroad age began in the United States, with groundbreaking for the Baltimore and Ohio line. Twelve years later, there were about 3000 miles of rail line in the nation, most of it consisting of short stretches radiating out, like wheel spokes, from major cities. By 1850, however, there were 8879 miles of track laid and the beginnings of a network that pulled the entire nation closer together. What the railroad and the steamboat meant was that the huge empty spaces of eastern North America could be quickly populated—by trains moving at up to 40 miles an hour or by boats that traveled more slowly but that were independent of winds and currents.

In addition, a number of inventions in farming made it possible to produce bumper crops to send to market over the new routes. Most notable were the cotton gin of 1793 and the McCormick reaper, successfully demonstrated in 1831. These made the large-scale growing of cotton and wheat profitable and, therefore, hugely increased the desirability of virgin acres in the Gulf South and the Great Lakes Northwest. They built the thrones of King Cotton and King

---

*CHRONOLOGY*

| | |
|---|---|
| 1807 | *Fulton's steamboat,* Clermont, *makes first successful voyage* |
| 1825 | *Erie Canal, from Albany to Buffalo, New York, completed* |
| 1828 | *Baltimore and Ohio Railroad started; first in United States* |
| 1830 | *Start of removal of Indians to west of the Mississippi River* |
| 1832 | *McCormick's reaper demonstrated* |
| 1836 | *Texas declares independence from Mexico* |
| 1846–1848 | *Mexican War* |
| 1862 | *Homestead Act* |

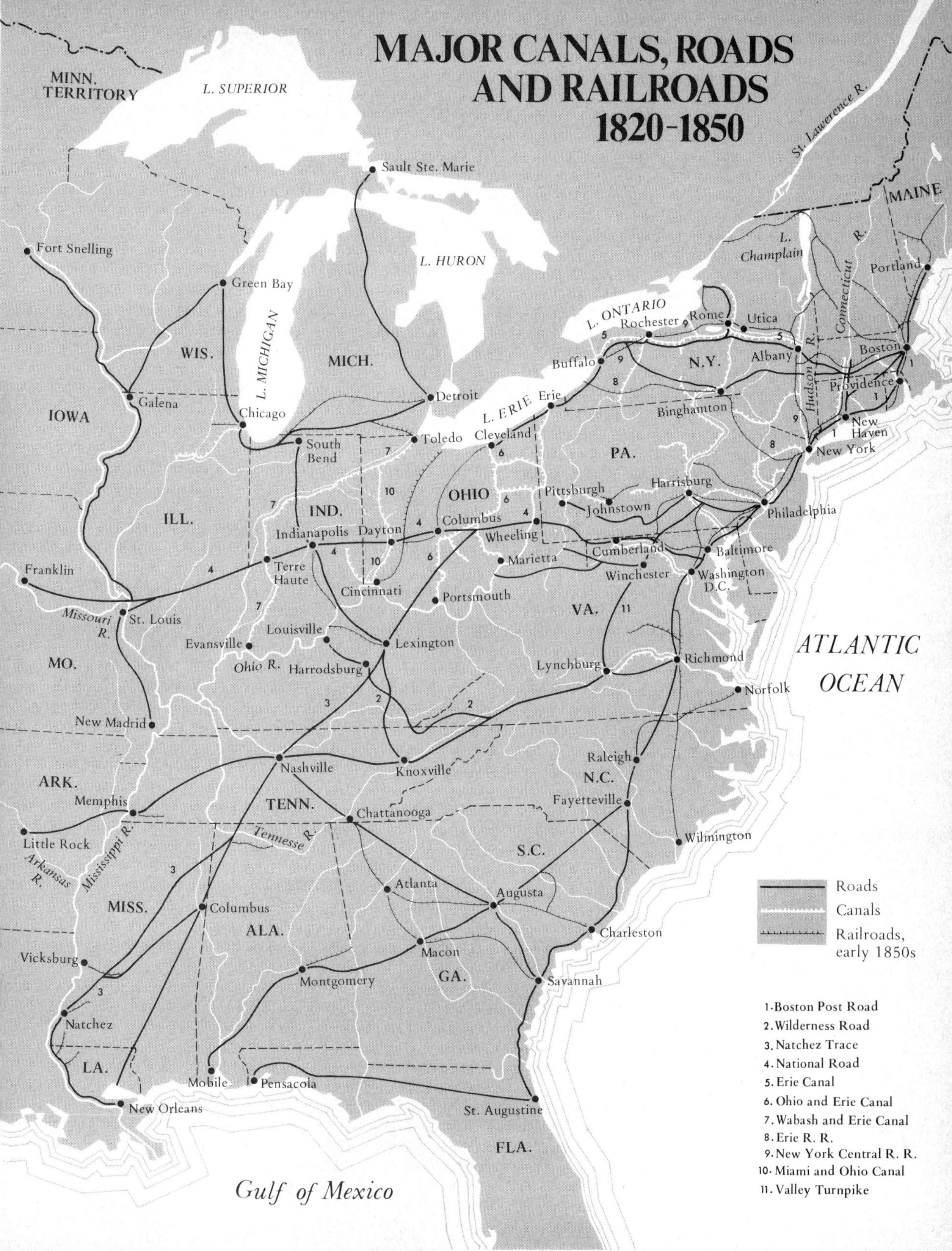

MAJOR CANALS, ROADS AND RAILROADS 1820-1850
MINN. TERRITORY
L. SUPERIOR
Sault Ste. Marie
Fort Snelling
Green Bay
L. HURON
L. MICHIGAN
WIS.
MICH.
IOWA
Galena
Chicago
Detroit
L. ERIE
Erie
Toledo
Cleveland
South Bend
L. ONTARIO
Rochester
Rome
Utica
Buffalo
Albany
N.Y.
Binghamton
St. Lawrence R.
MAINE
L. Champlain
Connecticut R.
Hudson R.
Portland
Boston
Providence
New Haven
New York
PA.
Harrisburg
Pittsburgh
Johnstown
Philadelphia
OHIO
IND.
ILL.
Indianapolis
Dayton
Columbus
Wheeling
Cumberland
Baltimore
Terre Haute
Marietta
Winchester
Washington D.C.
Franklin
Missouri R.
St. Louis
Cincinnati
Portsmouth
VA.
Evansville
Louisville
Lexington
Ohio R.
Harrodsburg
MO.
Lynchburg
Richmond
Norfolk
ATLANTIC OCEAN
New Madrid
Raleigh
Nashville
Knoxville
N.C.
ARK.
Memphis
TENN.
Chattanooga
Fayetteville
Little Rock
Tennessee R.
Mississippi R.
Arkansas R.
Wilmington
S.C.
Atlanta
Augusta
MISS.
Columbus
ALA.
Charleston
Vicksburg
Macon
Montgomery
GA.
Savannah
Natchez
LA.
Mobile
Pensacola
New Orleans
St. Augustine
FLA.
Gulf of Mexico
Roads
Canals
Railroads, early 1850s
1. Boston Post Road
2. Wilderness Road
3. Natchez Trace
4. National Road
5. Erie Canal
6. Ohio and Erie Canal
7. Wabash and Erie Canal
8. Erie R. R.
9. New York Central R. R.
10. Miami and Ohio Canal
11. Valley Turnpike

Wheat. In addition, came improved plows, methods of planting, cultivating, and fertilizing lands, and improvements in the breed and strength of draft animals. All these forces opened wide the doors of opportunity in the West. Through them poured a stream of moving families, who were soon sending back torrents of meat, grain, wool, and cotton for home and foreign markets.

*The East in Upheaval*

But this success story had a dark side for the America that was being left behind. Crops from the West were cheaper to produce and move, so that, thanks to the new inventions, the eastern farmer was undersold in his own markets. The center of wheat, corn, and cotton production moved steadily westward. Agricultural depressions, from 1816 on through the thirties, shook the older states. Settled families, and particularly younger children, no longer able to wrestle a living out of their ancestral acres, pulled up stakes and joined the migration. Rural counties began to lose population. Townships faced a decline in wealth unless they could attract industries or stimulate experiments with new crops in the surrounding countryside. Yankee farmers struggled valiantly to convert to vegetable, poultry, and dairy farming. Southerners banded in agricultural associations to spread the good word of crop rotation and natural fertilizers. The 1830s and 1840s saw an agricultural revolution in the older United States that was a remarkable adaptation to crisis.

But, nonetheless, there were still columns of newspaper advertisements listing mortgaged farms and homes for sale. There were new faces in the state legislatures and in political offices, as the farm population declined in size and importance. A new breed was now speaking for rural America, made up of small-town businessmen and the lawyers who worked with and for them. Likewise, there was a new kind of commoner in the Northeast, too, the industrial worker. Increasingly he (or she) was a Catholic and of French-Canadian or Irish nationality. Yankee America, land of the Pilgrims' pride, was changing her entire pattern.

That was one example of an old region breaking up. The social meaning of such changes was spelled out in a loosening of the bonds of community, tradition, and authority. Organization and written law tended to replace custom and tradition. The family itself was placed in a new framework. Fathers, for example, had traditionally employed their sons on their own farms or found land for them in neighboring areas. Now there was more of a tendency for children to move many miles onward and outward to new territories. That dispersal undercut parental authority and made each generation, more or less, stand on its own feet. This was especially true when only infrequent letters linked widely scattered clans.

Those youngsters who did not strike out for new farms often sought work in the factory towns or the coastal ports where whalers and merchant vessels offered the historic lure of the sea to wanderers. A new element entered the scene in the 1820s when textile factories began to hire women workers. Now even unmarried daughters could leave the family fireside for independent living. They were no longer dependent on a male breadwinner. A few could even take a more radical step: They might attend school and hope to qualify as teachers. This emergence of women into the world of work was the start of a whole new pattern of changing ideas about sex roles. And the whole nineteenth-century tendency of American family life to make home a nest out of which the young were pushed or from which they fled as early as possible was given a strenuous boost by the westward rushes.

Another kind of "family" was similarly affected. The old plantations of the upper South could not compete with new lands in growing cotton. Their owners had to turn to general agriculture, to raising crops like hay and hemp and horses. But this meant belt tightening and smaller work forces. The result was the reduction of the slave population by selling "extra" hands to western planters. The breakup of the slave family was even sadder than of the free family, for possible reunion and communication were almost totally out of the question for the blacks. So the westward movement, in the cotton states, emphasized the ugliest part of slavery, the auction block, and may have helped spur the attack on it.

Local government and local churches also suffered disruption. Congregations were systematically stripped of many of their older members. Preachers were forced, as we saw earlier, to become engineers of revivals or managers of do-good societies. As various denominations founded colleges and newspapers, their far-off influence became more important than the word of local parsons in deciding what made a good Christian. Townships found themselves playing minor parts in the drama of politics. The big issues that touched people's lives now were not whether to build a new poorhouse or fix a stretch of bridge but whether or not a railroad should be chartered by the state or paper money be issued by the banks in Boston. Only individuals who thought small were attracted to local government. The state legislatures, like Congress later, became the scenes of the really important debates, and fewer farmers were involved in them. The national parties, as we saw, were unifying forces, but they too, took a broad rather than a purely local, or *parochial*, outlook. So villagers thought of themselves as less important and took less interest in the things that once bound them together.

And on the frontier itself a new kind of individual was celebrated. Like Johnson Hooper's comic character Simon Suggs, this new individual had learned that it is "good to be shifty in a new country." A slick-tongued operator with no training could go through several "occupations" such as preacher, doctor, lawyer, land salesman, or newspaper editor and fail in each but start again unknown, and with fresh credit only a short distance away. It was, in fact, to guard against such frauds that professional standards of training began to be erected. In a small, unchanging society a so-called professional who was no good could be spotted and dealt with by group pressure. Now formal controls were necessary. True, there was another side to the coin. Honest failure did not wreck a life. A person might, like Abraham Lincoln, be unsuccessful as a surveyor and grocer, then switch to law and rise to new plateaus of respect. But freedom of opportunity, however good, left a problem. How was society to hold together? A nation full of free-floating individuals needed some kinds of binders, some recognized authorities, some guidelines of what was not allowed, to keep from flying apart in so many directions, as there were energetic, aggressive, hungry individuals "on the make."

There were some methods of social control. Public education later played an important part. But the early overall adjustment to the bewilderment of life in an America breaking up and moving westward took the form of the rise of brand-new attitudes. If these attitudes were shared nationwide, they could hold a scattered community of millions of Americans together, especially if spread through a popular press, political speeches, and a common school system. Those who shared the right ideas could be trusted and accepted. Those whose efforts added up to the right results were doing the proper American thing. The views of the majority in a fast-moving land were the new yardstick of right and wrong.

### *The New American Faith: Getting Ahead*

What were some of these new ideas, which were attached to or grew out of old ones? First of all, the technology that made quick growth possible was itself almost worshiped. Each new invention that shrank distances or multiplied muscle power was hailed as a sign of progress. And progress became the nineteenth-century American's idea of what God intended for humanity. The early colonists saw God as presiding over an unchanging universe and giving man the gift of reason to understand his place and duty in it. But nineteenth-century Americans who cheered for steam power argued that if man could use his reasoning powers—for example, to discover the laws of physics and then to apply them to a practical problem like getting from place to place more quickly—then the transportation revolution, had, in a sense, been God's intent. He *wanted* people to travel by rail, or He would not have given human beings the insight to produce the steam engine. Change was good. It was part of the overall plan. That was the answer to stand-pat thinkers who said that if God intended people to cover ground at 15 or 20 miles an hour, He could have given them the legs of antelopes. It was also American society's reply to critics like the writer Henry David Thoreau, who asked what good inventions did if they did not help humans to understand themselves better. (Learning, in 1845, that Maine and Texas were linked by the newly invented telegraph line, Thoreau wondered aloud what they had to say to each other.)

Progress, then, under God's inspiration, allowed for the acceptance and celebration of change. But by making it God's idea, Americans kept Him comfortably in the frame, providing the bridge from the old community of "saints" to the new one of "hustlers." Perhaps you can see, however, how God's image might be changed in the process.

A second attitude change put a new meaning into the word "plenty." Puritan settlers delighted in regarding their new Zion as flowing with "milk and honey." The prospects of wealth, as we saw, had also guided settlers to all the other colonies. But it is doubtful that the seventeenth century, when it cheered the "fruitfulness and fertility" of North America, foresaw what the production revolution in agriculture and industry would bring about. A goodly land for a township or a colony was one that would yield each family enough to feed itself well, clothe itself decently, house itself comfortably. It might also yield a surplus for the world's markets. The profits would be used to build improvements such as town halls and universities, and so cause civic pride and learning to thrive. But to make quantity production in itself a sign of godly favor and to feel that the bigger the surplus, the bigger the blessing, were not ideas that sat well in the American colonial mind.

However, when bushels of corn and wheat and bales of cotton began to be counted in the hundreds of thousands, when tariff officials and census takers began to list yards of cloth produced or miles of roadway built with the same pride that new parents took in presenting handsome offspring, the situation changed. The piling up of wealth was no longer something that carried the risk of worldly vanity and sin. Instead, it was a sign of the success of the American system. Boosterism, the numbers game, the dizzying triumphs of quantity became important values. Communities strove to outboast each other. The original seventeenth-century attitude favored diligence and believed that it would be rewarded in a fertile land. The new one was almost a pure glorification of surplus. Gradually, "more" came to mean "better" in the American vocabulary.

Out of these two beliefs—one in the virtues of progress, the other in the excellence of quantity—grew a new conception of man's relationship to Nature. Before, he had been one with the God-made creatures of the earth, even though given "dominion" over them. Now he more or less stood outside Nature and dominated it for his own benefit. The Declaration of Independence had spoken of a people assuming the station to which "the laws of Nature and of Nature's God" entitled them. But to Jefferson natural law ranked all things from God down to the smallest insect and prescribed a use and place for each. That was not what Americans of the nineteenth-century understood. To them the world of Nature was one of natural resources. Animals, trees, waters were to be used and transformed into the evidences of progress. They were to make way for "civilization," meaning to make natural things *civil,* that is, orderly, organized, and serving the purposes of a manufactured community.

Finally, the breakup of family and community hatched new ideas of what it meant to be an individual. True, the West was community oriented. It demanded joint efforts for survival. That was why frontiersmen took part in associations of "squatters" (new settlers who did not own their lands) and church congregations, camp meetings, militia musters, barn raisings, and other common endeavors. But these young communities were essentially collections of loners. They were to help individuals become joiners and cooperators but not to submerge individual ambitions in those of the group as a whole.

Every member of an eighteenth-century New England township and congregation was very conscious of his need to act in fraternity with his fellows under God's law as interpreted through the church. The nineteenth century, on the other hand, encouraged competitiveness and individual striving. It seemed necessary to get ahead in a tough, fast new life. Each individual was supposed to be a success, stake out a new claim, find his fortune, "make his pile," or simply "make it." The duty of the state was to equip each individual with the needed education for the task. That of the church was to teach him commonly agreed-on principles. (Theft and murder, for example, were clearly outlawed!) But once these basics were established, each person was on his own. What pulled communities together now would be each member's willingness to share the faith that life was a race and that the *common* good was best served by letting *each* person strive to do the best he could for himself. Failure then, if it was permanent, became a sin against everybody. The binding value was that everyone had an equal duty to show that he was special.

## *Progress in Action: The Case of the Indian*

These points become clearer when we see them applied in concrete cases. Let us examine Indian policy, land policy, and foreign policy in the era of Jackson and his successors. In each case the sequence of events will show the underlying value pattern that we have been discussing, as it looked when it was guiding actual decisions.

No one can accuse colonial Americans of having excessive sympathy toward the Indians. The horrors of frontier warfare, bristling with atrocities on both sides, were an old story by 1815. But between then and 1860 occasional clashes followed by treaties that wrung more land out of the Indians, a tribe at a time, were replaced with an overall plan to get rid of Indians altogether. Once, treaty making had been a colorful process in which the State Department treated the tribes like separate nations. At formal meetings presents were exchanged, flowery speeches delivered, and plenty of whiskey provided by the United States was poured. After that, the hungover chiefs, sometimes wearing parts of U.S. army uniforms that they had gotten as gifts, would make their mark on a handsomely inscribed paper, and several hundred thousand acres more of Indian hunting land would be yielded to speculators and farmers.

Gradually, however, the management of the Indian "problem," which was only a problem from the white man's point of view, was centered in the War Department. A Bureau of Indian Affairs was set up there in 1824. Its officials soon decided to abandon the treaty system bit by bit, to move *all* Indians out of the settled regions of the United States, and to get them into the almost empty region of the Great Plains. There, west of the Mississippi, they might pursue their hunting existence undisturbed, while the white race made the East flourish. There were two cultural assumptions behind this policy. One was that hunting was a "primitive" social occupation, inferior to farming because it could only keep a smaller population alive. The other was that it was right and proper, therefore, for the Americans, a more "advanced" people, to take over Indian lands. The willingness to let the Indians have the trans-Mississippi West was based on a mistaken idea, only corrected after midcentury, that agriculture was impossible on the plains, which lacked trees and heavy rainfalls. Needless to say, no one asked the Indians *already* living west of the Mississippi for their opinions on any of these decisions.

In 1830 a national law passed with Jackson's blessing; it authorized removal of almost all Indians east of the Mississippi, a process already begun by individual negotiation. The 1830 enactment provided that the army should conduct the removal. It did provide for some compensation to the Indians for their tribal property and called for funds to issue rations to the Indians en route and to help them resettle on new lands in "Indian Territory."

The tribes that were removed, for the most part, went without resistance, which they had sadly learned was futile. But there were some exceptions. The Sacs and Foxes of Wisconsin and northern Illinois fought back in 1832, and the result was a small campaign known as the Black Hawk War, in which Abraham Lincoln served as a captain of Illinois militia. It ended with a heavy slaughter of Indians of all ages and sexes. The Seminoles of Florida fought back from the swamps for nearly seven years, starting in 1835. After an expenditure of $20 million the United States managed to get most of them removed, though a few die-hards hung on and were left to themselves.

The Seminoles along with the Choctaws, Chickasaws, Creeks, and Cherokees were part of the so-called Five Civilized Tribes. The expulsion of these peoples was hard to justify even by American standards of the time. This was

*Looking like an eighteenth-century philosopher, the Cherokee leader Se-Quo-Yah points to the written alphabet which he devised for his people. They also possessed a constitution and a settled pattern of agriculture, but none of these prevented Americans in the 1830s from seeing the Cherokees as "savage redskins," and driving them from land that whites coveted.*

especially true of the Cherokees, scattered through Georgia, Alabama, and Mississippi. They had turned to agriculture. Some of their leaders were developing a written language, drafting a tribal constitution, and teaching the tribespeople skills such as the building of mills to grind corn and other grains. They even had a newspaper in English and were clearly adapting to the world around them. Despite this, whites in Georgia, hungry for Cherokee lands, got the state legislature to speed up the Cherokees' ouster. When two New England missionaries to the tribe challenged Georgia's action, the case went to the Supreme Court in 1832 as *Worcester* v. *Georgia*. The Indians won. But Jackson provided a lesson in the limits of the Supreme Court's power by declaring: "[Chief Justice] John Marshall has made his decision: now let him enforce it." Of course, Marshall could not. Only the president could deploy federal pressure against Georgia, and without his willingness to do so, the Cherokees were powerless.

Removal of the southern tribes took place over a long period of time. The road the Indians took westward came to be known, justifiably, as "The Trail of Tears." The Indian families shepherded along by the army suffered dreadfully. Often the rations provided were inadequate or spoiled. Shelter and medical care were nonexistent. Loafers and bullies harassed the moving columns and looted the Indians. Many whites also presented "claims" against the departing Indians and used them as justification to take away livestock and other property that various Indians had bought. The Cherokees, after selling their properties at heavy losses, struggled along toward Oklahoma except for a few who escaped and were allowed to stay in North Carolina. According to one estimate, 4000 of them died along the way.

The justification for this policy was the need for "improvement." William Henry Harrison, one day to be president of the United States, asked whether "one of the fairest portions of the globe" should remain "the haunt of a few wretched savages" when it was clearly "destined by the Creator to give support to a large population and to be the seat of civilization." Clearly the answer was no. A western editor described the Indians as "a useless and, perhaps, dangerous population," leaving the definition of "useless" to the imagination. A few Americans fought for humane treatment of the Indians, especially missionaries, who toiled to raise donations to teach Indian children how to read the Bible and to farm (knowledge that had done the Cherokees no good whatever). But for the most part, viewpoints like Harrison's prevailed. And shrewd individuals knew that if whites some day wanted the trans-Mississippi lands guaranteed "forever" to the Indians, the tribes would not long be safe there either.

In any case, what is important to see is how the Indians were thought unfit to have land because they did not "improve" it. Seventeenth-century New Englanders had denied the Indians souls and slain them because they were "heathen." Nineteenth-century southerners and westerners thought that because the Indians did not believe in the new gods of progress, that justified their virtual slaughter. True, the Indians removed to the West were not actually killed. But they lost their tribal independence. They were denied the right to practice their customs, and their resulting poverty became a scar on the national record. Being too close to Nature in nineteenth-century America was a dangerous invitation to be wiped out.

*Raiding the Public Domain*

The same kind of thinking was behind the tremendous pressure to get the public domain into private hands. The vast extent of federally owned land in existence at the beginning of the Union's life could have been dealt with in a number of ways. It could have been held as a resource for future generations and doled out to communities in the way that New England colonies had originally given grants to whole townships, as you will recall from Chapter 2. Or it could have been sold in huge tracts to land companies. They would take the responsibility for developing it by making surveys and building roads (like a modern suburban developer bringing in sewers and playgrounds). They would then sell it to individual settlers at a profit. Alexander Hamilton was known to favor a scheme like this, which was the pattern followed in some states, especially his own New York. The great speculators in land would be part of that business community whose loyalty to the nation would guarantee its strength. They would lead in opening the West. Their heavy payments to the national treasury for land would be a substantial source of public income. In the nation's first land law of 1796, which was Hamilton inspired, the minimum tract that could be sold was a square mile, 640 acres, at a minimum price of $2 per acre. This would have required a more substantial cash outlay than most individual families taking up western lands possessed, even though they could put a quarter of the money down and take three more years to pay the whole amount due.

But this one gesture toward a conservative land-sale policy by the national government was its last. Land continued to be sold and given to speculators in gigantic quantities within the states. The states also used it to endow schools, charitable institutions, and other worthy causes. That is, they would give land to the institution, which could then raise money by selling it. Land was also bestowed on companies that promised to build canals, roads, and railroads. The reason was simple. It was the most easily available form of donation, bound to rise in value as the population spread, but costing the giver almost nothing in its underdeveloped state.

But these large-scale donations by the states (later matched by huge federal land grants to railroad companies) were only part of the overall national policy. Increasingly, the federal government acted to sell or give land directly to individual families. The pressure to do this grew and continued growing as each new western state was admitted to Congress. In 1800 the minimum tract was reduced to 160 acres and in 1820 to 80 acres. The minimum price was reduced to $1.25 in the latter year, but the tract minimum was raised again to 160 acres. All the land was supposed to be bought at public auction, but would-be buyers often got together and agreed that no one would bid above the minimum, which therefore became the going rate. Under this 1804 law, too many people made down payments on more land than they would afford. This led to heavy borrowing and, later, failure to pay, which spelled national economic trouble. So in 1820 the law was revised to require a cash down payment. The rush to buy land was not entirely based on the urge to farm on a larger scale. Even small buyers hoped to have a little extra that they might sell off. The western attitude was that land was something that could be turned into money quickly. This was in contrast with the feeling of a European peasant that his land was a part of his family's life, passed on from generation to generation.

Even a 160-acre minimum tract and a minimum auction price of $1.25 was not enough for the West. It was soon demanding the principle of preemption, that is, a legal recognition of the right of a squatter to land he actually cultivated. Under federal policy, public lands were barred to settlement until officially surveyed and declared open for bidding. This was supposed to be done gradually, so as to control the flow of settlement. But thousands of families went out into new areas before they were legally authorized and began to farm parcels of their choice. They then argued that, as they had faced the risks and done the work of clearing the land and making it yield crops, it was unfair that someone else should be able to walk into a land office, buy "their" tract, and show up with a legal deed of title to throw them out. Congress eventually accepted this argument, through a General Pre-Emption Law of 1841. It allowed such settlers to bid for and get any lands they had under actual cultivation at the minimum price. In effect, preemption wiped out, for the aggressive and enterprising, the waiting period of survey and auction.

Even this was not the final step. In the 1820s a small band of reformers began to advocate "homestead" laws under which the government would *give* to each family head a farm-sized tract. The arguments for this came partly from labor reformers as well as from would-be farmers. They held that ownership of one's own acres was a sure road to independence. The government should therefore guarantee, out of its wealth of unsold land, the potential right of such independence to any American bold enough to claim it. The farmer, working his own acres with his own family, would never know unemployment; so the more farmers there were, the less hard times would hurt. And, finally, free homesteads would not be a giveaway. The land lying "idle" was worthless, whereas under cultivation it would yield crops and profits and taxes.

Homestead acts were passed by Congress in the 1850s, but vetoed by Democratic presidents Franklin Pierce and James Buchanan, mostly because of the opposition of large slaveowners, who believed that homesteaders would seize all available free land in the West and leave none for the development of plantations. Resentment over this helped to line up western votes for the Republican Party in 1856. It made free homesteads part of its platform, and one of its most potent slogans was: "Vote yourself a farm." The Homestead Act was finally passed in 1862. It did not fulfill the dreams of its backers for many reasons, but it was a logical outgrowth of national thought that exalted the profitable use of land by individuals as a high principle.

Whether, in short, government was endowing farm families, railroads, veterans, state universities, or mining and lumbering companies with land, the idea was the same. To conserve land was not considered. The national goal was growth through turning the bounty of Nature into revenue-producing goods. That concept linked national policies toward the Indians, the land they lived on, and, in our final story, toward a weak Latin neighbor.

### *Mexico and Manifest Destiny*

In 1820 the government of Mexico, then only recently freed from Spain, granted to Moses Austin, a Connecticut-born Yankee then running a Missouri lead mine, permission to settle 300 families in the Mexican province of Texas. Austin himself had planned the exodus but died before it was completed. His son, Stephen, took over his role. Soon the little colony of Americans was settled in Texas, busily engaged in ranching and in cotton raising, just as the elder Austin, a promoter at heart, had planned. Though they were now technically Mexican citizens, the Texan Yankees were every bit as aggressive in the pursuit of prosperity as their American kinfolk back home. And like such other Americans, they had contempt for their Spanish, Catholic "rulers" in faraway Mexico City. A typical Texan view was expressed in a letter that one of them wrote: "The Mexicans are never long at peace with each other; ignorant and degraded as many of them are, they are not capable of ruling, nor yet of being ruled." Various quarrels led to a demand on the part of the Texans for more autonomy. Finally, armed conflict broke out and ended with a victorous Texan declaration of independence in 1836.

From the start it was clear that the United States wanted to pluck the fruit of this "war of liberation" of Americans against their foreign "oppressors." The Texans expected it, asked for it, and it was bound to come in time, despite the opposition of antislavery Americans, various diplomatic complications, and Mexican objection. But finally, in 1845, the deed was done, and in the waning days of John Tyler's administration, Texas was annexed. As expected, Mexico reacted belligerently, just as the United States would have had the British annexed the seceding states in 1860.

A quarrel broke out over boundaries between the two nations, followed by an armed clash, which was provoked by the Americans, in April of 1846. A two-year war ensued, during which the youthful American army marched all the way to Mexico City and finally compelled a negotiated peace. Under it the annexation of Texas was recognized by Mexico. Moreover, she gave up her rich province of California, whose cattle lands, fruitful valleys, and Pacific ports had been long coveted by Americans. The middle of 1848 saw the United States not only in possession of California but also of Oregon, by treaty with Great Britain. A Pacific coast frontier had been gained; America was a nation that faced two oceans at last. But Oregon, owned by a strong Britain, we had gotten by negotiation. California, owned by weak Mexico, we had merely grabbed.

The justification for this double standard of international conduct was stated by a writer named John O'Sullivan, who spoke of the Manifest Destiny of the United States to expand. California, he said, could not be held by Mexico.

> The Anglo-Saxon foot is already on its borders. Already, the advance guard of the irresistible army of Anglo-Saxon emigration has begun to pour down upon it, armed with the plough and the rifle, and marking its trail with schools and colleges, courts and representative halls, mills and meeting houses. A population will soon be in actual occupation of California, over which it will be idle for Mexico to dream of dominion.

Mexico, a "weak" and "imbecile" nation, could not resist progress, as defined by "Anglo-Saxon" culture. Cheap lands, Indian removal, and war with Mexico all stemmed from a basic American, expansionist outlook on life. That same enchantment with the possibilities of growth had many other applications and results. Some were in the field of reforming society. Some, which we will now look at, touched the eastern world of factories, owners, and workers.

---

## *FOR FURTHER READING*

There is so much literature on the West that the only problem is one of selecting examples. For an overall view of the whole era, see Richard A. Bartlett, *The New Country: A Social History of the American Frontier* (1975). And for a thoughtful look at what people *thought* about the West, read Henry Nash Smith's classic, *Virgin Land: The American West as Symbol and Myth* (1948). Getting into special subjects, Madeline Waggoner, *The Long Haul West* (1958) is a good, popular history of canals; Louis C. Hunter, *Steamboats on the Western Rivers* (1949) is rich in interesting material on side-and-stern wheelers; the early railroad story is summarized in John Stover, *American Railroads* (1961); and, the interest of New England traders in fast routes to the Pacific is touched on in Norman Graebner, *Empire on the Pacific* (1955), all about Yankee interest in California.

There is no better introduction to the robust and rip-roaring fur trade than Bernard De Voto, *Across the Wide Missouri* (1947). For the effect of the frontier on uprooting older communities, read Stewart Holbrook, *Yankee Exodus* (1950). The sad story of Indian mistreatment is handled very well in Grant Foreman, *Indian Removal: The Emigration of the Five Civilized Tribes* (1953), and in a recent, popular history by Dee Brown, *Bury My Heart at Wounded Knee* (1972). A very good account of the revolt of Texas is found in an old biography by Marquis James, *The Raven: A Biography of Sam Houston* (1927). A recent account of the struggle with Mexico is Otis Singletary's *The Mexican War* (1960); but once more for adventuresome reading, try Bernard De Voto's Pulitzer-Prize-winning *The Year of Decision* (1943).

Firsthand tales not to be missed (all in various reprint editions) include Samuel Clemens (Mark Twain), *Life on the Mississippi* (1883); Joseph G. Baldwin, *The Flush Times of Alabama and Mississippi* (1959); and, Frances Trollope, *Domestic Manners of the Americans* (1832; reprinted ed., 1949). Fictitious but funny are Samuel Hopkins Adams' *Grandfather Stories* (1959), about life on the Erie Canal in early times and Charles Dickens' matchless *Martin Chuzzlewit*, a novel with an unflattering episode set in America. Dickens' *American Notes* (1841) is also extremely interesting, and critical of Yankeeland.

# *chapter 9*
# *Industry: disrupter or unifier?*

They were all individuals, the business pioneers of the new century. Most of them began with little; they had few links to the classes that had dominated commerce and trade in two centuries of colonial life. Their connections were with the future.

There was Eli Whitney, for example. In 1792 he graduated from Yale as a bright young Yankee with no special prospects. Through a friend he got a job as a tutor on a Georgia plantation, owned by the widow of a revolutionary general. While coaxing the children through their spelling and multiplication tables, he worked on a little machine that would clean the seeds out of cotton 50 times as efficiently as slave fingers could do it. It was a simple affair. He whittled out, in a few days, a wooden model of a cylinder with teeth that pulled the cotton through a comb that tore out the seeds. A revolving brush then whisked away the cleaned cotton. Simple! But it made possible mass production of cotton textiles. The cotton crop shot from 2 million pounds in 1790 to 2 billion in 1860, and Southern history was set on a new course.

Whitney was not yet finished as an inventor. He worked out a system of building firearms, made from parts that were cut out of metal by machines. The machines could precisely duplicate the size and shape of every part they made, so that all the parts were interchangeable. The musket or other firearm needed only to be assembled to be ready for use and could be repaired with a simple replacement. Applied to other kinds of manufacturing, the technique produced floods of finished articles and made America a nation of workshops as well as farms.

Then there was Samuel Slater, an Englishman born in 1768, who trained to build and repair the new machines for automatically spinning wool and cotton thread that piled up huge profits for British clothmakers. Seeking new opportunities in America, Slater memorized the designs of "throstles," "mules," and "jennies," disguised himself as a farmer, and sailed for New York. In 1790 he made a deal with the firm of Almy and Brown, threadmakers of Providence, Rhode Island. For half the profits the twenty-two-year-old immigrant built the machines and powered them with water wheels turning in the swift currents of New England streams. Before long, Slater and Almy and Brown were rich men, and textile manufacturing was a basic, booming U.S. industry.

There were many, many others. John Jacob Astor, a penniless immigrant from Germany, who arrived in New York to sell flutes, became a fur trader and real-estate dealer worth millions of dollars. And Cornelius Vanderbilt, a nearly illiterate Staten Island ferryboat skipper, would one day be king of the New York Central Railroad. And Samuel Colt, another Yankee, whittled out a model of a quick-firing "six-shooter" that won the West and made him a fortune.

If a revolution is any swift, massive change in the way people live and work and think, these individuals, who brought industry to America, were our leading revolutionaries.

## *The Forces of Pull Together and Push-Apart*

The coming of industry, just as we saw with westward expansion, was a tidal wave that washed out old social landmarks. But for every custom and tradition overwhelmed in the flood of time, there was often a new one to replace it. Historical change sometimes seems to be exactly like a rampaging river. The soil it washes away in one place cannot be destroyed. It is simply deposited somewhere else. This is an illustration of the general theory of conservation of matter.

---

*CHRONOLOGY*

1828 *Early working people's political parties*
1820s–1850s *"Lowell system," using young women as textile laborers*
1834 *First attempt at a National Trades Union, not successful*
1840 *Ten-hour day for federal employees*

Applying any "scientific" theory to history is risky. Human behavior is hard to measure and predict. But it could be interesting to set up a hypothesis and call it the principle of conservation of cohesion. Swift changes tend to disrupt societies by dissolving their binding forces, embodied in institutions like the family or the town. But the need for cooperation is so powerful that new forms of old institutions keep arising to dispel the fear and powerlessness of being alone. Every period of social change has disruptive and integrative energies, those that push people apart and those that pull them together. The happenings of an era visually embody at least a small amount of both forces.

If we try this hypothesis in the story of early American industrialism, we can find a key to organizing and understanding events. We can look at the coming of the factory system to New England and ask: How did it change family life for women, and what did it put in its place to give them group roles? Next we can examine labor unions. Why did early ones waver as industry grew, and how did they reach out for new members and new meaning? Finally, we can study patterns of business ownership and see how they changed to keep up with growth, while doing their basic job of providing capital and direction for the economy. In each story there is evidence of concentration and dispersion, and there are opportunities for you to consider the rewards and dangers of each.

## *The Mill Girls: From Hearthside to Picket Line*

Unlike the business founding fathers mentioned in the chapter opening, Francis Cabot Lowell was no stranger to reputation in New England. His family had already contributed outstanding judges and preachers to American history and would go on doing so. As one of the members of the clan who looked after its investments, Lowell knew, in 1810, with war approaching, that trade was going to suffer and that manufacturing would become basic. So he made a trip to Britain for a private survey of British textile-making processes. He was impressed especially with the way in which British producers were grouping spinning and weaving machines under one roof, so that raw wool and cotton went in at one end and finished cloth poured out of the other.

Lowell returned to the United States, gathered capital from family and friends, and started the Boston Manufacturing Company in 1813 to make fabrics from start to finish. He died soon afterward. But the business was doing well, and when its partners bought new land farther from the city for expansion, they named the factory town they built after him.

Lowell turned out to be a spectacular economic success story. Almost uninhabited in 1820, by 1827 it had 25 factories. In 1835 it was producing 45 million yards of cloth annually. Ten years later it had a populace of 30,000, one-third of them at work in 33 mills; each single week they turned more than

F. GLEASON, {CORNER OF BROMFIELD AND TREMONT STREETS. BOSTON, SATURDAY, MAY 29, 1852. $2 00 PER VOLUME. 10 CTS. SINGLE COPY. {NO. 22.—VOL. II.

**LOWELL FACTORIES.**

Lowell, in the rapidity of its growth and the extent of its manufactures, stands unrivalled in the United States, and well deserves the appellation of the Manchester of America. The buildings, which our artist has sketched for us below, are called the Boott Cotton Mills; they consist of five mills, the remaining two are exactly the same as the two in the front of the picture. The two mills in front are used for the purpose of carding the cotton, spinning it into yarn, forming the thread, and weaving it into cloth. The building in the rear is joined to the buildings in front by means of small suspension bridges. It is used almost entirely for spinning the cloth. There are in this building about 900 looms—all attended by girls; one girl has the superintendence of four looms; each loom will weave about twenty-five yards per day. There are employed in these mills about 1200 operatives, of which the greater part are girls. A high brick wall encloses the works. The grounds within are laid out in grass plats, and ornamented by a number of trees. There are connected with the mills other workshops, for preparing the smaller pieces of machinery required in the mills, manufacturing starch, storing cotton, etc. The town of Lowell was incorporated by the Legislature of Massachusetts in 1826, and was chartered as a city in 1836. It lies on the south side of Merrimac River, below Pawtucket Falls, at the junction of Concord River with the Merrimac; and it possesses a great amount of water-power, easily available. This is produced by a canal, 60 feet wide, 8 feet deep, and 1 1-2 miles long, commencing at the head of Pawtucket Falls, and extending to Concord River. By locks at its outlet into Concord River, it forms a boatable passage round the falls of the Merrimac. From the main canal, the water is carried by lateral canals to mills and manufactories where it is needed, and is discharged either into Merrimac or Concord River. The entire fall is 31 feet. Visitors will be agreeably impressed with the neat and respectable appearance of the operatives of this industrious city; and equally so with their moral condition. One-third of the entire population of the city is connected with the Sunday-schools established by the various religious societies; and there is less intemperance and crime than in most other places of its size in New England.

*Though English poet William Blake spoke of the "dark Satanic mills," the founders of the American textile industry tried at first to create little industrial paradises. This view of a neat, cheerful, almost smokeless factory town is a bit idealized, but conveys the intention well.*

30 million pounds of cotton (about 10,000 bales per workday) into more than 1.5 million yards of cloth. Besides using water power, the factories used, for heating and lighting, thousands of tons of coal, cords of wood, and gallons of oil.

But the most interesting aspect of Lowell was its labor force. The town founders deliberately sought a new kind of working population. They knew that it would be hard to get enough men to work in their factories, since so many young Yankees went West or to sea. They hoped, however, to make up this labor shortage by employing the "surplus women" of New England's farm families. These were the unmarried daughters, the childless widows, the maiden aunts who, without men, had never had any means of support.

But the European experience with factories offered a discouraging model. The working classes of France and Britain of both sexes were generally poverty-stricken, illiterate, diseased, drunken. Many of the men took to crime, and the women to prostitution. No American wanted such a fate for the nation's daughters. But it seemed bound to happen if girls were taken from the purifying influences of Christian homes. How could the owners cope with the results of this kind of dispersion?

The solution was a special creation, the "Lowell system" boardinghouse. Young women were recruited and brought to Lowell. There they shared living accommodations in buildings that were like dormitories. They were supervised by matrons, followed strict rules of conduct, and went to compulsory church services (which they almost surely would have done anyway). Confining as this may sound, it was not a great inroad into the girls' free time, for there was little of that. The workday ran from sunrise to sunset in summer and longer in winter, averaging about fourteen and one-half hours per day, six days a week, with only brief meal breaks. For this the workers got salaries that, in the 1820s and 1830s, hovered around $3.50 a week.

Yet to them this was not exploitation but liberation. The workweek in a farm household was even longer. Spinning, sewing, milking, feeding, churning, weaving, gardening, nursing, baking, and mending were dawn-to-bedtime activities. It was a relief to work a precisely limited day. It was pleasant to be surrounded by many friends instead of the same faces unendingly. And since board and lodging in the houses were a mere $1.25 to $1.50 a week, a girl had spending money left on payday. She could buy a book or a bonnet or even save $75 or $100 a year toward a long-range goal like a dowry or tuition at a "normal" school that might make her a teacher some day. Money was freedom. As one mill girl put it: "For the first time in this country . . . woman had begun to earn and hold her own money, and through its aid had learned to think and to act for herself."

These early workingwomen did some extraordinary thinking for themselves. After factory hours they plunged, with New England seriousness, into self-improvement. They combined funds to buy books and magazines. Some chipped in to purchase pianos. Finally, in 1840, a group began to issue its own magazine, the *Lowell Offering*, written and edited entirely by the workers. Sometimes the boardinghouses seemed less like industrial living quarters than like girls' schools. Lowell was a showplace. Foreign visitors, like Charles Dickens, came to marvel at working-class women who could produce the solid pages of the *Offering*, which he took home to read. Politicians also came to watch the girls at work, and Jackson allegedly swore that "by the Eternal" he had never seen such pretty women.

But beneath the surface trouble was developing. As competition became fiercer, mill owners stepped up the number of machines that each worker had to tend. They raised boardinghouse rents and in that way cut real wages. The "select young ladies" of Lowell organized in a Factory Girls' Association, and, in the late 1830s and early 1840s, went on strike. In their "picket lines" they marched, waving handkerchiefs and singing songs that said they would not be slaves. But in the end these strikes failed. The bosses began to replace the Yankee farm girls with French-Canadian and Irish immigrants. By 1860 one-fifth of the population of Rhode Island and Massachusetts was of foreign birth. These newcomers were vulnerable in ways that the early mill girls were not. They had no farm homes to retreat to or possibilities of professional education. Gradually, these easily abused laborers filled the ranks.

Lowell was not typical of all early American factory labor practices. But it was interesting as a brief experiment in avoiding some of the debasement that early industrialism inflicted on workers. It broke up the old family pattern when it removed the "surplus" women from the nest. It placed the girls in a new, less secure setting. They were now free of the chores and humiliations that often fell to unmarried women. But they were also deprived of the familiar and the expected. As always, independence was frightening.

But factory employment also created some new group self-awareness. The factory girls had new, larger "families." They now saw themselves as part of womankind as a whole. And they had loyalties to their fellow workers. The home ties of kinship were replaced or enlarged by membership in a larger social grouping. Just as we saw parochial, provincial, and state loyalties challenged by nationalism in political history at this period, we can see the same broadening-out process in the world of work. That development becomes clearer in the saga of early trade unionism. Here the record shows a move from small groups that were like fraternities of the self-employed to larger and more complicated organizations, with differing, hotly debated goals. The transfer of loyalties from early to later unions also shows how economic growth gave new meaning to words like "association."

## *Union: From Brotherhood to Ballots*

Early unions resembled clubs of skilled craftsmen who owned their own shops or hoped to do so and who often bought their own raw materials and did work only to order. Between 1792 and 1815, in the growing cities of Boston, New York, Philadelphia, Baltimore, and Pittsburgh, such associations of shoemakers, printers, and carpenters were born. Part of their job was purely benevolent: They bought insurance or burial plots at reduced group rates and helped each other with loans in tight times of personal distress. But partly they were out to keep up the quality and prices of their work. They wanted limits on the number of apprentices in their trades, long training periods, and minimum rates. Their way of putting pressure on craftsmen who would not go along with them was by persuading the public to boycott such "miserable botchers."

These societies had some clear resemblances to modern unions, which also make economic demands, try to win public support, and control admission to their ranks. But there was a difference. The early "mechanics' societies" often counted both employers and employees in their ranks. They did not simply involve workers against bosses. In the small cities of the 1790s, members also knew each other face to face. They had a special kind of fraternity. All of them had once been apprentices, and an apprentice actually lived with his master's family from early boyhood. He got whatever general education he could from the master and was fed and nursed through illnesses by the master's wife. If the master was a kind man, his own children acted almost as the apprentice's brothers and sisters. When the trainee graduated to being a journeyman, now qualified in the craft but still working for someone else, he left the family setting of apprenticeship. The association of others trained like him was something of a replacement for that lost closeness. The world of work, in the 1790s, was still involved with determining ways of life, not simply with wages. The unions were forms of basic social togetherness.

But the early unions were rocked by industrial change, just as we saw families shaken by migration. As the factory system grew, working people's organizations had to change their strategy and style. Their membership became confined to those who worked with tools and at machines owned by others. They no longer reflected employers' viewpoints. They expanded to the point where decisions could not be made by the entire membership gathered in a single, informal meeting. And as business grew national in scope, it grew more difficult to set prices and conditions locally, since a town's craftsmen were competing with goods shipped in from other cities.

The workers' organizations, to be effective, had to move in new directions. An obvious one was to broaden their bargaining power by combining into larger units so as to control conditions in many cities at the same time. Beyond that were choices. Should unions accept the new organization of industry as it was and simply try to better conditions within it? Or should they try to change the whole social setting of production by pushing for changes in the basic economic system, such as by trying to end wage work entirely? Each of these steps had or could have important long-range results.

For example, there was the result of consolidating small workers' associations into larger ones. Philadelphia and New York had citywide labor federations by the late 1820s, made up of many craft unions. In 1834 the New York federation took the lead in trying to connect several such bodies in what was called the National Trades Union. But it was born about a half-century too soon. Few working delegates could afford to travel to its three annual meetings, and it soon died. But efforts went on to join many local unions in the same trade into national bodies. There was a trend in that direction, and the 1850s saw the birth of national unions of hatters, machinists, and printers. These early stirrings of nationalization strengthened the workers' position, because their leaders could speak for thousands, not merely dozens or hundreds of members. But direct participation in big decisions by the average worker was cut down. Strong leaders who could speak well to a nationwide audience through the press and on the lecture platform outshone grass-roots heroes. Money was handled by bookkeepers, in large sums. Policies were set by committees and approved in infrequent formal conventions. All these diluted fraternalism, even though national union officials would still address each other formally as "brother." The large-scale organization was more impersonal than the small, even though it engaged in the same tasks.

The early drive simply to improve working conditions had clear and sharp targets. Besides better pay, unions wanted laws limiting the legal workday to ten hours. They also demanded that employers in financial trouble be forced to pay wages before meeting other debts; and they wanted to end the legal practice of seizing a worker's tools when he was in debt, thus leaving him no way to work himself free. The ten-hour demand made the slowest progress. But in 1840 President Martin Van Buren set it as standard for federal employees on public works. By 1847 New Hampshire had a ten-hour law; Rhode Island passed one in 1853; in other states, by the time of the Civil War, it was at least forbidden to hire children under twelve for unlimited hours of work. These victories came through protests, lobbying, and strikes. But they required political education and action and led unions in directions that further changed their nature.

### *From Strikes to Politics*

In order to get favorable actions from legislatures, workers needed the franchise. Politicians are not noted for actions on behalf of the voteless. So most spokesmen for workers clamored for universal suffrage. The unions, in that way, played a part in building up momentum for Jackson. But it was necessary to prepare an informed class of voting workers if the ballot was to mean anything. Therefore, pressure for tax-supported public schools for children of working-class parents also became a union goal. The need to get government help in controlling industrial conditions had pushed labor into politics and also into long-range social planning for the education of future generations. Now, in a sense, the whole nation was part of the workers' "family."

At least that was the thinking of leaders of special Workingmen's Parties formed in 1828 in New York and Philadelphia. They had come to believe that more was necessary than simply bettering the conditions of the industrial worker. They feared that society was falling apart, and they wanted to knit it together by reforms that went beyond wages and hours. In their efforts to combine brotherhood, individual freedom, and economic growth, they grew overly ambitious and confused. They were like the Lowell owners who with their blue-ribbon factory girls tried to mate progress and morality. The problem for all was to preserve human scale and connections in an exploding economy.

The leaders of these workingmen's parties voiced a growing fear that industrialization was driving wedges between the haves and have-nots that would make the functioning of the American system impossible. Of course, there had been class distinctions, both in the colonies and the young nation. But the farmer or mechanic of 1800 depended on no other person for the simple chance to earn his bread. He had his land or his tools—or at least the possibility of getting them glowed in his hopeful mind. The industrial worker, however, was totally vulnerable. If bad times closed the factory doors or if he was fired for any reason, starvation threatened. That gave the factory owner frightening power. What good was it to adopt a Constitution that banned aristocratic privilege and then adopt an economic system that, in a pungent phrase of the day, put the living of the many into the hands of the few? A Philadelphia Workingman's Party newspaper, the *Workingman's Advocate*, lamented in 1829 that: "We are fast approaching . . . extremes of wealth and extravagance on the one hand, and ignorance, poverty and wretchedness on the other," a situation bound to lead to the "oppressive distinctions which exist in the corrupt governments of the old world." In 1830 a committee of Pennsylvania working men put it even more sharply:

> There appear to exist two distinct classes, the rich and the poor; the oppressor and the oppressed; those that live by their own labour, and they that live by the labour of others; the aristocratic, and the democratic; the despotic, and republican, who are in direct opposition to one another in their objects and pursuits.

Concerning themselves with equality, these protesters were going beyond dollars-and-cents questions and getting into the broader area of how the new organization of industry was dividing society into the powerful and the helpless. They were coping with the breakup of old rules and habits. One way of reacting was to stick to simple issues of labor's fair reward within "the system." The other was to criticize the entire new social structure and try to change it so as to redefine everyone's place in society. To those "radicals" of the labor movement who thought in broad social terms, any efforts by laborers to better themselves had to get to the very roots of injustice to do any good. The most "radical" labor spokesmen of the 1830s was a faction of New York State's Democratic Party known as the Locofocos. (The name came from a rough-and-tumble moment of political warfare. The radical Democrats of New York City were holding a meeting one evening in a gaslit hall. The "regular" organization found a way to turn off the gas. In the darkness and confusion, however, some of the radicals produced safety matches, then new and known as locofocos. They lit candles and continued their meeting.)

The Locofocos started with the eighteenth-century idea that work itself was valuable. It enriched the earth and strengthened the characters of those who performed it. In preindustrial times, they thought, workers had shared closeness and responsibility for each other in small shops where masters, their families, journeymen, and apprentices ate at the same table. They had been brothers and sisters, and equals. But equality seemed to be the victim of growth.

Locofoco papers and speeches complained that "our fathers" had created a government that "prohibited the creation of monopolies and exclusive privileges." But later generations permitted a favored few "the more than princely privilege of taking houses, lands and labour, while they built no houses and give no labour in return." This backsliding, as they saw it, ignored the basic truth that "the true foundation of Republican Government is the Equal Right of every citizen." In a just land "the blessings of government, like the dews of heaven, should descend equally upon the poor and the rich."

But that sentiment showed a contradiction in early American labor radicalism. In a perfectly balanced society perhaps there would be no poor and no rich. Yet the Workingmen's Parties did not see it that way. As Americans, they shared the desire to prosper. Their idea of equality was an equal chance for some to get ahead. They wanted equality before the law, which meant, as we saw in the preceding chapter, an equal opportunity to get ahead in life, which was a race. Equality of opportunity was not the same as fraternal equality or equality of condition. It was not meant to make society one big barracks or monastery.

When they translated equality as they saw it into political programs, the Workingmen's Parties seized on two objectives. One was reform of the money and banking system, the other was the grant of free homesteads to all who wanted them, an idea discussed in the preceding chapter. When labor reformers threw their weight behind laws making it easier to charter new banks, their idea was that loans and credit should be freely available to all, not merely a favored few with political connections. And in the 1830s they favored "hard money"—gold and silver—as the medium of exchange, because paper money at that time was put out by banks, not the Treasury. It fluctuated in value so much that the worker paid in it could not count on getting the same purchasing power each week.

Behind the homestead crusade, too, stood the idea of the destruction of privilege. If any willing and able family could get a free slice of the public domain to farm, they did not need to fear any employer. The idea overlooked several inconvenient facts: (1) the high cash cost of seed, tools, and animals needed to start a farm even *with* free land, and (2) that most industrial workers and their children never had or soon lost agricultural skills and could only fit into an urban setting.

Both the homestead and easy-banking movements soon blended into the general pattern of American capitalist expansion. "Labor" reformers like George Henry Evans, Robert Dale Owen, Frances Wright, and Ely Moore simply wanted to make it easy for everyone to join in the parade of middle-class ambition for successful ownership of property. They often found themselves in political partnership with investors and small businessmen who also wanted steady money and readily available loans to promote their plans for towns, factories, and railroads. In the end they drifted away from both the utopian reformers who wanted to end capitalism (who will be introduced in the next chapter) and the "bread-and-butter" unionists who only wanted to better the setting of factory work and who did not get their full chance until after the Civil War.

Yet the fact remains that the leaders of the early unions and the Workingmen's Parties had been searching for principles that would restore among the producing classes the unity and importance that modern industry was taking away. They were trying to pull people together behind a common dream of opportunity for the uncommon.

## *Business: From Clan to Corporation*

The most usual form of business organization in the eighteenth and early nineteenth centuries was the partnership. Often, the several partners were members of the same family or soon became closely knit by marriage. And the social significance of this was that even business life was always tinged with personal feelings and loyalties, clan solidarity, in-law feuds, and the sense of responsibility felt by differing generations for taking care of each other. "Merchants," as all kinds of businessmen were called, may have believed that economic forces could be blind and impersonal. But the effect of such forces on people was emotional and spiritual. So moral duties to others were just as important in the office as in the church. Although single examples to support general statements are a dangerous practice, a sense of the personal style of early mercantile life can be gotten through a look at one "typical" family, the Lows of Salem.

Seth Low, born in 1782, was the son of a merchant. He married a Salem neighbor, Mary Porter, who was a merchant's daughter. Both their fathers were later lost at sea. In the wake of Jefferson's embargo and the troubles preceding the War of 1812, Salem's trade was hard-hit, so that Seth looked for a new base. First he went into a partnership with the Boston firm of Russell and Company, taking with him a young friend named Abiel Abbott. Russell and Company were involved in trading for tea and silk with Chinese merchants in Canton. One of the first results of the merger was that Seth's brother William went to Canton to take over the company's dealings with the Chinese there.

Among the other American merchants whom he met there were John Cushing and Thomas Forbes, members of old Boston families. Forbes was managing the interests of a trading company founded by Boston's Thomas Perkins. After a while, some time in the 1820s, the Perkins and Cushing firms were merged. Later, Russell and Company joined the firm, so that the Lows of Salem were now connected to the Perkins, Cushing, and Forbes families of Boston. When New York began to take on importance as a port out of which square-riggers sailed for China, the Low-Perkins-Forbes-Russell combination opened offices and built homes there.

So the three worlds in which young Lows and Forbes and Russells grew up were those of Boston (and nearby Salem), bustling New York, and exotic Canton. There were constant transfers of personnel among these three places. When Thomas Forbes died of illness in Canton, his two younger brothers went there to take over his tasks. One, John Forbes, obediently accepted a clerkship with the promise that he would one day become a partner. But brother Robert, with a soul not fettered to an office stool, insisted after a time on going to sea.

After a while, Seth Low's brother William was ready to come back. Abiel Abbott went to take his place. By now, Seth's own sons were reaching maturity and picking up their roles. Francis, fourth oldest, was sent to Canton in hopes that the sea voyage would clear an early case of tuberculosis. But it did not, and he died in the far-off city. Next William, Seth's number-two son, went to Canton, replacing the uncle for whom he was named. Charles, baby among the boys, went into the New York office, but insisted (like Charles Forbes) on an early release to go to sea, either as captain of a company ship or as supercargo, the company agent responsible for buying and selling whatever the vessel carried. When he finally got his wish, his older brother Josiah took his place. This allowed Josiah to do a favor for his father's old friend, Abiel Abbott. Abiel, after his time in Canton, had been sent back to Salem. But he had met and fallen in love with a girl in Brooklyn named Ann Bedell. Though duty sent Abiel to New England, Josiah, in New York, carried messages of courtship to Ann for him.

Abiel finally was sent to New York. But the course of romance did not run smooth. Josiah's brother William now returned from Canton, wooed Ann, and married her. But the story does not end there. William later became despondent over personal setbacks, and, on a trip home from Canton threw himself overboard. Abiel at last married his Ann. And yet another Low brother, Edward, replaced William in China.

All of these comings and goings, including marriages, illnesses, and suicides, may seem of interest only to those whose hobby in life is tracing the twigs on family trees. But the doings of the Lows—Seth, William, Charles, Abiel, Francis and Josiah—and their children indicate something else. These partnerships were really extended families. When their members talked of benevolence, charity, good works, the obligations of the rich to the poor, and of Christian character as shown in absolute business honesty, they were not merely making self-serving noises. Their profits might be large; they might be conservative in politics, hate unions, fear to see political power extended to the lower classes, and distrust immigrants and Catholics. They might believe that the gates of heaven opened only to members of their church. But despite these feelings, they thought of society as a close-knit fabric weaving the lives of many kinds of men and women together, and they were aware that gaps and rips in one part of it weakened another. So they tried to maintain what they saw as proper standards of honesty in their business dealings and compassion in their relationships with dependents. In any case, truthfulness was necessary. In a business world where families knew each other so well, a really heartless scoundrel would have had trouble securing credit and customers. Reputation meant something. Not that every pre-1830 business individual was the soul of honor. But human connections among all parts of community were still very evident and tight.

The early founders of New England's factories often were partners in this old style. Many were related to each other. They often undertook their new ventures with the clear intention of improving their local communities' economic lives. But the growing scale and cost of industry changed that. New factories, banks, insurance companies, canals, and railroads that cost millions instead of thousands drove more and more entrepreneurs toward the corporate form of organization. Under it hundreds or thousands of stockholders, unknown to each other, held shares. Policies and plans were made by boards of directors, responsible mainly to a few majority holders, who had little day-to-day connection with the running of the business. The advantage of the corporate form of organization was that it could raise large sums of money. Increasingly, it took over as the basic American business model. By the era of the Civil War the corporation had triumphed and was ready for the next stage, the combination of many corporations into superorganizations.

But the result was depersonalization. A corporation with assets in millions and shareholders in the thousands, many of them banks and other business firms, had no personality in the sense that a family partnership did. It was a legal "person," but in the popular phrase it had neither a soul to be damned nor a body to be kicked. Making this legal "creature" part of the community was no easy job.

So the family partnership, like the small shop or the Yankee farm family knit by a common need for survival, also fell a victim to progress. It, too, was disrupted by industrial growth. It was the constant pattern of disruption in families, towns, churches, and every institution bursting with growth that made Americans fear that society was flying apart.

Yet there was an ironic side to the coin. Actually, physically, industrial growth made everyone in the nation *more* interdependent, *less* disconnected. The spread of the telegraph and rail lines made Maine and Texas neighbors, even without their having anything to say to each other. The new economy of the 1840s sold Cincinnati-packed pork from Indiana hogs to Boston homemakers; spun cotton from a Mississippi plantation was made into coarse shirts in Lowell, which were then put on the backs of slaves in Georgia. A national marketplace was a fact of life in the new industrial order.

And another common bond was a general feeling that all Americans shared in the glittering march toward the future. The worship of material growth and the "booster's" triumphant figures were an economic counterpart to the nationalizing forces embodied in political parties. Americans were brothers and sisters in banishing scarcity. That shared belief was a foundation stone of the culture. Even the complaining "toilers" in the unions held to the faith that the factory was of social benefit. For most of them, just as much as for their bosses, the profit system was a noble spur to effort. Mutual participation of all classes in industrial growth was a binding force among them. Profit itself became a kind of "social glue." At least, the idea of it did, even for many who saw little of it

## *FOR FURTHER READING*

Suppose you wanted to begin with a history of technology in America? A good book would be Roger Burlingame, *March of the Iron Men* (1938). For a close-up of an important builder of engines, see Allan Nevins and Jeanette Mirsky, *The World of Eli Whitney* (1952). There are many good illustrations of early factories and machines in Marshall Davidson, *Life in America* (1974), and pictures tell the industrial story very well indeed. For a long time it was assumed that invention brought only benefits and never problems, but a new and thoughtful look at that proposition is taken in Elting E. Morison, *From Know-How to Nowhere* (1975).

There are several good sources on the life of the early industrial worker. An overall look is found in Norman Ware, *The Industrial Worker*, 1840–1860 (1924). If you want the interesting experience of reading actual records involving early labor practices, and your library has it, you may browse in the nine volumes of John R. Commons *et al*, eds., *A Documentary History of American Labor* (1918).

The mill girls of Lowell are extensively researched in Hannah Josephson, *Golden Threads: New England's Magnates and Mill Girls* (1967). An insider's view is revealed in Lucy Larcom, *A New England Girlhood* (1875), she was there and she wrote well.

The story of the Low family and the China trade is in Helen Augur, *Tall Ships to Cathay* (1951), while a fine general book on seagoing America is Samuel E. Morison, *The Maritime History of Massachusetts* (1921). Richard Henry Dana's *Two Years Before the Mast* (1972) is adventurous reading—the recollections of a young Harvard man who sailed as a foremast hand to California in the 1840s. Kenneth Porter's *John Jacob Astor* (1966) is good reading on the role of the fur trade in our Pacific expansion; and for the general story of business practices, see Stuart Bruchey, *The Roots of American Economic Growth* (1965).

# *chapter* 10

# *What can reformers do?*

When Noah's flood came upon the earth, say the Scriptures, the fountains of the great deep were broken up and the windows of heaven were opened. And the waters that covered the face of the earth wiped out the past, as God destroyed His first, flawed experimental model of humanity.

To nineteenth-century Americans it must sometimes have seemed that a new great deluge was taking place. A flood of inventions and changes was wiping out all traces of yesterday. As it did so, it dissolved the sense of connection with and dependence upon the human race's experience in all the preceding eras of time. This gave rise to a "freedom" that was both exhilarating and frightening. It is exciting to believe that anything is possible. At the same time, it is disturbing to realize that comfortable and familiar patterns are no longer useful to guide behavior. Progress opened magic windows on fantasy-lands of imagination for people. It also slammed doors firmly behind them. It created hope and fear. Out of the meeting of these two feelings came the concept of reform. Reformers feared the results of letting evils go unchecked, and they hoped that improvement was possible.

There was plenty of reason to dream that the world could be remade. The steam engine and the electric wire fascinated young America. Crude locomotives only appeared around 1830, yet by 1846 a New York merchant, Asa Whitney, was talking about a railroad that would run from the Atlantic to the

Pacific and bring Oriental goods to the marketplaces of American towns in a matter of days. The first message by telegraph was clicked out between Washington and Baltimore in 1844. "What hath God wrought?" it asked. The answer might have been "ambition," for only fourteen years later an underwater telegraph line across the Atlantic linked Britain and America electrically. It broke after a few messages but was successfully replaced in 1866. In 1819 the *Savannah*, powered partly by steam, had made the first Atlantic crossing; her sails and paddle wheels got her from the New World to the Old in twenty-nine days. Forty years later, a man named John Wise was laying plans, which never matured, to cross the same ocean in a free balloon, riding favorable wind currents and taking perhaps forty-eight hours. Technology seemed to bestride the earth; lightning grasped in one fist, steam power in the other, ready to shrink continents, dry up oceans, and banish scarcity.

But there was also the other side. A depression in 1819 brought plummeting prices and ruin to sturdy New England farmers and Virginia planters. Then, in 1837, there was another panic. Men stood in line for charity soup in New York, Philadelphia, and other bright cities of America's promise. In the middle of the 1840s Boston authorities looked grimly at the social debris of a flood of recent Irish immigration. They found the "paddies" living in cellars and hovels, diseased, illiterate, filling the poorhouses and jails. Even in the brand-new West there were problems. In the 1850s in the youthful Great Lakes port of Chicago there was a district known as "the Sands," where no one sensible dared walk at night for fear of violence in the saloon-bordered streets. Were all these scenes part of the price of progress?

Social problems themselves were not new. Wickedness and suffering existed in the colonies and were thought to be part of humanity's fate. But in the light of nineteenth-century optimism about the individual's power to change the world, wickedness and suffering did not seem so inescapable. Thousands of thinking Americans now believed that the same divinely inspired human intelligence that harnessed steam and electricity could create a society without evil.

But exactly how was this to be done? What blueprints were to guide the architects of a better human society? The answers depended partly on what particular reformers thought about human nature, what they regarded as the key weaknesses of society, and what kind of changes were possible.

### *Reform Sources: Reason, God, and History*

There were several ideas about what made humans ready for reform. One was the eighteenth-century faith in reason. That power had made possible the discovery of orderly and sensible patterns governing the physical universe, to which humanity gave the name of scientific laws. The obvious next step was simply to assume that similar laws ruled human behavior and then to find and use them. If the "laws" of heat and expansion made the steam engine possible, then the "laws" of human interaction could also make good government or world peace possible. This "rationalistic" view usually held that human reason worked best without taking things on faith, and therefore those who held it were doubtful about the value of religion.

But reform and religion did not always have to war. In the America of the 1830s and 1840s, there were preachers who were sure that God smiled on progress, too. Scientific facts like electromagnetism were His creation. He had "revealed" their workings to certain individuals in this exciting new century, and His next step would be to teach Adam and Eve's descendants to be spiritually perfect, even as He Himself was. Some reforming American clergymen thought that the exciting new developments of the era signaled the birth of a millennium, a 1000-year reign of peace and justice before the world would end, to begin right in the United States.

And even without a belief in reason or God, a reformer of the 1800s had simple historical example to back his dreams. The American Revolution had shown that swift, important changes in the form of government were possible. Only a few years later, the French Revolution had begun. By the time it and the Napoleonic Wars that followed were over, most of Europe's 1000-year-old feudal customs were dead or dying, wiped out in a very short time.

Though all reformers shared a common interest in improving life, their basic outlooks separated them by style. Whether a reform movement was inspired by God, reason, or history made a difference, for example, in whether

---

*CHRONOLOGY*

1816 *American Colonization Society to resettle freed slaves in Africa*
1819 *The* Savannah *makes first transatlantic crossing, powered partly by steam*
1825 *Founding of the New Harmony, Indiana, utopian community by Robert Owen*
1826 *American Temperance Union founded*
1831 *William Lloyd Garrison publishes the* Liberator, *his abolitionist newspaper*
1847 *Oneida, New York, religious community founded by John H. Noyes*
1837 *Severe financial panic*
1844 *First telegraph message, Washington to Baltimore*
1846 *Maine passes first state law prohibiting alcoholic beverages*
1848 *Seneca Falls Convention, first meeting of U.S. women's rights advocates*
1854 *Republican Party founded out of the Free Soil Party*
1865 *Thirteenth Amendment to the Constitution abolishes slavery*

it had authoritarian leaders or whether it was willing to compromise with existing patterns. Of course, reformers did not neatly label themselves or jump briskly into historical pigeonholes. Their motives were often mixed and cloudy. But there were very clear distinctions, which often were clearest in matters of tactics.

Reformers had to decide first how to proceed. Should they and their followers withdraw from society and its pressures and build little private working models of a better world? There were both advantages and limits to such utopianism.

Or, if they did not abandon the world, should they seek to change it by first changing the minds and hearts of the individuals who peopled it? Should "moral suasion," or persuasion, as we would now call it, be the key to change?

Or should they use the coercive power of law? That would involve political action to win over a majority of legislators; then, the hope was, that after a period when people were compelled to good behavior by courts and constables, such conduct would eventually become habitual and natural. "Human nature" would be altered.

The best way to show how some of these questions were answered and what then happened is to follow some particular reforms. To begin with, we will look at two utopian experiments, one rationalistic and the other religious: New Harmony and Oneida.

### *New Harmony: Paternalist Paradise*

The founders of all reform communities that separated themselves from society believed that the serpent in humanity's possible paradise was *individualism*. Others saw competition as the engine of social progress. It provided the energies for the race of life. But communitarians saw the spirit of competition as simply glorified selfishness. They believed that in order to find their true brotherly and sisterly selves, men and women had to escape from the pressures of trying to outstrip their neighbors. Or, in the words of Robert Owen, the existing system made "strife and contention . . . unavoidable" and banned the "love [and] good will . . . necesssary to the comfort and happiness of the human race."

Owen was ready to change the system, starting in the little town of New Harmony in Posey County, Indiana, in 1825. Owen brimmed with enthusiasm for the idea of operating a successful social experiment in new, unspoiled America, where he was a temporary immigrant. He was used to controversy, unique notions, and success. He was a self-made English millionaire textile manufacturer, and early in life he had gotten from his wide reading the idea that all conduct was the result of environment and conditioning. There was no inborn tendency toward good or evil, nor any universal definition of them, as all churches falsely taught. Owen set out to create a model humanity through model surroundings, starting with a model factory at New Lanark in Scotland. His workers were well paid, provided with neat and clean lodgings, and allowed to send their children to a private school where pupils were never beaten, were encouraged to ask questions, had no required subjects, and had ample opportunities for play. Like the fathers of the Lowell system, Owen was a paternalist, a believer in employer-provided incentives to improvement. Like them, too, his experiment was a success at first, and visitors flocked from everywhere to see his happy, sober, self-reliant working-class families.

Owen sold his factory and looked for new worlds to conquer. He thought, in the 1820s, that the ideal community was one in which a limited number of people shared a rationally planned set of buildings and institutions. To the land he bought in Indiana he brought about 800 people. Eventually, they were supposed to live in a set of buildings laid out in a neat rectangle around an open space. Some floors would be devoted to living quarters for individual families. But no children would live there, for at the age of two they would be taken from their parents' contaminating prejudices and educated in a community school to use their reason. No wasteful individual duplication of social tasks would be allowed, such as many families cooking. Instead, meals would be made and served in a common kitchen and dining room. The basic activity of the community would be communal agriculture. There would also be a commonly owned printing shop, a smithy, a sawmill, a gristmill and other "manufactories."

Yet the community would not be a herd or an army. People would, insofar as possible, choose the work they liked. They would be paid in notes, which recorded the time they spent on the job. These notes would be exchangeable for supplies and goods of individual choice. But the "New Harmonists" would be encouraged not to work all the time. Instead, they should express themselves in nature study, reading, writing, drawing, making music, and dancing. Lectures, concerts, and business meetings would fill the evenings.

It was an enchanting vision to lively minds. Soon after the community was opened, a canal boat deposited a so-called boatload of brains at New Harmony, including a zoologist, some writers, a poet, and several free-spirited ladies (for women were the equals of men in Owen's world). They all apparently had a marvelous time. Owen himself was rarely present. He was busy trying to raise capital in Britain to expand the community, or explaining to the U.S. Congress, and other solemn bodies how, once New Harmony proved workable, all Britain and America would rush to form similar "villages of cooperation." Society would be reborn on harmonious lines.

Unfortunately, just the opposite proved true. The worldly sins of quarrelsomeness and jealousy pursued the New Harmonists into their oasis of reason.

The property of the community was jointly owned, with members joining by buying shares. In time, disagreements erupted over who was entitled to how much of what. Owen himself dropped out of the picture early to devote time to other improvement schemes in Britain. He left his son, Robert Dale Owen, in charge, and the young man eventually became a congressman from Indiana. But after 1828 New Harmony suffered several major secessions by angry groups. The leadership changed hands. In 1855 the property was divided among the remaining individual shareholders, and in 1858 the community was dissolved. In that same year Robert Owen, a believer in intelligent planning to produce a pain-free humanity, also died.

*Oneida: Yankee Heaven*

In sharp contrast to Owen's faith in reason was the religious zeal of John Humphrey Noyes. Described by one biographer as a "Yankee saint," Noyes was a Yale graduate from Vermont who became convinced that the spiritual perfection of Christ in human form was possible to all men and women. Such talk outraged fellow ministers. So Noyes withdrew, not only from the profession of minister but from society. He took a group of his converts, or Perfectionists, with him to set up a commune in Oneida, New York, in 1847.

What distinguished Oneida was the intense closeness among the members and the absolute obedience to Noyes' strong leadership, something Owen had not demanded. Like the New Harmonists, the Oneidans shared common quarters and the tasks of making a living. Noyes realized that agriculture alone offered an uncertain economic base, and he got his "saints" into the modern world by having them make steel traps, luggage, and silverware for general sale.

But the Oneidans were more hivelike than Owen's followers. Members not only gave up all private property on entering but also the idea of individual families and, in a sense, their private egos. "We all have one home and one family relation," ran one of the community's songs, and they meant it literally. All members were considered to be "married" to all other members. Sexual relations were not confined to an exclusive possessive relationship between one man and one woman for life. Instead, members would change sexual partners—but only with mutual consent and community approval. The children of such unions, like all children who came into Oneida, were communally reared and educated. These practices in particular outraged mid-nineteenth century America and kept Noyes in constant legal hot water for permitting "free love." Private sex was even more hotly defended by the outside world than private property.

The most unusual part of life at Oneida was constant, strong, collective self-criticism. All members met frequently to find out if they had conquered such snares of Satan as vanity, selfishness, pride, and anger. A member with

Oneida community of Free Lovers—In the library at night.

*Despite the sobriety and studiousness of these readers from the Oneida community, the caption on this contemporary magazine illustration remorselessly singles out the one feature of the group's life which conventional Americans would not forgive—there was no ear for reformers who were "Free Lovers."*

a grievance would bring it up in a general meeting, often to find, however, that his trouble lay in too much concern for personal feelings, too little for the group. One member, after being made the subject of such a discussion, wrote that "after . . . being turned inside out and thoroughly inspected, I was, metaphorically, stood upon my head and allowed to drain till all the self-righteousness had dripped out of me." The Oneidans gave up not only meat, tobacco, and alcohol to purify body and soul but also individual control over children, spouses, and selves. What they got in return was escape from loneliness and the fear of responsibility for individual errors. Actually, Oneida could not keep itself going and finally dissolved in 1881. It became a simple corporation, owning the silverware and other factories. But many members voluntarily stayed on. As late as 1962, 57 people still lived in the former Mansion House, and 85 descendants of the Oneidans still made their homes in the immediate vicinity.

Oneida's intense cultivation of self-criticism would be understood by a Chinese Communist today. And in fact the whole experience of new nations in Africa and Asia is interesting to compare with that of the young United States. But more to the point is the fact that Oneida and New Harmony, though only two examples of planned American communities, clearly show some of the limits of "patent-office models of the good society." For one thing, such utopias require strong leadership and intense member commitment. Both qualities are hard to find and harder to keep alive. They thrive best, sometimes, in isolation from distractions of the outside world. Strong-minded people often disturb their neighbors and need to get away in order "to do their thing." Yet this very isolation makes the economic and physical survival of a utopian community more difficult. It also reduces the likelihood that the communitarians will have much influence outside of their own tight circle.

There were many communities that had brief lives in America between 1830 and 1860. There was Nashoba, run by a freethinking feminist, Frances Wright. Fruitlands was the creation of Bronson Alcott, father of the author of *Little Women.* The best known, Brook Farm, near Concord, Massachusetts, attracted a company of New England thinkers who liked the idea of farming by day and philosophizing by night. Amana, founded by pious Germans in Iowa, lasted until recent times. Like Oneida, it ran a factory that still exists today. It once made stoves and now turns out freezers.

All were "failures" in the sense that they did not stave off the world's seductions for long or bend the world into their own patterns. But the fact that they existed at all says much about the hopeful atmosphere of the United States a century and one-half ago.

## *The Battles Against Rum, Sexism, and Slavery*

Let us now turn from the "come-outers" who fled society to those who worked inside it. There was a wide variety of crusades chosen by those who hoped to work "within the system": crusades for better schools, more humane care of the insane, prisons that rehabilitated as well as punished, and an end to war. These are still live and recognizable issues. Others, like the efforts to multiply Sunday schools and missionaries, are now social antiques. Still others, like changing humanity's evil nature by eliminating meat from its diet were regarded as moderately eccentric, then as now.

Three deserve special examination. They are movements for temperance, women's rights, and the aboliton of slavery. They share one common characteristic. Each began primarily as an attempt to change things by reshaping attitudes. The founders of the movements believed that proper information would kindle the light of reason and that men and women would see their behavior differently by that light and freely change it.

In time, however, each gave up on sheer persuasion and moved toward concrete changes in the law to win its points. And the law is a form of peaceable coercion. It says "you must" instead of "you should." That being so, it is not easy, in a free and pluralistic society—that is, one hospitable to many viewpoints—to secure majority consent to legal change. Thus when a reform movement shifted from general propaganda to winning votes, it had to change its tactics, expectations, and perhaps its basic nature.

There were also important differences among these three crusades. The temperance movement had little trouble winning support, especially from the churches, which strongly shaped public opinion. The women's rights movement had the hardest struggle against the tide. It had virtually no organized religious or political sponsorship. As for the antislavery cause, it began with a reservoir of good will as long as it set no time deadlines and especially if it proposed to send freed slaves out of the country. But as it moved toward concrete targets and timetables, it created shock waves that eventually split churches, parties, and the nation.

These differences stemmed from variations in the root questions that each movement asked about the basic values of American society. The closer a reform drive came to changing society's central, unspoken beliefs, the more opposition piled up before it. It could then succeed only by adjusting its programs to reality. Whether this process is called compromise, realism, or surrender is a question you may want to debate. How much idealism should be given up to get power to make improvements in society? Also take note that the hardest changes to make were those that asked people to change their ideas about sex roles and race.

## *From Temperance to Prohibition*

When Lyman Beecher (whom we met in an earlier chapter) was a young man in the 1790s, christenings, weddings, and funerals were celebrated with plenty of rum and hard cider, and the officiating preachers drank their share. Farm workers often got part of their pay in beer or other liquors. Gentlemen, especially Southern gentlemen, were expected to put away a bottle or more of wine with their dinners. Drunkenness was not encouraged, especially the riotous behavior of frontiersmen full of fiery corn liquor. But drinking and even mild intoxication were not altogether disgraceful.

But drunkenness disturbed the young generation of ministers who, like Beecher, began careers around 1800. To them intoxication simply did not go with the expected behavior of the convert to true Christianity. Such a person

*This young man and the white-gowned daughter of virtue (offering him the pure and crystal cup instead of the poisoned and fatal wine glass) look a bit out of this world. That, unfortunately, was the dominant mode of much early reform thinking.*

needed a clear head and boundless energies for good works and self-examination. Progressive medical people, too, like Philadelphia's Dr. Benjamin Rush, a signer of the Declaration of Independence, worried about the health of those who underwent the "nervous excitement" of heavy drinking. In any case, it befuddled the important power of thought.

Both of these men, and others like them, saw no place for overindulgence in alcohol in the dawning, enlightened nineteenth century. Both led in the formation of temperance societies between 1800 and 1830. These organizations simply aimed at encouraging reasonable men and women through pamphlets, lectures, sermons, and newspaper articles not to drink too heavily. The idea behind it all was that sensible people could be trusted to regulate their appetites for their own and everyone else's good. There was faith in the same kind of self-control that would keep democracy from sliding into mob rule, or business competition from becoming economic war.

But by the 1840s a change came. Temperance societies still used revivalistic and political techniques like banners, badges, pledges, special meetings, and parades to spread the word. But now the "cold water armies" called for total abstinence. They wished all alcohol banished to Satan's kingdom. And they no longer trusted "voluntarism" and community consensus to do the job. For those who would not control themselves, they proposed stronger measures than propaganda: a ban on all liquor sales. From temperance they had moved to prohibition.

Why this change? One reason was that immigration and industrialization were filling the growing cities with a new lower class. Drunkenness was being spoken of as a special vice of this group, instead of a general problem. Among the new supporters of the war on "the demon rum" were many employers who wanted a sober, hangover-free working force. And merchants grew enthused over the prospect of whiskey money being spent instead for clothes and furniture. Public officials pointed out how taxes would drop in a city without drunkenness—less crime and less need to spend on police forces, courts, and jails.

More and more, antiliquor crusaders linked heavy drinking to foreigners, especially Catholic foreigners. These included many Germans who spent relaxing Sundays in beer gardens instead of in prayer meetings and the "carousing" Irish and French-Canadians. These strangers to true Americanism, said the prohibitionists, got their political ideas from machine bosses, whose headquarters were in saloons. So corruption as well as crime and poverty could be traced to the poisoned cup!

By the 1850s the prohibitionists were an embattled group, trying to get legislatures to impose the virtues of the older America on the lower classes, especially in the cities. Their biggest victory was the Maine law in 1852. It banned sale of liquor in that state in less than ten-gallon quantities, far more than any poor person could afford. After the Civil War the goal of prohibitionists was a constitutional amendment against liquor. That was finally achieved in 1919, and it lasted until 1933.

The early spokesmen of temperance, like Rush and Beecher, had been persons of progress. To them, abandoning drunkenness was part of the march toward perfection. By contrast, the national champion of prohibition in the 1850s was Maine's Neal Dow. He was better known for what he hated than for what he hoped. He was, for a time, a Know-Nothing, a member of an anti-Catholic, antiforeign party that flourished in the 1850s. And he disliked Democrats and slaveholders almost as much as Irish and other "papists."

Yet Dow was a successful antiliquor politician. He fell into step with a process that changed the movement against drunkenness from a purely personal and moral affair to a class issue. As a crusade against social evils created by newcomers and outsiders, prohibition won votes from those who, like Dow, clung to old ways. The "politicizing" of temperance probably made it more effective, if effectiveness is measured in laws passed. But it changed its nature. It geared the movement to social stability instead of social change.

### *From Women's Rights to Women's Votes*

Elizabeth Cady, born in 1815, grew up in a New York State that was rural but far from backward. In the 1820s and 1830s revivalists barnstormed it calling sinners to repentance. They always brought news from the outside world. Newspapers, religious and reform societies, and political clubs were also lively sources for learning about the changes of modern times: the Texas revolution, Jackson, the locomotive, and the swift-growing Union. Cady shared these stimulations. In addition, her father, a judge, had a well-stocked library of ancient classics. She was allowed to roam freely among these and among books of history, philosophy, and politics.

From the library and the daily life around her, Cady learned several things by her twenties. One was that even as a freeborn American young woman, she was far from independent. Like criminals, lunatics, and minor children, she had no vote. She could neither serve on juries nor hold public offices. If she married, any property she owned passed under the absolute control of her husband. In theory nothing prevented her from studying law or medicine, but there was not a college in the country that would admit her. Society expected her to marry, keep a good home, raise healthy children, and obey her husband. And nothing else.

But Cady also read the works of radical thinkers of the French and American revolutions such as Paine. Already resentful of the chains that custom clamped on her, she was inspired by the writings of liberated Englishwomen like Harriet Shelley and Frances Wright. Burying her young head in the pages of Franklin and Jefferson, she came to feel that humanity, since the late 1700s, had been struggling out of the dark cellar of the past. Progress was doing away with blind authority. It was freeing each individual human to achieve the tremendous potential that was in him or her. This historic surge toward liberation, thought Cady, should develop its fullest power in the United States, so new, so open, so much the child of revolution.

Filled with these radical ideas, Cady declared war on her "inferior" status. She came to learn, through the network of reform and other journals, that other American women were developing similar ideas—women like Susan B. Anthony, Amelia Bloomer, Antoinette Brown, first woman to enter Oberlin College (established in 1833) and to be ordained a minister, Lucy Stone, whose sister-in-law, Elizabeth Blackwell, became the first woman doctor in America. She even shared her ideas with the man she married, himself a likable reformer, Henry B. Stanton. Like other early feminists, Elizabeth Cady Stanton did not disdain marriage and children. She had the energy for them. She only objected to the idea that they alone were supposed to be a woman's life targets.

In 1848 Stanton and a number of other men and women reformers met in a convention at Seneca Falls, New York. There they issued a Declaration of Women's Rights. Its opening paragraph was that of the Declaration of Independence, with only one change: "We hold these truths to be self-evident: all men *and women* are created equal." The document demanded that women receive each and every right accorded to every other human being. Its list of grievances spelled out the ways in which men had long cheated women of such rights.

When it came to corrective action, the growing "women's movement" faced specific choices. It could play a simple educational and propagandistic role. It could try to teach people to see every human as a separate being, with no compulsory design for living dictated by the biological fact of "himness" or "herness."

But the traps of that approach were illustrated by the simple story of the bloomer. One way of freeing woman to take part in the world's work was to get her out of clinging, hampering long skirts and petticoats. Amelia Bloomer, an important feminist, therefore designed a costume consisting of a short tunic and a skirt divided and gathered up at each ankle. Howls of laughter and outrage greeted this "immodest" outfit, which shockingly showed that woman was a two-legged animal. Finally, Bloomer gave up her model dress. As she wrote a friend, people were so busy looking at what she wore that they were paying no attention to what she said. People's ideas on "proper" behavior as a woman or a man were simply too deeprooted. If bloomers raised such a storm, there was no way to underestimate the resistance to other ideas such as a woman's right to limit the number of children she should bear.

*In 1859, as at present, male chauvinists enjoyed fun at the expense of women seeking their rights. The conflict between mocking males and self-righteous females was a natural subject for a cartoonist's pen.*

It was easier to pursue short-range legal goals that did not change basic patterns. Women needed laws protecting them from husbands who beat or abandoned them. Divorce laws needed to be loosened to permit women escape from such brutish mates. Workingwomen needed laws that kept bosses from insisting that they work long, health-wrecking hours. Trustees of colleges might be more ready to admit women students under pressure of court orders.

Such changes demanded political action and skill. And soon the movement began to learn a political truth. Politicians listened attentively to voters, and only voters. When conditions in a monarchy needed changing, reformers had to win over the king. In America they had to court the sovereign people at the polling place.

Gradually, simply getting the vote for women loomed larger and larger as the number-one goal. Votelessness was a roadblock to any real progress. And the crusade for votes was a good one for gaining sympathy. Why should women, like the colonists of 1776, obey laws made for them by assemblies in which they had no voice? Even conservatives found that argument hard to fight. So, while there were advances for women on the educational and professional fronts, the main battle shifted to voting rights. Once women had the ballot, it was thought things would change. State by state the barriers fell, and finally there came a national constitutional amendment, the Nineteenth, nailing down the victory. But that was not until 1919. It was the same year the prohibitionists dried up the land.

The importance of suffrage could not be denied. But the shift in emphasis had important results. The "suffragists" left basic assumptions about woman's "role" untouched. Men continued to argue, and many women to believe, that women had a special sphere, the home. Woman was naturally pure, gentle, good with children, sensitive to the weak, protective of the male ego. She was too delicate and easily bruised by the world in which men daily struggled for livelihoods. So, in the early 1900s, when women did emerge from the home, it was only in limited ways. They might enter the world of work as teachers and social workers but not engineers and judges. They could be in business offices as secretaries and office managers but not corporation presidents. And always, their work was a secondary function ranking behind their duties to their families. And even when women finally had the vote, their early assignments in politics were to lick stamps, not to run for office.

By swinging away from their early revolutionary thinking, feminist leaders had limited the horizons of possibility. A crusade that was part of the whole onward march of humanity became instead a demand for a single political privilege: the vote. Perhaps any other course was impossible. But the change showed the price of realism in reform movements.

## *From Abolition to Free Soil*

By 1800 Europeans had been carrying kidnapped and enslaved Africans to work in their New World possessions for almost 400 years. The original kidnappers were other Africans, but they sent their victims to a European-created market.

But nineteenth-century European and American minds began to forsake slavery. It was not only unjust, but it was out of tune with economic reality. Growing capitalist economies did better with wage workers. And consciences as well as pocketbooks said no to slavery. New religious and political views made the world a little less ironbound and more interested in the freedom and growth of all people. Time was undermining the ideas by which Europeans had defended the enslavement of dark "heathens."

The antislavery movement in the United States began among religious leaders. They were found both in the North, which had imported the slaves in its ships, and the South, which had bought most of them. A few vocal clergymen, before the Revolution, blasted the "stealing" of God's African children, who had souls to be saved within their dark skins.

Antislavery had gathered enough momentum by the 1780s so that the Northwest Ordinance of 1787 reserved the territory north of the Ohio River for free labor. Sentiment against the African slave trade was also growing. In the Constitutional Convention, the South only managed to postpone the federal government's banning further importation of slaves until 1808. Then, in 1817, a national society appeared, one of the many reform bodies we have seen joining together well-wishers to progress in many states. This was the American Colonization Society. It pledged itself to urge private citizens and lawmaking bodies to donate money for buying land in Africa. There it would send any slaves whose masters could be talked into setting them free. Like the early temperance movement, the Colonization Society hoped to reason people into good behavior. And, it assumed that good behavior for blacks would be to remove themselves from white society and return to their "home" in Africa, even though most of them were two or three centuries removed from it.

It took only fourteen years for the American Colonization Society to prove itself a failure. The expected pace of *manumissions* (the freeing of slaves) was nowhere near reached. African land was bought for a new nation, Liberia, to receive the homecoming freed people. But farm tools, schools, and churches were not provided as quickly as expected. In the end, though the society limped on until the end of the century, only a few thousand blacks made the trip.

Meanwhile, the cotton boom had created a great demand for slaves. Prices for field hands rose, and the black population kept growing. A few slave revolts, meanwhile, badly frightened Southerners. In dread of a general slave uprising, they began to tighten up on the rules governing manumission and the movement to free blacks. Slavery had been abolished in all the Northern states by 1820. It seemed to be on its deathbed in the country at large. But ten years later it was more alive than ever, and Southerners were ominously insisting that they could not live without it.

At this point new voices were heard in the land. A fresh antislavery movement was born in 1831. Its best-known voice was that of William Lloyd Garrison. The American Antislavery Society, which he led in founding in 1833, demanded that the slaves be emancipated *immediately*, not gradually as owners might see fit. Nor should owners be paid for their lost investments as the colonization societies had suggested. Slaveholders had been "paid" well enough by the free labor of their slaves already. Slavery was a national sin—to be rooted out as totally as any other crime. Did churches recognize it? Then they must go back and reread the Scriptures and find their errors. Did the Constitution protect it? Then the Constitution must be condemned as "a covenant with Death and a league with Hell." As Garrison said in a oft-quoted passage, he did not wish to speak, think, or write with moderation. Reproached for being so fiery, he declared that he had need to be, for he had mountains of ice around him to melt.

In spite of this zeal, Garrison did not mean to use any method except rousing public opinion. He expected to stir such an uproar against slavery that Southern slaveholders would be forced to bow to it. He did not, however, reckon on the raging resistance he provoked. Immediate emancipation would confront the nation with the problem of actually living with the blacks as equals, under the Declaration of Independence, or as brothers under God's Bible. The South responded with furious attacks on abolitionists, as the new antislavery advocates were called. The North was basically no different in its unwillingness to abandon white superiority and live up to the national image. Northern editorials, speeches, and sermons thundered against Garrison. Once, in Boston, he was nearly lynched by a band of respectable citizens, a mob in broadcloth.

Such resistance provoked counterfanaticism. Disciples of the American Antislavery Society roamed up and down small-town byways. At meetings in churches and town halls they denounced slaveholders as individuals who defied God's command to earn bread in the sweat of their own brows. They claimed that idle white Southerners, with their minds not anchored in duty, wallowed in drunkenness, lusted after their black women, and put their mulatto bastards up on the auction block. And, said the speakers, Northerners were just as guilty for tolerating the evils.

Outraged audiences tarred and feathered abolitionist speakers, dumped them in wells, filled their waiting carriages with horse manure while they spoke. But the lecturers, men and women, were only encouraged in their zeal. Yet by 1840 it was clear that they were not speeding the pace of freedom. Part of the fault was in their enemy-making tone. People do not willingly listen to those who tell them that they are carriers of moral disease. But part of the fault was in the general resistance to facing the race question. And there were politically explosive consequences of abolitionism. If continued, it was almost certain to provoke the South to secession.

Nonetheless, the abolitionists were gaining some ground. They were getting experience as propagandists. Moreover, their arguments did touch basic popular chords. Americans became more aware of the injustices of slavery and especially concerned that it was holding back Southern and national economic growth.

In 1840 some abolitionists tried to capitalize on these assets. They formed the Liberty Party and ran James G. Birney, a Kentucky slaveholder converted to abolitionism, for president. They picked up only about 7,059 votes; in 1844 they managed to increase this total to 62,300. Yet most voters, like most politicians, shied away from abolitionism.

But in 1848 a change took place. A new group, the Free Soil Party, was created. Its platform was to leave slavery alone in the states where it existed (that change outraged genuine abolitionists). But the Free-Soilers would ban slaves in all new territories, including those just won from Mexico. We shall say more about this movement in Chapter 12. The key point here is that free soil succeeded in politics where abolitionism failed. An American could be for it and still claim loyalty to the Constitution, which protected slavery. An American could defend free soil as a way to preserve the West for free labor, sobriety, progress, and economic development. That path allowed its followers to avoid criticizing Southern morals and also to ignore the racial issues of slavery. In fact, an American could oppose slavery in the new territories for the reason that blacks should stay out of them. Like colonization, free soil made it possible for antislavery and racism to coexist.

Free soil became the basis of the new Republican Party, founded in 1854. Six years after its birth, Republicans won the election of 1860 and led the nation to victory in the Civil War that followed. Finally, slavery was abolished by the Thirteenth Amendment in 1865. Yet free soil, like votes for women or like legal prohibition, was something of a retreat from the dreams of the men and women who began the movements. They hoped that they could help humanity to self-betterment through mutual consent, without tainting their own principles through compromise or force. But it was not to be so.

Temperance fought against the inertia of human habit. It survived by changing its nature and becoming an instrument of class and social control. Women's rights had to retreat when it reached basic feelings about sex. Antislavery ran head on into the immovable obstacle of irrational race fear. So all three movements had to shift ground, make adjustments, and sacrifice long-range idealisms for short-term possibilities.

Is this the human condition? It is hard to say. Reform theorists write in an intellectual vacuum. Reform activists practice amid the stubborn realities of society. That is the difference between them. What America gained or lost by the change from ideal hopes to practical programs of social change is something you may discuss. In any case, the change was made. And three constitutional amendments arose out of the glowing age of 1830 to 1860, full of "freedom's ferment."

## *FOR FURTHER READING*

An old, but not yet replaced general study of reform movements is Alice Felt Tyler, *Freedom's Ferment* (1944). From this one can go on to particular subjects of interest like Arthur Bestor, *Backwoods Utopias* (1950), a book on the patent office models of the good society set up by reformers. New Harmony is dealt with in J. F. C. Harrison, *The New Moral World of Robert Owen* (1970), which is "heavy" but informative. Good recent information on the Oneida colony is found in Rosabeth M. Kanter's *Commitment and Community* (1973), which studies nineteenth- and twentieth-century communes in a comparative fashion.

The best early material on temperance is John A. Krout's *The Origins of Prohibition* (1967). Frank Byrne's *Prophet of Prohibition: Neal Dow* (1961) covers the life of a man who made the trip from temperance to legal prohibition.

Abolitionism has a gigantic literature. A good overview is Louis Filler, *The Crusade Against Slavery* (1960). Focusing on New England leads to Lawrence Lader, *The Bold Brahmins: New England's War Against Slavery* (1973). And there is a good study of New England's boldest antislavery leader in John L. Thomas' *The Liberator: William Lloyd Garrison* (1963). The hero of the western wing of abolitionism is studied in Benjamin P. Thomas' *Theodore Weld* (1950). Weld was married to the daughter of a Southern slaveholder who turned abolitionist, and she is the subject of Gerda Lerner, *The Grimké Sisters from South Carolina* (1967). Do not overlook Benjamin Quarles, *Black Abolitionists* (1969).

Reform leads to women's rights and Eleanor Flexner, *Century of Struggle: The Women's Rights Movement in the United States* (1959). For firsthand flavor and biography, try to find Harriet S. Blatch, ed., *The Life and Letters of Elizabeth Cady Stanton* (1922), it will repay you. A short biography of Mrs. Stanton is that by Alma Lutz (1940). Elizabeth Stanton's husband, Henry M. Stanton wrote a book called *Random Recollections* (1887) (which only large libraries are likely to have) that tells much about abolitionists. Frederick Douglass' *Narrative of the Life of an American Slave* (1968) is more about abolitionists than slaves, but very worthwhile. Louis Ruchames, *The Abolitionists* (1963) also contains firsthand writings full of fire.

# chapter II

# *The world of slaves and owners*

In a 1941 book, *The Mind of the South*, a young Southern writer named Wilbur J. Cash wrote this passage:

> And in this society in which the infant son of the planter was commonly suckled by a black mammy, in which gray old black men were his most loved story-tellers, in which black stalwarts were among the chiefest heroes and mentors of his boyhood, and in which his usual, often practically his only, companions until he was past the age of puberty were the black boys (and girls) of the plantation—in this society . . . the relationship between the two groups was . . . nothing less than organic. Negro entered into white man as profoundly as white man entered into Negro—subtly influencing every gesture, every word, every emotion and idea, every attitude.

Cash was describing plantation life in the pre–Civil War South. He was trying hard to understand why, in some way, his section was different from the rest of the United States. He rejected legends about Southern chivalry and the glorious "lost cause" of the Confederacy. They took no account of certain grim realities that he saw around him: rural poverty and ignorance, segregation and lynching. Defeat in 1865 could not, all by itself, explain them, nor pleasant parts of Southern life, either. The deeper Cash probed into the Southern past, the more he kept running into the central fact of race. In ways that we cannot ever know now, the encounter disturbed him. Shortly after the publication of his book, he killed himself.

*Organizing the Evidence of Slavery*

To approach the question of the South's differentness, we, too, must try to sift legends and stereotypes for kernels of fact. From time to time, so far, we have looked at mixed or changing communities. We saw the Spaniard and the Indian touch each other's life-styles. We read how seventeenth-century English emigrants built villages in the wilderness. We watched youthful industrial towns being turned into laboratories for contact between a new working class and a new owning class. *All* of these social mixtures made their times and places special and distinct, but they also taught general lessons about human behavior.

In the pre–Civil War South, history shows us still another society of unequals. This time we are dealing with Americans and Afro-Americans, masters and slaves, instead of conquistadores and Aztecs or merchants and mill hands. It is difficult to get at the meaning of American slavery, however, because the subject is in the shadow of many legends that arose in the battle to destroy it.

But perhaps we can turn this into an advantage. One of the tasks of historians is to select, from the huge array of facts before them, a limited number that they can arrange so as to tell a story. In slavery's case, the facts are so numerous and varied that it is hard to make sweeping statements about how it worked and how it created a Southern identity. Slavery lasted in the United States over 200 years. It was spread, in 1860, from Maryland to west Texas, covering many different regions and economies. Until just after the Revolution, it existed in the northern as well as the southern colonies. When it began, the enslavement of Africans by Europeans was common, but the United States was the last Western power to give it up. The first blacks brought to the colonies were not defined as slaves, and there were always at least a few free blacks living in slaveholding territory. Slave imports from Africa were banned in 1808, but slavery itself went on for another half-century. Clearly, any simple explanation of an institution so widespread and long lasting would be incomplete. There is no one answer to the question: "What was slavery in the South like?"

However, we can break the question down into manageable segments. First, we can sum up the facts about Southern American whites and blacks that we are sure of. Then we can examine some of the legends that veil those facts and show where the facts pierce and shred them. In that way we have created,

*CHRONOLOGY*

1808 *African slave trade banned by Congress*
1831 *Nat Turner's slave rebellion, Southampton County, Virginia*
1852 Uncle Tom's Cabin *written by Harriet Beecher Stowe*

as historians do, an order of inquiry, a road map through the mass of evidence. Then, finally, we can try our hand at some general judgments about the connections among blacks, whites, the mind of the South, and the whole course of the United States as a land of more than one race.



*The Different South*

To begin with, there is little doubt that the South, until very recently and especially before 1860, simply *was* different. It kept slavery after the Northern states had abandoned it. It clung to an almost exclusively agrarian way of life while industry was spreading its network of chimneys and wires over the North. The South had, by 1860, few railroad lines, few cities of notable size, few ships registered in its ports, few factories, immigrants, millionaires, businessmen, banking, insurance, and trading companies. Southern life moved at a tempo of cotton-piled wagons on back-country roads and swinging hoes, not of locomotives and belt lines.

Inevitably, this was reflected in Southern culture. A Southern accent drawled its way through lengthy stories with no hint that time was money. Southern hospitality invited the guest to spend time, not only to eat well but to linger. Southerners were more apt than others to know and care who their distant kinfolk and cousins were. Southerners were likelier to be Baptists or Methodists and saw fewer Catholics, Jews, Quakers, and Unitarians than Northerners did. As a group, Southerners read fewer newspapers, had fewer schools to attend and fewer local chapters of national societies to join. They spent much of their recreational life outdoors, gun or fishing pole in hand. They were rural people.

Of course, there were millions of rural Americans in the North before 1860. But whereas Northerners tended to welcome the changing countryside as it was shaped by progress, Southern society resisted newness. A "Bible" of Southern thought, George Fitzhugh's *Cannibals All! or, Slaves Without Masters,* published in 1857, denounced progress, individualism, and liberalism. Those things led, said Fitzhugh, only to the making of millionaires and paupers, to political manipulation of the masses, to riots and unrest in the streets, to making people restless and unhappy in their roles.

Each of the preceding statements is, of course, a generalization having many possible exceptions. In the "tropic" South there were freezes and snowstorms. In the "easy-going" South there were hustlers and defenders of factories, tariffs, and dollar piling. But overall, as traveler after traveler reported, the pre-1860 South did have a sense of separateness. The most telling proof is that the section left the Union and fought for four bitter years for independence. No other region in the United States, however proud of its local customs, did that.

If Southern white Americans were special, so were the South's American blacks. The proof is in their children. Today, most of the black populace of the United States live in cities outside of the Old South. Yet only a few moments in a black immigrant neighborhood reveal deep differences in language, religion, music, food, amusements, and style between U.S.-born black men and women and those from Haiti, Jamaica, Brazil, or almost any Caribbean or African country. American blacks are descendants of slaves held in a region that stamped its mark on both races. For them, as for white migrants from Appalachia to the cities, the South is, in black novelist James Baldwin's wording, "the old country." Beginning with the 20 dropped off in Virginia in 1619, blacks were part of Southern life in growing numbers. There were 4 million in 1860. In no other New World country did such an increase take place. That fact alone is worth bearing in mind when considering the realities and the false beliefs about American slavery.

*Legend 1. Most Southerners held numerous slaves and lived on plantations long held by the family*

The facts are quite the opposite. Of some 8 million white Southerners counted in the 1860 census, only about one in four families owned slaves. And of those who did, only an extremely tiny fraction held more than 20. The "typical" slaveholder was not an owner of 200 or more slaves. There were fewer than 250 of those in the nation. It was, instead, someone like James Burroughs of Virginia, who, in 1860, owned only a couple of slave families—including a four-year-old boy named Booker, who would one day become Booker T. Washington. The "typical" farm was not George Washington's Mount Vernon. It was a place where a few white and few black men, women, and children, with a few animals to help, raised a cash crop, plus all their own necessities, on a modest-sized piece of land.

And most Southern farms in 1860 were relatively "new." The great cotton-producing regions of western Georgia, Alabama, Mississippi, Louisiana, and Arkansas were wilderness in 1820. Farms were hacked out there by hard pioneer labor. That was why it was hard for a slave to be sold "down the river," away from the Old South, where much of the toughest work was finished. The "white-pillared plantation house" in the new area was apt to be a double log cabin, to which whitewash and a porch had been added as the master prospered. And his ancestors were themselves likely to have been small farmers rather than aristocrats.

Most of the "gracious old slaveholding South" was neither gracious, old, nor slaveholding. But that did not prevent slaveholders from dominating the region's life. The biggest part of the South's vital cotton crop was produced on large plantations. So the people who owned them had an importance in society that was far beyond their numbers. Almost every Southern figure of note held at least some slaves: almost every judge, every church official, every governor, every senator and representative, every Southern president and cabinet member. Even more than the factory owners of the North, they were the elite of elites.

Southern small businessmen, middle-sized farmers, and professionals (like lawyers and doctors) now and then criticized the power and arrogance of great slaveholders. But their attack rarely aimed at slavery itself. The reasons were two. White Southerners defended slavery primarily because it guaranteed their control of an "inferior" race. Even the most dogged critic of wealthy slaveowners wanted no competition with "free niggers."

In addition, most Southerners shared the American dream of success. For them this meant getting more slaves of their own some day. This actually became less likely as the years passed. The growing demand for slaves to cultivate new lands pushed the price to somewhere between $1000 and $2000 for a prime field hand in 1860. But just as many Northern workers refused to give up the idea of eventual self-employment, as we saw in the last chapter, so few slaveless or almost slaveless Southerners gave up *their* goals of advancing within the economic system. They looked to the great slaveowners as models for their own futures.

So the influence of the slaveholders was magnified. Out of it they created a distinctive world. They were strong believers in authority, tradition, self-sufficiency. They tried to run the plantations like little feudal baronies. They got service from their black "serfs" and power (through election to local offices) over their poorer white neighbors. They were captains and colonels in the local militia, sponsors of private schools, pillars of the church. Their loyalties were clannish. They set the social tone, and it was that of paternalism. Yet they lived in an expanding United States in which the personal contacts necessary for paternalism were getting harder to keep up every year, as the mill owners of Lowell discovered before the slaveowners did.

What the plantation slave saw was a system in which power and respect went to the wealthiest whites. He himself had most to fear from the poorer whites, who despised *him* because they needed someone to look down on from their own bottom rung on the ladder. Northerners, especially abolitionists, charged that the social ranks created in a slaveholding society flouted the American system. To the slave that *was* the American system.

*Legend 2. Africans brought no native culture with them or else were brutally stripped of their cultural heritage and family life in the process of acclimatization*

The first argument was often used by defenders of slavery. They claimed that in teaching the "savage" blacks the orderly practices of agriculture, they were raising them from the brute level of the jungle. This view rested on the nineteenth-century American notion that all Africa was the Dark Continent, populated exclusively by naked cannibal tribes and wild animals.

In fact, however, most slaves brought to the New World came from the West African area around the Gulf of Guinea. This region had been the scene of mighty black empires and civilizations. It had known great cities, rich caravans, and centers of learning. In the 1600s it was still the home of tribes such as the Yoruba, and the Ibo, which produced beautiful art objects in wood, bronze, and stone.

The peoples of West Africa were villagers and farmers. They had a rich store of folk legends, songs, ritual dances, and games. They had devised, like the Indian peoples of the Americas whom we met in the opening chapter, intricate patterns of life that added up to separate cultures. Today, anthropologists recognize such cultures as human creations equal in ingenuity to cathedrals or factories. But until very recent years, Western whites recognized only such cultural creations of their own as respectable.

So the Africans brought to American shores were not "primitive" savages. Once here, a deliberate effort was made to erase their tribal identities. Fearful owners did not want their "property" plotting escapes or uprisings. They forbade the Africans to speak their languages, gather in large groups, practice their religious ceremonies, or communicate as they once had by drums or homemade horns and whistles.

Nevertheless, there seems little doubt that an African culture existed and was passed on to American-born slaves. Words of African dialect remained embedded in the broken English of the quarters. There, too, some slaves told tales of cunning foxes who outwitted lions, sly rabbits who escaped wolves, and other weak but clever beasts who overcame their enemies. Such stories, it is now known, had strong resemblances to similar tales in African folklore.

And more. Black "uncles" and "aunties" told children, both black and white, chilling tales of spooks, "haunts," ghosts, witches, and other fearful creatures. Some of those stories, too, were reworkings of tribal folklore. They touched a basic human sense of mystery and wonder that surfaces in fairy tales of all nations. Likewise, in the slave quarters, there were "conjure" men and women who used herbs and barks to brew up medicines probably as effective as many home remedies then in use.

Finally, in their little free time, some slaves made tambourines, castanets, banjoes, and rattles and beat out the rhythms for strutting, shuffling dances that almost certainly repeated old tribal patterns. White observers marveled, too, at the black ability to make up work chants and songs whose strong, pulsing beats could pull tired muscles through a day's work.

In short, there obviously was a slave community with skills, values, and leaders of its own. The slave could turn to it for strength and affirmation and so resist the destruction of his personality. A good singer, a skilled "yarb" (herb) doctor, a popular storyteller—all possessed a standing and dignity that did not depend on the white masters' approval. In such ways blacks resisted and survived total absorption. In addition, slaves adopted some white institutions to their own needs. A good example is to be found in black Christianity. Some masters did try hard to provide a religious life for their "servants." Naturally, they stressed those parts of Christian doctrine that told believers to be obedient in this world and get their rewards in the next. For that reason many slaves resisted Christianization and regarded it as a hypocritical white man's religion that only taught the nonwhite to hug his chains. But some individual slaves found the idea that they had immortal souls as good as their masters' a source of considerable strength. The term "Uncle Tom" has come to mean a subservient and pliable black. But, in fact, *Uncle Tom's Cabin* (though written in 1852 by a white woman) tells a different and significant story. Uncle Tom, who is not a white-haired old man but in the prime of life and power, is a good Christian. He will give his owners any lawful service, since God has chosen to make him a slave. But he will do no evil. In the end he resists the orders of his owner, Simon Legree, to become a brutal overseer and punish other blacks. He resists, in fact, until he himself is beaten to death.

It is hard to say whether there were many black "Toms" who used Christianity to strengthen their inner selves. But all observers of black religious ceremonies agreed that the spirituals, the poetic sermons, and the shouted rhythmic responses of the congregations all added to Christianity a special note of emotion and passion that was clearly black. And white Southern revival meetings show a similar pattern. Not only did blacks in slavery keep some style of their own, but in some ways they very probably influenced white behavior. As we saw with Spaniard and Indian, cultural exchange is a two-way street.

It has also been said that slavery destroyed black American family life because masters could and did separate wives and husbands by sale. A slave mating had no legal standing. But even though this dreadful occurrence did occasionally happen (and recent evidence is that it was far from common), it is not certain, as some have suggested, that it wiped out a sense of responsibility among slave fathers. It is true that when a slave family was broken up, the children stayed with the mother and the father lost his role in their lives. But surviving accounts of plantation life by freed or escaped slaves show that black fathers who were allowed to stay with their sons and daughters did many traditional things that made fatherhood important, like whittling toys, settling quarrels, reciting stories and poems, or, when allowed, doing extra work to earn a few ginger cakes or bright-colored kerchiefs for the family.

To say this is not to soften the face of slavery. It is only to say that even in slavery there was an Afro-American culture. It had qualities of dignity, tragedy, suffering, poetry, humor, and loyalty all its own. There seems little question that Southern whites, reared by black servants and playing with black children, as Cash notes, picked up many of the "vibrations" of this style. That was one root of their distinctiveness.

*Legend 3. Slavery was (1) a benign and patriarchal institution or (2) a savage and crippling experience for an entire race*

The first statement was another staple of the proslavery argument. The slave, said Southerners, unlike the wage worker, was housed, fed, doctored, and supported in childhood and old age by the master. That view ignores the gritty facts of what slave labor actually *was.* Most slaves were field workers. They were planting, weeding, or picking the crop almost the year round from sunup to sundown. Breakfast was snatched before work started. There was only a very brief pause to eat the midday meal right in the sunbaked furrows. When they were not working on the cotton or corn, they were carrying water, feeding stock, clearing ground, mending, painting, or carrying on other bone-wearying chores. The work was done by men, women and all but the very youngest children. Only the desperately sick were excused. Pregnant women worked almost until delivery. Nursing mothers carried their babies into the fields on their backs.

The slave clothing was usually shirt, jacket, and pants for the men and a dress for the women, both of very cheap, rough cloth. There was little time to wash them, and they soon stiffened with sweat and dirt. They were in tatters, before long, but only replaced about once a year. Wool hats and head scarves were also issued, as were heavy coarse shoes, worn only when weather or rough ground forbade bare feet.

Food was mainly corn bread and fat pork. Rations were issued and cooked weekly. Meals were snatched up, catch as catch can, without knives, forks, or spoons. Living quarters were crude. The slave cabin had a cornshuck mattress and a few stools, perhaps, but otherwise its furnishings were nonexistent. Its floor was the bare dirt, and it consisted of one large room for the whole family. Through its logs chinked with mud, the drafts and rain blew in the winters, and in the summers the never-extinguished fireplace added to the blazing and bug-swarming heat. In a sense, the slave cabins were human stables. So, at least, Booker T. Washington remembered. Nothing in his childhood "home" encouraged a sense of humanity or privacy.

That was the boasted "care" of the slave. Yet a positive word can be added without appearing to defend slavery. Its basic concept was repulsive. But it must be seen as a whole to understand the black life that emerged from it.

First, compared with other slaveholding countries, the American mortality record was good. The food was simple and monotonous but adequate. Slaves probably were as healthy, on the average, as Southern poor whites who ate the same diet. The clothing and housing were minimal but sufficient for the climate. A slaveholder had no wish to see his valuable "stock" starved or hit by chills and fevers. A sick or injured slave was lost income. When slaves did fall ill, they were dosed with the same simple medicines, mostly strong laxatives, plasters, and liniments that whites got. In short, their care probably was at least as good as what early industrial workers could afford. The level in both cases was low but life sustaining.

In addition, a number of masters allowed slaves, in their little free time, to raise vegetables and poultry in garden plots and add them to their diet. Sometimes the slaves were even permitted to sell any surplus for a little pocket money.

And some slaves learned crafts, as well. In the isolated plantation world—especially in the eighteenth century—stonecutters, bricklayers, blacksmiths, harness makers, cooks, bakers, barbers, shoemakers, carpenters, and a variety of other craftsmen and women had to be, and were, home trained. The black child who showed aptitude at a particular job could grow into an important member of the work force. A skilled slave added to the master's status and might be rewarded with special privileges, such as passes to visit in town. Sometimes, especially in the older slave states, masters even found themselves with surplus black craftsmen on hand. They could then "hire out" such workers to neighbors or to city businessmen. The "rent" for the slave was paid to the owner, of course. But in some cases the slave was allowed to keep part of his hire. Some even saved enough money to "buy themselves" from their owners and be free. By the last days of slavery, there were even groups of hired-out slaves living in the few Southern cities and working in places like tobacco factories.

But there was also the dark side of the record. The system rested, basically, on punishment and fear. Even on "good" plantations, slaves were frequently beaten with ropes, whips, and paddles. Children looked on in horror as their parents were flung down to the ground, stripped, and mercilessly lashed. And that was not the worst. Slaves could be and were branded, mutilated, tortured, shot, and hanged by angry whites. There were laws on the books to ban such outrages, but no slave could force a white into court. In reality, all that held the planter in check was his own conscience and the opinion of his neighbors. For some brutal owners, that was not enough. Slave women were at the mercy, sexually speaking, not only of their masters but of any white overseer or neighbor who demanded their bodies.

Slaves could not bear arms; could not leave the plantation without permission; could not be taught to read or write; could not rely on self-defense or hope for self-advancement. And the worst horror was being a piece of salable

Is it possible that we of the North have been so deceived by false Reports? Why did we not visit the South before we caused this trouble between the North and South, and so much hard feelings amongst our friends at home!
Is this the way that Slaves are treated at the South!
It is as a general thing, some few exceptions, after mine have done a certain amount of Labor which they finish by 4 or 5 P.M. I allow them to enjoy themselves in any reasonable way.
I think our Visitors will tell a different Story when they return to the North, the thoughts of this Union being dissolved is to dreadful a thing to be contemplated, but we must stand up for our rights let the consequence be as it may.
SLAVERY AS IT EXISTS IN AMERICA.
PUBLISHED BY J. HAVEN 86 STATE ST. BOSTON, 1850.
Ah! Farmer we operatives are fast men, and generally die of old age at Forty.
Why my Dear Friend, how is it that you look so old? you know we were playmates when boys.
I say Bill, I am going to run away from the Factory, and go to the Coal Mines where they have to work only 14 hours a Day instead of 17 as you do here.
Oh! how I would like to have such a comfortable place. Wont you speak a good word for me Tom?
Oh Dear! what wretched Slaves, this Factory Life makes me & my children.
CLOTH FACTORY
TYTHES
Thank God my Factory Slavery will soon be over
SLAVERY AS IT EXISTS IN ENGLAND.
(See Bulwers "England and the English"
THOMPSON
THE ENGLISH ANTI-SLAVERY AGITATOR.
"I am proud to boast that Slavery does not breathe in England"
(See his speech at the African Church in Belknap St.)

*The myth of the "happy darkies" (top left) was a staple of the proslavery argument and it was often coupled, as shown here, with an assault on the evils of industrial capitalism—in this case, England's. The other side of the coin (above) is this romantic abolitionist version of a slave sale, with mother and child being torn apart. Virtue and vice are clearly separated as well by the artist.*

merchandise. In a twinkling the slave could theoretically pass from the hands of the best white owner to those of the worst. Slaves lived without hope of controlling their own futures. That was the cruelly blighting fact. Even the worst-abused free worker could daydream that some day if he could break the chains of poverty, he might be free from drudgery and exploitation. The slave could not nurse that dream until and unless his owner consented.

The flinty bedrock of American slavery was the central fact of race. The slave was damned, not merely for being a slave, but for being black in a white world. In ancient times, and in Africa itself, captives in war or unlucky debtors were enslaved, but they were not necessarily considered inferior. The slave was merely unlucky and had to live with his fate. A Greek or Roman slave might rise to a highly responsible position. A slave in Africa, owned by another

African, kept his own culture, gods, family, and self-image. All he owed to his master was unpaid labor.

The root curse of American slavery, however, was the antiblack prejudice that sustained it and lasted after it disappeared in 1865. A feeling of white superiority made even kind masters, and people who knew in their souls that slavery was evil, spring to its defense. Moreover, American law and custom recognized only blackness and whiteness.

In the countries of Latin America the situation was somewhat different. Various degrees of "color" were recognized, and lighter skins meant greater liberty. Besides, final ownership of all lands and slaves rested with the king, who would not permit overabuse of his black or Indian subjects. The Catholic church, too, insisted on teaching blacks enough to understand their duties to God and on supervising their morality through strict rules about slave marriages. In short, the Latin American view of all individuals as subject to church and the king acted to erase some of the distinctions between slave and master. In the United States, however, Protestant individualism allowed owners to treat their slaves simply like any other property.

This is not to say that slavery was kind in Latin America. It had its terrible cruelties there, too. But it was not quite so tightly sealed to the prejudice of race. When it was finally wiped out there in the nineteenth century, the ex-slaves did not face as grim a problem of adjustment as American blacks.

### *Legend 4. Slaves were childlike and submissive or in a constant state of simmering rebellion*

Each of these statements represents a *stereotype*, a rigid general statement supposed to describe the behavior of every member of a given group. Stereotypes are made to comfort the hearts of those who utter them, not to describe their subjects accurately. These two are no exception. Slavery's defenders constantly claimed that the basic nature of the Afro-American was affectionate, docile, and emotionally shallow. Their stock figure was "Sambo," the grinning field hand, contented with his lot provided that he could occasionally enjoy a feast of watermelon or "possum" and a nighttime dance to the banjo. Or else it was the faithful, pious Mammy or Uncle frequently exclaiming "bless Jesus!" as they went about making life comfortable for beloved "white folks."

To blast back at these humiliating images, abolitionists, and some modern black scholars, created a counterclaim. They held that almost all the slaves lived in a state of barely suppressed mutiny. It took many forms. The mildest was secretly laughing at the whites and aggravating them by sloppy or negligent work. The most severe was murder of the master or actual rebellion. In between was running away, a form of protest with the feet.

It is easy enough to say that, as always, truth lies somewhere between two

*Slavery "had qualities of dignity, tragedy, suffering, poetry, humor, and loyalty all its own." A black father goes off to work in the fields.*

flawed portraits. But it is much more difficult to demonstrate the truth exactly. Most of what we know about slavery comes from whites. Only a handful of runaway slaves or ex-slaves learned to write and left books for us. They were obviously exceptional people. It is in white society's plantation journals, court records, newspaper advertisements, letters, diaries, and travelers' tales that we find most of what we know about the average slave. In those documents there is plenty of evidence that there were good-humored patient blacks as well as less bright and not very brave blacks who could be easily managed. Men and women who made the best of life kept their discontents cool and looked for what rewards they could get within the system. Such personality types exist in every race.

Of course, there is almost no way of knowing how much blacks disguised their real feelings and went about "puttin' on ole massa," stringing the whites along for whatever advantages it brought. Every powerless group, starting with small children, does this sometimes. One white historian, Stanley Elkins, even tried, in 1960, to compare slaves with another helpless group, the prisoners in Germany's Nazi concentration camps of the 1940s. He found that inmates of the camps sometimes adopted "Sambo" behavior—childlike, pliant, and imitative of the "masters," the guards, and camp officials. He suggested that slavery might have had a similar impact. Critics pointed out, however, that it was hard to match plantations with concentration camps. The plantation was a loosely run place where the owner wanted mainly to get labor from the "inmates." The camp was deliberately designed by twentieth-century European experts to destroy the spirits of the prisoners.

The Elkins thesis and its antagonists are mentioned here simply to show one possible way in which a historian can think imaginatively and the pitfalls that lie in wait for him. No two events or institutions in history are exactly the same, so comparison is difficult. Yet if there are no useful parallels between past and present, there is not much to learn from history. This is a dilemma that makes the historian's work complicated but enjoyable.

What of the counterstereotype to Sambo? Was there widespread slave resistance? The evidence of this view is somewhat better. There were not many organized slave revolts. The last, and best known, was Nat Turner's rebellion in Southampton County, Virginia, in the summer of 1831. Turner, a powerful figure in the slave community, could read and had religious visions. In several of them the heavens commanded him to be the leader in a mighty struggle between blacks and whites. Turner obeyed. On an August night he killed his master and then led some 60 followers on a rampage through neighboring plantations. They killed over 50 whites before they were finally captured. Turner was executed, along with 16 others.

But full-scale revolts are not the only signs of resistance. Newspapers and public records show hundreds of cases of individual blacks who poisoned, shot, or stabbed their owners or other whites. Thousands of advertisements describe runaways who bore the scars of earlier punishments. Obviously, some slaves just could not be kept down. Most of these runaways (who often stole arms, horses, and property in their flight) were recaptured. Others hid out, however, sometimes in groups. They lurked in swamps and forests for months at a time, now and then raiding plantations for supplies.

Finally, plantation records tell of slaves who resisted discipline so hard that it was easier for overseers to woo them to work than to threaten them. And much "irresponsible" black behavior, such as the breaking of tools or the mislaying of goods, was clearly a form of resistance.

When we realize that all these acts took place in a situation in which the cards were heavily stacked against runaways and rebels, with terrible punishment sure to follow capture, we can assume something else. For every black brave enough or desperate enough to try to break free with a 1-in-100 chance, there must have been ten others who wanted to do so but lacked the nerve. So the evidence of day-to-day resistance to slavery is powerful.

*Slavery's Psychological Price for Whites*

What did the Southern whites actually believe about their slaves? It was, after all, the Southerners who invented the "happy darky" and the other caricatures designed to show that the blacks did not feel the pain of enslavement. Yet the South really seems to have feared that the slave nursed murder in his "savage" heart.

There are two ways of showing this. One was the constant harping of Southerners on the danger of slave rebellion. Whenever antislavery spokesmen seemed to be encouraging ideas of black liberation, Southerners worried aloud about a possible repetition of what had happened in Haiti and Santo Domingo in the 1790s. Tremendous black uprisings had taken place, some with indiscriminate killings, burning, and looting. Obviously, Southerners would have had no such fears if they truly believed that all of their blacks were faithful, loyal, and simple-minded. What they really thought was that behind the mask of "Sambo" was a semianimal being, full of base passions. This, more than anything, interprets certain patterns of Southern behavior.

The second way to illustrate Southern fear of the rage of their slaves is to show the high psychological and social price they paid to keep the blacks down. Southerners resisted whatever might give the blacks dangerous notions. Not only were slaves barred from learning to read, but as the defense of slavery hardened, even free blacks were likewise denied school opportunities. But this meant that a large part of the South's potentially productive population was locked in poverty and ignorance. The whole section paid. And the hostility toward anything that spread newfangled ideas among the blacks spilled over into a general Southern resistance to almost any kind of new thought. Booker T. Washington once wrote that to keep a man in the gutter, one had to get down there with him. It was true. Southern enmity to liberal racial ideas eventually led the South to discourage almost all original social thinking in its few universities as well as its churches and other institutions.

Southern emphasis on military valor owed something to the fact that the South was rather like an armed camp. In the rural North, too, guns for hunting were commonplace. But uncounted numbers of Southerners, long after the frontier was pacified, still acted like people in a besieged fort. They never retired, according to some accounts, without arms nearby. They organized local militia companies to patrol the roads in search of runaway blacks. They lived constantly on close terms with weapons and violence. More Southerners than Northerners went to military schools, including West Point.

Even the exaggerated Southern "chivalry" toward women was partly a result of the garrison mentality. Southern whites both scorned and envied what seemed to be the easygoing sexual habits of the blacks. But if this relaxed and guiltless approach to sex was the mark of a "passionate" people, then it was all the more important for white Anglo-Saxons to show their self-control by exalting the "purity" of their women, the mothers of the "superior" race.

So the South became a defensive region, which saw change as threatening to upset its social balances. As a distinguished Southern-born historian (Ulrich B. Phillips) once put it frankly, the central theme of Southern history was to maintain it as a white man's country. Race pride, plus fear, had bred a regional subculture. That was what made the South special. That, as Cash learned, was slavery's legacy to the whites who lived with it.

## *FOR FURTHER READING*

Since the chapter opens with a mention of this book, you may well want to read W. J. Cash, *The Mind of the South* (1940) as a starting point. A more standard historical overview of how the South came to see itself as another country is Avery Craven, *The Growth of Southern Nationalism* (1953).

But the Old South cannot be separated from slavery, and it is there that the story must be pursued. A general description of how slavery worked is Kenneth M. Stampp, *The Peculiar Institution* (1956). More popular and lively is J. C. Furnas, *Goodbye to Uncle Tom* (1964). With the start of the movement for black liberation in the 1960s, a number of new interpretations appeared. An interesting, if controversial, one is Stanley Elkins, *Slavery* (1959), which tries to determine whether and why there was a "Negro personality" on the plantation. More recently, scholars have been interested in the question of whether blacks under slavery were able to keep a culture and life-style of their own. Two works say yes. One, by a black historian, is John Blassingame, *The Slave Community* (1972); the other, by a white, is Eugene D. Genovese, *Roll, Jordan, Roll: The World the Slaves Made* (1974). An earlier study by Genovese speculates on the life-style and influence of the planter class, *The Political Economy of Slavery* (1965). And a very provocative look at the subject is taken by two "cliometricians"—economic historians who try to use scientific, computerized, statistical studies as the basis of their findings: Robert Fogel and Stanley Engerman in *Time on the Cross* (1973) claim new, positive, and unusual findings about the efficiency and behavior of the slaves.

Do not overlook firsthand materials. Some, but by no means all, of the best include the following: First, for narratives supposedly written by ex-slaves, try Gilbert Osofsky, ed., *Puttin' On Ole Massa* (1969); second, read firsthand reports, both pro and con. These include an antislavery account by Frances Kemble (an English actress married to a slaveholder), *Journal of Residence on a Georgia Plantation* (1969). A defense by a Southern belle is Mary B. Chesnut, *A Diary from Dixie* (1961). A classic criticism of the North's free labor system by a proslavery spokesman, George Fitzhugh, *Cannibals All* (1960) will make you think twice. If you have not read *Uncle Tom's Cabin* by Harriet Beecher Stowe, most recently reprinted in 1972, you will find it rewarding to do so, and to meet the original Uncle Tom, Simon Legree, and Little Eva, who may surprise you.

# THOUGHT PROVOKERS

*By the time a man or woman born in 1815 had reached middle age, life would have been very different from their cradle days. The United States would have achieved the continental boundaries it still possesses by adding to its territories Florida, Texas, and most of the Far West, from the Rockies to the Pacific. Railroads would link most cities in the area bounded by the Atlantic, the Mississippi, and the Gulf of Mexico. Steamers (with help from sails) would be plying ocean routes. The telegraph would whisk messages to every corner of the developed part of the Union. Nearly a billion dollars' worth of products, mostly foodstuffs and textiles, would be flowing through the channels of commerce each year after 1850. The population would jump from a little over 7 million in 1810 to more than 31 million fifty years later. It was fed not only by a sturdy birth rate but by substantial immigration.*

*This is the background of the broad changes studied in Part Three. Specific questions about the impact of those changes take us into the area where economic change and social thought affect each other. For example, did the size of the United States alone encourage railroad building? Or did the stimulus to railroads come mainly from business classes with goods to move? You may wish to approach this question by comparing railroad development in the North and the South. And how did mobility affect the way people thought about their ancestors? Could the United States have developed a pattern like that of the Vietnamese, for example, who do not like to leave their home villages because the spirits of their forefathers are there?*

*Or let us take the interplay of religious, political, and economic ideas. In earlier chapters we saw, in revivalism, a drive for "equal rights" in the kingdom of heaven. And we have also seen the drive for universal suffrage and a broader base for political authority. How did the drive for cheap lands and homesteads compare to these movements? Did it use the same arguments? Lead to the same conclusions? How did it affect sectional line-ups in national politics?*

*The chapter on technology shows how a new kind of economic organization touched on family roles and expectations. How did entering the factory change the picture of "ideal womanhood"? What happened to basic notions of a woman's "duty" when she became a breadwinner? Was that connected, do you think, with the quest for votes for women? In the same way was there a link between the breakdown of the apprentice system and the demand for public education? Remember that the workshop had been the apprenticed child's school. What changes were brought about in education when that school had to be replaced by a larger and more impersonal one? And, finally, in considering the family-run business as compared with the corporate-run business, what effect did the change have on fixing responsibility for business behavior? Would consumer protection agencies have been as necessary under the old system as they are today?*

*In studying the ideal communities of the reform era, what can you learn by comparing them with Puritan Massachusetts and Quaker Pennsylvania? What limits did these earlier "commonwealths" set on themselves that reform societies might not? How did the reformers' belief in human perfectibility affect what they did? And how did it make the utopian community different from those established in the seventeenth century? How did the political needs and goals of the reform movements differ from those of "ordinary" politicians as we saw them at work in Chapter 7? What were the limits on each kind of political operation?*

*Finally, in looking at the South and slavery, what were some key differences between the ways in which sixteenth-century Spaniards dealt with Indians and nineteenth-century Americans dealt with blacks? In other words, can you compare the mission and the plantation in terms of what they were set up to do economically, how their rules were made, and what their leaders thought of their nonwhite laborers? What differences are there, and why?*

*If the North was basically as racist as the South, why did slavery die out there relatively easily? Do racial feelings become more intense when greater numbers of the so-called inferior race are present? Or do they become stronger when they are needed to justify economic exploitation? Northern workers generally were hostile to abolitionists. Why do you think this was the case?*

*And was slavery possible in a machine age society? Could blacks have been used to provide labor for the textile factories? If so, what changes in the slavery system might have been necessary? Particularly, what changes would be needed in education, diet, work rules, and laws governing the association of groups of blacks? Was slavery the enemy of industrial progress? (If you choose and have the time, you might do some research on modern slave labor in Europe during World War II to help give broader perspective to your answer.)*

# part four: Division and Reunion

*Engineers and research scientists know that not every model or experiment must work in order to be an educational success. Failures can teach a great deal, too. They can show limits. Or they can send researchers back to thinking out their questions again. They cannot always prevent future errors, but they can discourage the repetition of particular, clearly evident mistakes.*

*It is in this spirit that Part Four looks at one of the outstanding failures of our national history, the Civil War. Just seventy-two years, or one long lifetime after the Constitution was put into effect, it could not keep the country from splitting. Americans of North and South who shared a common history and common prosperity looked at each other over gun muzzles for four brutal years. Unity was finally won by Northern victory, but it was a reunion based on force, not persuasion. At the heart of the war lay the inability of the two sections to agree on many questions, but chiefly the future of black slavery in America. Yet, ironically, the white majorities in each region almost certainly were united in a low estimate of the black race. And after the war was ended, the struggle for racial justice remained as harsh and unfinished as before.*

*Why then did the war happen? Chapter 12 raises the issue and uses it to probe the whole question of historical theory. There is no single cause for a complex chain of historical happenings. Yet most historians with imagination look for some pattern of explanation. "Why do we behave as we do?" is the root question of all the social studies. It can be focused sharply enough to yield some possible replies when looking at a past disaster. Each answer will use certain evidence and rest on certain ideas about humanity's collective experiences. Was the war the result of blind chance? Destiny? Error? Or evil? We look at some of the answers and their supporting arguments.*

*The twelve years following the war's end were full of high hopes and keen disappointments. Having won the war, a victorious North attempted to remake the parts of Southern life that it blamed for having created conflict. It shook up the old plantation society studied in Chapter 11 from top to bottom. The process left some lasting changes. But other parts of it were rather swiftly undone. With the ink on the amendments giving blacks freedom, citizenship and the vote hardly dry in 1870, the political control of the South was allowed to fall back into the hands of the white master class.*

*But was it exactly the same class as before the war? Or did it have new connections and new ambitions? And were all the gains of blacks erased? Obviously, a total revolution in social patterns could not take place in a short time. Why not? Was it because not enough force was applied? Or because the groundwork was not properly laid? Or because, when it came to matters of race, at least, there were barriers to the extent and speed of change that simply could not be broken? Are there, in fact, some areas of belief and action (say, sexual, racial, and religious) that cannot be reached by political compromise or even by force? Chapter 13 does not, like Chapter 12, contrast various historians' opinions on these matters. Instead, it introduces the evidence so that you yourself may try to find answers.*

*Finally, the part's last chapter digs into underlying economic forces of reunion. After 1870 the country* was *knit together with dazzling speed—not by political decisions but rather by the relentless growth of a nationwide market. With a common interest in wealth, Americans of every background flung themselves into the work of settling the Far West. A busy generation plowed up millions of acres of fresh soil, tunneled into the mountains for coal, iron, silver, and gold, felled trees by the millions for lumber, and grazed herds of cattle on land that a mere few years before had known only the hooves of Indian ponies. The final surge of westward expansion helped to power an industrial boom in the Northeast. And a spreading railroad network joined ranchers, miners, meat packers, factory hands, bankers, grocers, and immigrants in a common economic destiny.*

*What did this do to old political geographies? Which sections emerged on top? How was this rapid growth financed, and how much power did those who did the bankrolling exercise? As society became more complex, more interdependent, and more dominated by large-scale, multimillion-dollar investments like the railroads, what happened to the republic of the founding fathers? To Jacksonian democracy? To the self-sufficient small communities of the pre–Civil War years? How did the conquest of the last frontier—a work of giants—affect national institutions that were not built for giants? These are the themes with which the unit, and the first half of the volume, will close.*

# chapter 12
# The limits of compromise

The Civil War has always been a tormenting puzzle to historians of the United States. The reason is not difficult to find. It is a knife thrust into the heart of a strong national belief that our history is a sunny success story. The American people supposedly have moved from wilderness colonists to global leaders, getting stronger, richer, and more democratic all the time. Other peoples may commit political crimes and follies, but the United States has had a special immunity from the miseries of humanity.

And yet we had a Civil War, one of the most savage and disastrous of modern times. It killed 600,000 young men, destroyed millions of dollars' worth of property, and only stopped because one side was exhausted. And why? European lands had known civil wars, too. They blazed between groups speaking different languages, between Catholics and Protestants, between rival heirs to thrones, between lords and peasants. But in the United States there was a common language, no rigidly fixed classes to struggle against each other, no bloodshed over alternate routes to God, except for some occasional, temporary outbursts against Catholic immigrants.

How did it happen *here?* Such a painful mystery has challenged historical thinking almost constantly, though the war is more than a century behind us. No magic answer can be furnished in the next few pages. What we can do, however, is to use various explanations of the war as showcases of how historical theories are formed. What assumptions do they involve? Where may they lead in general efforts to explain the human condition? How is the study of history just one of many possible ways to try to make sense of life's experiences?

To begin with, we will briefly survey those events leading up to the war whose importance all historians recognize. Then we will discuss the general problems of explanatory theory. Finally, we will examine, sort out, and analyze the major theories explaining the disaster. If the project sounds discouragingly heavy, think of it merely as an unfinished mystery story told to an audience. Each member then supplies his own guess as to who and why? The fun of the game sometimes lies, not in guessing correctly (which may be impossible) but in second-guessing the other guessers.

*Missouri Lights the Fuse*

"This momentous question," wrote the aging Jefferson in a letter, "like a firebell in the night, filled me with alarm." The "firebell" was the 1819 crisis over the admission of Missouri as a state. It began when a New York congressman introduced an amendment to the bill granting statehood to Missouri, which would have banned slavery there. The battle that followed was long, complex, and touched on many issues not connected with slavery. Among them were the rights of Westerners to control their own societies and whether or not Congress could make different rules for admitting new states than it had for old ones.

But through all the storm of debate ran the thread of slavery. Southerner after Southerner rose to deny the right of the North to ban the South's "peculiar institution" from the lands of the Louisiana Purchase, bought with tax money raised in *all* the states. And Northerner after Northerner pointed out the discordant note of slaveholding in a nation founded on the principle that all men are created equal. Slavery, they argued, had been accepted where it existed when the Constitution was formed, as a necessary evil, a dark legacy from the past. But why give it a new lease on life by planting it in the West? (The idealism of this argument was in some cases bluntly mixed with racism: Why let blacks into a rich, new area clearly reserved by God for white Americans?)

Basic positions were being taken. They came as something of a surprise, for until then nationalism seemed to be growing and slavery dying. Between 1787 and 1819, slavery had been banned in the Northwest Territory, the foreign slave trade had been ended, the Northern states had abolished the institution, and the American Colonization Society been founded—all without much Southern objection. At the same time, Southern votes had usually supported nationalistic measures. During the War of 1812, remember, it was in New England that there was talk of secession.

But now, like a photograph taking form in a developing tank, the outlines of a new sectionalism were emerging. Slavery was localized in the South. The

South regarded an attack upon slavery as an attack upon the South itself. And the North looked doubtfully on slavery's spreading into the new territories that would shape the national future. An antagonism between the interests of slave states and free states was set up. The Missouri debates programmed a future political contest between the two.

The actual settlement of the question, therefore, was a way station. The solution adopted was urged by Kentucky's Henry Clay, an 1811 war hawk and an 1821 champion of compromise. Missouri would come in as a slave state. But all other territory in the Louisiana Purchase north of Missouri's *southern* boundary would be closed to slavery. And Maine, until then a district of Massachusetts, would also enter the Union as a free state, for balance. It seemed a triumph of compromise, a victory for the federal system. Each side gave up a little principle and got something it wanted. No one was completely triumphant or totally beaten. Such deals were the price of union. And time had been bought.

But time for what? If time did not settle the basic issue, what was gained? Only more strife? Doubts pricked the mind of John Quincy Adams, secretary of state in 1820. One day he talked the situation over with John C. Calhoun, secretary of war. Calhoun, then a strong nationalist, believed that the Missouri question would have to be compromised. It could not be allowed to disturb the destined expansion of the United States. But Adams went home and confided his private feelings to his diary. Slavery was a curse that must someday be wiped out. Otherwise, it would bring down fateful wrath on the nation. If the Union had to break, he mused, perhaps now was the right time and issue.

In the end, however, Adams also accepted the compromise. But from then on, there were increasing strains on the bonds of union. True, national growth marched on. Population swelled, tax revenues increased, and states continued

---

*CHRONOLOGY*

| | |
|---|---|
| 1820 | *The Missouri Compromise* |
| 1832–1833 | *South Carolina nullification crisis* |
| 1848 | *Gold discovered in California* |
| 1850 | *Compromise of 1850* |
| 1854 | *Kansas-Nebraska Act* |
| 1857 | *Dred Scott case* |
| 1859 | *John Brown's attack on federal arsenal at Harpers Ferry* |
| 1861 | *In April, Civil War begins* |
| 1863 | *Emancipation Proclamation takes effect on January 1* |

to be admitted (usually in pairs, a slave and a free). But contests kept arising, and even when they did not concern slavery, their outcomes were always weighed in public opinion for what they contributed to a Northern or Southern victory. More and more, people had to take positions—pro-North, pro-South, or moderate—on every controversial question, with the leeway for "moderates" always shrinking. Though hundreds of leaders made decisions without regard to sectional feeling, thoughtful people saw that the nation was drifting toward polarization.



### *The Turbulent Thirties, Nullification, and the Gag Rule*

The 1820s saw no fresh outbreaks of sectional strife. But in the 1830s two major developments changed that picture. One was the birth of the new abolitionism, which called for immediate action but only made the South more defensive—especially after Nat Turner's rebellion.

In 1833 there was a related crisis. South Carolina had been stung by the tariff of 1832. It argued that the cotton states were forced by the tariff to buy manufactured goods from the North instead of from cheaper foreign suppliers. In effect, the Carolinians claimed the tariff was like the old British Navigation Acts, hampering Southern free trade. Calhoun, abandoning his earlier nationalism, wrote that by benefiting factory states at the expense of farming states, the tariff destroyed the spirit of the Union. South Carolina therefore sought a remedy by falling back on the right of a sovereign and equal state to nullify an act harmful to its citizens. It would not permit the federal customs houses to operate in its parts.

President Jackson promptly threatened to send troops to enforce the law. No sister state offered to join South Carolina in resistance. South Carolina was in a tight spot. When a graceful way out was offered through a compromise that would gradually reduce the tariff, she accepted it and backed off. The crisis was over. But it had raised a question in Southern minds bigger than dollars and cents. If the federal government could "force" a tariff on the South by majority vote, might it not some day force anything else, including the end of slavery?

The slavery question also colored the nation's reaction to Texas. As we saw in Chapter 8, the Texans, after winning independence in 1836, hoped eventually to join the United States. But increasing numbers of Northerners had no desire to see an annexation that might add several slave states to the Union. So annexation was delayed until 1845.

Meantime, in the early 1830s, antislavery societies poured petitions into Congress demanding the death of slavery. Southerners were outraged at hearing their system denounced in the halls of the House and Senate, especially since the Constitution protected slavery in the states. On the grounds that Congress should not waste time in debating actions it could not take, they pushed through a so-called gag rule in 1836. It prevented the discussion of such petitions. Up rose Adams, who by this time had served a term as president, retired, and then been elected to the House of Representatives. To him and others it seemed plain that to protect slavery from attack Southerners would sacrifice the civil liberties of *all* Americans. What better proof was there of how slavery slowly corrupted the institutions of free government? So Adams led a long, divisive, bitter fight that finally got the gag rule repealed in 1844.

The 1840s, the third decade of "coexistence" under the Missouri Compromise, pulsed with economic growth. Thousands of miles of new railroad and canal lines were built. New factories rose, cities swelled, and heavy waves of immigration broke on American shores. But most of this development went on in the North. The South found it an alarming warning of minority status. Soon the House of Representatives would have a Northern majority. Equality in the Senate therefore became even more critical. So Southerners became more anxious than ever to secure new slave states. Westward expansion, like national industrial progress, became a threat to them unless protection for slavery went along with it.

### *The "Poison" of the Mexican War Spoils*

The event most damaging to the Union in the long run took place in the administration of James K. Polk, from March 1845 to March 1849. Polk was a nationalist, an expansionist, a slaveholder, a Southerner, and a Democrat. All of his actions were fairly consistent with this background. He wanted to annex California and New Mexico. So, as we saw, he accepted Texas into the Union and took on the war with Mexico that followed inevitably. Among many antislavery Northerners who were outraged opponents of the war with Mexico was Ralph Waldo Emerson. "The United States will swallow Mexico," he warned, "but it will be as the strong man swallows the poison which will bring him down." Events would prove him right.

Polk also negotiated a treaty with Britain, gaining for the United States about half of the jointly occupied Oregon territory. And, in the name of economy, he vetoed bills to spend money improving Northern rivers and harbors. These actions were consistent with Polk's basic ideas, but we shall see presently that they opened him up to charges of favoring the South at the expense of the North. Meanwhile, trouble was brewing over the future of the lands being won from Mexico. The idea of free soil or no slavery in the territories was taking shape. Though a formal party embodying that idea would not appear until 1848, as early as 1846 various Whigs and Democrats in the North were trying to get legislation to keep any annexed Mexican land free. Resolutions of that kind were repeatedly passed in the House, only to be killed in the Senate. Each debate aroused fresh gusts of passion. When the war ended in the spring of 1848, the issue was unsettled.

No breathing time was left to put it to rest. Gold was found in California. Thousands rushed there, and within a year the once nearly empty Mexican borderland had a population, almost exclusively of nonslaveholders, big enough to petition for admission as a free state. When the Congress elected in 1848 met in December of 1849, it faced a crisis. Many Southerners had already loudly announced that California was won for the Union by the blood and treasure of *both* sections. If the South was humiliated by having slavery shut out of the new state, it would secede. A convention of delegates sharing this view was called to meet in Nashville, Tennessee, early in 1850. So the third ten-year span following 1820 ended with a greatly enlarged Union. Its flag flew on both oceans, but it was on the verge of disruption. The spoils of Mexico had proved poisonous, as predicted.

It was time to engineer another adjustment. The giants of the early republic had their say. A dying Calhoun rose to announce that the old Union of equal sections was gone, thanks to abolitionism and Northern wealth. It could only be preserved by a new arrangement, with each section's consent needed for any common action. Clay pleaded once more for compromise. So did Daniel Webster, once New England's best-admired voice, now an old man. The pick-and-shovel work of writing and getting votes for the several measures that became the Compromise of 1850 was mostly done by Illinois' chunky little senator, Stephen A. Douglas.

The terms of the compromise seemed sensible so far as the territorial issue went. California was granted admission as a free state. In the rest of the lands taken from Mexico no decision was to be made until they were ready for statehood. That would be long in the future, since they were mainly desert and mountain and would only gain population slowly.

But two other provisions showed how deeply feelings about slavery ran. The slave trade—though not slavery itself—was abolished in the District of Columbia, so that visitors to the capital should not see ugly things such as slave pens, chains, and bars. But the South wanted an emotional concession, too, and got it in the form of a strengthened Fugitive Slave Act. But it was at a cost.

The new law strengthened the requirement that all law officers, North as well as South, had to help pursue runaway slaves. What was more, if any Southerner or his agent claimed that a black person was his escaped slave, the black was to be hustled before a federal commissioner and given a quick one-sided hearing with no appeal if the commissioner decided for the white claimant. Even Northerners indifferent to slavery found this outrageous. Many fugitives were living decent lives in the North. Moreover, many a free black could be mistaken for a runaway. Under the new law, men and women like these could be virtually kidnapped and sent South to a life of hell. Northern law-enforcement agencies were under orders to help in the dirty work. Though the Fugitive Slave Law was constitutional, it only made numerous fresh enemies for the Southern viewpoint.

### *From Compromise to Collapse via Kansas, Dred Scott, and John Brown*

Yet the compromise was achieved. The Nashville convention fizzled out. Once more, the Union was saved. But in the 1850s this final "deal" between sections swiftly unraveled. The nonpolitical ties between North and South were disintegrating fast. The Methodist church split into Northern and Southern branches over the slavery question in 1844; the Presbyterians followed suit in 1852. Southerners stopped reading Northern newspapers, which were full of irritating antislavery news and views. For the same reason they gave up participation in many of the national missionary and temperance societies formed earlier.

The basic conflict of the decade had now become one of the control and direction of expansion. A strong move developed to give federal money to help build a railroad to the Pacific. But Congress did not act, unable to agree on whether the line should follow a northerly or southerly route. Northern and western votes in Congress twice passed homestead laws. Slaveholders objected that these acts gave small farmers an unfair edge, and Democratic presidents twice obediently vetoed the bills. Proposals for subsidies or tariff hikes ran afoul of slaveholding fears of a powerful national authority. More and more, the South seemed to be standing in the way of progress.

But the North could obstruct, too. American interest in the Caribbean was growing. Moves were afoot to buy (or simply seize) Cuba from Spain. There were also schemes to have Americans move in on countries south of Mexico and stage uprisings in them. But while Northern capitalists were interested in controlling the economies of Central America, the general feeling of the North was that annexation of fresh southern lands would provide new breeding grounds for slavery. So Congress blocked all moves to add any more "Texases" to the Union.

National expansion was thwarted by the persistent slavery issue. There was a strong political desire to remove it from the national agenda, and since a final "victory" for the Northern or Southern viewpoint seemed impossible, some party leaders searched for a formula that would not agitate the subject further. One of these was Douglas. In the fateful year 1854 he introduced a bill to organize governments for the territories of Kansas and Nebraska (part of the Louisiana Purchase). It was necessary to do this before serious settlement could begin. In order to win Southern votes for this measure, the Illinois senator consented to a provision "repealing" the Missouri Compromise and providing instead that the question of slavery should be decided by the actual settlers when ready for statehood. Douglas was interested in seeing Kansas and Nebraska rapidly developed and in a Pacific rail line being built through them. He judged that the North, which would benefit economically from such growth, would be indifferent to the question of slavery as the profits piled up. He was totally wrong!

Surges of outrage rocked the North. The Kansas-Nebraska Act was fiercely denounced. People called it a backdown, under proslavery pressure, from a solemn pact. Thousands of disgruntled Democrats and Whigs deserted their old standards to join a new organization, the Republican Party. Its general disposition was to favor homesteads, railroads, and the tariff, but its one thundering specific demand was the absolute banning of slavery in the territories. Slavery might be left alone in the states, there to die a natural death or not. But it must stay out of the West. On this platform, the Republicans came within striking distance of winning the presidency in 1856.

Vainly, Douglas protested. Leaving the actual settlers to decide the questions, he argued, was the democratic way, the American practice of local decision making that went back to the first town meeting. Besides, climate and geography made it fairly clear that Kansas would not become a slave state in any case. (This prophecy turned out to be true, but not until after a bitter, small-scale civil war between proslavery and free-soil settlers.) Above all, Douglas insisted, his program of "popular sovereignty" would take the slavery question out of national politics and open the way for growth once more. The morals of slavery were not a possible subject for congressional debate. He did not care "whether slavery was voted up or voted down," so long as it made way for expansion.

In 1857 came another bombshell. This time, a pro-Southern majority on the Supreme Court (encouraged by a pro-Southern president, James Buchanan) tried to take the issue out of politics by a "final" ruling. The Court announced its decision in the case of *Dred Scott v. Sandford.* Scott was a Missouri slave who, with abolitionist help, sued for his freedom. His claim was that he had once been taken into Illinois and then into Wisconsin Territory, into a "free" part of the Louisiana Purchase under the Missouri Compromise. Scott's lawyers said that he should have been liberated then. In effect, he was claiming that when a Southerner settled temporarily with his slaves outside a slave state, he had a chance of losing them.

Instead of upholding this view, Chief Justice Roger B. Taney, a Maryland slaveholder, speaking for a 5-to-2 majority, completely turned the tables. First, he denied Scott's right to sue in federal courts, since Scott was not a citizen of his state and, therefore, not a U.S. citizen. Next Taney added a long argument insisting that the founding fathers had never foreseen or intended that blacks should become citizens. The crux of the decision was not merely that the United States was a white person's country but that Congress had no power to discriminate among the property rights of citizens of different states. A Southerner had as much right to go to a territory and have his black property protected as a Northerner did with his livestock or farming tools. The shocking final conclusion was that the Missouri Compromise had been unconstitutional in the first place.

Buchanan thought that respect for the Supreme Court was such that people would accept the Dred Scott verdict as the final (and proslavery) word on slavery in the territories. Instead, Republicans violently denounced the opinion and continued to call for the outlawing of territorial slavery, unconstitutional or not. To Southerners this was one more proof that Republicans cared nothing for the rights of their political enemies. Could there be any safety for Southerners in a Union governed by such Northern "fanatics"?

The question seemed to be answered with an explosive "No!" in October 1859. John Brown, a half-demented antislavery crusader—a saint or a murderer, depending on the viewpoint—led some two dozen black and white followers into the little town of Harpers Ferry, Virginia, and seized the federal arsenal there. His plan was to distribute the captured weapons to slaves on neighboring plantations. Then they would all escape to a hideout in the mountains and set up a free, interracial republic. Slaves everywhere, Brown believed, would run away to join it. Slavery at last would come crashing down under one firm push. So God would use Brown as His agent to doom the evil thing.

But Brown never got out of Harpers Ferry except as a prisoner. Inside of two days local militiamen (and some U.S. troops under Colonel Robert E. Lee) surrounded Brown's band and recaptured the town. Most of the insurgents were killed. Brown himself was speedily tried and hanged. But during the trial it emerged that Brown had had white financial backers in the North, Republicans as well as abolitionists. And although the Republican Party officially repudiated Brown, individual Northerners praised him as a brave man who had struck the blow necessary to arouse the nation from its moral sleep. Though such pro-Brown spokesmen were few, an unmeasurable number of Southerners now became convinced that "most" Northerners approved of someone who planned to put weapons in black hands. After that, unreasoning fear dominated the Southern outlook.

This was the background to the final crisis of 1860. The Republicans ran Abraham Lincoln for president on their free-soil platform. The Democrats fatally split, between those who still followed Douglas in efforts to "denationalize" the slavery question, and hard-line proslavery advocates who wanted a guarantee of protection for slavery in the territories. Two Democratic candi-

*This unusual portrait of Lincoln, in which his clothing is created out of the words of his Gettysburg Address and a biographical sketch, is only one of the thousands that show his enormous grip on the American imagination. To the North, he stood for the Union—which had an almost mystical meaning that went beyond politics.*

dates ran—Douglas and the pro-Southern John C. Breckenridge. In the border slave states of Missouri, Kentucky, Maryland, and Delaware many votes went to the ticket of a Constitutional Union Party, which attempted neutrality on the issue.

When the votes were counted, Lincoln had a clear majority in the electoral college. South Carolina immediately seceded. Within sixty days, six other cotton states followed. Douglas and other Northern Democrats deplored this move. They warned that the Union had become invested in Northern eyes with an almost mystical, sacred character as the guardian of prosperity, the ensurer of freedom, the provider of an American identity. Northerners who did not care a twig about slavery would fight to restore the Union. Lincoln, too, repeated that he had no intention of touching slavery in the states themselves. But he could not yield on the free-soil question without, in effect, reversing the verdict of the election under pressure. That would make a mockery of the voting process.

From election day, 1860, to April 12, 1861, the nation lingered in crisis. Then a concrete issue arose in the harbor of Charleston, South Carolina. Union troops stayed in Fort Sumter, an island garrison whose cannons were part of the U.S. coastal defenses. South Carolina demanded an end to the occupation of this portion of its "sovereign" territory by a "foreign" power. After long debate Lincoln sent an expedition to reprovision the outpost, believing that he could not let it be starved into surrender without seeming to recognize South Carolina's claim. In his eyes that was not possible. The Union was, and had to stay, undivided.

The relief ship headed for Sumter was fired on. Lincoln then called for 75,000 volunteers. Four more Southern states, protesting this attempt to "coerce" South Carolina, now joined the newly formed Confederate States of America. The battle was on. As Lincoln himself said, one side would make war rather than preserve the Union, and the other would accept war rather than destroy it. And the war came.

Four slave states remained in the Union. Because of that, Lincoln made it clear that his objective was the restoration of the Union and *not* the extinction of slavery, though he would be glad if it could disappear voluntarily and peacefully. But as the war raged on, Southern society's framework buckled under the strain of battle and occupation. More and more slaves ran away, into Union army camps, or were left without masters. Then in September 1862 Lincoln gave slavery a further blow by issuing the Emancipation Proclamation. It warned that in ninety days any slaves in a state still in rebellion would be set free. Theoretically, it was a wartime step to uproot the Southern labor force and cripple its economy. The proclamation only had force where Union armies could back it up. But it meant that wherever the bluecoats advanced after January 1, 1863, they carried freedom with them. By 1864 it was clear that there would be no sense or justice in restoring slavery to life once the war was won. So a constitutional antislavery amendment, the Thirteenth, was proposed and finally ratified at the war's end. And slavery at last lay dead in the ruins of the conquered South.

Though it may seem lengthy, the foregoing is a brutally brief condensation of the events leading up to the tragedy. But it offers enough to illustrate the problem of historical explanation. All historians choose what they consider their important facts from among the infinite number available to them. (Remember that the wart on Lincoln's cheek is as much a fact as the date of his election!) And all arrange them in some order, even if only that of simple chronology: First. . . . And then. . . . And after. . . . And next. . . . Even when they claim simply to be telling a story, not seeking an explanation, this very process of selection and arrangement involves historians in judgments about meaning and significance.

But when any historian explicitly attempts to go further and explain *why* something happened, his work becomes more complex. His theory of cause must meet certain standards.

1. It must neither violate known facts nor invent new ones.

2. It must be internally consistent. That is, we cannot explain a person's behavior in one year by one generalization and in the next by an altogether different and contradictory one.

3. It must also square with general data about human behavior. That is, for example, the historian cannot believe that all people act on purely idealistic motives, but only slaveholders, for some peculiar reason, were selfish.

4. It must be comprehensive enough not to allow too many exceptions. If it must constantly apologize for itself, it is apt to be inadequate.

5. Finally, it must have some logical qualities that make it satisfying. That is, it must meet a basic human urge to make sense of things and to apply some order to the messiness of experience. Everyone, as he recalls a day or week of his life, is a kind of historian, making order of many memories, adding them up to answer the questions of who we think we are and where we think we are going. History is a kind of group memory.

With these standards in mind, let us look at some theories of the causes of the Civil War. They are grouped in categories. Along with each theory goes a summary of the evidence that appears to support it, the basic assumptions behind it, and some of the possible difficulties with it. After finishing the chapter, you may wish to add to the pool of criticisms—or of theories.

*Category I. Great overriding forces*

*The will of God prevails.* This theory argues that God was somehow either testing the American people through the Civil War or punishing them for the sin of slavery. It was expressed most eloquently by Lincoln, who was himself not a formally religious man. In his second inaugural address he reflected on the strange fact that each side read the same Bible and prayed to the same God. Yet God allowed the struggle to go on for some purpose. Was it justice? The war

# CAMPAIGNS IN THE EAST (VA., MD., PA.)

*The opening skirmishes of the war (June 1861) were little noticed, but they resulted in the Union conquest of West Virginia. The showcase battle of 1861—the Battle of Bull Run ①—was fought in July when a Union army that moved confidently in to rout the "rebs" (under the gaze of visiting dignitaries from Washington, in a holiday mood) was itself routed and driven back to the capital city. The balance of that year was spent building up the Union army of the Potomac. In March 1862 its commander, General George McClellan, took it by sea to Richmond, at the mouth of the James River. The slow advance to within sight of the Confederate capital was checked in the fighting of the Seven Days' battles in June of 1862, when the forces of Robert E. Lee and "Stonewall" Jackson drove McClellan's men back to their base camps, ending the Peninsula Campaign ② in a Union reversal. McClellan withdrew to Washington, and a confident Lee swung northward in an invasion of Maryland. On September 17, 1862, in a bloody battle at Antietam ③, the Southern advance was halted. Three months later the Union army, under new leadership, tried to drive southward but was mauled at the battle of Fredericksburg. A similar attempt in May 1863 also came to frustration at Chancellorsville. Once more emboldened, Lee Launched a second drive northward. He reached southern Pennsylvania, but in the three-day struggle at Gettysburg ④ Confederate attacks were beaten off, and Lee pulled his battered forces southward once more.*

*Though early 1864 found the north discouraged and war-weary, the handwriting for the South was on the wall. The tightening Union blockade, growing stockpiles of Union supplies, and swelling Union armies meant that the Confederacy could not withstand sustained, punishing attacks forever. Such an assault was launched by the new Union overall commander, General Ulysses S. Grant, in May of 1864. Taking tremendous punishment, but also inflicting it, Grant took about two months to move into a position in which he could besiege Richmond ⑤. Though the South held on through a nine-month campaign of wearing-down, Union forces took the offensive again late in March 1865, captured Richmond on April 2, and finally pocketed Lee's army and compelled his official surrender at Appomattox ⑥ on April 9—exactly three days before the fourth anniversary of the war's outbreak.*

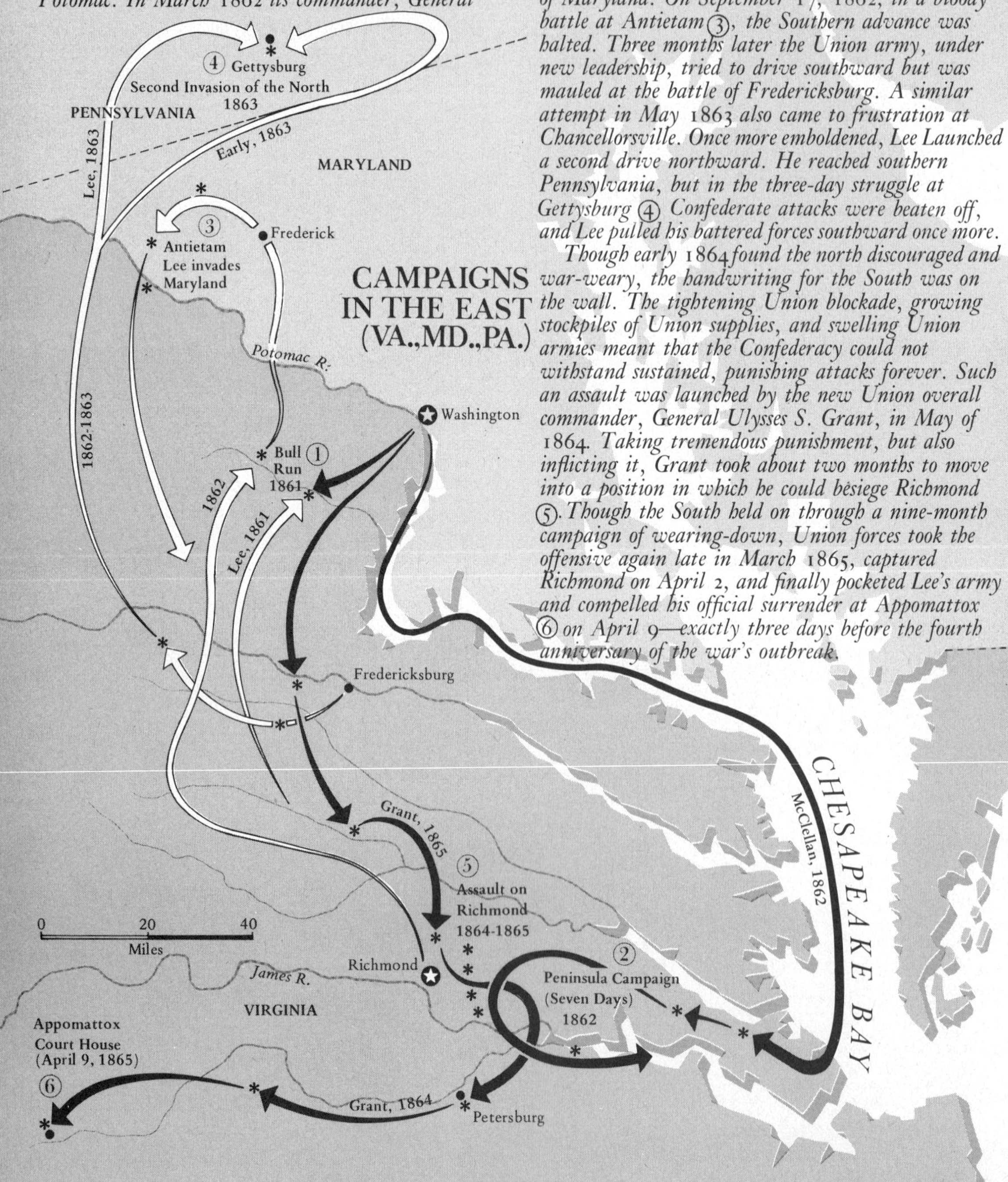

# THE CIVIL WAR

During most of the war national attention centered on the fate of Washington and Richmond, only about 100 miles apart. But despite the psychological importance of the two capitals, it is possible that the most important struggles of the war took place in the western theater, where Union armies methodically sliced up and occupied the Confederate "heartland" which furnished the indispensable economic underpinnings of the Southern war effort. The Union drive southward into Tennessee began early in 1862 and was checked, but not halted, at Shiloh ① in April of that year. At the same time that Union gunboats and land forces slugged their way down the Mississippi, a joint army-navy expedition captured New Orleans ② in February. During a year of hard fighting, the two Union expeditions on the mighty central river approached each other. Finally, with the capture of Vicksburg ③ in July of 1863, under the generalship of Ulysses S. Grant, they linked up, cutting the Confederacy in half and restoring to the northwest a free transit down the "Father of Waters."

During the remainder of 1863 Union troops completed the occupation of Tennessee and northern Georgia (despite a setback at Chickamauga, Tennessee in September). In the spring of 1864, General William T. Sherman launched an irresistible drive that took the manufacturing and railroad center of Atlanta ④ by September. Sherman's men than harrowed their way through Georgia, seizing or destroying rail lines and foodstuffs, until, just before Christmas, they reached the sea at Savannah and divided the Confederacy once more. Early in 1865 they turned northward, marching through the Carolinas ⑤. Sherman was approaching Raleigh and eventually a junction with the Union armies in Virginia where, Jointly, they planned to destroy the last spark of Confederate resistance. All that stopped them was word of Lee's surrender to Grant in April of 1865. The war was over at last.

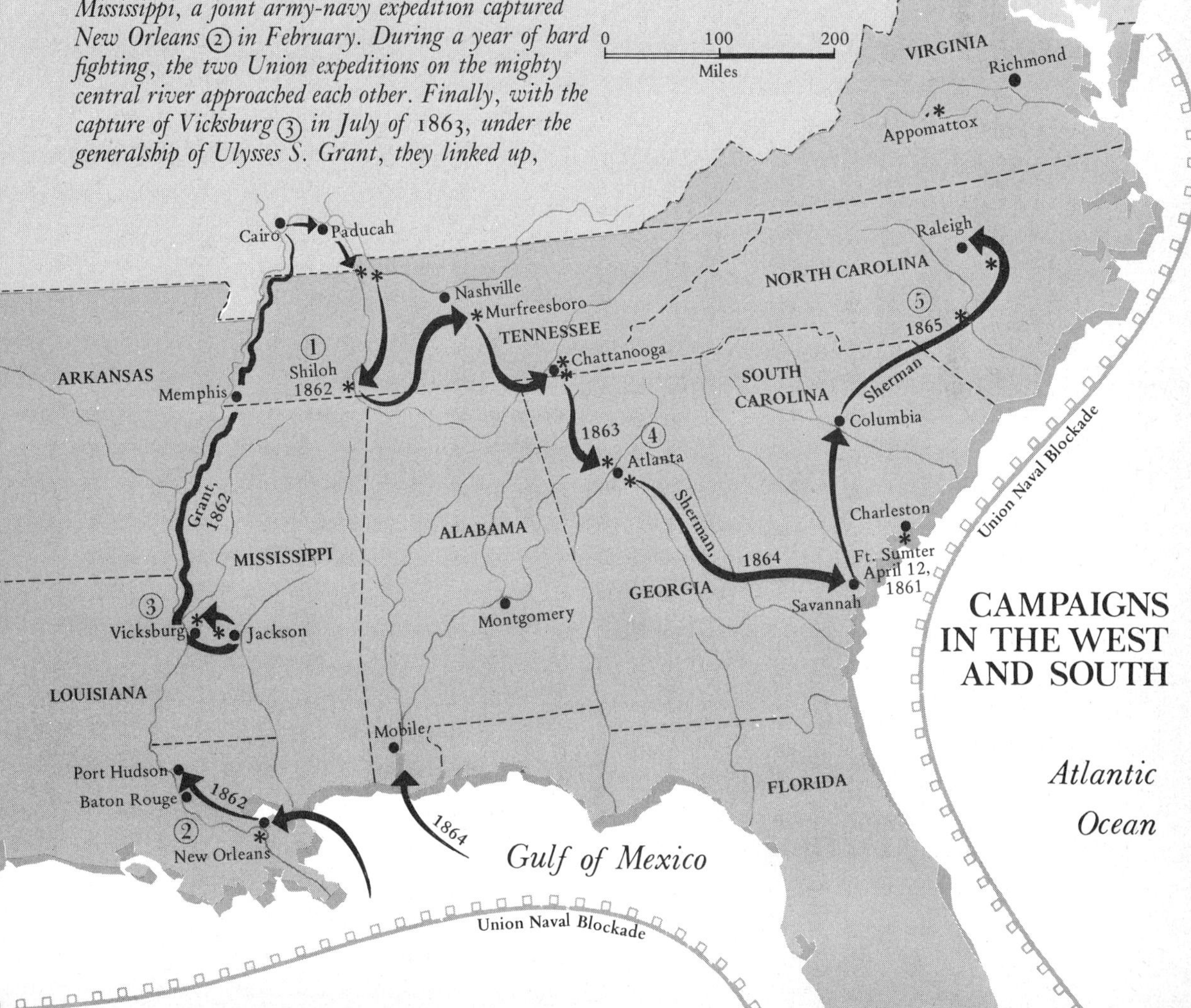


## CAMPAIGNS IN THE WEST AND SOUTH

might continue until every drop of blood drawn by the lash was paid for with one drawn by the sword and every bit of wealth earned by the stolen toil of slaves was consumed. In that case, all that could be said was: "The judgments of the Lord are true and righteous altogether."

Such a view is satisfying on some levels. It ties things together. It explains the sparrow's fall and the nation's agony by the same rule of God's decision. Its problem is that it leaves little room for judging the qualities of different kinds of evidence. If all was preordained in the mind of the Almighty, then Clay and Calhoun and Douglas and Lincoln, and every slave and master, were all acting out a prepared script. No single individual made a difference in the final outcome. The historian reading the record, then, must look for cues and indications of God's will. Perhaps they are in symbolic moments such as, for example, Lincoln's digust with slavery on first seeing a group of chained blacks on a river boat. These moments are "providences," as the Puritans called them. Small events had great meaning, in their eyes, when they bared the mind of God. Colorful history can be written that way, of course—but on what basis do historians then choose their "providences"?

*The triumph of nationalism.* This idea, popular early in this century, simply argues that the push toward centralized nation-states in the nineteenth century was almost irresistible. The South, in trying to reverse the tide and break one nation into two, was attempting the impossible. Much of the evidence for this point of view has to be selected from outside of American history. It uses facts such as the breakdown of the strength of the provincial aristocracy in France and Britain and the completion of nationhood for Germany and Italy. These last two were welded out of a number of separate kingdoms and duchies in 1870. The nationalistic interpretation puts U.S. history in a world setting, which is a valuable approach.

But it leaves some unanswered riddles. Why did the South go along with the nationalizing trend so readily until 1820? And why was it not able to create a workable nation in the Confederate States of America? Why could it not repeat, in its own way, the story of 1776? Was military defeat the only reason?

Moreover, if the South was doomed to lose, then its statesmen can and should be judged on how well they read the signs of the times. It is logical, if this view is adopted, to see Southern spokesmen of secession as misguided individuals who did harm to their section. The forlorn defenders of keeping the South in the Union then became unsung heroes. In short, the inevitable triumph-of-nationalism theory, like any kind of *determinism* (a doctrine that history *must* work out in a certain way), tends to push the historian into the role of a pseudoscientific moralist. He approves those who understood and followed the operations of historical "law." He consigns those in "error" to the "dustbin of history." Early and crude Marxist historians did this often.

*Category II. Human choices: conspiracy and crusade*

*Conspiracy.* This theory, popular in the North at the time of the war, flourished in books such as Horace Greeley's *The American Conflict.* It rested on the idea of a plot. When slaveholders saw, around 1820, that the growing strength of the North would eventually break their domination, they set up moves to get and keep control of the national government. First, the slaveholding Tennesseean Jackson encouraged the Texan independence movement and urged annexation. The job was completed when the Virginian John Tyler signed the resolution admitting Texas to the Union. After him the Southerner Polk went to work. He took the country into a war to seize a good part of Mexico for slavery. He also vetoed economic legislation that would strengthen the North for its contest with the growing slave power. Next the slave power, which by now ran the Democratic Party, got Stephen A. Douglas to force through the repeal of the Missouri Compromise. It also got Presidents Pierce and Buchanan to try to force slavery on Kansas. It got a Southern chief justice, Taney, to issue the Dred Scott decision. The scheme was to open the territories to slavery and drive out free laborers. Then there would be a drive to conquer a huge empire to the south and make the free states a minority. When this plan was threatened by Lincoln's election, the "slavocrats," determined to ruin what they could not rule, broke up the Union by force.

Before examining this theory, one may well turn to the opposite side of it, as follows.

*The great crusade.* In this abolitionist version the North made a fatal agreement to share common nationality with the slaveholding states in 1787. It knew it was doing wrong but wanted the political and economic advantages of the Union. It stuck to its immoral bargain by the Missouri Compromise. But the section was rallied from its complacency by the brave men and women of the abolitionist crusade. Scorned, mocked, assaulted, and even murdered by slavocrats and their pliant Northern tools, they nevertheless persisted in raising the alarm. Gradually, they won politicians to their side. Mighty works of propaganda like *Uncle Tom's Cabin* brushed the cobwebs from Northern eyes and made them see the evil thing for what it was. Brown's shining martyrdom aroused the land to a final sense of its painful duty. (In Emerson's words, Brown made the gallows as glorious as the Cross.) Only eleven years after the North had shamefully consented to the Fugitive Slave Act, Union volunteer regiments marched out to give slavery the death blow.

Both of these explanations have flaws so obvious that to pick at them is disgracefully easy. The conspiracy theory simply does not rest on any of the kind of evidence used either in history books or in courts. There are no documents in which the "plotters" exchange their views or map their strategies. The whole notion of a deliberate plan to make the Union solidly composed of slave states rests on implication. Lincoln himself made one stab at the theory; in an 1857 speech in Illinois he hinted that there had been a conscious effort to destroy the Missouri Compromise step by step, from the enactment of the Kansas-Nebraska bill to the Dred Scott decision. When "Stephen [Douglas] and Franklin [Pierce] and James [Buchanan] and Roger [Taney]" each brought a plank to a place, he said, and the planks turned out to be perfectly carpentered to fit together into a house, it was safe to assume that they had had the building of a house in mind. But is that always a reasonable assumption? Would you, as historical jurors, condemn Stephen and Franklin and James and Roger on that basis?

The crusade theory, likewise, faces inconvenient facts. The Civil War was in no way a crusade against slavery at the start. The "morally aroused" North never gave pure abolitionism more than a tiny vote. Even Lincoln, elected solely on a free-soil platform, did not have a majority of popular votes in the North. The war began merely as a war for the Union, with four slave states on the Union side. What is more, several Northern states had in their lawbooks statutes barring the immigration of free blacks. The crusade theory must explain how a racist nation made war on behalf of a despised race.

But both these theories do have a comfort. They tend to assume that human will and human choice are significant. They suggest that individuals pursue goals instead of stumbling blindly in the dark. And to that extent they are sometimes reassuring in a world where we seem more and more the victims of forces we cannot control. Is it better to be a passive rider on historical currents? Or a tormented chooser, uncertain of what is right? These questions bedevil all thinking individuals, and historians sometimes choose theories on the basis of their answers to them! Whether one accepts historical determinism or historical free will can be a personal as well as an intellectual choice.

Actually, another argument against the crusade theory is that while individuals may have consciences, huge social aggregations like sections or nations rarely do. They simply obey some laws of development that bring them into collision. That in itself is still another form of determinism.

*Category III. Institutional explanations*

*Failure of the machinery of compromise.* This theory has several variations but runs more or less as follows. Conflict is natural to any nation or any society. To avoid constant bloodshed, they create institutions (courts, for example) to settle differences peaceably. When those institutions are poorly designed or pushed beyond their stress limits by unforeseen forces, they buckle, and riots or civil war follows. Two versions of this approach have been expressed.

The first is a favorite Southern argument. It holds that the real problem lay in the breakdown of respect for the Constitution. Originally, it was a compact among sovereign communities made for their mutual benefit. A common government of clearly limited powers was created. Each state had equal rights, powers, and duties. But to work, the machinery had to be respected in spirit as well as in letter. Gradual growth of power in the central government, for whatever reasons, wore away the habit of jealously guarding state privileges. Laws like the tariff acts, which received a majority in Congress but actually helped one section more than another, also weakened the spirit of the Constitution. Finally, and above all, the constant assault by the people of one section against the morals, character, and habits of another (that is, the abolitionist assault on slavery) completed the destruction. The shell of the Constitution was there, but it was hollow within. When Southern states moved, by secession, to reclaim their independent rights, the North moved in and conquered them. The post-1865 Union was "pinned together with bayonets," not knit by compromise.

Echoes of this argument ring in the writings of a school of so-called revisionists of the 1930s. These historians held that the American party system was a splendid device for tying differing groups and regions together. Platforms were intentionally vague and principles deliberately loose, so that urban workers, small farmers, great planters, and middling manufacturers might all be drawn together in common hopes of victory and spoils. Once elected to Congress, party members fought the opposition but also relied on traditional "logrolling" to keep government in motion: "Scratch my back, and I'll scratch yours." "Vote for my tariff bill, and I'll vote for your free land." "Give me a bank, and I'll vote you a railroad."

Such deals enabled a diverse society to function. But they demanded that all political issues should be capable of compromise on the basis of self-interest: some for me, some for you. But once moral issues, questions of right and wrong, were introduced into politics (the revisionist argument ran), the system could not function. Leaders could not barter away freedom or Southern rights or split the differences where noble principles were concerned. The nonmoral character of politics was sacrificed. The parties, as agents of compromise, could no longer work.

For the revisionists, historical villains were the "extremists" of both abolitionism and secession. Their heroes were the moderates and compromisers, like Douglas. They assumed that great humanitarian and emotional drives can be barred from the political process. They also dodged the question of admitting new groups, from time to time, to the compromises of democracy. How would minorities, for example, become enfranchised without appeals to principle? A changing society requires constant rethinking about the fairness of the machinery of government. And that leads inescapably to aroused feelings.

Revisionists might answer that such a readiness to choke off the emotionalism in us is the price of quietly existing in a society of many conflicting group interests. But what would the price of that sacrifice be? Would it be a government deaf to injustice?

*Cultures at war.* Another kind of institutional theory holds that cultures, which we have defined elsewhere as the total expression of a society's style and outlooks, can change with circumstances. Therefore, two cultures can sometimes arise within one nation and find themselves on collision course. This, they say, is what happened in the United States between 1820 and 1860. There is some evidence to support this view. Certainly the rural, slaveholding, paternalistic, conservative South was very different from the urban, progressive, competitive North—perhaps as different as, for example, Britain was from Russia.

But there are two drawbacks. One is obvious. If the two cultures were different, why did they have to fight? Why was a power struggle under the Constitution not solved by peaceable secession? Why was there such resistance to a split-up? Was it because the North alone insisted on one American nation instead of two? Perhaps. But if so, we have another problem to face.

That one is that the South, too, was not totally unlike the North. The South had its own prophets of industrialism and tariffs and railroads. The South enthusiastically supported the nation's expansion westward and was fighting for a share of it. And the South knew that its prosperity depended on modernity—on booming cotton mills, growing consumer populations, better networks of transportation to market. Many Southerners held that the South's best way to protect itself was, in fact, to diversify its own economy with more industry and build independent economic strength within the Union.

That point of view existed in the pre-1860 South; it cropped up again in Reconstruction and became dominant in the 1880s. So to assume that the South was a "foreign" culture in the 1850s, we must assume that this culture contained a considerable number of "deviants" who emulated the Northern style and that these "deviants" became the spokesmen for the culture shortly after the war. That assumption considerably shakes the separate culture theory. If the South and the North were two peoples in 1860 (like the British and the colonists in 1776), they certainly behaved suspiciously like a single people not very long after the South staged its "revolution."

*Category IV. Economic explanations*

There are two general kinds of explanatory theory that make economic issues central.

*The "second American revolution."* This version, made popular in the 1920s by Charles A. Beard, holds that the distinguishing mark of American life between 1820 and 1860 was the emergence of two competing kinds of capitalist leadership. On the one hand were the great planter capitalists. They needed plenty of cheap semitropical land, a good supply of slave labor, free trade with all the world, and a rather simple and weak federal government. On the other hand stood the merchant and manufacturing capitalists of the North. They needed protection from foreign competition, good routes to market, abundant credit, a growing population to consume factory-made goods, and a large force of laborers educated in factory skills and discipline and in city living. So they required tariffs, railroads, shipping subsidies, a widespread banking system, immigration, growing cities, inventions, and public education.

These two outlooks were at war. Gradually, using the abolition movement as a lever and their growing strength in numbers as the ultimate weapon, the Northern capitalists politically isolated their Southern enemies. They forced them to leave the Union, and once they were absent, the Northerners triumphantly enacted an economic program of tariffs, railroad subsidies, and homestead and banking legislation that laid the foundation for America's industrial growth. This "second American revolution" was the true goal and meaning of the Civil War.

While not a follower of Karl Marx, Beard's theory shared Marx's stress on analyzing history in terms of economic conflict. You will see that it has some of the problems of the conspiracy theory. It assumes that when people talked of antislavery, they willfully or unconsciously meant banks and tariffs. It also suggests that the two competing capitalist groups *saw* themselves as linked by common interest and tended to follow long-range strategies to serve their needs. In short, it assumes a kind of determinism on one hand, by saying that underlying economic forces govern human beings' behavior. And it endorses a kind of free will on the other, by saying that spokesmen for economic positions could plan their futures. To what extent do these propositions seem justifiable to you?

There are some modern sophisticated forms of the basic economic interpretation. Eugene Genovese, a modern Marxist, holds that a region's economic style creates social patterns with a life of their own. The great slaveholders ruled their section because they controlled the basic means of economic production—the land. But the world of personal loyalties and patriarchal responsibility they created was then defended when it made no economic sense to do so, for the South was clearly bound to lose. Another recent scholar, Barrington Moore, thinks that the Southerners were reacting against a modern world of impersonal forces. The North was moving in the direction of many things now familiar: multimillion-dollar corporations, high finance, boards of directors, big government bureaus, crowded cities, and problems too big for anyone but committees of technical experts. Southern leaders rejected this drift and believed that they could change it or break away from it. So, Moore says, the secessionist planters, enemies of mass society, were the last revolutionaries. They were the heirs of

England in 1688, France in 1789, and America in 1776. They were the last to believe that intelligent middle-class leadership could successfully take arms against its troubles.

Interpretations such as these last two are more subtle, rich, and harmonic than some of the cruder ones described earlier. But they both hold that the key element in Southern leadership was the economic self-interest of the ruling class. They both argue that the productive organization of society sets up the basic relationships of power and social behavior. They both may underplay the historical roles of noneconomic forces like the lust for power, sex, fraternity, and fulfillment of God's will.

If you are confused because none of these theories is "right" or because there are no "answers," be comforted. Freedom may, after all, only consist in the fact of uncertainty—that anyone may be right or wrong. And anyone with a reasonable idea that he or she does not force on others, therefore, deserves respect and attention. That is one of the humane lessons of honest scholarship.

## *FOR FURTHER READING*

Theories of how the Civil War came to pass are developed in a number of books, some of them of great antiquity. A workable summary, however, is contained in Thomas J. Pressly, *Americans Interpret Their Civil War* (1954), which can lead you to some of the original works cited. A general rundown of the facts of the period leading up to 1861 is contained, in brief compass, in Elbert B. Smith, *The Death of Slavery* (1967). Particular moments of crises are well studied in T. Glover Moore, *The Missouri Controversy* (1953); in Bernard De Voto's *The Year of Decision* (1943), which handles the opening of the War with Mexico; and in Stephen B. Oates, *To Purge This Land with Blood: A Biography of John Brown* (1970), which is a good source for the modern views of the Kansas struggle and the Harpers Ferry raid.

The biographical route is a good one to take in any case. The best one-volume life of Lincoln is that by Benjamin P. Thomas, *Abraham Lincoln* (1952). His great Northern adversary is dealt with in Robert P. Johanssen, *Stephen A. Douglas* (1973). A leading political abolitionist is well handled in David Donald, *Charles Sumner and the Coming of the Civil War* (1960). Hudson Strode, *Jefferson Davis* (1955) describes the chief Southern statesman.

Three imaginative works should be mentioned here. The first is an old-timer, but still powerful: Stephen Vincent Benet's poem, *John Brown's Body* (1926), a verse history of the war. Second is a novel by a Civil War veteran, John W. De Forest, *Miss Ravenel's Conversion from Secession to Loyalty* (1867). And third is a classic brief novel about what the war was like, Stephen Crane's *The Red Badge of Courage* (1894).

# *chapter 13*
# *Reconstruction: revolution from the top down?*

On Sunday morning, April 9, 1865, Robert E. Lee surrendered what was left of his army in Virginia. Though some ragged, hungry Confederate forces were still under arms in North Carolina and in Texas, everyone knew the war was over. On Wednesday, the 12th, newspapers noted the fourth anniversary of the firing on Fort Sumter. On Friday, the 14th, Lincoln was shot. In one week the finale to four bitter years was written. An era had ended. An entirely new chapter in national history would now begin.

That chapter, the reconstruction of the Union, usually written with a capital *R*, was one of the most turbulent in American history. It has been the subject of some of the most testy writing by historians. Few episodes in the national past churned up such violent passions. Reconstruction was more of an upheaval than the war itself. Its issues are harder to deal with. Eventually, the passions of war cooled, and forgiveness wrapped both Confederate and Union dead. But the hates of Reconstruction lived on. For Reconstruction came closer to being a genuine social revolution than any other development in American life. And because societies do not easily accept quick, forcible change, the anger left behind by Reconstruction ran to the deepest roots of feeling.

*The "History" That Hate Wrote*

One of the best evidences of this anger lies in the semiofficial version of Reconstruction that dominated American history textbooks from around 1900 until very recent years. It was generally pro-Southern. It was also powerful and widely spread through films like *Birth of a Nation* and books (and films) like *Gone with the Wind*. A brief restatement of it runs like this:

*In 1865 North and South seemed ready to forgive and forget. Former Confederates were ready to return to the Union and bid slavery a final farewell. Both Lincoln and his successor, Andrew Johnson, were ready to back a generous and forgiving policy.*

*But enemies arose in the form of the Radical Republicans. These were individuals like Thaddeus Stevens and Charles Sumner, who wanted to punish the slaveholders and exalt the blacks. They challenged Johnson's leadership, overrode his vetoes, impeached him, and came within one vote of throwing him out of office. Meanwhile, they tore up his Reconstruction policy.*

*The South was divided into military districts. The Radicals ordered new elections supervised by the army. The voters in them were to be blacks and Southerners who had taken no part in the Confederacy's war. All ex-Confederate officials, namely, the South's best leaders, were banned from the polls. The new voters were loyal to the Republican Party from self-interest of course. The blacks especially were lined up by agents of the Freedmen's Bureau. This was supposed to be a relief organization to help them begin their new lives but was often a political front.*

*For twelve long years the South groaned under occupation. Its new rulers were the ignorant ex-slaves, "carpetbaggers"—Northerners who had come in after the war to pick the South's carcass—and "scalawags," or low-born Southerners enjoying revenge and advancement through the discomfort of their betters. Dominating the legislatures and statehouses, these scoundrels voted themselves huge salaries, gave fat public contracts to cronies and people who bribed them, and ran up huge debts. To pay them they pitilessly hiked taxes on the war-ravaged plantations.*

*On these plantations things went from bad to worse. Unsupervised blacks left work undone while they frolicked at Republican picnics or waited for the free "forty acres and a mule," which, they were told, would soon be coming. Many idle blacks turned to crime. Respectable whites, in self-protection, organized the Ku Klux Klan. It administered a few beatings and perhaps even killed a few unruly blacks who deserved punishment. But it worked harmlessly in the main, only using its outlandish hoods and masks to frighten the superstitious blacks into good behavior.*

*Gradually, painfully, things righted themselves. The North tired of the sad spectacle. More Democrats were elected to Congress. Decent people in the South banded*

---

*CHRONOLOGY*

1865 *April 9, Robert E. Lee surrenders at Appomattox, Virginia*
*April 14, Abraham Lincoln is assassinated*

1867 *Reconstruction Acts*

1868 *Fourteenth Amendment ratified*

*together to persuade, to insist on their rights, and to win over voters. As time went by, whole classes of ex-Confederates had the franchise restored to them by lawmakers. Eventually, the Radical governments were toppled in every state but South Carolina, Florida, and Louisiana. In 1876 there was a disputed election for the presidency. The result hinged on the electoral vote of these three states. In each, both sides claimed victory. Congress had to make the final decision. A deal was swung, in which the Democrats in Congress, who had a majority, agreed to hold still while all the contested votes were awarded to the Republican candidate, Rutherford B. Hayes. In return Hayes, early in 1877, withdrew the remaining troops in the South. Soon after that, the last three Southern states were liberated. Poor, but in control of their section once more, the South's former leaders rejoined the Union. To the blacks they showed kindness but firmness; to Northerners, willingness to bury the past; to the memories of their heroic dead, reverence.*

*The Question of Social Revolution*

The preceding story, somewhat slightly overstated, is what historian Kenneth Stampp calls the "tragic legend of Reconstruction." To pick it apart, thread by thread, would fill a complete book. Better than a mere recital of the "facts" of the era, however, is an attempt to see it for what it was and to learn from it. We have seen, in other chapters, how communities were organized by their members. And we have seen how community life was sometimes changed by outside economic forces that members could not control. In the case of the South from 1865 to 1877 we will see sweeping changes in the relationships between groups and classes in the community, brought about by the insistence of outsiders. Does such a change deserve the term "revolution"? Or must a revolution be self-starting? And if the South did undergo an enforced revolution, how long lasting was it, and how deep did it go? Did it succeed or fail, and what do we mean by these terms? Here, as always, the facts themselves are like bits of a puzzle. The answers we find, if any, depend upon their arrangement.

But first, there must be a brief glance at least at some of the distortions of the "tragic legend." In that way the facts on which interpretation rests will emerge.

*The Period of Southern Control: 1865–1866*

To begin with, there is the matter of time. Reconstruction, Radical style, did not last very long. For the first two years after the war's end, the rebuilding of the Southern states went on under a very liberal policy of pardon. The result was that each seceded state held new elections and chose substantial numbers of pardoned former Confederate officials to high office. Though Congress refused to seat the representatives and senators elected under these state authorities, the one-time "rebels" were not ousted from control of state affairs until the spring of

1867. Then a period of military rule and Radical control followed, which ended when Democrats regained control. In Georgia and Virginia that period was less than two years; in six other states it was less than seven. Only in South Carolina, Florida, and Louisiana did it take ten years.

During their first postwar period back in the saddle, the ex-Confederates provoked some of their own later troubles. True, they did duly ratify the Thirteenth Amendment and repeal or otherwise repudiate their acts of secession. In their eyes that was enough to satisfy the terms of surrender. They had accepted the Union's continued life and slavery's death.

But they went further. For one thing, they enacted a series of so-called Black Codes to govern the relationships between the freed people and the whites. Generally speaking, these laws clamped tight controls on black movements and behavior. For a variety of offenses, such as carrying arms or public drunkenness or vagrancy (which might simply mean being broke and between jobs), blacks could be fined and arrested. If they had no money, their fines might be paid by a planter. But they would then have to work for him, free, until the debt was repaid. That date often was postponed again and again. If any blacks complained, unsympathetic sheriffs tended to throw the book at them. Moreover, all black farm and other laborers had to sign contracts to work for employers for periods of a year or more. They could not leave before their times were up, no matter how outrageous conditions might be or even when better jobs were elsewhere. White Southerners defended the codes as necessary to train ex-slaves to be responsible. But to outside eyes they looked suspiciously like attempts to reestablish the controls of slavery, without its legal form.

Besides, the Johnson governments in the South had little use for whites who were outsiders. They held back jobs and patronage from Southerners who had been loyal to the Union. They also made life difficult for Northerners who had come South at the war's end to help blacks. This group included volunteer teachers who set up schools for the blacks, usually financed by Northern churches. It also numbered agents of the Freedmen's Bureau. The bureau was supposed to help *all* Southerners, black and white, who were dislocated or ruined by the war, to get back on their feet. But most of its efforts consisted of furnishing rations to blacks without jobs, handling contract disputes between blacks and planters, and setting up savings banks and other services for the freed blacks. The bureau's officials and the missionary teachers were hated, threatened and thwarted by local whites, and not protected by ex-Confederate state officials between 1865 and 1867.

The "Confederate-style" Reconstruction governments also did little to discourage threats of violence to blacks. In the spring and summer of 1866 two savage race riots tore Memphis and New Orleans. They were responses to black efforts at political organization and were meant to intimidate. But neither Tennessee nor Louisiana made any effort to punish anyone responsible for the riot-caused murders of dozens of freed blacks. Nor, of course, did any of the new state governments speak of giving the vote to any blacks—not even those who had been free before the war and who had both education and property.

By such behavior Southerners brought forced change on themselves. All these facts led many Northerners to believe that arrogant Southern leaders were denying their defeat. The North had lost over a quarter of a million men and spent some $5 billion to subdue the planter "aristocrats." Its only friends in the South during the war had been the blacks and the white Unionists. Now it appeared as if the enemy captains had simply jumped back into the saddle. Soon they would be in Congress again, with all their old power—with more power, in fact, because the freed blacks would now count in full for representation in the House. It was this fear that helped Radical Republicans to win a majority in the elections of 1866. After that they could put through their proposals for a hard line on Reconstruction, beginning with the Fourteenth Amendment.

### *The Turnabout of 1867: Black and White Newcomers to Power*

The Fourteenth Amendment declared that blacks were U.S. citizens, with all the rights of U.S. citizens. It proposed to reduce a state's representation in Congress if it denied any class of its citizens the vote. (This cumbersome way of encouraging black suffrage was, in 1870, replaced by the simpler Fifteenth Amendment. It forbade a state to deny anyone the vote on racial grounds.) The Fourteenth Amendment also barred from federal office and state legislatures anyone who had first taken an oath to uphold the federal government and then served the Confederacy. This meant any important Southerners who had held national office before 1861. The ban would last until Congress chose to lift it.

The amendment had been proposed in 1866 and was bluntly rejected by the Johnson state governments. That was what led in 1867 to the Reconstruction Acts. The Radicals wiped out the existing state governments and set up new elections limited only to those, black or white, who could swear they had never in any way aided or comforted the "rebellion." The idea behind the amendment and the acts was the same: to sift out a Southern electorate of unimpeachable loyalty to the Union. That was the only way, it seemed to the Radicals, that the South could safely be let back into the national fold. The goal of the Radicals' "revolution" was security for the victory of 1865. The problem was that only a minority of Southern whites would be part of this body of loyal voters. And any Southern government without heavy white support was doomed. But the Radicals believed their own wartime propaganda. They thought there was a silent majority of Southern loyalists that had been sup-

*The important thing to note about Blanche K. Bruce, one of Mississippi's two black Senators during Reconstruction, is how little he resembles the stereotype of the "ignorant slave" catapulted into political power. Educated and successful, Bruce looked—except for his skin—like any other plump man of affairs in the age of General Grant.*

pressed, up to 1867, only by terrorism. They thought that the newcomers whom they were putting in power had a more solid base than was in fact the case.

In each state the new voters first elected bodies that wrote new constitutions. Then they chose new state officials and legislatures. When these ratified the Fourteenth (and later the Fifteenth) Amendment, the state was readmitted to the Union. That process was used from 1868 to 1870 for all but two of the former Confederate states. Readmission formally opened the era of Radical supremacy in each state. It is this period of so-called Negro-carpetbagger-scalawag dominance that deserves the closest look.

First of all, "Negro rule" was purely a white supremacist fighting phrase. It was in no way a reality. Only in the lower house of the state legislature of South Carolina did blacks even briefly have a majority. In Mississippi and Louisiana the 40 or so blacks in the first Reconstruction legislatures were a voting minority. No black ever became a governor (except in a temporary emergency in Louisiana). Those who held important state offices such as treasurer or superintendent of education, or county posts such as sheriff were always few in number. So the black "revolutionaries," to begin with, never really held the reins.

It is well to remember, too, that the blacks who did hold office were not uneducated field hands, as legend hints. Most were formerly free and educated. Pinckney B. S. Pinchback, lieutenant governor of Louisiana (who served for six weeks as governor when the incumbent governor was impeached), was an example. He had a high-school education in Cincinnati and was a successful businessman and newspaper publisher in New Orleans. It is possible that he was not the world's most honest man, but he was able and brainy. Of the two black men to sit in the Senate during Reconstruction, both from Mississippi, Hiram Revels was a minister, educated at Knox College in Illinois. Blanche K. Bruce, though an ex-slave, had some Northern schooling before his election. The fourteen blacks elected to the House of Representatives at various times also had prior political experience. There is little doubt that the real objection to blacks in authority was not what they did, but rather that they were in public life at all.

And what of the new class of white leaders made prominent overnight by the social and political earthquake? They, too, were not necessarily seedy adventurers. Some of the carpetbaggers had settled in the South before 1860. Hundreds were Union soldiers who had liked what they saw in their wartime travels and came back to settle. Hundreds more simply felt, like all Americans, that they should show business initiative and "hustle" whenever new opportunities opened. They came South to open printing shops or sawmills or iron foundries or to buy farms or to practice law, just as they would have done in the states of the "undeveloped" West. That was the American way. Many of them held to political neutrality. Some became Democrats. These rarely had any trouble. But others entered Republican politics because they thought the Republicans stood for economic progress. Once they did that, and especially if they worked with black Republicans in the process, they often aroused hostility, and this led them to take further political action to protect themselves.

Albert T. Morgan, a Mississippi carpetbagger who held local offices, swore that his only motive was to protect himself and his lumber business from harassment after he spoke up for the Union, which he had served in uniform. Henry Clay Warmoth, an ex-captain from Illinois in his twenties, settled in New Orleans to practice law. Ambition of the same kind he would have shown in the North led him into Republican politics. He rose to become governor—and be impeached for alleged corruption. Yet after Reconstruction ended, he managed a sugar plantation that he had bought with his "winnings" and was respected by neighbors as a solid contributor to Southern economic growth. Some light is thrown on Southern attitudes by the fact that Warmoth, though he worked politically with blacks, did not mingle with them socially and married a Southern white woman of good family. That, too, was a key to his post-Reconstruction acceptance in Louisiana. But Morgan married a black woman and had to flee for his life.

A black carpetbagger like Pinchback shows a strong streak of adventurousness, too. Pinchback, almost white in complexion, was the son of a planter and a partially white slave woman. Before enlisting in the Union army, he had been a chief steward on Mississippi river boats. It was an important responsible job, involving the purchase of thousands of dollars' worth of supplies for the vessels. After Reconstruction Pinchback managed various investments with equal skill, well enough to live comfortably until his death in 1921.

The scalawags, too, often became Republicans because that party encouraged manufacturers, railroads, and banking. They had been a minority in Southern political life during the era when it was dominated by the planter leadership. Reconstruction made them eligible to vote and serve while their old foes were helpless, and they used the opportunity. A few were no more interested in blacks' rights than any other Southerners. Most successfully became Democrats after Reconstruction began to disintegrate. In short, both Northerners and Southerners who rose rapidly in this period were aggressive and willing to take risks and face the anger of some of their neighbors. They did so either because of faith in their own ideals or self-centered individualism or both. Perhaps there is a kind of "revolutionary" personality that is most successful in communities that are being torn apart and built anew instead of being begun from scratch. It may be an interesting research exercise for you to compare those who got ahead in a colony like Massachusetts with those who were assertive on the frontier, in a reform movement, and during Reconstruction.

## *Achievements and Costs of Revolution*

The so-called extravagance of the Radical regimes was exaggerated. Rapid changeovers are costly. Almost all the Radical state constitutions, to begin with, provided for new or expanded systems of public education. Many, in addition, created boards of charities and corrections. These were supposed to modernize and improve prisons, poorhouses, hospitals, and orphan asylums. All these functions of the modern world had been ignored by the planter leaders. All of them, even on the small scale on which they were operated in the South, required funds.

All the occupied states likewise faced major rebuilding problems. Roads rutted by thousands of army wagons had never been repaired. The South's few rail and telegraph lines had been ripped up and torn down by the invaders. Thousands of bridges had been burned. So had captured dockyards, arsenals, repair shops, and factories. Sunken steamboats made river navigation difficult. Simply getting the basic transportation network back in shape would have saddled the Radical governments, even if composed of nothing but angels, with heavy debts. There was no way to pay, moreover, except by taxing the plantations or by ever-heavier borrowing.

The Radical state governments, for their part, did more than repair the war's ravages. They encouraged a virtual orgy of railroad building. It was done by private companies, but the states made substantial loans to them, as well as gifts of land and other resources, such as timber or coal, along the right of way. The section's new rail mileage jumped dramatically between 1865 and 1885. But many companies went bankrupt, leaving the states' taxpayers stuck with their bad debts.

Yet this same process of government backing for railroad construction was taking place in virtually every state in the West. The railroad was *the* key to progress. Both in reality and as a symbol, its presence seemed to spell, to communities of the 1870s, the difference between success and stagnation. Governments were eager to pledge future income to bring rails and economic life to their peoples. Buying a future of prosperity, on credit, was also the American way. It went back to the time the Pilgrim fathers of Plymouth borrowed money to outfit the *Mayflower* and promised to repay it with the first profits from fishing, lumbering, and trapping. The new transportation boom was characterized by Henry Adams, New England descendant of two presidents, when he wrote that he belonged to a generation mortgaged to the railroads. Southerners—radical and "Conservative" alike—were part of that generation, too. The economic side of Reconstruction as a revolution was simply putting the South in step with the rest of the nation.

There was, of course, corruption, particularly in the granting of contracts to mine the iron and coal or cut the timber of the "backward" South. Bribery was rampant. But "respectable" Southerners were often part owners of the companies tainted by scandal. And bribing public officials, overcharging public treasuries, and issuing phony stocks and bonds were unlawful but nationwide business practices. The cost of modernization is always paid for in some way. In the case of modern revolutions in Russia, China, and Cuba, for example, payment came from robbed landlords or overtaxed peasants or forced labor. In the United States of the 1870s, and especially in the South, it came from many sources, including underpaid farmers, overworked laborers, and cheated taxpayers.

The whole process of Reconstruction must be seen in its historical context. The historian's facts render different meanings each time we enlarge the frame in which they are placed. Reconstruction's record of unscrupulousness, risk, and growth reflected the values of the whole nation. And even as a defeated people, Southerners made some postwar gains. By 1880 cotton production surpassed pre-1860 levels. Everyone—planters, carpetbaggers, Union veterans, Klansmen, blacks and whites—had supported the revival of the South's major cash crop. And some of the money spent in Reconstruction went into Southern cities that rose quickly out of their wartime ashes. By the early 1880s Richmond was humming with activity, much of it in cigarette factories controlled by a genuine Southern big-time industrialist, James Buchanan ("Buck") Duke. Atlanta was again the railroad center it had been before Sherman's men tore up rails, heated them on bonfires of ties, and twisted them like taffy around telephone poles. New Orleans' levees were busy and piled high with bales and boxes of cotton, semitropical fruits, refined sugar and other items in the Latin American trade. Its "sinful" streets were among the first in the nation to have electric lighting, just as Richmond was home to the first successful electric streetcar.

### *Failures and Unfinished Business*

There was, however, another side to the story. Reconstruction did too well in restoring King Cotton to his throne. The South continued to rely too heavily on cotton production. There was still very little industry to provide jobs and revenue when cotton prices fell, as they did in the 1890s. And outside investors took the profits of the railroads, the mines, the iron mills of spanking-new Birmingham. All paid tribute to Northern banks. So behind the few showcase cities of the new South was harsh rural poverty.

Of more long-range importance, perhaps, was the fact that farming was not democratized. The ideal of the American agricultural system was to guarantee every farmer the ownership of adequate land. Yet neither blacks nor poor whites got land at the war's end, despite some Radical talk of breaking up the great plantations. The plantations sometimes changed owners but stayed undivided. The commonest system of farming became sharecrop tenancy. The cash-poor owner furnished each tenant, black and white, with a plot of land, a cabin, some livestock and farming tools. At the year's end the tenants kept a part of the crop they raised for themselves and gave the rest to the landlord as rent. In theory it sounded reasonable. In practice it was abominable.

*Whatever happened politically, one result of Reconstruction was to tie the South into the booming post-Civil War economy. This 1881 drawing from a Latin American magazine shows a New Orleans that is bustling, hustling, and thriving as much as Chicago or Pittsburgh.*

The reason was that the owner of a large farm lacked motivation and money to improve his holdings. The sharecroppers lacked responsibility for the care of the property they did not own. Both planter and/or croppers were heavy borrowers. The planter bought equipment and luxuries by borrowing from banks or cotton merchants. The cropper got credit at the local store for meat, corn meal, molasses, and other necessities. Both pledged their cotton for security. And both stayed in debt as cotton prices fell through overproduction. Though the planter lived better, he was as fully enmeshed in the system as the tenants.

The tenants themselves remained at the bottom of the social ladder. To stay alive whole families had to work. There was no sparing of children for school. Illiteracy flourished—and so did sickness, on a meager diet of fatty meat, starchy corn, and overcooked greens. The cabins of tenants were not much above the level of slave quarters. It was a system of guaranteed annual poverty, from which there was no breaking out. It lasted until well into the twentieth century. And efforts to change it met the same kind of resistance that the antislavery movement had encountered, for the same reasons: Change might benefit blacks and whites, but it would give the blacks the idea that they could do better! Racism remained a barrier to real progress.

### *Counterrevolution and Race*

Any story of Reconstruction must take honest account of race and violence as forces in the recapture of power by Southern whites. It is true that disgust with some Radicals' corruption turned voters toward the Democratic ticket. But, more importantly, Radical rule rested on a coalition that was bound to unravel. The blacks, the Northerners who had recently come South, and the Southerners who had taken no part in the Confederate revolt were three very different groups. Often they were united only by their common enemies. The demands of sudden change and the shared role of outsiders had joined them for a time. But they were not revolutionaries linked by joint faith. It was inevitable that in every state they should split over various issues. The Democrats profited from these ruptures. And, as time went by and more and more ex-Confederates were pardoned, the Democratic voting rolls grew bigger. The old white leaders were more readily able to make deals and demands. It is difficult to keep a former ruling class out of the political arena, as a comparison of Reconstruction and the post-1945 attempts to "de-Nazify" Germany would show.

But behind all these reasons for Reconstruction's ending was simple violence. Unnumbered thousands of blacks and some white sympathizers were beaten up, shot, hung, horsewhipped, and burned when they tried to exercise their political rights or complained about conditions. Thick volumes of congressional hearings on Ku Klux Klan violence prove it. And the Klan was only one of many terrorist organizations. Terror, always justified even in modern times as a weapon of the oppressed, was used to oppress others. The only protection for blacks and their friends lay with soldiers and friendly law-enforcement officials. But as Radicals lost control of the statehouses, sheriffs and state militia became the agents of white supremacy. Federal troops, once a strong source of support, dwindled in number as Northern concern over the fate of the freed blacks faded and cutbacks were made. After a depression hit the country in 1873, the North's will to remake the South almost entirely vanished.

So nothing stood between the blacks and intimidation except their own willingness to vainly fight back. Some did, as was the case under slavery. They were soon killed. The rest had to submit. As a result, there is no way of knowing what truly honest, federally supervised elections in the early 1870s would have done to slow down or change the white counterrevolution.

The violence was not needed. There were many other ways to force blacks either not to vote or to vote Democratic. There were no secret ballots in the 1870s, so a voter's choice was easily known to others at the polls. A voter had to take a printed ballot of one party or the other, and, before all eyes, put it in the box. If a black man voted Republican, landowners could drive his family off the farm. Storekeepers could deny him credit. Employers could fire any of the women working as servants. All these techniques have been used in modern times to persuade Southern blacks to "know their place." Through them alone the Fourteenth and Fifteenth Amendments could have been effectively nullified.

But such acts do not paralyze the will to fight back as dramatically as fire and whip and rope and gun. Nor do they express the deepest racist emotions. The purpose of holding the threat of pain and death over blacks was to prevent their even thinking of going to court with any grievances. The old slave system had rested, in the end, on fear. And so did the new system of subjugation.

But to generate the paralysis of the blacks' will the "proper" Southerners paid a social price. "Gentlemanly" leaders who would not themselves have used a whip or gun on a helpless black looked the other way when poor whites did so. And they felt they had to lie to federal investigators about what was done. Their honor was stretched almost to the limits to meet the needs of keeping the South "a white man's country."

The individuals who won back control of the South called themselves Redeemers and Conservatives. The first word suggests a purifying process. The second is the opposite of Radical. But true conservatism had a deep respect for law and order. The Southerners who accepted ballot-box stuffing and savagery to get their way, no matter what their reasons, were also acting in a manner that made force more important than custom or respect for courts and judges. The counterrevolution against Reconstruction had its price, too. We may ask the same questions of both Radicals and Redeemers who gained their ends by using the threat of raw power instead of by waiting for time and popular education and consent. Were the results worth it? Was there another way?

### *Observations on the Limits of Revolution*

It is this final question that has the greatest interest for our time. The twentieth century, ushered in with bright promises, has been one of the bloodiest in history. It has been dominated by wars and the violent overthrow of past patterns. We all have, therefore, a special interest in trying to find useful general observations that can teach us to understand and survive our era. Here, to stimulate your own thought, are three.

First, if Reconstruction is any guide, existing patterns and habits persist strongly even in an admittedly revolutionary situation. Despite all the turmoil and intense feeling, both the Radicals in Congress and the states wanted the states readmitted as soon as possible under the Constitution. No new form of political organization for the South was suggested for long. Both Radicals and Redeemers in politics used the same kinds of party appeals and tactics that custom had taught them. Republican "revolutionaries" and Democratic "reactionaries" worked through the same system of conventions, state and local committees, and election machinery that were in use before 1860 and are in use today. No one seemed to feel that the basic apparatus of politics was in need of any change.

Likewise, those on both sides who rose to the top in the revolutionized South were remarkably like others who were succeeding elsewhere in national life. They were popular, good speakers, socially amiable. They were mainly lawyers and businessmen. They preached economic development. They were full of initiative, restless, and willing to move quickly from one project or one town to another.

America had, by the 1870s, produced a class of popular leaders rooted in no tradition and no locality. Both in business and politics, the persons at the wheel were adventurous but not individualistic in social style. They all conformed to majority tastes in religion, family behavior, and home surroundings. They all were raised in small towns from which they rushed away as youths to build their fortunes. The top figures in Reconstruction of both parties (even of both races) tended to fit this mold.

The second generalization seems to contradict the first slightly. Southern "go-getters" in business and "favorite sons" in politics did seem to be tailored to a nationwide pattern as the region grew modernized. But ordinary Southerners did not change some of the folkways that had so intrigued prewar visitors. There was hustle and talk of deals in cottonseed oil in Memphis and Little Rock. But outside the major towns the rural calm of the plantation era seemed to prevail. The South was still, in many ways, a separate cultural province. Like a foreign country tapped by imperialist powers, it did not experience modernization at the level of ordinary day-to-day behavior until a modern age of mass communications began to rub out its folk habits. Only movies, radio, television, and supermarkets began to dilute Southern accents or replace Southern cooking with "fast-food" items. And that was nearly a century after Reconstruction. The point to be noted is that revolutions may change political patterns or the distribution of wealth but culture changes slowly, if at all.

The third observation concerns the blacks. For them the revolution was a partial failure. They got freedom, the vote, and some educational basics. In the Radical view that was enough to guarantee them success. The liberal faith of the nineteenth century was that anyone with gumption needed only a chance in order to get ahead. When ex-slaves failed to emerge in ten years after 1865 as small businessmen or prosperous farmers, many Radicals disgustedly accepted the worst of racist stereotypes about them.

Of course, blacks had gotten nothing like an equal chance. The ballot was soon taken from them by force. Their education was a dead end after the earliest grades. Above all, there was almost no assistance in economic rehabilitation. Some were turned off the plantations, as one of them put it, like stray animals. Even the Freedmen's Bureau only helped by getting them contracts with planters, not land of their own. And, as we noted, sharecropping for blacks was not a great step up from slavery. It left black families still propertyless, still without basic skills in living. Nothing in the Radical program really made up for those lacks. So keeping blacks down was not difficult.

Reconstruction seemed to prove that a revolution that does not touch the economic system by which a class is exploited cannot long be effective in improving their lives. Oddly enough, it was Booker T. Washington, a very conservative black leader, who most vigorously preached this. In the 1890s he tried to win white support for a program of black agricultural and vocational education. To court white backers he appeared to echo antiblack stereotypes of the Reconstruction legend. He also proposed that blacks should for the time being forgo pressure for social and political rights. He may have been badly mistaken in such tactics. But he did realize that economic self-sufficiency was the first need of Southern blacks and that Reconstruction had not filled that need.

The era was not a total loss for justice. The nation did go on record, through the Fourteenth and Fifteenth Amendments, as supporting black civil and political equality. It had to try to make good on its promise, from time to time. And even the limited "freedom" of rural poverty offered a foundation for the future that could not exist under slavery's destructive self-image. Some blacks forged ahead even after 1877 and built a future for children who were now legally their own. Each year more of them were gaining literacy, even in the South's unbelievably poor black schools. Many urban blacks were forming neighborhoods, starting small businesses, from hairdressing to undertaking, and earning recognition and pride. Even a segregated society was not quite as ego-scarring as slavery. And, especially through their churches, blacks went on forging a cultural identity, more easily than they had under slavery, as Chapter 11 showed. All these gains were building blocks for the future. But the future remained a very long way away. Both black and white Southerners paid with frustration for the failure of Reconstruction to swiftly and directly tackle and solve Southern problems.

Perhaps such quick answers were impossible. The final overall generalization about Reconstruction is this: It seems to suggest that a revolution, to succeed, may have to come from *within*. If it does not rise from a society's voluntary sense of the need for change, shared by all classes, its results will not be long lasting. Revolutions imposed from outside, like Reconstruction, are unfinished, imperfect, and leave slow-healing wounds. But perhaps change can sometimes come in no other way.

## *FOR FURTHER READING*

There are good summaries of the old-fashioned view of Reconstruction and of modern changes in it in Kenneth Stampp, *The Era of Reconstruction* (1964). But if you want the flavor of Reconstruction mythology hot, strong, and original, read Claude G. Bowers, *The Tragic Era* (1929); or, in fictional form, Margaret Mitchell, *Gone With the Wind* (1934).

A fine firsthand account of how the Freedmen's Bureau worked is John W. De Forest, *A Union Officer in the Reconstruction* (1948). A more general view of that agency is in W. S. McFeely, *Yankee Stepfather: Oliver O. Howard and the Freedmen's Bureau* (1968).

The best all-around history of Reconstruction from the point of view of a black scholar is W. E. B. Du Bois, *Black Reconstruction in America* (1935). Much remains to be written describing actual life among blacks in those years, but a sample of what is possible is Joel Williamson, *After Slavery: The Negro in South Carolina During Reconstruction* (1965). A scholarly book on the Ku Klux Klan is Allen Trelease, *White Terror: The Ku Klux Klan Conspiracy and Southern Reconstruction* (1971). An old and passionate anti-KKK novel by a "carpetbagger" is Albion W. Tourgee, *A Fool's Errand* (1961), which you will find lurid and enjoyable, but probably untrustworthy.

The political deal which ended Reconstruction is best described in C. Vann Woodward, *Reunion and Reaction* (1951). Biographies of leading political figures are usually helpful. Among recent and interesting ones are Fawn Brodie, *Thaddeus Stevens: Scourge of the South* (1959); Eric McKittrick, *Andrew Johnson and Reconstruction* (1960); and David Donald, *Charles Sumner and the Rights of Man* (1970). For the pure fun of meeting a principled scoundrel, try Jonathan Daniels, *Prince of Carpetbaggers* (1959).

# *chapter* 14

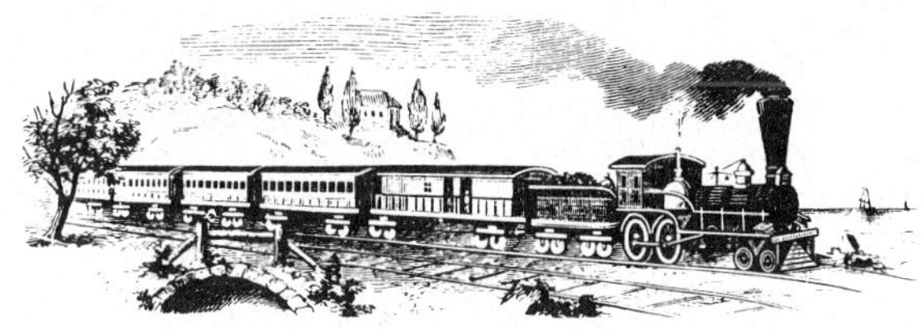

# *The last frontier falls*

On May 10, 1869, on a bare stretch of Utah land called Promontory Point the United States celebrated its most exciting ritual of completion up to then. Two old-fashioned steam locomotives stood hissing, cowcatcher to cowcatcher, on a single track stretching from horizon to horizon. Around them was a crowd of officials, newspaper reporters, and workers. While telegraph keys clicked, one of the well-dressed dignitaries took up a sledge hammer and gave three formal taps to a golden spike that nailed a rail to a wooden crosstie. As he finished, the train whistles broke into hoarse screeching, while people cheered, flung up hats and upended champagne bottles (later discreetly brushed out in official photos). The news of the last tap, telegraphed to San Francisco, New York, and other major cities, set off hurrahs, fireworks, bells, and binges there, too.

Why? Because the rail was the final one in a line linking Sacramento, California, and Omaha, Nebraska. But since both those cities had train connections to the Atlantic and Pacific coasts, the driving of that final spike meant that the oceans were now linked by rail. Some forty years after the first crude "steam carriages" had appeared in the United States and only twenty-one years after California was taken, amazing new possibilities had opened. Ordinary people could follow the heartbreak-haunted tracks of trappers, army scouts, and pioneers in a comfortable seat at 30 miles an hour. Any family with the fare could relive a basic experience of the nation by going from coast to coast, doing in a week what had taken some American people centuries.

This was what the technology of steam and iron had made possible. The elation of Americans in that spring of 1869 came from a sense of their power over space and time. That conquest would change their world in ways they could not foresee. They believed that all such changes were bound to be good. Though comparisons are hard to make, they were probably more excited, because they lived in a more hopeful time, than their great-grandchildren were exactly one century later, when an American set foot on the surface of the moon.

## *Westward Growth: From Trickle to Avalanche*

The first impact of the transcontinental railroad was felt almost at once. In only twenty-five years it led in a rush that wiped out Western isolation. By 1894 major rail lines linked the Pacific coast to the Mississippi Valley, the Gulf of Mexico, and the Great Lakes. In fact, a web of feeder lines was weaving the whole nation into a single economic unit.

In 1894 there was still a steady march of new settlers into empty prairie lands, but the 1890 census report could no longer draw a single, continuous line dividing areas where population was less than two per square mile from the rest of the country. That boundary—the frontier—was vanishing.

In 1894 there were still small sputters of Indian resistance in the Southwest, but the last claimed Indian "uprising" had been settled when 200 Sioux were mowed down by army guns at Wounded Knee, South Dakota.

In 1894 only four areas west of the Mississippi had not yet achieved statehood: Oklahoma, New Mexico, Utah, and Arizona.

### *CHRONOLOGY*

| | |
|---|---|
| 1859 | *Oil discovered in Pennsylvania* |
| 1862 | *Pacific Railway Act allows land grants and U.S. loans to transcontinental railroads* |
| 1867 | *First southwestern overland cattle drive* |
| 1869 | *Transcontinental rail link completed in Utah* |
| 1850s–1880s | *Western "bonanza" mining* |
| 1872 | *Crédit Mobilier scandal* |
| 1887 | *Severe winter virtually ruins northern cattle ranchers* |
| 1890 | *The frontier, as defined by the Census Bureau, is gone* |

In 1894 cities like Butte and Denver had opera houses and electric lights. They also had gold, silver, and copper mines run from office desks by the hired managers of large corporations. These mines employed a tough labor force that during strikes often fought violent battles, using guns and dynamite, with company and state police.

And, in 1894, steam-driven western sawmills were busy cutting up the trees that loggers cut down by the hundreds of thousands annually. Untouched timberland was going fast. Ugly piles of slag surrounded the mouths of overworked mines. The buffalo herds were gone. They had been shot in hundreds of thousands by "sportsmen," and their feeding grounds had become fenced-in farms or western Main Streets. Refineries that turned ore into metal spewed smoke into the air and waste into the rivers; no one cared too much about this yet. People believed in an endless supply of rivers and air. There were warning signs, however. Once the Great Plains, from Canada to Mexico, had been a sea of free grass for cattle. By in 1894 ranchers recognized a serious problem of overgrazing.

## *The Far Western Kingdom of Giants*

Not all these things were the direct result of the railroad. But the transcontinental line was the symbol of the time. It opened the period of rapid westward sweep. A movement that had gone on at the pace of oxen and riverboats now was wildly accelerated. What happens to national thought and behavior in a period of whirlwind growth? What happens when the natural limits to expansion are lifted? What happens when advance into unsettled country and the chewing up of its resources proceed at the pace of steam instead of muscle? What do such changes of pace and scale do to social organization and political beliefs? Now these questions, posed earlier in Chapter 8, may be posed again, but this time in the light of even faster and greater changes.

One question might well be: How does explosive expansion create new patterns of leadership and fame? The answer, for the years of far western occupation, is an interesting puzzle. The technology that made the emergence of railroad kings, mining lords, and cattle barons possible rested on the power of *organization.* It took much capital and long-range planning to build railroads or to extract silver and gold in commercial quantities from underground vaults. And organizations tend to downplay the importance of each separate person. Yet the focus of attention of the country was on a few key leaders in the development of the West. The spotlight hit the rich, the powerful, and the lucky.

Partly, it was because they were colorful, and color is always eye catching. But also they seemed themselves to bend Nature to their will. Their success was apparent proof that America was the land where the able *individual* could flourish. They were thought to be the true creators of growth, and society appeared to do best by not restraining them.

What happened, then, was that the West especially became a place where individualism was glorified as it had rarely been in the East. The heroes of western economic expansion resisted government supervision and control of their activities with great vigor and much popular approval. They fought labor unions, Indians, and natural obstacles with the same energy. Those whom they used or abused—like Chinese or Mexican laborers, for example—were thought of as exploitable resources, like the grass, lucky to contribute to progress. In these attitudes the new conquistadores of the West were like most other Americans. But they had a larger stage for their virtues and vices. In the more urbanized regions special problems and old community traditions softened individualism. In the West that quality stood out stark and gigantic, like silhouetted mountains. Yet the basic story of western growth was one in which, more and more, *corporate* effort, involving associations of people and money, became necessary for success.

### *The Great Iron Trail*

The railroad story is the first example and the foundation. All through the 1850s Congress had wrangled over how best to support the building of a transcontinental line. When it finally took action in 1862, it chose a financing system that was a mixture of private and public enterprise. There was almost no sentiment in favor of simply having the railroad built and owned by the United States. The tradition of private enterprise was too strong. On the other hand, even the wealthiest private investors could not raise the millions necessary to build 2000 miles of railroad through empty country.

Earlier lines had been built piece by piece. As each stretch was opened, its earnings helped pay for succeeding mileage. But it would be years before the deserts, plateaus, and prairies of the Far West would be settled enough to provide freight traffic and profits. How, then, could government help?

The answer was: with land and loans. Congress adopted a plan that called for chartering two companies. One, the Central Pacific, would build eastward; the other, the Union Pacific, westward. Eventually, the lines would meet. Each company would have the right to choose every alternate square-mile section of public lands in a checkerboard pattern along the right of way. A square mile contains 640 acres, and the land donations ran into millions of acres, which the companies could sell. In addition, the government would lend the companies money—$16,000 for every mile built on level ground, $32,000 per mile in more difficult country, and $48,000 per mile in mountainous terrain. The loans were in the form of U.S. bonds, which the builders could sell for ready cash. And, of course, with land and loans behind them, the promoters could also easily sell the stocks and bonds of their own companies. They were supposed to repay the government loans within a fixed time period, both in cash and by hauling troops and mail at reduced rates.

A few critics at once denounced what appeared to be a gigantic giveaway. They charged that private individuals, the railroad owners, were allowed to profit by the resale of public lands created by God and won by American arms for the benefit of all the people. The railroad land grants flouted the principle of the Homestead Act of 1862 which, as Chapter 8 relates, gave farms to willing and working citizens who asked for them. But defenders of the railroads and land grants argued back that, without the settlement made possible by the railroads' existence, the West would remain empty and valueless for years. It would grow no crops and create no profits and taxes. The government had simply given away part of its huge stock of empty lands in order to increase tenfold the worth of the rest. The bonds were merely loans. And land grants to finance public improvements were already a longstanding state practice.

Such answers blunted criticism slightly, though the federal government did stop major land grants to railroads after the 1870s. But the land grants aside, one major result of the congressional plan was emphasis on speed of construction. By offering large sums to those who would create the railroad, the government encouraged businessmen who looked for quick dollars in the building process, not the slow rewards of year-in-year-out operation. Directors of the rail companies could make immediate private gains by selling their own stocks. They could cut themselves into the profits of furnishing the building materials by secret deals with the companies from whom they bought supplies. They could rush construction in order to collect their loans per mile, leaving a great deal of cleanup work, like strengthening bridges, to be done later. They could use the cash in hand for personal speculations. Before a train rolled or an acre of land was sold, the builders could be rich, regardless of how well the line was planned. A national tendency to get quick results and ignore long-range problems was shown fully in the rush to finish the first transcontinental lines.

The pattern of federal financing also encouraged the overnight millionaire. Only a little working capital was needed to get things into motion. Once the contract to build the line was won, grants and loans would carry things along. Newcomers to the game of high finance had a chance. It was not necessary to begin with a gigantic personal fortune. The implication of this was democratic; anyone with the right combination of luck, energy, and connections might wind up as a railroad president. But such a person was also unlikely to operate within the restraints and traditions of a family with "old" money, a name to protect, a commitment to local good works, and relatives in politics with reputations to guard. Millionaires new on the scene might be less concerned with the long-run results of their actions.

So it seemed to turn out. The original leaders of the Union Pacific got involved in a scandal that did not surface until 1872. They set up a construction corporation called the Crédit Mobilier and paid themselves inflated sums for work performed on the line. Then, when possible congressional investigation was in the offing, they tried clumsily to head if off by giving stock to some senators and representatives.

The Union Pacific's directors were eventually displaced by businessmen who were shrewder about getting their way. In 1874 the line fell under the thumb of Jay Gould. He was a rural New York-born ex-surveyor whose talent was not to build and run railroads but to buy control of them. He would then use his inside position to make millions in buying and selling their stock.

Gould withdrew in a few years. Neither he nor the early directors gave much thought to setting aside money for repairs, modernization, expansion, or routine rises in the costs of operation. Instead, they piled up huge debts as they issued new stocks and bonds and tried to pay dividends on old issues. But, eventually, there was a day of reckoning. Managers after Gould could not repay the government and private lenders and still meet normal expenses without actions that brought public outcry, such as rate hikes, wage cuts, or illegal stifling of competition. In 1893 the Union Pacific, like many other lines, went bankrupt during a depression. It was then taken over by Edward H. Harriman, not a railroad builder at all but a stockbroker. In one way or another, customers, lenders, and even future generations paid a price for building the railroads quickly by offering boom profits to financial adventurers.

The true individual hero of the Union Pacific was General Grenville M. Dodge. He was a Union veteran who became the line's chief construction engineer. He faced enormous supply difficulties. Almost everything from nails to locomotives had to be hauled thousands of miles to the workplace. But Dodge arranged it and kept his crews of though Irish workers blasting, sledge-hammering, and hauling across the central North American highlands at a steady gait. He kept them in military order to withstand occasional Indian raids and to accept the discipline of living together many miles from civilization with few diversions except drinking and gambling. He also triumphed over blizzards, floods, landslides, mountain chasms almost impossible to span with timber bridges, and occasional halts while massive herds of buffalo crossed the right of way.

Yet once again there is a strange contradiction. Dodge was an outstanding individual; yet his success in overcoming these obstacles suggested that the pattern of any large-scale engineering undertaking was almost bound to be semimilitary. In modern times supercorporations and the armed services have shown a certain resemblance to each other in the demands for conformity and dedication that they make on their officers. In addition, top-level military personnel have often settled on retirement into corporation executives' chairs. Huge enterprises seem to rub distinctive rough edges off those who work for them. The Union Pacific may have been a dim forerunner of this development.

*The Southern Pacific: From Achievement to Octopus*

The story of the Central Pacific was equally colorful when it came to leadership. The chief organizers of the company were Charles Crocker, Mark Hopkins, Leland Stanford, and Collis P. Huntington, sometimes known in California as the Big Four. All had been small-town storekeepers in the East. All had come to California in the gold rush and found that real money was to be made by selling tools, food, blasting powder, hardware, and other supplies to the miners. Along with other Sacramento businessmen, they were approached before 1862 by an enthusiastic young engineer named Theodore D. Judah. He wanted them to put money into a proposed transcontinental line. They went along, not really thinking in transcontinental terms but only that if they ran the line as far as the mining camps, it would help their business.

But Congress's generosity changed things. The Big Four suddenly realized that they could really build a line through the incredibly difficult Sierra Nevada mountains, then across the desert of northern Nevada, and on to the link-up with the eastward-moving Union Pacific tracks. They would have to meet the engineering challenge without Judah, who died of a fever in 1863. And their logistic problem was even harsher than Dodge's. Every rail, every spike, every barrel of blasting powder or oil they used had to come from the eastern United States by the long water route around Cape Horn or by a difficult sea and land journey through Central America.

The job would take great drive, persistence, a nose for hiring good specialists, and a talent for raising emergency money when cash was low and federal funds were slow in coming. Crocker, Hopkins, Stanford, and Huntington rose to the task. One example of their ingenuity was their solution to a labor shortage as the line crept toward the "diggings." Workers kept dropping out to try their luck in the mines. Crocker, according to legend, had an idea. California already had a small population of Chinese. They had also come to the state to find gold, but white hostility drove them from the camps and into menial jobs. Crocker thought of recruiting his work force from among them. He was reminded that the "coolies" were too thin and frail for heavy construction work. Supposedly, he replied: "They built the Great Wall of China, didn't they?"

Whether Crocker said that or not, it *is* true that by 1867 thousands of "Crocker's pets" were shoveling, blasting, and pounding energetically without

*Building the first transcontinental rail line across mountains, deserts, and prairies was truly, in one author's phrase, "a work of giants." But some of the heroic "giants" were frail-looking Chinese laborers imported wholesale from the Celestial Kingdom.*

the fighting and drinking common among Caucasian crews. Thousands more were recruited from their homeland by Chinese already in California. They built snowsheds, bridges, and cliffside ledges for the tracks, which made a ride through the Sierras one of the nation's most breathtaking experiences.

When the Central Pacific was finished, the Big Four built thousands of miles of additional line in California. The whole network was renamed the Southern Pacific. Labor came, first from China, and, after Chinese immigration was stopped in 1882, heavily from Mexico. That is an illustration of how growth in a technological society has a magnetic effect on the peoples of yet undeveloped areas.

The lives of the Big Four were changed as well. Hopkins and Crocker more or less retired to fancy residences on San Francisco's Nob Hill. Stanford remained active in business. Then he went into politics to protect his interests. He became a senator from California and governor of the state. He spent handsomely on luxuries like fine horses, but he also gave to good causes. The best example was Stanford University, opened in 1891 thanks to generous gifts from the rail king. In one generation Stanford had gone from store clerk to patron of learning. That is part of the answer to the question of how the rush to settle the last frontier affected American society.

Huntington remained the chief business director of the Southern Pacific. Eventually, he moved its headquarters to New York, the nation's financial capital. Many other southern and western businesses found it convenient to be close to bankers. Huntington became known as a lobbyist and a stern defender of management's rights. In California he grew to be the favored target of everyone who objected to the Southern Pacific's policies.

Those policies left much room for objection. They included heavy charges for the railroad-owned lands, steep freight rates, harsh labor practices, and even threats to cut off rail service and thereby ruin communities that opposed the Southern Pacific politically.

The railroad in California had changed, in thirty years, from a promising highway to the future to an "octopus," as novelist Frank Norris called it in 1901. It controlled the lives of farmers and shippers who depended on it, and they resented that rule. As the twentieth century dawned, control of the railroads' power was a major national issue.

The railroads continued to be important and respected. But, increasingly, the tributes were not paid to railroad leaders but to the locomotives themselves. Between 1895 and 1915 elaborate and often beautiful terminals were raised in major cities to house crack "flyers" and their passengers. They were palaces for the machines rather than the individuals who made railroading.

The transcontinental line had, in its first thirty years of life, made a deep impact on America and the West. It had brought settlers thronging into the trans-Mississippi region, and that created the "need" for the army to make the West safe by wiping out the last pockets of Indian resistance. So the railroad helped to wipe out independent tribal life by 1890. It hastened the extinction of the buffalo. It helped to introduce the Chinese on a large scale to the West. So it shaped many thousands of lives, bringing hope, defeat, opportunity, and pain, like a mechanical agent of fate. It stood for the tremendous forces that surrounded nineteenth-century men and women. This gave it, in addition to its tremendous economic role, an important place in America's imagination.

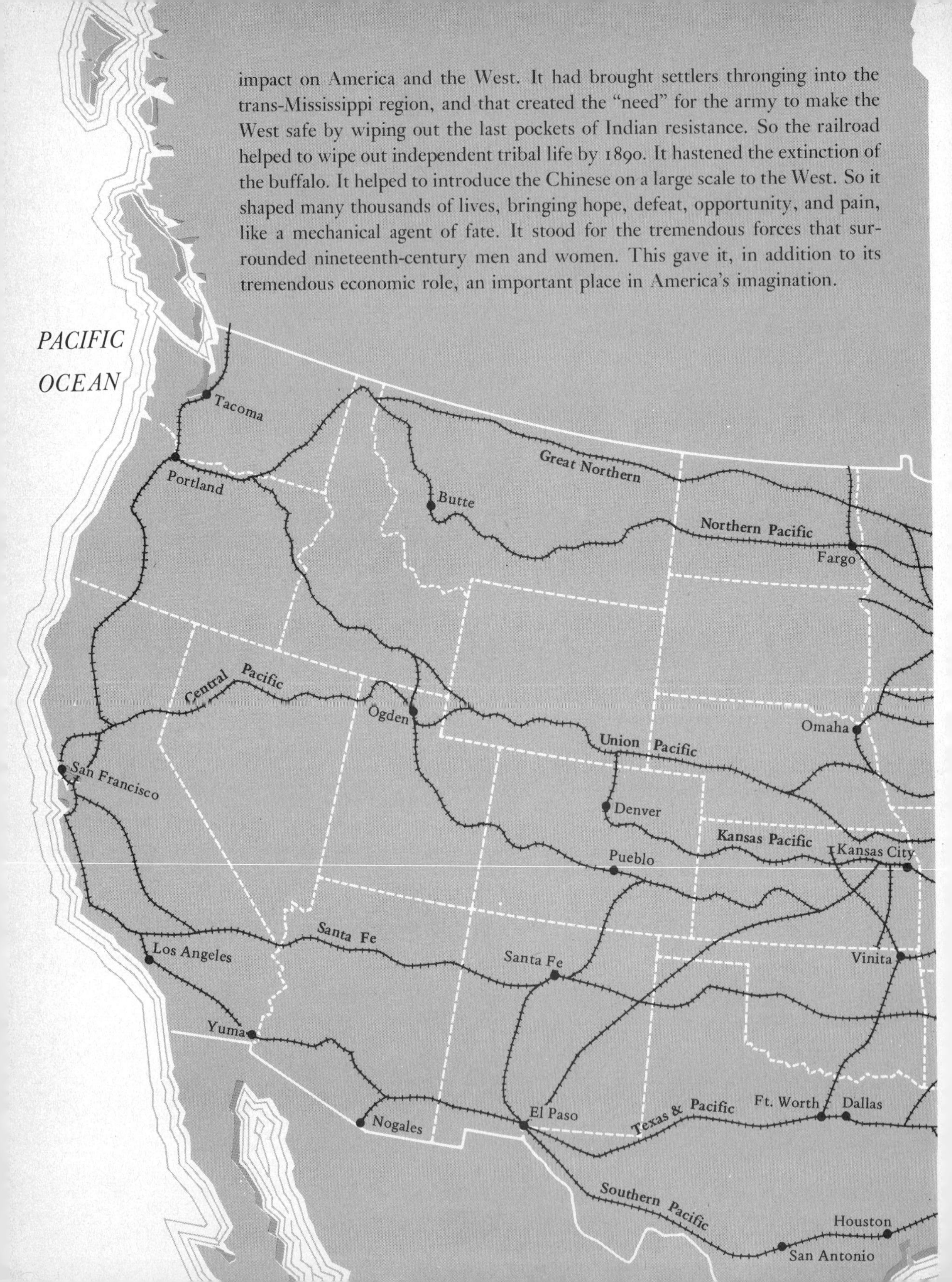

*Mining: The Lucky, the Powerful, and the Violent*

To a young Missourian named Samuel Clemens, Virginia City, Nevada, in 1864 was a wild but fascinating place. Ever since a fortunate handful of men had stumbled on rich veins of silver, running deep into the earth, the area had swarmed with prospectors. Each was obsessed with one idea: to find and claim another Comstock Lode, the great strike that had made millions for its discoverers. Prospectors did their digging along narrow strips called ledges, which were subdivided into "feet" that could be bought and sold. Chance ruled the day. An unlucky group could blast away at its ledge and get nothing but piles of rock. But if they hit a vein, every day's work could yield thousands of dollars.

Faced with this gamble, thousands of optimistic pilgrims had come to muddy Virginia City and caused a boom town to mushroom there. Hotels, assay offices (where the gold or silver content of rock samples were determined), refineries, a newspaper office, stores, courthouses, dance halls, saloons, livery stables, express company headquarters, and jails ran at full tilt around the clock.

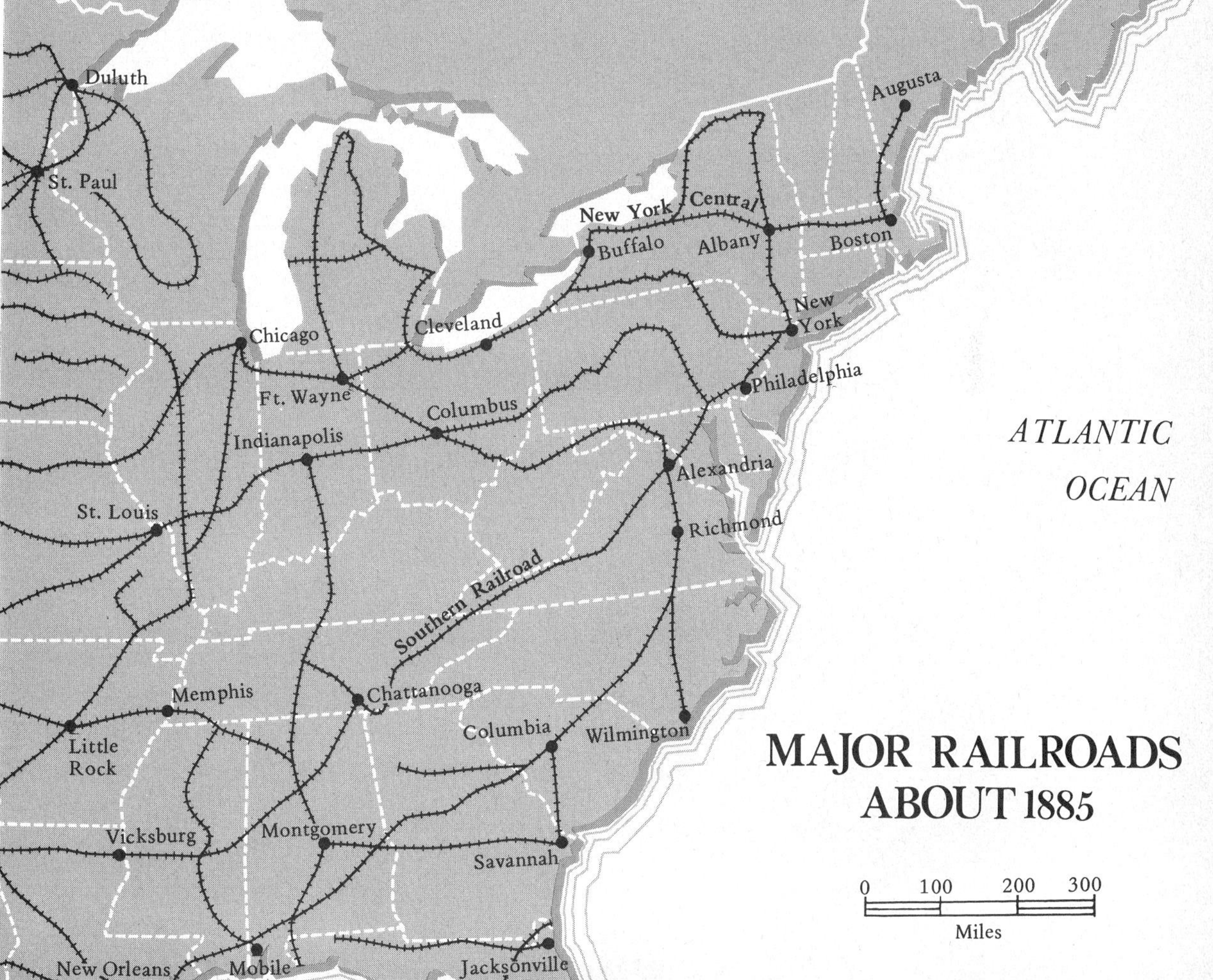


## MAJOR RAILROADS ABOUT 1885

It was a scene that was noisy, violent, and alive with the fever of expectation that sets a race-track crowd to cheering. Clemens, then a reporter in his twenties, kept his ears open in the saloons and restaurants and wherever people gathered. He wrote, later, about the excited talk of new veins, and the loud, unending flow of argument as prospectors formed and broke partnerships, swapped "feet" in good claims, or begged others for enough of a stake to buy a few more weeks' supplies. Virginia City, like other mining capitals, lived in the shadow of the always-possible miracle.

The early mining kingdom had a short, riotous rich history. After the California gold rush, new strikes were made in Nevada and in Colorado in the late 1850s. These two states were first settled in the resultant rushes to the mines. Only later did they get a grazing and farming population. There were other small "rushes," the last in the Black Hills area of South Dakota in 1878. Through the period from 1850 to about 1880, the silver and gold fields produced billions of dollars worth of precious metals. The great New World silver and gold discoveries of the sixteenth century had had a tremendous impact on the world's economy. But it had been felt slowly. The great bonanzas of the late nineteenth century were exploited much more quickly. In only a few years they had a powerful effect in raising prices and stimulating growth.

Their heaviest impact, however, may have been psychological. The whole idea of a bonanza is that of a sudden, overnight flood of plenty. The sheer size of the mining strikes forced a rethinking of conventional seventeenth- and eighteenth-century attitudes toward the way to wealth. The Puritans had seen America as a new promised land, flowing with milk and honey. But they expected that its fruits could be gathered only by hard toil. *Poor Richard's Almanack*, a hundred years after, also suggested that riches went to those who were careful, orderly, and reasonable. In the 1870s that theme was again expressed in the popular novels of Horatio Alger. His heroes were boys who went from rags to riches. Often they were helped by a chance "break." But they could take advantage of it only because of their clean, manly characters, which kept them away from idleness and costly pleasures.

But for the mining kings, neither piety nor thrift were important virtues. They knew that there was a simple element of luck in their good fortune. It may be for this reason that some of them were unabashedly showy in their spending habits. They were not trying to set a pattern of frugality and sobriety for others. They almost acted, sometimes, as if they expected to lose all their winnings as quickly as they had made them.

Some, by unwise investments, did just that. Others simply spent gorgeously, like James Flood, the Irish miner who became one of the "silver kings" of California; or like H. A. W. Tabor, who built opera houses and hotels in Denver and swaggered into them, resplendent with diamonds on his fingers and

*Overnight mining millionaire H. A. W. Tabor spent, gambled, and caroused lavishly. He left his first wife to marry the beautiful, divorced Elizabeth "Baby" Doe. They lived handsomely, invested foolishly, and died in poverty—a golden, romantic, American saga of the dream that came true and then turned to ashes.*

with his mistress, Baby Doe, on his arm; or like George Hearst of California, who bought himself an election to the Senate and passed on several hundred million dollars and an appetite for extravagance to his son, William Randolph Hearst. When young "Willie" went on to become a very successful newspaper publisher, he astonished twentieth-century Americans with his spending. He had a whole castle in California, San Simeon—crammed with precious art objects from all over the world—in which to amuse himself and show his splendor. But in building it, he was only following the pattern of his miner father, while other modern millionaires were becoming less showy.

Yet the age when a lucky individual like the elder Hearst or Tabor could suddenly strike it rich was short. As the easily available surface veins of silver and gold were used up, it became necessary to tunnel deeper into the mountains. That took capital. It demanded whole gangs of workers, teams of draft animals, thousands of feet of timber to prop up the tunnels, expensive ventilation systems, rails to haul the ore cars back and forth. Likewise, lower-grade ores needed more complicated mechanical and chemical processes to make them yield pure metal.

So, by the 1870s, more mines were being bought by corporations that could put together the enormous sums required for searching for mines, developing them, and processing the ores. Banks became indispensable allies. As it turned out, the mining kings of the end of the century were not ex-prospectors but the Guggenheims. They were a family descended from a patriarch named Meyer Guggenheim, an immigrant from Switzerland in 1847. They began their business career as peddlers. Then they branched successfully into the manufacture and sale of stove polish. By the 1880s the Guggenheims were looking for new investment opportunities, when someone interested Meyer in a pair of up-to-then unproductive mineshafts in Colorado. He took the plunge, made money, and soon was buying new mining lands. Success led to success. By 1910 the Guggenheims owned mines worth millions of dollars in the United States, Africa, Latin America, and Alaska. It was all made possible by careful research, planning, and investment. As an example, the Guggenheims would hire expensively trained engineers to survey potential mine sites and top-flight chemists to improve refineries. They tried to anticipate world needs for various metals, and they also tried to cut costs and raise profits by combining with other producers to fix prices. As little as possible was left to luck, once the prospectors' goddess.

The same shift from individual initiative to combination and planning pervaded the whole minerals industry. The discovery of oil in Pennsylvania in 1859 led to an oil boom. Fortunes were made and lost dizzyingly. But the rip-roaring industry was soon tamed by John D. Rockefeller of Cleveland. He came to dominate refining and eventually, through his Standard Oil trust, to dictate oil pricing and marketing patterns. Or, as another illustration, Montana copper made the fortune of a lucky man or two like Marcus A. Daly. He was an Irish prospector who started with nothing but bare hands and energy. But by the end of the century a giant combine known as Anaconda Copper controlled the mines.

Yet despite the march of organization, the extractive industries in the West and Southwest kept a flavor of individualism and violence. Texas oilmen to this day are among the sharpest foes of social planning. Labor disputes in the coal fields of Colorado, Illinois, Kentucky, and West Virginia, in the copper mines of Montana, and in the silver mines of Idaho have tended to be unusually brutal. Shotguns, sheriffs' clubs, and dynamite were in frequent use in strife-torn mountain towns between 1895 and 1915. A climax came in 1914, when a coal strike in mines owned by the Rockefellers at Ludlow, Colorado, flared into

*Here, in Butte, Montana in 1895, sits the "richest hill on earth." Ugly but full of copper, it nourished bonanza kings, governors, and senators, and ultimately the gigantic Anaconda copper trust.*

guerrilla war. Miners and their families were machine-gunned by National Guardsmen as they huddled in tents after being thrown out of company-owned houses.

Perhaps the violence of the mining kingdom came about because of a general loosening of social controls at the beginning. The region's wealth did not seem to be created by the organized effort of communities to use God's gifts of soil and climate. It came instead from the energies of daring individuals. Once they achieved success, they regarded what they owned as theirs and theirs exclusively, to do with as they wished. Their workers very often understood and resented the "bosses'" claim to raw power. They protested in dramatic, explosive fashion. One of the most violent labor organizations of the early twentieth century was the Western Federation of Miners. Some of its leaders believed that its mission was not simply to win concessions from owners but to blast capitalism (sometimes literally) out of existence.

In the mining kingdom the environment was not coaxed into productivity by patient effort. It was assaulted, and treasures were gouged from it. That pattern affected the social style of all involved. Another, and different, illustration of the social results of the far western boom was visible in the story of the cattleman's frontier.

## *The Cowman's World: Heroic Legend Versus Economic Reality*

Cattle raising is an American economic activity that goes back to colonial times. Most beef animals were slaughtered and eaten on the farm. Surplus meat could not be shipped far without great cost and risks of spoilage. But some animals were driven live to market. Drovers, on foot, accompanied the bawling herds along country lanes to city marketplaces to be slaughtered and sold.

In the early days of the Southwest, settlers in Texas found that the grasslands around them made excellent free feed for cattle. So, like their Mexican neighbors, they took to raising livestock. To handle large numbers of animals spread over a wide area, however, it was necessary now that the drovers be mounted. The Mexicans had a name for the men who roped, branded, castrated, and coaxed the steaks-on-the-hoof from place to place: *vaqueros*, or cowboys. Americans who did the same work adopted the name and the uniform. This included the broad-brimmed, sun-defying sombrero, the chaps to protect the trousers from tearing in cactus and sagebrush, and the elegantly wrought leather boots and saddles.

But Texas cattle raising, until the late 1860s, was not a large-scale operation. It was still limited by the small size of the local markets. To move the herds any great distance involved great risks. Many of the animals would stray. Some would be picked off by raiding Indians. Some would die of diseases picked up en route. All the survivors would be thin, tough, and not very marketable.

The coming of the railroad changed this, however. Shortly after the Civil War, rail lines pushed out from the meat-packing centers of Milwaukee, Chicago, and Kansas City into the western parts of Missouri and Kansas. A few far-sighted ranchers saw mighty possibilities in this fact. They argued that, with care, large herds could be driven northward from Texas to towns having railroad connections eastward. There would be some losses, certainly. But an animal that cost a Texas rancher only $5 to raise might fetch $40 or better in a Missouri or Kansas market. At that margin of profit, reasonable losses could be absorbed. The buyers in Sedalia or Abilene or Dodge City could then rest and fatten the animals and ship them to the packing houses.

The first overland drives took place in the spring of 1867. When they proved successful, a trickle, then a flood of would-be ranchers rushed southwestward. The basic elements in creating the cattle boom were three. First, there was the gift of Nature, abundant fodder. The great, unsurveyed public domain of the Southwest was head deep in prairie grass. There was not a fence in sight for thousands of miles. No one needed a license to pasture animals on it. It was a kind of national "common," like the pastures shared by the settlers in New England townships, only on a vaster scale. The beginning cattleman needed only a small "starter" herd and a few acres of his own for a home. He could turn his cattle out at any time to munch contentedly in the mild southwestern climate. Soon the cows would calve and increase his wealth without any effort or expense on his part.

Next came technology's contribution, the rails. They were as important as the free grazing land. They moved the cattle swiftly to packing centers, where improved, belt-line techniques reduced them quickly to choice cuts. Then the rails moved them again, with equal swiftness, to the meat-hungry cities of a growing nation. The coming of refrigerated cars made the progress even easier, safer, and more profitable.

Finally, there was the social system's contribution, the profit motive and its lure in an expanding economy on the frontier. Americans had always enjoyed an ample supply of pork; but beef, which could not be raised as easily in the wilderness, had been expensive and less common. Now it appeared on the tables of urban workingmen and women, at good prices. The thousands of steers and oxen, daily shuffling and lowing in the crowded stockyards of Chicago, Milwaukee, and St. Louis sang a song of dollars.

What was in process was actually a food-producing revolution, still going on, in which a few intensively cultivated areas raised enough for a gigantic nonfarm population. Around 1870 the southwestern American in the cattle business was in a position to profit especially by this revolution.

There were, of course, problems of organization. They were solved by self-initiated cooperative effort. That was part of a pattern of frontier cooperation that offset its individualism. Associations of stockmen got together to agree on brands to identify each owner's cattle among the thousands on the open grasslands. They made pacts for sharing the calves born each year. They arranged for common use of precious water sources. And to some extent, they tried to set territorial boundaries to grazing areas and to keep out newcomers, just like other businessmen aiming to control competition.

But even though they were compared to feudal lords and called cattle barons, the stockmen had no power to enforce their rules. Within a very short time an inevitable process of expansion set in. Despite efforts at restriction, more and more individual entrepreneurs entered the business. The number of cattle shipped eastward grew from thousands to millions. Each new herd put a greater burden on the grasslands. They had had thousands of years to grow and renew themselves naturally, nibbled only by the buffalo and later by a few Indian ponies. Now they were swiftly worn out.

The westward-moving transportation lines brought thousands of farmers into the West. These rapidly crisscrossed it with fences and plowed under the grasses to plant future market crops. A battle raged over whether the public domain should be a great pasture or a vast farm. The farmers began to win politically by weight of numbers. And, to the disgust of cattle raisers, sheep ranchers even began to claim their share of virgin land and to reduce further the elbowroom available for the open-ranch system of cattle raising.

Transition came gradually but irresistibly. As newcomers entered the field, the price of an initial herd and lands went up, so that large-scale investments were required. There was more of a tendency for the business to be conducted by companies, often formed abroad. There were no great combines of cattle growers comparable to those in industry or mining. Yet the way of the loner became more difficult. Finally, crowding of the southwestern ranges drove cattlemen ever northward in search of fresh free acres. But in Wyoming and Montana and the Dakotas, winter could be a savage enemy. In 1887 great blizzards virtually wiped out the northern herds. The feeding grounds, after snow melted, were strewn thickly with frozen carcasses.

Thus by the century's end, survival in the cattle business meant more businesslike organization. It meant buying large tracts of land; building pens and barns to stock through the winter; applying science through improved feeding techniques, and the beginning of selective breeding. It meant digging deep wells and building windmills to pump and store water. It meant taking the steps necessary to make meat growing frankly a business, not a sporting venture or a romantic struggle with Nature.

Nonetheless, the cattle kingdom, in its brief life, created a basic American folk figure, the cowboy. Actually, he was a mounted agricultural worker. His job, after the long drives and the open-range system ended, was more or less prosaic. And from the start it was clear that railroad extension would eventually make the overland drives needless.

But the cowpoke who rides through a thousand Western novels and filmed "horse operas," stopping stampedes, fighting off rustlers and Indians, did exist in a special dimension. He is a culture creation, a figure of popular art who embodies qualities that we desire to have.

In a society of crowds the fictionalized cowboy appears as the attractive "loner." He is loyal to his comrades but always an individualist. He has no family ties or lasting romantic attachments. In a world of hard moral choices, he is never in doubt as to the distinction between good and evil. He does not wait to see what others do. When confronted with evil in the form of the bad man, he is direct in his opposition and quick to remove the "problem" with his fist or his gun.

Novels about cowboy heroes began to appear as early as 1903. Was it because he was close to the last frontier? Being far from cities and settlements, was he thought of as the American closest to Nature and therefore, most natural? And was it not Nature who was the patron deity of America, the virgin continent, the New World?

It all makes sense. Yet it is ironic that, in fact, the cowboy's mission, like that of earlier lone heroes, the fur trappers, was to help use up Nature's resources quickly and convert them to the form in which "civilization" could use them. The cowboy and trapper loved unspoiled Nature—and both went down to doom with her as civilization followed their own efforts.

As students, you may enjoy pondering such questions and meditating on the strange American relationship with Nature—one of love for the primitive and unspoiled, on the one hand, and of admiration for those who are the flagbearers of progress (and thus change what is primitive and unspoiled), on the other.

The history of the frontier is a paradox. A paradox is a situation that presents two reasonable but actually contradictory impressions. The rush to settle the mountain and prairie West presented just such a situation. The swift civilizing of the West seemed a triumph for all the American virtues of energy, will, drive, and individual initiative. It was a proof of progress and of God's grand plan of expansion for the American people.

Yet the end result, in a short time, was the creation of great wealth. Progress brought pain and poverty with it. It brought huge and powerful corporations, bitter struggles between labor and capital, dwindling opportunities for individuals to enter economic competition on their own. The thrust of the age swelled the power of organizations and shrank that of unorganized people. The West of the Southern Pacific and Anaconda Copper and the King ranch might produce politicians and tycoons who were still markedly individualistic in behavior. But it was different. It began as a land of prospectors and pioneers. It ended tied to the banks and insurance companies of New York.

People had to adjust their thinking to this paradox in a short time. And that need to deal with swiftly changing realities is part of the entire modern age. It links the booming days of the last frontier to our own time.

---

## *FOR FURTHER READING*

For a lively history of the first transcontinental railroad read Robert West Howard, *The Great Iron Trail* (1965), and then, if the later careers of the builders interests you, try Oscar Lewis, *The Big Four* (1938).

The mining kingdom is dealt with in many works by experts, but a good general overview is in Irving Stone, *Men to Match My Mountains* (1956). Nothing beats an intelligent eyewitness and, therefore, no one with an interest in the silver boom in Nevada should miss *Roughing It* (1875) by Mark Twain, who was there.

The best scholarly history of the cattle business is Ernest L. Osgood, *The Day of the Cattleman* (1929), rich in facts and figures. A charming book that has the real aroma of sagebrush in its pages is by a cowboy-turned-scholar, Edward Everett Dale's *Cow Country* (1974). A reprinted classic is Andy Adams' *Log of a Cowboy* (1927). A forgotten aspect of the cowboy legend is the presence of many blacks on the job; their story is told in Philip Durham and Everett L. Jones, *The Negro Cowboy* (1965). You might find interesting the first modern "western" novel, from which most of the others stem: Owen Wister, *The Virginian* (1903).

As for the humble sod-busters who went to homestead the prairie, the most thorough and detailed examination of their economic and political lives is Fred A. Shannon, *The Farmer's Last Frontier* (1945). But once again fiction can enrich your feeling for the times, so consider Ole Rolvaag, *Giants in the Earth* (1927), a moving story of pioneering hardships. Reinforcing Rolvaag's picture is a memoir by a boy who grew up on a prairie farm, Hamlin Garland, *A Son of the Middle Border* (1962). A cheerier view, in a children's classic, is Laura Ingalls Wilder, *The Little House on the Prairie* (1941), good-natured, but not false to the facts.

# Thought provokers

*By 1898, when a new war with Spain occupied the nation's attention, the Civil War's passions had largely burned out. In fact, a former Confederate general named Joseph Wheeler accepted a commission in the U.S. army and fought gallantly for the Stars and Stripes against which he had battled in the 1860s. (There is a legend, however, that when a Spanish force retreated before him, he absentmindedly shouted, "Hurrah, boys, we've got the damn Yankees on the run.")*

*If the goals of the war other than the preservation of the Union were considered, the process of forgiving and forgetting was possible only because they were buried. Slavery was gone. But American blacks remained at the bottom of the Southern economic heap, with rare exceptions. They were segregated by law, banned from the ballot box by threat, and forgotten by both political parties in the North.*

*Moreover, Lincoln had mobilized Americans against the slaveholding "aristocracy" by claiming that the true meaning of free soil was equality of opportunity. The battle cry of 1860 Republicanism was that unsettled territory must not be carved into plantations but kept open for every person to have a fair chance to get ahead. Yet in the 1890s huge corporations loomed over the national scene, small farmers were in dire trouble, and laboring men and women suffered from exploitation and from the knowledge that they would always work for hire.*

*If the war had not "worked" as a factor in changing American life for the better, then the people who fought it did not understand the limits of their power. Or else they misunderstood their own underlying motives. It is to questions such as these that you may now wish to address yourselves.*

*For example, were Southerners correct in actually seeing themselves as a separate people exploited by "outsiders"? How do you now evaluate a favorite Southern argument that they were in the position of the colonies in the 1770s with the North playing the part of London? Does the comparison hold? Was Northern economic policy like mercantilism? Was the South as helplessly exploited economically as the colonies? Were the political situations of the Southern states and the colonies the same?*

*We saw that many Northerners thought of the slaveowners as being part of a conspiracy. One element in that plot, they believed, was the drive to take all of Mexico. From what you have read in Chapters 7 and 8, however, do you see the Mexican War as anything that required plotting? Or as an outgrowth of certain basic American drives? Was it any more Southern in inspiration than Western or even Northern? And what does your answer suggest to you about the validity of conspiracy theories in general?*

*And if the real key to the Civil War was the failure of institutions such as the political parties or the courts to hold the Union together, why did some break down and others work? That is, was not the spread of abolitionism a proof that the national exchange of ideas through newspapers and improved communications was successful? Was not the winning over of church bodies to a sense of Christian duty toward the downtrodden proof that the church was actually a living institution in touch with realities? Or is the function of a church to unite believers by ignoring social issues? In any case, can you compare the performances of the Supreme Court, the Congress, the popular press, the churches, and the parties and say that they all failed to do "their jobs" in exactly the same way? Review the record of each and see what the evidence suggests.*

*In regard to Reconstruction, one obvious question to raise is why the abolitionists, having fought so hard for the Thirteenth and Fourteenth Amendments, did not try very hard to enforce them after 1877. But more than that, you may want to look at underlying social attitudes that shaped Reconstruction policy. For example, why was there no move to do what some Radicals suggested, that is, to break up the plantations and give small plots to the freed blacks? Was it because of racial feelings only? Or did it have to do with feelings about property in general? Was there any time in American history when there had been heavy seizures of property and its redistribution? (As a hint to research, look at what happened to Tory estates after the Revolution, and ask why the same thing did not happen after the Civil War.)*

*And did the carpetbaggers and scalawags have anything in common besides the fact of their being newcomers to power? What prevented them from staying on top of the heap? Were their objectives the same? And on the whole question of objectives, what do you think is the connection between the ending of Reconstruction and the rush of economic development described in Chapter 14?*

*Finally, what gains did the blacks manage to keep after 1877? Why could whites in the South accept the end of slavery but not the end of white supremacy? Did it reflect a change in their thoughts about modernization of the economy and about how it might help them? What did the efforts to evade the Reconstruction laws of racial fairness do to the Southerners' traditional conservatism and respect for law? And looking at the black leaders in Reconstruction, which black institutions seemed most likely to produce black men and women who would lead their race upward after 1877?*

*With regard to the economic material in the final chapter of Part Four, one of the interesting facts about a modern social and economic order is how tightly woven its parts are and how growth or decline in one area is felt in many others. What other kinds of economic growth did the railroads stimulate? What raw materials and resources did they require? What kinds of investment and invention did they encourage? What made them the key industry in modernization? One handy trick of economic analysis is to look at certain indicators of economic performance to judge the overall health of an economy. Why was the railroad such an indicator?*

*And, in terms of social history, earlier chapters have shown us how old mercantile families kept and used their power. Likewise, we saw how the plantation lords got and held theirs. How did the cattle barons and mining millionaires compare with these earlier moneyed "aristocracies"? Think of areas such as interest in the rest of the world, responsibility for their workers, and concern for preserving the monuments of the past and the natural resources needed by the future. Did big-time industrialism and the quick conquest of the frontier create a whole new kind of social outlook and class? And if so, how did that change the political order? Were the financiers who later moved into the western picture comparable to any of the aforementioned groups?*

*And, finally, speaking of politics, where do you think the center of gravity of the political parties came to rest by the 1890s? Here is something for you to study: The first six presidents came from Massachusetts or Virginia. Of the next ten, two were from Tennessee, one from Illinois; two were generals who made reputations in Indiana and in Mexico; one was a Virginian; and four were from the Pennsylvania-New York-New England region. Try to account for this. Then take the presidents from 1868 through 1896, find out where they came from, and explain why none were from the Deep South or the Far West, despite the economic importance of gold, wheat, cattle, and cotton. What does your study tell you about the centers of population and political financing and how they are connected to economic growth? What sections contributed resources to the boom? And what section controlled it? Answering such questions makes you a student of large-scale political and economic movements and their interactions.*

# part five:

# The Machine Age

*With fireworks, speeches, parades, band concerts, and quantities of bad poetry written for the occasion, the United States celebrated the hundredth anniversary of independence in* 1876. *In the thirty-five years after that—a period selected simply because it is so brief—the country rushed, along with the rest of the world, into a complex modern era. The speed of change was breathtaking. In that short span of years these are a few of the things that happened: The use of electricity as a power source, petroleum products as fuels, and steel as a basic building material became common. Inventions either introduced or developed more fully during this period included the telephone, electric lighting and railways, photography, moving pictures, sound recordings, the radio, the automobile, the airplane, and the X-ray—and also the machine gun, TNT, ironclad warships, and the submarine. The time to travel around the world was reduced to a few weeks, and to cross the Atlantic, to a few days. Millions of Europeans and Asians left their homelands in search of jobs; and about* 13 *million of them came to the United States. Ideas like evolution, socialism, psychoanalysis, trade unionism, and women's rights were discussed. Almost every "rule" in the arts—harmony in music, rhyme in poetry, imitation of reality in painting—was successfully broken.*

*How did the men and women who lived through this whirlwind of change cope with its impact on their lives? We touched on that problem in the third part of this book, dealing with the first outburst of American growth. Now we will look at it again, on a larger scale. How did turn-of-the-century Americans, who like all other humans were creatures of habit and custom, adjust to the shocks of having customs become outdated almost overnight in area after area of life?*

*The opening chapter of this part, Chapter* 15, *will examine a particular set of inventions, namely, the skyscraper, the typewriter and telephone, the cheap camera, and the automobile. Each has often been discussed in terms of its economic impact. But what of its effect on behavior? These inventions changed the looks of cities and the feelings of city dwellers about the importance of various parts of their urban environment. How? They also changed the nature of work and gave it new meanings, while opening the world of business to women. How did that begin to dissolve certain hard-and-fast beliefs about the "proper" life-style of each sex? The camera and the automobile revolutionized patterns of leisure, broke down boundaries between country and city, and allowed individuals to sample a wider variety of surroundings without leaving their homes permanently. What did that do to ideas about the wisdom of local authorities, the value of work, or the advantages of rural rather than urban life? And what was the overall impact of so many inventions on people's views of the future toward which they were heading? Did they find it threatening or promising? In their control or out of it? Something to work for or just to wait for?*

*Chapter* 16 *deals with one particular aspect of modern life, the great metropolis. Early in the book, we looked at some European settlers' efforts to create communities in the wilderness. We also studied model communities in Chapter 10. Here we will look at what became of urban communities that were as populous as entire states. How did it become physically possible to deal with the physical requirements—food, heat, light, water, sewage disposal—of one-half million people living in a few square miles? How was the power of the community gathered and used for agreed-on ends? Once, a "fellow townsman" was someone known by face and family history. Neighbors were as members of a family. We saw, in fact, how the Puritan village was set up to create a political imitation of the congregation of religious worshipers. But how did a town work when it contained hundreds of mini-nations, separate congregations, families who would spend a lifetime, sometimes, not even knowing people who lived a few blocks away? What were the special devices, good and bad, that furnished unity and leadership to such hive-like towns?*

*The final two chapters of this part present another particular dilemma of modern life, namely, the getting and using of power, from two different angles. In theory the American political system distributed power reasonably among all elements of the population. But economic and cultural facts of life do not always agree with political theories. The industrial worker and the Southern black were burdened with mighty handicaps. For different reasons, simple political remedies were unusable or unworkable. And the American woman was not only barred from political activity but hobbled by custom as well. These three "victims of disadvantage" had very different problems but were linked by one common need: to find ways to change their conditions for the better. How did they go about that? The specific stories of three "underdog" leaders are used to illustrate some general problems of peaceful change in modern society.*

*And there was also the question of the state and the economy. In the modern world the great corporations that controlled the machinery of industry came to be little "states" in themselves. Thousands depended on them for a livelihood. Whole communities and classes could be helped or damaged by decisions that boards of directors made, decisions that affected the cost of living, the chances of employment or of business success, and, therefore, the root elements of life itself. How could such enormous centers of economic decision making be brought under the democratic control of the voters, without destroying the system of private management of business? How could giant concerns be made efficient and responsible, successful and fair? And how, in an economy of giant organizations that made possible mass production and nationwide distribution of cheap goods, were the doors of opportunity to be kept open for new business leaders to emerge?*

*All of these chapters, in short, try to show how the American people attempted to shape their ways of life, thought, and political operation to the age of crowds, speed, and abundant energy. These are still living questions, though the men and women who faced them in their modern form are now passed away. Issues outlive people, which is one link between past and present, and another reason to dig into history.*

# chapter 15
# Invention and men's minds

In 1876 the nation celebrated its first hundred years of independence with a mammoth fair in Philadelphia. Among many other poets, Walt Whitman composed some lines inspired by the marvels of invention on display. These included steam engines, special high-speed printing presses, sewing machines, an early model of the telephone, the typewriter, a great many devices to help farmers to sow and reap, and hundreds of machines that could automatically and swiftly stamp, grind, cut, smooth, twist, bend, and mold metal, glass, wood, leather, and other materials into objects of use and beauty.

"This, this and these, America, shall be *your* pyramids and obelisks," Whitman sang. And he went on to hymn: "These triumphs of our time, the Atlantic's delicate cable, the Pacific railroad, the Suez Canal, the Brooklyn Bridge, this earth all spann'd with iron rails, with lines of steamship threading every sea." All these marvels, he believed, should inspire modern poets to forget the traditional subjects of rhyme and write heroic verses about industry.

A quarter of a century later a *New York Times* editorial tried to sum up the achievements of the passing nineteenth century. It had been "marked by greater progress," the newspaper declared, "in all that pertains to the material well-being and enlightenment of mankind than all the previous history of the race; and the political, social and moral advancement has been hardly less striking."

### *A Love Affair with Technology*

In these two quotations the spirit of the period following the Civil War shines like a lamp illuminating social history. Invention was linked to a rebirth of art in Whitman's mind. It was responsible for humanity's political and social advancement according to the *Times* editor. America, like other "advanced" nations, rushed joyously into the twentieth century. Her people were convinced that technological achievement was a guarantee that all earthly life was about to be changed for the better.

Praise of invention colored all the patterns of national thinking. Not only did those who created "works of the mind"—poets, artists, philosophers, and preachers—weigh the impact of scientific and technical breakthroughs. Ordinary people, too, were affected. Progress in applied science affected the whole culture. As we have said before, that is the sum total of all of a people's conscious activities as a group.

Two broad areas of technology's impact on life are immediately evident. In the matter of life-style the key word was "urbanization." Between 1875 and 1915 new devices and improvements on old ones seemed to tread on each others' heels. They included electric lights, street railways, iron and steel bridges, elevators, telephones, and high-rise steel-framed buildings. All of them made it possible to concentrate huge masses of people in a small area, move them back and forth between home and work daily, feed them, light their streets, provide them with water, dispose of their wastes, and keep them warm in winter. The urban revolution, which is still at work gathering the American people into great metropolitan centers, rested directly on the successes of technology. And in those cities, despite some obvious disadvantages of crowding, most residents were in better material circumstances than their rural ancestors. They were better fed, better clad, and better housed, with less effort. The discomforts of modern living were not those of scarcity.

### *Social Darwinism: Explaining It All*

A second commonly noticed result of the surge in invention was the birth of a popular outlook to make people feel at home with modernity. Oddly, though the basic sciences underlying the machine age were physics and chemistry, the roots of the philosophy that justified late nineteenth-century progress were found in biology. Darwin's theory of evolution, gaining steadily in popularity after its publication in 1859, seemed to explain it all.

Darwin had argued, from his field observations, that countless species of living things are always being created at random. They are all in competition for food, water, and other vital needs. Life is a struggle for existence. Those best adapted to their environment win that struggle by surviving. Others become extinct. At any given time, all life on the planet is the result of this continuing process of natural selection. Birds, beasts, fishes, and man alike "evolved" from the play of natural forces. Life is forever in flow and development.

Darwin's ideas were adopted almost at once by others to explain the workings of human society as well. Writers in Britain and the United States took the constant movement implied in Darwin's biology and gave it a direction and a goal. They declared that societies evolved from the simple to the complex, from "backward" to "advanced," from "lower" levels of organization and intelligence to "higher." Individual institutions within society, such as governments and churches, followed identical laws of growth. At any given time, therefore, a country's characteristic patterns represented survivals from an earlier past, in which cruder ways of behavior had been tried and discarded. And all the world was moving, though at an uneven pace, toward higher stages of development.

Christian churches resisted Darwinism at first. It seemed to clash with the idea that the world and its creatures had not changed ever since God made them all in a week. But most American denominations managed, after a while, to swallow evolution. They accepted the biblical account of creation as merely being poetic. After all, a "day" to God might well be a million years to humans. And they now depicted God as the driving force behind evolution, bringing all of His creatures, through an infinite amount of time, to final perfection. By this adaptation, all but a few of the churches avoided a conflict in which they pitted their authority against that of science. They had to, for science, the bringer of new marvels, was too widely respected to be put down by religion any longer.

This casting of social history into an evolutionary mold was known as social Darwinism. In the United States of the 1890s it was a convenient doctrine for justifying almost any argument. Conservatives could warn, for example, that it was wrong to break up great business monopolies, because those monopolies had survived in the struggle for existence amid the beasts of the economic jungle. They were, therefore, results of the workings of natural law, which could not be tampered with. But their opponents could argue back that one sign

---

*CHRONOLOGY*

1859 *Charles Darwin's* Origin of Species *published*
1875 *A practical typewriter invented*
1876 *U.S. centennial*
1888 *George Eastman's Kodak camera put on the market*
1889 *Home Building, Chicago, nation's first skyscraper*
1903 Great Train Robbery, *first feature movie*
1903 *First flight of Wright brothers' airplane*
1908 *Henry Ford introduces Model T car*

of evolutionary advance in society was the replacement of individual, selfish effort by overall planning. Therefore, the government was following the script of evolution in regulating monopolies for the common good. Or, as another example, it was common to defend racism and imperialism by pointing out that nonwhite people were clearly lower on the evolutionary scale than more civilized folk who knew of steam power, ironclad warships, and high explosives. The "backward" races needed the leadership of advanced civilizations. But anti imperialists tried to point out that compassion and nonviolence were the true signs of higher development and that conquest was therefore wrong.

The important thing was that evolution colored almost everyone's thinking. Social Darwinism lent the prestige of the scientific view of the world to a variety of arguments. Pride in the technological revolution forced almost everyone with a cause to plead to find some scientific framework within which to form his case.

Urbanization and social Darwinism, then, are two broad illustrations of how technological change molded society. But how was everyday life touched by the era? In an earlier chapter we looked at the social impact of invention on the New England family, on workers, and on businessmen. Now we will do so again for a later period. What effect did late nineteenth- and early twentieth-century invention have on how people saw themselves and dealt with each other? Toward the end of this book we will consider, for a third time, the effect of invention on an era—our own. At that time we will note that the onrush of the jet, the computer, TV, the nuclear bomb, and the birth-control pill brought anxieties and problems that seem to cloud the future. But between 1880 and 1920 the emergence or development of the skyscraper, the crack express train, the transoceanic cable, the ironclad ship, and the first primitive automobiles, airplanes, and squeaking radio sets seemed full of bright promise. A "revolution" caused by an outburst of invention may have one effect at one place and time and quite another effect in a different setting.

## *New Styles in Shelter and Their Meaning*

Let us look first at the field of building. In the mid-1880s two inventions changed the appearance of American cities. One was steel framing, which made it possible to raise buildings to hitherto unreachable heights. Formerly, the masonry walls of large structures carried all the weight. The higher they stood, the thicker they had to be at the bottom to compensate for the added load. But the weight of a steel-framed building is distributed evenly through strong, elastic, and relatively light girders. The sky, almost literally, was the limit. The other invention that moved office-dwelling humanity upward was the elevator, patented shortly before 1890.

Now it was possible for tall buildings to accept large numbers of office workers without spreading out over expensive downtown real estate. The first skyscraper is often said to have been the Home Insurance Building, raised in Chicago in 1885, to a height of ten stories. Others soon followed in a race to be tallest that is not yet ended. New York's Flatiron Building of 1902 was the wonder of the day, with 22 stories. The Chrysler Building, completed in the 1920s, had 77. In 1931 the Empire State Building, at 102 stories high, took the title. Forty years later it was topped by Chicago's Sears Tower and the twin 110-story towers of New York's World Trade Center.

What the skyscraper did was to give the downtown centers of big cities a special look. In every major urban center a business district cluster of office buildings, 10 to 30 or more stories high, reared against the skyline. This sharpened the distinction among the different areas of the city. Tall apartment houses are a recent development, and until very modern times residential neighborhoods had a low profile. So did factory districts, whose assembly lines did not fit easily into tall structures. So the skyscraper was used almost exclusively for offices. This meant that a division among the functions of living literally became visible. There were the places where people lived and where things were made. And there were the places where the papers were shuffled, the decisions made, and the money collected that enabled it all to happen. Those last places had the soaring spires. They were the showplaces of a commercial civilization, as cathedrals were monuments of medieval Christianity.

Skyscrapers emphasized the class advantages of white-collar over blue-collar workers. The business center was the best-maintained part of a city. Fashionable shops, theaters, and restaurants tended to be clustered near it. The residences of the rich were ornate and impressive, too. But usually they were on avenues out of the reach of busy throngs, like Chicago's Lake Shore Drive or New York's upper Fifth Avenue to give privacy to the owners of wealth. The cloud-touching downtown areas, however, were intentionally where the densest crowds gathered.

Another illustration of technology's effect on how people lived is seen in the fullness of American Victorian furnishings. In the age when Grant was president, the widespread use of the jigsaw made it possible to cut facing and exterior lumber in fancy shapes. So the homes of well-off Americans who wanted to be up with the times abounded in curly eaves, ornamented cornices, pierced balustrades, and porch rails, gates, fences, bays, and spires with borders of hearts, loops, leaves, and whatever else the architect's imagination could suggest. The house was a hymn to the power of mechanical woodcutting.

Inside, dutiful homemakers filled every available inch of space. Rugs covered every speck of floor, pictures and mirrors crowded each papered wall, ottomans, sofas and side chairs, tables, desks, buffets, sidebays, and whatnot shelves, all plush and varnished, gleamed in lamplight when the heavy drapes were closed, as they usually were. Everywhere stood figurines of china and plaster, and vases, jars, lamps, trays, and bowls covered with designs. Naturally, the women who ruled these surroundings wore many layers of clothing, flaunting ribbons, bows, and bustles.

What the furniture and the clothing both were saying was that relatively inexpensive mass-produced goods were largely available. Society could show off its mechanical prowess and enjoy a feast of objects. The home showed the same pride in the machine age that was behind the popularity of evolutionary thought.

Later on, architects and decorators could think in simpler terms or aim for cleaner lines and simpler statements of industrial power. A stainless steel knife, after all, is as much a credit to the machine that made it as a mass-produced wrought-iron gate full of metallic vines and berries. But until the end of the nineteenth century, heaviness continued to be the theme. Government buildings were often in the so-called neo-Renaissance style, best shown in the new Library of Congress building built in Washington in the 1890s. It was and is overpowering—with great columns, high-vaulted ceilings, inlaid floors, and other exuberant proofs that Americans could take the models of Greece and Rome or of Florence and Paris and copy them on an immensely grander scale. Imitation of old models was very plain in the buildings of the Chicago World's Fair of 1893. Everything was there, from Japanese pagodas to Venetian palaces. In wood, stone, steel, and glass architects were joining in Walt Whitman's boast that democratic, machine-age human beings could beat anything done before.

As an exercise, you may wish to look at pictures of modern cities and fairs and discuss what they show about our present-day feelings toward the machine age.

### *Of Telephones, Typewriters, and Women*

Let us choose some examples, now, from the field of communications. The modern typewriter was patented by Christopher L. Sholes in 1868. It was a modest-looking machine, but its results were to be enormously powerful. The same could be said of the telephone. Both machines, first of all, greatly eased the work of offices. No longer was it necessary to laboriously handwrite business communications. Now they could be swiftly typed, in many copies, or by-passed altogether by telephone calls. This speeding-up process was indispensable in helping businessmen to operate on the great scale of the post-1865 industrial boom.

But in addition, soon after their introduction, typewriters began to be "manned" by feminine hands. In the 1880s most private secretaries were still men. But by the time of World War I the office girl pounding her keys was as much of a fixture as desks and file cabinets. Likewise, telephone switchboards were at first run by men. Yet soon after 1900, when a subscriber rang and asked for "Central" to connect him with a number, it was a female voice that would answer. Earlier we saw how the first textile factories brought Yankee farm girls out of their isolation and into the boarding houses and milltowns. Later, factory work became less of an opportunity and more of a necessary drudgery. Then the first female operatives were replaced by lower-class women, who had to be less choosy about their jobs.

In a sense, office work repeated the pattern. It opened doors of mobility to girls who had enough education to avoid factory labor, but not enough to aspire to the few professions open to late nineteenth-century women, such as nursing. Work at a telephone switchboard or at a typewriter was in the zone between unskilled and highly skilled labor, respectable and within reach. Unmarried girls continued to escape from dependence into jobs. They moved out of the circle of expectations that limited them entirely to cookery and childbearing, thanks to a second phase of the onset of modernity. The first industrial revolution made it possible for women, at machines, to take part in the manufacturing process. The second, still in progress, began to reduce the number of workers at production machines and increase the number handling the output of the machines. Each year, to this day, the number of employees in the sales, service, and managerial fields grows larger, and the number of those in manufacturing shrinks. As that change takes place, the number of jobs that women can fill grows steadily larger.

Modern advocates of women's liberation resent women's being frozen into clerical and secretarial jobs. They argue that the time has now come to think of women in business as executives and engineers as well as stenographers. But in the early 1900s, routine office jobs, like the factory jobs in the Lowell textile plants, were an upward step.

There were still other results of the "office revolution" symbolized by the typewriter and the girl who plied its keys. For one thing, the involvement of women in the business system gave them a loyalty to its ways that strengthened its general acceptance in the United States.

In addition, the educational system felt the impact of the steady demand for an enlarged supply of clerks, bookkeepers, stenographers, filing and billing clerks, and low-level managers who could handle correspondence and make out orders. Commercial courses became more popular in the high schools. The high-school population itself rose steadily in the half century from 1900, when only 6.4 percent of the population 17 years old and over had completed twelve years of education, to 1950, when the comparable figure was 59 percent. Great corporations needed small armies of employees whose job was to keep inventories, orders, plans, and records under control, and American society through its public schools rose to answer the need. This was one more example of how in a business-oriented culture, technical, commercial, and social developments were linked.



*Prelude to the Age of the Image: Kodak*

Let us consider another invention or cluster of inventions that literally altered people's images of themselves. A giant step in photography was undertaken with the introduction of the Kodak camera, first patented and marketed by Rochester industrialist George Eastman in the 1880s. Cameras had been in existence since the 1840s. They were large, bulky affairs, needing tripods, a portable darkroom, and bottles of chemicals to develop immediately the wet glass plates on which they recorded what their lenses saw. Eastman, a serious, ambitious young bachelor gave up a good job as a bank clerk in order to spend years of experimenting (some of it in his mother's kitchen) to perfect a simpler system. First, he devised a way of making dry plates, which did not require instant development. Then, after becoming a successful plate manufacturer, he put a research staff to work on a roll film that could be contained entirely within the camera. His success allowed him to market a boxlike piece of photographic apparatus that took no special skill or strength to use. Eastman invented the name Kodak, because it was easy to remember, though it had no meaning in any language. The owner of a Kodak camera had only to point it at his subject and snap. He wound a crank to advance the film. When it was all exposed, he sent the entire camera to Rochester and got it back, freshly loaded. Eastman's sublimely simple advertising phrase was: "You Press the Button: We Do the Rest."

Eastman was a genius at the modern technique of simplifying the product, lowering its price, advertising it widely, and getting it into the widest possible number of hands. By the time of World War I he was marketing a "Brownie" for $2. The Eastman Kodak Company still continues to dominate the field of popular photography. What did its saga of business triumph mean?

For one thing, it increased people's self-awareness. In recording their own family histories, vacations, celebrations, and the like, they stood outside of themselves, in a sense. They became observers of their own lives as well as actors in them. The beginning of modern concern with how we function as human beings—the age of analysis and anxiety, so to speak—owes something to this process. There is a tendency to stop taking inherited patterns for granted when we step back and deliberately watch ourselves playing them out.

Secondly, the most common popular use of the camera quickly became the recording of holidays and trips. Photography was one of the earliest industries devoted to helping Americans fill up their leisure time. Leisure itself, for everyone, was a modern development. An earlier, hard-working nation had

THE
KODAK CAMERA
"YOU
PRESS
THE
BUTTON
WE
DO THE
REST."
AN APPROPRIATE WEDDING PRESENT
THE EASTMAN Co
·ROCHESTER·N·Y·

little time to invest in play, unless the play was also productive, such as corn husking or a cabin raising, when jokes and drinking helped people along in the sharing of a chore. Even horse racing was a way of showing off the merits of animals that were always being bought or traded. It was serious business in a day when horsepower was not something under a hood. But simply looking for fun in hours left over after a "job" (itself a very different pattern from the steady, intertwined round of work and living on a farm) was simply for the "idle rich."

But in the twentieth century more middle-class Americans would travel to be amused. They would watch professional athletes play or actors perform. They would themselves play croquet or pitch horseshoes and would preserve the memories in their albums of snapshots. As time went on, they would, even while praising the "work ethic," demand shorter hours and longer vacations as part of their working conditions. And their standard of living would require more grown-up toys like cameras!

Eastman's success also had a complicated effect upon democratic social styles. Though the camera could be a means of expression for the serious artist and a useful tool for the scientific observer, when it became cheap, it also became the plaything of millions. And, like all other mass-produced products, the popular camera both increased and cut down individuality. The proud owner of a Kodak was his *own* private portrait artist, his *own* picture historian. He saw himself preserved, in all his uniqueness, in a way that had never been possible to him before. On the other hand, he was achieving this advance in exactly the same fashion as millions around him. At a scenic place like Niagara Falls, one could see tourists from every state and every social class all busily snapping the same views with the same camera. It was a kind of lock step to identity.

Another impact of the dawning age of photography was felt when it went beyond the single shot taken by an amateur and into the areas of news and entertainment. During the period from 1860 to 1920, a number of striking improvements were made in the technology of printing newspapers and magazines. Among them were techniques for transmitting and printing news photos. Rare and expensive at first, they gradually became more common. By the time of World War I every big-town newspaper usually had at least one photo on its lead pages. In 1919 a new paper was born, the *New York Daily News.* It carried so many photos that it called itself "New York's picture newspaper." Within a few years it had many imitators in other cities. In 1936, to carry the story forward, Henry R. Luce brought out the first issue of *Life.* This magazine consisted almost exclusively of pictures, and so pioneered what Luce called photojournalism.

Meanwhile, another kind of pictorial revolution was going on. Eastman received a request in the 1880s from the inventor Thomas A. Edison. Edison was working on a camera that would automatically open and close its shutter at high speed to take a series of shots separated by only fractions of a second. When printed and projected back rapidly, these "moving pictures" gave the illusion of continuous action. Edison needed a film tough enough to be whirled rapidly on rollers, in the camera, and in the projector. Eastman created it for him, and the first brief, unconnected movie shots of dancers and scenery were shown in New York in 1893. Ten years later, the first feature film, *The Great Train Robbery*, had been made. By 1910, movie houses known as "nickelodeons," from the cost of admission, were a standard feature of urban life. Hollywood was soon flourishing as a movie capital. Then came the introduction of sound in 1927. "Newsreels" presented the "real" (or "reel") world in all its true drama, and then the audience settled back to ninety minutes of celluloid dreams.

Television, though experimented with in the 1920s and 1930s, did not reach the public until after World War II. Yet television simply married the camera to the electron gun in order to open an entire new universe of instantaneous transmission of images. The quick spread of the medium was possible because there was a mass audience already conditioned to seeing the world in pictures by sixty years of exposure to photos and the movies. There is a kind of unbroken flow from the first photograph in 1839, through the crude Kodak of the eighties, and then through the movies to the age of the tube.

We will look at the impact of television later. But even before its arrival, news photos, newsreels, and movies had a powerful leverage in changing American life. They went far toward breaking the limitations of local cultures on people. They brought the great world beyond the horizon, of which country boys and girls only dreamed, to life. One unfolding development in national life in the twentieth century was the end of America's supposed isolation from the world. Many economic and political factors created that change. But one cultural force was almost certainly the increased familiarity of almost every American, through pictures, with the events and the people of Europe, Africa, Latin America, and Asia. The history of those areas became a drama played out before American audiences, who formed opinions on the merits of the various villains, heroes, and victims. This became important psychological preparation for Americans to play a part of their own.

Photojournalism, and especially movies, also had a dissolving effect on "old-fashioned" manners and morals. Between 1910 and 1945, "going to the pictures" became a form of entertainment that involved almost every American. Millions saw as many as three a week. The ways of eating, dressing, playing, and behaving that the films portrayed inspired nationwide imitation. Boys and girls in prairie towns, urban slums, and mountain mining hollows—all picked up the mannerisms of their heroes and heroines. Nationally advertised products

*The movies, made possible by combining Eastman and Edison inventions, became the projected fantasies of entire generations of Americans. From Hollywood's "dream factory" emerged figures as real and evocative as any history book heroes—among them, the unforgettable Count Dracula, the polished vampire (America's idea of Europe?), played by Hungarian-born Bela Lugosi.*

enjoyed sales boosts when endorsed as favorites of the stars. Main Street furniture stores and dress shops stocked the styles shown in the most recent hits.

As this nationalization of behavior went on, the force of local custom and tradition was weakened. The movies (and television after 1950) were not the only factor involved. Swift transportation and quick distribution of identically packaged goods through national chains of stores were also doing their bit for uniformity. The mass production of images, however, was an especially strong magnet in turning youth away from the conventional wisdom of village elders such as the judge, the school principal, and the preacher. Once, the ambitious youngsters of a town ran away to the frontier or the city or the sea to get broadened outlooks and new ideas. But the communications revolution of which photojournalism was a part brought the frontier, the city, and foreign ports to the stay-at-homes, too.

## *A Nation on Wheels*

Let us finally glance at the invention that had perhaps the greatest long-range impact on America, the automobile. It has been customary to split the story of this invention off from the general history of transportation improvements since 1815 and treat it as a new page. But this is an artificial separation, caused by a tendency to shift mental gears at the appearance of a new century.

Actually, a study of transportation in the fifty-year period from 1876 to 1926 shows an unbroken process of knitting the nation together. The post-1865 surge of railroad building, lasting until 1910, made the West a working part of the national economy. Texas beef and Kansas wheat made hamburger sandwiches in Los Angeles and Boston. The railroad boom also made small towns satellites of the large urban centers. It became increasingly common to take a one- or two-hour train trip to the nearest big city to get legal advice or an operation or simply to shop.

Then, in the 1880s, came electric streetcars, first successfully tried in Richmond, Virginia. They tied together city neighborhoods in the way that steam railroads had joined cities and states. Locomotives had not worked for in-city transportation, due to their size, noise, and fire hazards. But the electric streetcars were perfect for short runs on narrow, curving, or hilly streets. They made it possible for cities to grow outward. "Streetcar suburbs" sprang into existence as families sought space, light, and air by fleeing the factory districts on the trolley cars. By 1920 or so, in the nation's biggest cities, streetcars were supplemented by elevated and subway lines, new landmarks on the urban map.

Against these earlier developments, the automobile can be seen simply as a final step in a process that saw the power of steam, then of electricity, and finally of gasoline applied to moving people and goods quickly from place to place. The "horseless carriage" first appeared in the United States in 1893. What it quickly did was to give every family its own train or streetcar. It was a personal share of an improved transportation network. On a self-chosen schedule, drivers could travel to work, shopping, or, on weekends, several hundred miles away from home to see what there was to be seen.

The rapid popularization of autos required a production revolution. The chief "radical" of that revolution was Henry Ford, who was to the car what Eastman was to the camera. Born on a Michigan farm in 1863 (where he died

*The automobile itself was not only an invention that worked revolutionary changes in the way people lived, worked, played, and thought; but in addition, its assembly line method of manufacture seemed the very essence of machine-age orderliness. Here is an assembly line making Model T cars for Henry Ford, who was, in the popular mind, the representative and master of mechanization.*

almost eighty-four years later), Ford showed an early knack for mechanics. It led him to do what many handy young people were doing in the 1890s, to work on a gasoline-driven "buggy," like those just appearing in Europe. In 1896 he had built a workable model in a shed behind his house in Detroit, where he had gone to work as an engineer for the Edison electric power company. When it was finished, he found that he could not get it out of the shed without knocking down the wall. It was not the first obstacle that he would deal with in that way.

In 1903 Ford found ten partners who would help him raise the capital to found the Ford Motor Company. That was the same year in which the Wright brothers first flew, marking still another transportation breakthrough. (It was two years after the first transatlantic wireless signals were sent.) Ford's cars were neither the first nor the best nor the only ones being looked at by Americans eager for gadgets and movement. But he did have an original and powerful idea.

It was to make the motor car a truly mass-used invention. In 1908 he had his engineering staff help him work out the Model T. It was a starkly plain vehicle, with a four-cylinder engine that could usually be repaired by home-workshop experts using hardware-store parts. It came only in black, had a crank to start it, a top speed of under 50 miles per hour, and very little in the way of class.

Over the years, it changed remarkably little—except to decline steadily in price. But that was the basic point. Ford's goal was to put the Model T into the barnyard or garage of every American. He kept prodding his engineers to cut expenses and simplify procedures. And he kept plowing the company's profits back into enlarged facilities, which enabled ever more massive production at a lower per-unit cost. By 1926, 15 million "Tin Lizzies" had been made.

But they were not the only cars on the road. The success of Model T also proved its undoing. Other companies, too, had begun to mass-produce cars. Moreover, they began to change their products to suit different markets. Luxury cars, family sedans, and sporty models began to roll off the assembly lines of General Motors and other Ford rivals. As the populace became used to the automobile, they were tempted by cars that changed looks each year, cars in color, cars with electric starters and other costly "optionals," cars that were not merely transportation but also signs of status.

Ford, a stubborn man, was trying to create an automobile as practical and earthy as his vision of the American past. He clung to his insistence on concentrating on the Model T. But in 1927 he had to give in, and Ford factories began to diversify production. But he had already played a key part in making auto ownership a basic fact of life for almost every American family.

### *Motion and Mental States*

What did the automobile do to American social patterns as well as to the country's economic life? In the first place, the coming of the automobile hastened the dispersion to suburbia. As we shall see later, that became one of the most significant developments of twentieth-century America.

In the second, it reinforced the revolution in manners and morals. Just as the communications revolution broke down traditional authority, so the power of people to whisk themselves quickly from place to place further weakened the role of custom in controlling behavior. This was particularly true for the young. In the 1920s, when automobiles grew quite common, boys and girls no longer "courted" in the parlor under watchful parents' eyes. Instead, they took to the road and freedom.

Thirdly, the automobile helped expedite the assault on natural resources, which we saw was part of the American frontier from earliest days. Huge quantities of steel, rubber, glass, and other materials went into the millions of cars made yearly. The auto industry became the backbone of the economy. But the depletion of reserves, especially of the oil that produced the voraciously used gasoline, went on relentlessly. And another disappearing resource turned out to be pure air, which was relentlessly fouled by eternally active exhaust pipes.

The automobile also spawned the highways. They seemed at first to improve the landscape by replacing rutted muddy lanes with neat concrete ribbons. And they helped to end the isolation of the farmers. But they too, were heavy users of resources, including open, green space.

Finally, the auto changed American thrift patterns. It quickly became a family's second most expensive possession, next to the home. As a result, installment buying became for most the only possible way to get an automobile. This meant that the old middle-class ideal of saving for the future, of not spending money on personal luxuries, of investing it instead in productive uses, took a beating. Respectable families came to live in a constant state of indebtedness for their auto, paying off one, and immediately buying another. As the pattern spread to other purchases, Americans became dependent for their continued prosperity on the hope of endless growth, better-paying tomorrows.

Thus, if we look over the entire period from 1876 to 1926, it is clear that the impact of invention on the lives and thought of ordinary Americans went far beyond formal intellectual statements like social Darwinism. Invention reached into the very marrow of contemporary civilization. Many of its fruits were most visible when gathered together in the framework of the city. It is to the city that we must now turn for further lessons in how the present came to be.

---

## *FOR FURTHER READING*

E. C. Kirkland, *Industry Comes of Age* (1961) is a closely-knit and somewhat hard to read work, but is absolutely indispensable for the facts on industry's forward leap after the Civil War. A more general survey of invention and how it affected society is John A. Garraty, *The New Commonwealth* (1968). An older work that covers the same ground from different angles is Allan Nevins, *The Emergence of Modern America* (1927).

The best book describing the way thinkers wedded science and God to industrialism is Richard Hofstadter, *Social Darwinism in American Thought* (1944). Lewis Mumford attempts to put the whole question of machinery and behavior into some worldwide historical framework in *Technics and Civilization* (1934). An interesting comparison between the British and American experiences can be found in H. J. Habakkuk, *American and British Technology in the Nineteenth Century* (1962). A recent and lively look at how our machinery sometimes seems to be managing us, instead of the other way around, is Elting E. Morison, *From Know-How to Nowhere* (1975), previously mentioned at the end of Chapter 9.

Specific histories of inventors and inventions are numerous and interesting. The standard biography of the inventor of the "Kodak" is *George Eastman* (1931) by Carl

Ackerman. A history of photography in America by Beaumont Newhall, *History of Photography: 1839 to the Present Day* (1972) is also worth a look. But the impact of photography is best studied through pictures themselves, and a highly interesting collection is Oliver Jensen's *American Album* (1968). The effect of motion pictures is dealt with nicely in Hortense Powdermaker, *Hollywood: The Dream Factory* (1950). And the inventor of movies, records, the electric light, and so many other things, Thomas Edison, is well depicted in a biography simply entitled *Edison* (1959), by Matthew Josephson.

For the origin of the typewriter, see Bruce Bliven, *The Wonderful Writing Machine* (1954). And the saga of the telephone is best told in Robert V. Bruce, *Alexander Graham Bell* (1973). John B. Rae's *The American Automobile* (1965), tells the general auto story, but for a lively look at the superstar of auto making, read Keith Sward, *The Legend of Henry Ford* (1948).

# *chapter* 16

# *Cities as human habitats*

*You are going far away*
*But remember what I say*
*When you are in the city's giddy whirl;*
*From temptations, crimes and follies,*
*Buses, hansom cabs and trolleys,*
*Heaven will protect the working girl!*

Thus, in a popular song of the 1890s, a mother warned her daughter who was off to the urban frontier. The lyrics to music-hall ballads are not the usual raw materials of deep social analysis. Yet these do express one aspect of the nation's wary attitudes toward the metropolis. From the early days of the republic onward, there was a strong belief that only those in close contact with the earth could truly know, taste, and use independence. They predicted that a humanity huddled together in mazes of streets, cut off from the sky, and deafened by the crash of machinery would grow artificial, mannered, and wicked. Jefferson has said that cities added just as much strength to the body politic as sores did to the human body. He had hoped that Americans, so long as they had land to till, would never walk in the urban ways of Europe.

And yet the city has been part of U.S. history from the beginning. Boston, Philadelphia, and Savannah were laid out and inhabited when most of Massachusetts, Pennsylvania, and Georgia existed only as wilderness. In the whole westward movement the city did not, as sometimes thought, come as the last stage in development. In the Mississippi and Missouri valleys, for example, St. Louis (founded in 1764) and New Orleans (1718) were fur-trading, sugar-refining, and shipping centers when the areas all around them were still mainly in Indian hands. Cincinnati and Louisville, both born around the 1790s, were actively dealing in flour, pork, and whiskey long before Ohio and Kentucky were fully settled.

City merchants often "staked" the pioneer farmer to what he needed for his first harsh year of grubbing. City businessmen put up capital for the roads, bridges, and mills that made rural settlement possible. Naturally, they profited by the investments, but they were creators of the West as much as soldiers, trappers, and explorers.

The cities had their supporters, too. In many a speech they praised the town as the place where learning, opportunity, and the arts flourished as nowhere else. The argument was almost as old as history itself. Jokes about country innocence and clumsiness versus urban sophistication and sinfulness go back to Greece, where poets and playwrights wrote about the Athenians and their bumpkin neighbors, the Boeotians. But two things especially sharpened the debate in the United States late in the nineteenth century. One was that the long existence of the open frontier had given unusual importance to the pioneer farmer and his claim to be the best example of American ideals. The other was that after midcentury, the American city grew with almost terrifying speed. Unlike other industrializing nations, the United States had a strong tradition of identifying its best characteristics with rural ways. But once it started the headlong rush toward metropolitan culture, it went faster than most.

### *The Urban Portrait: From What Angle?*

There are a number of ways to deal with the urban history of the period from approximately 1890 to 1920. A conventional method is to count noses and record the steadily swelling mass of Americans whom the census takers found to be living in places of over 50,000 or 100,000 or 500,000 or 1 million inhabitants.

---

*CHRONOLOGY*

1869 *Professional baseball begins in Cincinnati*
1893 *World's "Columbian Exposition," Chicago*
1898 *Five boroughs combined into New York City*
1901 *Lincoln Steffens' exposé of municipal corruption*
1904 *Interborough Rapid Transit (IRT) Company subway, New York City*

Such figures can be dramatic. When Lincoln was elected president, only 1 American in 5 lived in a place with more than 2500 people. Sixty years afterward, it was every second American; 110 years later, approximately 1 American in 3 lived in "a metropolitan area" with 1000 times that population—over 2.5 million.

Another way to dramatize municipal growth would be to record the steady annexation of independent little towns by their giant neighbors. There is a lively story of community politics in how the costs and benefits were divided when small school systems, water works, police departments, and other urban services were absorbed into gigantic ones.

Still another approach is to describe how city streets gradually were changed by the coming of power lines and transit systems and to examine the men who authorized them, built them, and raised money for them. This approach leads to the historical area where technology, economics, and politics meet and mingle.

Each of these ways of studying urban growth is useful. But we will choose here to focus on some of the problems of human community as they were affected by urban growth. We have talked about seventeenth-century plantations and nineteenth-century communes. We have looked at nation-making in the 1780s and nation-splitting in the 1860s. Our focus has always been on the problems of human interaction. We can see them through another lens if we concentrate on a few special areas of urban history.

### *Close-up Shots: Neighborhoods, Politicians, and Monuments*

We can learn much, for example, from a study of neighborhoods and neighborhood institutions. For most city dwellers the few square blocks surrounding their homes or apartments were the equivalent of the small towns they had left. Their churches, stores, restaurants, and saloons were often psychological first-aid centers. They served as message centers, marriage and employment bureaus, and clubs. The texture of a city's life depended on the variety and style of its neighborhoods. And it changed as neighborhoods were created or wiped out by immigration, hard times, or new construction. Urban historians have usually taken the bird's-eye view of a city, looking at it as a complete beehive. But they have ignored the richness of life in each separate cell where the honey of neighborliness was stored.

Another way to weigh the impact of urban growth on human behavior is to examine shifting patterns of civic leadership. What kinds of "elites" emerged as mud streets gave way to cobbles, then to asphalt, while the skyline thrust itself higher against the clouds? Who controlled the direction of city growth, and how? Was there more than one "ruling class"? Did power belong to those who owned the shipping lines or factories or banks on which a city's economic foundations were laid? Or to those who furnished the critical services of lighting and transportation? Were the owners of those services from the same background as the businessmen whose ventures had built up the city? And what of another top-drawer group, the technicians who ran the power plants, kept the drinking water pure, supervised schools and hospitals, or managed the complex bookkeeping of big-time taxation and spending? What kind of power did they enjoy? And where did they stand on the ladder of influence and respect?

Another fresh angle of vision looks at urban politics from the viewpoint of the politician as an arranger of deals among various groups or subcommunities within city boundaries. "Boss rule" was an unhealthy growth in some respects. But it also filled some needs. True, the bribes and kickbacks that political machines took in return for favors came out of taxpayers' pockets in one way or another. And machines also regularly broke election laws and got away with it thanks to their control of judges and district attorneys, creating the dangerous situation of having some powerful officials operating outside the law.

Yet the machine workers knew the demands of all of a city's districts, high and low. And machine power made joint action possible for wards and precincts of widely differing ethnic and economic backgrounds. In the formal setting of a city council or a board of aldermen, for instance, delegates from different districts might be deadlocked until word from the boss pulled them together. The machine speeded up work on important projects too. It slipped contractors through the nets and mazes of official inspection and review (for a price, naturally) in a way that saved many months of waiting. Finally, the machine wooed votes by putting improvements in populous but poor neighborhoods that respectable upper-class politicians often neglected.

Without romanticizing the various bosses of the nation's city halls, it is still safe to say that they exercised a communal function, worth observing. As cities grew bigger, face-to-face contact of elected leaders and plain citizens was lost. Old-fashioned government by town meeting or by informal consensus became impossible. New institutions had to be "invented" both by law and habit to help the many subcultures and pressure groups within the faceless mass of the whole city's population to fit together. To look at a political machine as a means of meshing interests in a big community is another useful way to learn from and about the history of cities.

Finally, what were some of the cultural means of forging a sense of civic unity? People were brought together in stadiums and music halls, libraries, parks, and other recreational and educational settings. One of the effects of such places was to give those who used them a sense of a common stake in their cities. This was especially true of highly visible and attractive buildings raised by city governments. In a metropolis of many neighborhoods there was always a tendency to forget the wholeness of the community. But well-used public places offset this fragmenting pull. They helped people who were squeezed together in great clusters to fight off feelings of being meaningless in the asphalt jungle.

*Urban Villages: New York's Neighborhoods*

Big-city neighborhoods tended to fall, with minor variations, into set patterns. There were showplace areas for the rich; bohemian blocks that were favored by artistic types; solid working- and middle-class home neighborhoods; slums and precincts known for high vice and crime rates; and miniature "foreign" villages where there were high concentrations of immigrants. There were local variations from place to place, but the long-range sociological maps of all major urban places looked alike.

New York City is often used as a model for studying urban growth. Between 1880 and 1920 it clearly showed the contrast and variety that lured young people from the isolation and monotony of life "down on the farm." New York's "plush" area at the turn of the century was the strip of Fifth Avenue bordering Central Park. There Cornelius Vanderbilt, the railroad mogul, had built himself a mansion. There, in time, came others: John D. Rockefeller, the oil king; Henry Clay Frick, the steel baron; James J. Hill, the emperor of the Great Northern line; J. P. Morgan, the superbanker; and others. Some of Fifth Avenue's millionaires, like Morgan, had made their fortunes in New York itself. Others, like Hill, were drawn there from the West because New York, the country's financial capital, required their business presence.

Some of the moneyed new aristocrats took an active part in the support of local institutions such as the Metropolitan Museum of Art, the New York Philharmonic Society, or Trinity Church. Others, however, remained tied to their midwestern backgrounds. Though living in New York, they were also immortalized in buildings raised with their donations in Chicago, where Rockefeller helped to found the University of Chicago, or Pittsburgh, where Frick gave numerous benefactions. In this way great American fortunes became national charitable resources.

The millionaires gave New York great style. Tourists and natives alike enjoyed gaping at their handsome brownstone residences and the spanking rigs that they drove in the park on Sundays. But they were not, for the most part, a local aristocracy with roots that went far back into the city's past. As a result, their interest in local conditions and politics was uneven. Some strongly backed efforts to improve the metropolis, while others took only as much interest as their investments required.

A city where, in contrast, the millionaire class was predominantly a class of long-time residents was Philadelphia. There the Drinkers, Chews, Bowens, Shippens, Mitchells, Willings, and Baldwins, who controlled the banking, insurance, railroad, coal, iron, and shipping firms that provided the city's wealth, were largely the descendants of eighteenth-century Philadelphians. This did not always make them fond of civic improvement. They lived in the better suburbs of the city, in homes and clubs remote from the prying eyes of passersby, and let many downtown trouble spots fester. But they took a possessive pride in the museums, libraries, and concert halls that they founded.

Therefore, although Philadelphia was often corruptly governed and beset by poverty problems, it was always culturally well-off.

By 1914, visitors who came to New York to marvel at the Interborough Rapid Transit (IRT) Company's ten-year-old subway or the Flatiron Building (twelve years old and 22 stories high) or the four recent bridges spanning the East River were apt to be drawn to still another kind of attraction. This was Greenwich Village, an area of a few square blocks on the city's lower West side, quietly removed from business and shopping areas. Once it was a neighborhood dominated by Italian immigrants. Its low rents and plentiful cheap but good restaurants attracted a number of poets and artists whose free-swinging life-style and political and artistic radicalism both shocked and fascinated ordinary people. It was lived in or often visited by rebels such as "Big Bill" Haywood, leader of the Industrial Workers of the World, a labor organization dedicated to class war; or by John Reed, an Oregon-born graduate of Harvard who was to die in Russia in 1920 and be buried inside the Kremlin. It was where Mabel Dodge, a "new woman," made her house the headquarters for writers and talkers, men and women who smoked, drank, lived together out of wedlock, and spoke of changing America's values and replacing its dedication to business with a love of beauty and freedom. "The Village" could only exist within the anonymity of a large urban setting. Rebellious sons and daughters could try their wings there, far from prying family eyes. In some ways, it was the urban, twentieth-century version of early "reform" communities, without the tight framework.

### *"Cops," "Workers," and "Greenhorns"*

East and north of Greenwich Village lay two of New York's tough districts, the Bowery and the Tenderloin. Both carried on an early, harsh nineteenth-century tradition. They had been the haunts of tough gangs who ruled their unlit streets, lined with brothels, saloons, flophouses, and gambling dives. The Bowery was losing some of its hard reputation by 1900, but the Tenderloin, divided from the rest of the city by railroad tracks running up Tenth Avenue, was still a vice capital. It was a training ground of gangsters of the 1930s. It was also a fruitful source of police corruption, as officers took graft from owners of gin mills and houses of prostitution and were lax in arresting "toughs" with the right connections. It was not simply a case of police wickedness. Every major city had such problems, because every major city bred a special kind of relationship between lawbreakers and police forces.

In a huge community there was always bound to be some criminal activity. It could never be brought entirely under control, nor reduced to a scale in which every chronic offender in town was known to every police officer. Crime was a continuing affair. The police were enlisted in a kind of never-ending war in which they could not always be active on all fronts. Moreover, they were paid poorly by the society they protected, and they were constantly exposed to temptation. In addition, police appointments and promotions were often controlled by politics. So the police departments, in many cases, were under the thumb of the machine that ran the city—the same machine that accepted graft from large-scale criminals who controlled the traffic in narcotics, liquor, and prostitution. In short, the "cops" got their jobs and the "crooks" got their favors from the same dishonest politicians. Finally, police officers knew that many "respectable" citizens—those with slum properties, for example—made payoffs to the machine in order to avoid inconvenient inspections for violations of housing laws and other codes.

The result of all these factors was to encourage a certain amount of police corruption. The police officer, no matter how honest, knew that at best "the force" could only contain but not destroy the wicked. It was not an unthinkable violation of conscience to come to occasional, limited, and temporary truce terms with the underworld. The police officer was an underpaid public servant who often badly needed his small bribes and knew that some of the "best people" also stepped outside of legal bounds now and then. And the police officer who was too scrupulously honest might find that, in making an arrest, he had hauled in a friend of some political boss who could wreck *his* career in the department. It paid to be careful, to get one's small piece of the action, or at least not to notice too noisily if one's fellow officers did. Not every officer felt this way. But those who did were as much a result of urbanism as the streetcar.

The neighborhoods where people of middle incomes and large families lived were widely scattered. Blocks of delicatessens, lunch counters, newspaper stands, nickelodeons, soda parlors, groceries, tailor shops, meat and fish markets, laundries, and barber shops, all mingled with modest lawyers', doctors', and dentists' offices and apartment houses, were found in various places on Manhattan Island. They were the world in which the children of working people and low-paid white-collar and professional employees grew up. They were the city's backbone, self-contained and secure.

Far out, in the other four boroughs joined with Manhattan to encompass "Greater New York" in 1898, were open spaces where modest homes stood, belonging to workers and their families who were willing to pay with a long subway or trolley ride for some air and light and gardening space. Queens, the Bronx, and Staten Island were predominantly vast bedrooms. Brooklyn was different. It had been an independent city and a popular suburb before 1898. As a result, it had its own urban institutions, from libraries and museums to a baseball team and newspapers.

By 1914 a new kind of neighborhood resulted from the tidal wave of immigration surging into New York. On Manhattan's lower East side, tene-

*Most post-1890 immigrants settled in the nation's major cities and accounted for a good deal of urban growth, vitality, and difficulty. They gave to America the "foreign" neighborhood, the ethnic election slate, the energy of their dreams and the work of their hands, as well as the problem of absorbing a diversity of faiths and life-styles. Here some of them encounter the Statue of Liberty, symbol of a welcome that often varied in warmth.*

ment houses swelled with a population of Russian Jews, Italians, and representatives of all the nationalities of the sprawling Ottoman, Hapsburg, and Romanoff empires. There were Czechs, Poles, Hungarians, Rumanians, Slovaks, various kinds of Slavs, Syrians, and Greeks, as well as Chinese and Irish. In 1920 most residents of the great city had either been born abroad or had at least one parent so born.

New York's national enclaves lent enormous color and variety to the city's life, problems, and politics. Population density on the lower East side was the highest in the nation. Its people were mostly ordinary laborers in the construction, garment, and other trades, struggling to support large families. Sanitation, light, and air were absent from many tenements. Contagious diseases swept whole areas. Some had so many cases of tuberculosis that they were known as "lung blocks." Fires gutted tenements in a few moments, often burning to death those who were trapped on the blazing wooden staircases. Rats and vermin were often the first animals tenement infants knew. Tenement flats were often also sweatshops where whole families slaved.

But there was another side. The newcomers quickly filled their few square blocks with institutions and styles of their own—from the Italian grocery stores hung with Genoa salamis and provolone cheeses to the solid red-brick architecture and onion-shaped spires of Eastern Orthodox churches. Each of these mini-nations added one more dot of color to the urban landscape.

The Jewish lower East side was almost a world in itself. Pushcarts crammed with goods lined its streets. In tiny synagogues, often created from converted stores, worshipers swayed in age-old chants and rhythms. Cafés and restaurants provided places where young and old men and women played chess, drank tea, and debated philosophy, religion, ethics, socialism, trade unions, the theater, and such timeless topics as the failings of children, husbands, wives, and bosses. For the ambitious there were night classes in English and other subjects that led to Americanization and advancement.

There was vitality in the lower East side. It was a sociological disaster area. Ward politicians, social workers, public health and police officials knew how full it was of sickness, crime, broken families, despair, and superstition. But it also gave its inhabitants security, intimacy, connection to each other, human recognition, and hope. It lived as a community within a community. It could not have existed except within the larger setting of the city. It was one of many subcultures that showed to newcomers fresh possibilities of human interaction.

It did not necessarily take immigration from abroad to create a special cultural zone. Perhaps six miles north of the lower East side was a district known as Harlem. Once it had been a place where well-off New Yorkers got away to the country. In 1909 some real-estate dealers began trying to make it something new, a black neighborhood that would not be as run down as the "Bronzevilles" and "Darktowns" of other cities. They worked hard to attract migrant blacks from the South to buy or rent space in the pleasant homes and stores being vacated by white New Yorkers who were traveling to more distant suburban retreats.

By 1920 a virtual flood of Southern blacks had come northward in search of jobs in factories humming with World War I orders. And then Harlem achieved the special style predicted for it. It became the home of black jazz musicians, artists, poets and writers, entertainers and artists—a jewel of what was known, in the 1920s, as the Negro Renaissance. Harlem, too, proved that interesting things could happen when a sudden flow of people with a particular style was dammed and contained within one portion of a major city.

## *Tweed and Others: A Tale of More than Two Cities*

The best known of all nineteenth-century urban machines is New York's Tammany Hall. It went back to the 1790s, but it burst into fame in the late 1860s. At that time, its leader, William Marcy Tweed, had gained a dominating position in the life of New York City through his control of the "Hall." The mechanism of Tammany power was simple enough. In each ward and precinct of the city, members of the club recruited followers. They did so mainly through the arts of crowd leadership, which we saw practiced on the frontier in Chapter 7. Tammany precinct workers who were handy with their fists, generous with a treat, or quick with a loan or a favor soon had a group of loyal neighbors who would vote as they asked. With many such groups in hand, Tammany could control nominations and elections in the Democratic Party.

This meant that a large body of aldermen, city officials, judges, and state legislators owed their political lives to the Hall. As a result Tammany's ward leaders could promise jobs on the city payroll, "fix" court cases, and egg on or call off the police. They could determine which businessmen got licences to operate and which were harassed. They could often demand kickbacks and payments that swelled their war chest and financed goodwill-building operations. A Tammany ward leader always had money to help a deserving family burnt out by a fire, to buy new uniforms for the parish baseball team, pay medical bills for an injured worker, run a Fourth of July barbecue, or give free turkeys and coal to the needy at Christmas. The rewards came in gratitude, a fine old word in machine politics, translated into Election Day pro-Tammany ballots. If gratitude did not bring out enough votes, it was time for bribery, false counts, ballot-box stuffing, and "rough stuff."

At the higher levels Tammany used its control of city officialdom to see that franchises, building permits, and contracts for lighting and widening streets, digging sewers, and in other ways improving the urban landscape went to the right companies, those that paid for the service.

That was Tweed's game. Along with the mayor of New York, its chief officials, and the board of aldermen, all of whom were in his pocket, Tweed issued contracts for an ambitious program of buildings. The contractors who were chosen charged the city incredible sums, part of which went to Tweed's ring. Between 1869 and 1871 taxpayers were taken for some $45 million.

But Tweed was finally unhorsed. Usually, machines were only occasionally slowed down by coalitions of reformers. In his case it was different. One of his bookkeepers leaked the facts. The story was soon front-page material in *The New York Times* and in *Harper's Weekly*, an illustrated journal, whose chief cartoonist, Thomas Nast, drew merciless caricatures of Tweed and his gang as vultures and worse. Nast symbolized Tammany Hall itself as a tiger, jaws open and slavering, slitted eyes full of cruelty. The message was clear—*all* New Yorkers suffered under Tammany rule.

Tweed wailed that he did not mind what was in the papers; his constituents could not read. But, he noted, they could understand "those damned pictures." Moved in part by "those damned pictures," a jury convicted Tweed of various violations of the law and sent him to jail. He escaped and was recaptured. He was recognized in his flight because Nast had made his face so familiar. He died a prisoner.

His successor, "Honest John" Kelly, was a less flamboyant Tammany chief. And the man who succeeded Kelly at the helm of Tammany Hall, Richard Croker, was of a different breed. Much of his money went into legitimate business "fronts." Croker himself was a gentlemanly sort who escaped his political duties each year for a few months in his native Ireland, where he raised and raced thoroughbred horses. Styles in bosses varied. They were not all fat men wearing derbies and checkered vests. That image was created by Nast, with Tweed as a model. Many, like Croker or Philadelphia's James Manes or San Francisco's "Abe" Ruef, were well-dressed, cultivated men. In their own eyes they were only businessmen who smoothly ran a complex organization like a municipality and took a reasonable profit for themselves.

Machines were inseparable from urbanism. At one end of the big-city social scale was a large, often uneducated mass of poor voters. They had problems that required attention not provided for in town charters written for a simpler time. At the other end of the scale were businessmen who were modernizing the city and expected promptness and decisiveness and planning. But these qualities were not provided by old-fashioned local governments designed to be run by amateurs as cheaply as possible. Until progressive reforms in the twentieth century created social services for the poor and planning organizations to run cities efficiently, the machine filled a gap. It did so extralegally and expensively, but it was a natural response to the situation.

Chicago's machine politicians at the turn of the century were a colorful lot. They also made good newspaper copy and showed that ward bosses could have distinctive styles. Among the two best known were "Hinky Dink" Kenna and "Bathhouse John" Coughlin. They operated in a riotous section of the city known as the "Levee." Once a year they threw a huge party, to which their voters and contributors, along with a number of curious respectable citizens and reporters, were invited. It was usually distinguished by the lavish consumption of liquor, wild dancing, "abandoned" high jinks, and frequent arrests for brawling. But behind the amusing false front the serious business of machine rule went on as it did elsewhere. It had the same basic elements of control of votes, control of civic machinery, and high-level deals.

When a brilliant reporter, Lincoln Steffens, did a series of articles on corruption for *McClure's Magazine* in 1903 (later printed in a volume entitled *The*

*Shame of the Cities*), he pointed out these similarities. Steffens was one of the first to see that municipal corruption was not the creation of a few immoral individuals who only needed to be thrown out in order to end the problem. Instead, he saw that the system itself—of urban need and business ambition—made the bosses the middlemen in basic civic transactions. He saw how the machine was a clumsy but unavoidable means, until something better came along, of achieving the benefits of "community" within the metropolis.

### *Parks, Playgrounds, and Pleasure Palaces*

"The City Beautiful" was a label that civic planners liked to give to their dreams. What they often had in mind was an American community made lovely by the palaces, gardens, and fountains once created only by an aristocracy. They hoped for places to please the eye, impress visitors, and give every citizen pride in his home. There should be areas for gathering, gossip swapping, self-improvement, and relaxation as well as public business. The ideal blueprint of urban planners of the 1890s included plazas, boulevards, parks, libraries, concert halls, museums, and handsome courthouses, and city halls.

The actual American city had only a small resemblance to such a fanciful drawing. Most of the business "aristocrats" of the United States paid more attention to bookkeeping than palace building. And most city governments hated to spend tax money for anything as unproductive as decoration. So most American big cities stayed basically plain looking and even dreary. Yet a few did show touches of the public beautification that had been so common in Renaissance Italy or ancient Greece. Some grand structures were put up by private charities. And some parts of cities were beautified by cities with out-of-the-ordinary foresight. Taken together, they all created a distinctive surrounding for the city dweller.

Chicago celebrated the 400th anniversary of Columbus' voyage with a mammoth World's Fair along part of its Lake Michigan shorefront. The sight of a "White City" of imposing buildings on the "Columbian Exposition" grounds proved inspiring to the city's leading citizens. Within twenty-five years after the fair had closed its doors, three castles of learning had been put up: the Field Museum of Natural History, the Adler Planetarium, and the Museum of Science and Industry. Each was both privately and publicly funded. The city furnished the necessary land, free of taxes, and private donors (like Marshall Field, owner of Chicago's largest department store) paid the actual construction costs. Twentieth-century Chicago also boasted a handsome Chicago Public Library, on wide Michigan Boulevard, which carried traffic briskly north and south along the edge of a lakefront park. Another Chicago monument was the Art Institute, done in grand style with a sweeping staircase and a great façade with columns and carvings facing the boulevard. In the 1920s Samuel Insull, a

*The 400th anniversary of America's discovery was the occasion for an "Exposition" in Chicago in which the United States celebrated its new power in many ways. Some were architectural, as here in a triumphant administration building of neo-Renaissance style. No republican simplicity here, but domes, pillars, balconies, statues and staircases, richly ornamented and carved, all advertising a taste for splendor.*

czar of electric power companies, financed a gigantic opera house along the Chicago River. Money to add to the libraries and museums came from other lords of industry like the Ryersons, McCormicks, and Pullmans, makers of steel, harvesters, and railroad cars.

New York, Philadelphia, Boston, San Francisco, and other cities aiming at greatness raised new libraries and art institutes. Many of them are still urban landmarks, even under years-old layers of city grime. The New York Public Library, built with donations from real-estate and other millionaires like William B. Astor, seemed so much a part of the city that people hardly realized how it depended on private gifts. It stood next to a small, once gemlike piece of greenery in the heart of Manhattan's busiest district, named Bryant Park, like a jewel on green satin. As another example of civic beauty, Philadelphia's Museum of Art rose at one end of a great, open plaza.

Such buildings owed their existence to private wealth. But they also had a public meaning. Even the most nonartistic citizen knew of them as landmarks, boasted of their size to out-of-town relatives, and was proud to "possess" such treasures. In addition, they furnished a learning experience that was each city's alone. Millions of schoolboys and schoolgirls were taken on trips to the museums. They were led, giggling, past the statues of nudes or, open mouthed, along the rows of glass cases holding mastodon bones, arrowheads, and meteorite fragments. For most of them the experience ended there. But thousands were, as planned, spurred to intellectual adventures and even careers of learning of their own. For them the great museums and libraries and concert halls became a place of discovery shared with others like them. For them any drawbacks of city life paled beside the wonders such centers offered. An urban culture took root among a whole generation of children raised in cities.

The public park was another civic feature that defined a whole new style of life. When Frederic Law Olmsted and Calvert Vaux laid out New York's Central Park in the 1850s, they had two goals in mind. One was to save some green beauty from the onrush of paved streets. The other was to provide a piece of decorated landscape, like an eighteenth-century squire's gardens, for "the public" to enjoy as though "the public" was the squire—was, so to speak, democracy personified. So along with "wild" spots there were quaint bridges, little ponds, twisting walks, and many nooks for private sitting.

But the park became more than an artificial rural retreat. It also became the place where nurses walked children from expensive homes and slum youngsters played stickball or touch football. It became the place where immigrant and "American," white-collar and blue-collar families, took the Sunday air, gawked at animals in the zoo, ate peanuts and ices, dressed easily, and acted not like country gentlemen but like common folk having a good time. Central Park, like Brooklyn's Prospect Park and like Chicago's lakefront Grant Park, became a crowded, popular playground. It kept some of its aristocratic touches, like the bridle paths, but it surrounded them with playgrounds, skating rinks, trees for swinging, rocks for climbing, and other pleasant helps to ordinary leisure. The parks did not make American cities resemble royal grounds like Versailles—all promenades and splashing fountains. They did, however, have fountains and statues dedicated by groups that had heroes to worship in stone as well as influence at city hall. And they did, moreover, make the cities vital. It is sad to report that many of these parks, in modern times, have become dirty and unsafe.

Besides the monuments, educational establishments, and parks, there were other city centers where people collected. There were settlement houses,

*The magic of the city was that it brought people together in crowds. Even if they were unknown to each other, they shared a stake in the city's mass-populated places of culture, information, and recreation. The happy, leisurely Sunday idlers here in San Francisco are having a community experience different from that of a few dozen families on the village green, but similar in essentials. The differences are those between the old and the new America.*

playgrounds, public pools, and downtown universities scattered through neighborhoods. But besides these the rise of popular amusements created still other gathering centers. Professional baseball began in Cincinnati in 1869. Up to then it was a game for gentlemen amateurs' "Base Ball Clubs." But Cincinnati's Red Stockings, who all played for pay, bred imitation. By the late 1880s there were already franchises in most big cities and the National League had been born. By 1910 the American League was in the picture. In 12 of what were then the country's biggest cities (all of them east of the Mississippi except for St. Louis), 10,000 to 40,000 people could gather daily to watch their heroes perform and share the joys and agonies of pennant races.

The baseball park was only one place of "lower-class" amusement. There were also beer gardens, burlesque and vaudeville and legitimate theaters, and the indoor arenas where prize fights, circuses, and other such events were held.

Democratic public entertainment was part of many developments that brought urbanites together for common purposes. True, ladies and gentlemen went to the opera and the theater. Ordinary people went to vaudeville, movies, ball games, and fights. But there was some spillover from one to the other. As we saw, plain people knew of and admired the monumental centers where the arts flourished, and the well-off were not above following the local baseball teams or visiting the music hall.

The modern American city was a special creation with a life of its own. Each one had a distinctive mixture of basic business activities and special neighborhoods. Various urban interests and regions were knit together by newspapers, political machines, and shared landmarks. The overall similarities among cities did not bar individual differences. These came from some geographic feature (San Francisco Bay), some key industry (Pittsburgh steel mills), some historic feature (St. Louis' position as gateway to the West). Each city, with its wealth and its scars, was too big to be a planned community, yet too closely knit to be just an accidental collection of many peoples in one political unit. All of them together made the United States distinctively urban by the time of World War I. Jefferson's hope never to see Americans huddled in cities was unrealized a century after his death. But the "huddling" produced great warmth and growth in its way.

## *FOR FURTHER READING*

There are many recent books on the way in which we became a nation of cities: one of the latest is Zane L. Miller, *The Urbanization of Modern America* (1973). Although, like other new works, Miller incorporates much modern research, it does not displace an earlier classic by Arthur M. Schlesinger, *The Rise of the City* (1933).

There are many biographies of individual cities and special studies of the aspects of urban living. Among the studies, two by Sam B. Warner, Jr. stand out: *Streetcar Suburbs* (1962) and *The Urban Wilderness* (1973). *Wilderness* shows the many forces at work which give each city its special shape and texture. Stephan Thernstrom, *Poverty and Progress* (1964) studies the residential patterns of working-class families and tries to connect them with certain long-held American ideas about social mobility.

"Ethnic" neighborhoods are a story in themselves and a sampling of the fare should include: St. Clair Drake and Horace Cayton's *Black Metropolis* (1945), exploring Chicago's Negro world; Gilbert Osofsky, *Harlem: The Making of a Ghetto* (1965); Humbert Nelli, *The Italians of Chicago* (1973); Herbert Gans, *The Urban Villagers* (1962), which deals with Boston's modern Italian enclaves; and Moses Rischin, *The Promised City: New York's Jews*, 1870–1914 (1962).

The age of the urban bosses is full of interest and is best revealed by firsthand accounts. Lincoln Steffens, *The Shame of The Cities* (1957) is still a classic, and his *Autobiography* (1931) repays reading. *How The Other Half Lives* (1890) is an 1890s account of New York's slums and sins by Jacob Riis, a reporter. Jane Addams, *Twenty Years at Hull House* (1910) shows Chicago from the viewpoint of a turn-of-the-century reformer and social worker. Brand Whitlock, *Forty Years of It* (1914) tells of the efforts to clean up Cleveland. For the look and feel of American cities, however, there is no substitute for photographic collections or simply walking the streets of your own town.

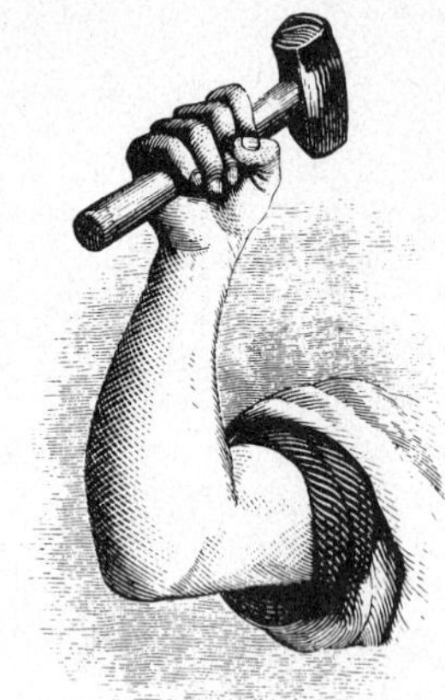

# chapter 17
# Power to the powerless in modern America: workers, blacks, women

One of Samuel Gompers' earliest lessons in the perils of weakness was almost fatal. It came on a bitter winter day in January 1874 in New York's Tompkins Square. Thousands, thrown out of work by a deepening economic depression, had gathered to demand food and shelter for their hungry families and public works projects to provide jobs. The rally was technically against the law, since the frightened mayor had given it no permit. Gompers, an immigrant cigarmaker, twenty-four years old, mingled with the crowd, listened to the speeches, and glanced now and then at the mounted police ringing the area.

Suddenly, without warning, they charged, clubs swinging. Men and women screamed and struggled to escape the pounding hooves and the heavy night sticks that could crush a skull. Panting, Gompers tumbled into a doorway and safety. He was heartsick as well as scared. The United States had seemed a haven of hope for men and women who worked. But it was clear now that without power to challenge the authorities, the grievances of labor would go uncorrected forever. Gompers would spend a lifetime helping in the search for that kind of power. He would find it in organization.

For Booker T. Washington the lesson was learned as soon as he became aware of himself as a separate being, for Washington was born a slave. As a small boy, he lived with his mother, brother, and sister in a cabin on a Virginia farm. It had a dirt floor, no furnishings, no scrap of comfort or beauty. It was a human barn, and Washington's family slept on the floor and ate with their hands like the two-legged work animals they were. When he was still under ten, slavery ended, and Washington became "free" in the sense of not being owned by another. But he knew that without escape from poverty and ignorance there would be no true liberation, no growth toward humanity. He would seek for the power to make that escape, which was doubly difficult for blacks in a white world, and find it in education.

When Carrie Lane first became convinced of woman's need for power is not certain. She was born with advantages. Her father was well-off enough to send her to college, a rarity for girls in the late 1870s. By the time she was the age at which Gompers escaped a beating in Tompkins Square, she was superintendent of schools in the midwestern town of Mason City, Iowa. But despite her achievements, she knew that, like all others born female, she faced obstacles. Legally, she was still barred from full control of her own property and even her own person. Doors of professional and educational advancement were firmly closed to her—for woman's "destiny" was to marry and rear a family, and nothing else. The most basic privileges of citizenship were not hers. She would seek for the key to correct these injustices and find it in the struggle to vote. But she, being a woman, would become famous in that struggle not under the name she was born with, but through the names of two husbands she outlived. She would go into history as Carrie Chapman Catt.

### *Problems of Idealists*

Gompers was born in 1850, Washington in 1856, and Carrie Lane in 1859. They all grew up during the post–Civil War rush to industrialism and reached the height of their maturity and influence when the twentieth century was young. Each had a dream of achievement for the underprivileged group with which they were identified. But those who were strangers to power in the new, modern America faced special problems in making their ideals come true.

They started with some strengths on their side. The nation officially endorsed freedom and equality. Though the promises of the Constitution and the Declaration of Independence were often ignored in practice, the fact that they existed at all was a powerful propaganda lever. It opened the way for appeals to conscience. White workingmen, too, had the vote at their disposal. And educated women were almost always listened to respectfully because of their position in society, even if their message was ignored.

On the other hand, the obstacles were high. For working-class Americans the vote was apt to be meaningless without job security and decent wages. Polling-place power did not always translate into economic power. John D. Rockefeller might be outnumbered on Election Day, but his "vote" in the marketplace was decisive. Blacks and women, in different ways to be sure, had to battle against deep-grained stereotypes that existed outside the law and could not be reached by the law or changed by money.

Those who hoped to lead the powerless toward improvement had practical decisions to weigh. Their "armies" were divided. Who should be the shock troops? Should a labor movement be built around skilled craftsmen or the unskilled who had greater numbers but were more easily replaced? Should movements to upgrade blacks aim to find and train future doctors, lawyers, and other professionals? Or should they better the lot of the struggling sharecropper? Was it possible to build a women's movement that would find common ground among the lonely, isolated farm wife, the seamstress huddled in a sweatshop, and the comfortable—but still powerless—daughter of an upper middle-class family?

And there was the question of tactics. We saw that emerge in our look at early reform movements in Chapter 10. Was it best for underdog groups to combine forces and attack oppression together? Or was it better to work in isolation, so that the disadvantages of one group did not weigh down another? Was it not hard enough to win sympathy for black rights, for example, without having to demand women's equality as well?

Was it best to work peaceably through persuasion? Or through militant tactics like strikes, boycotts, demonstrations, and court challenges? Or was the best method the tested route of political lobbying? Which worked better, militancy or moderation?

And what should the goals of a movement be? How broad or narrow? Should workers get only a better wage or a share of the ownership of industry? Should blacks struggle for full social equality or only for a chance at an equal paycheck? And should women be content with the right to vote and hold office,

---

*CHRONOLOGY*

1869 *National Women's Suffrage Association founded*
1881 *Booker T. Washington becomes president of Tuskegee Institute in Alabama*
1885 *The American Federation of Labor started, Samuel Gompers, President*
1894 *Pullman Palace Car Company strike*
1895 *Booker T. Washington proposes "Atlanta Compromise"*
1896 *William Jennings Bryan runs for president on Populist and Democratic tickets*
1905 *Industrial Workers of the World (IWW) founded*
1909 *National Association for the Advancement of Colored People (NAACP) founded*
1919 *The Nineteenth Amendment gives women the vote*

or should they try to overturn the whole idea of "family" that kept them, too often, prisoners in the home?

Gompers, Washington, and Catt were all leaders who chose the conservative answer to such questions. Each eventually focused on using moderate means to win limited victories for one particular group. And each was successful to a surprising degree. But all three were bitterly criticized by fellow reformers and charged with "selling out" their followers by settling for the half-loaf. And, in fact, for whatever power they did bring to workers, blacks, and women through alliances with the established order, they paid a price. Your judgment on whether that price was too high can be a valuable part of your own education. But you must make it fairly, not only on the basis of your hindsight and knowledge of modern times but also with some understanding of what the world looked like in your great-grandparents' day. The good historian, like the good novelist, is not afraid to show his characters in the wrong, but he must also show them in the round, and do so with compassion.

## *The Battle for Bread-and-Butter Unionism*

To Gompers first, then, emerging from his doorway in 1874. As a cigarmaker, he worked in a trade that was not yet under the control of a few large corporations. Cigar "factories" were often lofts or basements that held only a few dozen workers. Thousands of cigars were made in tenement rooms (under unspeakably filthy conditions) by newly arrived immigrants under contract. No politicians were willing to crusade to ban this practice by law as a public health measure. There was a Cigarmakers Union (of which Gompers was a member and an officer), but it could not coordinate or control the actions of its members scattered through many shops. Strikes began when a disgruntled worker slammed down his tools and walked out, urging others to follow. They ended, as often as not, when hungry cigarmakers were forced back to the benches by need or were replaced by new hands.

In 1877 New York's cigarmakers went out in a lengthy strike. Sometimes workers won these fights because an employer was eager to get back into production and beat his competitors. But this time the bosses stuck together, and after bitter months of starvation the cigarmakers straggled back, beaten. Union leaders like Gompers, whose wife had almost died in childbirth for lack of money to buy medicine for her, were for a time blacklisted (that is, barred from all shops) and sometimes could only work by taking aliases.

Emerging from the wreckage, Gompers and a fellow union official, Adolph Strasser, analyzed their defeat. They blamed it on bad planning, lack of resources, and unclear targets. Patiently and forcefully, they worked to create a new kind of union. A structure was created that gave power to a central executive committee. It had the power to make assessments on the shop locals

*For many of the urban poor, life in the land of opportunity became a bitter struggle which consumed even the lives of tiny children, as this scene of a family doing piecework at home shows. It was anger at such betrayals of the American promise that fueled the early labor movement as it pursued "liberty and justice for all."*

and to give or withold its approval for strikes. If there was no approval, then no strike benefits were paid out to keep the workers going. What Gompers and Strasser wanted was a union that would plan industry-wide action, have enough money to finance a long strike, and enough organized, vocal members to make lawmakers listen to demands for regulation. And when they had built such a union, they would not use its power loosely or casually, risking defeat on matters of high principle. They would create a unionism as efficient as the corporations it fought—business unionism, as they called it. And they would use it only for limited ends that would gain general approval, a policy known as "bread-and-butter" unionism.

To win these battles Gompers, a man of tireless energies, had to fight off the challenges of other bidders for leadership. They included numerous Socialists, who argued that justice could only come for the working class when private ownership of factories, protected by the middle-class state, was replaced with a government of, by, and for laborers. To these prophets of socialism the main job of unions was to educate and train workers for the "revolution," which might come peaceably or otherwise but which would end capitalism. Gompers found those expectations ridiculously unrealistic. He realized how deeply Americans were wedded to the capitalistic system and how much public support was needed to help unions survive. His job within the Cigarmakers Union was to beat out the many talented and energetic Socialists who contributed to the building of the union, without driving them into destructive countermovements. By the early 1880s he and Strasser had succeeded in doing that. It was then time to move upward.

*The AFL, the Knights, and the Populists*

Since the late 1860s, trade unionists had been trying to weld a nationwide league of unions to create a major pressure group for cherished reforms such as the eight-hour day. Several such efforts had died young. One that had not was the Knights of Labor. Founded in 1869 in Philadelphia as a secret society of garment cutters, it was provided with elaborate fraternity-like rituals by its originator, an ex-ministerial student named Uriah Stephens. Members took poetic initiation oaths, celebrating brotherhood and productiveness, and officers had titles like Worthy Foreman and Venerable Sage.

But the Knights meant business, too. In 1879 under a new leader, a bespectacled, lawyerlike former machinist named Terence V. Powderly, they emerged into the open and launched heavy organizing drives. Basically, the Knights were organized along shopwide lines, linking the skilled and the unskilled together in local units. Such units, from many different trades, were then joined in regional assemblies, which therefore spoke for "labor" in general rather than for particular crafts. Under Powderly the Knights of Labor pushed for general changes in the industrial system that would roll back the wave of consolidation that created armies of wage workers. They wanted easy credit and free land (to encourage more workers to become small businessmen and farmers), cooperatively owned and run workshops, and tight control of "monopolies." Powderly actually disliked strikes, which interfered with production. His war was with the bankers, landlords, and other "middlemen" who took an unfair share of what labor produced.

Gompers and other "pure and simple" trade unionists rejected all these ideas. But they saw the Knights growing in membership as workers looked anxiously for mutual support and direction. Gompers was one of those who took the lead in setting up a new organization in 1881, known as the Federation of Organized Trades and Labor Unions. In 1886 it was reorganized and renamed the American Federation of Labor (AFL). Gompers became its first president and, except for one year, 1895, held that office until his death in 1924. It was deeply and uniquely his creation.

The AFL was built around strong, nationwide unions of skilled workers—brickmakers, carpenters, brewers, and the like—who had the most power to hit the economy hard by strike action. Its executive council would map joint strategies and select goals. But each union would be sovereign in its own field. More than one union in any craft would not be recognized. And the targets of action would be strictly of the bread-and-butter variety.

Within its first few years of life, AFL membership climbed satisfyingly to over a million, while the Knights dropped from a peak of about 700,000 in 1886 to virtual nothingness ten years later. American workers seemed ready to think of themselves as craftsmen first and federationists second, instead of the other way around as the Knights and Socialists demanded. And they seemed ready to take what gains they could within the industrial system. How well the AFL philosophy could work was proved when, in the first year of the 1890s, a series of carefully timed strikes of key unions won workers the eight-hour day, something that reform lobbyists had struggled in vain for fifteen years to enact into national law. (But, naturally, the "victory" only counted for the members of the unions that got the provision in their contracts with the employers.)

Gompers believed that further forward steps depended desperately on keeping public confidence in the "responsibility" of unions alive. Most Americans deplored strikes and feared "radical" assaults on the rights of property and management. So it was important to hold the AFL in the middle of the road. Gompers had witnessed one heavy reaction against organized labor in 1886 when, at a workers' rally in Haymarket Square in Chicago, a bomb supposedly thrown by an "anarchist" had wiped out a number of lives.

The middle road was not always easy in the turbulent, depression-ridden nineties. In 1894 workers at the Pullman Palace Car Company (railroad sleeping-car manufacturers) went on strike. They were followed, in sympathy, by members of the newly organized American Railroad Union (ARU), which linked skilled and unskilled members of train crews together. Participation by the ARU turned the Pullman walkout into a major rail tie-up. The federal government struck back by sending troops to guard scab-run trains. Within the labor movement there was a widespread feeling that this only proved that the national political machinery was the tool of the railroad barons, and demands were heard for the AFL to support the Pullman and rail workers with strikes of its own. But Gompers, hearing the ARU's leader, Eugene V. Debs, denounced in the wildest terms as an "anarchist," "fanatic," and "terrorist," stubbornly used his power to prevent any such action, except for a $500 donation to the walkout. (Debs, the Indiana-born son of Alsatian immigrants, came out of the broken strike a Socialist and ran for the presidency on that ticket five times.)

Again, in 1896, farm protest against hard times erupted in an enormous surge of strength for the People's, or Populist, Party, formed only four years earlier. Raging against the domination of the United States by "plutocrats," the Populists cried for what were sweeping reforms in the nineties: government management of the currency, farm loans, public ownership of railroads, telephones and telegraphs, an income tax, the recall by ballot of corrupt officials, and the direct election of senators. They headed their ticket with William Jennings Bryan, a Bible-quoting prairie spellbinder, also nominated by the Democrats.

Though Bryan was in fact no true radical, once more the respectable elements of the country smelled revolution in the air and warned that factories would close, the stock market would collapse, and catastrophe would overwhelm America if Bryan were chosen. The Populists, in turn, looked for support from all elements who had grievances against the system. Specifically, they sought help in what one of their leaders called raising "more hell" from labor. They got it from the remnant of the Knights. But Samuel Gompers kept the AFL neutral and refused to endorse Bryan. His instinct for popular sentiment proved right, when the orator from Nebraska was swept to defeat in November.

## *Fighting "Wobblies" and Reaching Respectability*

From 1900 to 1916 the AFL under Gompers gained new vigor and numbers. In 1903 Gompers and two other AFL leaders were invited to join the National Civic Federation, an organization founded by big businessmen and designed to encourage the arbitration of strikes. Around 1910 the AFL also began to abandon its traditionally hands-off stance toward politics. It went, instead, for a policy of supporting candidates favorable to labor aims (such as restricting immigration and providing for safety inspection and workers' sickness and accident compensation) and opposing those who were critical. The policy was one of rewarding friends and punishing enemies. By 1912 Gompers had decided that most of labor's friends were to be found in the Democratic Party. He became openly supportive of the Democratic candidate, Woodrow Wilson. In turn, when Wilson was elected, he was happy to work with the AFL leadership. Wilson spoke eloquently at the dedication of a new AFL building in Washington in 1916. He named to the new cabinet post of secretary of labor a candidate approved by Gompers. And when, in 1916, with war clouds in the sky, he created a Council of National Defense to plan economic mobilization, Wilson named Gompers to it.

In thirty years Gompers and his organization had come a long way. In the AFL's first days Gompers had made his tiny apartment into his office—his desk being an empty crate for canned tomatoes and his entire staff consisting of his teenage son. Rarely collecting his $1000-a-year salary, Gompers traveled by train, stayed at the cheapest hotels, and punished his sturdy frame with an endless round of speeches, letters, and meetings.

But by 1916, though the endless activity went on, the circumstances were different. Gompers lived in a pleasant, though modest, home in Washington. He was seen at the theater and the best restaurants. And above all, this cigarmaker who had begun life in America as a thirteen-year-old immigrant living in an East side New York tenement near a slaughterhouse, sat at the planning table with corporation executives, millionaires, and presidents of the United States of America.

It was not a path trodden without enemies. Conservative businessmen continued to snipe at Gompers. The National Association of Manufacturers launched a major union-busting campaign in the early 1900s. As part of it, they secured a court injunction—that is, a legal prohibition—against messages in the *American Federationist*, the AFL's official magazine, urging boycotts of antiunion firms. When Gompers defied the injunction, he came close to going to jail; he was, in fact, sentenced, but won a reversal on appeal to the Supreme Court.

Meantime, foes on the left were active, too. In 1905 a new, militantly radical labor federation, the Industrial Workers of the World (IWW), was born. Its members, nicknamed "Wobblies," rejected the entire AFL approach of organizing the skilled aristocrats of labor, negotiating contracts with employers, and hiring lobbyists and lawyers to work with business-loving politicians. For them there could be no peace between the employing and the working classes. They were "Socialists with working clothes on," hoping for a new society, which they would build within the shell of the old. It would be one in which workers' councils determined what, how, and how much to produce with America's industrial machinery.

Until then the Wobblies worked among the unorganized, particularly miners, harvest hands, loggers, and dockworkers. They also made some headway among immigrant textile workers. They had a flaming ingroup spirit, expressed in songs from the *Little Red Song-Book*, which set pro-Wobbly messages to familiar tunes. And, because they were so militant and advocated violent tactics like sabotage when feasible, they were hated and feared and in constant trouble with the police. During World War I, which they opposed, they were virtually smashed by the federal government.

Wobbly organizers never threatened the AFL's domination of the labor movement. But their vigorous barbs at Gompers and his allies stung. They claimed that the AFL left the great mass of workers ununionized and unprotected. And they argued that the AFL's limitation of demand to a simple larger slice of the pie still allowed the owning classes to walk away with far more than a just share of the value created by the workers' toil at machines. They said that the AFL system encouraged elitism among the leadership and corrupt deals with politicians and bosses and, moreover, that it bred apathy and indifference among the rank and file.

All these charges would be repeated many times after 1916. Some had, and have, a measure of truth. By giving up large dreams of brotherhood and universal justice for the power to make some gradual changes, Gompers had made a bargain that would always be open to scrutiny, imitation, and debate.

*Booker T. Washington Defines the Black Problem for Himself*

For Booker T. Washington the end of slavery did not mean the end of poverty and degradation. He was taken with his brother and sister to West Virginia, and there his black stepfather put him to work in a coal mine. (Booker's actual father was unknown but certainly white.) The boy hated the darkness and the drudgery and found little joy of life in a slumlike shack that was no improvement on the slave cabin as a home. Ambition and a sense of unusual ability that was going to waste combined to gnaw at him. But opportunity opened the door widely enough for him to slip through. He managed to pick up some educational rudiments from a spelling book acquired by his helpful mother and from brief attendance at a "school" kept by a black Civil War veteran for the black children of the little mining town of Malden. And he was hired as a houseboy by the white wife of the local superintendent of the mines. This woman, a New Englander named Viola Ruffner, gave him a merciless grounding in the fundamentals of respectability: orderliness, punctuality, cleanliness, thrift, reliability.

As a young teenager, Washington walked halfway across Virginia to enroll in Hampton Institute. This was a school set up for ex-slaves by the Freedmen's Bureau and northern charitable and church bodies. Its aim was to teach useful skills and trades, plus the elements of citizenship, to prepare the former slaves for life as independent people. A penniless charity case dressed in hand-me-downs, Washington worked his way through the institution, visibly impressing its staff with his energy and brightness. A few years after his graduation, a request came to the institute for a candidate to head a new "normal" (that is, teacher-training) school to be set up for blacks by the state of Alabama at Tuskegee. The superintendent unhesitatingly named his star graduate. That was early in 1881.

In the short period after leaving Hampton, Washington had taught school at Malden, done some graduate study in Washington, and thought briefly about using his persuasive speechmaking skills as a lawyer or politician. But by late 1880 he had rejected that course. He found himself out of sympathy with eloquent or well-educated or financially successful urban blacks like those whom he met in Washington. His race, he believed, needed no more of them.

Nor did it need more black officeholders, since the doors of public life were being closed to blacks everywhere as Reconstruction faded.

The basic problem of the American black was that he was an illiterate and unskilled peasant who owned neither tools nor land and had no resources for self-improvement. Black poverty, ignorance, and disease not only held down the ex-slaves but also slowed the economic development of the entire South. What Washington decided to do with his life was to find ways of educating blacks to be successful farmers, craftsmen, and businessmen. This meant breaking them away from the stereotype of the "shiftless darky" by teaching them the schoolbook virtues of the America of the 1880s. And this cultural reeducation would be aimed at producing producers, not intellectuals or artists.

Taking over Tuskegee on July 4, 1881, Washington began to implement his plan. The beginnings were small. The school's "campus" was a rundown farmhouse and henhouse, through whose tattered roof rain poured on Washington as he lectured. He was, at first, the entire faculty. But he was undiscourageable and unstoppable. He set his "scholars" to work clearing brush, chopping trees, making bricks, and digging foundation trenches after their morning encounters with arithmetic and geography. And he tirelessly made the rounds of wealthy white homes, especially in the North, beseeching money to train a generation of self-disciplined ex-slaves who would buy goods, have bank accounts, pay taxes, and justify their emancipation.

It worked. By 1900 Tuskegee was a major institution. Its hundreds of students, of both sexes, were learning animal husbandry and soil chemistry, home nursing, carpentry, brickmaking, and the management of laundries, dining rooms, wagon repair shops, and power plants. Their school had property worth nearly $1 million, a model demonstration farm, and dozens of shops, laboratories, and classroom buildings, all student built. Dignitaries came to visit and to admire, and one of them spoke a widely held view when he was asked whether he had seen "Booker Washington's school": "School!" he said, "I have seen Booker Washington's city."

### *The Atlanta Compromise and National Leadership*

But by 1890 Washington's mind was ranging beyond the neatly kept grounds of Tuskegee and its young future leaders. The school was putting back into Southern life a small but steady supply of black teachers, business operators, and successful farmers. But it was only making a dent in black problems. Black per-capita income and grade-school education still lagged. Black ownership of land and property was still severely limited. And racism continued to cripple black spirits.

Washington wanted an expanded program of education and job opportuni-

*Right or wrong, it was Booker T. Washington's assumption that if blacks worked hard at practical tasks that America needed, then racial prejudice would disappear of itself without "agitation." In this classroom at Tuskegee Institute that philosophy radiates from the very walls, as black leader Frederick Douglass joins Franklin and Washington (between flags) soberly regarding the youngsters learning the useful trades depicted on the blackboards. Can you see here how Yankee culture—or any culture—is transmitted?*

ties for blacks. And he believed that support for it would have to come from the South, where 90 percent of America's blacks then lived, if gains were to be lasting. But winning Southern support meant coming to terms with the firm resistance of the white South to anything that threatened its control of the section's life. The fear and hatred built up in Reconstruction days was still a living force in the old Confederacy.

Washington devised a formula, which he got a chance to present before a major audience in September 1895. He was placed on the opening day program of an industrial "fair" at Atlanta to show off Southern economic progress. He was supposed to introduce an exhibition of products manufactured by blacks. In so doing, he gave a concise, but superbly effective, speech. One-third of the Southern population, he said, was black. It could make up one-third of the crime and ignorance of the section or "contribute one-third to the business and industrial prosperity of the South." If Southerners would help blacks achieve education of "head, hand and heart," the ex-slaves would "buy your surplus land, make blossom the waste places in your fields, and run your factories." Together, Southern blacks and whites would bring to "our beloved South a new heaven and a new earth."

But to tempt his white listeners to embrace that vision, Washington catered to the belief that blacks had gotten "too much" after Reconstruction. He said that blacks must learn to begin "at the bottom of life," must forget the pursuit of "ornamental gewgaws" (by which he meant advanced degrees), and must learn that there was as much dignity in tilling a field as in writing a poem. He implied that the search for political power must be postponed until industrial skills were achieved. He raised his hand in the air, looked down at the audience bathed in the declining sun's reddish light, and spread his fingers as he said: "In all things . . . purely social we can be as separate as the fingers,"; then he clenched his fist and finished: "yet one as the hand in all things essential to mutual progress."

Applause echoed in roaring waves through the hall. The governor of Georgia rushed to shake Washington's hand. He had said precisely what white Americans wished to hear—that blacks would stay in the "humbler" stations of life, making no inconvenient political and social demands, provided they received economic opportunities, or, as it was often put then, "a man's chance." This speech was what came to be known as the Atlanta Compromise.

The speech, reprinted in newspapers throughout the nation, gave Washington coast-to-coast fame. In 1901 he was invited by Theodore Roosevelt to the White House to discuss ways and means of improving federal political appointments in the South. (Under Republican presidents they had previously gone to undistinguished white and black political hacks.) The research staff at Tuskegee was asked to pour out, under Washington's name, a flood of books and articles about black leaders, problems, and achievements. Washington's advice was sought by anyone with money to donate to a new black school. His approval was virtually required for any important appointment of a black to a governmental post. His counsel was asked by missionaries trying to found little Tuskegee-type schools in colonies all over the world, as if he had a magic key for transforming "backward" peoples into model citizens. He was, at least until 1910 or thereabouts, the virtual czar of black life in America, appointed by the white leadership.

*The Anti-Washington Reaction*

Washington used his power and the money he controlled to build a "Tuskegee machine" that kept him on top of most happenings in America's black community. What was not known then was that he also funneled some of it secretly into legal actions challenging the various laws that were thrusting blacks into Jim Crow public accommodations and denying them the vote. Washington had never said that he would accept segregation and disfranchisement forever. And there is ample evidence that he honestly believed that whites would be color-blind to the dollar, in other words, that they would admit to the voting booth, and even to social equality, those blacks who were successful, diligent, and obeyed all the rules of good behavior by which middle-class America lived.

But in public he moved with the caution of a scout in hostile territory, rarely challenging antiblack stereotypes and practices. Moreover, he was genuinely conservative himself and out of sympathy with labor radicalism or any other movements that went against the views of the turn-of-the-century industrialists who were his patrons.

As a result, currents of anti-Washington rebellion soon were running high among educated blacks like Monroe Trotter of Boston or a young doctor of philosophy from Harvard named William E. B. Du Bois. They had a long bill of complaints against the superintendent of Tuskegee. For one thing, they believed that Washington's emphasis on training blacksmiths at the expense of educating scholars and artists reinforced white ideas that blacks were only good for menial jobs. For another, they believed that giving up the struggle for political power took away an important weapon in the fight for advancement. And they also thought that accepting segregation, in order to cultivate white goodwill, saddled black men and women with an unbearable burden of humiliation. No people with a negative self-image, they argued, could achieve dignity. No people who accepted "one jot or tittle less than . . . full manhood rights," as stated in a manifesto by young black intellectuals in 1905, was worthy of freedom. A landmark of the reaction against Washington was the founding, in 1909, of the National Association for the Advancement of Colored People (NAACP). It was dedicated to peaceful, legal action—but action!—against racial discrimination in any form.

Perhaps what hit hardest at Washington's position was that, in many ways, black life in America grew worse after the Atlanta Compromise. Segregation laws swept every Southern state. The last blacks were driven from the ballot box. The ugly practice of lynching, primarily used against blacks, swelled to its highest proportions, claiming 2394 lives between 1890 and 1918. Most of all, the white South betrayed Washington by not keeping its part of the bargain. Despite the abandonment of black claims for the "privilege" of equal treatment, there was no sizable increase in school budgets or job openings for blacks in the South.

Washington's supporters could claim, nonetheless, that some progress had been made. If he trained and encouraged thousands of black farmers, carpenters, insurance agents, laundry and barbershop owners to raise themselves "up from slavery," he had certainly improved the situation that existed in his youth. If he argued, in effect, that economic independence must come before protest could have any lasting meaning, that argument was worth hearing. It would be repeated in later days by other blacks.

But whether these few steps had been too slow or taken at too great a cost in pride—whether they caused damage that outweighed the progress—remained a point of controversy among historians, black and white, sixty years after Washington's death in 1915.

## *The Question of "Woman's Place"*

The women whom we met in Chapter 10, struggling to improve their condition in life, remained a divided army until well after 1900. Many of them, like the pioneer leader, Susan B. Anthony, had expected that with the toppling of slavery, the barriers blocking women would also fall soon. Susan Anthony, in fact, at first refused to crusade for a specific amendment to the Constitution authorizing women to vote. She believed that the Fourteenth, guaranteeing that no state should abridge the rights of U.S. citizens, contained within it the right to vote. When the courts threw out this interpretation (and caused Anthony, who had tried to register, to be indicted for a crime), she drafted what was known as the Anthony Amendment, specifically forbidding the states to deny the vote to anyone on grounds of sex.

Yet she was condemned to watch while Congress passed the Fifteenth Amendment, specifically giving blacks the vote, and, year after year, buried the question of woman suffrage. Dutifully trying to follow the example of the abolitionist crusade, which had finally gotten the amendment it wanted, she continued, until her death in 1906, to press for a constitutional change to gain her end. Her instrument was the National Women's Suffrage Association, founded in 1869.

As the eighties and nineties slipped by, however, the association fell on hard times. Disputes among leaders caused it to split and then be reunited under the name of the National American Women's Suffrage Association. But even with technical harmony restored, it continued to be plagued by tactical disputes. Some women, outside the organization, belittled its work entirely. They believed that it was more important, for example, to educate women to independent professional life than to win them the right to participate in the often empty rituals of party politics. Charlotte Perkins Gilman, a well-known feminist writer, was one of those who felt that women's dependence on male breadwinners was the main handicap that would have to be erased.

Others felt that women would have to "prove" their capacity for understanding public issues by emerging from the home and taking part in the progressive crusade to humanize industrialism. This viewpoint underlay the work of many distinguished women. Among them were social workers like Jane Addams, doctors like Alice Hamilton, and thousands of other upper-class, educated graduates of colleges (mainly women's), who formed the backbone of the General Federation of Women's Clubs. This approach to female emancipation sometimes caused friction among feminists. It rested heavily on the argument that women had particularly tender social consciences and a particularly high moral sense. Women should, therefore, be taking the lead in cleaning up the mess that men had made of life. But this elevation of women to a pedestal could make them prisoners, too. They could be told that they were too "pure" for the hurly-burly of business and politics or that their "wholesome" influence was so needed in the nurseries and schoolrooms that their first jobs were to be mothers and teachers. So women who got out into the world of progressive reform often did it with an apologetic defense that they had knowingly given up their "highest duty" of motherhood for the benefit of society at large.

Even within the ranks of those who put getting the vote first, there were differences of opinion. The first of these dealt with whether or not to try to get votes for women passed state by state or to push for a national amendment. The state-by-state approach could point to some victories by 1900. Wyoming, Colorado, Idaho, and Utah had admitted women to the polling place. Others might follow in time. But it was clear that it would be a slow process to achieve that goal in 45 separate political communities (the total number of states in 1900). And it would take an enormous duplication of funds and efforts.

A battle opened up within the ranks of the association on this question. When Carrie Catt was named its president in 1900, she made it clear that she favored the most efficient use of the organization's power—and that meant a federal amendment. She was defeated for the presidency in 1904 but would return in 1915 for the final "push." It came naturally to her to argue for the least wasteful approach. Her experience as an administrator had taught her the values of order and concentration. She represented a new breed of woman leader, not a speechmaker or a crusader like the founders of feminism. Nor was she a doer of good and charitable deeds, with a reputation as a public "angel," like Jane Addams. She was, rather, a bureaucratic-minded administrator with a great capacity to focus on the central question.

If concentrating on Washington meant depriving the state feminist organizations of grass-roots enthusiasm and loyalty, no matter. There were other problems to face that required more attention. One was whether or not the

*Western territories led the way in granting women the vote, but apparently not always with boldness. It seems that these female citizens in Cheyenne, in 1888, had to remain outside the polling place and slip their ballots in through the window, lest the impure political atmosphere within defile them. Thus was the suffragists' battle "won," compromise by compromise.*

women's suffrage movement should strike a bargain with one political party or the other. There was strong pressure to do so from wealthy Republican women like O. H. Belmont. Heartened by Theodore Roosevelt's interest in the cause in 1912, she wanted to abandon political neutrality. But Catt managed, in a number of crucial meetings, debates, and votes, to hold the association to the middle of the road as Gompers had held the AFL in 1896.

There was also the question of tactics. Some feminists had been impressed with the example of English women seeking the vote. They had organized mass parades and demonstrations, picketed public buildings, and trapped officials in their offices and besieged them with questions. Arrested for "trespass," they had conducted hunger strikes in prison and dramatized their sufferings in a way that won widespread sympathy. Two young women, Alice Paul and Harriot Blatch, attempted to take the American movement on this course in the early 1900s. They rejected the new and moderate leadership of women like Catt or Anna Howard Shaw, a minister who had tried to give the whole drive for the vote the flavor of a crusade for purity. Abandoning the posture of being "ladylike," Harriot Blatch (the daughter of feminist pioneer Elizabeth Cady Stanton) set up a radical Women's Political Union and organized massive suffrage parades in Washington in 1912 and 1913. Alice Paul founded a Congressional Union and undertook similar tactics. There were arrests and imprisonments. And there were lively scenes when President Wilson was ambushed by suffragettes (as the press called them) on the golf course or when congressional offices were invaded by women demanding a favorable vote on suffrage.

These tactics seemed less effective to Catt, however, than a step-up in lobbying efforts. She publicly kept her distance from militant tactics. And she insisted, in 1916, on remaining politically neutral in that campaign. The organizations of Blatch and Paul, now merged in the Women's Party, tried hard to defeat Wilson. The idea was, like the AFL's "punishing its enemies," to make the politicians see reason. But Catt held to the nonpartisan course.

And events rewarded her, as they did Gompers. A grateful Wilson named her to the women's division of the Council of National Defense. When war came, in recognition of the heavy participation of women in war-bond and propaganda drives, he finally emerged as a proponent of women's suffrage. The Republicans, already eager to tap a potential source of new strength, also swung into line. In 1919 the Republican-led Congress elected the preceding fall—with plenty of Democratic votes—passed and sent to the states the Nineteenth Amendment. It was quickly ratified. In 1920 American women got the vote, a full fifty years after it had been given to ex-slaves.

Much of the credit went to the whirlwind campaign of Catt between 1915 and 1919. Her cautious tactics, narrow in focus, had added 2 million members to the association in two years. Politicians listened to that kind of language. She had put the movement in step with the main currents of American politics. And recognizing the danger of tight linkage with one party, she had kept to the midroad. The National American Women's Suffrage Association was renamed the League of Women Voters in 1920. And it remained nonpartisan then and thereafter.

Yet the achievement of the vote along the conservative lines set by Catt was not the end of the story. Women entered the voting booths but did not substantially change the nature of American political life. The "revolt" of women in the twenties, which brought short skirts, bobbed hair, cigarettes, and sexual frankness to some upper-class young women, did not touch the deep problems of millions who were still expected (or chose) to perform in only traditional roles. The Depression of 1929 further set back the cause of emancipation. And in the aftermath of World War II there was a rebirth of a feminine mystique that once more glorified childbearing as women's highest calling.

Gompers, Washington, and Catt were all examples of conservative leaders who had sensed the main thrust of American life. They saw that most Americans accepted without major question the industrial and social and political systems that emerged after 1865. Certain arguments could be made in favor of workers, blacks, and women—but they had to be arguments acceptable to the political parties and the "leaders of society" who spoke for the most widely held values of the nation. Freedom had to be justified in terms of advancing the American ideal of prosperity, individual striving, family stability, social harmony, and gradual progress.

By understanding this and by battling radicals who called for a fundamental rebuilding of values, the conservative reformers had gotten some of the power they needed. But they had left certain areas untouched and traditional centers of authority intact. Limited power was not a final answer to the problems of "outsiders." Yet unlimited power could not be gained. It was a dilemma that remained to confront future generations seeking social change.

## *FOR FURTHER READING*

The story of Gompers and the AFL is well covered in Bernard Mandel, *Samuel Gompers* (1963), which also has much to say about business unionism. But Gompers' various "enemies" should be studied, too, to understand why they lost out to him. Gerald Grob, *Workers and Utopia* (1961) is the story of the Knights of Labor. Although there are several general histories of the Socialists in America, the most readable approach may be through Ray Ginger's *The Bending Cross* (1949)—a biography of the four-time Socialist presidential candidate, Eugene V. Debs. As for the Industrial Workers of the World, their story is well told in Melvyn Dubofsky, *We Shall Be All* (1969).

Booker T. Washington is thoroughly covered in a modern biography by Louis Harlan, *Booker T. Washington* (1973). A shrewd evaluation of Washington is contained in August Meier, *Negro Thought in America, 1880–1915* (1963). Washington himself was a prolific writer, and his mixture of conciliation, directness, energy, tactical shrewdness, and meaningful silences can best be experienced in his *Up From Slavery* (1901).

The story of women's fight for emancipation is told in Eleanor Flexner, *A Century of Struggle* (1959), already mentioned in Chapter 10. A more popular version is Andrew Sinclair's *The Better Half* (1970). Provocative in its interpretation of why suffrage activity was a "setback" for true women's liberation is William O'Neill, *Everyone Was Brave: The Rise and Fall of Feminism in America* (1969). M. G. Peck, *Carrie Chapman Catt* (1944) is straightforward and there are thoughtful looks into conflicts in the women's movement in Allen Davis, *Jane Addams* (1973).

# chapter 18 Business and government: antagonists, allies, or twins?

"The law," according to the seventeenth-century English political thinker Thomas Hobbes, "is the public conscience." Few people have been so willing as Americans to take that statement for granted. Few have so firmly believed that a statement of conscience automatically solves difficult social problems. In a preceding chapter we saw how early nineteenth-century reformers thought that the mere exposure of a national "sin," joined with calls to righteousness, was enough to cure the wrong. We also observed how this faith had to yield to facts. The actual, gritty business of changing society, rather than fleeing from it to mini-utopias, required legislation, lobbying, endless work, and, in the end, compromise.

If the way of the reformer was difficult when he dealt with flaws in personal conduct, it was doubly so when he got into the area of an entire society's behavior. At the nineteenth century's end this was dramatically shown. The nation defined a particular economic "sin"—the creation of trusts—and moved to purge and punish it. But it proved enormously hard to act on idealistic statements, as the economic machinery of the nation proved both complicated and rewarding even when unfair. The ups and downs of trust regulation revealed a great deal about the nation's basic purposes, as well as some conflicts in "the public conscience."

Americans worshiped the new machines that were lifting them from a rural age into one of industrial power and leadership. But the price of enjoying that abundance was a departure from cherished notions of how economic life should work. Railroads, power plants, and factories that rumbled and quivered with the noise of thousands of machines could not be created by small sums saved by a few individuals. Nor could they be managed on a small scale. They demanded millions in capital. That meant floating stocks and bonds. It meant control by bankers and dealers in securities, who themselves were not industrial managers but individuals whose "work" was manipulating pieces of paper.

In addition, modern factories demanded a high degree of coordinated planning and organization. That caused them, to an ever larger degree, to be managed by teams of specialists who required unusual skill and training. Above all, the enormous costs of large-scale industry drove these managers into constant, relentless search for economies in production and distribution. One route to that goal was to cut down on waste and uncertainty by eliminating competition. Perhaps monopoly was not the highest form of business efficiency. But it was undeniable that free rivalry among individual firms was inconsistent with smooth planning. It was far better to control prices, output, and costs of labor and materials by not having many firms try to outbid and outsell each other. In the long run, monopolists argued, that way was cheapest for consumers.

But, leaving economic theory aside, the idea of stifling competition was not an easy one to promote. Americans liked the fruits of industrial bigness. But they did not easily lose their worship of the Jacksonian idea of equality of opportunity. If life was a race in which all began on an equal footing and in which a smart person made and deserved his pile, then competition was essential. The issue was not only economic. It was social, moral, political, and psychological. The race had to be real, with a genuine chance to win, and the prizes had to have honest value.

But how was that possible in a modern world? It was, after 1877, becoming absolutely clear that the only real chance a lone individual had in competing with a corporation worth millions of dollars was the chance to go broke. Once, an ambitious new arrival in a community might set up a rival newspaper, department store, or law office to challenge the local establishment. But he was not going to set up a rival blast furnace or oil refinery.

It became even worse when large economic organizations not only overwhelmed individual competitors but then erased even competition among themselves. Such actions aroused a sense of betrayal among ordinary Americans. Their outrage was an emotional reality, whether or not economic logic was on their side. The anger was hard to handle sensibly, too, because it had no clear targets. Bigness alone did not seem to be a fault. And individual villains were not easy to find. An occasional industry, by 1900, might still be personified in one individual, as oil was in Rockefeller. But for the most part, the directors of major corporations were unknown to the general public. Citizens wryly recalled the popular phrase that the corporation had neither a soul to be damned nor a body to be kicked. Or as a distinguished sociologist, Edward A. Ross, put it in a 1907 book, *Sin and Society*, villains were no longer wicked men who breathed forth curses and an odor of gin. Wickedness might be seen in a railroad company that refused to spend money to put fences around a dangerous crossing. That decision might take a child's life. Yet each company director who voted for it might be a flawless family man at home. His business judgment belonged in a different moral framework.

So there the conflict-ridden national mind stood. The monster firm, run by financiers, that devoured business "enemies" offended the American democratic ideology. But, as we just saw, it also worked miracles of modernization that Americans worshiped. What legal machinery could emerge from such contradictory ideas? The answer provided by the political system was twofold. Congress devised policies of "trust control" that reflected popular criticism of big business. Then these policies were not applied. Or else, they were applied in such a way as to guarantee the survival of bigness.

Was this conscious hypocrisy? We now are in the shadowy area of explaining group thought. Do nations, like people, try to behave in such a way as to get what they want, while keeping a positive self-image and earning the admiration of others? It is a good subject for debate. We saw a similar situation in Chapter 8. Americans reveled in the openness and opportunity of the unspoiled frontier. It made freedom and equality possible. Yet they could hardly wait to "use up" that frontier by gorging themselves on its natural resources. Out of that conflict

---

*CHRONOLOGY*

| | |
|---|---|
| 1890 | *Sherman Antitrust Act passed by Congress* |
| 1895 | United States *v.* E. C. Knight Company *decision weakens antitrust laws* |
| 1901 | *U.S. Steel Corporation assembled by J. P. Morgan* |
| 1901 | *Theodore Roosevelt becomes president after McKinley's assassination* |
| 1911 | *Standard Oil Company trust ordered broken up by Supreme Court decision* |
| 1913 | *Establishment of Federal Reserve Board to control nation's banks* |
| 1914 | *Clayton Antitrust Act passed* |
| 1917 | *U.S. economy mobilized to increase production to fight World War I* |

of values came twisted cultural patterns. Romantic fiction of the West exalted the nobility of the trapper and the backwoodsman. But the gritty realities of westward expansion included Indian killing, land speculation, and province grabbing from Mexico. Likewise, in the case of the assault on the trusts, similar discordant notes were sounded by parties, Congress, the courts, and presidents.

*High Tide for Moral Talk: the 1890s*

The language of the early anti-big business movement was not known for exactness. Few voices were raised, for example, against a simple kind of collusion (or illegal agreement) among railroads known as a "pool." Under it, lines serving the same areas divided up traffic among themselves, shifting consignments from one to another when necessary. Then they split the profits. It was a convenient way for the roads to plan their schedules and equipment needs. But it clearly deprived customers of the benefits of competing rates and services. Yet no one could condemn a pool with quite the emotional force that he could muster in assailing the most hated word of the 1880s, "monopoly."

True monopoly, the absolute control of a product by one supplier, was rare. It might exist in pure form in a few areas, as, for example, when a single rail line linked a small community to market. But sharp definition did not matter. Even if a trade was controlled by a small handful of firms, instead of one, the effect on equality of opportunity was just as grim. The pain could be better expressed by the cry of "monopoly," which implied a single being full of selfishness and power.

The word "trust" next came into vogue. A trust was a legal device, which began to appear in the 1880s. Under it, the managers of a number of firms in the same business turned over their stock to "trustees." The trustees then ran these technically independent companies as a unified noncompetitive operation.

The trust was a lawyer's device, later outmoded by other forms of combination. But the word was short, fit easily into headlines, and had as much punch as "monopoly." It soon became the definition of any group of firms strong enough to set the conditions of an industry. By the 1890s there were such trusts in many diverse fields. They included meat, whiskey, sugar, flour, petroleum products, cordage, iron, steel, and matches, to name only a few.

Both "trust" and "monopoly" were emotional substitutes for the more accurate term "combinations." But whatever word they chose to describe the enemy, the opponents of bigness and concentration followed a clear line of argument. They painted a dramatic struggle between the evil and powerful and the good and weak. A New York State legislative committee, studying the problem in the mid-1880s, reported that combinations in dozens of industries all had the same goal: "the acquisition or destruction of competitive properties" in order to "fix the price at which they would purchase . . . raw material . . . and

*"The only thing that worries me is that he won't go back into the bottle. How can I stop him?" Little explanation is needed for this cartoon of the 1880s that depicts Uncle Sam's Aladdin-like dilemma—how to control the power at his disposal. Aladdin's luck at rebottling his genie was better than America's.*

at which they would sell." Workers, suppliers, and consumers were to be placed at the mercy of the syndicate, combination, or trust.

A history of farm protest movements written in 1889 shouted that: "Individual effort is fruitless. The relentless, remorseless, and unyielding grasp of monopoly is upon every avenue of trade and commerce." Powderly, the powerful union spokesman, declared: "He is a true Knight of Labor who with one hand clutches anarchy by the throat, and with the other strangles monopoly." An Antimonopoly Party, formed in 1884, lamented that all the key elements of trade were "mercilessly controlled by giant monopolies." By 1888 even the two major parties, usually slow to adopt inflammatory language, were joining in moral denunications. The Republican platform spurned those who would "control arbitrarily the condition of trade among our citizens." More bluntly, the Democrats said that people were "betrayed" by combinations that "rob the body of our citizens by depriving them of the benefits of natural competition."

Such statements were obviously not clear-cut descriptions of the economic functioning of large corporations or groups of corporations. It followed, therefore, that the actions demanded by such protesters were also not specific about how to curb particular bad practices. Trust control was on the congressional agenda all through the 1880s. But the discussion was mainly in moralistic terms, and so were the resulting actions.

The legal precedents for antitrust enactments were found in certain English statutes (and common-law court decisions) against monopolies. They arose from the medieval idea of society as a closed, small band of brothers under God and king. The monopolist in that case was a sinner against his fellows, and the law aimed to punish him rather than to deal with the situation that allowed him to get a monopoly of some needed good. When Congress finally passed the Sherman Antitrust Act in 1890, it took this ancient track. The new law simply declared that every "contract, combination . . . or conspiracy, in restraint of trade or commerce among the several States, or with foreign nations, is hereby declared to be illegal." Every member of any such combination or conspiracy was guilty of a "misdemeanor" and liable to a $5000 fine. There was no enforcement machinery. And there were no guidelines to help courts decide just what words like "restraint" meant. Presumably, in the age of transcontinental railroads and multimillion-dollar corporations, they could use the same standards as in fourteenth-century England. In fact, few congressmen cared. The real purport of the bill was guessed at by Connecticut's Senator Orville Platt. He said that the idea was not honestly to prohibit trusts but to get "some bill with that title that we might go to the country with. The questions of whether the bill would be operative, or how it would operate . . . have been whistled down the wind."

*The Futile First Years of the Sherman Act*

Nevertheless, the bill was on the books. But its first fifteen years of life showed plainly that passage of a law is only the first step in effecting a social change. Sometimes it is an almost meaningless one if no one has the responsibility or will to use it. No special agency within the federal Department of Justice in 1890 had the job of finding violations. And in 1895 Attorney General Richard Olney, a conservative Massachusetts corporation lawyer, wrote genially to a friend that he would not prosecute cases under a law that he deemed to be "no good."

The courts themselves interpreted the statute in a way that favored continued corporate growth. A landmark decision in 1895 put the Supreme Court in the position of virtually nullifying the Sherman Act. A suit was brought against the E. C. Knight Company, which was one of the member companies of the sugar trust. It had bought control of four refineries, responsible for more than 90 percent of sugar manufacture in the country. But a Court majority held that the Sherman Act only gave the United States the right to bar combinations hampering *interstate* commerce. Since the refineries involved were all in Pennsylvania, strictly speaking the Sherman Act had not been broken at all. Justice John Marshall Harlan, in a strong dissent, pointed out that the commodities produced by giant combinations all found their way into commerce among the states. To allow monopolization and price rigging to continue so long as the deals involved took place within a state's boundaries, therefore, was really to license trust building in a nationalized economy.

But this was a minority view. Where the courts *did* apply the Sherman Act was in a traditional area. They used it to cudgel striking labor unions by holding that strikes and boycotts were "conspiracies in restraint of trade." In the Danbury Hatters case of 1902 a federal district court imposed a crippling fine on striking hat workers. In 1907, in the Bucks Stove and Range case, another court charged Gompers and the AFL leadership with lawbreaking for urging a boycott of products made by the union-busting Bucks Company.

Nonprosecution and hostile court interpretation limited the reach of the new law. While the depression of 1893 lingered, there was still an anticombination outcry. But the return of prosperity and the coming of a new century sent consolidation racing ahead. There were only 86 industrial combinations formed between 1887 and 1897, according to one economist's count. But by 1904 there were 318, with a capitalization of over $7 billion.

Symbolic of the new age of giants was the formation, in 1901, of the U.S. Steel Corporation. It was a combination of firms put together by the nation's most powerful banker, J. P. Morgan. It was the first billion-dollar corporation. Though its monopoly was not complete, from the start it set steel prices in the industry. Its few competitors could only challenge its prices at the risk of being ruined. The birth of such corporate giants was defended by Morgan's publicity agents as a forward step in progress, efficiency, and the scientific creation of new wealth.

Yet combination showed a seamy side that was all too plain. It was a cause of rising consumer prices, fading opportunities for individual economic effort, and labor strife. While consolidation rolled along a seemingly clear track in the first decade of the new century, new and sharp criticisms were heard. Once more the federal government stirred itself to cope with the problem.

### *Sound and Fury: TR, Progressives, and Trusts*

The year 1900 saw the arrival of the "progressive" attack on combinations. It spoke a different language from that of the antimonopolists of the 1880s. Moral urgency was still there. But the essence of the twentieth-century reform leadership that took the name of "Progressive" was, simply, that it accepted "progress." It did not look wistfully back to a lost golden age. And it hoped to apply information and intelligence to the solution of modern problems.

Progressives were convinced that gigantic institutions were inseparable from economic advances that promised a better life for all. As they saw it, a healthy democracy began with an informed population. Voters would gather facts from an active and free press and form their opinions with the help of various reform groups that pointed out abuses and evaluated various proposals for their correction. Then, using a cleaned-up political process, this wise electorate would choose public officials to carry out its intentions. The jobs might be complicated ones, such as improving urban health facilities, building new schools, or conserving natural resources. But the elected leaders would then name nonpartisan experts to do the actual hard tasks of planning and operation. Thus bigness and freedom would somehow be reconciled.

It is understandable that this style of thinking would produce a new approach to the trust problem. Its outline was suggested in the first annual message of President Theodore Roosevelt to Congress in December 1901. At that time Roosevelt was a long distance from total progressivism. He also had a strong sense of how difficult it was to win sudden reforms, considering the natural caution of most people. Yet he was sure that the masters of mighty industries must not be permitted uncontrolled power. This view was perfectly in tune with the opinions of the rising urban middle class. What he actually said, therefore, was middle of the road.

Speaking of the "tremendous and highly complex industrial development" of the preceding era, Roosevelt paid tribute to the people who had led it.

> The captains of industry who have driven the railway systems across this continent, who have built up our commerce, who have developed out manufactures, have on the whole done great good to our people. Without them the material development of which we are so justly proud could never have taken place.

But, he later added, "it is also true that there are real and grave evils." He noted that "trusts are in certain of their features and tendencies hurtful to the general welfare." Therefore, "combination and concentration should be, not prohibited, but supervised and within reasonable limits controlled." First, there should be an exposure of the facts. "Publicity is the only sure remedy we can now invoke." Next, remedies through governmental regulation or special taxes should be determined "by process of law." Since state laws on corporations varied widely and trusts did business in many states, "the nation"—meaning the federal government—"should, without interfering with the power of the States . . . assume power of supervision."

This was a far more detailed program than the vague provisions of the Sherman Act. It was also a smooth piece of political blandness, natural in a new president, especially in Roosevelt, who had only gotten to the White House after McKinley's assassination in September 1901. It probably deserved the widely quoted satire of the earlier mentioned fictitious Irish barkeep, Mr. Dooley. Dooley's version of the message was irresistible. "Th' trusts . . . are heejoous [hideous] monsthers built up be th' enlightened intherprise iv th' men that have done so much to advance progress in our beloved country. . . . On wan hand I wud stamp them undher fut; on th' other hand not so fast."

Yet that was not really the whole story. Despite Dooley's well-aimed joke, Roosevelt was turning a corner in antitrust policy. True, he moved with toughness against notably sinful trusts. In 1902 he had his attorney general move against the Northern Securities Company, a combination of the major railroad networks in the Pacific Northwest, which was in a position of almost total monopoly. In March 1904 the Supreme Court ordered the breakup of the combine

But a less spectacular event of 1903 was the creation, on TR's urging, of a Bureau of Corporations within the newly created Department of Commerce and Labor. This bureau had the power to gather and sift information and prepare the groundwork for court cases. Its birth was a more significant step than the well-advertised victory over the Northern Securities railroad barons. It pointed to a growing pattern of fact accumulation and sifting before any action was taken. And that process meant that there would be fewer cases but more research and more pinpointing of problems.

Roosevelt himself set an example by reversing his field on antitrust prosecutions in 1907 and allowing the U.S. Steel Corporation to acquire a new subsidiary, the Tennessee Coal and Iron Company. The official excuse for the action was that it was necessary, during a financial panic, to raise the value of U.S. Steel's stocks and give an emergency shot in the arm to the sagging stock market. But it was clearly a case of the president's weighing the national interest as he saw it and deciding that *this* particular consolidation was allowable, whereas others might not be. Roosevelt was not howling down all sinners. He was making a judgment between "good" and "bad" trustbuilding. His example was soon to be followed by the Supreme Court.

Among the 40 or so antitrust prosecutions that Roosevelt started was one against the Standard Oil Company, which was in the popular mind the trust of trusts. The case reached the Supreme Court in 1911. The Court did, in fact, order Standard to be broken into smaller components. But its majority decision declared that only when the restraint of trade was "unreasonable" was the fragmenting of a great corporation justified. This "rule of reason," in effect, meant that the courts would review, with expert advice, the economic activities of large corporations and then apply the law selectively to particular abuses. Antimonopoly fury was to be replaced by judicial surgery.

This was, in fact, the general trend of congressional economic legislation between 1900 and 1914. Congress made several new moves to strengthen the position of the fairly young Interstate Commerce Commission (ICC) controlling the railroads. The Elkins Act of 1903, the Hepburn Act of 1906, and the Mann-Elkins Act of 1910 spelled out and forbade particular abuses in rate fixing. They also extended the commission's power over other forms of transportation, like ferries and pipelines. They also enabled the commissioners to get court orders forbidding the companies from carrying on challenged practices while their cases were being heard.

Such acts were not based on hostility to business. Many businessmen who used the railroads in fact favored the measures, because it was easier for them to calculate their transportation costs in a regulated industry than to bargain and connive with individual lines for special treatment. And many railroad leaders, too, though they formally opposed regulation, understood that there were some advantages to orderly procedures and rates. Monopoly and combination had been intended all along to achieve business dependability and regularity and so to make long-range planning possible. Rail trusts and mergers, simply to take one example, had moved toward standardized conditions, but without having to answer to the public. Now the government seemed to be encouraging such movement, but it was guiding the trusts in what it thought to be the public interest. Naturally, railroad owners and railroad commissioners tended to disagree on just what was fair, necessary, and "reasonable" in governing the lines.

### *Business and Government: Coming Together*

Yet owners and regulators *were* moving on parallel, if not identical, paths. And as the new laws went into effect, the ICC had to take more and more testimony concerning the technical workings of the industry; it assigned more and more specialists to the preparation of its cases. These specialists had the same training in engineering, law, and economics as the experts hired by the railroads to argue their case. Often they came *from* the railroad industry itself. It was inevitable that the commissioners themselves, in order to follow the arguments, would very often be veterans of railroad management. The public could only dimly understand the specific issues and demand "fairness." Industry and government together furnished the expertise that made the rules. They rationalized big business. The word *rationalize* is used here in two senses: to excuse a thing and to make it systematic and orderly.

In the years just before 1912 there were other progressive attempts to keep the freedom of political democracy but gain the economic advantages of large-scale planning. Progressive mayors and governors moved ahead with programs establishing regulatory panels and boards for streetcar lines and power companies or even making them publicly owned. Conservation commissioners were authorized to guard limited supplies of timber and minerals. New state laws guarded against fraud, not only on a small scale in retail stores but in the multimillion-dollar insurance and banking fields.

Each of these reforms called for a bureaucracy of engineers, attorneys, and administrators. When the objectives were to purify water and milk supplies or to wipe out tuberculosis and other diseases, then the payroll had to be enlarged with doctors, chemists, bacteriologists, and professors in various specialties. Universities became indispensable as the training grounds of a new elite of public servants.

But the same tendencies existed in big business. Giant corporations no longer entrusted the building of new plants to the rule-of-thumb methods of those who had begun at the bottom. Instead, they turned to the same educational establishment that was furnishing skilled civil servants. In government offices and business headquarters, it was not possible to make important decisions without the careful accumulation of data by technicians.

Business and government, in short, had somewhat differing objectives, but they were also showing recognizable similarities. Of course, politics was still the underlying force in governmental decision making, as profit was for the businessman. But modernization touched everywhere. Progressive attempts to fight boss rule through steps such as direct election of senators were defended as up-to-date ways of bringing government closer to the people. Corporations likewise tried to appear more responsive to social needs. A few giants like U.S. Steel, Standard Oil, Eastman Kodak, and Heinz Foods took tentative, paternalistic steps in the decade from 1910 to 1920 toward employee welfare and community relations programs. They sponsored company unions, profit-sharing and pension schemes, and other devices that were attempts at progressivism in management to match progressivism in politics. These did not prevent many of the great corporations from continuing with unfair labor practices or policies that hit the public pocketbook hard. Nor did they spread to many small business firms.

Nevertheless, it is still fair to say that a traditional image of politics in the Progressive era that pits high-minded reformers against reactionary plutocrats is oversimplified. Differences were not that clear-cut. The nation, in fact, recognized by 1912 that relations between business and government had a new sophistication. This awareness colored the political contest of 1912. In the presidential race Theodore Roosevelt ran as the candidate of a third party, the Progressives. His platform demanded what he called a New Nationalism. This was the doctrine that the federal government had a responsibility for maintaining the general welfare by accepting the corporation-dominated economy but holding its rulers to high standards of behavior. The whole nation was now one community, like a kind of hugely expanded Puritan village. The federal government, as the voice of that community, should guarantee things such as the purity of food and drugs, the safety of factories, the care of the sick, aged, and helpless, the fairness of prices, and the protection of natural resources. It should see that human rights, as well as property rights, were recognized.

*The 1912 Election and the Clayton Act*

Woodrow Wilson was running for the Democrats against Roosevelt and William Howard Taft, the Republican incumbent. He backed a set of measures called the New Freedom. In theory, they were distinct from what TR proposed. They aimed to curb the power of the trusts and guarantee more competition, leaving the individual to battle for his own welfare against the giants who would only be allowed to use their advantages fairly. But, in actuality, Wilson recognized that to cut Goliath down to size and give David a chance meant strengthening the hand of government, just as TR wished to do. When he won the election, Wilson's congressional allies took antitrust measures that simply carried on the trend toward regulating, not ruining, the trusts.

The Clayton Antitrust Act of 1914, the first major change in the Sherman Act, simply defined some new practices that were not allowable. One, for example, was the "interlocking directorate," in which the same individuals sat on the boards of many allegedly competing companies. In addition, the Clayton Act exempted unions from the Sherman Act's provisions. But the enforcement of the new measure was the key point. Another law, the Federal Trade Commission (FTC) Act, set up a five-member nonpartisan board appointed by the president. It had broad power to examine industrial practices and fight abuses of fair competition in the courts. Such abuses included false advertising, shoddy goods, price-fixing agreements, and plots to freeze out newcomers in a business field. The FTC began a long career of policing the industrial scene in order to protect the public.

But the FTC was a watchdog, not an executioner. It did not wipe out trusts and sow the seeds of small business on their ruins. And its staffs were not necessarily enemies of big business. Much of the FTC's information was developed in cooperation with the regulated industries.

In some ways the FTC was like another Wilson era creation, the Federal

*It was the blazing, focused energy of Theodore Roosevelt that captivated a whole generation of his Progressive followers. Yet for all his fierce demands for reform, he was basically a conservative who wanted to modify the American system only as much as necessary to spare it revolutionary shocks. This was the reason for his frequent changes of stance regarding industrial concentration, but this very inconsistency was itself distinctly American.*

Reserve Board. That agency was established in 1913 to break the grip of major banks on credit. It did so to some extent. Yet its governors were neither labor leaders, farmers, professional politicians, nor spokesmen for citizens' groups. Generally, they were bankers of long experience. They regarded their job as one of improving the private moneylending system for the public's benefit and their own. They were not exactly wolves set to guard the sheep, but they were not wolf killers either.

The FTC's future was shaped, not by rigid rules but by the play of events, as its first fifteen years of life revealed. The battle against monopoly, in that period, suffered two important setbacks. One was brought on by the nation's plunge into the most centralizing of all modern activities, war. The other came about when the business-regulating machinery in Washington was turned into an instrument to promote rather than to retard concentration.

Soon after the United States joined the ranks of the Allies in April 1917, the economic mobilization of the nation got under way. In area after area, increased production became the highest priority on the national agenda. To achieve it industry was organized from the top in a number of ways. A War Industries Board awarded contracts, decided who got first choice of scarce materials, and had a say on every aspect of expansion, from where to put new plants to setting up timetables for delivery. To speed creation of a wartime merchant marine an Emergency Fleet Corporation oversaw the nation's construction yards. The railroads were nationalized after a few months of war. The War Food Administration and the War Fuel Administration worked at stockpiling and conserving items such as grain and coal. They did this partly by urging nationwide campaigns of self-denial (meatless and wheatless and sugarless days) and also by boosting production through encouraging more efficiency.

But "efficiency" was exactly what came hard to small producers. They could not afford the savings of large-scale buying. They could not buy machines to replace scarce labor. They could not lump frequent small shipments into occasional big ones, so as not to "waste" freight cars. Small businessmen often could not get long-term credit. They had to live from day to day.

Making the economy more efficient, therefore, made it more concentrated. It was sensible to give major producers the big contracts for munitions, airplanes, or trucks and then to have them assign subassembly operations to smaller companies. It was sensible to locate new plants close to existing ones, where transportation was already available—even if that meant concentrating industry more tightly in big production centers: Pittsburgh for steel, Detroit for autos, and so on.

Even labor practices followed the pattern. A National War Labor Board tried to settle disputes without work stoppages. Its personnel included some union leaders from the AFL. That was Gompers' reward for a no-strike pledge. On the whole, the standards it set were fair. But the wage levels it required in war-related industry were those that could be managed by big concerns but that were difficult for smaller ones. What economists called the marginal producer, the one who could only stay in business when profits were high and costs were low, was being squeezed out in the wartime consolidation. Meanwhile, the lawyers and statisticians and engineers for both the corporations *and* the government departments were now on the same side of the table. The common enemies were "the Hun" and "inefficiency."

The war's end somewhat loosened the centralization of 1917–1918. But the administrations of Presidents Harding and Coolidge that followed showed an unexpected result of trying to control industrial bigness through government regulatory boards. If the board members themselves were not believers in an antitrust philosophy, they could actually use their powers to increase concentration.

There were two proofs of this in the twenties. For one thing, the monetary policies of Secretary of the Treasury Andrew Mellon, a Pittsburgh banking millionaire, sharply reduced taxes on major corporations, leaving them with more money for even greater expansion. For another, there was the activity of Herbert Hoover as secretary of commerce. Hoover deserves closer scrutiny as one model of an American modernizer. Born poor in West Branch, Iowa, in 1874, he had gone the rags-to-riches route. Gifted with a first-class technical mind, he did brilliantly at Stanford and by middle age was a millionaire mining engineer.

Hoover was a superb organizer of humanitarian activities. He came upon the national scene as a relief administrator. In 1914 he was called on to head a drive for Belgian war relief, aimed to help the victims of the German invasion. His success was outstanding. In 1917 he was named food administrator, and he performed triumphantly in that capacity as well. Just after the war, he headed another relief drive for famine sufferers in revolution-torn Russia (despite his distaste for the Bolshevik regime).

From 1921 to 1928 the side of Hoover that was most evident was his urge for tidiness and order in the industrial system. He wanted to increase productivity, so that all classes in a prospering America would know higher levels of income and enjoyment. But his method was to continue the encouragement of concentration under corporate leaders. As secretary of commerce, he urged businesses to form "trade associations" of firms in the same industries (such as trucking, textiles, petroleum products, and the like). These associations were provided with up-to-date marketing, credit, and other information by the Department of Commerce. They also were given every advantage in expanding their operations at home and abroad. In turn, they were supposed to adopt voluntary codes of quality control, fair pricing, and labor arbitration. It was all very highminded. But again, like the wartime mobilization, it turned out that the few giants in each associated industry set the terms that were best for them and hard on small competitors.

So, by 1930, when the Sherman Act was forty years old and the country had plunged into the Depression of 1929, antitrust action had been a very inconsistently applied national policy. In 1938, when the act had its forty-eighth birthday, Congress had a mild flurry of trust-busting activity. It created a Temporary National Economic Committee to look into and plan remedies for continued concentration of ownership in the economy.

But in 1940, on the half-century anniversary of the act, the nation undertook a new economic mobilization to prepare for its almost inevitable participation in World War II. With cries for an airplane production capacity of 10,000 planes per year and for a two-ocean navy ringing aloud in the land, the United States once more made the production of military hardware its overriding concern. Soon, an Office of Production Management and various other planning agencies, just like their predecessors in World War I, were busy bringing "order" in industry. Once more, the United States had gone to war and sacrificed democratic principles to achieve victory.

Soon the nation would emerge from that conflict, too. And new generations would grow up knowing that somehow the mighty names of American life included Gulf and Standard, ITT and ATT, GM and Bell, Anaconda and Alcoa, Monsanto and Dow, Sperry Rand and Boeing. Supertrusts and supergovernment marched on, hand in hand.

## *FOR FURTHER READING*

A standby introduction to the growth of trusts is Ida Tarbell, *The Nationalizing of Business* (1936), and a classic statement of antitrust outrage is Henry D. Lloyd, *Wealth Against Commonwealth* (1894). There is also much antitrust material in John D. Hicks, *The Populist Revolt* (1931).

A heavy but useful study of how the Sherman Act came into being and what happened afterward is Hans Thorelli, *The Federal Antitrust Policy* (1954). Interesting sidelights on Sherman are in Margaret Leech, *In the Days of McKinley* (1959), and a fine, fascinating look at J. P. Morgan, who went right on building trusts after the act was passed is Frederick L. Allen, *The Great Pierpont Morgan* (1949).

Theodore Roosevelt's back-and-forth wavering on the trust question is covered in a biography by William Harbaugh, *Power and Responsibility* (1961). Wilson's ambivalence is amply described in Arthur S. Link, *Woodrow Wilson and the Progressive Era* (1954).

Did the Progressives really distrust the trusts? Two recent studies answer negatively: Gabriel Kolko, *The Triumph of Conservatism* (1963) and Robert Wiebe's *The Search for Order* (1968).

What actually took place in the twenties—an increase in concentration of economic power—is well described in George Soule, *Prosperity Decade* (1947). Herbert Hoover's ideas on "associated activities" are covered in Albert U. Romasco, *The Poverty of Abundance* (1965). An amusing look at the whole problem by a trust-busting law professor of the 1930s is Thurman Arnold, *The Folklore of Capitalism* (1937).

# Thought provokers

*By the time the twentieth century was well under way, the United States had developed a new, semiofficial religion of optimism. Behind it lay many years of gradual acceptance of Darwinism. How did the social version of evolution come to be the national gospel? What things were going on that made people particularly ready to look for a scientific explanation of the march of events? Did they make a clear distinction in their minds between science, a way of organizing human experience and seeking truths that can be tested, and technology, the application of knowledge about the physical universe to solving practical problems? Did they really change their basic outlooks on the world so as to accommodate the scientific habits of doubting and questioning any proposition not laboratory proved? Or did they simply replace their old unreasoning faiths with new ones? How was the God of evolution different from the God of the Puritans? Why did so few thinkers read Darwinism pessimistically—that is, assume that human beings were helpless animals in the grip of forces they could not change? In sum, how did American culture change under the impact of scientific theory but also remain unchanged in certain ways and bend new theories to fit certain set habits of mind? To answer this question is to recognize that cultural change lags behind swift-moving events, a basic fact of behavioral life.*

*Such questions may seem rather remote and intellectual to some of you. To those who care for specific instances, it may be valuable to take a particular invention and follow through on its effect on society. How did the telephone, for example, give people a basic sense of being able to overcome the physical limitations of time and space? What difference does it make if, in order to get in touch with someone thousands of miles away, you have only to pick up an instrument and speak, instead of writing a letter and waiting many days and weeks for a reply? Would it increase your sense of humanity's power to determine the conditions under which it lives? Would it make you feel that an age of invention was a sign of superior wisdom on the part of your generation? And if it did, how would that affect your respect for the "lessons" of the past? And for rigid rules of behavior altogether? Try to ask the same questions about other inventions after thinking precisely and in detail of what it was that they made possible.*

*Next, you may find it useful to get into the social possibilities created by inventions. In addition to those mentioned in the chapter on city life, what other inventions made cities "work"? In order to manage the coming and going of hundreds of thousands of people daily and their living together without accidents, disease, or calamities, what kind of planning becomes necessary? Can such matters as care of the poor or control of crime be left to individual family efforts? What kinds of municipal regulations concerning the licensing of peddlers, for example, or garbage disposal can be traced to the needs of a big city as opposed to a small? What was the connection between the age of urbanism and the development of graduate schools to train experts in fields such as traffic engineering and water purification?*

*And if the face of a city reflects the powers it worships and the ideas it wishes to honor, what would you expect, in American cities, to replace the cathedrals and palaces of Europe? And what actually* did *replace them? What are the outstanding sights of your own city today, and what do they tell you about its values? What would you guess about the culture of the United States if you came across the perfectly preserved ruins of New York, for example, 500 years from now?*

*Turning finally to politics and power, what underlying forces toward order were at work in* all *parts of society? For example, does the work of Gompers in creating business unionism resemble, in any way, what the creators of trusts were doing in the world of business enterprise? And how would you compare the efforts of Gompers, an organizer of supercorporations like U.S. Steel, and an urban boss? Were they all trying to impose some systematic pattern on large-scale undertakings? In what ways did they differ? And in what ways were their tactics suited to, or out of step with, the officially expressed codes of behavior of American life? And especially of unions, businesses, and governments? Was there a gap between what had to be done or was done to keep large systems running and the official respect paid to individualism, democracy, and honesty? Did personal codes suit the needs of large organizations?*

*How did a changing world affect reformers? Look at Chapter 10 again, and then compare it with Chapters 17 and 18. Did the shift in antitrust efforts from the Sherman Act to the Clayton Act twenty-four years later resemble the shift from the moral zeal behind the amendment ending slavery, in 1865, to Booker T. Washington's hard-headed concern with industrial training for blacks in 1895? In other words, did the lapse of time in both cases shift the emphasis of reformers from idealism to efficiency? From the desirable to the possible?*

*Reacquaint yourselves with the four amendments to the Constitution added between 1913 and 1920—numbers Sixteen through Nineteen. They all are creations of the Progressive era. How do they show the progressive outlook? Do they try to combine "purifying" democracy with making it work more "scientifically"? Or do they merely express good intentions? Do they require complicated enforcement machinery? And how do they unite old and new values? That is, can you arrange a dialogue between a reformer of the 1830s (like Lyman Beecher or Susan B. Anthony) and a progressive like Theodore Roosevelt on the reasons for supporting income taxes, direct election of senators, votes for women, and national prohibition of alcoholic beverages?*

# part six: The World and Us

*The world we live in is divided into more than* 100 *separate, sovereign political communities, or nations. Each is the representative of "one people" who have taken, in the words of our Declaration of Independence, a "separate and equal station" among the "powers of the earth." They deal with each other through trade, diplomacy, and war. These dealings are called foreign relations. There comes a time when any historian of a country must tackle those relations. When he does, he finds himself moving, too often, in a world of undefined terms and agreed-on fairy tales.*

*Traditionally, histories of foreign relations are a long list of disputes, negotiations, treaties, and wars. The chief actors are ministers of state, generals, and ambassadors. Both story and cast are dull. For one thing, they often take official statements at face value. A little more hard-boiled skepticism would be helpful. (For example, all nations officially proclaim that they want peace. But an American humorist once said that for governments, peace was just "an interval of cheating between two periods of fighting.") In addition, some questions are never explored.*

*First and foremost, it is taken for granted that the goal of any government's foreign policy is to protect the national interest. But* what is the national interest? *Certainly, it includes independence; and beyond that, perhaps, protection of the national boundaries. But what should a nation's boundaries be? Natural barriers like rivers? Lines accidentally drawn by history? The places where language changes from one town to the next? Or simply the outer limits of what the country is strong enough to take and hold? The United States added to its territories by purchase or conquest in* 1803, 1810, 1819, 1845, 1852, 1867, 1898 *and* 1917. *With each step, then, the "national interest" of protection required heavier commitments of defense. Was this balanced off by some gain for the national interest? Or are there a number of national interests that can be weighed against each other? Could a national interest in economy ever tip the balance against a national interest in defending territories taken in war long ago?*

*Another good question often absent from the usual diplomatic history is that of* who defines the national interest. *Let us be specific again. In* 1871, *by treaty with Great Britain, the United States "won" the right for its citizens to fish in certain Canadian waters. (Note how the very terms of diplomacy, "winning" and "losing," suggest that the natural relationship among nations is one of contestants.) That "victory" was in the national interest, but those who gained most from it were the small numbers of Americans directly involved in commercial fishing.*

*It is true that this might have general benefits for others. The price of fish would come down in the marketplace. And if New England fishermen had a brighter economic future, their borrowing and spending boosted the prosperity of millions of other businessmen. Then, too, the psychological dividend of an American "victory" at the bargaining table was spread throughout the nation.*

*But the fact remains that a particular, select, small, and special group was the main beneficiary of that part of the treaty. Other groups profited by other parts of the treaty, and still others do by* all *American treaties. So it may be that the national interest is the total of a number of special interests, each demanding support in the name of* the *national interest. And the definition of* the *national interest may change, depending upon which groups are the closest to power.*

A third question that needs to be asked is: How does a nation officially describe its national interest? Governments are usually not very frank about their goals. They do not advertise desires to help their own citizens become prosperous. Instead, they adopt a rhetoric of explanation of their foreign policies. This rhetoric then becomes part of the self-image of a people. For example, for the past thirty years of its military growth, the United States has claimed that it is simply the guardian of a peaceful and stable world. France under Napoleon in the early 1800s said she was spreading the principles of democratic revolution throughout Europe, no more. Great Britain, late in the nineteenth century, explained that her worldwide empire was part of her mission of carrying civilization to the "backward" races.

By raising these three questions—who defines national interest, how the definition changes, and how it is defended in propaganda terms—we open up new ways of looking at foreign-relations history. The diplomatic record becomes one more tool for analyzing the large, artificial community known as a nation.

Learning who has most to say about the goals of diplomacy (protecting the national interest) tells us something about the distribution of power within a country. Finding out what the influences of foreign policy want tells something about their economic functions and needs. And seeing how they present their case furnishes a kind of psychological self-portrait of a people as they would like to be seen by others. Applying such analysis to the United States allows us to use the record of its foreign policies as we have used our other evidence. We can study the impact of change on American society, as we trace the chain of events from yesterday to today.

Three case studies are used here. The first chapter of this part, Chapter 19, contains a sketch of U.S. relations with China from 1784 almost to the present day. For most of that period China was a gigantic, ancient, "pagan," and weak country. American contacts with her illustrated how people in the United States felt about their rights, privileges, and duties with regard to the great riches and huge populations of Asia.

Chapter 20 will sweep over U.S. relations with Mexico from 1846 until 1933. Like the United States, Mexico had broken away from the mother country and set out to be independent. Her Hispanic-Indian culture and the Anglo culture of the United States had different meanings for North America. The two nations were in fairly steady conflict, with the United States usually emerging as the winner and the dominant influence. How this came to be explains a great deal about the elements of U.S. power as it grew to overshadow the entire western hemisphere.

Finally, in Chapter 21, on the United States and the rest of the world, there is a close-up examination of relations with Europe around the time of World War I. We will see how the United States got into that war, why it chose the side it did, and how it misunderstood the possibilities opened by victory. The great discussions of neutrality in 1914–1916 and of peacemaking in 1919 illuminated this country's ideas about the nature of European society and politics. They also highlighted how Americans regarded their own virtues as compared with the qualities of other peoples. The entire story is not merely one of submarines, torpedoes, trenches, and treaty signings. It is a look at America's early twentieth-century mentality. It shows the close, continuing relationships between foreign policies and problems at home.

# chapter 19

# China and the United States

In the beginning there was commerce. In 1784 a small vessel flying the colors of the two-year-old United States (still under the Articles of Confederation) left New York for Canton. One year later it returned with a cargo of silk and tea and a handsome profit for its owners. At last, it seemed, American merchants had something to replace their once-profitable voyages to the British West Indies, which were now closed to them, because they were no longer British subjects.

The China trade was part of a general boldness that took Yankee skippers deep into the eastern Mediterranean as well as into the Pacific in the late 1700s. The lure of high prices for exotic Oriental goods such as spices, porcelain, jade, tea, and silk drew all the seagoing powers of the world eastward. That was, after all, what had led to the discovery of the Americas in the first place.

*Young America Meets Old China*

Whatever the reasons, the *Empress of China*, that first American ship of 1784, was soon followed by others. By the 1840s the United States was well established in the trade. You will recall that in Chapter 9, on business beginnings, there was a portrait of the Low family, merchants in Canton. They were part of a complete and colorful way of life.

The Chinese at this time were still masters in their own land. They only allowed foreigners, whom they regarded as barbarians, to conduct trade through the one port of Canton. Americans unloaded furs, sandalwood (a fragrant wood used in cabinetworks and dyes), ginseng (a root that Chinese males thought would help their virility), and raw cotton. They lived, like other Western businessmen, in compounds known as "hongs." They could not travel outside of Canton, and they had no diplomatic representatives at the Imperial Court in Peking, which refused to admit the uncouth presence of uncivilized outsiders.

But life in the hongs was far from unpleasant. There were plenty of inexpensive servants. There were gardens to walk in, boat rides and picnics, and excellent meals. Even simply walking to work in the city brought the visitor a feast for the eye. Nowhere in Boston or New York could he see crowded streets full of babble and bustle, rickshaw coolies trotting with their two-wheeled vehicles, professional rat catchers walking the streets with their cages and traps, street entertainers doing acrobatic dances, and vendors' carts selling hot goodies. A young American named Low or Russell or Forbes might miss clam chowder or sleigh rides during his training period in China. But he could not complain of dull surroundings.

The Chinese dealt with the Americans and other foreigners through a "guild" of special merchants. These were themselves wealthy, educated men. They did not object to making friends with their "barbarian" business associates. They invited them to dinner, showed them where to shop for the best porcelains, silks, and jades, and gave them gifts. Many a scroll, fan, and lacquered box came to rest that way in New England parlors. In turn, the Westerners often helped their Chinese merchant friends with banking and investment matters outside of China, and kept up their part of the rituals of companionship. It was for both sides a personal kind of business dealing. If each side thought the other's civilization was inferior, they did not press the point.

A few Protestant missionaries appeared with the traders. They were not important enough to disturb the Chinese with the "insult" of their presence. The Chinese simply tolerated the Americans, British, Dutch, and Portuguese as necessary for purposes of trade. China simply opened one port as a back-door tradesmen's entrance and admitted only authorized visitors. She and she alone controlled the door. The point was made especially clear by devices such as those involved in the opium trade, mostly conducted by British ships. They could only bring opium from India to a point just off Canton's shores. There they had to transfer it to Chinese-owned craft for actual landing.

Opium, however, brought on the downfall of the old hong system. The balance between China and the West was upset by Western capitalism's explosive growth and drive to maximize every chance for profit. British traders wanted more traffic with China, especially in opium. The Chinese government, however, late in the 1830s, tried to ban the trade in the drug, whose growing use was becoming a problem. The British then fought what was called the Opium War. It quickly demonstrated the total inability of the Chinese to defend themselves against Western armaments. A treaty was signed in 1842, and under it the Chinese were forced to open four more treaty ports. This was the first of many such concessions they would have to make, once the West had tasted blood.

The United States took no part in the Opium War. But it also had no intention of passing up the fruits of victory. In 1843 an emissary, Caleb Cushing, was sent to negotiate a treaty with Chinese officials. It gave Americans the right to trade in the treaty ports on a "most-favored-nation" basis. This meant that any privileges granted by the Chinese to any other nation ("most favored") in the future would also be shared by the United States. The United States also got the privilege of "extraterritoriality," meaning, in the words of the agreement, that "citizens of the United States who may commit any crime in China, shall be subject to be tried and punished only by the Consul, or other public functionary of the United States . . . according to the laws of the United States."

Translated, all these terms meant that the Chinese could not bargain

---

*CHRONOLOGY*

| | |
|---|---|
| 1784 | *First U.S. trading voyage to China* |
| 1792 | *The ship* Columbia *discovers Columbia River for United States* |
| 1843 | *Caleb Cushing negotiates favorable trade treaty with China* |
| 1854 | *Matthew Perry establishes trade with Japan* |
| 1867 | *Alaska purchased at urging of Secretary of State W. H. Seward* |
| 1882 | *Chinese Exclusion Act passed by Congress* |
| 1890 | *Admiral Mahan's Book,* The Influence of Sea Power on History, *published* |
| 1899 | *Secretary of Stage John Hay starts Open Door policy* |
| 1900 | *Boxer Rebellion, siege of Peking* |
| 1911 | *Chinese republic created* |
| 1921 | *Nine-Power Treaty reaffirms Open Door policy* |
| 1931 | *Japan invades Manchuria, then China* |
| 1941 | *Japan bombs Pearl Harbor on December 7* |
| 1949 | *Communists takeover in China* |
| 1950–1953 | *United States and China on opposite sides in Korean War* |
| 1972 | *President Nixon visits the People's Republic of China (Communist China)* |

among Western powers for advantageous deals for themselves. What they gave to one, they had to give to all. Moreover, they had to allow foreigners the extraordinary right of not being bound by their laws. Later treaties spelled out other rights for foreigners, among them, permission to build churches, schools, hospitals, and cemeteries in parts of the treaty ports. Each such port eventually became, therefore, a small foreign settlement, a cluster of alien, sovereign outposts on Chinese soil. And most ordinary Chinese were admitted to these settlements, for the most part, only as servants. The treaty ports, extraterritoriality, and most-favored-nation clauses were three terms that spelled out for China the price of being powerless in the nineteenth century. They ended the old trading system in which Chinese were respected strangers.

The United States gained the advantages of the new system that subjugated China, without committing itself to conflict with the Empire. So the United States was able to argue officially that it was a traditional friend of the Chinese people, a statement that most Americans came to take for granted. That did not prevent the United States, however, from sharing in the advantages of still another harsh treaty imposed by France, Britain, and Russia on China in 1858.

### *Gazing Westward: Growth of an Idea of National Interest*

To make sense of the China story in this early period we must set it against the broad background of U.S. history. There lies the question of national interest and who was defining it. A rough answer is that the national interest of the United States from the 1790s to the 1850s was defined by expansionists, those who wanted the nation to grow and to move ever westward as part of a historic and heavenly mission. The trade with China was only one of a set of steps guided by that idea.

In 1792, only a few years after the voyage of the *Empress of China*, another little ship, the *Columbia*, nosed her way into the mouth of a huge river emptying into the Pacific from North America. Captain Robert Gray named the stream after his vessel. This established a claim by the United States to the territory later known as Oregon. The claim was strengthened in 1805, when Lewis and Clark reached the Columbia on their overland explorations. The main value of planting the American flag there was that it cut Americans in on the valuable trade in northwestern furs. In 1811 the king of the American fur trade, German-born John Jacob Astor, got permission from the U.S. government to set up a post at the Columbia's mouth and deal for furs with the local Indians. This establishment was named Astoria in his honor. Captured by the British in the War of 1812, it was restored by the peace treaty.

One prime reason for American interest in Oregon was that its sea-otter pelts were specially prized by the Cantonese merchants. So it made good economic sense to send ships around Cape Horn to the Oregon coast, to swap blankets, axes, kettles, powder, and traps for furs, which could then be taken on across the Pacific to China. But on the way there was an important stop in the Hâwaiian Islands. That stop opened another door to the American future.

Discovered in the 1770s by Captain James Cook of Britain, the islands, about halfway across the Pacific, were an ideal stopping place for repairs, fresh water, and food. This fact was known not only to the grateful crews of China-bound sailing ships but also to those of another set of far-ranging American vessels, the whalers. Yankee whalers, hunting for valuable sperm-whale oil to kindle the nation's lamps, had, by 1820, gotten all the way into the southern Pacific and Indian oceans. They made the Hawaiian Islands a frequently used base for refitting, and the China-bound vessels followed suit. Hawaii had still another asset for the China trade, a plentiful supply of sandalwood. So Hawaii soon was a regular American port of call and rapidly became an American satellite.

Hawaii, unlike China, was not an ancient and a civilized empire. It could not hold the Yankees, as China did until 1840, to a limited area around its docks and warehouses. Americans set up stores and shipyards to serve the needs of sailors and skippers. Other Americans looked with interest at the lush acres that could grow sugar and other valuable crops and began to buy and exploit them. And still other Americans, missionaries, set on fire by the blaze of revivalism seen in Chapter 7, got into the picture. They were convinced that it was their duty not only to save the souls of as many lost American sheep as possible, but to bring to millions of "heathens" the word that Christ had died for their sins. Some godly Americans even believed that God had raised up the United States especially for the purpose of getting that truth to the "benighted" parts of the world. That was how He *wanted* it done; and so, Lewis and Clark, the *Empress of China*, and, later on, steamships and locomotives were all part of His master plan.

Burning with such spirit, young ministers formed the American Board of Commissioners for Foreign Missions in 1810. Its first missionaries went to India. Others soon headed for Hawaii, where they found an easier situation than in India, China, or other nations where local authorities and customs were still strong. Hawaiian culture was disintegrating under the shock of Western penetration. The missionaries rapidly established themselves in positions of importance, not only as preachers but as doctors, builders of schools, landowners, newspaper publishers, and administrators of good works. By the 1840s, in fact, the "native" rulers of Hawaii had virtual "cabinets" of American business advisers. The islands were, in all but name, an American outpost.

The China trade, therefore, was part of a whole pattern of early American commercial imperialism that reached a crest in the 1850s. Inventions gave it new momentum. When railroads in America were less than twenty years old and few railroad companies operated more than 100 miles of line, Asa Whitney, a New York merchant with interests in the trade to the Orient, submitted a petition to Congress. He wanted the United States to build a railway from the Great Lakes to Oregon. Running for 2000 miles through barren country, it would seem on the surface to be an all-time white elephant. But Whitney saw it as a marvelous link for getting Asian products to U.S. markets in weeks instead of months: a quick voyage across the Pacific and then a dash across the continent at 30 or 40 miles per hour. As Missouri's Senator Thomas Hart Benton put it: "The rich commerce of Asia will flow through our centre. And where has that commerce ever flowed without carrying wealth and dominion with it?" (Ironically, the projected line was not built for another twenty-five years, but then, in part, with Chinese labor.)

*Pacific Manifest Destiny: Opening Japan*

Americans gradually looked for new golden openings in the western Pacific. In the 1840s an American missionary and doctor, Peter Parker (later a minister to China), proposed unsuccessfully that the United States annex the island of Formosa. Then in 1853 an even more weighty event took place. For centuries Japan had been even more restrictive than China about admitting Westerners. It permitted only one Dutch ship per year to trade at the port of Nagasaki. Foreign sailors who were shipwrecked on Japanese shores were immediately imprisoned, and, if lucky, later sent away. Then the United States, newest and youngest power in the Pacific, decided, all on its own, to do what older nations had not done—to challenge that policy. An expedition was sent under an American naval commander, Matthew C. Perry, to "open up" Japan.

Supposedly, Commodore Perry was sent to pave the way for a treaty covering the fate of American seamen shipwrecked on Japanese shores. Actually, his letter of instructions, drawn up late in 1852, said that he should try to get permission for American vessels to enter at least one or more Japanese ports to obtain water, fuel, supplies, and coal, as well as "for the purpose of disposing of their cargoes by sale or barter." The letter unflatteringly deplored that "the civilized nations of the world should for ages have submitted to such treatment by a weak and semi-barbarous people." It authorized Perry to say that the president of the United States entertained "the most friendly feelings toward Japan." If, nevertheless, the emperor should ignore the letter that Perry was to deliver and continue to deny "humane treatment of our shipwrecked seamen," then both the government and responsible Japanese individuals would be "severely chastised."

These instructions suited Perry well. He had large ambitions for the navy

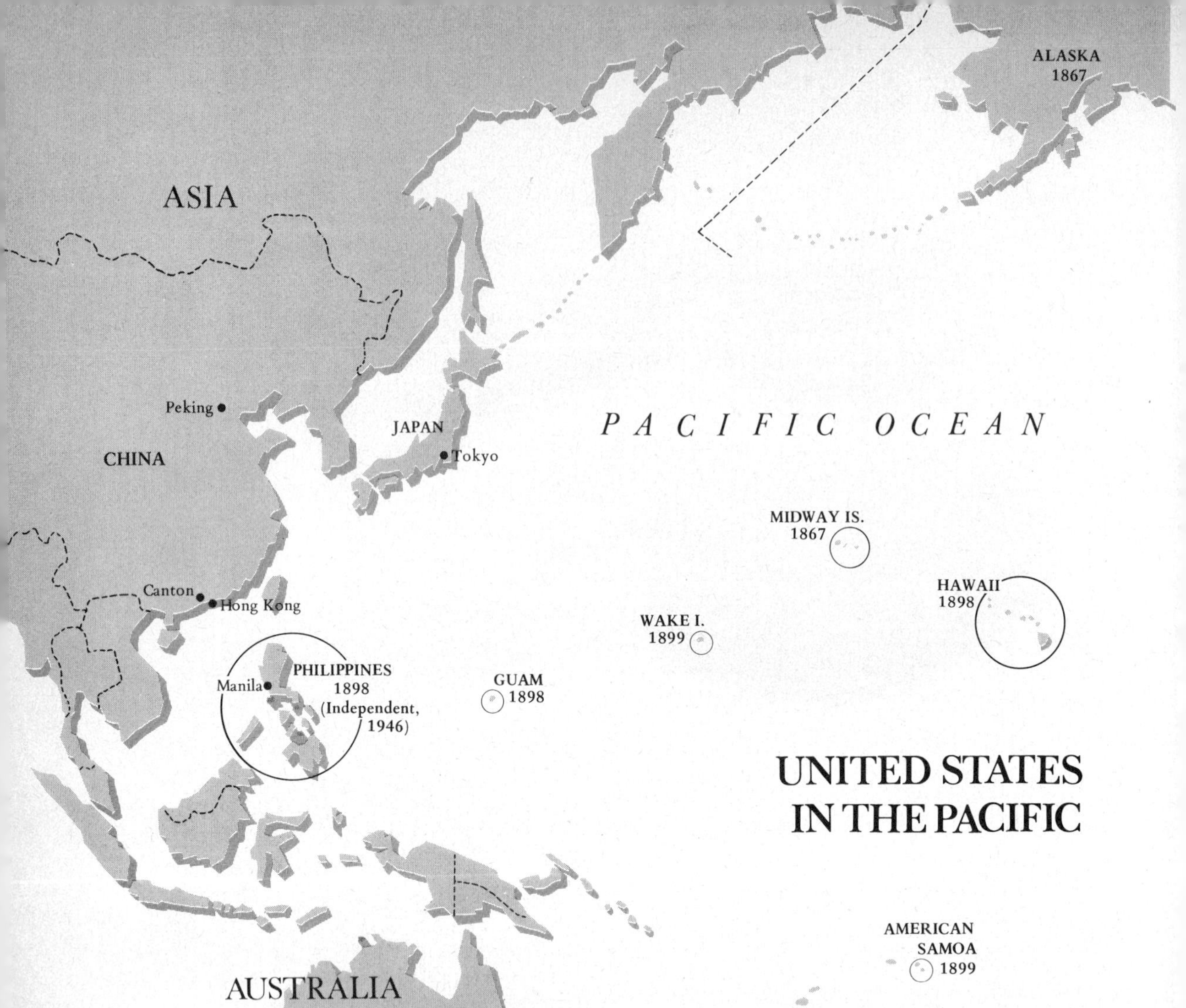

ALASKA 1867

ASIA

Peking

JAPAN

CHINA

Tokyo

PACIFIC OCEAN

MIDWAY IS. 1867

HAWAII 1898

Canton

Hong Kong

WAKE I. 1899

PHILIPPINES 1898 (Independent, 1946)

Manila

GUAM 1898

## UNITED STATES IN THE PACIFIC

AMERICAN SAMOA 1899

AUSTRALIA

and, like Parker, wanted the United States to have territory in the Pacific. His proposal was that the United States occupy the Ryukyu Islands, between Formosa and Japan. Though this idea was not acted on, forcing Japan, a free nation, to obey Western rules of trade seemed a reasonable alternative step.

Perry was no blusterer. He carried out his mission with an unusual amount of deftness. He sailed boldly into Tokyo Bay and insisted that he would only deal with the highest officials, who could take the president's message straight to the emperor. He kept himself majestically aloof. He also managed to keep his guns visible without making open threats and backing the Japanese into a corner where it appeared that they were being humiliated by going along with him. The Japanese, in fact, were greatly impressed with what they saw of the West both in the weapons on Perry's flagship and in the various gift products of

American industry that he presented. In 1854 they concluded the treaty he wanted and enlarged its provisions by another in 1858. Soon they were not only trading with the West but, unlike the hapless Chinese, rapidly industrializing and modernizing their entire nation, and building an up-to-date army and navy.

By the 1850s, therefore, the Americans were beginning to play an independent and forceful hand in the Pacific. Before that, they had contented themselves with following Britain's diplomatic and military leadership in the pursuit of the trade dollar. The change in policy, however, was gradual and did not involve threats to China. So the conviction remained fixed among Americans that the United States was not one of the imperialist powers active in the Orient.

Everything flowed together. What American Pacific policy actually stood for was a use of the nation's strength to force weak peoples to trade with Americans. It could be called mercantile imperialism. There was also a kind of agrarian imperialism alive in the 1840s, which we saw at work in the war with Mexico. It demanded land for the uses of "civilized" American farmers, not "backward" Mexican peasants or Indian hunters. Agrarian and mercantile imperialism were sometimes at cross-purposes, but sometimes they worked together. The conquest of California and the annexation of Oregon fulfilled the agrarian imperialist dream of fresh lands to occupy. But they also offered coastlines and harbors from which to carry on commerce with Asia, dear to the hearts of mercantile imperialists.

The politics of expansion touched foreign and domestic policies alike. By and large, it was the Democrats who were agrarian minded and the Whigs who favored commerce and industry. The first Whig administration sent Cushing out to China in 1843 to negotiate the initial Sino-American pact. The second, and only other one, signed Perry's treaty with Japan in 1854. In that same year one of the chief Whigs, New York's William Henry Seward, helped give birth to the new Republican Party. That party united various kinds of expansionism. To win agrarian votes it spoke up for free soil in the West. It proposed a tariff policy to aid industrialists with *their* kind of booming growth. And through Seward, who became its leading foreign-policy expert, it expressed dreams of a steady growth in overseas bases to nourish American trade.

Seward was Lincoln's secretary of state and stayed on under Johnson. He held office from 1861 to 1869. In that period he took a firm stand on preserving Mexico as a virtual American protectorate, as we will see in the next chapter. He also bought the Midway Islands and Alaska and tried to negotiate the purchase or takeover of the Galapagos Islands in the Pacific and of parts or all of Santo Domingo and the Virgin Islands in the Caribbean. He was the fully completed American Whig, turned Republican. He was the agent of land grabbers *and* missionaries, of merchants *and* inventors, of manufacturers *and* those reformers who wished to purify American life and extend its blessings everywhere.

So the China policy of the United States until about 1870 can only be understood as part of the story of revivalism and the tariff, of the fur trade and the iron horse, and of the ideas and power arrangements that those events and stories and objects symbolize. History is the story of culture, and all parts of a culture are bound together in some way.

American culture, early in our relations with China, did not threaten Chinese culture, even through the limited efforts of missionaries. Until the 1850s, China's rulers, though beginning to realize her weaknesses, thought they could get the benefits of trade with the West without giving in to Western values. China, unlike Japan, did not want to be "modernized." Nor did she want to go the way of India and become a satellite to the British or any other nation. The old hong system, of which the United States was a part, seemed to meet these Chinese hopes. The old-fashioned Western merchants involved in it demanded no revolutionary changes in Chinese folkways to secure their ends. But the hong system rapidly disintegrated as the twentieth century began to approach. China was to learn some new and brutal lessons, and her relations with the world, including the United States, were to change as Western power became far more demanding and shattering to her.

The story after 1868 is different in the way that a Pittsburgh steel mill is different from a fur-trading post or an armored battleship from a square-rigger. By 1899 China was no longer granting favors to "barbarians." She was threatened with extinction as an independent nation. The United States, by the same year, had become a modern naval and industrial power with bases in the western Pacific. Once more, the United States willingly took advantage of China's weakness. At the same time, it announced that a cornerstone of its Asian policy was the independence of China. That was something of a paradox, a situation containing apparent, built-in contradictions. It was not the only irony to imprint itself on Sino-American relations. At the very time that the United States became China's "protector," the trade with China became less important to American economic health. And at the time when American missionaries were busiest saving Chinese souls, most Americans at home shared a social Darwinist belief that Chinese minds were biologically inferior, and the American Congress barred Chinese laborers from admission to the country.

Between 1858 and 1882 China and America seemed to be drawing closer together. Under the 1858 Treaty of Tientsin, Americans were given new privileges of trade, travel, and extraterritoriality in China. In addition, the way was opened for an American representative to appear at the Chinese court in Peking. (A minor aside reflects the changing situation of China. She had always insisted that in case "barbarian" ambassadors were received by the emperor, they should honor him by the kowtow, which consisted of kneeling and knocking the head three or more times on the ground. The first American minister to Peking flatly refused, and by that time a weakening China could not insist.) In 1868 the one-time American minister to China, Anson Burlingame, negotiated a new treaty with the Peking government. It allowed almost total freedom for nationals of each country to travel in the other. This liberality had its economic motive. In granting the Chinese free access to U.S. territory, the Americans were assuring themselves of a continued supply of Oriental railroad labor in the West.

Within a few years, however, the situation began to change. A depression hit the United States from 1873 to 1878. There had long been anti-Chinese feelings in the Pacific states, and they now erupted in demands that the "coolie laborers" be barred from competing with American workers for scarce jobs. In 1882 Congress passed a Chinese Exclusion Act, banning any further entry of Chinese except for brief visits by diplomats, teachers, and businessmen. It also ordered U.S. courts to deny citizenship to Chinese immigrants already here. The exclusion law flatly violated the Burlingame Treaty. It was also passed when churchgoing people were dropping coins into collection plates so that missionaries might teach Chinese in China to behave like model Americans. It was not logical at all, but far western votes counted for more than logic in the House and Senate.

The Chinese government had more pressing matters to be concerned about. Between 1880 and 1900 European powers and Japan suddenly began to step up their demands upon Peking. The old imperialism had not required China to give up any of her own soil or much sovereignty outside the treaty ports. But in 1896 the Russians demanded the right to build a railroad in Manchuria and two years later extracted a twenty-five year lease on the harbor of Port Arthur. In 1898 the Germans demanded a ninety-nine year lease on Tsingtao, another Chinese port. They got it, of course; so did the British when they bid for Kowloon, on the South China coast, and Weihaiwei to the north. The French took a similar bite, grabbing control of Kwangchow, near Canton. Meanwhile, the Japanese beat the Chinese in a war in 1894 and took away the island of Formosa. Japan, too, began to make heavy investments in nearby Korea, which she would take over in 1910.

It looked as if China was becoming the victim of a new kind of imperial adventure, gobbling up East Asia. The British had consolidated various "independent" Indian states into the Empire of India in 1857; they added Burma to their colonies in 1886. The French annexed Indochina between 1897 and 1902. Both powers, along with Germany and Portugal, were also rapidly carving up Africa. Late nineteenth-century European imperialism did not mean simply setting up small trading posts on the margins of other continents to get out the slaves, ivory, tea, gold, or furs, while leaving "native" governments intact. Instead, it was industrially based. It aimed to open mines, build railroads and factories, and market mass-produced goods among the nonwhites.

This required stability and order *inside* the "backward" nations. It led to the overthrow of existing governments and the substitution of European-trained administrative planners. Under the new imperialism, in short, European powers first set up "spheres of influence" in Africa and Asia, within which their nationals ran the economy. Then, at leisure, they converted the spheres into actual colonies. The history of the 1890s seemed to predict that China would undergo this fatal process. Her ripest provinces were turning into Russian, British, French, German, and Japanese spheres of interest. It seemed logical that those powers, to avoid clashes with each other, might soon carve up China among themselves.

### *Propping Open China's Door*

It was at this point that the United States, which had just taken the Philippine Islands from Spain, stepped in with two significant notes. The first was a mild proposal that was circulated to the capitals of all nations concerned in 1899. It merely suggested that powers with spheres of interest in China keep the treaty ports open and give to citizens of other countries all the rights and privileges that the Chinese had given them. It said nothing about giving up

*It took an international expedition to rescue embassy personnel besieged in Peking in 1900 by antiforeign Chinese groups known as "the Boxers." American and European politicians often referred to the relief mission as an action on behalf of Western civilization against "Oriental barbarism." But they forgot or overlooked the participation of Japan, who was also industrialized, powerful, and hungry for influence in China. Naturally, the Japanese themselves saw it quite differently, as this illustration from one of their magazines shows. The same events are reflected differently in the mirrors of varied cultures.*

spheres of influence—only that all nations should go on enjoying the benefits of trade with China equally.

There was general agreement to this. But the next year, 1900, saw a sudden outbreak of antiforeign feeling in China. A patriotic society known as the Boxers (the foreign abbreviation for an organization known as the "righteous society of harmonious fists") launched an attack on the foreign legations in Peking. The Boxers were a sign of the rising discontent of young Chinese with the fumbling and decay of the empire. (In 1911 a revolution would replace it with a republic.) But the foreign powers simply saw Chinese nationalism as a threat to their pattern of having their way unopposed in China. They raised a 20,000-man joint expeditionary force, which included a detachment of American marines. It landed and fought its way into Peking to rescue the besieged foreigners, who, with their families, had fled into the embassy buildings. Now the stage seemed set to punish China for her sins by dismemberment.

At this point, the American secretary of state, Hay, issued the second of what came to be called the Open Door notes. This one announced that it would be American policy not merely to guarantee equal trading opportunities for all nations in China but to "preserve Chinese territorial and administrative entity." In short, the United States not only wanted the door kept open, but it wanted to make it clear that the Chinese should continue to own the whole house.

Historians have long mulled over what was behind this policy. It seems most likely that Hay simply wanted to continue Chinese independence because it had worked well for everyone for a long time. But the effect was to give the United States an apparent role as the "protector" of China. This fit the long-held American notion that we were special friends of the Chinese. It also dovetailed with the American decision to keep the Philippine Islands. Now the United States had both a colony and a policy in the Far East; keeping China whole and open, however, committed the United States to voyages on uncharted seas of diplomacy. It meant a heavy concern with the balance of power in the western Pacific and a growing number of confrontations with Japan. As Mr. Dooley put it, we had once simply held the stakes in the international card game. We cried "gentlemen, gentlemen!" when there was a threat of a fight, and, sometimes, when no one was looking, we grabbed part of someone else's sake. But now, as a player, "by hivins, we had no peace of mind."

From 1900 to 1931 American Far Eastern diplomacy focused on keeping China intact and protecting the Philippines. In 1905 President Roosevelt offered to mediate in a war between Russia and Japan. Part of the settlement he worked out involved both those countries' getting certain economic rights in Manchuria but staying out of each other's way. In the same year, the United States quietly recognized Japan's "special interests" in Korea, in return for an unspoken Japanese pledge not to try to move in on the Philippines.

There was an agreement of 1908, in which Japan once more agreed to the principle of the "independence and integrity of China," while the United States promised anew to understand Japanese interest in Manchuria. In 1910 the U.S. government tried to reduce rivalries in Manchuria by urging American bankers to join in an international loan to enable the Chinese government to buy up the various railways being developed by Russian, Japanese, and other foreign capitalists. They would then be "neutralized." But neither the great powers nor the bankers cared much for the risks. So this attempt at "dollar diplomacy" fizzled out.

In 1915, during World War I, Japan seized German holdings in China. She then confronted the Chinese with what were called the Twenty-one Demands. They would have made China a virtual Japanese satellite. The United States opposed them and once more managed to get Japan to agree to a joint statement in 1917. In a now-familiar ritual the United States admitted Japanese "special interests" in China, and the Japanese conceded the desirability of China's "integrity."

Finally, five years later, the United States, Japan, and other countries having interests in China, signed the Nine-Power Treaty in Washington, once more agreeing to respect the Open Door. By then, the situation had changed. Russia, torn by the revolution of 1917, was no longer in the picture. Nor was defeated Germany. Britain and France were exhausted. So in effect the United States and Japan were left to face each other alone in the Pacific. Japan resented American interference with her efforts to do in China what the United States had done in Latin America. The United States fretted over Japan's ambitions, which conflicted with America's "historic" interest in a free and sovereign China. Both nations eyed each other warily, kept up a vigorous naval race, and marched down the road toward Pearl Harbor.

### *Changing Cultures and Changing Diplomacy, 1890-1930*

What was going on in the United States that shaped the post-1890 American outlook on China in the way that revivalism and Manifest Destiny had shaped it earlier? What were the cultural and economic forces behind a new century's China policy? And how did the same forces affect Chinese thinking?

One change in American thought was a growing taste for a modern navy. Some leading Americans were impressed by a book that appeared in 1890, Alfred Thayer Mahan's *The Influence of Sea Power upon History*. Mahan, himself an admiral, tried to show that every great nation of the past had possessed a wide-ranging merchant marine and the naval muscle to protect it. In the 1890s Americans, aware of their country's mushrooming growth, were ready to see themselves as taking up the role of ancient Rome or of Spain in the days of Columbus or of nineteenth-century Britain. That would require an up-to-date armored steam fleet, which would need coaling stations, dry docks, and repair shops around the world. Such a navy—good for armor-plate suppliers and the national ego alike—was built by 1898, and its needs provided extra arguments for annexing Hawaii in that year and the Philippines in the next. The mere fact of having them, however, made us a full player in Pacific power games.

Secondly, a new kind of world-saving outlook was sweeping America.

Missionaries in China and elsewhere talked the old language of bringing the world to Christ. But social Darwinism, which we saw at work in Chapter 15, had its own way of justifying the imposition of American culture on others. It held that the races of humanity evolved from primitivism at a differential rate, as shown by the sophistication of their technology and political organization. The advanced nations were bound to plant their insitutions all over the globe, just as successful species of animal life outlasted weaker rivals. The undeveloped races were not expected to become extinct. But by losing their independence temporarily and adapting themselves to the ways of superior conquerors—their new "environment"—they, too, would eventually advance towards the uplands of progress. So in penetrating the backward areas, imperialists were only taking up the "white man's burden" of spreading progress.

You will note that this is the old missionary argument in some sense, with salvation and Jesus replaced by progress and biology. The flaws in comparing social and cultural skills, which are transmittable by teaching, with physical characteristics, which are transmittable by heredity, should be evident. It may take centuries for gills to develop into lungs, but people can be taught to use and repair automobiles in a single generation. Yet social Darwinism gave a powerful boost to the new imperialism by adding to biblical authority the power of science. And to Americans China seemed tailor-made for proof of the theory. Since the Chinese were already ahead of the "savages" of the African jungle or remote Pacific islands (so the theory ran), they were clearly most ready to be "civilized," and Western infiltration was most justified.

A third cultural prop of American activity in China after 1900 was, curiously enough, a progressive variation of social Darwinism. The progressives, whom we have seen at work in chapters on the city and on antitrust laws, did not always proclaim racial superiority and power. But they did have faith in the power of applied intelligence and sensible planning to transform people's lives. Looking out at a chaotic world, they yearned to replace trade competition with tidy plans for internationally financed economic development of backward areas. They itched to dismantle the ancient, graft-ridden regimes in Latin American or Asian nations and replace them with up-to-date bureaus that would drain swamps and build elementary schools. This Wilsonian vision has not altogether died in America. It partially explains the paradox of progressivism flourishing in the United States side by side with imperialism, despite progressivism's humanitarian emphasis and imperialism's frank worship of power.

Finally, the United States of the McKinley-Roosevelt-Taft era worried heavily about overproduction. During the depression of the 1890s, a common outcry was that farm prices were down because agricultural surpluses were piling up, and factories were closed because of a glut of unsold goods. Neither statement could be clearly proved. But both spurred a vigorous search for foreign markets.

American consuls in the Orient fed this quest by talking of the giant possibilities of trade with their part of the world. Helping such commercial expansion was part of a consul's job. China especially seemed to be a lush market. Once again, the Chinese were a special case. They were not heathens in loincloths. They wore cotton jackets and pants, traveled, lived in houses, and ate a varied diet. The temptations of having 400 million customers were overpowering. What would happen if every Chinese (or "Chinaman," as they were better known in the United States) bought one pair of Massachusetts ready-made shoes and two New York-woven shirts a year? Or if everyone ate fish canned in Pacific canneries from Pittsburgh steel? Or if everyone got to his job on American-produced streetcars, or burned American kerosene in American lamps?

The fact that British and Japanese manufacturers thought in the same way was no discouragement. There seemed to be plenty of room for all. And a new kind of China trade, in which the export of mass-produced consumer goods from the United States to China became as important as the import of exotic Chinese goods, did not exhaust the possibilities. Whose capital would build the rail lines and open the coal mines of China? Why should it not be American? America's economic destiny seemed to demand continuation of a supposed special closeness with China.

Ironically, China between 1900 and 1915 was not a great consumer of either American goods or investment capital. The trade of the United States with China amounted to no more than a small part of our trade with the world. Commerce within the western hemisphere and between Europe and the United States brought in many more dollars. And chances for investments in economic development were much better and easier to protect in nearby Latin America. If imperialism really rested entirely on the needs of a financial "ruling class" in the United States, as some Marxists claim, then there was no sense at all to the persistent interest in China.

Perhaps the answer to the riddle is that simply through its economic potential the United States was bound to play a positive hand in the world. An imperial-sized nation must protect itself by being in a position to control commerce with other nations, even if it does not actually exert such control. An imperial-sized nation needs to show the flag, maintain overseas bases, and have alliances that give it a role in maintaining world stability. Its self-image and its need to keep growing, and thus avoid problems, demand no less. It may generate economic interests to feed its constant search for large-scale activity to keep its system in order. It will take territory that *gives* it a stake in a new global area. The United States was bound to grow in Asia in this area, it can be argued, because a supernation is the prisoner of its own gigantism.

From the Chinese point of view, the history of these years might read quite differently. The swift crushing of China's power to refuse other nations' demands was deeply shocking to thoughtful young Chinese. It fed their discontent with their own authorities. It set them to thinking about ways in which they could, like the Japanese, get the benefits of modernization without paying the price of subjection. Whereas Americans tended to see the Chinese as weighing Christianity against their own religions or calculating what they could afford to spend on American-made goods, from the Chinese point of view the key issue was different. It revolved around what they had to do to regain their freedom of action and meet the challenges of a changing world. What was the price they must pay in the way of altering themselves? Chinese individuals faced this question in many ways directly and indirectly connected with Western penetration. Many of them went to growing Asian cities like Manila or Singapore, which were becoming important business centers. This mass migration tended to loosen the bonds of family tradition and local community authority, just as we saw it doing in the United States. In addition, Chinese youngsters who studied in missionary schools or who went abroad for training in American and other universities were exposed to new ways of thinking. They then had to reconcile these with their accustomed styles of behavior in the old-fashioned Chinese way. Strange prophets named Darwin and Marx and Freud and Einstein had given messages to the West. Western-trained Chinese had to square those teachings, which seemed to have helped the West to become so powerful, with ancient Chinese ways that seemed more intellectually comfortable, yet did not "pay off" in a world of gunboats.

We should also note that a historian of China's relations with the West who is looking at the facts from China's side would have to see the story as part of China's struggle to enter the modern world. That battle affected the way Peking dealt with Americans, just as changing American ways of life created different U.S. approaches to China. The history of the diplomatic relations between the two countries cannot be peeled away from their internal histories.

### *Postscript: China in War, Revolution, and Peace*

There are two more major periods in the story of China and America to date. From 1931 to 1949 China was gripped by foreign and civil war. The Japanese invaded and annexed Manchuria in 1931. In 1937 their armies stabbed deep into the heart of China, and they occupied most major population centers by 1941. The United States tried to slow this movement by official complaints, diplomatic moves, and, finally, the threat of economic pressure through embar-

*After World War II, China's Communist-led revolution against Chiang Kai-Shek drudged on to final victory and led to a bitter debate in the United States as to whether America had "lost" China. Here, red leader Mao Tse-Tung is shown with some of his troopers in 1947. Twenty-five years later, after a long rupture between America and Communist China, he would receive President Richard Nixon as a guest in Peking.*

goes of critical war materiel shipments to Japan. These steps only increased the tension that exploded into war between Japan and the United States on December 7, 1941.

Meanwhile, what of the Chinese? A major split had occurred in the 1920s in the revolutionary nationalist movement that had been trying to unify the nation since the creation of the republic in 1911. Chiang Kai-Shek, a strong figure in that movement, broke with the Chinese Communists. They moved themselves into China's northern provinces and dug in. Chiang, meanwhile, began to attempt to pull the nation together under his leadership. He had to win over or beat down the various provincial warlords who had seized power in the chaos following the revolution. Curiously, the Japanese invasion aided Chiang in this task. It showed the importance of unified leadership in resisting enemies, and it awakened a militant Chinese patriotism.

Sino-American friendship seemed to reach a peak during 1941 to 1945. American supplies kept China from collapsing entirely before the Japanese attack, and Americans trained and fought beside Chinese troops in Burma and in China herself. The year 1945 brought the beginning of a four-year period of change. War broke out between Chiang and the Communists. Both struggled to control the future of the gigantic nation. Both were aware of its great possibilities once it achieved unity, independence, and economic development. The United States, though still the ally of Chiang, first tried to mediate in the struggle. Then, for a number of reasons still historically debated, American policy lost control of the situation. Chiang was beaten. The Communists took over the mainland in 1949, while he fled to Formosa where he remained until his death in 1975. At that point the United States became firmly wedded to his cause and entered a period of isolation from, and enmity with, Communist China.

The second post-1930 period of Chinese-American relations from 1950 to 1972 saw a reversal of traditional Pacific line-ups. The United States moved closer to Japan, which it had helped to rebuild after defeating her in World War II. Official U.S. policy was to resist possible Communist expansion anywhere in Asia. That led to a situation in the Korean War (1950–1953) in which American and Chinese troops actually fought against each other. The Americans backed the anti-Communist government of South Korea, and the Chinese sent "volunteers" to help their red neighbor, North Korea. It also led, in the mid-1960s, to an ever-deepening American involvement in maintaining an anti-Communist government in Vietnam, on China's southern frontier. Meanwhile, the Chinese undertook a radical program of modernization along Communist lines and looked to Russia, the old Chinese foe of the early 1900s, for assistance and guidance.

Late in the 1960s, the Chinese-Soviet alliance began to unravel. Increasingly, the People's Republic of China seemed to be threatened with isolation. But then, in 1972, a dramatic development took place, opening a new and unfinished chapter. Reversing a twenty-year policy of hostility to the Communist government of China (and shocking the Japanese in the process), President Richard M. Nixon made a trip to Peking and announced the beginning of a new era of peace and collaboration with the Chinese. The full impact of this new phase is yet to be felt. What Nixon and his foreign-affairs adviser, Henry Kissinger, later secretary of state, seemed to have had in mind was some kind of great-power balance in the Pacific, involving the United States, Russia, Japan, *and* China.

Using the kind of cultural analysis employed to set the scene for the earlier periods, can you attempt your own interpretation of the past forty years? As you read onward and learn more about America in the roaring twenties, the depression-torn thirties, and the cold war fifties and sixties, can you relate domestic developments to our defense of China in the 1930s, our rupture with her from 1949 to 1972, and our "reunion"? If you can, you will be on your way to using history, not merely for perspective and pure entertainment but in a way that ties together many separate stories and threads. Political, cultural, economic, social, and diplomatic history do, eventually, form a pattern. You will quickly learn this when you begin to sort and handle their materials for yourself.

## *FOR FURTHER READING*

As a start, a general history of American foreign policy should be consulted. Alexander De Conde, *A History of American Foreign Policy* (1963) is very useful. An old but indispensable introduction to the early relationships of Americans and Chinese is Tyler Dennett, *Americans in East Asia* (1922). For the colorful background of the old China trade, see Samuel Eliot Morison, *The Maritime History of Massachusetts* (1921). Arthur Walworth, *Black Ships Off Japan* (1946) is the story of how the U.S. opened that country to Western penetration and explains the ins and outs of our Pacific involvements during the nineteenth century.

Tyler Dennett's *John Hay* (1938) has good material on the era of the Open Door. Our Far Eastern relations in the Progressive era are very well covered in Howard K. Beale, *Theodore Roosevelt and the Rise of America to World Power* (1956).

Studies that examine and reflect on our Pacific policies are numerous. An excellent short one is George F. Kennan, *American Diplomacy, 1900–1950* (1951). More critical and economically-oriented viewpoints are in William A. Williams, *The Tragedy of American Diplomacy* (1962) and Walter La Feber, *The New Empire* (1963).

China's convulsions in the 1920s and 1930s, and how they touched American life, are beautifully described in Barbara Tuchman, *General Stillwell and the American Experience in China* (1972). An examination of how we backed the losing side in the Chinese civil war that ended in a Communist victory in 1949 is Herbert Feis, *The China Tangle* (1953). A very recent summary is Warren Cohen, *America's Response to China* (1971).

# chapter 20

# *Latin America and us: the case of Mexico*

The pattern of history was beautifully simple to the generation that lived between the two instants of violence that marked off an era—the shots that cut down Lincoln in 1865 and McKinley in 1901. Consider, for a moment, the words of Massachusetts Senator Charles Sumner, speaking in 1867 on behalf of the treaty to buy Alaska from the czar of Russia. Sumner is fifty-six years old. When he was three, the British had burned Washington, and New England had almost left the Union. And it is only two years, in 1867, since the United States has emerged from the Civil War as a unified modern nation. Yet Sumner sees it marching toward empire:

> The present treaty is but a visible step in the occupation of the whole North American continent. As such it will be recognized by the world and accepted by the American people. But the treaty involves something more. We dismiss one other monarch from the continent. One by one they have retired—first France, then Spain, then France again, and now Russia—all giving way to the absorbing Unity declared in the national motto, *E pluribus unum*.

When Sumner made that speech, a five-year-old boy named Albert Beveridge was growing up in Indiana. In his youth he saw the settlement of the Far

West, the growth of cities, the rise of trusts. By 1900 he, too, was a senator. Here is how he defends the American seizure of the Philippines. Sumner, thirty-three years earlier, had seen the Stars and Stripes flying over all of North America. But for Beveridge, the world itself is the limit. The new century will be that of the American empire:

> God has not been preparing the English-speaking and Teutonic peoples for a thousand years for nothing but vain and idle self-contemplation and self-admiration. No! He has made us the master organizers of the world to establish system where chaos reigns. He has given us the spirit of progress to overwhelm the forces of reaction throughout the earth. He has made us adept in government that we may administer government among savage and senile peoples. Were it not for such a force as this the world would relapse into barbarism and night.

We have already seen some of Beveridge's ideas at work in the American penetration of the far Pacific. How did both men's visions of American destiny shape our relations with other continental neighbors? Canada, the chief remnant of the British king's North American possessions, remained safe from U.S. invasion behind the power of Britain (though not immune to economic penetration). But what of the various nations to the south, which had themselves helped to expel the king of Spain from North America? Specifically, what of Mexico? When Sumner spoke it was just nineteen years—less than some of your lifetimes—since the United States had amputated one-third of that nation's territory by the Treaty of Guadalupe Hidalgo.

Was Mexico, despite her breakaway from Spanish rule, still to be considered feudal, autocratic, Catholic? Was she, therefore, doomed to vanish as a force in North American history before the democratic, capitalistic, Protestant United States? Were her people, partly Hispanic and partly Indian, to be considered "senile" or "savage" or both or neither? Would she have a place on the continent as a neighbor? As a friend? Satellite? Colony? Would she simply disappear as a separably identifiable geographical unit?

The answer turned out to be different at different times. In the early years of the twentieth century Mexico, like all the other Latin American nations, was woven into a web of U.S. domination of the western hemisphere. The chronicle of Mexican-American relations from 1850 to 1933 is, however, more than a simple story of subjection. It is, like the other foreign-policy developments we examine, a story of shifting self-conceptions and of changing pressures on two differing states, peoples, cultures. For study purposes it can be divided into five phases: (1) the aftermath of the Mexican war, (2) the French intervention, (3) the era of the new Manifest Destiny, (4) the period of Mexican revolution, and (5) the emergence of maturity and stabilization.

*Phase I: The Aftermath of War: Would Mexico Last?*

For Mexicans the question of questions between 1848 and 1862 was whether or not the United States had satisfied its appetite for land with Texas and California or was it only pausing for digestion before taking fresh bites of Mexican territory. Many Americans went on proclaiming that liberty's eagle would soon spread its wings from the North Pole to the Isthmus of Panama. Texans loudly complained that the Mexican government could not control bands of marauding southwestern Indians, who hid out on Mexican soil. Southerners denounced Mexico for offering a potential safety zone to runaway slaves. Their sentiments were best put in a private letter by John Pickett, who became, in 1861, the ambassador of the Confederate States of America to Mexico City. He said that his hosts were "a race of degenerate monkeys . . . robbers, assassins, blackguards and lepers." (The letter somehow leaked out, which abruptly ended the undiplomatic Pickett's mission.)

All through the 1850s there were American voices in favor of pacifying northern Mexico by absorbing it. The United States did force Mexico to sell it another strip of land, known as the Gadsden Purchase, in 1852. Its purpose was to acquire a valley that offered the best route for a southern railroad to the Pacific. But it likewise appeared to support the view that American expansionists might be, in the words of one staunch congressional foe of the Mexican War, preparing "our anglo-saxon gastric juices . . . for another Cannibal breakfast."

No U.S. armed forces crossed the border in the 1850s. But there were several expeditions by filibusters, armed parties of Americans who hoped to seize a province, turn it into an "independent" republic, and then, like the Texans, ask for annexation to the United States. In 1855 and 1857 two such small companies of Americans entered the northern provinces of Mexico. They

---

*CHRONOLOGY*

| | |
|---|---|
| 1848 | *Treaty of Guadalupe Hidalgo* |
| 1852 | *Gadsden Purchase* |
| 1863–1867 | *French rule over Mexico* |
| 1877–1911 | *Porfirio Díaz rules as strong man* |
| 1898 | *United States takes Puerto Rico after Spanish-American War* |
| 1904 | *Roosevelt Corollary to Monroe Doctrine* |
| 1911 | *Mexican revolution begins* |
| 1914 | *Woodrow Wilson uses U.S. force at Veracruz* |
| 1916 | *U.S. troops raid Mexico* |

claimed to be hunting for fugitive slaves and thieving Comanche Indians, but there was a clear possibility that they might try to "Americanize" the Mexican states of Sonora, Chihuahua, or Lower California. They were turned back. In 1859, when a Mexican bandit named Cortina was troublesome to frontier settlements, some Americans did cross the border to try to catch him. This, too, could have been the seed of a new invasion. But 1860 was not the year for American foreign adventures. Washington only continued to demand damages for American citizens robbed or injured by outlaws and Indians. Angrily, American diplomacy scolded the "irresponsible" Mexicans for not controlling them.

Deep cultural and political differences separated the two nations. Mexico was, in fact, weakly governed; she lacked a strong army and bureaucracy and the tax moneys to pay for them. It was for just this reason that she was so susceptible to filibuster attack. If she had been able to guarantee order in her domains, she might never have lost Texas. But it was not mere lack of funds that kept Mexico decentralized. Many of her important citizens simply did not care to undertake the necessary investment and organization to knit their nation together by common schools, railroads, or the like. Mexican politicians could strut and boast as well as Yankees and were impressed with martial valor and the cult of *machismo*—proof of manhood through toughness and domination of others. But they did not want expansion. A provincial chieftain expected to be the unquestioned boss on *his* ground but not necessarily elsewhere. He craved riches for the fine horses, many servants, and splendid homes they bought. But he would not easily forgo today's pleasures to buy stocks that would yield him more wealth tomorrow. He could feel some loyalty toward a far-off government in the capital. But his loyalties and hates were mainly personal and revolved around neighbors, kinfolk, and friends. Ideas like "order" and "progress" were not at home in his mind.

In fact, both the Hispanic and Indian backgrounds, which you may recall from Chapter 1, supported a tragic view of life. It was full of pain and risk. It called for mercy and bravery in the shadow of ever-present evidence of humanity's weakness and fate. Such a view of existence can create heroes or saints but not planners. To live for the distant future, to put faith in money or machinery or organizational rules—these were alien values to nineteenth-century Mexicans.

But Americans, as we have seen, were deeply convinced that growth was good in its own right. Riches, they thought, were to be invested so that they might multiply. Technology's demands for self-discipline and order were more than repaid by technology's gifts of speed, abundance, and comfort. To such minds the Hispanic-American style of the 1850s was incomprehensible. It was not strange that Americans thought of Mexicans as superstitious semisavages.

What saved Mexico from total conquest, oddly enough, was that in the 1850s the United States itself had not yet jelled into a modern nation-state. The battle between Northern and Southern states, which was partly over centralization and progress, paralyzed vigorous foreign-policy action. So, as it turned out, undeveloped Mexico owed some safety to the fact that the United States was also still "unfinished."

*Phase II: The French Interlude*

In the brief seven-year period following 1860 a sudden turn of events changed the picture. For a time the United States became the friend and protector of an independent Mexico. There was no change in the value conflict, but there was a dramatic and rather romantic set of international events.

The president and ruler of Mexico in 1861 was a genuine national hero, Benito Juárez. He had come to power as a result of a revolution that overthrew the dictator Santa Anna, whom the United States had defeated in 1848. Juárez was a reformer who was interested in cutting down the influence of the great landlords and of the church. One of his first needs was for a solid financial basis, and in order to save money he temporarily suspended the payment of debts owed by the Mexican government to French, Spanish, and British bankers. These three nations, stung and alarmed, agreed in May 1862 to undertake an expedition to punish Juárez. He was able to reach an agreement with Spain and Britain, which dropped their invasion plans.

France, however, was then governed by the Emperor Napoleon III. He was trying to recapture some of the glory of his uncle, the conqueror of Europe. Accordingly, he proceeded with the plan. A French force disembarked at Veracruz and followed the historic tracks of Cortes and Winfield Scott up to Mexico City, which fell in June 1863. A year later, Napoleon III declared Mexico to be a French protectorate. He set it up as a satellite empire and named a young Austrian prince, Maximilian, and his Belgian-born wife, Carlota, as emperors. Both were innocent aristocrats, willing to play-act in Napoleon III's rerun of the drama of Europe from 1800 to 1812, when the first Napoleon threw many heirs of old families out of their royal palaces and replaced them with his own relatives.

Juárez, in exile, bided his time. Meanwhile, where was the United States while France was setting up a puppet state on its southern border? Comparative dates supply the answer. In May 1862, when the invasion of Mexico was first planned, Union forces were unsuccessfully battling the Confederates a few miles from Richmond. In June 1863, when Mexico City fell, the ragged regiments of Lee were marching northward into Pennsylvania, toward Gettysburg. In May 1864, when Maximilian was making a triumphal procession to his imperial capital, Grant had just launched the wilderness offensive, and his army was suffering thousands of casualties each week. Truly, as Seward said in

*Benito Juarez, part Indian and a thoroughgoing Mexican nationalist and patriot, became president of his country in the same year that Lincoln was inaugurated. Juarez was ousted from his capital by the French, but regained power with the behind-the-scenes help of the U.S. State Department. He died in 1872 and it was another half century before Mexico was finally and fully established as a neighbor, not a satellite, of the United States.*

response to sharp questioning about American inaction, "Why should we gasconade [boast] about Mexico when we are in a struggle for our own life?"

No sooner was the Union safe in 1865, however, than the picture changed. Now a victorious Union army, more than 1 million strong, was in position to lunge southward into Maximilian's "empire." Playing a cool hand, Seward made no threats. He simply asked Napoleon III, now that an "orderly" regime was established in Mexico, when he intended to pull out his troops. The French ruler had dreams of grandeur, but he was no fool. Without a navy or British cooperation—neither of which he had—he was not prepared to go to war with the United States. So he soon announced that the French forces would shortly embark for home. As soon as they did so, Juárez led a revolutionary army toward the capital. He easily overpowered Maximilian's few hired supporters. Maximilian could have fled and saved his skin. Yet he had taken it all seriously and insisted that he would stay in "his" country to the last. He was captured and shot in 1867. Carlota lived on, playing the role of banished empress for another half-century.

Seward's actions had made Juárez's victory possible. The United States had befriended a strong Mexican nationalist and popular leader. It seemed to have given up its ambitions of conquering its neighbor. In fact, Seward's motivation was somewhat less self-sacrificing. He was, as we saw in Chapter 19 an imperialist, but a sophisticated one, who knew that investments abroad were more effective spearheads of American penetration than armies. He also recognized that the technical sovereignty of a weak nation meant little when the strings of its economy were pulled by foreign bankers. And he foresaw a day, as he put it, when Mexico would be as "cheerfully" hospitable to American immigration "as Montana and Idaho"—and therefore as valuable to the U.S. economic system as those western territories. Americans, Seward noted, were coming to "value dollars more and dominion less."

By pushing out the French, Seward had guaranteed that Mexico would remain a safe preserve for American dollars. It was the first really vigorous U.S. enforcement of the Monroe Doctrine. From that turning point onward, U.S. invocation of the doctrine would become more frequent and combative. The nation had emerged unified and strong from civil war, and the taste of power was zesty and habit forming.

Mexico, meanwhile, had begun to develop more national self-consciousness as she struggled to overthrow the foreigner Maximilian. So the best summation of what happened from 1862 to 1867 was that growing Mexican nationalism and U.S. nationalism temporarily had found themselves on the same track. That fact explained the period of friendly association better than pages of official notes.

### *Phase III: Economic Penetration: The New Manifest Destiny*

In 1876 a new figure rose to the top in the scramble for power in Mexico City. This was Porfirio Díaz. He was a general who had once led an unsuccessful insurrection against Juárez in 1872. Four years after Juárez died, Díaz won the power he wanted. He was a strong man who permitted little democratic interference with his rule. Though his technical title was only president, he managed to control matters by patronage and force so that he remained in office for thirty-one years, except for one brief interlude when a subordinate filled the job. Díaz was a paternalistic "boss" who wanted to bring Mexico into the mainstream of modern life. Perhaps it was only to enhance his own stature. And perhaps there were some idealistic motives. It is not always easy to make judgments about why individuals seek power.

Díaz, like many other strong-man leaders of undeveloped nations, desired Mexico to have railway and port facilities, an export trade, and revenues from mine and mill that could go into building cities and other works to give him credit. He could, however, only manage this by inviting in foreign capital. So, like the "boss" of a Southern state offering low taxes to industries to settle there or the "boss" of an American city handing out favors to the builders of a streetcar system, Díaz extended an open hand to outside investors. They willingly took advantage of generous land grants, tax breaks, and cheap labor. Although British and other foreign capitalists were involved, the chief stream of dollars came from the United States.

To build rail lines in Mexico, Jay Gould, Collis Huntington, and Edward H. Harriman, masters of the U.S. transcontinental lines, laid out $650 million. By 1911 Americans were responsible for building two-thirds of Mexico's more than 12,000 rail miles. During this same period, thousands of Mexican immigrants came north to work on the completion of the American southwestern rail network. The border line on the map was crossed by Mexican laborers flowing northward and by Yankee dollars flowing in the opposite direction.

American mining combines like Anaconda Copper and U.S. Steel owned a quarter of a billion dollars' worth of property in Mexico in 1911. Ranching and cattle raising attracted the free-spending, free-drinking millionaires who had made their fortunes in Texas and were looking for new worlds to conquer. One land company owned 2 million acres in Chihuahua; another had 1.3 million acres in Sonora; and several others had spreads of more than a half-million acres each. Still other Mexican lands were blossoming, in 1911, with crops of sugar cane, rubber trees, cotton, coffee beans, and tropical fruits. They added up to some 80 million acres, into which investments of about $30 million had been poured.

Oil drilling was only beginning to come into its own as a southwestern industry in the early twentieth century. But by 1901 Gulf, Standard, Sinclair, and over 200 other U.S.-owned companies were bringing in Mexican wells and refining the petroleum that bubbled up, thick, black, and smelling of money. Their properties were worth about $15 million.

In all, when 1912 opened, American investments in Mexico were worth over a billion dollars. Americans owned 78 percent of the mines, 72 percent of the smelters, 58 percent of the oil businesses, and 68 percent of the rubber industry in Mexico. More than 77 percent of all Mexico's exports went to the United States, and just over 50 percent of her imports came from there. The

# MEXICO, CENTRAL AMERICA, AND THE CARIBBEAN

75,000 Americans living in Mexico, which included missionaries from some 600 Protestant church organizations, dwelt in what was an economic colony of their own motherland.

From the American viewpoint it fulfilled Seward's idea of a new kind of Manifest Destiny, according to which the United States did not fight wars and snatch lands but exerted American power through investments, sales, and bases abroad. Naturally, to protect the Yankee dollar where the Yankee flag did not fly, an occasional show of muscle was needed. And it was also necessary to control the politics of economically Americanized countries. Their governments must continue to be good to American property owners and must keep order, so that there would be no excuse for "foreign" intervention.

The whole Western Hemisphere was involved in the process. While Mexico was drawn into the U.S. economic orbit, the Monroe Doctrine was becoming the basis of claims by Washington to more or less rule Latin America. In 1898 the United States took Puerto Rico from Spain after a short war to free Cuba from Spain. But in 1901, by the so-called Platt Amendment to a military

appropriations bill, Cuba became an American protectorate. She could make no treaties granting foreign powers any bases on her soil. She had to give bases to the United States. She could borrow no money abroad beyond a set limit. Finally, the United States might intervene to assure the "maintenance of a government adequate for the protection of life, property, and individual liberty."

In 1903 the republic of Colombia would not make a deal with Washington to permit the building of the Panama Canal. Outraged by "that lot of jack rabbits in Bogotá," Roosevelt informally approved of a quiet arrangement with a group of Panamanian nationalists. They staged a "revolution" in Panama

City. A U.S. cruiser stood by to prevent Colombian troops from landing and breaking it up. Then the United States recognized the new republic of Panama, which promptly granted it the right to dig the canal. Years later, Roosevelt summed up the whole affair in three words: "I took Panama."

In 1904, when Santo Domingo was unable to pay European creditors, Roosevelt announced a "corollary" to the Monroe Doctrine. In a message to Congress he declared that if a nation in the hemisphere kept order and paid its debts, it had nothing to fear from the United States. But "chronic wrongdoing or an impotence which results in a general loosening of the ties of civilized society," he warned, might require "intervention by some civilized nation." Since the United States could not allow any other "civilized nation" to exercise power in the Americas, it might "reluctantly" have to exercise "an international police power." The explanation of what Roosevelt meant came in the following year. The United States took over the collection of the customs in Santo Domingo and used part of the receipts to pay off the debts. American marines also landed in Nicaragua in 1912 and in Haiti in 1915 for similar reasons.

That was the broad background of American policy toward Mexico. Elsewhere in Central America, American corporations were almost sovereign. They were the unofficial government behind the theoretical rulers of most "banana republics." Díaz, in fact, was more solidly in control of his country than many of his neighbor dictators. From the point of view of the Mexican people, his policy had both benefits and drawbacks. Díaz did lay the groundwork for economic growth. But like many other leaders of his kind who allowed foreign development of their national resources, Díaz paid little attention to the fair distribution of the profits reaped from Mexico's fields and mines. The lion's share went to the outside corporations. A second cut went to the favorites and protégés of Díaz who became the middlemen between the Americans and the Mexicans. These were the Mexican lawyers, supervisors, technicians, and government officials who helped with the management of local enterprises.

Practically nothing, however, went to those on the bottom, the peasants and workers who grunted and sweated their way through year after year of hard labor for pennies. Díaz invested little in facilities for public education, health, welfare, and recreation. He did not break up great landed estates. He counted on the common Mexican's pride in Mexico's growth to soften complaints. He depended on the Mexican church to continue assuring the poor that God would reward them in heaven. Like some American big businessmen and urban bosses, Díaz so enjoyed the use of power that he could forget to examine the ends to which it was put.

But by building Mexico's sense of nationhood, Díaz gave the Mexican poor a sense of their own importance and needs. Nationalism gives the lowest peasant or laborer a special identity. When it is joined to a demand for economic justice, a potent revolutionary force is created, as the history of non-Western nations in the past eighty years clearly shows. In Mexico, revolutionary energy exploded in 1910. The struggle to control the results went on for another fifteen years or more. American policy was put to new tests, first under a progressive president, and then during two administrations devoted to the gospel of efficient big business.

*Phase IV: The Day of Mexican Revolution*

Discontent with the Díaz regime had grown steadily during its final years. A class of educated, responsible Mexicans wanted the fruits of progress more fairly shared. They were eager to raise crops, not only of cocoa and sugar cane, but of trained and healthy citizens. A start would be made by restoring constitutional government, with a fair vote and an unbossed parliament.

One major spokesman for this viewpoint was a man named Francisco Madero. In 1911 Díaz was forced, by the threat of open revolt, to retire, and Madero was installed as president. To watching Americans this seemed an encouraging sign of Mexican progress. But they were unaware of two facts. One was that a genuine Mexican revolution would have to reduce American influence in the country. The other was that Madero's success had depended on the neutrality of the army. Unhappy with Díaz for various reasons, senior officers had not given him the backing to crush rebellion. But Madero's future rested, unsafely, as it turned out, with the generals.

No one was happier with Madero's emergence or more unaware of his weakness than Wilson. To this Southern-born ex-professor and college president, the first need of a young nation was for a responsible elite of high purpose. Under its leadership, civilization could develop. And civilization meant unity, productiveness, bullets instead of ballots, tidiness, and an end to waste. It meant large-scale industry and reform-minded government.

Naturally, therefore, Wilson was cheered by Madero's election. And just as naturally, he was horrified when, in February 1913, just a month before Wilson's own inauguration as president of the United States, General Victoriano Huerta staged a revolt that ousted and killed Madero. At that point Wilson showed a trait of his character that would later be critically important. This was what might simply be called the messianic motive, the urge to improve other peoples. Wilson argued, in various statements, that the United States must help Mexico and other hemispheric neighbors by helping the democratic elements within those nations to defeat their autocratic enemies.

We will see in the next chapter how Wilson translated this point of view into a peace policy at the end of World War I. And we saw the kind of progressive "imperialism of uplift" surfacing with regard to China in Chapter 19. It is important to spell out its basic ideas. One was that those who opposed tyranny in other societies were, like reformers in the United States, concerned mainly with order and progress and not with base matters such as winning power and settling old grudges. A second was that regulated capitalism and freely chosen governments were the forces emerging to the top in the modern world, so that to help them along was merely to keep step with history. And a third was that the United States, the most progressive nation, had a moral right and duty to encourage the growth of "civilization" in other lands even by meddling actively in their politics. Wilson had taken social Darwinism and missionary Protestantism and woven them into a foreign policy that claimed to have nothing to do with power, territory, and markets. He said that the United States was bound not only to set an example of public morality for the rest of the world but possibly to exert pressure on those who did not follow it. The fact that this outlook did not interfere with American investments did no harm to its chances for broad support in the United States.

Wilson began at once to execute his policy. On taking office, he withdrew diplomatic recognition of Huerta's regime, announcing that he would not deal with a "government of butchers." This reversed a traditional U.S. practice of doing diplomatic business with any government that exercised actual control of its territory and people. This is called de facto, practical, as against de jure, legal, recognition. But Wilson believed that isolating Huerta in this way would weaken him. It was part of his plan to "teach the South American republics to elect good men." He urged other nations to follow suit and got the British to do so. Meanwhile, he also tried to stop shipments of arms to Huerta. It was his hope that this would weaken the chief "butcher" against possible rebellion. Sooner or later, he felt, the pressure would squeeze out Huerta. Thus what Wilson called "watchful waiting" with regard to Mexico would be rewarded.

The trouble with this hope was that it ignored what was really going on in Mexico. Huerta did indeed have enemies, among them a fellow general, Venustiano Carranza. But Carranza was no more of a believer in liberty than Huerta. Yet the bedrock need for any move to throw out Huerta was power, and only military leaders had that. Carranza did stage an uprising against Huerta, and by the spring of 1914 was close to victory. But that was of little value to Wilson. Then Wilson muddled his own policy further by a blunt use of force.

It was April 1914, in Tampico, Mexico. A party of American sailors on shore leave was arrested by Huerta's officials for wandering into a forbidden area of the town. They were promptly released. The United States demanded an apology and a 21-gun salute to the American flag. We got the apology but not the salute. Wilson then, in punishment, ordered the occupation of the port of Veracruz. His motive was not only to "spank" Mexico but possibly to cut off foreign arms shipments to Huerta. The Mexicans resisted. The American naval forces opened a bombardment. When the fighting was over, they were in command of Veracruz. But fierce Mexican resistance cost 19 Americans dead and 21 wounded, while 126 were killed and 195 wounded on the Mexican side. Wilson was now on the verge of war with Mexico.

The result was to solidify Mexican opposition. Carranza himself objected bitterly. Since Wilson did not wish to invade Mexico, the United States submitted to arbitration by outside powers, and a financial settlement was made. Then Carranza, in August, finally ousted Huerta. But the Mexican revolution was still unfinished. Carranza himself was attacked by still other would-be strong men. Among them was a man named Doroteo Arango, better known as Pancho Villa. Whether Villa was a valiant guerrilla leader or a bandit who wrapped himself in the flag of Mexican nationalism is somewhat unclear, and perhaps the difference in the Mexico of 1915 was not easy to establish.

In any case, Villa wanted to get Carranza in trouble, and he apparently believed that a handy way to do it was to provoke an American intervention in Mexico. Partly for that purpose and partly to fill his own war chest, he conducted numerous raids on American properties in northern Mexico. He would then, in his view, requisition property for his revolutionary army or, in the eyes of the Americans, steal what he could and murder those who resisted. In January 1916 he shot down 16 U.S. citizens. In March his raiders swept into Columbus, New Mexico, with guns blazing and left a trail of dead and wounded behind them. For Americans, living near a revolution was a guarantee of danger.

Wilson, for the second time in two years, sent American armed forces to punish Mexicans. Over Carranza's objections he ordered a small detachment of New Mexico and Arizona National Guardsmen to chase into Mexico after Villa. Armed with such "modern armaments" as a handful of Model T Ford cars and a couple of rickety observation biplanes, the American citizen-soldiers on cavalry mounts struggled over 300 miles into Mexico. They suffered thirst and hardship, sampled the few fleshpots of tiny Mexican towns, and had several inconclusive skirmishes—but they did not find Villa. Finally, they were withdrawn, and the undeclared Mexican-American war of 1916 was over. (Villa was ambushed and shot down by enemies in a butcher shop in 1923.)

By the fall of 1916 Wilson's Mexican policy was in ruins. The attempt to uplift Mexico had led to two armed clashes. In trying to control the Mexican revolution, Wilson, the pacifist progressive, had used force to guarantee the property of great American corporations. Gathering European troubles led him to make peace with Carranza and recognize him before 1917.

But as late as 1919, some southwestern Americans were denouncing Mexico as "half-bandit and half-Bolshevik" and crying out, like New Mexico's Senator Albert B. Fall, for invasion. Fall was a thoroughgoing tool of oil interests. He was later to be indicted and tried in the Teapot Dome scandal of 1924, for joining, while secretary of the interior, in a scheme to let private

*Until the time of the first World War, the United States, whose citizens owned millions of dollars worth of business property in Mexico, freely asserted the right to intervene in Mexican affairs in order to protect those investments. Here, General John J. "Black Jack" Pershing is exercising that "right" as he leads U.S. calvarymen across the border in pursuit of the Mexican guerrilla leader known as Pancho Villa, with neither an invitation from Mexico's government nor a declaration of war.*

companies illegally tap U.S. navy oil reserves. Yet Fall had only followed a path trodden by reformer Wilson. The high-minded claim of the American right of intervention on behalf of progress had only strengthened U.S. business interests and rallied Mexico behind her generals.

*Phase V: Attempts at Stabilization*

It remained for the administrations of Warren G. Harding and Calvin Coolidge to reach a truce with Mexico. This was done when Alvaro Obregón, likewise a former general, took the reins of power in 1920. Obregon and his successor, Elías Calles (1924–1928), both wanted to continue the modernization programs of Díaz but also to make Mexico independent of foreign capital. Their job, as they saw it, was to keep the fruits both of the Díaz years and the revolutionary years. To do that they were willing to make deals with, rather than war upon, outside developers.

From the points of view of Harding and Coolidge, the situation was somewhat similar. Business-minded presidents both, they had no concern with the moral uplift of Mexico but only with the return of a safe environment for investors. If that meant settling for a half-loaf of higher Mexican taxes and more Mexican control, then so be it. Such a policy was more sensible and less costly than invasion and war. Therefore, in the early 1920s Secretary of State Charles Evans Hughes began negotiations that lasted for several years. They resulted in American recognition of Obregón's government, in return for Mexico's allowing some foreign ownership and management of her resources.

One stumbling block was both religious and political. The Mexican government pursued a strong policy of cutting down on the power and property of the Mexican church. This angered American Catholics and made American friendliness to Mexico City somewhat politically touchy. But a peaceable agreement was worked out in 1927, just sixty years after Maximilian's fall, by the efforts of Dwight Morrow, the American ambassador. He was a partner in the gigantic Morgan banking firm. The same American financial interests that had set the new Manifest Destiny in motion helped lay the groundwork for longterm peace with Mexico.

The needs of the American business community with interests in Mexico in the 1920s called for caution and compromise. And the interests of the Mexican postrevolutionary leadership, after a decade of anarchy and tempest, likewise called for caution and compromise. As in 1862 and 1867, the needs of the two nations—the strong and the weak—coincided. Neither messianism nor exploitation on the American side nor revolutionary ferment on the Mexican side was strong enough to disturb that harmony of interests. The stage was set for a new era, that of "good neighbors," after 1934.

---

## *FOR FURTHER READING*

For the pre-Civil War period, when we considered finishing our Mexican banquet, you should read an intriguing book by W. D. Scroggs, *Filibusters and Financiers* (1916). American diplomacy's tactics during the French occupation are covered in Glyndon Van Deusen, *William H. Seward* (1967), and American investments south of the border are carefully studied in Howard F. Cline, *The United States and Mexico* (1953).

The relationship of the United States to the Mexican revolution is given a thorough going over in Robert F. Smith, *The United States and Revolutionary Nationalism in Mexico*,

1916–1932 (1972); it picks up where Dana Munro, *Intervention and Dollar Diplomacy in the Caribbean*, 1900–1914 (1964) leaves off. The Wilson policies are discussed in a biography of his first secretary of state, Louis W. Koenig, *Bryan* (1971). But for a light, firsthand account of the bungling attempt to capture Pancho Villa in 1916, read Herbert G. Molloy, *The Great Pursuit* (1970); it is lively and rewarding.

American policy towards Mexico in the 1920s is touched on in Donald McCoy, *Calvin Coolidge* (1967). And for the final reconciliation under FDR, one of the best and most amusing sources of information is in E. David Cronon, *Josephus Daniels in Mexico* (1960)—Daniels was the ambassador charged with carrying out the Good Neighbor Policy there while placating American conservative opinion at home. For an imaginative fictional account of one American's involvement in the Mexican revolution, read the first volume of John Dos Passos' great trilogy of novels, *U.S.A.* (1937), entitled *The 42d Parallel.* Pay special attention to the parts dealing with "Fainey McCreary."

# *chapter* 21
# *Europe and us: peace, points of view, and politics*

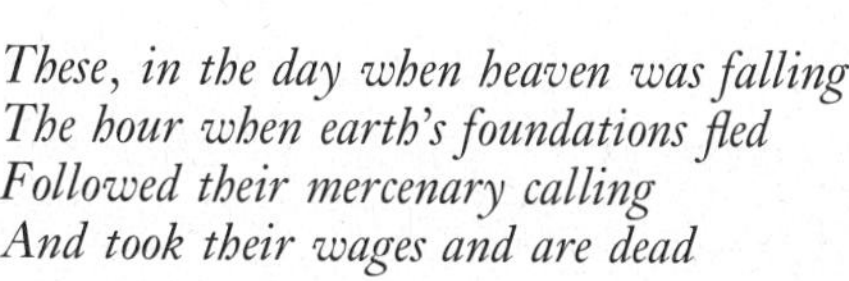

*These, in the day when heaven was falling*
*The hour when earth's foundations fled*
*Followed their mercenary calling*
*And took their wages and are dead*

A modern world has forgotten the subject of this poem, entitled "Epitaph on an Army of Mercenaries," by A. E. Housman. Its heroes are the men of the small, professional British force that was hastily flung into Belgium and northern France in the summer of 1914 to slow the advancing Germans. They were wiped out in the process. But the basic truth of the verse is deeper than a tribute to fallen heroes. It lies in the lines about collapsing heavens and a crumbling earth.

For 1914 was the opening year of a catastrophe for Western civilization, whose full effects we are still feeling. An entire generation was permanently scarred. Revolution toppled ancient regimes. Mighty nations were exhausted and bankrupted, and their overseas empires began to unravel. Millions of the best of Europe's youth fell before bullets and shells. Hunger and disease killed and stunted millions of innocents behind the lines. The "winners" in the struggle were as drained as the losers.

Many things not measurable in numbers also perished. Among them was Western humanity's faith that the world was automatically improving and that the twentieth century would soon make such barbarisms as war obsolete.

*Appearance and Reality: Which Makes History?*

Where does the United States enter this picture? How did Americans react to the collapse of the community of great nations? That community had no official overall authority. Each member was sovereign and independent. But each had an interest in avoiding violent and costly confrontation with the others. That had kept Europe from having a general war from 1815 to 1914. So Americans of the Wilson era had never truly faced the problem of living in a period of heavy international violence.

Our survey of Chinese-American relations showed how the United States profited through the penetration of a weak China by the strong, technologically sophisticated nations of the West. Next we saw how the United States, as the strongest and most advanced nation-state in the western hemisphere, imposed its version of order and stability on Latin American neighbors.

In the case of World War I, however, Americans were not dealing with helpless peoples on whom patterns could be forced. Instead, they were obliged to react to a death struggle among the great powers. For decades Americans had blandly prospered, without the need to arm heavily or to fear that each dawn might bring a disaster for which they must prepare. Suddenly, that calm was smashed. America faced a situation in which the strong states that usually kept order in the world were destroying each other, thereby leaving international society unpoliced.

How did this change touch the American people's vision of their national interest? What national self-images were reinforced and remade in the world's

---

*CHRONOLOGY*

| | |
|---|---|
| 1914 | *World War I begins in Europe* |
| 1915 | *British liner* Lusitania *torpedoed by German Submarine* |
| 1917 | *April 6, United States declares war* |
| 1917 | *Russian Revolution; Bolsheviks seize power in November* |
| 1918 | *Wilson proclaims Fourteen Points* |
| 1918 | *November 11, armistice declared* |
| 1919 | *Paris Peace conference* |
| 1919–1920 | *U.S. Senate rejects Treaty of Versailles and with it, League of Nations* |

crisis? What pressures were generated on American political and diplomatic leaders? Or to take a more basic question, did the American people realize what was happening? Or did they act on mistaken impressions and deal with a flawed image of international truth?

The fact is that in certain ways Americans of 1914 were not tuned in to the truth of disaster. And that not only explains some of their actions but opens up an entirely new line of thinking. If history "makes sense" and if there is some visible underlying pattern to the unfolding of a nation's story, based on long-term trends, then how is it that history is so often abruptly shaken up by the uninformed acts of miscalculating individuals? Our whole approach to the subject assumes an orderly flow of events based on reactions to reality. But do individuals and communities always know the "reality" of what they respond to? Or do error, whim, and even chance play a strong shaping role in what happens historically?

Such questions cannot be answered finally, but let us try an exercise. Let us look at three separate pages of the record, as historians now see them and as Americans of sixty or so years ago saw them. The first part of our examination deals with the period from 1904 to 1914, when the United States was basically ignorant of the fact that a general war was coming. The second will focus on the years from 1914 to 1917, when the American people mistakenly believed that they could remain neutral. Finally, comes the aftermath of the war, in 1919, when Americans took part in peacemaking and expected it to be much easier than in fact it was. In all three cases we will present the record of what was actually happening to the world. Then we will present the popular American ideas of how matters stood. And, finally, we will play Monday-morning quarterback and try to guess how mistaken notions actually guided U.S. behavior and what might have happened otherwise. At the very least, we will show the importance of getting facts straight before making judgments.

### *The Coming of Chaos: I—The Reality*

In the ten years prior to 1914 the world was, in fact, on a long downhill plunge. At least five areas of social and international conflict were heating up to emergency levels. First, there was the growing system of military alliances, each power jockeying to find partners to increase its war-making strength and overpower its potential enemies. By 1907 two major coalitions had emerged. One of them linked France, Russia, and Great Britain; the other, Germany, Austria-Hungary, and Italy. (Italy, in 1914, would stay neutral and then a year later join the Franco-British-Russian side.) Other nations were loosely linked to these power centers. Japan, for example, had an "understanding" with Britain. Turkey was almost a German satellite by 1912. The peril in the alliance system was that it made any small war a possible big one. The quarrel of one partner automatically drew in the others. Like climbers roped together, the major powers could not afford to have any one of them make a major mistake.

Next the race of the great European nations to colonize Asia and Africa kept sparking exactly those crises that the alliance network made so dangerous. In 1904, as Chapter 19 notes, Russia and Japan warred over their respective rights in China. That struggle was ended by the mediation of Roosevelt. In 1905, and again in 1911, the Germans and French came close to fighting over Morocco, and it took international conferences to settle things. In 1911 Italy attacked the crumbling Ottoman (Turkish) empire and won the north African province of Libya. That war, too, was over before it could spread.

Flammable material was also piling up as a result of a third twentieth-century development, the increasing fervor of nationalism among traditionally subject peoples. The Balkan Peninsula had once been almost totally divided between the multinational empires of Turkey and Austria-Hungary. But Greece broke away in 1830. New "Slavic" states—Serbia, Montenegro, Rumania, and Bulgaria—had been created after a Russo-Turkish war in 1878. In them there was a steadily growing enthusiasm for liberating fellow Slavs in Austria-Hungary, and that zeal was fed by the one great Slavic power, Russia. In 1908 Austrian annexation of two Slav-populated provinces brought on an alarm of war. In 1912 and 1913 the small Balkan states went to war, first against Turkey, and then with each other to divide the spoils. Nor was nationalism confined to southeastern Europe. The Irish independence movement was strong and active in 1914 and would explode in an actual unsuccessful uprising in April 1916. But Ireland's unrest did not involve other great powers.

Hotheaded nationalism, joined to great-power rivalry, explained a fourth ominous sign, the steady build-up of armaments. France, Russia, and Germany kept enlarging and modernizing their land forces. Each year they drafted and trained hundreds of thousands of reservists. From 1901 onwards Germany and Britain raced to outstrip each other in huge, deadly, and expensive warships.

The tax burdens of the arms races hobbled even willing governments in coping with a fifth area of potential explosiveness, the growing demand of underprivileged classes for power. Social revolts did not automatically bring war, but they created unrest and changes that made governments operate more unpredictably and unreasonably. Russia had a small revolution in 1905 that forced the czar to make unkept promises of reforms. Workers in France between 1902 and 1914 went out in numerous paralyzing strikes. In Britain the Labor Party gathered strength while the demand of women for the vote increased in volume. To add to this general picture of the breakdown of old patterns, there was a steady change in intellectual and artistic standards and values. It could be seen, but only by a far-sighted few, in the emergence of atonal music, symbolist poetry, abstract painting, and Freudian psychology.

Despite all these danger signs, most European thinkers remained comfortably optimistic. The upper and middle classes lived well on incomes of stable purchasing power. They rejoiced in inventions like the telephone and the electric light and the automobile. They were aware of the problems of the poor but could cheer themselves by noting a regular increase in social benefits provided by government. The colonial picture, it was felt, would improve as the "lesser breeds" were trained in civilized ways. The arms races and crises were disturbing, but there was wide belief that the future lay with the forces of peace. Modern nations would soon see the sheer wastefulness of war and abandon it. Machine guns would be shown in museum cases along with battle-axes and longbows. Most thinking Europeans were as convinced as Americans that progress was humanity's destiny.

Before turning to the question of how Americans saw these developments, it must be noted that the American people shared the underlying outlooks of the Western world. Inventions and ideas flowed both ways across the seas, as they had done since Europe had colonized the Americas.

The United States was in no real sense isolated. The products of American factories, from safety matches to locomotives, flowed steadily to Europe. America used European goods as diverse as chemical dyes and imported ales. Francs, marks, guilders, and pounds were still invested in American railways and mines. And most noticeably, in almost every year from 1900 to 1914, anywhere from one-half million to a million European immigrants entered the "promised land" as Americans-to-be. One-third of the American populace in 1910 was only a generation or two removed from the Old World.

In international dealings, too, America felt the forces that stirred great nations. She had her imperial enterprises in the Pacific and Latin America. She was also, like the British, the Germans, and the Japanese, building a modern navy. American representatives went to two conferences at the Hague, in 1899 and 1907, aimed at setting up international arbitration machinery and rules of warfare. And, without formal involvement in an alliance system, the United States had an unspoken deal with the British. They made no objection to the Panama Canal's being American controlled. In turn, the United States based most of its fleet in the Pacific, policing that ocean and leaving the British to do the same in the Atlantic.

## *The Coming of Chaos: II—American Images*

Despite these facts, however, Americans believed that they were special and separate. They moved to the drumbeat of a world marching towards war, but they *thought* they were doing something quite different. The American view of the U.S. role in the world as of 1914 was contained in several propositions. First, the United States was protected from the need for great armaments or "entangling alliances" because it was sheltered from attack by two mighty oceans. Secondly, the country was free of the dead weight of the past. For a century it had avoided involvement in the world's battles. Credit for this was not given to Europe's diplomats who had avoided general war but to American luck and virtue. It was through its free institutions that the United States had avoided the weight of conscription and high taxes and the passion of Europe's ancient tribal rivalries.

Americans did not think of European peoples (with the possible exception of the British) as really sharing a common human destiny and frailty with them. Europeans who poured in as immigrants were urged to forget their old loyalties, habits, and tongues as swiftly as possible and to "melt" into a new breed of 100-percent Americans. The best that popular opinion might say of Europe's governments was that they were getting better and in time might approach the perfection of elections, newspapers, and two-party systems.

European life was viewed in the stereotypes of operetta, full of sexy French people, heel-clicking Germans, and sad Russians. But there was nothing comic about this ignorance. The United States, wrapped in unawareness of how many benefits it owed to a prosperous and stable world, took no responsibility for maintaining such a world. Americans felt no obligation to help avoid war, except by moral statements about its wickedness, and were, with few exceptions, untroubled by the prospect that one might occur.

Historical might-have-beens are risky but irresistible. The United States might have taken an open role as a mediator in international crises simply because it *was* an outsider. Or it might have acknowledged its working relationship with Great Britain and admitted an interest in helping the British to keep control of the Atlantic. Other European nations might then have reconsidered the odds in a war between themselves and Britain and been more careful. In any case, American leaders might have tried to frame clear views of the national interest and of the steps the country would take to make the world a safe place for the United States. There might have been an effort to urge all industrial nations to negotiate solutions to outstanding colonial, economic, and social problems *before* a war came rather than after. American aloofness simply helped to make war more likely.

### *America in a World at War: I—The Reality*

At the beginning of the summer of 1914, Balkan nationalism and the alliance system combined to produce the disaster. The spark was struck when a Serbian nationalist assassinated the Austrian Archduke Franz Ferdinand, heir to the throne, at Sarajevo on June 28, 1914. Austria-Hungary then made demands on Serbia to control and punish pro-Slavic "terrorists" within her borders. To satisfy them would have seriously dented Serbian independence—

so Serbia refused. Austria-Hungary declared war on her on July 28. Russia then went to war against Austria to protect her Slavic brothers. Germany, true to her alliance, joined Austria against Russia, while France and Great Britain honored their pact with the czar and prepared to fight Germany. In one fatal week, July 28 to August 4, the system operated with deadly effectiveness. Millions of reservists rushed to arms, and Britain, France, and Russia, thereafter generally known as the Allies, were flung into war against Germany and Austria-Hungary, which were called the Central Powers.

The first thirty days set the pattern of desolation to follow. On the eastern front the Germans smashed a Russian invasion. In the west they launched a knockout blow at France under a war plan that sent their army plowing through Belgium, despite Germany's having signed an 1839 treaty guaranteeing that small country's neutrality. But this drive was stopped by the French, just outside Paris. By October 1914 the evenly balanced armies settled into a stalemate in France. Great land battles in Russia also did not bring a decision. The British fleet blockaded Germany. In 1915 Italy joined the Allies, and Turkey, the Central Powers. Their entry increased the bloodshed without changing the picture.

From 1914 to 1917 the great powers defied common sense by indulging in an insane carnival of self-destruction. Gigantic battles were fought to gain a few square miles of shell-pocked mud. New inventions such as poison gas, tanks, and air bombardment did not break the deadlock. Each day brought thousands of casualties and cost millions of dollars. Individual makers of war supplies grew rich, but national treasuries soon were approaching bankruptcy. Scarce goods like food and fuel were rationed to cold, hungry civilians. Bitterness grew as the war threatened to turn Europe into a vast cemetery. Propaganda makers did their best to turn the fury against the enemy instead of against the system that had produced the war.

By 1917, exhaustion was common. Governments could offer nothing but fresh sacrifices. Yet just because of that, each nation's people made a passionate demand for "victory," in order to justify their past agonies. The great powers were trapped. Each side was unable to win the war and unwilling to end it with an unheroic compromise that would seem to make the deaths and suffering in vain. The growing strain brought a revolution in Russia in March 1917. In November power was seized by the far-left Bolsheviks, and civil war between these "Reds" and their "White" enemies ravaged the country. The French army had serious mutinies in 1917. German Socialists called for an end to the struggle. The nations that had not yet suffered revolt wondered how much more popular rage and despair they could take.

The United States watched this from afar, with little understanding of how deep the tragedy was. (Not for another half-century would the American people know what it was like to be imprisoned in an unwinnable war.) An America of the Model T, the New Freedom, Greenwich Village, and gunboat diplomacy saw in the struggle only fresh cause to be glad that her people were not Europeans.

Wilson announced at the war's outset that the people of the United States must be neutral in word, thought, and deed. But by the time the war was a year and one-half old, any truly impartial observer would have seen that the nation was anything but neutral. Early in 1916 the United States was selling arms to the Allies, but not to Germany. Its bankers were lending money to the Allies, but not to Germany. And while still praising peace, America had entered on a crash program of arms build-up and manpower training that went under the name of "preparedness."

All of this did not come about because American policy makers thought that the national interest needed an Allied victory. Instead, we became a treasurer and supplier for the Allies through some unexpected circumstances. The first and most important was that the British controlled the sea's surface. In the first weeks of the war, Britain's navy cut off communication with Germany except by roundabout routes through neutral countries. Americans could not trade with the Germans, and their war news, which was heavily censored, came almost entirely from the Allied side.

In addition, despite neutrality, many American intellectual leaders were firmly pro-British. Preachers, professors, and editors, mostly of English stock, had long sung the praises of America's "Anglo-Saxon" past. Yet there were those who were not convinced. In the Midwest, especially, where Scandinavian and German immigrants were numerous, there was little zeal for the Allied cause. Nor were Irish Americans eager to aid the British. But among the makers of public opinion there was a strong bias toward London. France was also admired, though somewhat less, and Russia was not sympathized with at all, but Americans paid little attention to the war in eastern Europe. The Germans helped Allied propaganda by being clumsy. Their invasion of Belgium, which was harshly carried out, was hard to defend. Germany's military leaders, from the kaiser downward, were also unusually powerful and open in their contempt for both peace and democracy.

But most important in wrecking American neutrality was the submarine campaign. The Germans' answer to the British fleet's power was the undersea attack on cargo vessels bound for Britain. But a U-boat could not proceed in the old-fashioned way of sea war—fire a shot across the merchantman's bow, search it for goods of war, take off personnel for delivery to a neutral port, and then sink the ship. Submarines had no room for prisoners and were very vulnerable to attack even by light guns. They could only fire from subsurface concealment, without warning. Technology had provided Germany with a naval counterweapon. But it could only be used at the expense of humanitarian values. Faced with this conflict, all nations in the twentieth century have moved steadily in the direction of using whatever weapons were available. But Germany was the first country to face this twentieth-century dilemma and to take the consequences.

Americans were irritated by the British blockade, which also undercut traditional neutral rights. Ships with nonmilitary cargo for Germany or for neutral countries near Germany were stopped and held for weeks and months, awaiting search in British ports. The owners' losses from the delays and seizures mounted to the millions of dollars. The British also exerted unfair economic pressure through boycotts and blacklists against American firms lawfully doing business, as neutrals, with Germany. Angry notes of American protest crackled through the undersea cables to London. But when all was said and done, British policies did not take innocent lives.

Matters reached a first climax on a May morning in 1915, when a German U-boat torpedoed the Cunard liner *Lusitania* just off Ireland. The huge vessel sank in less than twenty minutes, drowning nearly 1200 of her passengers, including 128 Americans. The Wilson administration threatened to break diplomatic relations. For the time being, at least, the Germans agreed to suspend surprise attacks on passenger-carrying vessels. But after another six months of the war the Germans once again said that at the start of 1916 they would torpedo ships with war matériel bound for Britain. Late in March, a passenger-carrying liner, the *Sussex*, was sunk in the English Channel, with heavy loss of life. Again there was a strong and threatening U.S. note. Again, the Germans agreed to suspend such attacks. Finally, however, in January 1917, two and one-half years into the fruitless war, the Germans announced that as of February 1, they would once more throw a submarine blockade around the British Isles. The United States recalled its ambassador to Berlin, armed its cargo ships, and finally declared war on April 6, 1917.

In part, the submarine had only given the United States the motive to formalize its partnership with Britain and to prepare for war. After the *Lusitania* crisis, a nationwide campaign was set afoot to modernize the army. Pacifist sentiment was overwhelmed in a tide of cheers for men marching off to volunteer officer-training camps and in congressional votes for military spending. It was actually an indispensable program of mobilization for a modern war. And yet no one called the drive for "preparedness" a mobilization effort. It was another sign that illusion overshadowed fact in the American mind of 1916.

That was proved in the presidential campaign. It should have been clear that the Germans would not deny themselves the use of the submarine indefi-

"All the News That's Fit to Print."

# The New York Times.

EXTRA
5:30 A. M.

VOL. LXIV NO. 20,923. NEW YORK, SATURDAY, MAY 8, 1915.—TWENTY-FOUR PAGES. ONE CENT

## LUSITANIA SUNK BY A SUBMARINE, PROBABLY 1,260 DEAD; TWICE TORPEDOED OFF IRISH COAST; SINKS IN 15 MINUTES; CAPT. TURNER SAVED, FROHMAN AND VANDERBILT MISSING; WASHINGTON BELIEVES THAT A GRAVE CRISIS IS AT HAND

SHOCKS THE PRESIDENT

Washington Deeply Stirred by the Loss of American Lives.

BULLETINS AT WHITE HOUSE

Wilson Reads Them Closely, but Is Silent on the Nation's Course.

HINTS OF CONGRESS CALL

Loss of Lusitania Recalls Firm Tone of Our First Warning to Germany.

CAPITAL FULL OF RUMORS

Reports That Liner Was to be Sunk Were Heard Before Actual News Came.

The Lost Cunard Steamship Lusitania
X Where the First Torpedo Struck. XX Where the Second Torpedo Struck.

SOME DEAD TAKEN ASHORE

Several Hundred Survivors at Queenstown and Kinsale.

STEWARD TELLS OF DISASTER

One Torpedo Crashes Into the Doomed Liner's Bow, Another Into the Engine Room.

SHIP LISTS OVER TO PORT

Makes It Impossible to Lower Many Boats, So Hundreds Must Have Gone Down.

ATTACKED IN BROAD DAY

Passengers at Luncheon—Warning Had Been Given by Germans Before the Ship Left New York.

**Only 650 Were Saved, Few Cabin Passengers**

QUEENSTOWN, Saturday, May 8, 4:28 A. M.—Survivors of the Lusitania who have arrived here estimate that only about 650 of those aboard the steamer were saved, and say only a small proportion of those rescued were saloon passengers.

Official Confirmation

WASHINGTON, May 8.—A dispatch to the State Department early today

**Cunard Office Here Besieged for News; Fate of 1,918 on Lusitania Long in Doubt**

Nothing Heard from the Well-Known Passengers on Board—Story of Disaster Long Unconfirmed While Anxious Crowds Seek Details.

**List of Saved Includes Capt. Turner; Vanderbilt and Frohman Reported Lost**

**Saw the Submarine 100 Yards Off and Watched Torpedo as It Struck Ship**

Ernest Cowper, a Toronto Newspaper Man, Describes Attack, Seen from Ship's Rail—Poison Gas Used in Torpedoes, Say Other Passengers.

*The stunning news of the* Lusitania's *loss was a landmark in twentieth century United States history. Regardless of rights or wrongs, it brought home with stunning force (note the far-left column's description of Wilson's shock) what submarine warfare really meant—the inevitable killing of innocent civilians. In time, the American people came to accept, and to make, this kind of warfare, but it created quite an impact on the unprepared public mind of 1915. This "grave crisis" was temporarily resolved through diplomacy, but ended in war twenty-three months later.*

nitely if their military situation became desperate. By telling Germany that she must give up a major weapon, the United States had already gone halfway to war against Germany. Wilson knew this, and he also knew that the first renewal of submarine attacks would force the issue. Yet he campaigned and won on the slogan "He Kept Us Out of War." And Americans continued to believe in their innocence and peacefulness.

It took only ninety days after the election to bring reality into focus. The Germans resumed submarine warfare because they believed that a final, convulsive effort would knock out the Allies in 1917, before the Americans could develop a full-scale military effort against them. They left the United States no choice but to fight or back down, and they had little doubt of what the choice would be.



*America in a World at War: II—American Images*

In that first week of April, Americans had simply taken the final step in a long march to involvement. Yet it was not seen that way. A popularized version of events grew out of our own wartime propaganda and was most persuasively stated by Wilson. Perhaps he convinced himself. What he declared in speeches of 1917 and 1918 was that the United States had been truly neutral at the start. Gradually, however, it had become involved in defense of the historic principle of freedom of the seas. This principle was violated by Germany most outrageously of all the belligerents, through the use of a terror weapon, the submarine, which slew the innocent.

But, the Wilsonian summary continued, it became clear that this was to be expected from the Germans. Their rape of Belgium had shown their hand. Dominated by the military and autocratic mind, imperial Germany lusted to dominate others. In the end that was the root cause of the war itself—the spirit of raw power, expressed in tyranny at home and conquest abroad, the spirit embodied in the kaiser's court. The United States, in entering the war, therefore, was attacking the heartland of disregard for human rights. The end result would be good. The destruction of German militarism would pave the way for the destruction of the exaltation of power everywhere. The war would be a war to end wars and to "make the world safe for democracy."

Almost overnight, Wilson changed the clear process of going to war in pursuit of a limited objective, neutral rights, into a crusade to emancipate humanity from war and to guarantee self-government everywhere. Both these feats had never been achieved. And Wilson, a historian, should have known that his version of the causes of the war was oversimplified and distorted, as you yourselves know from the first pages of this chapter. Yet he managed, by his effort, to give the war moral and ideological meaning. Above all, his views were accepted because they confirmed Americans in the belief that their role from 1914 to 1917 had been one of innocence and isolation.

What were some of the costs of this mythologization? What might have happened had the American people been more realistically informed about their real position? For one thing, the United States might have recognized its stake in saving strong, responsible governments that could hold together the international order that had prevailed before 1914. That would have meant trying to shorten or end the war to avoid the exhaustion and weakening of the European belligerents.

Two American approaches could have been tried. One would have been a

*Mud, debris, vermin, constant fear, the smell of death—all these were part of the animal-like existence of millions of soldiers in the trench warfare of 1914–1918. Here two Americans aim a machine gun at the unseen enemy in the waste of "No-Man's Land" between the lines.*

frank lining up with the British, accompanied by a full American build-up to war status. Early in the war, this would have offset the impact of German land victories, evened the scales, and perhaps made the Germans receptive to seeking a negotiated peace.

A more truly neutral, but practical, stance, would have been to threaten an embargo of both sides, while offering inducements to them to bargain. In 1916 Wilson did twice make moves in this direction. First, he raised with the British the possibility of an American-summoned peace conference. Then he asked both sides for statements of war aims. By then, however, American support of the Allies made Germany suspicious of any American initiatives. And when at the year's end both sides did state war aims, each had to appease its war-weary peoples and honor secret treaties with demands for unrealistic terms. It was too late. Early in the war, all the major governments might have compromised an unwinnable war under the helpful prodding of the United States. Halfway through it, passions were too deep.

So the United States passed up all chances to speed the war's end before 1917. Then when America did enter, she did so on the basis of arguments that simply embraced Allied propaganda. These were two long-range results of this crusade against the "Hun." One was home-front hysteria. In a crusade dissent is intolerable. Strict espionage and sedition laws were passed. The United States, fighting for "democracy," jailed antiwar Socialist and labor leaders, muzzled papers, hunted for spies, and encouraged hatred of everything German from operas to sauerkraut. The climate of conformity and suspicion thus created furnished the seed of harsh developments in 1919 and the early 1920s. Among them was a great "red scare," a racist immigration law, and the revival of the Ku Klux Klan. Americans, like Europeans, lost their heads.

Another consequence of wartime passion was the demand for the destruction of the governments of the Central Powers. But encouraging revolt did not always mean spreading liberty. When established governments were overthrown in the war's turbulent aftermath, the results were not always an increase in democracy. Instead, there were merciless struggles for power. And from those bloody contests dictatorships emerged. By adopting the moralism of the warring powers, the United States managed to make the outcome more devastating.

*Peacemaking: I—The Reality*

The final phase of the story took place in 1918 and 1919. Early in 1918, Wilson announced a set of war aims that reflected his hopes for the postwar world. They were supposed to hearten the American and Allied peoples by creating a permanent peace that would seem to make the bitter years worth-

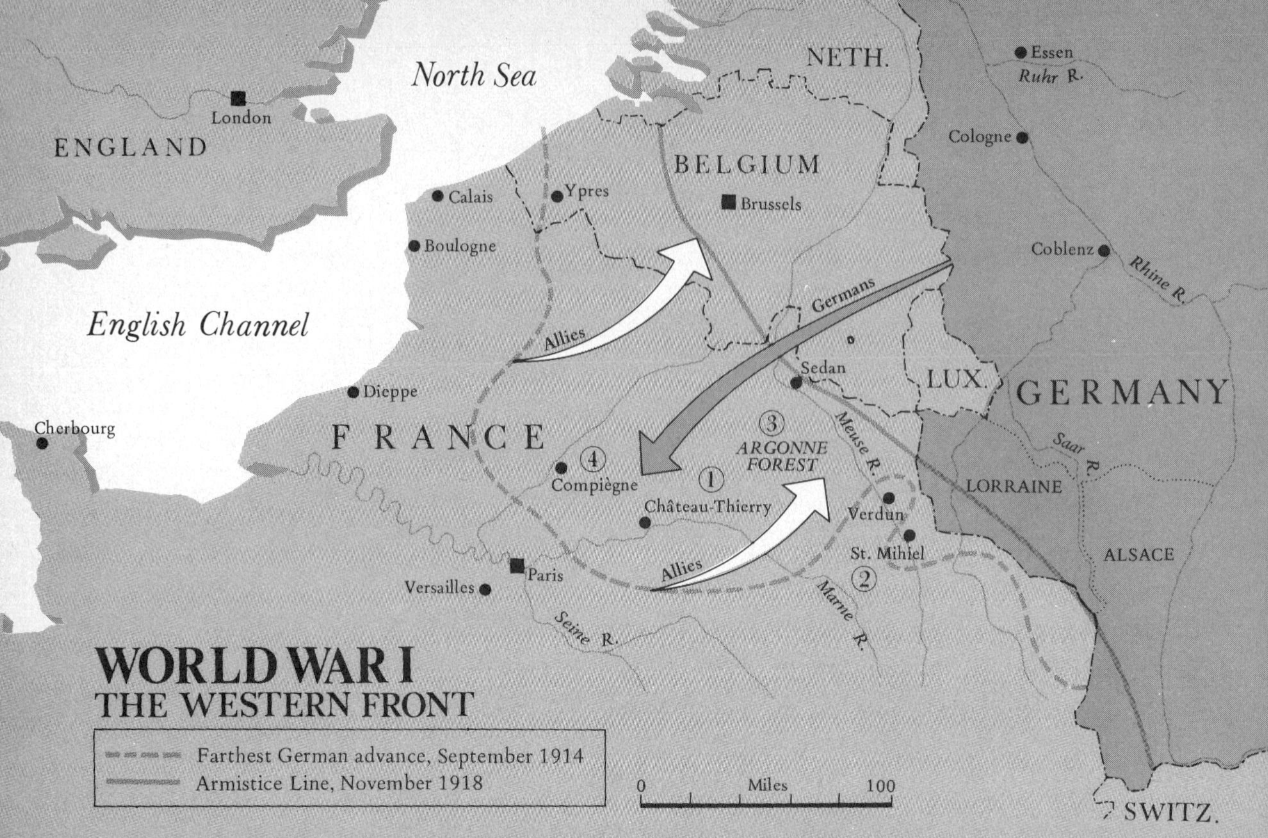


*Although the United States entered the war in April of 1917, it was not until more than a year later that her land forces saw combat in France. This was partly due to the American insistence that U.S. troops be organized as a separate army, rather than be quickly trained and fed as replacements to tired French and British divisions. Large numbers of "Yanks" got their baptism of battle in June and July of 1918, when the last, desperate German push in the west reached within fifty miles of Paris. The Germans were stopped by American contingents at Cantigny, Belleau Wood, and Château-Thierry* (1)*. German intelligence reported that the newcomers fought "with bravery and dash," in good part because their "nerves are not yet worn out."*

*August saw the French and British swing into a counteroffensive. The Americans did their part to destroy German fighting power, first by reducing a great "salient" or bulge in the Allied lines at St. Mihiel* (2) *in mid-September, and then, as the month ended, by launching an all-out drive through the Argonne Forest* (3)*. This campaign involved more than a million men, and was savagely resisted. In 47 days, the casualties of the American Expeditionary Force reached 120,000 or about 10 percent. But America was spared the horror of the endless months of bloodletting that the other combatants had endured. The weary German army, after four years, had had enough. The Kaiser's generals asked for a halt in the fighting; the Kaiser himself was forced to abdicate by a revolt in Berlin; so on November 11, 1918, an armistice was signed in a railroad car in the forest of Compiègne* (4)*. History's greatest war, until then, had ended—and soon, American occupiers' flags and uniforms would be seen in the unfamiliar setting of the Rhine.*

while. They were also intended to drive a wedge between the German people and their leaders. Since they contained no provisions that would be harmful to ordinary Germans, there was an implied invitation to the war-weary subjects of the kaiser to throw out their autocratic masters and deal themselves out of the war on decent terms.

Wilson's plans were contained in what came to be known as the Fourteen Points. The first five of these called for an end to secret treaties, freedom of the seas, reduction of tariffs and other trade barriers, limitation of armaments, and an "equitable adjustment" of colonial claims. The next eight specified abandonment of territories occupied by the Central Powers and a readjustment of boundaries so as to give every nationality a country of its own. A shorthand phrase for the concept was "self-determination of peoples." A specific illustration of it was the requirement for an independent Poland. The final point called for a League of Nations.

It was clear that Wilson now admitted that many factors had caused the war in 1914, among them colonial and economic rivalries, national jealousies, and arms races. It was clear, too, that he wanted to wipe them out and to create a kind of international "Congress" to see that they stayed wiped out. It was somewhat like a progressive plan for dealing with an American problem. First, have the trouble spots analyzed by experts. Next, legislate solutions. Finally, monitor the new arrangements by a commission. The Fourteen Points called for a progressive faith in intelligence, reason, and an ever-bettering world. In Wilson's words, they said to the world: "Here are the principles of freedom. Here are the things which we must do in order that mankind may be released from the intolerable things of the past."

But the past was not so lightly to be cast off. In October 1918 Wilson appeared to be triumphant. The Germans, their lines in France collapsing, asked for peace on the basis of the Fourteen Points. Early in November, a brief and relatively bloodless revolt threw out the kaiser and set up a provisional republic under the Social Democrats, the most liberal German party. On November 11, 1918, an armistice was signed, and the great bloodletting came to an end. Wilson then prepared to go in person to the forthcoming peace conference, accompanied by batteries of scholars who would help him blueprint the brave new world. When he got to Europe and toured the Allied capitals, thousands cheered him hysterically.

But, in fact, the Europe of 1919 was in no way ready for reconciliation and generosity. Each country, exhausted and fearful, demanded some kind of security for the future and revenge for the past. Britain wanted to see the whole financial burden of war costs shifted to the beaten Germans. France wanted to keep Germany forever weak. Italy wanted chunks of Austria-Hungary. New nations created out of the dismantled Austro-Hungarian empire—Yugoslavia, Poland, and Czechoslovakia—had demands of their own.

Rampant and outraged nationalism was one force on the loose in 1919. A second explosive kind of energy was the emergence of Communist revolution as a specter haunting Europe. Today, when the Soviet Union is a major power that behaves more or less like all others, it is difficult to realize the frightening radicalism of the Bolsheviks. They executed the czar and his family and promised to put all power in the hands of uneducated workers, peasants, soldiers, and sailors. They publicized the secret treaties between the czar and the Allies, refused to recognize czarist international debts, and nationalized all foreign-held property. They abolished ranks in their armies, and changed elemental social relationships such as marriage, by making divorce a simple matter. As it turned out, most or all of these steps were later abandoned, and Russia became, in fact, a dictatorship run by the head of the Communist Party, with the "normal" military, political, and diplomatic trappings.

But in 1919 that was not foreseeable. What the established classes of Europe saw was the emergence of a system that roundly denounced and promised to destroy parliamentary government, capitalism, and all the bases of authority and power on which nineteenth-century Europe had rested. Bolshevik leaders freely announced their aim of spreading the revolt to all nations. To rulers who had survived the 1914–1918 period, this seemed like a threat to complete the wreckage that the war had begun. In their fear many anti-Communist Europeans turned readily to repression of all potentially disruptive ideas and even to armed right-wing fanaticism as zealous as communism itself.

But the Wilsonian scheme of various national governments' sensibly planning a common future assumed that such governments would be composed of people of good will. It was not likely to work in nations where "red" revolutionaries fought pitched battles against die-hard defenders of church, property, and monarchy, with progressive liberals caught in the middle.

Against this background of fear and hate it was impossible for the peacemakers at the Paris conference to follow the Fourteen Points. In the end, despite Wilson's best efforts, they forced a harsh Treaty of Versailles on Germany, which she was forced to sign. She was formally made to accept the guilt for the war and to promise to pay reparations running into billions of German marks. Ten percent of her land area was taken away and given to Poland and France. All her colonies were likewise taken. Some of her most valuable mining regions were occupied by the French. Her merchant marine was reduced by seizures for "compensation" as well.

The Germans felt betrayed by Wilson's promises. Many of them came to believe a legend that Germany had not been beaten in the field but tricked into surrendering. The villains in this stab-in-the-back legend were the Social

Democrats who had accepted the armistice. These moderate politicians were hated by forces of the extreme right, which never forgave them for deposing the kaiser, and also by the German Communists. As a result, the democratic government they set up in Germany led a short and stormy life of only fifteen years before yielding to Adolf Hitler in 1933.

The year of "peace," 1919, saw a Europe that was hungry, cold, and torn by violence. In May a left-wing revolution in the German state of Bavaria briefly succeeded but was then smashed by its opponents, with thousands of executions following. That summer, Hungary, reduced now to a small state, was taken over by a Communist dictator, Bela Kun. Then he was pushed out by an invading Rumanian army. In Russia, Red and White armies clawed at each other. The Whites were encouraged by the former Allied powers. A small American-British expedition was sent to Murmansk, and a Japanese force landed at Vladivostok.

Americans, watching all this upheaval, grew more cynical about Europe and more fearful of radicalism and foreigners in their own midst. The year 1919 was a turbulent one of demobilization in America. Among its episodes were a general strike in Seattle, a great steel strike in the Pittsburgh area, and a strike of Boston policemen. All were broken, but all tended to increase anti-"red" hysteria. Race riots in Washington and Chicago also inflamed ugly mob feelings. As the year ended, with the red scare in full cry, the federal government staged the so-called Palmer raids. Named for the attorney general who ordered them, they were a series of hasty and arbitrary arrests of suspected radicals. Many of the victims were later deported, without evidence of any wrongs having been done by them. The social conflicts of Europe seemed to have washed onto American shores.

## *Peacemaking: II—American Images*

This was the framework for the rejection of the Treaty of Versailles in the United States. Wilson went to Paris, and did his best to bring about the kind of peace he had depicted. But he could not bar the imposition on Germany of the bitter final agreement with its plentiful seeds of future trouble. The cause was not that the statesmen of Europe were villains. There are few real heroes and villains in history. The Allied prime ministers faced enormous pressures to make the defeated enemy bear the entire burden of the war and to strengthen their own nations as much as possible. Wilson had to recognize these realities and salvage what he could. His chief comfort was in the League. Whatever problems the treaty might create, the League could peaceably straighten out in the future.

But on his return to the United States at the end of June, Wilson found the task of getting the necessary two-thirds Senate ratification more difficult than

*Woodrow Wilson received a hero's welcome when he arrived in Paris for the peace conference in December, 1918. The bearded, top-hatted gentleman with him in the horse-drawn carriage is President Poincaire of France. The carriage could serve as a symbol of the pre-1914 world that neither man realized was gone forever.*

anticipated. This was because of the pressures that *he* faced. He had no political consensus behind his peace plan. He had not enlisted major leaders of either party to join him in planning and publicizing American peacemaking strategy. The Republicans especially, therefore, were in an uncooperative and partisan mood. Nor were the Democrats solidly behind Wilson. The connections between domestic politics and foreign policy were clearly exposed that year. Irish Americans, usually Democrats, resented Wilson's refusal to put pressure on the British for Ireland's independence. Italian Americans resented Wilson's resistance to Italy's claims of territory also demanded by Yugoslavia. Other ethnic groups also had discontents with the treaty, which turned into abandonment of Wilson.

Many progressives, like the editors of the *New Republic*, were shaken by the vindictiveness of the treaty. They titled their first article after its text was released: "This Is not Peace." On the other side stood conservatives and isolationists who had always disliked and distrusted Europeans. They objected to the League especially, with its clear machinery for involving the United States in the destiny of the Old World.

Ordinarily, Wilson might have dealt with these problems in the usual way of American presidents. He could have granted political favors, built bases of support in Congress, involved important figures in activities connected with the League, and cultivated the press. But the summer of 1919 was no ordinary time, as we have seen. Problems were piled high, and feelings ran deep. And Wilson was busy and weary and, as a result, less of a politician and more of a stubborn, self-righteous man.

Accordingly, Wilson fumed while the Senate Foreign Relations Committee, led by Massachusetts Senator Henry Cabot Lodge, held up the treaty and slowly debated amendments to preserve American freedom of action. Finally, in September an angry Wilson decided on a nationwide speaking tour to rally the public behind him as he had done in wartime. But then came one of those accidents that history cannot foresee but that may change the balance in a struggle. Exhausted by the months of hard work, Wilson collapsed on the trip. He was rushed home to Washington and there suffered a paralytic stroke. For the remainder of his term he remained half paralyzed and unable to lead. For the first few months of his illness, he simply did not function as president at all. A prisoner of his helpless muscles and stricken nerves, he watched as events swung beyond his control.

The treaty came up twice for votes in the Senate. When it was presented without any amendments or changes, a combination of irreconcilables, who opposed it in any form, and reservationists, who opposed it as it stood, sent it down to defeat. When it came up again with various changes to suit the reservationists, the irreconcilables joined with the purists, who would accept no changes, to deny the two-thirds majority needed to ratify. And so American participation in the League died. The whole Wilsonian peace plan had rested on a progressive view of European life and politics that was wrong for 1919. And Wilson's defense of the treaty in the United States ignored the American political climate of 1919. Once again, a leader's misjudgments changed the course of history.

But Wilson's fellow Americans viewed his failure differently. For them the events of 1919 only reaffirmed the myth of American innocence and virtue. One popular legend was that Wilson had gone to Paris to battle for truth and justice and had been swindled by the crafty, power-mad statesmen of Europe. He was an innocent abroad or, as one writer put it, a virgin in a bawdy house, piteously calling for lemonade. Such a view only confirmed the popular desire for isolation.

In later years, and especially during and after World War II, another more pro-Wilsonian version of 1919 was spread. In this one Wilson far-sightedly saw that the League was critical in keeping future peace. But jealous and narrow-minded superpatriots at home had thwarted him. Where there was no vision, the people perished. That view, too, skimmed over the complex realities underlying international wars and also over the variety of currents in the stream of American politics. It echoed the old idea that following a good person's advice is the cure-all for human evils.

What are the "might-have-beens" if there had been more American realism? Little could be done to make quick repairs of European society in 1919. An informed American policy would have merely gone slowly. Wilson could have gotten the United States to sign a separate pact ending hostilities with Germany, which later was done. Then—assuming he had not become ill—he could have edged America toward participation in the League by first joining its international economic and social reconstruction agencies. Full membership could be a possible climax when American public opinion was ready. And the United States, on its own, might have called for conferences on colonialism, disarmament, and tariff reduction.

In fact, two conservative Republican administrations that followed Wilson's did some of those very things. The United States did not lapse back into total isolation. But the American people, in overreacting to Wilson's and their own fundamental ignorance of the twisted maze of modern international life, *thought* that the United States could and should keep clear of a "hopeless" Europe. The belief that America was special, different, and a land on which God smiled especially fondly did not die. Even involvement in war and peace from 1914 to 1919 did not change it. Ideas change more slowly than circumstances. And, as we have seen, ideas have much to do with the making of foreign policy.

## *FOR FURTHER READING*

To begin with, it is useful to have a look at the European and American worlds in the early years of the twentieth century. Two books by Barbara Tuchman, *The Proud Tower* (1966) and *The Guns of August* (1962), beautifully describe how a confident Europe blundered its way into destruction. Meanwhile, Henry May's *The End of Innocence* (1959) deals with American thought in the first years of the twentieth century and shows how unprepared Americans were for its complexities. A more popular look at pre-1914 America is Walter Lord, *The Good Years* (1969).

The story of how the United States became involved is best approached through biographies of Wilson. The most thorough and massive one is in several volumes by Arthur Link. The volume on the war's approach, *Wilson: The Struggle for Neutrality* (1960), is enormously complete in detail. A shorter road to the same goal is to read John Garraty, *Woodrow Wilson* (1956), one of a series entitled Great Lives in Brief. For the firsthand flavor of life in America in those years, you should know of a series by Mark Sullivan, *Our Times: Over Here*, vol. 5, 1914–1918 (1926–1935). This is one of several volumes covering the period from 1900 to about 1929 in the same way—many newspaper and magazine excerpts, illustrations, cartoons, and interviews. Another very full and readable book that takes the point of view that we should have stayed out of the conflict is Walter Millis, *Road to War* (1935).

Finally, for the peacemaking, it is once again good to begin with the overall view of a professional historian. Thomas A. Bailey wrote two books on Wilson at Versailles, *Woodrow Wilson and the Great Betrayal* (1945) and *Woodrow Wilson and the Lost Peace* (1944). A popular but gripping history of Wilson's last, sick, sad years in the White House is Gene Smith, *When the Cheering Stopped* (1971). For inside looks at Paris in the spring of 1919, Ray Stannard Baker's *American Chronicle* (1945) and William Allen White's *Autobiography* (1946) will be colorful and helpful. Also, the first chapter of William E. Leuchtenburg, *The Perils of Prosperity* (1958) is a useful summary of 1919's America.

# Thought provokers

*One of the standard themes in textbooks of U.S. history was the claim that the pressure of "land-hungry" westerners drove us into the War of 1812 and the Mexican War and accounted for other attempts to enlarge our territory. Yet, in fact, it is difficult to separate geographical expansion, domestic economic growth, and the increase in American trade with the world. Do you see any significance in the fact that the first American minister to China, Cushing, was from Massachusetts? Do you see any connections among New England investors and railroad promoters, the annexation of California in 1848, and the addition of Hawaii to the United States just exactly fifty years after that? Were the economic centers of power in the country as important in supporting an expansionistic foreign policy as the southern and western regions, which raised the loudest cry for taking more territory?*

*When we studied the coming of the Civil War in Chapter 10 we noted how the free-soil program of the early Republican Party wanted to save the West from slavery and free it for economic development. What connections would you be able to draw between Seward's free-soil doctrines (he was one of the very first Republicans) and the policies he followed as secretary of state? What might his foreign policy show about his attitude toward dark-skinned people, in contrast to the attitudes he expressed as an antislavery man?*

*By the end of the nineteenth century the United States was a major manufacturing nation. How did this change Americans' desires when it came to making treaties and arrangements with China? What did the United States hope to gain from China in 1900 that it might not have wanted in 1800? Why did the United States show more willingness to become a western Pacific power after 1898 than in the early 1850s? Did it have to do with the spread of certain Darwinistic ideas in the United States? With the conversion of navies to steam and iron? Or with new ideas about what was necessary to the health of the U.S. economy—such as avoiding surpluses?*

*In dealing with American policy toward Mexico before the Civil War, the major fact of note is that American internal quarrels prevented further grabs of Mexican land. What were these quarrels? Were both Southern and Northern* economic *leaders in a position to gain from expansion into Mexico? If so, what political and ideological differences divided them on the issue? Are economic interests the strongest elements in making national policy? How, in short, would you use the story of Mexican-American relations in the 1850s to analyze the economic interpretation of history discussed in Chapter 12 (on the coming of the Civil War)?*

*Here is yet another question touching on apparent contradictions between foreign and domestic policies. When mining companies, oil companies, and railroads were making successful investments in Mexico between* 1890 *and* 1910, *were they under severe criticism for their business practices at home? Review Chapter* 18 *for your answer. Why was it possible for American corporations to enjoy the protection of their investments in Latin America under progressive administrations, which tried, at the same time, to restrict their growth in the United States? Why were the rules different?*

*How would an American progressive, admiring the modern, centralized, bureaucratic state—with modern Germany furnishing a prize example—have interpreted the factional battling that went on in Mexico City between* 1910 *and* 1916*? Would there be any similarity in his attitudes toward Mexicans, blacks, Indians, and immigrant voters and their "bosses"? And would progressives and their political opponents in the United States have been in agreement with such attitudes?*

*Finally, how did American ideas about their differences from Europeans reflect some earlier themes we have touched on? How many of them were due to the Puritan tradition discussed in Chapter* 2*? Or to the worship of the frontier touched upon in Chapter* 8*? Why were such attitudes not changed much by improved communications? Did American journalism, despite being able to get news from Europe more quickly, only give Americans the news that editors and the public expected and wanted to hear?*

*And how does the American effort to "reform" Europe in* 1919 *compare with the general kinds of reform efforts touched upon in Chapters* 16 *through* 18*? Was it similar in goals, means, and follow-through? Was Wilson, as a "world reformer," in the league of the abolitionists and commune builders of Chapter* 10*—or was he a pragmatist like Booker T. Washington and Gompers? Or was he some combination of both?*

# PART SEVEN: WHAT THE

# TWENTIETH CENTURY BROUGHT

*Time is a necessary dimension for all of us. We cannot function without a sense of past and present and the difference between them. A person who could not separate the past from the present would live in a world of confusion and ghosts of bygone days. And a victim of amnesia, who forgets everything known before a certain date, suffers a paralyzing loss of identity. We are the sum of our yesterdays.*

*Historians find time sequence a necessary beginning guide to their work. Faced with massive evidence on some subject, they can at least begin to arrange it in the simplest way, by organizing it chronologically: First, this happened. Then this. And then that. Are connections visible? How does one then proceed to explain them?*

*In fact, historians need a long time span in order to make sense of their evidence. Their information can only fall into patterns when it is spread over a number of years. The closer they get to the present, the harder it is to know what is important and what is not. We can each recall headlines of some years back that seemed world-shaking at the time but later turned out to have little impact. And we could, with a little work, find buried news stories, such as a fall in the birth rate or a warning that some natural resource was becoming scarce, that became important factors in our lives much later.*

*In dealing with the past fifty years of U.S. history, therefore, it is difficult for historians to be certain that the events they describe will really turn out to have been significant. So instead of trying to cover all the "major" happenings of the era, we will try another approach here. The remaining chapters will spell out certain key themes in the lives of the American people. They will deal with happenings and people who illustrate those themes. And they will try to lead you up various "pathways to the present" in such a way that you may be encouraged to look for still others, planting your own route markers as you go.*

*One basic fact of life has been the sudden surges of prosperity that have gone along with the steady growth of the modern economy. They have alternated with periods of depression, including one catastrophic era of hard times that took up almost all of the* 1930s. *It is worth asking certain questions about these boom and "bust" periods. Why do they happen? Are their effects evenly spread among the whole population? And what do they, in their swiftness, do to the normally slow-moving patterns of society? What expectations do they build among certain classes of people? How do they change the nature of family life? What leaders are likely to emerge in a period of good times, and which ones will last through a slump? What happens to old-fashioned values when new gadgets and luxuries become cheap and available? What groups in society use value changes as excuses to demand new freedoms? And what groups are most frightened by such changes? In the first chapter in this part, Chapter* 22, *we will look at the great prosperity decade, the* 1920s, *in search for answers to some of these general questions. There will also be a glance at the stock market crash and what followed it, with the same questions being posed.*

*Then we will turn our attention to politics. More and more, the presidential races have tended to become the all-absorbing focus of public attention for one year out of every four. Clearly, this is not because other elections are unimportant or even because great changes take place every time a new occupant enters the White House. But, somehow, the American people have come to feel that they express their attitudes on a variety of subjects in their choice of the chief executive. The presidency has become, for millions, a symbol of the nation. What symbol shall be chosen? In answering that question, the voters paint a self-portrait. They show what is on their minds, what qualities they admire and identify as best, and how they would like to be seen in the eyes of the world. Sometimes, in addition, the election registers a genuine choice of direction for the future. We will study three key presidential elections to demonstrate this style of analyzing the voters' choice.*

*Another general development of the past few decades has been the tremendous growth of the bureaucratic state. It is true that the government has always been in the business of doing things for people, from levying tariffs and selling lands to regulating weights and measures and protecting the public from disease, violence, and fraud. But since the* 1930s, *particularly, there has been an enormous increase in the number of agencies that, in the words of the Preamble to the Constitution, "promote the general welfare." Some regulate business dealings; others help to conserve the environment; still others promote the renewal of cities, the care of the aged and jobless, the training of specialists needed for national protection, and so on, through an endless variety of functions. What has this growth in "paternalism" done to the United States? Has it weakened individual responsibility? Has it destroyed the sense of local initiative in communities? Has it, as many charge, increased the cost of government, encouraged the multiplication of government decrees, and narrowed citizens' liberties? Or has it been a needed response to a larger, more complex society? Has it made the national government, with its vast, collected resources, a partner in helping individuals and communities adapt to change?*

*Finally, we will take a close look at American society since the* 1950s, *under the impact of new inventions that were truly revolutionary. Devices such as jet aircraft, television, and computers—to name just three—enable humanity to leap previously impossible boundaries of time and space. They have extended the range of human consciousness and had heavy impact on the natural environment and on the political arrangements under which peoples live. We shall study some of these impacts. How does the modern technological age make itself felt in educational systems? In churches and families? What kinds of social organizations are needed to spread inventions through a mass market? Are mighty corporations the only possible agencies for handling technological growth? And what do they do to the political ideal of equality? How are the bounties of invention spread through various classes? Must the rules of fairness and opportunity be rewritten in an age of giants? In short, how did the amazing technological breakthroughs of the post-*1945 *era affect the American scene that had emerged in the preceding century and a half?*

# chapter 22

# Boom and depression: a study of culture shock

It is the fall of 1928. There is the inevitable sweep of leaves turning scarlet. Election-year orators mow down opponents with the hot winds of their oratory. Presidential candidate Herbert Hoover stands before an audience in New York's Madison Square Garden and celebrates the American system. It has been good to him, raising him from a modest rural Iowa boyhood to the Republican nominee for the highest office in the land. So it is with genuine loyalty that he ticks off the record:

> Today there are almost nine automobiles for each ten families, where seven and a half years ago only enough automobiles were running to average less than four for each ten families. The slogan of progress is changing from the full dinner pail to the full garage. Our people have more to eat, better things to wear, and better homes. We have even gained in elbow room, for the increase of residential floor space is over 25 per cent, with less than 10 per cent increase in our number of people. Wages have increased, the cost of living has decreased. . . . We have in this short period decreased the fear of poverty, the fear of unemployment, the fear of old age; and these are fears that are the greatest calamities of human kind. . . .

Almost exactly four years later, President Hoover is in his fourth and final year of office. A national business magazine, surveying life in a United States lurching into a third winter of the Depression, provides the history of 1932:

There were ten million unemployed, and going by average family size, that meant some 25 million people—perhaps one-fifth of the entire population—whose source of livelihood was cut off, and who either needed relief or would need it as soon as their meager savings were exhausted.

Public and private welfare organizations, overwhelmed by applications, could barely provide families with enough money for food—and with nothing for shoes, clothing, rent or medical bills. Weekly allowances per family had fallen as low as $2.39 in New York, with $3 and $4 the rule in most cities and $5 a high figure.

32,000 families in New York, waiting to receive relief—with a normal average earnings of $141.50 a month before the Depression—were now averaging an income of $8.20 a month.

Chicago teachers, in May 1932, had received only 5 months' cash in the preceding 13. 3,177 had lost $2,367,000 in bank failures, 2,278 of them had lost $7,800,000 in lapsed policies, and 759 had lost their homes.

In Philadelphia there had been one eleven day period in April, 1932, when both private and public charitable funds were not available. A study of 91 families, undertaken to see just what they did, revealed that one woman borrowed fifty cents, bought stale bread for 3½ cents a loaf, and the family lived on it for the 11 days; another put the last food order into soup stock and vegetables, which the family ate as sparingly and infrequently as possible for 11 days; another family lived on dandelions; another on potatoes; and another had simply done without food for two and one half days.

Seldom has there been such a dramatic downfall in so short a time. Of course, nothing in history is ever totally black and white. Hoover was not a fool. When he spoke in 1928, his optimism was shared by most of his fellow Americans. But he should have been more aware that even in that palmy year millions of Americans were still in the grip of want. On the other hand, even in the disastrous winter of 1932–1933, there were those families that suffered only a little or not at all.

The boom of the twenties was not universal. Nor was the misery of the thirties. Nevertheless, the facts speak for themselves. A nation on a protracted economic joy ride in 1928 was shattered by the biggest crash of its history only a few years later. The twenties would properly go down in the history books as the prosperity decade. The thirties would be the haunted age of the Depression.

In that violent opposition of moods and settings there is good opportunity for social analysis. We have spoken often, in earlier chapters, about culture under various pressures. We have, from time to time, looked at how urbanization, expansion, technological breakthroughs, and war touched on culture and how cultural attitudes, in turn, shaped political and diplomatic behavior.

What is the impact of sudden new kinds of wealth or of instant poverty on culture? Do dizzying roller-coaster rides on the graph of economic progress have a deeper impact on society than slower-paced changes? Can sudden economic shocks reveal dangerous stress patterns in a culture? To attempt to answer such questions requires a close, detailed look at the economy of the twenties and thirties.

### *The Big Boom in Consumer Goods*

The boom of the twenties rested on several props. One was a steadily increasing productivity per worker. Another was a shift of productive energies toward consumer and luxury goods. A third was a tendency to gamble on the future that was reflected in a "bullish" stock market, in which heavy buying pushed the price of shares steadily upward, creating paper fortunes.

A few figures out of many tell the tale. The overall index of manufacturing output between 1920 and 1929 increased over 50 percent. This took place while the number of workers in the manufacturing industries was only increasing by about 23 percent. Each industrial worker was creating a greater volume of goods. And so was every agricultural worker. Huge crops were produced by a shrinking number of farmers. Their number sank to 10 million between 1920 and 1929.

Production statistics showed a shift toward a new kind of economy. It provided more goods for high living as well as heavy industry. Residential construction soared, with heavy outlays going for office buildings, apartment houses, and suburban "bungalows," the key features of the modern urban landscape. The biggest boom of all was in automobiles. Whereas 1920 saw just under 2 million turned out by the assembly lines, 4.4 million rolled onto the

*CHRONOLOGY*

| | |
|---|---|
| 1920 | *First national radio stations, WWJ and KDKA* |
| 1922 | *Height of revival of Ku Klux Klan* |
| 1924 | *Immigration Act sets quotas* |
| 1926 | *Scopes "monkey trial"* |
| 1927 | *Lindbergh's nonstop transatlantic solo flight* |
| 1929 | *Stock market crashes in late October* |
| 1933 | *Franklin D. Roosevelt inaugurated as president* |
| 1933–1940 | *New Deal era* |

highways in 1929. As Chapter 15 shows, automobile prosperity triggered waves of profit in related fields: in earth-moving equipment to build the roads for the cars, in the making of the rubber, steel, glass, and textiles that went into them, in the refining of the gasoline that fueled them.

The squeaky sounds of early radio signals soon turned into the words and music of a broadcasting industry that sang lyrics of high dividends. By the end of the decade there were some 700 AM radio stations, many already linked in a few major networks. Radio sets and parts were made in increasing quantities. The value of all such products in 1920 was $17 million. By 1929 the comparable figure was $366 million.

Electrical appliances also fed the boom. Telephones, phonographs, washing machines, vacuum cleaners, and refrigerators became more and more common. Each spawned new businesses, providing parts and repairs. The demand for electrical power in the home soared. So did industrial electricity consumption as more and more factories switched to compact, clean, efficient electrical engines. Naturally, then, the manufacture of electrical equipment zoomed from $46 million in 1920 to $976 million nine years later.

Cameras and films, both for home snapshot makers and the growing movie industry, were big items. Chemicals of various kinds, for use in industry, agricultural fertilizers, and synthetic products like rayon and cellophane, also led in the production parade. Cigarettes, considered sissyish before World War I, when he-men smoked cigars and pipes or "chawed" and no lady used tobacco, also became a major consumption item. The commercial aviation industry also took off.

All of this expansion took credit and kept bankers busy. Busy bankers, in turn, meant more work for lawyers and insurance people. And against this background of gold-rush-days optimism, the stock market continued to rise. Everyone wanted to own a share of a profitable corporation. One could collect dividends on it or perhaps sell it at a profit and reinvest in fresh stocks and so climb on the escalator again at a higher floor. Everyone with even a little cash to spare wanted some action. They were encouraged by liberal loans from stockbrokers to put their small stakes into the pot along with the giants of banking. As a result of such encouragement, the number of shares traded on Wall Street rose from 282 million in 1924 to 920 million in 1928. And brokers' loans to their customers went from $3.5 billion in 1927 alone to $8 billion early in 1929.

The big beneficiaries of the boom were, of course, the great corporations who dominated production—GM, RCA, Westinghouse, Standard Oil, American Tobacco, and the others whose names ring out in Chapter 18 as evidence of the failure of antitrust reform. But some blessings rained down on the average person. Average annual wages rose from $1238 in 1921 to $1449 in 1928. Average real per-capita income (each person's share of the total national income)

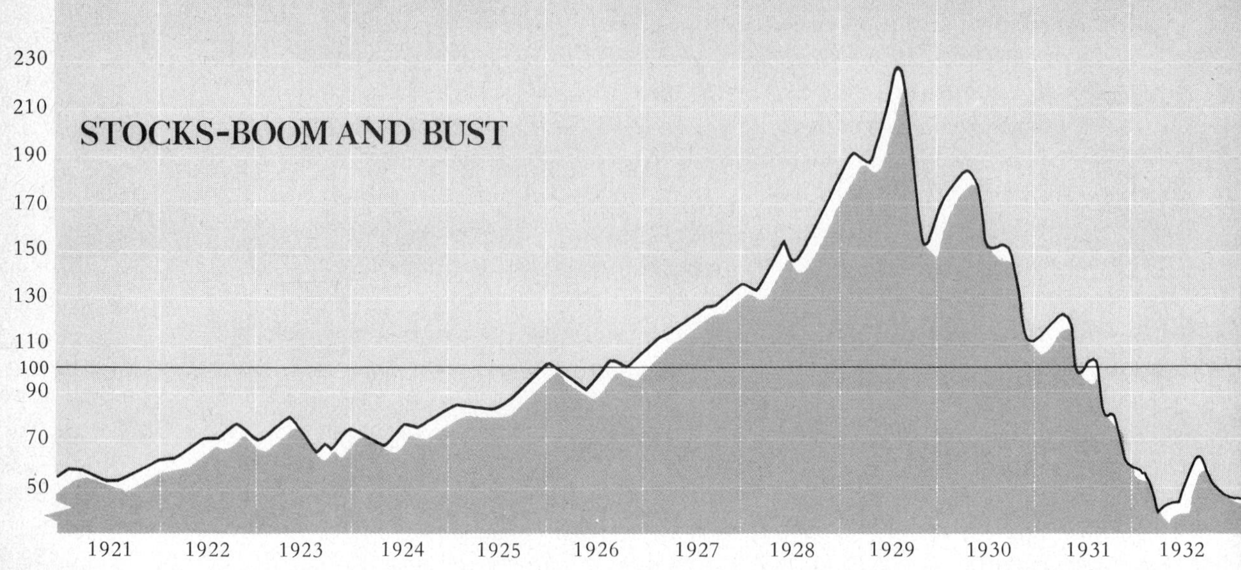


*The chart shows the rise and fall of a representative sample of 421 common stocks. The 1926 average price was 100 and is the base for the other relative figures.*

went from $543 to $716 in the same period. These statistics mean that millions of Americans, many of them your grandparents and great-grandparents, were enjoying a better life and more real purchasing power than *their* grandparents. More worked an eight-hour day, owned their homes and cars, and kept their children in school through the 12th grade. Hoover was not entirely wrong.

Yet the picture was not as perfect as public-relations people for "the American way" made it seem. As progress by-passed the old nineteenth-century industrial giants like rails, coal, and textiles, workers in those fields of the economy were laid off. They suffered, unnoticed amid the ballyhoo. Less than 12 percent of the labor force of some 49 millions in 1929 were unionized, and therefore without protection and power. In places like the cotton mills of North Carolina or the harvest fields of New Mexico, men, women, and children still worked ten- and twelve-hour days for less than a dollar. The national income was not fairly distributed. In 1929 the top 5 percent of the 27.5 million American families received 26.5 percent of the total national income. The top 1 percent received 14.5 percent of it. More than half of all American families received less than $2000 in annual income. Four in ten, in fact, received less than $1500. Every fifth one received less than $1000 annually.

The greatest number of poor families were concentrated in agriculture. The rising costs of equipment plus the falling prices for crops combined to force more and more individual farmers off the farm, leaving the field to large-scale operators. In addition, small businesses disappeared into large ones at a fearsome rate. Over 8000 businesses in manufacturing and mining alone vanished between 1919 and 1930. The 200 largest corporations owned almost half of the wealth of *all* corporations. So in the prosperous twenties, the independent farmer and businessman, the backbone of society according to America's official economic mythology, were going the way of the buffalo and the Indian.

Yet the nation did not complain. It approved of what looked like a great surge of population into the middle class, and it applauded basic changes in ways of life that resulted.

Let us begin with a large, overall generalization, then trace it to individual areas of life. The biggest fact of life was the shift to an economy in which a high level of consumption was a social necessity. The nineteenth-century industrial boom had provided farm machines and locomotives to break the isolation of the West and make it yield crops. It had provided the machinery to turn natural resources into exportable commodities like steel ingots and copper wire. It had fed and housed the millions of workers needed to build cities. The emphasis was on working hard to harness the power of Nature and create more materially productive human communities.

Now, in what was called the New Era, the forces of material creativity were spewing out an avalanche of goods that had to be bought, used up, and renewed in order to keep the wheels spinning.

## *Status, Work, and Style in a Consumer Culture*

A first sign of this new truth was in the make-up of the labor force. Since it was essential to keep customers spending, salesmanship and advertising became tremendously important. The dollar volume of advertising increased from $2,935,000 in 1920 to $3,426,000 in 1929. The number of men and women employed in advertising and selling likewise jumped. Though the total number of workers in industrial jobs increased, a greater *percentage* of all the employed went into the categories described by the census takers as "sales, service, clerical and managerial" work.

There was a new definition of work itself. No longer was a working person a "producer." The assembly line had already robbed workers of the satisfaction of creating an entire item from beginning to end. Now millions of employed men and women never even handled part of a product. They simply typed statements, added figures, wrote inventories and purchase orders, or talked others into buying. Americans had long preached a "work ethic," which made labor necessary, dignified, and honorable. But the Puritans who founded that ethic used the word "work" to mean something more productive than what many twentieth-century white-collar Americans did for a living. Socialist theorists, too, had definition problems. They divided the world into capitalists and workers. But now millions of workers, though depending on wages, lived, dressed, and behaved like capitalists and sometimes owned shares in capitalistic corporations.

Still another impact of the changing economy was the growing importance of schooling. Enrollments expanded, and longer periods of schooling were completed. The reason was that a simple, old-fashioned reading-writing-arithmetic-geography curriculum, completed in six years, would not supply America with enough salesmen, bookkeepers, department heads, personnel managers, accountants, secretaries, designers, technical assistants, and the like, to keep the consumer economy healthy and running. So high-school diplomas became more common. Opportunities for self-improvement by advance into white-collar ranks increased. But the other side of the coin was that those, who for whatever reason did not get through school, a number that ranged from 20 to 40 percent of the pupils, were largely condemned to low-level employment, if any.

They became part of the industrial working class. And despite official worship of the value of labor, expressed in Labor Day political speeches, the foot soldiers of the production line, the people who got their fingernails dirty and carried lunchboxes were looked on as being less "successful" than those who earned their living by using words and numbers in offices. One way in which the blue-collar worker could regain some equality, however, was to buy the same goods as the foreman, the professional man, or the employer himself. His urge to consume for the sake of status also helped to keep the system working.

Appearances grew more and more important. "Keeping up with the Joneses" is a human trait in all cultures. But now the Joneses were not next-door neighbors but artificial creations of the world of image making. Newspapers and magazines filled their pages with pictures of chic women and elegant men smoking brand-name cigarettes, lounging on finely made furniture, driving in sleek cars. Ordinary people were encouraged to imitate these models. The movies, too, were especially influential. Boys and girls from little crossroads hamlets tried to make up, dress, dance, and talk like their favorite stars. The power of film in the marketplace was shown when, in a 1934 movie, *It Happened One Night*, the hero took off his shirt and revealed his bare chest. Undershirt makers unhappily reported an immediate drop in sales throughout the nation.

The whole thrust of newspaper and radio advertising was to build psychological needs that could be appeased by purchases. Appearances became as important as substance. We have seen how Ford mass-produced the Model T in the belief that Americans were a down-to-earth lot who wanted the cheapest, simplest, and most efficient basic automobile possible. But by 1926 he was losing business to rivals who were providing yearly model changes, color, streamlining, new interior trim, engine options, and other novelties that would become part of Detroit's standard trade-in promoting package. For by then the family car was not simply transportation. It was part of a family's life-style. Americans therefore wanted it to express their tastes and attitudes and to look custom made. Ford's surrender to "normal" auto industry practice in 1927 was a victory for the age of advertising.

## *Thrift, Family, and God in a Consumer Culture*

A third revolutionary reworking of American values also came as part of the culture of consumption. Like the early machine age, which changed people's homespun clothes into store-bought ones, the twenties replaced the era of cash on the line with that of installment credit. Purchases of new gadgets, starting with the automobile, took many weeks' wages. They could only be managed on the installment plan. Millions of families dutifully put their few dollars down and promised to pay their few dollars weekly, without quite thinking of themselves as being in debt. Yet in debt they were, and in being so, they were violating the old American rule that a penny saved was a penny earned. Early America had not frowned on borrowing for *business* purposes. But in order to create investment capital saving was necessary. A well-trained American, therefore, did not even spend today's income, much less promise tomorrow's, to buy personal luxuries. In colonial and early national times, progress depended upon postponing gratification, delaying consumption. The new economy reversed the rules. The need of the twenties was for everyone to buy and to keep buying, to guarantee jobs to themselves and others. Duty called for the constant planning of future purchases. Optimism was a national necessity. The "booster" was praised to the skies, while the worst thing one could do was to be a "knocker," or a critic, or one who warned of social or environmental dangers in future growth.

The big boom also labeled the word "family" with a new meaning. And it entered the ancient relationship between Americans and their God, changing it in ways that would have startled the Pilgrim fathers and the Founding Fathers.

The American family seemed to be in crisis in the twenties. The divorce rate rose, slowly but unmistakably. And young people charlestoned, drank, and petted their way out of the taboos of their parents. Behind these developments stood certain economic and cultural facts. One was the automobile, which allowed young people to enact their courtship rituals in restaurants, roadhouses, dance halls, theaters, and other places safe from watchful eyes. Another was the popularity of the movies. They emphasized romantic love and caused long-married couples to be discontented if it was missing from their lives.

Even more important was the weakening of the family's productive function. Once, it had been an indispensable economic unit. Father and grown sons brought in the crops, tended the stock, and did the outdoor chores. Mother and daughters made the food and clothing. Everyone, young *and* old, shared in basic tasks such as making ink, candles, soap, baskets, and dozens of items of humble, daily use. This basis of family unity had been weakening ever since the frontier age gave way to the factory era. Still, faced with common problems of survival in a hard world, working-class and immigrant families had tended to remain solid until the twenties.

But, increasingly, even for the poor, "automobility" made it possible for teenage children to move out of the family circle to distant places to find work. And for those who made some money, the strength of family bonds lessened. True, some purchases—a boat, a vacation cottage, a radio—were family shared. But mutual dependence, mutual need, mutual cooperation to produce—all vanished. Each family member was, to some extent, set apart by his or her personal purchases.

Then there was the God of the marketplace. Popular religious teachings of the New Era stressed over and over again that prayer and positive thinking led to promotions and business rewards. Perhaps the most astonishing book of the twenties, *The Man Nobody Knows,* suggested that the central figure of Christianity himself was a kind of superexecutive. Its author, Bruce Barton, was one of the founders of a powerful advertising agency. He announced that the meek and gentle Jesus of his childhood Sunday-School books was a fraud. Barton's own reading of the Gospels as an adult had revealed to him that Jesus was actually a go-getter who had taken 12 men from "the bottom ranks of business" and forged them into an organization that conquered the world. Likewise, Jesus was "the most popular dinner guest in Jerusalem."

In fairness it should be said that lining up Christ behind a social viewpoint was not a monopoly of advertisers. The essence of a movement known as Christian Socialism was that Christ's teachings were meant to be applied to life on this earth and that they were hostile to the spirit of capitalist competition. Progressives, too, often defended their reforms as putting Christianity into action. One poet, Sarah Cleghorn, even made Christ a labor agitator:

*Thanks to St. Matthew, who had been*
*At mass meetings in Palestine*
*We know whose side was spoken for*
*When Comrade Jesus had the floor*

But in the twenties, few important people publicly accepted the social gospel. Instead, a business civilization made Barton's book a best seller. And so the awesome Jehovah of Puritanism, who could undo the work of humanity in lightning and thunder and tempest and drought and so teach the children of

Adam their limits, was replaced by a great Chief Optimist, whose message was to lay up treasures on earth through buying growth stocks. Whoever remained poor, it seemed, remained disgraced.

### *Heroes, Patriots, and Old-Time Religion*

Yet no matter which way a cultural mainstream flows, countercurrents are sometimes set up. There are swirls that appear to move in an opposing direction. They actually make the true direction more noticeable. In the American twenties the movement of culture was toward a semireligious faith in the goodness of the business system. People reverenced its prophets, the corporation directors, and took part in rituals of consumption around the rolling altar, the auto, or in the dim cathedrals of movie houses. But there were contrasting forces of three kinds.

One was a celebration of certain values that were traditional but that actually ran counter to the needs of the system, such as individualism. Three heroes of the twenties—Babe Ruth, Charles A. Lindbergh, and Calvin Coolidge—show the contrast between image and reality. Ruth, the mighty "Sultan of Swat," whose homers electrified crowds of thousands, was idolized during a so-called golden age of sports because he stood out from the mass. The thrill was in "the Babe's" solitary duel with the pitcher, all neatly framed within the rules of fairness—the strike zone clearly limited, the precise number of balls and strikes allowed unchangeable by whim or collusion or pressure, the two players trying to outguess each other—and then the ecstatic moment of resolution when the bat cracked and the ball took off like a holy object soaring homeward to heaven. It was a gigantic individual victory. And off the field Ruth played his part well, too. He had huge appetites and unschooled, roughneck ways as far removed as possible from polite, organization behavior.

And yet the reality was that Ruth was an entertainer in a mass-audience enterprise. His fame was made possible by the well-organized machinery of press coverage. His large salaries could only be paid by owners who were multimillionaire business people and whose ball teams were profitable investments. He was a hero of a game that was born in cow pastures and played originally by amateurs but that turned into a big-time enterprise played in urban stadiums and broadcast over national networks to enrich owners and advertisers.

Charles A. Lindbergh was another example of the popular hero. One May morning in 1927 he took off from New York's Roosevelt Field and spent thirty-three lonely hours, fighting off sleep, guiding his tiny Ryan monoplane, the *Spirit of St. Louis*, through Atlantic weather systems, to safe touchdown at Paris' Le Bourget airport. It was the first nonstop transatlantic flight and a shining

*After one game-winning clout by "the Babe," columnist Heywood Broun wrote, "the Ruth is mighty, and shall prevail." Mighty indeed was George Herman Ruth, shown here knocking out his 60th home run in the 154-game season of 1927—a record still unmatched for that number of games. The excitement generated by the long-ball hitting of the "sultan of Swat" turned baseball into a major financial success in the twenties, the so-called Golden Age of Sport.*

achievement. Yet the almost hysterical applause for "Lindy" laid bare some troubled nerves of a mass society. He was cheered as the "Lone Eagle," the solo adventurer who, in a prepackaged and preplanned world, had pitted himself against the dangers of sea and sky, and won.

Lindbergh filled the frame well. He *was* a shy, deeply private, individualistic young man, just the kind of "loner" America wanted to idolize. Yet he himself knew that his flight was not a victory *over* the machine but *of* the machine. He had calculated every drop of gas consumption and every pound of extra weight beforehand. He had studied weather charts with the devotion of a scholar. He had tuned his engine again and again to milk the utmost performance from cylinder and spark plug. He ran the risk of unexpected problems, to be sure. But in his own view his flight was simply a laboratory proof of what he had worked out on paper: the possibility of a single-engine flight of over 3000 miles. The real winner was the technology that had created his plane.

Finally, there was the case of Calvin Coolidge. Supporters hailed him as a frugal, prim, waste-no-words type of Vermont Yankee, the very man to symbolize America after the good-natured but corrupted Harding. This image was strangely reassuring to a nation that, as we have seen, would have been in deep trouble if people had decided to be truly sparing and spend no money on luxuries or if the advertising agencies had stopped talking endlessly about products.

But Coolidge himself was, in fact, no Green Mountain State "hayseed." His father was a well-off farmer who could and did send Calvin to Amherst. It was a college for the rising sons of professionals and business people. After graduation, Coolidge became an attorney in the city of Northampton, Massachusetts. There he served his industrial clients so well that he was rewarded with support when he ran for the state legislature. From there he worked his way up to lieutenant governor, then to governor of the Bay State, and finally to the vice presidency of the United States. He was as rural as a supermarket "country" ham pumped full of water and chemical preservatives.

A second countercurrent to the business culture was conservative reaction against swift change and against uniformity. One example of it was the rebirth of the post–Civil War Ku Klux Klan. This time it surfaced as a predominantly midwestern, as well as Southern, organization, though it had followers in most Northern cities. Its new program called for the preservation of pure Americanism against the threats posed by Catholics, Jews, and Bolsheviks, as well as by blacks. Hundreds of thousands of Americans marched in its hooded ranks in the 1920s. There was an ugly side to the Klan that expressed itself in beatings, harassment, and boycotts of innocent merchants of the "wrong" religion, or in political pressure on lawmakers to crack down on the rights of free speech and press. Such activities grew in part from an urge to restore the joy-riding society to a simpler day when the United States was united under white, Protestant, small-town-minded leadership.

Similarly, it was a search for a lost, "pure" America that underlay the passage of the Immigration Act of 1924. This legislation set a top limit of 150,000 per year on immigration from Europe and divided that total number among nationalities by a quota system. These quotas were based on various nations' supposed contributions to the "American stock." They were drawn up in such a way as to limit the entry of southern and eastern Europeans and to encourage those from the British Isles, Germany, and Scandinavia. Orientals were barred altogether. The whole purpose was to freeze white Anglo-Saxon Protestant (WASP) America in her existing mold, free from those disturbing elements, the "honkies" and "spics" and "wops" and "kikes" who filled the cities and the factories and were thought in rural America to be either Bolsheviks, criminals, or both.

And there was the celebrated Scopes trial, or "monkey trial," of 1925 in the Appalachian mountain hamlet of Dayton, Tennessee. The Tennessee state legislature passed a statute forbidding the teaching of the doctrine of evolution, because it denied the biblical account of the world's creation in six days. The five-year-old American Civil Liberties Union (the ACLU was organized in 1920) decided to challenge the limit on religious and intellectual freedom by seeking a test case. They found a young school teacher, John T. Scopes, who knowingly broke the law and was tried. Legally, the case came to nothing. Scopes was found guilty and fined, but on appeal a higher court reversed the finding on technical grounds.

The trial itself, however, was a national sensation. Tennessee brought in a potent volunteer for the prosecution in William Jennings Bryan, three-time Democratic nominee for president. Bryan publicly mocked the idea that humans were not descended from Adam and Eve but shared a common ancestry with the great apes (hence the name of "monkey trial"). Against Bryan the ACLU ranged several trial lawyers. The best known, Clarence Darrow, was a brilliant defender of unorthodox and unpopular views. In blazing heat in a tiny courthouse packed with national press representatives, Bryan and Darrow clashed in a battle of "old-time religion" versus progressive views. Bryan tried valiantly to defend the literal interpretation of the Bible against Darrow's questions. Darrow asked: "If all the creatures on earth were drowned in the Great Flood, what about the fish?" Bryan angrily denounced Darrow's attack on the foundations of faith. Darrow in turn shouted assaults on Bryan's "fool religion," which no "intelligent Christian" could stomach.

What was really at stake? For the ACLU it was the right of inquiring minds, young and old, to be given whatever information they might need in order to grow. But for Dayton there was something at stake, too, blurred by jokes about "rubes" and monkeys. Dayton was asking that a community be given the right to hold back the modern world, to cling to the old ways, and to save its children from the age of Ford and Freud as well as Darwin. The issue deserved debate in less of a carnival setting. It exposed some of the real social rifts that prosperity had created.

*The Great Crash and After*

To turn, then, from the twenties to the thirties is to go from a tropical landscape of hothouse economic growth to one of desert barrenness. For a number of reasons there was a mighty collapse of the stock market in October 1929. Prices of shares fell to almost nothing during waves of selling. Millions of dollars in paper values were lost. While it was "only paper" that vanished, paper had a great impact on life. Banks that had lost millions of dollars demanded repayment of the loans they had made to companies. Companies could only repay the loans by abandoning future expansion plans and shutting down some production operations. This threw people out of work. They in turn soon stopped making installment, mortgage, and other payments. This knocked other businesses into bankruptcy. Soon real-estate values were plummeting, factories were closing, the unemployment rolls were swelling, and with each new addition to them the sad cycle of "no pay" began afresh. Taxes and investments dried up. The economy was sick. By 1933 the odd thing was that all the marvelous productive machinery behind the boom of the twenties remained in existence, but no one knew how to put it back to work.

The Depression sank its talons deeper into the United States until early 1933. Then Franklin D. Roosevelt replaced Hoover as president. Roosevelt launched a major program of reform, recovery, and relief measures, which we shall consider in a future chapter. One key element in all of them was public subsidy. To the unemployed went relief payments and jobs on government-run public works projects. Small businesses and homeowners got guarantees of federal repayment of loans made to them, so that they were able to get credit. The construction industries were helped by heavy federally financed building efforts. Farmers received loans to help them market their crops, as well as payments for soil conservation and supported prices—that is, guaranteed minimum amounts for certain agricultural programs. The aging benefited by the Social Security system of retirement insurance. Organized labor won strong federal support.

The New Deal, as these measures taken all together were called, ran its course for some seven years. No one can say whether it cured the Depression. There were ups and downs of unemployment and investment. But in 1939, with war breaking out in Europe, a huge program of defense spending was

*The faces of Herbert Hoover and Franklin D. Roosevelt mirror their dominant moods as they ride from the White House to the Capitol for Roosevelt's inauguration on March 4, 1933. Hoover was somber, weighed by memories of the crash and depression that doomed and haunted his expiring presidency. FDR, buoyant, was preparing to launch a swift, broad-gauge program of recovery and reform and to tell the nation: "The only thing we have to fear is fear itself."*

launched. A year later, the nation went into war and full-time military production. Those surges of activity definitely ended the Depression. It is almost impossible to know how, when and if full recovery could otherwise have taken place.

### *People, Politicians, and Togetherness in Economic Collapse*

But that is all a brief overview. The questions that remain are: How did sudden poverty affect the culture? Did it have the same or different effects as sudden affluence?

To answer in detail would require as many pages as have already been spent on the twenties. But some general statements can be made and the outline of a specific example or two presented. You may then choose some areas of your own to investigate as you look for answers.

The great crash and its aftermath did not wipe out respect for a business civilization. But they did somewhat reduce the nation's faith in the overall wisdom of business leaders. The destruction of prosperity reduced them to human size. Morgans, Rockefellers, Harrimans, and others like them would continue to have great power and influence through their money. They would carry political weight through contributions to the party war chests, and some would seek and win high office. But chairmen of the board were no longer listened to as oracles about the future, simply because their quarterly earnings reports had been good. In hard times, captains of industry were not quite the culture heroes they had once been.

Individualism, too, declined further. Though some people stubbornly insisted that anyone wanting work could find it, by 1933 most people had come to a new realization. Economic security could not be guaranteed in a complex, interrelated modern economy, even by dedicated individual efforts to work hard and to save. Millions not only took relief when they had to but came to accept the idea that old-age or unemployment insurance and other forms of social payments in times of misfortune were not charity, but rather a simple return for taxes and contributions paid during times of work. Old-fashioned reliance on private savings, local charity, and even local taxes as the source of help in times of trouble was replaced by a more "collective" outlook. There was a tendency to turn toward the city hall or the state capital or, more and more, to Washington for help with economic problems. One lasting effect of the Depression was to step up the speed with which a national outlook took shape. In that way, the era of poverty actually continued a long-term trend.

In the further adventures of the American family, too, the Depression continued the pressure toward redefinition of family roles begun by prosperity. The loss of income by family heads further eroded their authority with their children. And often, fathers had to "take to the road" in search of work, leading to a pattern of absenteeism that enlarged women's roles and left children with less control. Migrant laborers became more numerous, and that led to a jump in the number of "unstable" families, those without permanent roots in any community and with children who developed learning problems because of constant shifts from school to school. Furthermore, as more wives and daughters went to work to maintain family incomes, the unrecognized strides toward women's liberation began to cover more ground. Some families, it is true, were driven into greater closeness by hard times, as they were forced to share housing and income to survive. But, generally, poverty led to a shaking up of certainties about "proper" behavior of husbands, wives, children, and other relatives.

Finally, the old-fashioned political boss who won loyalty through handouts found his power limited in certain ways by the Depression. Many factors entered into his slow decline. Among them were the rise of unions with their own systems of benefits and security and the migration to the suburbs, which weakened the political strength of the central cities, which the bosses controlled.

But especially noticeable was how the growth of federal relief programs undercut the traditional boss role of providing jobs for the jobless, coal and food for the destitute, and recreation for poor neighborhoods. Relief programs, unemployment insurance, public works jobs, public housing—all made urban masses less dependent on machine-provided favors. The age of barbecues and Christmas baskets gave way to that of relief checks and government benefits. These required time-consuming procedures and bureaucratic forms. But they did not have to be repaid by a specific vote on Election Day.

Local loyalties, personal dependencies, the handshake deal, the family-and-neighbor network of political influence—these things survived to some extent but in weakened form. The passing of the old-time precinct boss was a sign of that. And so, out of adversity, one more phase of an older America, for good or ill, had disappeared.

## *FOR FURTHER READING*

Two general surveys of the twenties are valuable and readable. William E. Leuchtenburg, *The Perils of Prosperity* (1958) is a brief, scholarly overview. Frederick Lewis Allen, *Only Yesterday* (1931) is a journalist's summary of highlights of the decade, written right after its conclusion, and is notably lively.

There are several biographies of Warren G. Harding which deal with the boom times over which he presided; a recent one is Andrew Sinclair, *The Available Man* (1965). As for his successor, Coolidge, the best book is still an old one, William Allen White's *A Puritan in Babylon* (1938).

Special studies of particular episodes throw a good deal of light on how people felt about life. Andrew Sinclair, *Prohibition: The Era of Excess* (1962) is a good history of Prohibition. Francis Russell, *Tragedy in Dedham* (1962) is the latest book on the case of Sacco and Vanzetti, two Italian radicals executed for an alleged holdup and murder. Lawrence W. Levine, *Defender of the Faith: William J. Bryan, 1915–1925* (1965), is a study of William Jennings Bryan's last years that covers the Scopes trial well. There is another good summary in Ray Ginger, *Six Days or Forever* (1958). For the revival of the Ku Klux Klan you should look at David Chalmers' *Hooded Americanism* (1965). A good look at the general distrust of "foreigners" that led to immigrant restriction is in Jethro Lieberman, *Are Americans Extinct* (1973).

Lindbergh is beautifully dealt with in Kenneth Davis, *The Hero: Charles A. Lindbergh and the American Dream* (1959). As for Babe Ruth, he is nicely handled in a neglected but fine book on the golden age of athletics, Paul Gallico, *Farewell to Sport* (1938). See also Robert W. Creamer, *Babe* (1974) for the life of "The Sultan of Swat."

Finally, no one can understand the twenties without wide reading in the fiction of

Hemingway, Dos Passos, and F. Scott Fitzgerald. Dos Passos' trilogy *U.S.A.* (1937) has already been mentioned; Hemingway's *The Sun Also Rises* (1926) (though it deals with Americans in Europe) is important for expressing certain attitudes of the era. And Fitzgerald's *The Great Gatsby* (1925) is an experience you owe yourself. The last two are easily available in several paperback editions.

For a look at the Depression era, a standard history is Dixon Wecter, *The Age of the Great Depression* (1948). Caroline Bird's *The Invisible Scar* (1965) studies the effect of the Depression on its survivors (your grandparents). And a relatively lighthearted history is Robert Bendiner, *Just Around the Corner* (1967). Fascinating firsthand reminiscences of what it was like to live through the Depression are in Studs Terkel's *Hard Times* (1971).

# chapter 23

# Politics and parties: from stump to studio

*There were truths eternal in the gab and tittle-tattle.*
*There were real heads broken in the fustian and the rattle.*

So runs a couplet in Vachel Lindsay's "Bryan, Bryan, Bryan, Bryan," a poem about the election that broke his sixteen-year-old heart in 1896. The whole poem could well be quoted as an illustration of one set of meanings to a presidential election. It shows the symbolic significance of the contest, and young Lindsay's belief that the world was truly changed by Bryan's loss. (He wrote it, in fact, some years after the election.) It also highlights the deep sense of participation in stirring events; the excitement, unity, and march rhythm of campaigning—"And torchlights down the street, to the end of the world."

Excitement and involvement are only two aspects of the mixture of carnival, ritual, and decision making that add up to a national presidential election. Much American history has been told in terms of these contests and their results. It is, in one way, a somewhat limited view. The race for the presidency is not the only demonstration of self-government at work. Every other year, the voters choose one third of the Senate, the entire House of Representatives, and, usually, their state legislatures. In addition, they elect governors, mayors, judges, and hundreds of other officials who have a great deal to do with the daily mechanics of living. Nor is every presidential contest stormy or ringing with debate over important issues. The party machinery that grinds out candidates and platforms goes methodically about its work, year in and year out, with professional political managers on both "teams" unchanged. Newspaper reporters, lobbyists, members of Congress, and civil servants go about their tasks as before. Only high-level, appointed bureaucrats depart with a departing president. In short, the focus of attention on the presidency is not justified by any deep change in the political system that automatically follows a change of presidents. Moreover, certain underlying economic and social trends go on at a pace of their own. And so, to try to tell the story of national evolution in four-year segments is to falsify its rhythms.

Yet on the other hand certain acts spotlight the presidency. The presidential election is the single one in which every American voter, from a tiny islet in the Hawaiian chain to the heart of an East Coast urban ghetto, finds the same names to choose from. No other public official can say that he is elected by 30 or 40 million or more votes.

Furthermore, throughout the span of history the president has been the official to make swift and dramatic decisions—to buy Louisiana, fire on Fort Sumter, "take" Panama. There is always a fateful possibility in every choice of president. Though there are limits on his power, set by the Constitution, by the political situation, or the simple size of the bureaucracy he runs, the president is someone who can dramatically change the course of events with the stroke of a pen. The voters know it. They therefore feel that they are registering a historic choice when they pull the voting-machine lever.

Then, too, the president has come to be not only a spokesman for the nation but a living symbol of the attitudes and values that the mass of Americans have or wish they had. This identification of president and people account for the ever greater publicity given to the president's public *and* private behavior. It is why he must participate in various regional and ethnic ceremonies and say correct and predictable things on Thanksgiving, Labor Day, and Mother's Day. It is why so much media space and time is devoted to the First Family. Americans have come to believe that they are making a major statement about themselves and their national character when they choose a president.

Since what people believe in is often as important to the historian as the facts themselves, we can therefore learn certain things about American history at a given time by looking at the presidential elections. They can be important barometers of opinion, change, and social pressures. Let us test this notion by looking at a handful of specific elections (with some passing reference to others), so that we can see what real "truths eternal" were in the "gab and tittle-tattle."

*Presidential Choice: Mirror of National Issues and Emotions*

Each of the two major parties, if it hopes to win, must reach out for as broad a segment of the electorate as possible. It must try to find what the elusive national "consensus," the generally held opinion, is on the issues of the day and stay as close to it as possible. Since both candidates are chosen for their appeal to the great middle-of-the-road mass of voters, it often does appear, in the words of third-party candidate George Wallace in 1968, that there is not "a dime's worth of difference" between Republicans and Democrats. Both of them have been almost certain to nominate white, middle-aged, middle-class Protestant males, with some political experience, who will run on platforms full of inoffensive promises. It is therefore natural that the vote will usually be split about evenly between the two. But landslides *do* occur when one party names a candidate who seems to stand outside of the popular consensus. For this reason lopsided elections can measure the limits of that consensus or show sudden changes in it. We will look at one such election, that of 1936.

In studying the electoral vote, we learn a second lesson from the study of elections. Generally, the winner's share of the popular vote is only a tiny bit more than half. But the electoral college system often disguises the closeness of the people's choice. Theoretically, a candidate could win by a tiny margin in every state and, under the winner-take-all electoral system, have only a 1 percent lead in the popular tally but score a complete electoral wipeout of his opponent. That has not happened, though in Richard Nixon's 49-state sweep over George McGovern in 1972, his popular-vote lead was only about 2 to 1 compared to his 520-to-17 electoral-vote score. A candidate can also win heavily in states having few electoral votes and lose closely in states having more electoral votes and thus come out ahead in the popular vote but still lose the election. That happened only once in modern times, to Grover Cleveland when he ran against Benjamin Harrison in 1888.

Yet the very nature of the electoral college effectively measures shifts in

---

*CHRONOLOGY*

1928 *Herbert Hoover defeats Al Smith in presidential race*
1933 *Tennessee Valley Authority (TVA) established*
1935 *Social Security Act sets up federal old-age insurance*
1936 *FDR is reelected in a landslide victory over Alfred Landon*
1948 *Whittaker Chambers accuses Alger Hiss of secret communism and treason*
1950 *Korean War starts*
1952 *Dwight Eisenhower swept to victory over Adlai Stevenson*

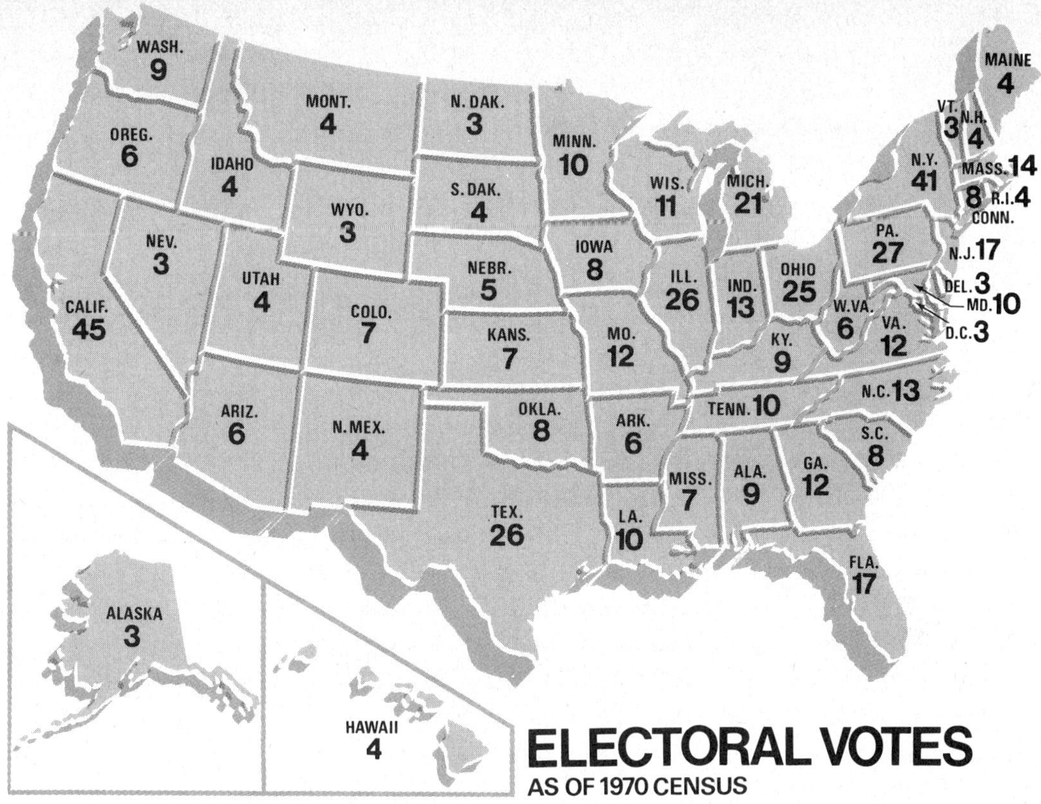


centers of voting power. The key states become those with large populations. (A state's electoral vote, remember, is equal to its number of senators and representatives.) Since these popular states are the most heavily urbanized and industrialized, a look at the states in the winner's column tells which sections of the country experience the greatest economic growth. Parties have always tended to nominate those who are identified with these centers. The "Virginia dynasty" that named four of the first five presidents gave way to a wave of candidates from the then new West. Between 1900 and 1972 the election-year residence of 11 of the 13 winners in 19 presidential elections turned out to be in the Northeast. The two exceptions, Harry Truman and Lyndon Johnson, both won nomination only after being vice presidents who took over a predecessor's term.

The presidential elections offer still another opportunity for analyzing society. Each party, as we noted, tries to build a coalition of as many diverse interest groups as possible. The national party conventions are super showcases for the process at work. All of their back-room hammering and nailing together of alliances requires considerable effort—in some years more effort than in others. The problems of candidate selection and platform making highlight the various tension points in the society. Is it easy to unite urban food buyers and rural food growers? Blue-collar "workers" and white-collar "employees"? Suburbanites and inner-city residents? Yankee and Southerner, recent immigrant and old-stock westerner?

The answer depends on the issues of the moment. In the United States in 1940, for example, many Scandinavian- and German-descended farmers in Wisconsin and Minnesota who had readily supported Franklin Roosevelt in 1936 changed their minds and switched sides. It was not because they had lost faith in Roosevelt's agricultural program but because they were hostile to his open sympathy for the British side in World War II. In the 1972 election some Jewish voters, lifelong Democrats, turned to Nixon because they believed, rightly or wrongly, that he would take a tougher line than McGovern in defending the state of Israel. Other examples could be cited. The issues and nominees of the national campaign do test how well society is "hanging together." If diverse groups can get their various needs reconciled, the system is cohesive and healthy. If not, it is troubled.

Finally, as one speaks of presidential personalities, it is clear that a great deal of social history is reflected in the various images of leadership that popular presidents have embodied. Rail splitter, "Rough Rider," country squire, honest soldier—these are more than styles adopted by Lincoln, Theodore Roosevelt, Franklin Roosevelt, and Eisenhower. They are guideposts to popular feelings in 1860, 1904, 1932, and 1952 about what human qualities Americans respected. So important are candidates' images, in fact, that by 1968 the designing and "selling" of them to voters had become an expensive and corrupting element in the election process.

### 1928: *Great Engineer Versus Brown Derby: Modernism Wins*

In 1928 Coolidge prosperity was in full swing. Republicans and Democrats got set for political combat. We have already seen, in Chapter 22, Hoover's ringing defense of the American business system. His opponent, Alfred Emanuel Smith, was governor of New York, city-born and bred, of Irish, English, German, and Italian ancestry. Smith did not challenge the goodness of the business civilization. Instead, he concentrated on his own record as a progressive governor of New York and on his support for the repeal of the Eighteenth (antiliquor) Amendment.

Smith spent much time fighting off a handicap that no other candidate had then faced. He was a Roman Catholic running for the presidency of a predominantly Protestant nation. He did not succeed in that battle. The election went decidedly to Hoover. Smith carried only two states outside the solidly Democratic South—Massachusetts and Rhode Island—and Hoover even cracked the South, winning Virginia, North Carolina, Tennessee, Florida, and Texas. The rural South, where faith in the Ku Klux Klan, prohibition, and old-time religion ran strong, turned against a Democrat for the first time since Reconstruction.

But that is not the entire story. For the issue was not simply "wet" against "dry" or Rome versus Luther or country versus city. They were not the main issues in the nation as a whole. In fact, both candidates represented a thoroughly modernized America. Both believed in the business system, with a limited amount of government management. The election was, if anything, simply a referendum on who would continue to be caretaker of Coolidge prosperity. Hoover may have gained the winning margin on the issues of liquor and religion, but his real strength was that he was so closely identified with the big boom. Hoover was no simple-minded all-out defender of the business system. In the public mind he was neither a businessman nor a politician but an expert who could offer wise guidance to both. As secretary of commerce his fundamental credo was productivity and efficiency. His goal was to bring order, planning, and forethought into large-scale industrial operations. As we observed, in Chapter 18, he encouraged trade associations, which were suspiciously like supertrusts.

But for Hoover the end product of efficiency was not the mere enrichment of individual capitalists. He regarded it as the Progressives did, namely, as a way to make the economic system produce more of everything for everybody. He did assume that the normal distribution pattern of the free market would provide fairly for everyone's needs. The key to abolishing poverty was to expand the productive powers of the economy and see that its leaders were dedicated to service to the community.

The other element of his faith was a deep trust of the local communities' strength and wisdom. He believed that they could spell out their own needs and bear their own burdens. Thus he was not in favor of large-scale intervention by the central government in the economy to help distressed groups. But he *was* in favor of an activist government, providing industry with whatever it needed to take full advantage of technology and to march forward.

These were not the ideas of a McKinley or a Harding. Those two Republican presidents were mild and likable small towners who still thought of business in terms of small productive units. Their view of government's role was confined to levying tariffs, issuing antilabor injunctions, using foreign policy to build foreign markets. The choice of Hoover by the Republicans in 1928, therefore, was actually a step away from simple-minded Grand Old Party (GOP) traditions. He was chosen as the great engineer, in fact as a kind of city manager for the nation as a whole.

With Smith, the Democratic Party, too, turned a corner. Historically, it had found much of its strength in the rural South and West. Democratic managers built an alliance among these sections and the big cities, with backing from businessmen outside the Republican fold. From 1884 on, Democratic candidates had represented the countryside, the financial centers, or the forces of reform. Never had one come directly from the city streets, which provided so many Democratic votes. Cleveland had three times been the Democratic choice (1884, 1888, and 1892). He was a New York governor from "upstate" and was known for financial caution and stubborn honesty. In 1896, 1900, and 1908 it was Bryan, Nebraska's voice of prairie evangelism. In 1904 the loser had been Alton B. Parker, a conservative New York State figure who pleased the bankers on the Democratic National Committee. In 1912 and 1916 it was Wilson and in 1920 another progressive, the Ohioan James M. Cox. In 1924 it was a conservative corporation lawyer, John W. Davis. By then, the city was demanding its share, and the Davis nomination came at the end of a convention deadlocked over whether or not to support the Eighteenth Amendment and condemn the Klan. In the end it did neither, but the struggle was dragged out by the Democratic rule, which prevailed until 1936, of requiring a two-thirds majority for the nomination. This in effect gave the South a virtual veto on the choices.

So Smith, coming in as a "wet," Catholic, former Tammany man, and unabashed urbanite, was a new voice, whose theme song was "The Sidewalks of New York." Smith had worked in the city's fish market as a youth, rung doorbells in local elections, sported a "city-dude's" brown derby, and rasped his speeches over the "raddio." But Smith was more. As governor, he had supported public health services and conservation and expanded public school, highway, and park systems. He was personally honest and was as fully self-made and proud of it as Hoover. He was no more a cartoon city ward boss than Hoover was an honest farm boy. Smith would have been more ready than the Republican candidate to work with farmers, labor unions, and other discontented outcasts from Coolidge prosperity. But he had no basic quarrel with the economic system of the twenties.

Both men, to sum up, were old-fashioned liberals, representing two modern forces, superorganization and urbanism, as well as the two traditional parties. The vote itself simply showed a tendency to support the "ins" in time of prosperity, and it showed the disastrous effects of Smith's Catholicism in some traditional Democratic areas where the Pope and the devil were considered one and the same. The long-range significance of 1928 lay in the choice of candi-

*After paying homage to rural virtues by electing Vermont's "Silent Cal" Coolidge in 1924, the nation was ready to accept presidential candidates who represented modern, urban-industrial realities. Above is the Democratic choice of 1928, Al Smith, a progressive governor "from the sidewalks of New York." Appropriately, he is speaking into a camera that makes the breathtaking new "talking movies." Smith also frequently made speeches on what he called "the raddio."*

dates and in a big Smith vote in the cities. There, a whole new generation of voters, the children of the immigrants, was rising.

## 1936: *A New Direction Taken*

In 1936 Franklin Delano Roosevelt had been in office for four action-filled years. Elected in 1932, he seemed to be simply a Democratic gentleman-reformer. Born to a well-off family in the Hudson River valley, he had traveled a pleasant route to success before 1921: Groton (a gentleman's prep school), then Harvard, then Columbia Law School. From there he went into politics and was elected to the New York State legislature. There he soon joined with a coalition of progressives and Tammany-backed lawmakers who were working for laws to limit child labor and otherwise help the "outs." Roosevelt at thirty was handsome and well connected, and carrying the name of the ex-president and Rough Rider, his fifth cousin, did not harm him. He was named assistant secretary of the navy by Wilson and served through the war. He got the Democratic vice-presidential nomination in 1920 and took a beating like a loyal party man.

Then in 1921 infantile paralysis crippled him. His mother and some friends urged him to retire to a life of respectable hobbies. But he loved the hurly-burly of politics. And other friends believed that there was a touch of the giant in him that could overcome the handicap of being locked in braces and a wheelchair. They persuaded him to reenter political life. He did so, ran for governor of New York in 1928 to succeed Smith, and won. After two terms of an excellent progressive administration, he was a leading candidate for the presidential nomination in 1932 and won.

During the campaign itself, he spelled out few specific remedies for the Depression. Instead, he conventionally attacked Hoover. But there were a few hints of a dynamic future. In one memorable address in San Francisco he spoke of a new philosophy of government. Under it something would be done for the American who, through no fault of his own, suffered disaster in the collapse of the economy.

Such an individual could no longer begin life anew like some frontier farmer who, when wiped out by locusts or Indians, could move on to a fresh 40 acres of opportunity. Individual effort would not help protect the jobholder dependent on the nation's economic health, if that health failed. Individual savings could not guard against ruin by illness or old age, if a depression could wipe out those savings overnight. Some kind of government action was called for to help "the forgotten man at the foot of the economic pyramid" whose toil had built a nation.

Such talk was scarcely socialistic or even radical sounding. Roosevelt was elected by a big majority, as the voters punished the party in power for the hard times. In March 1933 Roosevelt took office, at the very bottom of the Depression. He immediately launched into a vigorous and far-reaching program, so new as a whole (though each part had been suggested before) that by 1936 he had presented the country with a truly different political system. It was this system that the voters were called upon to approve or reject when he ran for a second term. So the campaign of 1936 became one of genuine choice, one of the few in the record even though, on paper, the two platforms bore much of their usual similarity. To understand this it is necessary to summarize what FDR had done and what the political results were. The Roosevelt program, called the New Deal, was improvised under pressure and often hastily modified to win congressional support. But its various measures to promote relief, recovery, and reform added up to sweeping changes in American life.

*The federal government had created, first, a Federal Emergency Relief program, followed by a Public Works Administration and a Works Progress Administration. These filled empty local relief chests and committed the federal government to help build post offices, bridges, dams, airports, municipal buildings, and hundreds of other projects that put people to work. There was also a Civilian Conservation Corps, in which jobless youths, living in semimilitary camps, furnished the muscle for a big program of reforestation, conservation, and improvement of public parklands. There were even short-lived federal projects that used writers, artists, actors, and musicians to provide guidebooks, murals, plays, and concerts.*

*The federal government created a Securities and Exchange Commission to regulate the stock market, a Federal Deposit Insurance Corporation to guarantee the safety of bank deposits, and a Federal Housing Administration to help citizens finance the purchases of their own homes. It began or expanded regulation of airways, communications, and the electric power industry. In the Tennessee Valley Act the federal government undertook a vast program of building dams and creating hydroelectric plants in a depressed area stretching through parts of five Southern states.*

*With the Social Security Act of 1935 the federal government set up a broad-ranging program of old-age and unemployment insurance and assistance to widows, orphans, the blind, and those otherwise handicapped. In the same year, through the Wagner Act, the New Deal set up machinery to give workers the chance to organize and bargain collectively. This gave the trade union movement its biggest boost in American history.*

*The federal government, through the Agricultural Adjustment Administration (AAA), began to pay farmers to reduce production and so raise prices. The AAA was thrown out by the Supreme Court in 1936. But it paved the way for later acts that did virtually the same thing and survived legal challenge. The federal government also moved drought- and Depression-stricken farmers off unproductive lands and resettled them in new areas where they could find work.*

*For city dwellers the New Deal not only furnished many public works projects but began to lend money to cities that they could use to replace slums with modern housing for families living in the belly of poverty.*

This condensed summary only touches the highlights of New Deal activities. They were designed by a strange combination of aging ex-progressives,

*Reactions to hard times dominated American politics throughout the thirties and for many years after. To understand why, it is necessary to visualize a United States dominated by scenes like this one of a miner's child in West Virginia, with a chunk of stolen coal that will help keep his ragged, hungry body warm. To end such misery, Americans reevaluated their ideas and accepted many changes in government's responsibility for the general welfare.*

young and old academic dreamers, ambitious lawyers, and improvement-minded businessmen, who wanted the profit system to work better. They were brilliantly defended and promoted by Roosevelt, who displayed an uncanny skill in communicating directly with the person in the street. Historians still debate whether they show a jagged revolutionary break with the American past or simply completed trends begun in the time of the earlier Roosevelt and of Wilson.

It is not easy to answer that question. But it can be said for sure that the New Deal spelled out a whole new set of relationships among the national government, the states, the cities, and the people. It ushered in the era of multibillion-dollar budgets. It opened the way to a massive growth in the federal bureaucracy, whose impact the next chapter will weigh. And it made Washington a partner in hundreds of new enterprises: a partner with the homeowner signing a mortgage bond, with the farmer plowing under cotton or corn, with the union organizer hitting a new shop, with the governor and the mayor planning a bridge, a tunnel, a highway, or an office building.

It was a kind of unsocialistic socialism in action, aimed at salvaging the private enterprise system. And it built a new political coalition behind the Democratic Party. The children of working-class immigrants liked what the New Deal did for unions. Private homeowners and bank depositors were grateful for rescue. Blacks, traditionally followers of the party of Lincoln, shifted their allegiance, not because FDR broke with the racist but Democratic South but because federal relief programs for the jobless and the dispossessed were administered in such a way that blacks got a share. Farmers who had been casting Republican ballots since the Homestead Act appreciated the New Deal's subsidy programs. Whoever benefited from the spending programs to fight the Depression looked kindly on the party that FDR headed.

In 1936 the Republicans did not formally reject everything that had been done since Roosevelt's inauguration. Their platform actually called for expanded programs of federal assistance to agriculture, for example, and legislation against sweatshops. In turn, the Democrats made pledges of economy in government. The Republican candidate, Alfred M. Landon, was not a full member of his party's Old Guard, which was suspicious of everything that had happened since McKinley's assassination.

But in the campaign itself the flavor of conflict was clear. Most Republican orators hit at New Deal spending and its tendency to make localities dependent on Washington for the solution of problems. The essence of the Republican position was objection to what the New Deal had done. And when confronted with this position, the voters gave a clear answer in favor of Roosevelt. He had spent the campaign denouncing "economic royalists" and promising an even brighter future of federal help in modernizing and humanizing society. He got about 60 percent of the vote—some 27.5 million—to Landon's 37 percent, with minor-party candidates picking up 3 percent. In the words of one of FDR's speeches, the generation of 1936 had made a rendezvous with destiny.

*"Ike," the Healer*

Four elections later, Americans entered another significant election campaign. The year 1952 was a war year, with young Americans dying along the 38th parallel as they confronted North Korean and Chinese armies. But whereas the wartime election of 1944 had swept Roosevelt to a fourth term on a surge of patriotic unity, that of 1952 reflected a sharp conflict in the nation's spirit. Its final result was an act of faith in the powers of a popular, nonpolitical leader to repair that split.

Like at least five presidents before him, Dwight D. Eisenhower came to the presidential campaign trail via a military career. Born in the Midwest and West Point trained, he earned a reputation as an expert in planning and organization during the lean peacetime years. Pearl Harbor saw him immediately placed by Chief of Staff George C. Marshall in the War Plans Division to help oversee, mobilize, and assign American armed strength. In the autumn of 1942 he was put in charge of the Allied landings in North Africa. In the summer of 1943 he was named head of the forthcoming assault on Nazi-held Europe. On June 6, 1944, five divisions stormed the beaches of Normandy. Eleven months later, almost to the day, May 7, 1945, a battered Germany surrendered.

Eisenhower was the hero of the European war. His reputation was of a special kind. A big share of his job had been to coordinate the efforts of British, Free French and American commanders. He was expert at smoothing national jealousies. Eisenhower was not cast as the swaggering combat cavalryman, like the Civil War's George Custer or World War II's tank-riding George S. Patton, Jr. Nor was his image that of the godlike military leader with a higher sense of national honor than that of civilian "politicians." That part was played by the bemedaled, aloof, egotistical Douglas MacArthur.

Eisenhower, by contrast, seemed open and approachable. He was readily known to the press and public by his nickname of "Ike." His grin was businesslike but friendly. In addition, he was also a good soldier who could work within the American political system. He was particularly good at sensing what Congress would and would not pay for. And he carefully avoided any partisan identification until early in 1952. In fact, some Democrats had even talked of nominating him in 1948.

After a peacetime stint as president of Columbia University, Eisenhower went back into uniform. He was made head of the armed forces of the North Atlantic Treaty Organization, the alliance of western Europe and the United States created in 1949 to counterweigh the power of Russia. "Ike" was now representing a new American stance, namely, worldwide commitments to maintaining international security. At the same time, he was the head of the world's foremost anti-Communist army. He was acceptable both to those who saw a need for immediate war on the "red menace" and to those who hoped that international cooperation would make armed combat unnecessary. He was also a man with a vast talent for administering an army that had become a multibillion-dollar enterprise. He thus spoke the language of the chairmen of the boards of the great corporations that were organizing the American and world marketplaces. He stood, as Hoover had in 1928, for a combination of the old American virtues with the expertise of a new America that was the world's richest, most powerful nation.

Eisenhower won the Republican nomination in July 1952 after a hard primary fight in a divided Republican Party. His chief rival was Robert Taft, a hard-working, intelligent Ohio conservative. Taft was basically isolationist in foreign affairs; domestically, he was a standpatter as well, favoring antiunion legislation, severe restrictions on federal spending programs, and a tight rein on the president's power to regulate business or take the initiative in social change.

insurance and another of large-scale federal assistance to public and private schools to help them modernize. But Congress, dominated by conservative Republicans and Southern Democrats, rejected these last proposals, though it did agree to a raise in the minimum wage and a widening of Social Security coverage. Yet under the stimulus of war, or rather dealing with war's aftermath, it passed two historic and far-reaching statutes. One, the so-called GI Bill of Rights of 1944, allowed the government to pay the cost of higher education or special on-the-job training for veterans. In that way, it added millions to the pool of skilled and professional workers. The bill also provided veterans with unemployment benefits while they were getting resettled. In addition, the United States guaranteed loans that enabled ex-soldiers to buy or improve homes, farms, and businesses. This pumped billions of dollars worth of buying power into the economy and helped lay the foundation of prosperity. The bill as a whole was a rather sweeping piece of "socialism."

But it was equaled if not exceeded by the Atomic Energy Act of 1946. It, too, grew out of World War II. Because of the mighty military power of the atomic bomb, the government would not trust the development of atomic energy to private capitalism. It had to be kept safe in national hands. So Congress created an Atomic Energy Commission. This presidentially appointed body had total responsibility for research and production in all areas relating to nuclear energy and its applications. The commission alone had the right to find, make, and store "fissionable materials" that released such energy. It alone could license their use in medicine, scientific experiments, the production of electric power, or any other area. From the beginning, therefore, the "atom industry," unlike any other, would be government owned and controlled.

Both the GI Bill of Rights and the Atomic Energy Act were proof of how the dramatic changes of wartime cracked old molds. The Fair Deal package of legislation would have added to the U.S. government's continuing responsibility for the health, economic security, job opportunities, and living conditions of millions. Though it did not say so in plain English, behind it was the notion that private investors would never find it profitable to meet such needs for the poor. The slack had to be taken up by government, both for humanitarian reasons and to guarantee the continued buying power that made the whole profit system work. That idea challenged the traditional American faith that the solution to all social ills was to stimulate further business productivity, which would in turn cause a burst of employment that would solve all welfare problems.

Arguments against the increase in the size and function of the welfare state carried weight. They represented a kind of social inertia, the tendency of a system to remain at rest, unchanged. But other forces, like economic ups and downs, technological change, population movements, wars, and arms races, worked to keep up the steady expansion of caretaker government. These represented momentum, the forces working toward movement and change. In the end, inertia had its brief triumphs, but momentum won out.

### *Eisenhower and Modern Republicanism*

This was shown in the eight years of the Eisenhower administration. The popular general took office after having expressed a deep distaste for increased government manipulation of the economy. He called it creeping socialism. Yet "Ike" could not and did not try to fight for the repeal of a number of existing programs that poured Treasury funds into the economy. For one thing, the ending of federal programs of assistance to the aged, the unemployed, the dependent, and the handicapped under the Social Security system would have caused social chaos. It would have led as well to a sharp drop in the private spending that spelled prosperity. Payments to keep a minimum level of buying power were indispensable to keeping society on an even keel, and by the 1950s even most states had such assistance programs in action.

There were other benefits, too, that had, almost unnoticed, become part of the basic texture of American life. During the Depression, the New Deal had made payments to farmers to maintain their incomes on a level of equality, or "parity," with those of workers in other sectors of the economy. Moreover, to boost farm prices and guard against future disasters the government bought surplus agricultural commodities such as wheat, cotton, corn, soybeans, and sugar. Bursting warehouses of foodstuffs supposedly made the United States famine-proof.

These subsidies to a stricken farm populace changed in character during the 1950s. Steady improvements in farm technology allowed a shrinking number of farmers to produce ever-larger crops. There were still some small farmers wringing a living out of meager acres. But most of the nation's food was being produced by successful farmers who were pioneers in "agribusiness." They spent freely on automatic equipment, new fertilizers, and special livestock feeds full of hormones, vitamins, and chemicals. These allowed them to grow more food on less land, with fewer workers, and to bring in a good return on large investments. The government continued to spend billions of dollars buying and storing the ever-mounting surpluses produced by such "food factories," as if their owners were still struggling pioneers.

Eisenhower's secretary of agriculture, Ezra T. Benson, tentatively tried to reduce the level of such payments. He found it politically impossible. The farm vote in Congress was too powerful. Then the Eisenhower administration tried to reduce surpluses by creating a "soil bank" and paying farmers to leave some acres unplanted. But this meant that the largest farmers, who could afford not to use all their lands, were getting paid thousands of dollars that they little

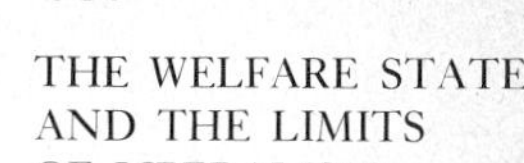

*Date palms in Coachella Valley. The agricultural subsidy programs of the 1930s were aimed at preserving the American family farm as an on-going economic unit because such farms had been thought, since frontier days, to have uniquely American social values. But, ironically, agriculture in the twentieth century was going the way of industry in the nineteenth—becoming mechanized and hugely expanded. So the government found itself bestowing largesse on the lords of "agribusiness"—corporate, mass-producing farm operations. Above is an example of one, date palms in ordered ranks in California whose fruit will soon be in plastic packages on supermarket shelves.*

needed. In short, the agricultural subsidy program had become what some called a kind of socialism for the rich.

There was some concern for the poor shown, too. To dispose of the mounting surpluses, Congress, in the Eisenhower years, introduced programs to give some of the stored commodities at cut rates to families on welfare. The price of school lunches was also reduced by gifts of federal milk and other foodstuffs. In this way a program to support farmers "spun off" some humanitarian gains. The federal role in welfare continued to grow. And as a sign of recognition, Eisenhower asked Congress, in 1953, for authority to create a new cabinet department, Health, Education, and Welfare, to pull together the many federal agencies already involved in those three areas.

But not all federal growth was due to humane efforts. The escalating military establishment was now creating a kind of super-public works program. Its scope was far greater than that of any New Deal agency. New missile bases, air bases, dockyards, arsenals, and training centers kept construction workers busy and made opportunities for business people. And the planes, ships, vehicles, and military hardware that the Defense Department consumed kept assembly lines moving. The umbrella of "defense needs" spread to cover other projects, too. Partly on the plea of how vital a modern road system would be in a national military emergency and partly under pressure from the oil and auto lobbies, Congress authorized a federal highway-building program. Under it the nation took over up to 90 percent of the cost of building a network of modern interstate expressways, four to six lanes wide, looping around congested urban centers. The money came from a highway fund, created by setting aside receipts from federal gasoline taxes. This fund proved to be a gigantic bonanza not only to road builders, car makers, and the petroleum industry but also to a whole chain of road-based businesses, like motels, ski resorts, fast-food chains, and drive-in theaters. And the bonanza was stamped "Made in Washington."

The needs of a booming economy and swelling armed forces, therefore, demanded more federal machinery than Eisenhower liked to operate. But the logic of growth left no choice. In another area, that of civil rights, events also forced him into presidential activism. By 1953 a mood of assertiveness was growing among American blacks. They were ready to tackle, head-on, a nationwide system of both legal and unofficial discrimination that had kept them down for a century. In 1954, an important breakthrough came when the Supreme Court decided that segregation by race in the public schools was an automatic badge of inferiority and a denial of the constitutional rights of black citizens. Three years after that ruling was handed down, Eisenhower was compelled to enforce it. Obeying the court requirement, the school board of Little Rock, Arkansas, worked out a desegregation plan that would bring a small number of black youngsters into that city's previously all-white Central High School.



Just before opening day, Governor Orval Faubus of Arkansas ordered troops from the state's National Guard to surround the school and prevent integration. He called it a move "to avoid violence," ignoring his own obligation to prevent violent resistance to lawful court orders. This was a flat slap at the authority of the federal judiciary. Eisenhower was a constitutional conservative, not at all pleased with the Supreme Court ruling. But he knew a challenge to the Union when he saw one. He promptly had the Arkansas Guard mustered into federal service. Its new orders were to do precisely the opposite of what the governor had commanded—that is, to protect the black students from the jeering, howling, spitting mob rather than to bar their entry.

When the crunch came, both Governor Faubus and Alabama's governor, George Wallace, who tried similar resistance in 1963 when orders came to admit a black student to the state university, backed down. But the lesson that emerged from those stormy hours was that the national government had become an active partner in the search for racial justice and equality. The Eisenhower administration went on to support the passage of two Civil Rights Acts, in 1957 and 1960, which provided federal machinery for hearing and evaluating black complaints that constitutional freedoms were being denied to them.

Thus in the Eisenhower fifties, as in the Roosevelt and Truman forties, the federal government continued to expand. That did not necessarily mean an increase in anti-big business liberalism. In fact, Eisenhower appointees to various federal regulatory commissions, such as the Federal Trade Commission (FTC) and the Interstate Commerce Commission (ICC), were drawn from the managerial ranks of the great corporations. They generally tried to follow the philosophy expressed by Eisenhower's secretary of defense, Charles E. Wilson, past president of General Motors: "What's good for General Motors is good for the country." The federal establishment, it appeared, could be good as well as bad for GM. The tendency toward centralization brought on by modern communications and technology was proving irresistible.

## *The New Frontier: The Sixties Open with Optimism*

Yet centralization itself did not solve social problems. When John F. Kennedy took office on January 20, 1961, he pledged to get the nation moving and open a New Frontier. There was plenty of work to be done. Black income, health, and educational standards still lagged disproportionately behind those of whites. The spreading superhighways had helped enlarge that special kind of American noncommunity, "suburbia." To its neat lawns and gadget-filled homes, millions of productive middle-class taxpayers fled each evening at 60 miles an hour. Behind them in the central cities they left their emptied office buildings and an urban populace consisting heavily of the poor who could not afford to move and a few wealthy people who enjoyed city life. These alone could not provide enough money and leadership to stop decay in school and sanitation systems and deterioration in police and fire services and in housing.

Besides sick cities, there were also sick regions, like the Appalachian heartland, where coal mining and small farming no longer supported the population. There was also a growing concern about the pollution of air and water resources, which we will touch on in the next chapter. And there was still a federal budget swollen by huge defense costs, subsidy payments to farmers, and highway-building programs. All in all, there were many problems to deal with. Yet Kennedy's election campaign was keyed to the idea that vigorous action could correct the situation and "get this country moving again." Though he won election by only a slim margin, the young and the well-educated believed him. The New Frontier appeared to some onlookers as a rebirth of the active years of progressivism and the New Deal.

Yet Kennedy's tragically cut-short administration could not, would not, or did not meet many of these problems, which, like the 40 million or so poor people of the nation, showed the underside of the prosperity of the fifties. Faced with a slim election mandate, distracted by crises in Berlin and Cuba, and met by a cautious Congress, Kennedy's planners managed to press through an Area Redevelopment bill providing money for Appalachian communities to retrain their people for new jobs, attract new industries to the region, and in other ways rebuild their crippled economies. Congress also raised the minimum wage once more to keep up with the steady march of inflation. Some increases in public housing were voted. So was a manpower development and training program for the cities. But the lawmakers struck down proposals to increase federal aid to public schools and for a nationwide health-care plan that would insure citizens against rising medical costs.

As always it was easier to find money for purposes other than social change. Kennedy had little trouble winning funds to launch a space program designed to put a man on the moon by 1970 or to strengthen the armed forces to deal with Communist "insurgency" in places like Vietnam. Whether he could have focused more attention on domestic needs as time went on can never be known. Kennedy was murdered in Dallas on November 22, 1963.

But in one domestic area his administration continued to press hard. The black restlessness of the 1950s had blossomed into a full-scale "revolt" in the 1960s. Young blacks and white sympathizers were challenging segregation laws in places of public accommodations and in interstate transport by "sit-ins" and "freedom rides." The Justice Department persistently supported their cause in the courts, and sent federal marshals to monitor the behavior of Southern officials and crowds. Both Kennedys—the president and his younger brother Robert, the attorney general—openly befriended Dr. Martin Luther King, Jr., the black leader of the Southern Christian Leadership Conference, when King was conducting demonstrations for civil rights in Birmingham, Alabama, and Albany, Georgia. In October 1962 came an echo of Civil War days. A court ordered the University of Mississippi to admit a black student, James Meredith. Mobs gathered to prevent Meredith's appearance on campus, and Mississippi's Governor, Ross Barnett, backed down on an earlier promise and refused to provide state protection. Thereupon, federal marshals and troops were flown in. In a bloody night of tear-gassing, rock throwing, and sporadic shooting in which two civilians died, the "battle of Oxford" (Mississippi) was fought and won by the North.

### *The Great Society: Completion of the New Deal*

Kennedy's death brought Lyndon B. Johnson to power. In the last fourteen months of the Kennedy term and in the first two years of his own, Johnson pushed federal welfare policies to their furthest limits yet. Himself a Texas rancher and businessman, Johnson had known childhood poverty. He had come to maturity as a young Democrat in Washington in the thick of the New Deal days. While fundamentally wanting to preserve the American system as it stood, Johnson dreamed of completing the work of Roosevelt by creating a Great Society, which he described as "a place where men are more concerned for the quality of their goals than the quantity of their goods."

Johnson had extraordinary political skills, gotten and sharpened in more than twenty years of Congress, the final few of them as leader of the Democratic majority in the Senate. He also had a monarchical ego, which prompted him into furious bouts of activity that carried him relentlessly toward whatever goal he set. He yearned to be the chief personal architect of the Great Society, and he thrust himself into the building work with the drive that had carried pioneer ancestors, uprooting and planting, into the wilderness heartland.

In the immediate aftermath of Kennedy's death, Johnson had a honeymoon period with Congress of which he took full advantage. That his plans were basically in tune with the national mood was shown in the 1964 election, when he ran against Senator Barry Goldwater. Goldwater, an Arizona ultraconservative, flatly and openly preached the gospel of decentralization and individualism. He did not, however, extend his idea to the point of calling for a reduction of the defense establishment. Only welfare programs were a threat to liberty, it seemed. He was snowed under by Johnson's 61 percent of the popular vote.

Johnson's programs were sweeping and can only be listed briefly to avoid a heavy mass of detail. They included the following key pieces of legislation and creations:

1. An Economic Opportunity Act, dubbed the charter of a "War On Poverty." It created an Office of Economic Opportunity (OEO) to sponsor and coordinate the work of various agencies that dealt with the unemployed, the aged, the handicapped, the unskilled, and the other faceless millions of "the poor."

2. A law creating a Department of Housing and Urban Development to tighten links between the cities and Washington.

3. Under OEO control, a series of Community Action Programs designed to mobilize the urban poor to determine their own most pressing needs.

4. A Domestic Peace Corps, comparable to the corps that had sent young Americans abroad to help the peoples of underdeveloped nations learn agricultural, technical, medical, and other skills. Volunteers in Service to America (VISTA) hoped to recruit middle-class youths to undertake the same kind of work in the slums of American cities.

5. A Youth Corps and a Job Corps, both modeled roughly on the New Deal's Civilian Conservation Corps. They were supposed to furnish employment and training for out-of-work young people.

6. A Model Cities program to finance slum clearance, rebuilding abandoned downtown shopping districts, and in other ways improving the urban living environment.

7. A law setting up Medicare. It aimed to provide health care for the aged and was financed through the Social Security system. It raised the contributions paid by both employers and workers and included medical payments among the benefits that followed retirement.

8. An act to set environmental standards, helping communities attack air and water pollution problems, and to landscape and beautify highways.

9. A new Immigration Act, which replaced the 1924 law that set quotas by nationality as Chapter 22 shows. The new statute limited overall immigration. It also set up preference categories of who might be admitted, how many, and in what order. But these were keyed to the immigrants' having relatives in the United States or professional skills or being refugees from totalitarianism, instead of to race or birthplace.

10. Laws pumping well over a billion dollars in federal aid into public educational systems.

11. A Mass Transit Act to help finance urban rapid-transit systems.

12. And, in the field of civil rights, two major pieces of lawmaking:

a. The Civil Rights Act of 1964, outlawing most discrimination in public places, in the training and hiring of workers, and in almost any institution that in one way or another was licensed, regulated, or touched by federal *or* state laws.

b. A Voting Rights Act in 1965, allowing federal registrars to enroll black voters and supervise elections in any area where evidence showed a persistent pattern of banning people from the polls.

These two laws (which applied to all minorities, including women, of course), once more put teeth into the century-old Fourteenth and Fifteenth Amendments. They represented an enormous step for a country whose Congress, only twenty years earlier, had refused to outlaw poll taxes or lynching.

The Great Society never quite came out of the blueprint stage. It was booby-trapped by the Vietnam War, which took away needed funds and attention. In addition, many of its programs would take years—and billions of dollars—to fulfill. It was easier for Congress and the president to launch them, with appropriate political fanfare, than to continue the grubby year-in and year-out work of taxing and spending to keep them going. It would not be long before a number of them, starved for funds, would be accused of "failure." Under the Nixon administrations of 1969 through 1974, many were totally or partly scrapped.

But even without Great Society plans, the nation had moved steadily toward a centralized, bureaucratic system. By 1968 the federal government was the nation's single biggest spender and biggest employer. Its annual budgets were moving past the $80 billion mark. It had millions of employees. Its hand and presence were felt everywhere.

The motorist sped over roads paid for mostly with federal funds, to a home that he had bought with a loan guaranteed by the federal government. The retired worker collected his monthly check from Washington and signed forms at the hospital that let Washington pay his doctors and nurses a portion of his bill. Grade-school children drank milk in their lunch periods partly paid for by the federal government. At the other end of the educational ladder, graduate students in mathematics or military Russian lived on federal fellowships, and would-be doctors, lawyers, and teachers paid their tuition with federal loans.

Federal money provided the lights along the runways down which modern planes roared and also the ground equipment that guaranteed their safe flight. Federal dollars financed sewage treatment plants and municipal clinics. They put some groceries in the welfare client's supermarket shopping cart and computers in the great university's research laboratory. The sudden drying up of the rivers of federal money would have paralyzed the American economy, terrified every statehouse and city hall in the land, and had earth-shaking effects on almost every citizen's life. That was why, although many Americans agreed with Goldwater in principle, they voted against him in practice.

All of this had taken place under a Constitution that more or less planned to restrict the federal government's operations to maintaining the army, navy, diplomatic corps, and postal system. It had not happened so much by design but in response to the gigantic growth of the nation into a "community" of nearly 200 million people, living in a complex changing society. It could be defended as a kind of inevitable response to growth and the only means whereby so many people could manage their essential business together.

But it could also be criticized on a variety of grounds. The history of the country under supergovernment showed that it created as many dilemmas as it solved.

*Limits of Liberalism, or Problems That Do Not Go Away*

There were, to begin with, the obvious disadvantages. The enormous costs of the caretaker state, even eliminating military expense, raised everyone's tax bill to levels that would have been unthinkable in 1913 when the income tax first took effect. It could be claimed that in a modern society, people simply had to count on paying more of their earned dollars for public services. The days were gone when a few cents per citizen per week maintained the local jail and almshouse and the county road. But it was undeniable that part of the increased price of government was due to a swelling army of officials, building paper mountains of forms. There was some truth to the charge that Washington tax collectors took the citizen's dollar and then "gave" it back to him in services, only after taking out a huge slash for administrative costs.

It was also undeniable that bureaucratic officialdom was frustrating to deal with. Anyone who tried to get a delayed check from the Veterans Administration or the Social Security office knew that. Great private corporations were often as difficult to deal with, but they could be threatened theoretically, at least, with the loss of the complainant's business. Uncivil civil servants were unmoved by such warnings.

More than that, the huge and layered labyrinth of federal programs was such that, without organized help, many individuals and communities were unable to make use of funds lawfully due them. Cities, universities, unions, hospitals, and welfare organizations found that they often needed to establish offices in Washington simply to deal with the jungle of regulations that had to be met before funds could be secured. To get anything done took experts, usually lawyers and ex-government officials, who knew their way around and could call on the right people. Industries had known this for a long time, and their capital-city lobbies had, long before the 1960s, become staffed with such experts as well as with public-relations people. But all of this added up to a situation in which the best-organized claimants had the best chance of getting money. The unorganized, such as the poor or consumers, had much smaller opportunities. The general welfare activities of the federal government too often served only special groups.

It was also true that the constant practice of looking to Washington for assistance took some toll on local governments. Certainly, many problems were too big to be dealt with on the state and local levels. That explained the rise in special interstate and intercity "authorities" for improving mass transportation or cleaning up rivers, often with funds raised by borrowing and by federal grants. But though there were logical reasons for dependence on the central government, the result was a lack of attention to the workings of municipal or state officialdom. Since the cities and states still held wide powers over people, lack of interest in how they were governed was damaging in the extreme.

Corruption increased. Good individuals were not eager to seek obscure public office. Initiative was lacking to devise plans at the local level for dealing with local problems. The cure for overcentralization was vigor at the grass roots. But those roots were often planted in the soil of apathy and cynicism.



### *Built-in Conflicts of the Welfare State*

In addition, the bounty of Washington was not equally spread. Washington's right hand often unwittingly worked against its left. Society was so interrelated and so complex that what was done to one of its organs often produced pain in another. Some specific examples illustrate these conflicts.

*Racial backlash.* Of necessity, most programs aimed at helping the poor found themselves dealing largely with nonwhites. This was natural, since nonwhites had been left behind in the race toward affluence. But it sparked resentment among many working white people who were fighting a hard battle with the rising cost of living. Any tendency toward racism that they had was, in some cases, made more intense by the feeling that the government was "giving things" to blacks and other minorities and ignoring their needs.

This antagonism flared again and again in particular settings. When federal public-housing authorities tried to create new projects outside central-city slums, they often located them in nearby working-class areas. But the residents resisted, fearing that their new neighbors would bring drugs and street crime along with them. Though this fear blamed slum dwellers for problems of which they were the victims and not the cause, it was real and powerful.

Programs to achieve racial balance in the schools sometimes also created turbulent conflict in city districts, which already had problems of overcrowded and underequipped classrooms. Federal insistence on quotas for minority hiring in federally funded projects also filled some white workers with worry that jobs would be denied them and their children to benefit others. The same anger was aroused by government pressure on unions to open up their ranks to minorities, on colleges to admit more nonwhite and female applicants, and on all institutions to change past patterns of racism or sexism.

These resentments led to a growing "backlash" of hostility to school, housing, and job integration. Much of it centered on the bussing of children in and out of neighborhoods to balance school populations by race. By the mid-1970s the backlash was strong enough to threaten a sharp reduction in such efforts. It was easy enough to condemn such feelings if one did not live in the cities and share the problems. It was more difficult to confront the dilemma of fairness. The federal government had moved into the area of equal opportunity because other institutions and local governments had not done so. But correcting decades of injustice to nonwhites, women, and others who had been

*The welfare state may legislate, but social change—and the realization of such high ideals as equality—move at their own slow pace. Above, National Guardsmen in Little Rock, Arkansas (1957) protect black students entering Central High School in response to a judicial desegregation order based on the Supreme Court's 1954* Brown *vs.* Board of Education *decision.*

*Angry Bostonians demonstrate (1974) against a court-ordered busing plan issued to achieve racial balance in the schools. Racism is not the exclusive property of any one part of the country, and solving the problems of racism and quality education for all cannot help but be a slow and aggravating affair. Where does that leave the optimism of the liberal mind?*

handicapped by prejudice often meant apparently handicapping others. The liberal state found it easy to preach a just rule but hard to achieve one with evenhandedness.

*City versus suburb.* The federal government also discovered other contradictions in its policies. For example, aid to highways encouraged the rush to suburbia. But this rush undercut the purposes of urban renewal, the rebuilding of the central cities so as to attract residents, merchants, and industries back into them. Mass-transit programs and highway development programs often ran head-on into each others' goals. Programs to attract industries into decaying areas often conflicted with the campaign to preserve the environment, clean up dirtied air and water, reduce noise, and avoid heavy traffic.

Some programs helped cities to buy and clear "downtown" and sell it to those who would build shopping centers and other attractions that would bring business to rundown areas. But the land chosen was often the site of substandard housing serving the poor and the small merchants who dealt with them. When the ugly slums were torn down, these people were left homeless. They rarely could afford to move their homes and businesses to other parts of the city where rents were higher. And they were not anxious to move far from their old jobs and schools. So the federally financed wrecking machinery that wiped out slums to make way for expensive stores and apartment and office buildings or for expressways made new headaches for the federal agencies trying to cope with the problems of housing the poor.

*Taxes, subsidies, and inequality.* Curiously enough, many of the central government's moves to stimulate the economy and raise purchasing power widened the gaps among classes. For example, as we saw earlier, agricultural subsidy payments were based on the size of the harvest. Therefore, they went largely to the successful "bonanza" farmer, who was equipped with a multitude of expensive ways to raise his productivity per acre, while the unfortunate dirt farmer still scrabbled for a bare living.

The federal government spent only a modest amount on public-housing projects. But it gave the private home-building industry an enormous boost through the device of loans whose payment was guaranteed by the Federal Housing Administration. This government backing enabled banks to lend as much as 90 percent of the cost of a house to a buyer. That meant that less cash for a down payment was needed. So millions of middle-income families were able to own their homes, But, as always, these homes were in suburbia, and the rush to suburbia, sometimes called "white flight," helped to aggravate the woes of the abandoned central city. In addition, homeowning taxpayers could deduct the interest payments on their mortgage loans (a loan to buy property) from their income taxes, a privilege not shared by apartment dwellers. So the fine idea of helping the construction industry and encouraging thrifty souls to buy homes and plant good solid community roots partly backfired. It made life harder for the low-income urban public and set up political tension between them and suburbanites.

*The inflation dilemma.* Through the years the government did raise minimum-wage and Social Security payments and, through its labor mediation machinery, encouraged contracts that gave organized workers wage boosts. Yet all of these gains were eaten away by the higher cost of living. But the higher cost of living was a result of inflation. And inflation came about in part because of the enormous pressure of government spending. Government money in circulation created a demand for goods and services, made business boom, and led to easier credit and higher prices. That was the reason why government spending programs had been undertaken during the Depression. Washington was then following the general outlines of the economic theories of John Maynard Keynes. And Keynesian economics—that is, government spending to "prime the pump" even if it means borrowing—had dominated the thinking of most administrations from Roosevelt's onward.

But the problem was that rising prices tended to wipe out the gains. The orthodox remedy for that, according to Keynesians and others, was to raise taxes. That would mop up excess purchasing power and slow down the rate of inflation and growth. The extra money in the Treasury could pay off old government debts and prepare for the next round of pump priming.

Unfortunately, two things were difficult about that remedy. One was political: Politicians found it much easier to cut taxes and give away money than to raise taxes. But beyond that, care was required. If government took too many vigorously anti-inflationary steps—raising taxes, raising interest rates through the Federal Reserve system, cutting back its own spending—it could cause too quick a deflationary spiral. The rate of growth would slow down. New jobs and businesses would not absorb a growing population. Unemployment would rise, and, as it did so, payments would not be met, new purchases would not be made, and the country would roller-coast downward into depression. Efforts in the Eisenhower administration to "cool down" the overheated economy had brought two recessions. By the mid-1970s, inflation had reached frightening proportions. But at the beginning of 1975, various other forces had also created the severest slump in twenty-five years. The dilemma of matching policies to fight depression with those to combat inflation showed no sign of shrinking.

Solutions to such built-in conflicts were not easy. Some conservatives argued that the answer lay in a return to the free competitive market. That hardly seemed possible in an age when a few supercorporations dominated whole industries. Socialists continued to insist that the answer was in outright replacement of private economic goals by socially determined ones through ending the profit system. And some argued that *any* gigantic system was bound to break down. They said that human beings must find the path back to sanity by reorganizing into smaller social units. Otherwise, dehumanization and the exhaustion of resources loomed. But such doomsday pronouncements drew little practical support.



The nation had to find some way of taming the superstate, for in realistic terms the return to a decentralized America was technologically impossible. The challenge was to make opposites work in harmony; to make local government lively but allow for nationwide cooperation; to mate economic growth and jobs with sparing resources; to get the benefits of technology but share them equally. It was a set of dilemmas faced by all modern nations in a swiftly changing world. These dilemmas were cast in political terms. But they stemmed basically from technological revolutions that we will now examine.

## *FOR FURTHER READING*

The most helpful kinds of reading on this subject are general studies of part or all of American society from about 1945 to 1970. A start can be made with a broad survey, George Mowry, *The Urban Nation* (1965). From there one goes to books that are a kind of special pleading and must be matched with others to get a rounded picture. For example, C. Wright Mills' *White Collar* (1951) describes a new kind of middle class in America; but, Mills goes on to argue in *The Power Elite* (1962) that the class he describes does not really have much say about how the United States is run. Samuel Lubell, however, in *Revolt of the Moderates* (1956) holds that the great group of voters at the center is a controlling influence.

John K. Galbraith has written several books that were "bibles" of liberalism. In *American Capitalism: The Theory of Countervailing Power* (1952) he challenges the assumption that a few top corporations were all-powerful in shaping public policy; in *The Affluent Society* (1958) he seems to suggest that some of the gross problems of poverty were cured, or rather that they could be cured, by wise public expenditure, while private capital catered to the desires of a growing class of well-off citizens. Galbraith's *The New Industrial State* (1967) describes an alliance of business, government, and universities that was producing a managerial elite of planners.

These ideas were challenged from several quarters. Notably, Michael Harrington, *The Other America* (1960) insisted that poverty was still widespread and painful in the United States. Conservative objections to government manipulation of the economy were voiced not only in Barry Goldwater's *The Conscience of a Conservative* (1964), a book which helped Goldwater win the Republican 1964 presidential nomination, but in a number of readable works by William F. Buckley, of which *Up From Liberalism* (1968) and *The Jeweller's Eye* (1969) are typical.

Likewise, in the era of civil rights controversy, Louis Lomax's *The Negro Revolt* (1963) summarizes happenings in this area, and James Baldwin, *The Fire Next Time* (1963) eloquently explains the feelings behind the black protest. Two black leaders' self-portraits are also critical: Martin Luther King, Jr., *Stride Toward Freedom* (1958) and *The Autobiography of Malcolm X* (1966). But Michael Novak, in *The Rise of the Unmeltable Ethnics* (1972), says that the focus on the black struggle led "liberal" white Americans to ignore the plight of lower-class whites of Polish, Irish, Italian, Greek, and Slavic descent, with disastrous political consequences.

Finally, good social "snapshots" of the issues racking liberal America are contained in the volumes of Theodore H. White entitled *The Making of the President* (1961, 1965, 1969, 1973). Each covers a campaign for the top office; they begin with a study of the campaign of 1960 and extend through 1972.

# *chapter* 25 *Society, technology, and human fate: America in the* 1950s *and* 1960s

We begin with a symbolic scene set in tomorrow.

*On a launching pad somewhere stands a gigantic rocket. Twenty or more stories in height, it gleams in the floodlights. It is wreathed in the vapors of its fuel tanks. A network of power cables still ties it to earth. But in a few moments the cables will fall away, and amid a terrifying storm of sound and fire the rocket will hurtle toward the moon, the other planets, or into the darkness of deep space.*

*In the nose capsule are three or four or five people. Perhaps the crew is international. These astronauts are human beings. They have a sense of time that tells them their own ages, a sense of the place from which they came. They are conscious of themselves as men and women, fathers and husbands, daughters and sisters, Russians or Chinese or Americans. Their minds are crammed with memories, faiths, dreams.*

*But once they begin rushing into space, all of that will change. Time, the measure of earth revolutions, has no real meaning there. Nor is their fragment of metal, pulled here and there by other bodies' gravitational forces, in a particular geographical place. Their "selves," they become increasingly aware, are a collection of biological systems—respiratory, circulatory, excretory—all wired to electrical sensors for monitoring and all capable of being swiftly changed by emergency medications. Their contact with their fellow humans outside the capsule is impersonal. Their voices and pictures may be transmitted through space by electrical impulses. But a slight mishap may maroon them forever, so that even their dead bodies will probably never again be touched by human hands.*

Our imaginary rocket is a towering achievement of the human mind. Yet, at the same time, it can totally change the landmarks of human existence. It is used here as a symbol for all our modern technology, which takes us on new voyages in unknown directions.

In previous chapters we spoke of some of the sweeping effects of invention on American life in the eras following 1815 and 1865. Now we return to that theme again. The inventions we study now, however, are so different from some of the earlier ones, that a few scholars speak of them (and us) as belonging to a "postindustrial" age. The inventions of the earlier "industrial revolutions" multiplied humanity's power to convert natural resources into goods with less effort. The scientific and technical discoveries made after 1945 went further. They actually could work directly on people's minds instead of merely increasing the output of their muscles. This had a mighty effect on humanity's self-image and social machinery.

If we watch the changes we are speaking of at work in the United States, we must bear in mind certain facts. From 1945 almost until the present moment of writing, the United States was in another of its periods of swift, prosperous growth. The population was rising. So were the gross national product and the national income. Larger families meant more of everything—more houses, more automobiles, more schools, more demand for every kind of commodity, and hence more jobs. As always, not every American shared in the flush times, but the tendency was for the national mood and tone to be set by those who did. Invention and prosperity remained linked in the popular mind.

In addition, Americans tended to forget that most of humanity remained bound to the grim struggle for livelihood that sets iron limits on hope. They thought of their affluence as something that all humanity might one day

---

*CHRONOLOGY*

| | |
|---|---|
| 1945 | *July 16, first atomic bomb exploded at Alamogordo, New Mexico* |
| 1949 | *Early commercial TV sets* |
| 1950 | *Miltown tranquilizer developed and put into wide use* |
| early 1950s | *First practical electronic computers* |
| late 1950s | *Birth-control pill comes into general use* |
| 1959 | *First commercial transatlantic jet flight* |
| 1963 | *Betty Friedan's* The Feminine Mystique *published* |
| 1964 | *Free speech demonstrations at University of California, Berkeley* |
| 1965 | *Martin Luther King leads march in Montgomery, Alabama* |

achieve. And they saw their problems as the future problems of the whole human race. They still believed that America was the cutting edge of the future.

So Americans remained full of pride and optimism. But some of them also worried that world society was in trouble as a result of progress. Three centuries after the Puritans, there were moderns who feared, as they had done, that pride might in fact go before a fall, that children were straying, that Nature might take revenge for the penetration of her secrets. These anxieties were stirred because progress was making such radical changes in human activity and institutions. Let us simply suggest the kinds of problems that were arising from the new discoveries, and you may debate among yourselves whether the fears were well founded or not. The new world being discovered by science was like the physical New World found by explorers in the 1500s and 1600s. It had treasures and opportunities as well as wild, unknown regions full of traps and dangers. Which of these would determine the future?



*The bomb*

An entire new age of human history was born on a July day in 1945 when American scientists detonated an atomic test bomb, hung from a steel tower in the desert near Alamogordo, New Mexico. As a gigantic fireball rose into the sky, "brighter than a thousand suns" in the words of a watching reporter, he was filled with a sense of wonder and terror. The incredible destructive power of the new weapon was demonstrated only a few weeks later at Hiroshima and Nagasaki.

For a few years after the war, the United States possessed an atomic monopoly. But by 1949 Russia had developed a bomb of her own. Both nations then moved into a terrifying arms race. A new kind of nuclear weapon was developed, the hydrogen bomb. It relied on the fusion of nuclear elements, rather than on the splitting of atoms, to generate its incredible energy. H-bombs had far more lethal power. The Hiroshima A-bomb had only the force of 20,000 tons (kilotons) of high explosive, but by the 1960s America and Russia had the capability of making and testing H-bombs in the range of 50 million tons (megatons).

Estimates were that in any war between the two powers, casualties of 20 million to a 100 million on each side could be immediately expected. Amid this sobering news, both powers concentrated on improved, protected delivery systems for their bombs. Then they made the warheads of missiles capable of speeding halfway around the globe in a very short time. Those missiles were placed in buried underground silos or in submarines on constant patrol, or they were carried in supersonic bombers, always on the alert. Both sides possessed what was called second-strike capability. Even if seared by a surprise bombing, each could automatically strike back. The situation was made more dangerous by the early 1970s, when Britain, France, China, and India, with weapons of their own, joined the "nuclear club."

The world could literally be destroyed in a nuclear clash. And this fact was bound to have an impact on conventional ideas of patriotism. The old idea had been that war was justifiable to save one's nation from disgrace or loss of independence. But in a nuclear war nothing would be "saved." "Winners" and "losers" would present to the pitiless skies the same picture of radioactive desolation and corpse-strewn rubble. Though the world did not seem to be ready for the lesson yet, the nuclear bomb was proof that a world community without arms might be humanity's only hope of survival. But such a development was not in sight thirty years after that first A-bomb was detonated.

Human beings held the power to wipe themselves out of existence. But they had no new political machinery to handle that power. That brutal fact not only changed the meaning of nationhood, but it also blasted the almost religious faith of Americans in a better future. Children born after 1945—you, your children, and theirs—lived and would live as their parents never had. They would have the constant awareness that at any moment the future might not be. That made them resist the traditional advice of their elders to plan for tomorrow. And so the bomb not only redefined the behavior of nations but made its contribution to what would, by the sixties, be called the generation gap.

*The jet*

Jet engines first made their appearance on German military aircraft late in World War II. By then it was too late for their superspeed to do Hitler any substantial good. During the 1950s, every up-to-date military power equipped itself with jetcraft. Meanwhile, passenger airlines prepared for the jet age. For the United States it came in 1958, when Pan American introduced Boeing 707s on its New York-Paris route. In 1970 the same line put into service the first giant Boeing 747, able to carry up to 450 passengers on the New York-London run. By late 1973 most American cities of any size had jetports. Millions of passengers flew round trips of 1400 or 1500 miles in an ordinary business day (New York to Chicago, as an example). Millions shot airborne across the continent, covering it at over 600 miles per hour, the same trip that had taken covered wagons six painful months. Millions sipped cocktails and ate frozen dinners eight miles high, as their Europe-bound jetliners made child's play of traveling the lonely, risky route of Lindbergh. Provided one had the fare, no place in the world was more than a two-day trip away.

Every jet traveler suffering the fatigue and stomach upset of leaving New York, for example, at 9 A.M. and arriving six hours later in San Francisco to find that clocks read only 11 A.M. and lunches were being readied knew that jet

*The power, the gigantic size, the blinding speed of jet-age technology are all implicit in this picture of a 600-mile-an-hour, 400-passenger Boeing 747 jumbo jet. How will it make the life of the small boy staring at it different from that of his grandfather?*

travel created problems for the human system. But there were broader social consequences as well.

*The case of the foot-loose young.* For children of the middle class—a small but highly educated percentage—travel outside the United States became progressively easier. Though even low fares excluded the majority of the nation's young men and women, who were from working homes, millions of young people spent time in the Old World. It is not easy to say how much this had to do with a decline in conventional patriotism among middle-class youngsters, but it certainly created a sense of international identification. Educated youth of all nations seemed to share a common culture. It was based not only on jet travel to each others' countries but on commonly admired clothing styles, films, and music. In 1968, when there were numerous campus uprisings in the United States, they were matched by similar upheavals in France, West Germany, and Japan. To some disturbed conservative elders this smacked of an international conspiracy led by Communists. It was more likely the consequence of a shrinking globe.

*The case of the foot-loose builders.* The jet could also whisk lawyers, business people, and technical experts from continent to continent within the space of a working day. One consequence of this was to smooth the way for the outward spread of American corporations. At jet speeds it was easy to oversee the building of American-owned oil refineries in Saudi Arabia and Venezuela, American car-assembly plants in Britain and the Philippines, American-financed dams in Thailand, and sewage-treatment plants in Korea. Other prospering industrial nations—primarily Japan and West Germany—were doing likewise. By 1970 people, money, and equipment seemed to recognize no national boundaries.

A sign of this was in the architecture of air terminals and business districts of all major cities. They were built by architectural firms that did an international business and found little or no difficulty at all in shuttling key personnel around the globe. All of them used plenty of glass, plastics, and prefabricated parts. All had to make room for air conditioning and for great quantities of electrically driven equipment. Since they all faced common problems of space use, a kind of "international modern" style arose. In any modern air terminal, then, one found the same plastic furniture, the same glass-encased corridors, the same layouts of counter and baggage-handling and boarding spaces, and the same electrical departure-and-arrival display boards. And in downtown London, Rome, New York, or Tokyo one found tall, glass and chrome and steel office buildings, with the same kinds of fluorescent lights, reception desks, switchboards, and elevator banks—all seemingly indistinguishable.

All this changed the face of nationalism. It perhaps erased conflicts, but it also erased differentness in urban centers. The pagoda, the cathedral, and the palace all expressed different styles of power in sixteenth-century Europe and Asia. The skyscraper looked the same in all three places. And the skyscraper, as we observed in Chapter 15, was a characteristically American temple.

*The case of the foot-loose diplomats.* Eisenhower's secretary of state, John Foster Dulles, dreamed of building anti-Communist alliances around the world. In pursuit of that vision he became the most traveled secretary in American history up to that date. Constantly shuttling back and forth between Washington and Paris, London, Bonn, Rome, Tokyo, Saigon, Bangkok, Manila, and Singapore, he logged millions of air miles. Those who followed him in that office after 1959 traveled widely, too, though somewhat less. In 1973 Henry Kissinger became secretary of state and soon seemed to be matching the Dulles record.

Where secretaries of state went, presidents themselves followed. When Wilson personally traveled to Paris in 1919, it worried Congress that the chief of state should be so far away from his work in the White House. Between 1942 and 1945 Franklin D. Roosevelt's trips to Casablanca, Teheran, and Yalta and Truman's to Potsdam were all considered extraordinary World War II emergency missions. But the pattern of negotiations "at the summit," or between the heads of state of allied nations, was riveted permanently into American diplomacy by the arrival of the jet age. Eisenhower went to Korea in December 1952 and later to European capitals. Kennedy visited the hot spot of West Berlin in 1961. Johnson personally visited the Pacific to discuss the Vietnam War with his field commanders in 1966 and came back promising the American people that they would "bring home the coonskin" of victory. And Nixon, in what he clearly saw as his own finest hour, personally journeyed to Peking in 1972 to drown twenty-four years of Sino-American hostility in a flood of toasts with Mao Tse-tung and Chou En-lai.

The traffic in leaders worked the other way, too. Nikita Khrushchev came to see the United States in 1959. Alexei Kosygin conferred with Johnson in Glassboro, New Jersey, eight years later. After 1970 almost every chief of state in the world who had dealings with the United States made at least one trip to Washington.

All of this changed diplomacy almost beyond recognition. Nations, the United States included, had long dealt with each other through staffs of ambassadors. These representatives were, in the case of European and Asian nations, veteran observers of the countries with which they were accredited. American ambassadors were often political appointees, but they were backed up by teams of career foreign-service officers. Ambassadors negotiated slowly, by mail, with lengthy pauses for instructions. These became breathing spaces for tensions to cool or new policies to be considered. And ambassadors were interpreters between the cultures of their own land and others. Governments counted on their embassies' opinions on political, military, and economic situations abroad.

But in the 1960s such information was gathered by professional intelligence agencies in every country, manned by teams of technicians with electronic gimmicks. When negotiations became serious, ambassadors were replaced at the conference table by the secretary of state or the number-one man himself. Presidents and their foreign-policy aides and staffs were like top corporate executives, negotiating across a table with their foreign counterparts. Once more, the lines between nations and cultures tended to be obliterated. That might be a hopeful step toward a peaceful world. But it could also condition peoples to expect too much too soon. It could lead them to look for a rabbit in every hat and to turn in fury on a president or other leaders who did not produce one.

## *The Elements of Community: Changes in Class and Group Relationships*

### *Automated machinery and the computer*

Automatic devices—those that operate to replace human hands in some way or another—were an old story by the early twentieth century. Automated machinery, which replaces some functions of the human mind, only began to develop its full impact after World War II. The differences are hard to explain, but an example might be found in a steel mill. There, around 1940, one might see workers at the controls of various cranes, lifts, shears, rollers, and hammers. These automatically poured molten steel into troughs, cooled it, lifted out the bars, and cut and rolled them into sheets, rails, and beams. Workers turned the machinery on and off. One might decide when the furnace was ready for pouring; another would decide when a bar was cool enough to handle; and yet another when the metal had to pass from one set of rollers to another.

But in an automated steel mill of 1970, pouring, cooling, lifting, rolling, and cutting might all be done without a worker in sight. The machines would be preset to make "their own" judgments of when to perform their functions, to correct those judgments when needed, and to check on their accuracy. A very few technicians at an elaborate panel of instruments that monitored the machines' sensors were the "manpower" of this new kind of laboratory-smock industrialism.

Automated machinery was visible everywhere. It was as sophisticated as that required to bring parts in proper order to an auto assembly line. And it was as unnoticeable as office-building elevators that remembered a whole series of floors at which to stop and knew how long to "rest" between trips, depending on whether it was time for the incoming or outgoing rush.

The general results of automated machinery were to displace a great many workers and to increase the productivity of those who remained. Some of the unemployment caused by automation was "sopped up" as new jobs opened, thanks to rising production and population curves. But few of those new jobs were for the unskilled. More and more of the labor force went into the fields known as technical, sales, service, clerical, and managerial. More of the "working class" worked with their heads, not their hands. For those without the chance or ability to learn at least elementary mathematics, business English, or practical physics in some form, life was grim. They stayed unemployable, a potential permanent "underclass." Moreover, for those who still remained in overalled jobs on the assembly line, there was a fear that they simply represented the parts of the production process that could not yet be mechanized. So the gap between skilled and unskilled, blue-collar and white-collar workers widened and grew more cruel.

At the same time, another development was extending the range of human thought by creating new problems of human relationships. This was the coming of the computer. It began to appear in the 1950s. By 1970 it had reached new heights of complexity and was spread throughout the economy. The computer is basically a device capable of storing enormous amounts of "memorized" material within its magnetic mind, working on it mathematically in seconds, and producing visible information. It is an "analytical engine" that multiplies the speed and power of the human brain in the way that steam expanded the function of muscle. Among just a few of its uses (you yourselves may quickly think of more) are:

1. Making possible the immense mathematical calculations that allowed us to reach the moon. Computers constantly calculated and fed course and power settings and corrections to the astronauts or directly to the engines and guidance systems.

2. At a more earthy level, computers underpin the credit-card economy. Banks, gasoline companies, department stores, and businesses of every variety can handle hundreds of thousands or millions of transactions, keep track of balances, and submit bills monthly. This possibility alone was one of the factors underlying the enormous business expansion of the fifties and sixties. Though it created problems, a credit-card economy was a stimulus to growth, as cash was when it first replaced barter.

3. Computers were indispensable in the behavioral sciences. A particularly noticeable application was their use in political forecasting. By analyzing past votes in sample districts, storing the information, comparing it instantaneously with early voting results, and then extrapolating the revealed trends, computers could allow newscasters to predict results early on election evenings. And pollsters and market researchers also found the new machine indispensable in surveys to guide what they said and did.

Computers did hundreds of other things. They punched out licenses and airline tickets, helped census takers, planned material orders for complex building projects, inventoried multibillion-dollar stocks of supplies. But in forecasting votes and buying habits, they showed a worrisome tendency to

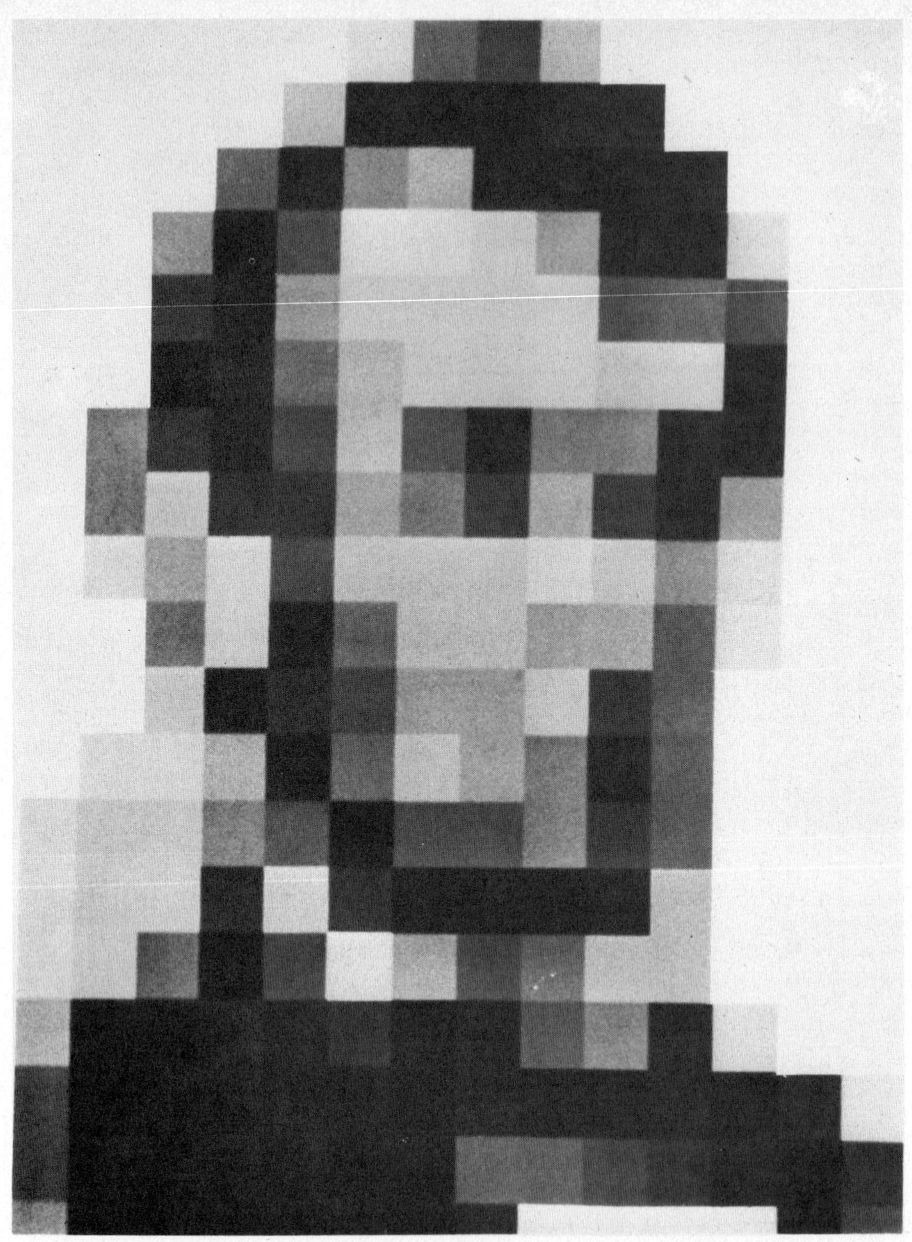

*Look closely at this picture, then step back at least 15 feet and look again. Do you recognize the subject? (If you can't work it out, the answer is on page 501.) Is this an abstract painter's trick on the viewer's eye? No. It is done by a computer that divided the original picture into squares, each one rendered in an even tone from one of 16 intensities of brown. Can we humanize our machines before they dehumanize us? Or is some kind of new mating of human and machine in the offing?*

dehumanize. They reduced individuals to ciphers whose behavior, in the mass, could be accurately pinpointed. The ego we all cherish is somewhat deflated to discover how much it is like a thousand others, contained in people of similar birth, breeding, background, or training!

What are some examples of the impact of automation and computation? Here are just a few.

*The case of the restless blue-collar workers.* Increasingly, in labor-management negotiations the issues that arose did not confine themselves to wages, hours, pensions, vacations, and other benefits. In assembly-line industries, especially auto making, there were new demands for more humanized working conditions. Workers wanted cleaner surroundings, more rest periods, and, above all, the option to set their own pace from time to time or even to change jobs on the line. There existed a strong possibility that this attitude was a protest against the dehumanization of work. Workers were protesting not only dirt, noise, and monotony but also the manipulation of people by decisions that were made without regard to human values, but rather dictated by cost data supplied by the "analytical engines."

*The case of the restless white-collar workers.* At the same time, white-collar workers, including those in the "salaried professions," such as teaching, were becoming increasingly restless in their jobs. They, too, were beginning to unionize, something done up to then almost entirely by manual workers. Various office, professional, technical, and clerical workers' unions came to life in the 1950s. Perhaps the most striking development was the rising tide of unionization among teachers. City after city was shocked when men and women who had long refused to strike walked out to protest contracts.

Leaving aside the rights and wrongs of whether teachers should strike, it is clear that behind their restlessness was a change in nature of their work. Once they had felt very close to the superintendents and principals who made policy. But by 1970 bureaucratization was becoming more and more the order of the day in large school systems. Routines, schedules, books, and lesson plans were determined at the top and communicated by printed form to the "troops." What teachers wanted was not merely better salaries to keep pace with inflation but also a sense of having a personal relationship with authority. Like the assembly-line workers, they wanted some control over their lives and work; that is, they wanted autonomy. The loss of autonomy in teaching could be traced to many factors. But the increasing big-city reliance upon machine-processed forms in dealing with remote "headquarters" in the Board of Education was a specially irritating kind of "automation" of what was once personally rewarding work. It was only one teacher grievance, but it had great emotional sting.

*The case of the absentee professors and the alienated students.* In December 1964 the United States witnessed a spectacle new in its history. Thousands of students on the campus of the University of California at Berkeley went on strike against a university ban on certain political activities. Later, as we shall see, student unrest over the Vietnam War led, in 1968, 1969, and 1970, to other campus rebellions, at Columbia, Harvard, Wisconsin, Chicago, and dozens of other campuses.

Again, setting aside momentarily the debate over whether student tactics such as the seizure of campus buildings were justified, it seems plain that turbulence amid the ivy was also a partial response to a steady growth in factory-style organization of education. As classrooms became filled to bursting with an ever-rising student population, registrars turned to computerized forms to keep track. Section assignments and grades came on the familiar "printouts" that seemed to have no visible connection with a human mind that saw the student as an individual. In the large universities, classes numbering hundreds of students became commonplace. A student attended a mass lecture given by a professor whom he might never meet personally, or he simply watched him on a closed-circuit TV screen. He discussed his assignments with a laboratory or teaching assistant and fed back his knowledge in a test that might only ask that he fill in blanks with a pencil, to facilitate electronic scoring.

Professors, too, became increasingly concerned with introducing their students to the advanced techniques of data collection, measurement, and analysis, which were becoming the basic work of the social and natural sciences. There was enormous pressure on students to specialize early and a drift away from concern with moral issues and artistic expression. One special grievance was that many professors with unusual skills were constantly on call as visiting experts for government or private industry. That was possible because jet transportation allowed a specialist to be summoned from as far as 2000 miles away on a day's notice. Such professors were, therefore, rarely present for formal or informal conferences with students.

Once, the college had been a place where young people and their elders had occupied a common moral universe. The faculty, as temporary "parents," made rules for student behavior and were supposed to be concerned with character development. In the classrooms, small groups of students demonstrated their increasing maturity to professors who knew them as distinct faces and voices. Gradually, they were admitted to the world of learning. At least that was the theoretical ideal.

By the 1960s, however, professors were ready to abandon responsibility for students' drinking and sexual habits. This allowed the young greater freedom, which they wanted. But teachers were now only in contact with that corner of the young person's mind devoted to their specialty. The sense of community shrank. The university, too, was becoming an automated educational factory. This was at least one great stimulus to the flare-ups.

*The tube*

The theoretical work behind television was done in the 1920s, and crude apparatus was on display at the New York World's Fair of 1939. But commercial models did not appear until the late 1940s. Their spread thereafter was one of the most amazing of industrial success stories, from a few thousand sets in 1949 to millions in 1970. An entire generation has now come to maturity that began, at age five or younger, to watch television anywhere from seven to thirty-five hours or more a week. It is almost impossible to grasp the cultural impact of such an overwhelming fact. But simply for purposes of analysis, we will focus on one aspect, the power of the successful TV show to unite 20 or 30 or 40 million people in watching one event for an hour or two. Here are merely two illustrations of what that could lead to.

*Cultural homogenization and the destruction of local community enterprise: the case of the vanishing minor leagues.* Once upon a time, there were only sixteen major-league baseball teams. At the time our story begins, in 1949, just before television's great leap forward, they had been in their home cities anywhere from forty to eighty years. Each of these teams was known, loved, and argued over locally. Each was fed by a network of minor-league teams from those cities of less than one-half million or so that could not turn out crowds large enough to support big-league ball.

Minor-league teams of the forties like the San Francisco Seals, Jersey City Giants, Milwaukee Brewers, Rochester Red Wings, Toledo Mud Hens, or Kansas City Blues had vigorous lives of their own. They, too, had local fans who supported them through thick and thin and who liked to follow the big-league progress of their stars who made it upward and to welcome big leaguers past their prime who used minor-league teams as a ladder of descent out of baseball.

But soon TV stations began to broadcast major-league games in minor-league towns. Even loyal fans could not resist watching the national stars on their screens instead of their local favorites. More and more Jersey City or Rochester sets were tuned into the Giants and Yankees. Fewer and fewer people went to the park. A big TV audience meant more advertising revenue for the major-league owners of the minor-league teams. So they kept piping games into farm-team towns and quietly destroyed the audience for small-town ball. By the 1970s the minor-league game was played in fewer places, at night, to tiny crowds.

Nor did it end there. Major-league owners, wanting more TV money, ran national telecasts of important contests and pooled the revenues. But this hurt the attendance of weak teams. No one went to the ball park to watch, let us say, the eighth-place Boston Red Sox, when they might catch, on television, a collision between the pennant-bound Yanks and second-place Cleveland Indians. So major-league attendance, too, slumped.

Then the stricken owners began to listen to bids from communities without big-league teams. These cities promised new stadiums, tax breaks, and ripe new markets for telecasting. Beginning in 1958, when the New York Giants and Brooklyn Dodgers moved to San Francisco and Los Angeles respectively, major-league baseball embarked on a career of expansion and "franchise hopping" that is still in full swing.

The world would not necessarily be poorer. But baseball had been something essentially local. It was a cow-pasture game that mobilized city residents to mutual pride in the accomplishments of "their" Dodgers or Pirates. Each of its teams had a local style and image. Now it was a nationwide spectacle, played for the entertainment dollar. The crowning irony was that, although it did well enough, actually baseball as a TV show was inferior to professional football. It was the fast-moving collision-filled gridiron game that became most watched on home and barroom screens.

*Homogenization and reform: the case of Selma.* Television, in short, tended to reduce the force of local loyalties and customs by replacing local audiences with a national one. Yet not all local customs deserved immortality. Midway through the 1960s, another aspect of TV power was dramatically shown.

On March 7, 1965, a small group of blacks from Selma, Alabama, under the leadership of the Reverend Dr. Martin Luther King's Southern Christian Leadership Conference, set out on a 70-mile "march" to the state capital at Montgomery. Their purpose was to petition Governor George Wallace for more respect for their voting rights. As the group crossed a bridge over the river at the town's edge, they found double lines of local police and state troopers drawn up awaiting them. Through a bull horn Colonel "Al" Lingo, commander of the state forces, informed them that their march was an illegal threat to "highway safety" and that they must disperse.

The group paused to consider: Some knelt to pray. Then, before TV cameras from the national networks, the state troopers advanced, firing tear-gas grenades and swinging their billy clubs. In seconds the march was a scene of weeping, bleeding blacks struggling to flee the savagery of the Alabama police. And within hours the scene was being played before the horrified eyes of millions who were watching the evening newscasts in the nation's big cities.

The next day, King asked for all those who wished to "bear witness" of their support of black Alabama citizens to come to Selma. A great outpouring of people took place. Within a few weeks U.S. court orders had legalized the march to Montgomery. It turned into a major public-relations triumph for King's movement and generated pressures on Congress that led to passage of the Voting Rights Act of 1965.

This could hardly have come about without television, which had also showed, in 1963, Birmingham police dogs and fire hoses turned upon black demonstrators. The unblinking eye of national attention caught Southern sheriffs in its glare and made it impossible for the worst of them to continue their "local customs" of a century. Television did not convert the nation to racial liberalism. It simply made the open and violent forms of racism visible, and it dramatized the struggle against them that helped bring them to a halt.

*The plastic gadget*

Along with the computer, the jet, and the TV camera came a series of inventions of the fifties that brought down the costs of a number of consumer items to the point where they could attract a wholly new set of customers. Some examples and their impact follow.

*Transistors, plastics, and youth cult.* The development of transistors (tiny amplifying devices that took up much less space than the traditional vacuum tube) along with various kinds of plastics that replaced costly metal and wood in the cabinets underlay the great boom in the so-called audio industry. In 1939 radios were almost always heavy objects, sitting in splendid majesty in living rooms as one of a family's most prized and costly purchases. Phonographs were likewise heavy and costly. They played thick, 78 rpm records that gave only a few minutes of music on a side.

By 1969, however, the shirt-pocket radio, retailing at under $10, was a commonplace. And while phonograph equipment could run into the hundreds of dollars for expensive speakers, tape decks, and amplifiers, it was possible, for $100 or so, to buy a compact set that could easily be taken to a college dormitory or (with batteries) to a beach. A large supply of plastic long-playing records was well within the range of a middle-class youngster's pocket money.

Youth is stressed, because it was this technological development that underlay the enormous spread of popular music—rock, folk, country, and western—whose audience was not yet adult. For the first time, youth as a distinctive group had found a voice of its own. It was the eight-to-eighteen, or at least the twelve-to-twenty-one group, that tuned in its transistor radios to find out what was going on in the musical world and then rushed to the stores to buy the latest hits. This was something they could afford even when cars, trailers, boats, expensive cameras, and the other toys of their parents were still beyond them. Once, young people had had to stand in line awaiting admission to the world of adult culture. Now they were sustaining a culture of their own. So technology, too, contributed to the developing problem of communication between generations.

*The world of abundance and the looters.* The cheapening of component parts through the discovery of synthetics also made it possible for manufacturers to increase enormously the range of goods supplied to the middle class. As in the twenties, installment buying spurred people to a carnival of consumption. In suburban developments row on row of cheaply built houses arose. And in each of them could be found nylon carpeting and drapes and plastic dishware made to look like imitations of fine china. And in each there were electric washers and dryers, toasters, hair dryers and curlers, toothbrushes, mixers, blenders, power saws, movie projectors, ice-cream makers, hot lather dispensers, and whatever else engineers could create and TV pitchmen sell. And in the garages stood not only cars but also fiberglass boats, camping tents and trailers, snowmobiles, fishing rods, skis, and other items to amuse people on their two-to-four-week vacations and during the long holiday weekends, which sent almost the entire population churning out onto the roads.

All of this was a tremendous drain on energy and resources, first severely felt in the oil pinch of early 1974. It also had painful social results. It defined people by their possessions. It made "keeping up with the Joneses" a constant struggle, as there were always more things that the Joneses could get, which you then had to have. The "rat race" was the appropriate name for that nerve-racking business. Moreover, although it *appeared* to reduce the gap between classes by putting the one-time luxuries of the rich in the homes of the middle class, it widened the differences between the middle class and the poor.

For ghetto dwellers and rural pensioners saw, on television each night, the model homes of "typical" Americans, bursting with consumer goods that were beyond them. They burned with a hostility and self-hate that is not yet fully measured. Perhaps its extent was suggested, however, during the riots in the black ghettos of Watts, Newark, New York, Detroit, and other cities between 1965 and 1967. One of the commonplace sights of those explosions was that of parades of rioters breaking into appliance stores and carting away TV sets, fans, air conditioners, and electric frying pans.

Part of the motive was possibly to resell these commodities for cash. But many of those who took them were simply acting from a longstanding desire to have what "whitey" seemed to have as a matter of course. The rioters did not rush to the courthouses or the business buildings to smash the legal and institutional structures of racism. Instead, culture patterns directed them unerringly, first, to set fire to their own dispiriting decayed homes and, secondly, to try to lay hold of the goods that filled the homes of their "oppressors."

*The throwaway economy: the case of the foaming rivers.* Finally, we come to one more example of how inventions changed relationships among localities and classes. A throwaway culture, which wrapped everything in plastic bags and metal cans, was creating enormous disposal problems. Sewage plants and factories also discharged more and more poisonous wastes into lakes and streams. And the areas polluted by garbage were not always the areas that created it.

A good example arose in the sixties. It was discovered that many lakes and

*"O, beautiful, for spacious skies . . .*
*. . .*
*O beautiful, for patriot's dream*
*Across the busy years*
*Thine alabaster cities gleam*
*Undimm'd by human tears"*

*One kind of patriots' dream—of a mighty America—has been fulfilled by growth and technology. But what happened to the spacious skies, the alabaster cities, and the shining sea? Here is Los Angeles, a city of celluloid dreams and freeways. What answer does it give?*

rivers were beginning to be covered with foamy scum and to lose their fish populations. Research showed that the answer lay in a strange chain of events. Laundry-detergent manufacturers had been putting new chemicals, including phosphates, into their products, to "guarantee whiter washes." Many of these chemicals did not break down as they were washed through sewage systems in the waste water. They poured into lakes and streams unaltered. The high phosphates nourished algae in the lakes. The algae multiplied and consumed oxygen. The lack of oxygen killed fish. City housewives doing their laundry might be ruining not only their own water supply but also fishing spots and natural scenery for countryfolk hundreds of miles away.

Ecological destruction of that kind was a national problem, but its immediate impact was only felt in some places. As another example, strip mining of coal in Appalachia was undertaken to feed the huge fuel appetites of power plants churning out kilowatts of electric power for city apartments. Ugly scars and wasted lands were the result in the mining areas. The issue posed was well put in the title of a magazine article in August 1973: "Shall We Strip Mine Illinois and Kentucky to Air Condition New York?"

Nation and nation, section and section, class and class—all had their relationships altered. There was, finally, a third category of relationships touched by affluence and technological revolution.

## *Changes in Relationships of Individuals to Themselves and Their Families*

The last set of changes we shall look at stem from revolutionary discoveries in chemistry, particularly the chemistry of the body. How did these change the nature and quality of life for modern Americans? Here are some key points, to which you may be able to add others that you have observed. The changes in this area opened up deep questions of personal morality for continuing debate.

### *The pill*

Beginning in the late 1950s, drug companies put on the market birth-control pills that were not very costly and almost always were effective. Though they required a doctor's prescription, such prescriptions were not difficult to obtain. What this meant was that women, both married and single, had greatly increased control over whether or not they would conceive a child as a result of sexual intercourse. They did not have to depend upon male initiative in contraception. Nor did they have to rely on mechanical and other devices that were not always immediately available. Provided they remained "on the pill," they were as free to indulge in sex without pregnancy as any male. Some of the though-provoking results that might be traced to this development follow.

*The case of the new morality and the new pornography.* Freed from worries about pregnancy, young men and women began in small, but significant, numbers to live together without marriage. Since marriage was already under siege from rising divorce rate, this practice seemed to be another attack on it. Setting aside for the moment the religious and ethical questions involved, any real weakening of marriage raised urgent social questions. The whole pattern of a young person's life had been childhood, then work, marriage, and the responsibility for raising a family. With that changed, basic views of how people should behave might be changed. And marriage was more than romantic coupling. It was also a community-recognized arrangement for carrying on family names and identities and for sharing property and passing it on to new generations. What would be the long-range consequences of making it obsolete? Or of creating a situation in which fewer marriages resulted in children? Or in which many people went through several marriages in their lifetimes? Would the end product be new freedom? Or moral decay? The biochemical possibility of easy contraception opened the whole subject of human mating to new questions. They might be asked by only a few, but they had not been asked at all previously.

Some claimed, too, that an increasing concern with sex in films and literature was a partial by-product of the pill. When sex had primarily been regarded as a potential source of the creation of new life, it had serious emotional and cultural overtones. Of course, there had been extramarital sex and casual sex before the pill. But the sex act was still connected to the possible carrying on of the chain of human existence. Divorcing sex from procreation, some said, made the act shallower. It forced the partners to expect more in emotional and physical pleasure from sex. It released a flood of previously repressed fantasies that equated sex with possession, power, and many things other than the continuation of life.

*The case of women's liberation.* A "new feminism" was given a great push forward by the publication, early in the 1960s, of a number of books such as Betty Friedan's *The Feminine Mystique.* They insisted that women take a new look at themselves and recognize that they had a full range of human potentialities that went beyond wifehood and motherhood. Many forces shaped the women's movement. But clearly it could not have received its new injection of life without the impact of easy contraception. Contraception made motherhood a choice, not a necessity. And once choice was opened up to women, it was natural for them to examine the reasons for their choices, the social framework within which they had been contained and limited. So the biochemical revolution had altered one of the most fundamental of human perceptions—one's view of one's self as a being with a particular gender.

### *Consciousness altering from Miltown to LSD*

In the fifties, medical researchers discovered that certain special substances could be manufactured in laboratories. They had a soothing effect on emotional states such as nervousness, depression, anxiety, and the like. Presently, a number of "tranquilizers" emerged. Fundamentally, these were drugs that altered states of consciousness. There is no direct line from the tranquilizer culture of the 1950s to the drug culture of the 1960s. There had long been a "drug problem" (and alcohol was a kind of drug, too) but it was usually confined to the lower and "criminal" classes. It only took on a new dimension when it spread to middle-class youth and was defended as a necessary breakaway from the rational, calculating kind of mentality that was producing the dehumanized and horrible world of the bomb and people-processing machines.

But alcohol and tranquilizers and other drugs had one thing in common. They changed, by chemical means, human awareness and consciousness. New drug research tended to show that the capacity of people to feel and think and to recognize what they were feeling and thinking was only a biochemical and electrical function. It could be controlled and manipulated. That raised the possibilities of deliberate adventures in sensation. And it also opened possibilities that were terrifying. These included mass control of people through required drug injections or insertion of chemicals into food and water supplies. Or it meant, possibly, the creation of a race of human robots managed by a superstate, through these means or by electrodes implanted in the brain.

*Medical miracles and the definition of life*

The 1950s and 1960s also saw the coming of miracle antibiotics that swept old diseases out of existence. There were new machines such as artifical kidneys and heart pacemakers that could prolong life in cases in which it once would have been impossible. And, finally, there were important breakthroughs in life-prolonging organ transplants. But these, too, raised difficult questions.

1. Antibiotic miracle drugs were not universally available throughout the world. What would happen when mortality rates fell in developed countries but not in underdeveloped ones? Would there be have-not nations condemned to watch others evade mass death while they themselves had no escape? Alternatively, if such drugs became widely available in underdeveloped nations to reduce mortality and if there were no corresponding reductions in the birth rates due to cultural or other inhibitions, what would happen to the already rising world population, which was threatening intolerable pressure on the world's resources and foodstuffs? Medical miracles might be the source of a new Malthusianism—the doctrine that if natural checks on population (wars, famines, diseases) are eliminated, human beings will crowd themselves off the planet.

2. Within the United States itself, the cost of miracle drugs and medical machinery escalated until only a tiny handful of the very rich could afford them. (What kept the poor and middle class in the competition for such services at all was the availability of clinics and insurance plans.) But, ultimately, decisions would have to be made about who should get to use a limited number of such devices. What should such decisions be based on? On the ability to pay? If the shocked answer was "certainly not!" then what *was* the answer?

3. The possible prolongation of life through artificial means raised the question of "human vegetables." It was possible for the dying to be kept alive technically—that is, with heartbeats and respiration but without consciousness—for months and years at tremendous costs to their families and indirectly, of course, to society. It seemed wrong to do this, and yet who could decide

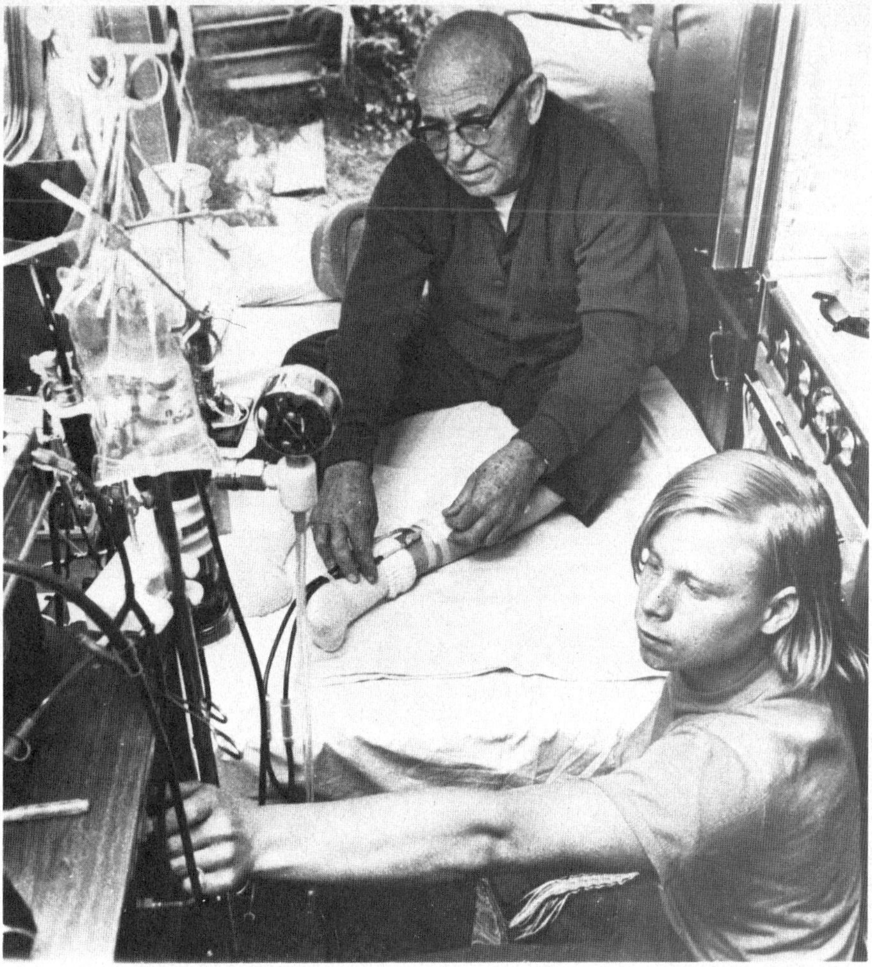

*The dialysis machine, the contemporary medical miracle of the artificial kidney, becomes almost commonplace for this man who travels with the machine in a special truck. A young grandson helps him get set for a six-hour session that will clean the life-threatening poisons from his bloodstream.*

when to "pull the plug" and terminate life? Doctors? Families? Society, through some kinds of committees?

4. In fact, the whole nature of the vital process was in question. With the possibility of easy abortions in the 1960s, an argument had sprung up as to when and whether, in fetal development, the fetus really begins to be "human" as we interpret the term. Abortion before that moment—if in fact that moment did not occur at the instant of fertilization, as antiabortionists claimed—might be defended. After that moment, even proabortionists conceded, it was possibly

murder. So, in effect, society and humanity really found themselves faced with choices about when life *begins* and *ends*, concerns that had previously been beyond their need to consider. Ultimate decisions once thought to be Nature's or God's were now those of men and women.

## *Conclusion*

Those were exhilarating and frightening prospects. Much of what we have studied in this chapter seems to have little to do with conventional history. Yet conventional history itself—the record of governments and their doings—might be in the process of becoming an obsolete method of explaining human development. The fact was that the post-1945 era was one in which the very elements of human self-definition were being changed. Was humanity climbing to new heights of godhood? Was it making a Faustian bargain? Faust was given knowledge of all things and the magical power to change the natural order of space and time. But in return for such godlike abilities, he had to surrender his soul to the devil.

Faust does not have to be the model. It is still possible to take a nineteenth-century optimistic, religious view and say that these innovations were steps toward final unity with God, when each individual's mind would see what only His mind had seen. But however a man or woman thought these problems through, it was necessary to recognize that new human powers were straining old frameworks. Humanity still lived with institutions created in different times. Much of the stress on old habits came not from the mistakes and follies of human beings but from the triumphs of the mind. That was the irony of the twentieth century!

## *FOR FURTHER READING*

There are so many books that discuss our contemporary problems that the only difficulty is in choosing the right handful. To begin with, some of the appalling potentialities of nuclear weaponry are dealt with in the official history of the Atomic Energy Commission by Richard Hewlett and E. L. Anderson. Its first volume, *A History of the U.S. Atomic Energy Commission: The New World*, 1939–1946, vol. 1 (1962), is a good introduction to the theoretical problems and limits of the bomb. As for the media, Marshall McLuhan's *The Global Village* (1968) presents a challenging interpretation of how the TV "revolution" changes the entire structure of human thought.

Computers and their meaning are dealt with in Jeremy Bernstein, *The Analytical Engine* (1963) and a groundbreaking work on the impact of our modern life-style on the environment is Rachel Carson's *Silent Spring* (1962).

The complexities of urban "sprawl" are handled thoughtfully in Jane Jacobs, *The Death and Life of Great American Cities* (1962), but some attention should be paid to an earlier survey by the editors of *Fortune* magazine entitled *The Exploding Metropolis* (1958).

The revolt of women made possible by "the pill" has produced a large literature, but the groundbreaking study that started it all was Betty Friedan, *The Feminine Mystique* (1963). Likewise, the revolt of youth, made possible by the inventions that nourished a separate youth culture, is treated in many works. Some made a stir in their time: Charles Reich, *The Greening of America* (1971) and Theodore Roszak, *The Making of a Counter Culture* (1969). To get the full flavor of disaffected youth in the sixties, though, read James S. Kunen, *The Strawberry Statement* (1969).

The fullest thrust of the technological revolution was felt in the sixties, and is dealt with in William O'Neill, *Coming Apart: An Informal History of the 1960s* (1971).

---

*Computer photo subject: Abraham Lincoln*

# THOUGHT PROVOKERS

*The period of quick and drastic change that began after 1920 seemed to have no end to it. There was prosperity, then depression, then war, then renewed prosperity—all to the relentless tempo of growth and invention. Almost all of the basic beliefs that America had officially endorsed in the preceding centuries underwent some weathering. Men, women, families, and institutions changed their behavior in many significant ways, but often they failed to recognize or to acknowledge what they were doing. And it was often the degree of acceptance of new styles of existence that earmarked groups. "Old" and "new" Americans, educated and uneducated, blue collar and white collar, were distinguished from each other by their embracing or rejecting certain modern attitudes. This can be studied in many ways by focusing on the social shifts that followed economic ups and downs or on the introduction of wonder gadgets to the marketplace.*

*For example, you might ask what the stock market boom of the twenties, in which small investors were encouraged to plunge, did to the old Puritan prohibition on gambling? Or again, given the strong emphasis of the "work ethic" on the value of production, how did the growing number of sales, clerical, and administrative workers justify their economic function? What did they claim to "produce"?*

*How did the image presented by Coolidge illustrate that millions of Americans were still tuned into the values defended by Tennessee and Bryan in the "monkey trial"? And how would you evaluate this proposition: The real final blow to traditional authority, embodied in figures such as ministers, educators, and fathers, was given by the Depression, which finished off the work of prosperity in eroding confidence in the past? How does the story of the twenties and thirties show the connection between a society's economic health and its patterns of respect or its accepted social goals?*

*In politics, class, locality, and style have much to do with a candidate's acceptance. If Al Smith had been a Catholic from an old, established family dating back to colonial days, like the Carrolls of Maryland, would the reaction to him have been the same? What had to happen in the United States between 1928 and 1960 to make it possible, finally, for a Roman Catholic, John F. Kennedy, to be elected president?*

*Some elections are not particularly divisive or decisive; others are. Four particularly significant ones were those of 1828, 1860, 1896, and 1936. All are discussed in earlier chapters and the last is studied in Part Seven. What did they have in common that might account for their being characterized as turning points?*

*Turning to the growth of the modern, bureaucratic state, how would you compare the role of government in creating the atomic energy and space programs with the role of the English government in the 1600s in fostering colonization (discussed in Chapter 20)? And that of the*

*United States in the* 1860s *in helping to build the first transcontinental railroad? (The process was described in Chapter* 14.*) What conditions tend to involve governments of so-called free-enterprise nations in economic activities? When, in other words, do such governments abandon free enterprise? And for whose benefit?*

*Finally, as an exercise in measuring the pervasive growth of federal power, try for one day to keep a record of every reminder of that government that you see. Here are some hints: An obvious place to begin is to look in your wallet or purse. Next try your mailbox. And do not forget to read the gasoline pump information carefully the next time you fill up your car.*

*The chapter on the technological breakthroughs of the fifties poses most of its own questions. But you might look for a few comparisons and connections between the* 1920s *(discussed in Chapter* 22*) and the* 1950s *and* 1960s. *How did the "youth revolt" in the first case compare with that in the second? Was there a difference between jazz and rock, drinking prohibition liquor and smoking pot, wearing short skirts and wearing jeans? If so, what accounted for them? How did the credit-card economy, made possible by the computer, compare in its social results with the introduction of the installment plan? Did the nature of entertainment and advertising change as it shifted from newspapers to radio to movies to television? How did television watching affect family life, in comparison with going to the movies? And as a final thought provoker, how did some of the "conscious-raising" experiments of the* 1960s *(with drugs, for example, or Eastern cults) compare with the religious revivalism of the early* 1800s *described in Chapter* 7*? Do things really stay the same the more they change?*

# PART EIGHT: SMALL WORLD,

BIG POWER

*The most overpowering fact of American life in the past generation has been the deep engagement of the United States with the rest of the world, which for so long it seemed to be ignoring. Only twenty-six years after rejecting the Treaty of Versailles, the United States emerged from World War II as the world's superpower. It was undamaged by conflict, possessed billions of dollars, and controlled the world's most terrible weapon.*

*The nation that had been a child of European settlement and immigration now undertook the job of maintaining international order. It soon found itself confronting the Soviet Union in a test of power and will. And that confrontation committed Americans to what they had once deeply feared. They had to sustain a large standing army. They had to ally themselves with other nations all over the globe. And, in addition, they were forced to give massive economic help to "client" nations, in order to keep them from falling into the grip of communism. Or at least so it was believed.*

*Along with a global economic-assistance and alliance program, and a mighty fleet, air force, and army, went a deep concern with "security." Fears that once would have been strange to Americans now haunted them. Would allies or neutral nations be subverted stealthily by internal conspiracies? Would our atomic and defense secrets be stolen from us by spies? Such fears were deepened when the Soviet Union emerged with nuclear weapons in 1949. In the climate of terror the United States created agencies of political surveillance and counterrevolution. It set up part of the apparatus of a police state, in order, it was claimed, to protect itself.*

*How did the sudden expansion of the military, intelligence, and security agencies of the United States affect national life? And what did it do to our own self-image and to our role abroad? Were we seen by other nations as we once had been? Were we considered a model experiment in democracy? Or a pillar of stability, even at the expense of other people's desire for freedom and change? Or as the last defender of freedom in a troubled world? And how did the American people react to these various possible new identities?*

*Chapter 26 discusses these and other questions: How did the enormous global outreach of the American economy affect American life? What happened when American engineers and attorneys, salespeople and government experts were at work in territories stretching from the Andes to Saudi Arabia? Was there really what some critics called a Coca-colonization of the world by Americans? What did that do to the heirs of those who founded a tiny coastal republic in the 1780s, called it the United States of America, and hoped it would be a beacon to humanity?*

*Chapter 27 looks at an actual episode that weaves together the answers to many of these questions. Beginning in the late 1950s, the United States found itself involved in the support of an anti-Communist government in the small Indo-Chinese state of "South Vietnam"—itself an artificial creation of nationalist revolt in Asia combined with cold war politics. That American concern for the fate of a particular political group in Saigon somehow broadened into a deep commitment. By* 1965 *the commitment led to a full-scale undeclared war that lasted for eight years. At least two American presidents insisted that the whole future security of the United States was involved deeply enough to warrant continuing the fighting, even at a heavy toll in lives and resources. This viewpoint was challenged by a number of Americans. Tension over the issue led to some of the most bitter episodes in national political history since the Civil War. When the war ended for America with the withdrawal of U.S. troops early in* 1973, *there was not even agreement on whether victory, defeat, or a draw had been achieved. The collapse of South Vietnam in April of* 1975 *left American still arguing about where the responsibility lay.*

*The chapter on the war will not try to settle those disputes, but it will attempt to show how they grew out of different interpretations of the needs and responsibilities of the United States as a world power. We will see what forces led different groups in society to adopt clashing positions on the war, instead of adopting the near unanimity that had marked the home front in World War II. As in our earlier chapters on the United States and the world, we will try to draw the connections between a people's behavior among themselves and with regard to other national communities.*

*Our final chapter, Chapter* 28, *attempts to show how the evidence of the past can be read in many different ways. Just as the hard facts of an individual life may be undisputed but yield different interpretations to friends, relatives, and enemies, a nation has an "objective" history of events that happened and a number of "past portraits." The experiences and achievements of the American people as a whole can look differently to a young person or to an old one, a black or a white, a woman or a man, a "success" or an "outsider." Some have argued that a single vision of the past, shared in by everyone, is an absolutely necessary condition of national unity. (History of that kind has been cynically described as "a pack of lies agreed upon.") But there is another view, which holds that true unity can only come when every citizen respects the right of every other to seek his own truth in his own way. In such a society men and women would agree only on the necessity of continuing to ask difficult questions about the meaning of past and present experience. And people would also agree to live together* peaceably *just because there are no "final" answers to be forced on life.*

*Western peoples have come to adopt this attitude about religion and science in modern times. They have yet to embrace it in other areas, such as political life. And national history has long been taught as a means of educating young people to endorse the political machinery under which they live. Part Eight attempts to open your minds to the possibility of other approaches.*

# *chapter* 26

# *From isolation to Coca-colonization and beyond*

Platform speakers loved to quote the following advice, especially in the Midwest, where the currents of isolationism ran strong, where "foreigners" were believed to be touched with a bit of the devil, and where even eastern cities like New York and Boston seemed slightly un-American. And its terseness and strength made it quotable indeed:

> Europe has a set of primary interests which to us have none, or a very remote relation. Hence she must be engaged in frequent controversies, the causes of which are essentially foreign to our concerns. . . .
>
> Why forgo the advantages of so peculiar a situation? Why quit our own to stand upon foreign ground? Why, by interweaving our destiny with that of any part of Europe, entangle our peace and prosperity in the toils of European ambition, rivalship, interest, humor, or caprice.

The author was George Washington, warning his countrymen of the perils of mutual defense treaties in his Farewell Address in 1796. But, always prudent, he went on to add that "we may safely trust to temporary alliances for extraordinary emergencies." Isolationist orators in the 1920s and 1930s tended to ignore that part. They focused instead on the emotional core of the message: Americans were special, different, better than the Old World's warring, greedy nations.

And yet, 170 years after the Farewell Address, in 1966, the United States had become a partner or associate in three major alliance networks in Europe, the Middle East, and Southeast Asia. It also had bilateral (two-power only) treaties with dozens of other countries providing for "mutual assistance." But the assistance was almost all from the United States to the other partners. In order to provide it 275 major American bases rose in 31 countries. The descendants of Washington's audience were maintaining more than a million soldiers, sailors, and airmen in places as diverse as Ethiopia, the Ryukyu Islands, the Azores, Thailand, West Germany, South Korea, and Turkey. And about one-half million of those were in active combat in Indochina.

*Wide-Gauge Questions of Diplomatic History*

What caused such a stunning turnabout? To answer that question in full would plunge us into a bitter historical debate. Some writers who support the official declarations of our government believe it was a fatal necessity. The United States was forced to answer the threats of aggressor nations who were sworn enemies to American ideas of freedom. We could not allow Fascist powers in the 1940s or Communist powers in the 1950s and 1960s to destroy other democracies, or else we ourselves would someday stand alone and in danger. So we took up arms, despite our love of peace.

Other historians find that interpretation is moralistic and self-serving, especially for the period after 1945. They claim that the biggest fact of international life in the 1950s and 1960s was the huge growth of the American economy's outreach. American products and American investment dollars marched steadily over the globe to the drumbeat set by the boom at home. The United States had to make sure, then, that as much of the world as possible would stay under governments sympathetic to the hopes and plans of American capitalism—that is, governments that would not bar American products or grab American properties within their boundaries. The umbrella of American power was spread over an economic empire created by gigantic U.S. corporations.

Most of the debate centers on the post-1945 confrontation with Soviet Russia, and later with Communist China, which came to be known as the cold war. Between the "cold war apologists" who take a pro-American position and their opponents, the "cold war revisionists," there is a third possible interpretation. Without blaming or moralizing, it only notes that the growth of Russian and American power was inevitable. After 1945, world stability collapsed. Pieces of the old French, British, and Dutch empires in Africa and Asia floated free on a tide of revolutionary nationalism. Germany, Japan, and Italy, the losers, were broken and exhausted, but so were France and Britain. Thus there was a power vacuum that would naturally be filled by strong nations that found security in situations they could control. The United States, unhurt by the war, was chief among these. The Soviet Union—badly hurt but strong enough to recover—was another and, in 1945, the only other. Each country struggled to create a world safe for its own needs as it saw them.

This last theory simply sees that despite differences between Communist and capitalist "imperialism," they are both reflections of the way great nations automatically operate in a world of uncertainty. But if it avoids the issue of cold war guilt, it raises another historical problem: the matter of determinism. If great industrial nations need a stable world and if the world as it is can only be peaceful under the control of a few superstates, then any great industrial nation must try to become such a state. And the United States was helplessly set on the road to great-power status as soon as its post–Civil War industrial boom began and as soon as some of the older powers of the world began to lose their grip on things.

All of these versions of the past are debatable. But, as we turn for the last time to foreign policy, the intention is to spur debate, not to announce impossible final truths. As we saw in Chapters 19 through 21, diplomatic history can open doors to many kinds of general thinking about human destiny. The pages that follow will try to set out the record of how the United States penetrated the world's markets and councils of power. They will provide material for many probes into the meaning of the American experience. There is, for example, the question just raised: Was our post-1945 leap to empire "inevitable"? If so, was

*CHRONOLOGY*

| | |
|---|---|
| 1933 | *Hitler comes to power in Germany* |
| 1935, 1936 | *Neutrality Acts forbid shipment of war goods to countries at war* |
| 1938 | *Germans seize Austria* |
| 1939 | *Germans take over Czechoslovakia* |
| 1939 | *All-out war begins in Europe in early September* |
| 1940 | *British evacuate their army from France; air "Battle of Britain"* |
| 1941 | *Germans invade Russia in June* |
| 1945 | *May 7, Germany surrenders; Japan surrenders in August* |
| 1945–1963 | *The cold war* |
| 1947 | *The Marshall Plan proposed to help rebuild Europe* |
| 1948 | *Berlin blockade and airlift* |
| 1949 | *North Atlantic Treaty Organization (NATO) formed* |
| 1962 | *Cuban missile crisis* |
| 1967 | *Israel wins the Six-Day War with Egypt and Syria* |

consisted mostly of foodstuffs. But by 1930 almost half of them were manufactured goods, including construction machinery, generators, trucks, autos, railroad cars, steel, and other heavy industrial goods. In turn, American industry depended on large imports of silk, rubber, tin, and copper.

Besides loans and exports, there were also what were called direct investments abroad. These were production centers overseas actually built, owned, or controlled by U.S. corporations. Even before 1914 some great American companies like Eastman Kodak, McCormick Harvester, and Singer Sewing Machines had built overseas plants. They were lured by cheap labor or resources and low taxes. The total of such investments rose from $3 billion in 1919 to $7.5 billion in 1929. Ford and General Motors assembly plants made autos in Canada. Gulf and Standard Oil put up rigs in Venezuela and Turkey. Liberians tapped rubber trees owned by Firestone in Africa. In Central America workers in Honduras harvested bananas on acres that belonged to United Fruit. American dollars and equipment were found all over the world. If proof was needed of how tightly America's economic destiny was tied to the rest of the globe, it was furnished when the Depression hit. It soon engulfed every major nation. When the American economy was sick, all other countries suffered.

## *A Collapsing Peace: The Thirties*

Despite official isolationism, therefore, the United States had a deep involvement with the world of the thirties. Though U.S. citizens did not always recognize it, American needs could be best met by nations that enjoyed orderly growth, stable governments, smooth transitions of power, and peaceful social change. All these things protected business as usual. And all were put in mortal danger by the Depression and a step-up in aggressive behavior by dissatisfied totalitarian nations in the 1930s.

In 1931 Japan, using the excuse of protecting her nationals from banditry, overran the rich Chinese province of Manchuria and set it up as a puppet state controlled by Tokyo. Six years later, finding a fresh "provocation," Japanese troops landed in Shanghai and other coastal cities and marched inland. By 1939 they occupied most of China's richest provinces, claiming that they were only behaving as the United States had done for a long time in the western hemisphere.

In Europe Adolf Hitler came to power in Germany in 1933. His militant and terrifying program exalted Germans as a master race and promised a crusade against "Bolshevism" (his term for all opponents) and the Jews. He wiped out all traces of German democracy, began a process of exterminating his enemies at home, and announced that he would rearm Germany and unite all Germans in Europe under the iron rule of his National Socialist (shortened to

Nazi) movement. Steadily, he moved ahead on his timetable. In 1936 he reoccupied the Rhineland, flinging aside the Treaty of Versailles. In 1938 he seized Austria. Early in 1939 he gobbled up Czechoslovakia. That summer, he demanded that Poland restore the German territories given to her in 1919. Nobody had any doubt that the powerful, rebuilt German army would soon smash into Poland if she resisted.

Hitler found an ally in Italy's dictator, Benito Mussolini. Mussolini came to power in 1922. His Fascist program was founded on an alliance of various enemies of liberalism to destroy "red" dissenters and put some order into Italian life. In twelve years fascism destroyed free thought and activity in Italy's society. Mussolini actually ruled the country through a cowed king and legislature. Early in the thirties, he decided that depression-hit Italy needed a crusade for empire to jolt the economy and soothe discontented workers with a sense of national glory. In 1935 he sent his legions to conquer and annex Ethiopia. In 1939 he seized Albania. Meantime, he and Hitler furnished support to a church- and army-led rebellion against the republican government of Spain. General Francisco Franco, using the aid in a three-year war, from 1936 to 1939, won and made himself dictator of that country. The thirties leaped from crisis to crisis. Great Britain and France, which were supposed to be protecting the Europe they had constructed in 1919, reacted with floundering confusion. They protested, but permitted the various takeovers. Japan contemptuously left the League in 1933. Both nations were hit hard by bad times at home. The British feared the cost of rearmament. The French, thinking themselves safe behind heavy fortifications on the frontier with Germany, were not inclined to help other nations. Conservative French and British politicians feared communism more than fascism or nazism. In power in Paris and London in 1938, they tried to turn Hitler eastward against the Russians. As part of that strategy, when Hitler demanded certain territories from Czechoslovakia in September, Britain and France forced the Czechs to yield after a conference at Munich. Munich thus became a symbol for any policy of "appeasing" a greedy power by feeding it someone else's territory.

But appeasement lasted less than a year. When Hitler marched into the rest of Czechoslovakia in March 1939, the British and French had to join in guarantees to defend Poland, or else lose what little standing they still had as protectors of the peace. Then, in August, Josef Stalin, the Soviet dictator, and Hitler stunned the world with a "nonaggression" treaty. Both found it temporarily profitable to thwart the British-French plan of pitting them against each other. The pact freed Hitler for quick action. He attacked Poland on September 1, 1939. France and Great Britain declared war on Germany two days later. But nothing could save the Poles. Inside of three weeks, invaded first by the Nazis and then by the Russians, the country was destroyed and divided.

*The downfall of Benito Mussolini and Adolf Hitler—shown here at their peak of power in the summer of 1941—was not brought about by cruelties to their own people. Rather, it was their strutting glorification of war and conquest that threatened the established pattern of international dealings on which statesmen and businessmen had learned to count. They were revolutionaries of the right. Eventually the Western democracies, at first seduced by Hitler and Mussolini's anti-Communism, realized their dangerous potential and, with United States help, fought back.*

The next spring saw a series of disasters. In April the Nazis invaded and occupied Denmark and Norway. On May 10, 1940, they smashed through Holland and Belgium into France. In thirty days they drove the British army there to the Channel coast. It escaped to England in an armada of small, civilian boats, leaving all its major equipment behind. Paris fell in mid-June. At the end of the month France surrendered. Through the autumn of 1940 Nazi bombers poured death and fire on British cities, but fierce resistance by fighters of the Royal Air Force kept them from gaining absolute control of the skies. Without that control the Germans did not risk a cross-Channel invasion, which the entire world expected.

In the spring of 1941 Hitler, thwarted at the Channel, turned against his Russian ally. In preparation, German troops, still unbeaten in any big test, overran Yugoslavia and Greece in April. In June, attacking without warning, they invaded Russia. By November 1941 German guns were pounding the suburbs of Moscow. The Japanese, meanwhile, signed a treaty of mutual support with Germany and Italy. Only twenty-two years after the Treaty of Versailles, the world was turned upside down. The winners of 1919, France and Britain, were down; one was beaten, and the other was fighting for life. The Rome-Berlin-Tokyo "Axis," as they called their alliance, was triumphant almost everywhere. How had the United States reacted to these astonishing upsets?

### *America and the Magnetic Pull of War*

We have already seen part of the answer in the Neutrality Acts. There was almost no popular sentiment for joining in any kind of collective-security agreement with the only other big democracies, Great Britain and France. Many Americans were disgusted by Hitler. But there was no majority for risking war to stop him. That lack of mandate for action against aggression was a problem to Franklin D. Roosevelt. For Roosevelt was staunchly anti-Nazi and pro-British. He believed that the safety of the United States would be worthless in a world controlled by Nazi Germany or by a combination of powers that behaved like Germany.

Roosevelt could not prevent passage of the Neutrality Acts. Nor could he try to delay the war before 1939 by joining the British and the French and raising the opposition that Hitler had to prepare against. But the Allied disasters in the war itself opened a conflict in the national mind. Public opinion polls showed that a majority still resisted American intervention but also did not want Britain to lose. There was a gap between the American desire for neutrality and the American wish to save Britain. Into it Roosevelt moved with deft, maneuvering strokes. In the fall of 1939 he got Congress to approve changes in the Neutrality Act that allowed cash sales of U.S. arms to the British and the French. After the fall of France, he used his authority as commander in chief to transfer "surplus" and "obsolete" weapons to the threatened British. Next he negotiated an executive agreement—not subject to Senate ratification—that exchanged 50 "overage" U.S. destroyers for British island bases to "strengthen defense of the Western Hemisphere." Stunned by Axis victories, Congress meanwhile passed a legislation for a crash program of building up land, sea, and air forces. It also enacted the first peacetime draft in our history.

In January 1941 Roosevelt handed Congress the outlines of a so-called Lend-Lease program. Under it the British, who by then no longer had money to buy American armaments, could be "lent" equipment, to be replaced in kind when the fighting was over. After it was passed, Roosevelt used presidential emergency powers to defend the hemisphere and ordered the U.S. navy to convoy Lend-Lease cargoes more than halfway across the Atlantic. German submarines did, in some cases, attack American ships and were in turn fired on. By November 1941 we were actually Britain's partner in an undeclared Atlantic naval war with Germany.

But it was in the Pacific that matters were decided. The Japanese, getting deeper and deeper into China, badly needed such raw materials as oil, rubber, and tin to sustain their war machine. They also had to have rice for their booming population and safe markets for their busy factories. After the summer of 1940 Japan looked hungrily at French Indochina and the Dutch East Indies. Both had what she needed—and all could no longer be protected by their European owners.

But the United States, as we have seen, was more or less committed to contain Japan. Washington made it clear that it would forbid Japanese moves against the Southeast Asian possessions of Hitler's beaten or on-the-ropes enemies. Worse, from the Japanese point of view, the United States kept insisting that the Japanese get out of China. As time went on, the United States began to back its words with economic action. It seized Japanese properties in America and made plans to slap an embargo on Japan-bound shipments of oil and scrap iron. In time, that step could strangle Tokyo's armies in China.

There were forces in the Japanese government that argued for caution. It was better to give a little in China, where the long war was becoming a costly trap, they said. It was better to use diplomatic and economic pressure to gain Japan's goals. But in the late 1930s a militaristic clique had come to dominate Japanese cabinets. They aimed, like American "hawks" in Vietnam thirty years later, for nothing less than a clear-cut victory. And they forced a gamble on the emperor: Strike a quick blow to paralyze the American fleet, move in and seize Southeast Asia while the shock lasted, and then trust that the Americans would make a deal rather than fight a long war. To carry out this design a Japanese carrier force secretly moved across the Pacific in November 1941 while negotia-

WORLD WAR II
EUROPEAN THEATER
Allied offensives
Maximum area of Axis control indicated by heavier line
ATLANTIC OCEAN
NORTH SEA
BALTIC SEA
NORWAY
SWEDEN
IRELAND
GREAT BRITAIN
DENMARK
EST.
LAT.
LITH.
(GER.)
Leningrad
London
4 Normandy Invasion, June 6, 1944
NETH.
GERMANY
Berlin
Warsaw
U.S.S.R.
POLAND
BELGIUM
Reims
Paris
6 V-E Day, May 7, 1945
CZECHOSLOVAKIA
FRANCE
SWITZ.
AUSTRIA
HUNGARY
ITALY
RUMANIA
PORTUGAL
SPAIN
5 Invasion, Aug., 1944
CORSICA
YUGOSLAVIA
BLACK SEA
BULGARIA
Rome
Anzio
ALBANIA
Istanbul
SARDINIA
3 Salerno
Invasion, Sept., 1943
GREECE
TURKEY
Casablanca
1 Africa Invasion Nov., 1942
Oran
Algiers
SICILY
Tunis
TUNISIA
MOROCCO
ALGERIA
CRETE
MEDITERRANEAN SEA
Tripoli
0 100 200 300 400 500
Miles
LIBYA
Alexandria
El Alamein
EGYPT

*When the United States officially entered the war in December, 1941, Hitler's armies had already overrun Norway, Denmark, Belgium, Holland, and France (in 1940), and Yugoslavia and Greece (in the spring of 1941). Forcing the other Balkan countries into neutrality or collaboration, Germany launched an invasion of her ex-ally, Soviet Russia, in June 1941, which reached the gates of Moscow by the year's end. Hitler's only failure until then was his inability to invade or break the spirit of Great Britain. In North Africa, Egypt-based British forces had fought seesaw battles, first with Italian, then German armies, alternately capturing and abandoning desert strongholds like Tobruk in Libya. During the summer of 1942 a massive German drive, coinciding with Japanese Pacific successes, brought the Axis powers to their peak expansion. The German Afrika Korps pushed to the point where it threatened Alexandria, while German armored divisions in Russia drove across the north shore of the Black Sea, and turned southward into the Caucasus Peninsula to link up with the Afrika Korps, hoping to make the Mediterranean an Axis lake, and cut off the Russians totally from the West.*

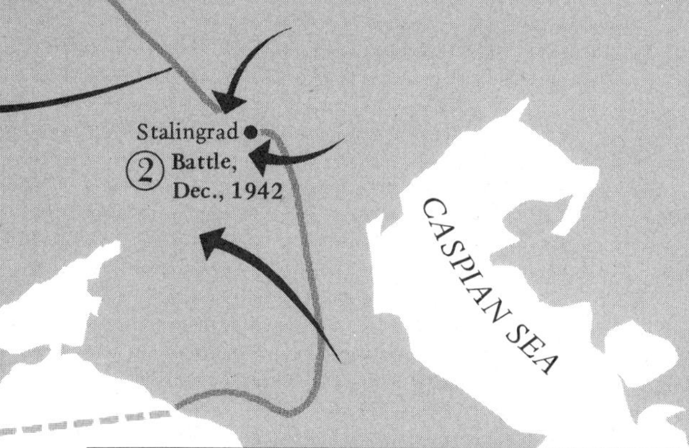


*But the Allies had been building their strength, and their long counterattack began in October. At El Alamein, the British hurled back General Erwin Rommel's Nazis, and began an advance that would carry them all the way to Tripoli in seven months. In November 1942 an American and British amphibious force stormed ashore at several points in Algeria and Morocco ①, and the pro-German French forces quickly surrendered. Within weeks, the Allies were driving eastward toward Tunis against hastily gathered German forces. Rommel was caught in the North African pincers and most of his army surrendered in May 1943. Meanwhile, the Germans reached their furthest point in Russia at Stalingrad ② on the Volga. In a gigantic battle fought in bitter winter weather, the Russians surrounded and captured an entire German army, went on the offensive, and began a slow, massive advance that resulted in the major land battles of the war—a point often forgotten by Western historians.*

*In July 1943, following the momentum of North African victory, British and American armies invaded and overran Sicily. Then, in September, under massive naval and air bombardment, they put ashore an expedition at Salerno ③ in southern Italy. Italy surrendered almost at once, but German armies rushed down the peninsula to contest the Allied advance, mile by mountainous and bloody mile. An attempt to get around the German flank by a landing at Anzio failed—but relentless, costly pressure finally brought the Allies to the capture of Rome in June 1944. By that time, however, a gigantic armada on the English channel was waiting to launch the invasion that would recapture Europe and send the Allies' columns slicing into the vitals of Hitler's realm. D-Day came on June 6, 1944 ④, and after an initial five-division beachhead was established and consolidated, the final phase of the war began. The Allies broke out of their beachhead in July and raced southward and westward. Paris was liberated in August and a fresh invasion force landed in southern France on August 15 ⑤. By September Germany's heartland was being pounded daily by huge American and British bomber fleets; the Russians were advancing steadily through central Europe; and the German armies in the west, exhausted and lacking in supplies, were doomed. A brief German counterattack in the Ardennes forest in December of 1944—the Battle of the Bulge—threw the Allied timetable off and caused a brief setback; but by the last week of April it was all over. The Russians were capturing Berlin street by street; Hitler supposedly committed suicide in his underground bunker; the remaining German forces in Italy surrendered; and on May 7, 1945, the German high command formally and unconditionally ordered all Nazi units to lay down their arms ⑥. V-E Day, the long-sought victory in Europe, had arrived.*

tions were still in progress in Washington. On December 7, 1941, Japanese planes hit Pearl Harbor in a devastating surprise attack that crippled the major American Pacific base.

The next day, as Japanese forces also poured into the Philippines and began operations that would soon conquer Burma, the Malay Peninsula, and the Dutch East Indies, President Roosevelt demanded and got a declaration of war. Within days, true to the terms of the Axis pact, Germany and Italy in turn declared war on the United States. So, in the end, the president had the United States involved in the war in Europe—a development he had been sure would come.

This is not the place to recapitulate World War II. But in sum the Japanese lost their gamble. The United States came back from defeat at Pearl Harbor and in four years fought its way into Tokyo harbor, where the Japanese surrendered in September 1945. In Europe, American forces bore the brunt of invasions that knocked Italy out of the war in 1943 and liberated France by the end of 1944. Then, while Russian armies (supplied heavily through Lend-Lease shipments) smashed into Germany from the east, Anglo-American armies battered their way in from the west. On May 8, 1945, a Germany almost totally occupied by Soviet and American forces surrendered. A few days earlier, Hitler had committed suicide in an underground bunker in Berlin, while the Russians smashed their way to control of the city.

## *Why We Fought and What Came of It*

This dosage of facts is necessary to understand historians' interpretations of how, for the second time in the century, America plunged into a world struggle. It also helps explain some of the results of that participation.

Official and popular writings during the war itself traced the event to aroused virtue. Americans distrusted the Axis powers, which tore up international agreements, exalted militarism and conquest, and invaded neighboring states. Though slow to see the danger at first, in due time they took action. Pearl Harbor convinced the last doubters that Germany, Italy, and Japan must be beaten to make the world a better place to live in. As in 1917, the war became a crusade for international democracy.

But, soon after 1945, these ideas were challenged by a World War II revisionist school, which charged that the war had been unnecessary. Japan, ran their argument, had legitimate interests in Asia, which American diplomats should have at least recognized. And however bad Hitler might have been, there was never any evidence produced that he intended to attack American possessions or interests. Nor did we show much interest in democracy when we allied ourselves with Stalin's Russia to beat Hitler. Why, then, had we gotten into the war? According to the revisionists, it was largely because Roosevelt hoped that a war boom would cure the Depression, which his New Deal program had failed to lift. Furthermore, an internationalist-minded clique, full of admiration for the British, wanted to make the world safe for Anglo-American investments. (It is clear that these arguments showed a midwestern suspicion of eastern, pro-British financial and intellectual leaders that went back to Populist days.) Roosevelt's needless war saddled the United States with debts, postponed attacks on social problems, and created a military and business autocracy.

Truth does not always lie exactly halfway between two positions. Yet it is possible to see some reason in both arguments. Those who criticize our steps toward intervention correctly point out the flaws in the "war-for-democracy" propaganda and the economic and political benefits gained by big business and FDR in the crusade against Hitlerism. But they may underestimate the revolutionary danger of Axis militarism. It was not likely that America could "do business" with powers who tore up treaties, seized the property of their own and other citizens, occupied other nations, and were contemptuous of all international rules. In effect, Roosevelt was claiming that the Axis nations were global gangsters, and society could not work under gang rule. Axis defenders might have answered that the rules were made up by the haves among nations to keep out challengers. Whoever is right in these arguments, it is important to glance at some of the consequences of our entry into World War II. They explain a great deal about the twenty-year period that followed victory. Among the most significant were these:

*The power of the presidency was enormously enhanced.* Roosevelt acted while Congress debated. He traded ships for bases, declared emergencies, held top-level meetings, and could always go on the air to defend his acts. He could keep secret whatever facts he chose in order to protect national security. He could release whichever bits of information helped him to build his case. Once the war was on, he controlled the generals who commanded the armies and armadas of the nation, and so had the same extensive authority as Lincoln and Wilson had had. World War II gave the trend toward the superpresidency another mighty boost.

*Americans adopted a new version of history, which reduced complex matters to stark outline.* They came to believe that war came because the democracies had not been firm enough in time. If all the powers had confronted Japan with an ultimatum in 1931, for example, if Britain had blockaded Italy in 1935, and if the French had opened up with artillery on Germans moving back into the Rhineland in 1936, then the unprepared aggressors would have been forced to back down and behave, and peace would have been guaranteed. The crime of crimes was the sellout at Munich. The "Munich analogy" would be applied again and again in postwar situations. Future demands by a Communist power

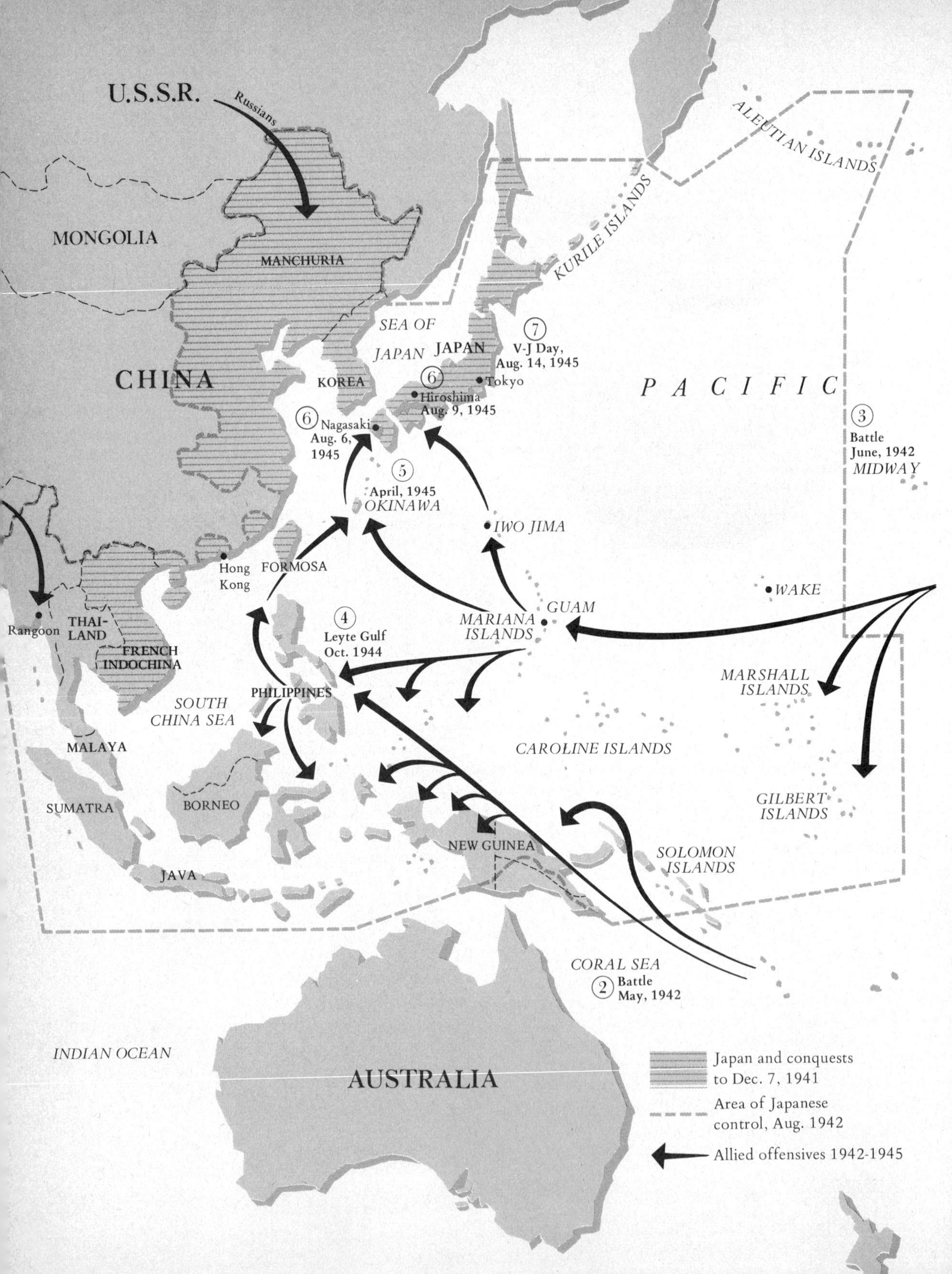

U.S.S.R.
Russians
MONGOLIA
MANCHURIA
CHINA
KOREA
SEA OF
JAPAN
JAPAN
ALEUTIAN ISLANDS
KURILE ISLANDS
7 V-J Day, Aug. 14, 1945
Tokyo
6 Hiroshima Aug. 9, 1945
6 Nagasaki Aug. 6, 1945
P A C I F I C
3 Battle June, 1942 MIDWAY
5 April, 1945 OKINAWA
IWO JIMA
Hong Kong
FORMOSA
WAKE
GUAM
MARIANA ISLANDS
4 Leyte Gulf Oct. 1944
Rangoon
THAI-LAND
FRENCH INDOCHINA
PHILIPPINES
SOUTH CHINA SEA
MARSHALL ISLANDS
MALAYA
CAROLINE ISLANDS
SUMATRA
BORNEO
GILBERT ISLANDS
NEW GUINEA
SOLOMON ISLANDS
JAVA
CORAL SEA
2 Battle May, 1942
INDIAN OCEAN
AUSTRALIA
Japan and conquests to Dec. 7, 1941
Area of Japanese control, Aug. 1942
Allied offensives 1942-1945

# WORLD WAR II PACIFIC THEATER

O C E A N

(1)
Attack
Dec. 7, 1941
Honolulu •
(Pearl Harbor)
HAWAIIAN
ISLANDS

*The lightning surprise attack of Japanese naval aircraft at Pearl Harbor (1) on December 7, 1941, accomplished one major goal. It neutralized the U.S. Pacific battle fleet for at least six months, even though it failed to destroy the four United States aircraft carriers based in Hawaii (they were away on a maneuver at the time). Given this free hand, Japanese forces swept on to numerous victories. In the next six months they occupied the Philippines, the Malay Peninsula, the Netherlands East Indies, and Burma. They landed forces in New Guinea and the Solomon Islands and there seemed a real chance that they might invade Australia; but during the spring and summer of 1942, they reached their limit.*

*In May, a fleet of Japanese transports heading south with reinforcements for New Guinea was intercepted and turned back in a savage fight that inflicted heavy losses in warships and personnel on the Japanese. This battle of the Coral Sea (2) was the first setback for Emperor Hirohito's forces, but it was soon followed by another. In June the Japanese launched a major naval thrust across the Pacific. But their plans were known to the Americans, who had broken the secret Japanese naval code. American carrier planes found the Japanese vessels near Midway Island and, in the June battle of Midway (3) , sank the entire Japanese carrier force making it impossible for them to continue. In a northern Pacific diversion, the Japanese captured the Aleutian islands of Attu and Kiska, but had to give them up in 1943. Then, in August, U.S. Marines landed on Guadalcanal in the Solomons. A devastating series of land and sea actions went on until early 1943, but finally the island was secured.*

*The summer of 1943 found the Japanese position weakening. Japan's main land armies were pinned down on the mainland of China. Her other forces, scattered over many islands, had to be supplied over long vulnerable sea lanes. American industrial power, now at its peak, was daily turning out more ships and planes. The U.S. strategy was to launch submarine war against the Japanese merchant marine and gradually move west from Hawaii and north from Australia seizing key island bases from which air assaults could be launched, meanwhile leaving other Japanese island garrisons to starve. This "island-hopping" technique took two years to bear fruit. In 1943 forces from General Douglas MacArthur's southwest Pacific command completed the reconquest of New Guinea and outlying islands, while marines and sea forces under the command of Admirals Chester Nimitz and William Halsey seized Tarawa in the Gilbert Islands. In June, 1944, amphibious landings planted the American flag over Saipan in the Marianas Islands. The Japanese navy tried to defend the Marianas but was badly mauled, had suffered huge casualties, and lost most of its air power. What was left was destroyed when the Americans invaded the Philippines that fall; the Battle of Leyte Gulf (4) completed the virtual destruction of the Japanese fleet.*

*Soon huge B-29 bombers, based in the Marianas, were hitting Japan itself with incendiary and high explosive bombs. The noose tightened in February of 1945 when U.S. marines captured Iwo Jima in the Bonins, and in April when army and navy forces landed on the island of Okinawa (5) and began their conquest. From Iwo Jima, fighters could fly "cover" missions to protect the bombers, while Okinawa offered a base for staging an eventual invasion of Japan.*

*August, 1945, found the Japanese with cities in ruin, no merchant marine, no fleet, and no hope of victory; but, there were thousands of loyal fighting troops in China and the main islands still ready to defend the Emperor with their lives. On August 6 and 9, however, the United States struck with the ultimate weapon—two atomic bombs which virtually wiped out the cities of Hiroshima and Nagasaki (6) causing hundreds of thousands of civilian casualties. To this day, some Americans doubt the wisdom of dropping the superbombs on a reeling enemy, while others say that it was the only way to prevent an invasion that would have been more costly. In any case, the Japanese asked for terms of surrender. On September 6, 1945, V-J day, Japan's diplomats signed a capitulation on the deck of the U.S.S.* Missouri, *in Tokyo Bay (7). The Emperor remained on the throne, but Japan was to be occupied by the United States and "ruled" by General MacArthur. The long agony had ended.*

would meet firm American resistance, because yielding would be considered "another Munich." A few voices noted that every historical situation is slightly different and that every nation must sometimes consider giving in on an issue. But thoughts of this kind troubled few Americans after 1945.

*Casting the war in ideological terms made for faith in easy solutions.* Anti-Fascist and anti-Nazi books and plays rightly aroused disgust with totalitarian regimes that ruled by torture, secret police, harassment of minorities, and suppression of dissent. But they implied that the war would end such ugly practices in all the world's nation-states. That was a dangerous assumption. It ignored such practices in countries on our side. It encouraged Americans to think that they could guarantee freedom to the whole world, a risky notion, since the world was a big place and freedom was always endangered somewhere on its surface. It gave the United States a sense of self-righteousness and encouraged its citizens to expect too much after the war, especially from the United Nations. We saw earlier how, in the Progressive era, citizens often voted in a reform administration, threw out the rascals, and expected all problems thereafter to solve themselves. The United Nations was seen by many Americans as a "good-government league." And, just as Americans proved impatient with their own reformers when perfection did not immediately follow the election, they became cynical about the United Nations.

*Finally, the war left an enormous economic and power vacuum into which the United States could not help but rush.* Even if isolationist sentiment had surfaced again in 1945, the facts were different from the way they were in 1919. All the European powers were exhausted. There could be no policing of the world without the intervention of the United States, which possessed a superweapon and untapped resources. Nor could the shattered world regain economic health without American help. Without such help, there would be no international customers to trade with the United States.

## *Cold War, 1945–1963: Europe*

For the rest of this chapter we will follow a track parallel to the first part. We will quickly summarize the leading events in the evolution of the cold war. Then, to discover the connections between diplomatic and economic developments, we will survey American business activity abroad. Next we will weigh different theories of what was happening. Finally, we will look at some of the domestic consequences of being a superpower.

It took less than two years for wartime cooperation between the Soviet Union and the United States to crumble. Stalin's forces occupied all Eastern Europe, and he was easily able to wipe out any opponents of communism and put puppet regimes in power. By late 1946 the operation was complete. In Winston Churchill's words an "iron curtain" had descended from the Baltic to the Adriatic. Behind it Soviet Russia dominated the peoples of half of Europe.

Though weakened by the war, Russia still had the world's greatest land forces. And, through her control of Communist parties in Western Europe, she could cause trouble in nations such as France and Italy. As 1947 dawned, American officials were convinced that the Russians might actively be planning a takeover of the rest of the European continent.

A danger point was reached in 1947. A civil war raged in Greece. The antigovernment rebels, allegedly Communist led, were reportedly getting supplies and reinforcements from neighboring Communist Yugoslavia. In March President Truman went before Congress to ask for a grant of $400 million. Part of it would be used to help the Athens government protect itself against this subtle form of invasion. Part of it would go to neighboring Turkey, to allow her to modernize her forces and withstand a possible Russian attack to open the way to the Mediterranean. Congress responded promptly with the money. With the so-called Truman Doctrine of aid for Communist-threatened governments, the United States took up the combative pose it had lacked in the 1930s. This time the "aggressor" would meet resistance, retreat, and keep the peace.

A few months after the Truman Doctrine was announced, the United States undertook the economic rebuilding of Western Europe. This was done through a heavy program of loans, known as the Marshall Plan, after Secretary of State George C. Marshall, who first publicly proposed it. There were good sound business reasons for such a step. But the plan was packaged as another "defense" measure. Americans were told by Truman that Communist parties made most headway among peoples who were hungry and miserable. Therefore, helping a cold, starving Western Europe to its feet was not only humanitarian, but it would also pull the rug out from under Communist plans for subverting other countries.

The year 1948 saw the scene of conflict transferred to Germany, which was divided among Britain, France, the United States, and Russia, pending a final peace treaty. The Russians had encouraged the creation of a Communist police state in the half of the country they held. Berlin was in their occupation zone but by wartime agreement was jointly occupied by all four powers. In midyear the Russians tested Western nerve. They allowed the East German authorities to shut off all road and rail access to the city, threatening it with starvation. The Allies countered with a massive, months-long airlift of food and fuel; and finally the Russians gave in and lifted the barriers. But each day had seen the possibility of a plane being fired on and a new war beginning. By 1949 all hope of peacefully reuniting Germany was gone. Two separate states were born. We recognized West Germany, and the Russians, East Germany.

In 1949, too, the United States took the lead in forming the North Atlantic Treaty Organization (NATO). It was a military alliance at first including Britain, France, Italy, Norway, Denmark, Belgium, the Netherlands (Holland), Luxembourg, Iceland, and Canada. Greece, Turkey, and Portugal later joined. Meantime, stunned to learn that the Russians had developed an atomic bomb, the United States pushed ahead with research to develop the more powerful hydrogen bomb. So did the Russians. They also forged a military alliance among their satellites, known as the Warsaw Pact. By 1955 each of the two superpowers, armed with weapons that could blow up the world, stood at the head of a linked system of dependent nations.

Not only did each country have its formal allies, but it furnished arms and technical assistance to "client" states in Africa and Asia. Latin America remained an exclusively American sphere until 1959. Then Fidel Castro, who had led a successful revolution in Cuba, openly announced his membership in the Communist camp.

*Cold War, 1945–1963: Asia and the Americas*

In Asia, as we saw earlier, the cold war burst into flame in Korea in 1950. In 1954 Eisenhower's secretary of state, John Foster Dulles, hammered together an Asian counterpart to NATO. The Southeast Asia Treaty Organization (SEATO) linked Australia, New Zealand, Thailand, Pakistan, and the Philippines in a defense pact with France, Britain, and the United States. The next year, Dulles gave American blessing to the Middle Eastern grouping known as the Central Treaty Organization (CENTO), in which Britain, Turkey, Iraq, Iran, and Pakistan joined hands to resist Communist expansionism. The United States was not a formal CENTO partner but clearly intended to help any of its members in trouble.

In the late 1950s the world seemed always teetering on the edge of doom. But neither of the two superpowers wanted the ultimate unthinkable moment of pulling the nuclear trigger. In head-on conflict, one side or the other always backed down. The Russians crushed anti-Soviet uprisings in East Germany in 1953, in Hungary in 1956, and in Czechoslovakia in 1968. The victims got no help from the United States. Despite much talk about desiring to liberate Eastern Europe, Washington wanted no involvements in Russia's front yard. In turn, the United States helped to overthrow a Communist government in Guatemala in 1954 and sent marines into the Dominican Republic in 1965—without raising a threat of war.

Only once in the western hemisphere was there a close call. In October 1962 President Kennedy learned that Russian advisers and technicians were building medium-range missile bases in Cuba. He ordered them removed and proclaimed a naval blockade of the island to prevent any more being landed. The world held its breath—until the Soviet head of state at the time, Nikita Khrushchev, gave up and withdrew the missiles.

Other collisions in the Middle East were likewise contained. The Russians befriended Egypt and in 1956 had a chance to show what that meant. The

Egyptian ruler Gamal Abdel Nasser nationalized the Suez Canal. Britain and France, who had once managed it, launched an invasion of Egypt. They were aided by Israel, which feared Egypt. But before the attack could succeed, the Russians threatened to intervene. This time the United States backed away from a face-to-face clash. By refusing to support the invaders, the United States brought the action to a halt.

In 1967 the Russians could not prevent the armies they furnished Egypt and Syria from being wiped out during a lightninglike six-day war with Israel. But when still another round of the continuing Middle Eastern war broke out in October 1973, both the Russians and the Americans, by agreement, pressured the parties into a truce and a peace conference.

As the 1960s dawned, a dangerously armed world was kept from destruction only by mutual fear of nuclear war. It was called the balance of terror. And the United States left the advice of the Farewell Address completely behind. America was deeply involved in arming and protecting dozens of other nations.

*American Multinationals: Investment Marches On*

Meanwhile, the economic reach of American industry grew worldwide. The investments of the 1920s shrank to the level of pocket money compared with those of thirty years later. In 1946 the total was up to $18.7 billion. In 1956 the figure was $49.5 billion. These sums included all types of investments, including American loans to foreigners. The *direct* investments of the United States, which, you will recall, included plants built or owned abroad by Americans, went from $7.5 billion of 1929 to slightly under $12 billion by 1950. Then they shot up to $22.2 billion in 1956, $49 billion in 1965, and a staggering $78 billion in 1970.

What caused the great boom in such investments? First, there was the readiness of hundreds of millions of customers to buy American-made goods. Secondly, it was often cheaper to manufacture abroad than at home, due to lower labor and raw-material costs and taxes. (This was exactly the logic that moved American textile firms from New England into the South between 1890 and 1930.) Every overseas sale of overseas-made items brought higher profit margins. In 1959, for example, Kodak reported that while its foreign sales were up 9 percent, its profits on those sales were up 51 percent.

Lured by such rewards, major American corporations began to become "multinational." At the beginning of the 1960s the Ford Motor Company had 40 percent of its assets (things it owned) and 36 percent of its sales scattered through 27 foreign countries. International Telephone and Telegraph was lodged in 60, Pepsico in 114. Standard Oil of New Jersey had 275 subsidiaries operating in 52 countries. Only one-third of its assets were located abroad, but they earned two-thirds of its overall profits. Some companies, like Heinz or

*The American corporate presence in the so-called developing nations is one of the central facts of world history in the second half of the twentieth century. It has had a profound effect, not only on the people of the United States, but on those of the entire globe. The impact is reflected here, in a single Asian street scene.*

Colgate-Palmolive, had more than half of either their assets or their total sales abroad. A French commentator, Jacques Servan-Schreiber, said that American multinational corporations were almost a world power all by themselves.

Matching private investments was a steady flow of government-provided dollars abroad. They were part of technical and economic assistance programs to underdeveloped or handicapped countries. The Marshall Plan of 1948, a Truman-inspired program known as Point Four in 1949, a Kennedy project called the Alliance for Progress—all poured money and goods into Europe, Africa, Asia, and Latin America. All of these public investments were supposed to help the recipients to banish poverty and fight Communism. "Foreign aid" became a regular annual element in American national budgets.

American money was made visible overseas in gleaming office buildings in foreign cities and in dams and power lines in rural areas. American dollars went into European cash registers when American soldiers and airmen shopped in the towns near their overseas bases. American goods, from motor oil and electric shavers to insecticides and cosmetics, crowded the world's shelves. The "Coca-colonization" of the other continents went on at a rapid clip.

The overall costs were gigantic. Besides the money Congress spent on foreign economic aid, it gave healthy yearly sums to the armed forces of client countries. There were also the costs of maintaining our own overseas military establishment. By 1965 the total of expenses was reaching over $100 billion annually. Even the healthy American economy felt the strain. All the billions spelled out an American interest in a stable world, an interest that was now greater than ever. The question was: How did Americans define a stable world? Was it simply a world under American subjection? Was America to create a new Roman Empire?

### *Wherefores and Results of the Cold War*

To defenders of the cold war, it was wrong to talk of American urges to dominate other nations. The official line of the American State Department remained constant. Our only aim was to have a world in which nations freely chose their own forms of government and were safe from attack by others. Our moves in 1947 had been responses to dangerous Soviet intentions. Only the shield of American power had kept "red" tanks and troops from clanking and crashing down the boulevards of Western European capitals.

In the 1960s such arguments were not accepted uncritically. Some scholars, young and old, reexamined the onset of the cold war. Though hobbled by the lack of nonsecret official records, they pointed out a lack of solid evidence of Russian plans to overthrow any Western government. They also noted that it was easier for the Truman and Eisenhower administrations to extract funds for foreign aid from Congress by dramatizing the threat of world communism.

They went on to say that the crisis atmosphere of the cold war made it easier for leaders to manipulate public opinion, bury mistakes in secrecy, and dodge the responsibilities of democracy. And they pointed out the facts and figures of worldwide American economic expansion, which we have just noted. Our real fear of Communist aggression, they suggested, was simply a glorified kind of greed. We feared that left-wing regimes would seize American properties and cripple American prospects. Our foreign policy was really only to protect nations and governments hospitable to our presence from revolutionary social changes within. Such changes might throw out the admirals, generals, landowners, managers, technicians, merchants, and lawyers who made up an affluent elite, which looked to Washington for inspiration and support.

The argument could not easily be settled, and it simply shows how different eyes may view the same "facts." All the facts may not be fished out of secret archives for years, if ever. But the results of the cold war in American government are clearly visible. And it was a growing awareness of the political and social casts of the cold war that led to a reaction against it.

Some of those costs were ideological and cultural. We noted in Chapter 23 the era of McCarthyism, when a deep suspicion of everything possibly tainted with communism darkened the landscape. That made some people afraid to argue honestly for different policies. And the cold war created pressure toward exaggeration and deceit. Official propaganda, which always had us ranged on the side of freedom and painted the Communists in pure black (or red), oversimplified issues and muddled thought. There were aspects of American life that were far from perfect, and there were countries on the American side that were in no way free. There were always two sides to quarrels between Communist and non-Communist powers. By putting all things in terms of good and bad, facts became easily distorted. And unrelated issues were forced into cold war molds just as, before the Civil War, questions of lands, tariffs, and expansion became mixed up with the slavery issue. Programs of space exploration or aid to education were debated in terms of whether they would help us against the Russians or Chinese.

Democracy in America has always had its share of hot air and error. But in order to thrive it needs open and frank debate over real issues.

The cold war deprived it of those assets. The cold war also sped the creation of superagencies that strained the Constitution. In 1947 Congress created the Central Intelligence Agency (CIA) and charged it with many duties. It was authorized to use whatever "dirty tricks" were necessary to accomplish its intelligence gathering and operational missions. To keep its work undercover it was given a broad shield of secrecy and not required to report its work and budget openly to Congress. Unlike other parts of the government, it did not have to account for what it received or spent.

And its expenditures went for some curious goals. The CIA financed spy flights of U-2 reconnaissance planes over Russia and satellite countries. The camera ships flew out of neutral countries, with civilian pilots at the controls. The CIA underwrote revolt in Guatemala in 1954. It trained Cuban exiles for an unsuccessful landing at the Bay of Pigs in Cuba in 1961 to overthrow Castro. The CIA funneled secret money into trade unions, student societies, cultural groups, and university research centers and used the organizations as "cover" for CIA activities. The members of the agency thought of themselves as loyal Americans doing a difficult and dangerous job. Nonetheless, they were members of a secret state within a state.

Finally, the economic costs of the cold war were full of long-range consequences. For one thing, defense orders and contracts strengthened the grip and dominant position of the largest corporations. In partnership with the huge Department of Defense, these companies made up part of a "military-industrial complex." That phrase was used by President Eisenhower in *his* farewell speech in 1961. He warned that Americans must "guard against the acquisition of unwarranted influence" by this alliance. "The potential for the disastrous use of misplaced power exists and will persist," was his warning.

The gigantic expenses of the warfare state also took resources from critically needed areas of development in the United States. They also affected the U.S. financial position abroad. In the 1940s European countries imported huge quantities of American goods and furnished little of their own in return. They suffered from a "dollar gap," a lack of earnings to convert into dollars to pay Americans. The dollar was prized and highly valued in European currency markets. But by 1969, American spending abroad to maintain U.S. military bases had helped to turn the flow in the other direction. The "balance of payments" was against us. We owed the world more than it owed us at each year's end and had to pay out gold and dollar reserves to make up the difference. The result was a decline in the value of the dollar abroad. This led to trade and banking problems, as it raised our costs of doing business abroad even further. The dollar was also a symbol: When it was in trouble, so was America.

## *The Sixties: High Hopes and Coming Disaster*

These costs and burdens led to a gathering move to reevaluate the cold war after 1960. Meantime, similar problems caused Soviet leaders to take a fresh look at the situation. The world itself was changing. For one thing, there were cracks in the Communist camp. China had broken with Russia in the early 1960s. Various other Communist nations balked at Russian leadership. American allies, too, were thinking matters over. France left NATO in 1966. Other countries thought of doing likewise to reduce their arms burdens and give themselves more flexibility of movement.

The recovered nations of Europe tried to move away from dependence on U.S. aid. They joined in multinational pacts to reduce tariffs among themselves, like the Common Market, created in 1957. The Third World nations of Asia, Africa, and Latin America also were seeking a position that did not tie them firmly to Russia or America.

The rise of new industrial powers, like an again booming Japan, suggested the possibility of a new kind of world order emerging in the seventies. It would have diffused centers of power and fresh kinds of international cooperation. It needed peace to survive, however.

So the old line-ups were faced with shuffling around in the mid-1960s. But before the United States could enter a smooth transition out of the cold war, it stumbled into its most agonizing cold war conflict. It entered a struggle that deepened all of the problems of the preceding twenty years and split and tested the nation down to its very roots. No history of modern America can escape the jolt of considering the Vietnam War.

---

## *FOR FURTHER READING*

American foreign policy in the twenties has often been dismissed as "merely" isolationist, but a different view is presented in two volumes describing Republican secretaries of state: Merlo J. Pusey, *Charles Evans Hughes* (1953) and Elting E. Morison, *Turmoil and Tradition: A Life of Henry L. Stimson* (1960).

As for American diplomacy in the thirties, much is covered in general biographies of Roosevelt. Friendly accounts are T. R. Fehrenbach, *FDR's Undeclared War* (1967) and the older, but beautifully written book by Robert Sherwood, *Roosevelt and Hopkins* (1948). Isolationist critiques are also plentiful, however, and a typical example is Charles A. Beard, *President Roosevelt and the Coming of the War: A Study in Appearances and Realities* (1948).

So far as the coming of the cold war is concerned, there are a number of conflicting accounts. A relatively balanced treatment is J. L. Gaddis, *The United States and the Origins of the Cold War* (1972). A primary source that gives the official version is the first volume of Harry Truman's scrappy memoirs, *Years of Decision* (1955); another source is the memoir of Dean Acheson, *Present at the Creation* (1970). Critical volumes are numerous, but among the sharpest are Donald F. Fleming, *The Cold War and its Origins* (1961) and Gar Alperovitz, *Atomic Diplomacy* (1965). A colorful account of the Potsdam Conference, in which Churchill, Roosevelt, and Stalin tried to redraw the world map is Charles L. Mee's *Meeting at Potsdam* (1975).

Eisenhower diplomacy is covered in Townsend Hoopes, *The Devil and John Foster Dulles* (1973); that of Kennedy in Arthur M. Schlesinger, Jr., *A Thousand Days* (1965); and that of Johnson in various works on Vietnam to be covered in the next chapter.

As for the outreach of American corporations, the best recent book is Richard J. Barnet and Ronald Müller, *Global Reach: The Power of the Multinational Corporations* (1974).

# chapter 27

# The Vietnam war: a recognizable turning point?

We have already noted that it is difficult for historians to interpret current events. They need some distance from the past in order to see its big patterns. But sometimes people are aware that the happenings of the moment fall into a clear arrangement that spells major change. The generation that fought the Civil War knew that, whatever the exact result, the United States would never quite be the same nation again. Lincoln captured that feeling in one of his best assertions: "We cannot escape history." Americans who suffered in the Depression of the 1930s were aware that, somehow, they were in the midst of what one survivor called an earthquake.

"Earthquake" is a good and vivid word for what we mean. The ground shifts. Cracks appear in structures that once were solid. Underground geysers erupt from long-buried pipes. Some buildings collapse, some are burned, some remain. The landscape is devastated. And those who have lived through an earthquake never again have a total sense of safety.

The Vietnam War was that kind of earthquake. No matter what differing opinions people may hold about it, it is easy to see that social and political structures were rocked by its impact. When one news development dominates public debate for years, destroys a president, wrenches the economy, splits parties and classes, and undercuts the Constitution, then that development is a turning point in history.

Let us examine the Vietnam years as a time of dramatic changes in American life and use them as a yardstick against which to judge other such episodes. How do we distinguish a turning point from a slight curve in the road? Mainly by the results, the echoes of events. How loud are they, and how long? After you have finished reading this chapter, you may want to try your hand at selecting and comparing other periods that were actually corridors of decision.

Throughout the story, which is somewhat lengthy and complex, keep in mind a pair of questions: (1) What did the war do to the elements of American society? And (2) how did the war itself represent a weaving together into a final pattern of tradegy the many threads spun in the 1950s and 1960s?

## *Background to Involvement, 1945–1954*

### *The end of the colonial era*

When victorious Japanese divisions poured into Burma and the Dutch East Indies in the spring of 1942, they broke the long grip of Europeans on nonwhite peoples. The rising sun of Japan was the setting sun of Western empire. Even after their victory in 1945, the old colonial powers could no longer meet the high costs of keeping control of their colonies. This was especially true when nationalist rebellions broke out or threatened to. Between 1946 and 1958 France gave up almost all her African colonies (not willingly), Britain yielded independence to most of her African possessions and to India, Burma and Malaya, and the Netherlands East Indies broke free. A few Portuguese, Spanish, and other European outposts in Africa and Asia remained. Like the tiny European footholds in South America and the Caribbean, they were remnants of Europe's great age of exploration.

*CHRONOLOGY*

| | |
|---|---|
| 1954 | *French surrender an army at Dien Bien Phu in Vietnam* |
| 1963 | *President Diem of South Vietnam assassinated* |
| 1964 | *Tonkin Gulf resolution; Congress gives president power to intercede in Vietnam* |
| 1965 | *Several U.S. ground army divisions sent to Vietnam* |
| 1968 | *January 1, 500,000 U.S. troops in Vietnam* |
| 1968 | *January 31, Vietcong start Tet (New Year's) offensive* |
| 1968 | *April, Martin Luther King shot to death in Memphis* |
| 1968 | *June, Robert Kennedy assassinated in Los Angeles* |
| 1968 | *November election, Nixon defeats McGovern for presidency* |
| 1973 | *Peace agreement between United States and North Vietnam* |

The changeover was not easy. One place where it was especially hard was in French Indochina. That was the name the French had given to three separate Asian states, Laos, Cambodia, and Vietnam, which they conquered and united in the 1880s. Returning after the Japanese surrender, the French found an established nationalist movement. Its leader was a wispy, bearded Vietnamese named Ho Chi Minh. Ho had been working for an independent Indochina since the end of World War I. As a young man, he had gone to France and there became a convert to Marxism. He had spent time in the Soviet Union and later in China. He was unquestionably both a Communist *and* a nationalist, and until he died in 1969 Americans were to argue about which of these loyalties came first.

The French negotiated a deal in 1946, whereby a Ho-led "Democratic Republic of Vietnam" was established, whose capital was in Hanoi. It called for a semifree status within a union of French dominions. But late in 1946 the agreement broke down. The French bombed Hanoi and began a struggle to wipe out Ho's army, known as the Vietminh. The fight lasted eight years. It ended in total French defeat.

The Americans' attitude in 1945 and 1946 was lukewarm toward helping Western European nations to reclaim Asian empires. In 1946, in fact, in obedience to a law passed twelve years earlier, the United States itself had granted independence to the Philippines. Franklin D. Roosevelt sympathized with anti-imperialist stirrings and said in 1944 to an associate that France had "milked" Indochina for a century and ought to get out.

### *The United States Goes from Anticolonialism to Anticommunism*

But the coming of the cold war, Communist victory in China, and then the Korean War suddenly changed things. Sympathy for anticolonial rebellions vanished when the anticolonial leaders were Communists. Communists had always been among the various groups within colonies struggling to take the lead in independence movements. After 1946 they were accused of being behind revolts against Asian governments already free. Two such outbreaks, in the Philippines and in Indonesia, were snuffed out with considerable bloodshed. Battles like these were power conflicts within the framework of nationalism.

But American official thinking from 1950 onward saw it differently. Washington insisted that there was a single "world Communist movement." At its head was the Soviet Union. Communist parties everywhere devotedly followed the Moscow line. Red China, dependent upon the Soviet Union for technical and economic aid, took orders from the Russians. And, in turn, Communist parties in small Asian nations followed the Peking line.

The chain of descent seemed clear. The Russians had "won" in China. They had plotted the North Korean attempt to seize all Korea. Whenever a

Communist force surfaced in Southeast Asia, it was following a blueprint for worldwide Communist takeover. And so, the cold war line of thought concluded, any Communist-led "war of liberation" anywhere was a threat to the United States.

Thus the Americans, by 1949, moved from a position of opposing the French reconquest to one of supporting the French war against Indo-Chinese Communists. But the French, it soon became clear, were fighting a losing battle. Though they gained strong footholds in the cities and in southern Vietnam, they discovered what Americans would discover a few years later. They could not control the countryside. Vietminh soldiers lived in every village and looked like innocent peasants. No sooner were French troops out of sight when they would emerge to blow up bridges, kill pro-French villagers, demand contributions of food and supplies, issue orders, and act like a government. While these guerrillas gnawed the French supply lines, formally organized Vietminh units, apparently using some Soviet-furnished equipment, pummeled France's armies in open battle.

Modern methods of war did not work well in Indochina. Aerial bombardment and artillery fire did not stop the flow of supplies carried, shell by shell, along jungle trails on the backs of patient peasants. The villages concealed, by dark, an "enemy" without uniform who, by day, hid his rifle in the mattress and looked like a friend. It was a new kind of war. Even the old rules of political battle did not hold. Fitting the Indo-Chinese situation into a clear-cut worldwide struggle between Communists and "democrats" ignored the real complications.

Vietnamese differed from Laotians and Cambodians and very much among themselves. There were Buddhists and Catholics. There were Vietnamese nationalists who had adopted French ways and skills and who were satisfied as lawyers, businessmen, landlords, and civil servants; they labeled any movement for change as "Communist." Other nationalists hoped to restore a true Vietnamese character by getting people out of the cities and back to village life and customs. There were great masses of rural Vietnamese, deeply rooted in their ancestral acres. They would accept whatever authority seemed to have the blessings of their traditional gods and would reflect "the will of heaven." The "winning side" in Vietnam would be the *Vietnamese* faction that unified this diverse society and made its program identifiable with traditional Vietnamese habits. When the French and, later, the Americans who came to Vietnam spoke of "democracy," "modernization," "reform," and "efficiency," they were talking a language that many Vietnamese rejected. The ordinary, non-Westernized Vietnamese certainly wanted his own land and ways, security from attack, better crops, and good public health facilities. But the country as a whole was not ready for the virtue *versus* vice context of the crusade against totalitarianism.

And so in 1954, eight costly, bloody years ended when a French army was surrounded and forced to surrender at Dien Bien Phu. American arms aid to France had been small. President Eisenhower, after 1952, resisted efforts to increase it. He correctly guessed that deep involvement in a jungle-style guerrilla war would hurt the United States far more than it could help. Besides, the lesson of Korea, that some wars are unwinnable, was fresh. Neither Secretary of State Dulles nor the chairman of the Joint Chiefs of Staff nor Vice President Nixon could persuade "Ike" to intervene at Dien Bien Phu. The French surrendered. A new French government asked for peace terms, and a fresh chapter began.

## *The "Best and the Brightest" Involve Us:* 1954–1963

### *The Geneva accords*

The United States did not participate in the Geneva conference of 1954, which ended the first Indo-Chinese War. But it became an unofficial party to enforcing the agreed-on settlements. Indochina would be divided into three states: Cambodia, Laos, and Vietnam. The neutrality of the first two would be internationally guaranteed. In Vietnam itself the picture was cloudy. Ho was firmly in control of its northern half. But the French had not lost control of the areas around cities in the south, to which, therefore, anti-Communist Vietnamese flocked. Temporarily, the country, though recognized as a single nation, was divided along the line of the 17th parallel. A demilitarized zone (DMZ) separated the two halves. Both sides were to respect it and to await free elections in 1956 to unify the country.

The two Vietnams began to develop in different directions. Ho proceeded to set up his Democratic Republic of North Vietnam as a tightly organized and disciplined Communist Asian state. Large numbers of Vietnamese fled from his regime. Some were Catholics; some had been friends of the French; and some were old political enemies of the Communists. But few outside observers denied that Ho was popular in the north and that he was widely respected in the south as a symbol of the long fight for Vietnamese independence.

Meanwhile, in the south, a republic of Vietnam appeared, with its capital in Saigon. It was headed by Ngo Dinh Diem, the former prime minister of the French puppet emperor. Its top officials and generals were almost all French trained. Diem announced a program of modernization and democratization. He would divide land among the peasants, end bribery and theft of public funds by high-ranking officers, raise health and educational standards, and build trade links with the Western world. But he said he needed time and a free hand to make it all work. So he had his police crack down on critics whom he called Communists and Communist sympathizers. And he indefinitely postponed the 1956 elections. (By almost all independent judgment, Ho would have won them.)

The anti-Diem forces were thwarted by press censorship and arrests.

Their members in the new but powerless parliament could do little. But in the countryside, anti-Diem groups were formed. They were soon linked into a new organization, the National Liberation Front. It began to build a revolutionary "army," the Vietcong (VC), which operated in the rural areas, as the Vietminh had done. The Diem government claimed that the VC was helped by troops from the north, plus Soviet and Chinese weapons. North Vietnam countered with charges that the south had broken the Geneva agreements. The war slowly escalated in the villages during Eisenhower's second administration.

Eisenhower played a careful game in Vietnam. We recognized South Vietnam as an independent state instead of as a temporary partitioned zone. We insisted that there were two Vietnams, and that "ours," belonging to the free world, was under attack by guerrillas trained and equipped in North Vietnam in a special kind of invasion. (Hanoi answered that it was only helping fellow Vietnamese to resist oppression.)

But though Eisenhower and Dulles insisted that the Vietcong were only agents of Hanoi, Peking, and Moscow and denied that the struggle was only a civil war, they did not back South Vietnam with much manpower. A small U.S. Military Assistant Advisory Group (USMAAG) was created in 1955. Plenty of military equipment was also sent to the government in Saigon. But the USMAAG's personnel had only reached 685 by 1960, although numerous American civilians worked in our embassy to Saigon, the Peace Corps, and in other aid programs.

*The Kennedy team takes over*

At the beginning of 1961 the situation changed. John F. Kennedy took office, with promises to "get this country moving." In foreign affairs his team of advisers had mixed objectives. On the one hand, they wanted to add to military aid more technical and economic assistance and people-to-people efforts (like the Peace Corps) to raise other nations' living standards. But, on the other hand, Kennedy continued to play on the theme of how necessary it was to be tough with the Soviets and show no weakness that would encourage more aggression. Eye-to-eye confrontations in Berlin and over the missiles in Cuba (as we saw in the preceding chapter) were part of that firm posture.

And part of that overall plan called for the defense of South Vietnam. The arguments in favor varied. Sometimes it was held that South Vietnam was one piece in a row of dominoes. If it went Communist, then Thailand, Malaya, Burma, and other Asian allies might topple next. Sometimes it was argued by Kennedy's secretary of state, Dean Rusk, that faith in America's word was at stake. And always there was a basic belief that a Vietcong victory would be a "win" for Russia, China, and all the Communist powers and that it would give them a psychological edge over the United States.

The Kennedy team was proud of its sophistication. Its members did not like the simple, moralistic slogans of Eisenhower years. Nor did they want to commit themselves to the risk of all-out war by butting head-on into Russia. No great crusades for them. Instead, they argued, the thing to do first was to analyze problems carefully, decide on what was needed for solution, and apply just the right amount of remedy without undue emotion.

South Vietnam, they said, was dealing, not with a Korean-type invasion, but with an insurgency. The United States could help by using techniques of "counterinsurgency," which included specially trained outfits to infiltrate guerrilla headquarters and commit espionage and sabotage; special equipment like infrared cameras and gunsights to catch Vietcong fighters and reinforcements from the north moving under cover of night; special defoliants and herbicides to destroy the jungle cover that offered shelter to infiltrators by day; helicopters to lift South Vietnamese forces quickly from place to place; electronic barriers that warned of anyone entering a guarded zone.

That was one side of the program. The other was to accentuate the positive and build up support for Diem in the villages. American experts would help Diem devise land reform programs. American economists would help train South Vietnamese officials to fight inflation, black marketing, and shortages. American "pacification teams" would move into hamlets and win the hearts and minds of the people with doctors, crop experts, and engineers to build dams, roads, bridges, rice mills. Americans, working on Diem's side, would make the Vietnamese people realize that the path to a better standard of living was not through Marx and Lenin but Yankee know-how. South Vietnam could become a showcase to the other underdeveloped nations of the blessings of freedom.

If you have followed earlier chapters closely, you will note how much this viewpoint owed to the "can-do" spirit of American progressivism. Progressives, too, thought that experts armed with good will could end age-old evils. In addition, the Kennedy advisers were young people who had done their basic growing up in the technology-saturated fifties. They believed in planning, computers, and the power of statistics. American culture had made them arrogant. Kennedy's secretary of defense, Robert McNamara, was a former president of the Ford Motor Company. He had a brilliant business record. He surrounded himself in the Pentagon with a staff of "Whiz Kids" dedicated to using the most up-to-date machinery possible to make the armed forces as efficient as possible, that is, with the greatest power and flexibility of response possible for the last investment. This cost-accounting approach often ran McNamara into head-on clashes with his older generals and admirals.

### *The "Whiz Kids" strike out*

The Kennedy advisers were, in one writer's words, "the best and the brightest" of their kind. They were proud of their combination of idealism and toughness. And their pride blinded them to possible flaws in their thinking.

They did not see that their plans for a Vietnam virtually run by American advisers really called for making South Vietnam a puppet state. Many South Vietnamese would resent and oppose that.

Secondly, they did not guess how little the South Vietnamese liked sudden change. The South Vietnamese population could only be won to support the Saigon government by appeals in Vietnamese terms. All the American technical assistance in the world could not buy loyalty for Diem, unless he convinced the peasants that he was carrying on Vietnamese practices, basically speaking. This he was unable to do.

Finally, the Kennedy team did not realize that there were limits to power. Despite all the detection devices, infiltration went on. Villagers continued, willingly or in fear, to shelter VC units. The Kennedy people's response was, therefore, in their jargon, to change the "input." They planned to beef up the South Vietnamese forces and perhaps even squeeze Hanoi by aerial bombardment of infiltration routes. The idea was to make the North Vietnamese and VC hurt enough so that, in *their* calculations, the continued war would not be worth it. The root idea was that the people in Hanoi thought like the people in Washington. They had a goal; they were willing to spend soldiers and effort to reach it; but if the price was made too high, they would abandon or change it.

But Hanoi, by 1961, was in its own eyes in the seventeenth year of a struggle for national unity and liberation. It would not settle for the half-loaf of North Vietnam, like a football coach taking a field goal and a tie in place of a touchdown and win. Its "game" had no final whistle. So, through the Kennedy years, the war dragged on. The South Vietnamese lost more and more control. The number of American advisers grew from a few hundred to 4,000 and then to 33,000. They created a new problem. Sooner or later, guerrilla attacks on South Vietnamese outposts would kill some of them. Then the question would arise of sending in more American forces to protect them.

Things were not working out. Reports showed that South Vietnam might fall without more American help. A hard turning point was reached. Should the United States operate on the line once stated by Kennedy, namely, that the war was basically South Vietnam's to win or lose? Or should it follow the advice of McNamara, who defined our task in 1963 as taking "all necessary measures within our capability to prevent a Communist victory"? In other words, should it pull out or fight to the end?

The full story of the debate of 1963 is not clear. Part of it was revealed in the so-called Pentagon Papers, made public by an administration insider in 1971. Part of it is still locked in secrecy. In any case, events exploded late in 1963. The Americans began to move away from support of Diem. This left him open to attack by a group of Saigon generals seeking to take over in Saigon. On November 1 they struck, assassinated Diem, and announced a tough, new line of war on Communists and all who would give in to the enemy.

How Kennedy reacted, given a little time, cannot be known. Three weeks and a day after Diem died, Lee Harvey Oswald's bullet shattered Kennedy's skull in Dallas. Soon thereafter, the Vietnamese War entered yet another new phase.

*Johnson goes all the way: Tonkin*

Eight and one-half months after Kennedy's death, Johnson was running for president on his own. And he was also receiving bad news from Vietnam. The new government, under General Nguyen Kanh, was not doing well. A shot in the arm was needed, a sign to Hanoi that the United States would refuse to quit. Perhaps it might be necessary to hurt Hanoi by dropping American bombs on North Vietnamese soil. Johnson bided his time. Then either chance gave him or else he manufactured—the facts are not clear—an opportunity to act. On August 4, 1964, he announced on nationwide television that two American destroyers on patrol in international waters in the Gulf of Tonkin had been attacked by North Vietnamese torpedo boats. As an answer, he was ordering American air raids on oil dumps and dockyards in the Hanoi-Haiphong area.

Johnson next went before Congress, asking for authority to take "all necessary steps including the use of armed force" to help any ally "in defense of its freedom." Congress promptly passed what was called the Tonkin Gulf Resolution. It practically gave Johnson full war powers without a declaration of war. It was carried by an incredible margin: no dissenting votes in the House, only two in the Senate.

But in fact the North Vietnamese "attack" was in no way clear-cut. Johnson had neglected to stress what Wayne Morse, one of the two senators voting nay, pointed out. South Vietnamese vessels were conducting operations nearby, and the American ships might have been part of a move to distract North Vietnamese attention. Moreover, in the pitch-black night, it was never certain that American ships did not mistake each other for supposed North Vietnamese attackers.

But the real lesson of the Tonkin Gulf resolution was not how hard it is to get at truth in history. Rather, it showed how, in foreign policy, Congress had given up its constitutional power to make war. The lawmakers believed that the president alone had the facts and that quick action was due. So they gave him a blank check. Tonkin Gulf capped a quarter of a century of thinking that the United States was in a permanent undeclared war that was directed from the White House.

What happened after 1964 in Vietnam showed the impact of American culture on our overseas policies. As we have already seen, Americans had great faith in the power of technology to solve any problem. They had a deeply ingrained idea of themselves as the defenders of world freedom. And, above all, in business, in sports, in school, in politics, everywhere, they were taught the importance of being competitive and of winning. Prizes, profits, honors, medals went to whoever was ahead of the final count. Nothing went to losers.

Johnson was especially cut out for winning. He was a tough, determined Texas millionaire. His legislative skill as Senate majority leader was legendary. He was the proud architect of the Great Society. He now dreamed that if he could win in Vietnam, he might even later coax from Congress a shower of American bounty to Vietnam to repair the wounds of war. A prosperous Vietnam would be valuable to the United States. But one way or another, Johnson would get a victory or, as he put it, "bring home the coonskin." That meant taking over the war.

In February 1965 several divisions of American ground troops were landed in Vietnam. They soon took over many of the missions of the South Vietnamese forces. Shortly afterward, a massive program of bombing of the north began. Again and again, Johnson was assured by the generals that the combination of U.S. air bombardment and ground fire power would wipe out the "enemy's" will to resist.

And none of it turned out to be true. For three years the war ground on. The North Vietnamese sent in enough of their "main force" troops to brace and support the Vietcong. China and the Soviet Union continued to supply just enough modern matériel, such as antiaircraft weapons, tanks, and trucks, to Hanoi to keep their fighting forces in contention. No matter how heavy the bombardments, North Vietnamese and Vietcong reinforcements and supplies kept moving in. And no matter how many pitched battles with North Vietnamese troops were fought and "won" in American communiqués, the "losers" seemed only to melt back into the landscape and reappear soon thereafter in the "cleared" areas. Meantime, the bill for the war kept mounting—up to $10, $20, and $30 billion a year in direct costs. And a more gruesome toll was seen as army transports at West Coast wharves unloaded "body bags" for burial. American casualties, by 1967, were approaching 1000 dead each month. And there was no end in sight. Invisible costs, such as growing disbelief in the truthfulness of the American government, kept climbing, too.

*Levels of destruction and atrocity increase*

Both Vietnams were pocked and pitted by an endless rain of American bombs. The destruction sent thousands of refugees flocking into hideous camps or into the overcrowded poverty-ridden cities. In addition, to solve the frustrating problem of separating "friendlies" from hostile Vietnamese, American forces began a program of moving certain village populations out of their homes. This was an enormous culture shock to Vietnamese who had to leave behind

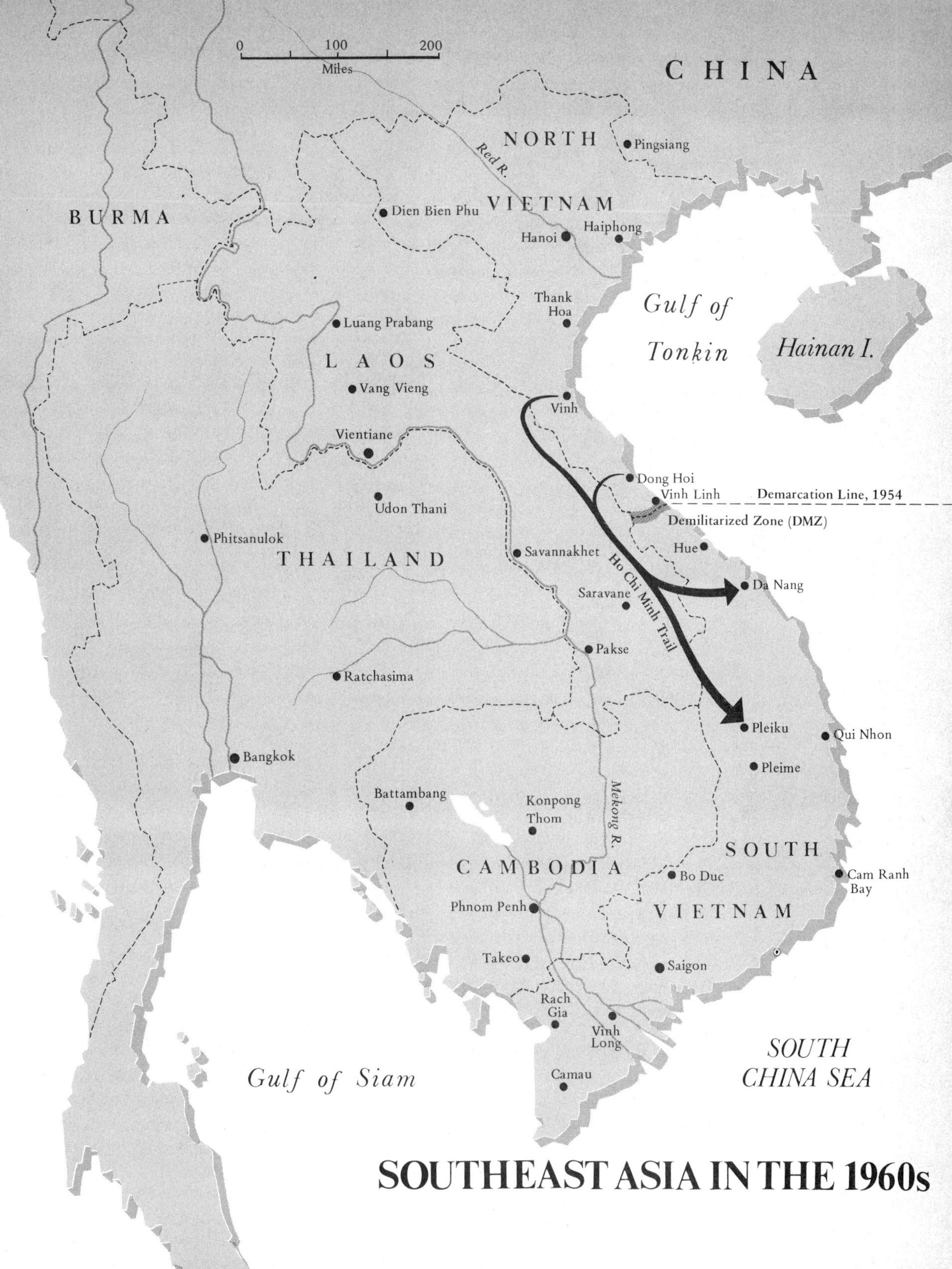


# SOUTHEAST ASIA IN THE 1960s

their sacred ancestral ghosts and fields. But it was done, and the Americans then shot any Vietnamese found in the cleared areas. The image of the American soldier abroad, smiling and giving away chewing gum, was now challenged by one in which he set fire to native homes to deny them to the Vietcong. Since units tended to report their successes in terms of numbers of Vietcong killed, great weight was given to "the body count." A heap of dead Vietnamese in a "free fire zone" became evidence of a completed mission.

We have already seen a tendency in American life to devalue and downgrade nonwhites. Vietnam reinforced it powerfully. Shocking proof came when it was learned in 1969 that a year earlier an army platoon in the village of My Lai had wantonly shot at least 22 unarmed civilians. Higher authorities who had tried to cover up the atrocity were brought to trial. So was the commander of the offending unit, Lieutenant William L. Calley, Jr. Only Calley was convicted.

Though his actions were appalling and a clear violation of official army regulations, Calley had his defenders. They pointed out that he was only the product of his situation. Americans had learned to distrust any Vietnamese who could bear arms as a possible enemy. And many women and youngsters were Vietcong members who ambushed and booby-trapped Americans. On the other hand, the "body count" had destroyed any sense, among some Americans, that Vietnamese lives were individually important. In Calley's words, the killings were "no big deal."

While it was possible to answer by pointing out that many American soldiers had kept their sense of humanity and refused to join in the shooting and that there were ways to check Vietnamese for weapons without killing them, it was hard to deny that some of Calley's guilt belonged with the war itself.

### *The end of "honor": official lying*

The United States was able to wage a war halfway around the globe. But officially it could not tell its own people the truth. As the war dragged on, the Saigon government became more and more dictatorial. General Khanh was succeeded by General Nguyen Cao Ky, an airman who suppressed "defeatism" in Saigon by jailing anyone who urged peace talks with the VC. In 1967 an "election" was held, which brought another general, Nguyen Van Thieu, to power. Thieu continued to hound opponents, often using American-furnished police equipment. He ignored the parliament, built a political machine for himself, and, finally, in 1971, ran for reelection under such one-sided rules that no one would contest him. Corruption continued to infect top levels of his regime.

So the statement that we were "defending democracy" in Vietnam became even more hollow. Yet American officials continued to repeat that plainly untrue statement. Prolonged propaganda eventually wears out the credit of governments with their own people. That began to happen in the United States by 1967. And the armed forces, too, once considered guardians of honor, fell into the habit of untruthfulness. Time and again, officials would announce that the government now controlled most of the countryside and that there was a "light at the end of the tunnel." And then the VC would reemerge in some new area. The official army briefings conducted for reporters in Saigon always reported such gigantic enemy casualties that reporters came to dub them "The Five O'Clock Follies." Eventually, lying became so embedded in army public-relations work that the whole system was tainted. After 1968, as we shall see, a halt in the bombing of North Vietnam was ordered. But in 1969, 1970, and 1971 American planes ran numerous bombing missions over North Vietnam and "neutral" Cambodia. Air force officials willfully falsified their records to hide such acts or called them reconnaissance flights.

It was small wonder that the average soldier, the "grunt" at the bottom of the heap, became demoralized. He was fighting a war against an invisible enemy, was surrounded by what seemed to him ungrateful "natives," and was criticized by many war protesters at home. He was led by generals who often seemed interested only in image making, not in protecting him. By the thousands, therefore, soldiers in Vietnam took drugs, dodged regulations, and disobeyed their officers. The war was beginning to destroy the American army by 1968.

## *The Developing Protest: 1965–1968*

A vigorous antiwar protest movement took shape. But it was met by an equally forceful resistance. Society divided sharply along lines of strain that had been developing for many years past, because of forces that we have seen at work in the preceding three or four chapters. Protest was fed from several sources:

*The apparent endlessness of the war.* By New Year's Day, 1968, American military and naval personnel in Vietnam totaled more than one-half million. Yet the war continued, with no victory in sight. The prospect of more years of the draft, high taxes, and casualties was a bitter one. Even those who believed the official line that the war was vital to the free world were discouraged. If the war was that important, surely, it was important to *win* it. What was holding Washington back? Why not plaster North Vietnam with nuclear weapons and napalm? Why not mine their harbors to cut off supplies from China and Russia?

The diplomatic answer was that there was a point at which the Chinese might be provoked to enter the war. Then the United States would have millions of red Asian troops to fight instead of hundreds of thousands. And, though Moscow and Peking had quarreled by 1966, the use of nuclear weapons might frighten the Russians into retaliation and bring on the unthinkable collision. But if the United States could not afford to win because of the threat of world war and could not afford to lose because of the threat to its alliance system, it was trapped. And the trap hurt. For conservative patriots Vietnam was becoming a painful lesson in frustration. It was equally harsh for liberals.

*Liberal woes: lagging priorities.* The liberals who had supported the Fair Deal, the New Frontier, and the Great Society divided on the question of the war. Many of them were vigorously anti-Communist. If the dominoes fell, they reasoned, the United States would be placed at an unacceptable disadvantage. A just society at home required an unthreatened world abroad.

But these individuals, who served Kennedy and Johnson, were challenged by others who held that the costs of rigid anti-Communism were too high. They noted that the Communist world was not single-minded. They argued that the constant armed readiness required by the cold war played into the hands of the military-industrial complex and thus strengthened conservatism. They insisted that however autocratic the Hanoi regime might be, it was no worse than that in Saigon. But, above all, they said, we were making a huge investment of our resources in a tiny country whose strategic importance was questionable. And our resources were not limited.

That, by 1967, was coming to be the key issue. Taxes and prices were moving steadily upward. Meantime, Great Society programs were gasping for funds. Urban woes mushroomed—riots, crime, slums, traffic, pollution, abandonment. Only some kind of massive federal aid could solve such problems. Only federal dollars could finance a national system of low-cost health care or modernize the schools—only federal funds, because only the federal government had money on the scale needed. But federal funds were going up in blast and smoke in Vietnam.

Discontent of all parties with the war was also nourished by the forces of technology that made a struggle so far away possible. Television, for the first time, was bringing combat directly into people's homes. A writer referred to it as "the living-room war." People became emotional about Vietnam when they saw its agonies on their screens. The Canadian scholar of communications Marshall McLuhan had once argued that television made the world a "global village." In that village, Vietnam was a war next door. It could not be pushed out of people's minds.

By 1968 the Vietnam War had become the most unpopular war in the nation's history, surpassing the War of 1812 and the Mexican War. Yet the protest against it did not jell into a universal demand for U.S. withdrawal. This was because antiwar feeling provoked counterfeelings and exposed deep splits in American society.

*Conflict and paradox: the war as divider.* The antiwar movement drew much of its early strength, originally, from professional intellectuals, especially those who lived in large eastern cities or taught on university campuses. This group included numerous scholars, writers, literary critics, journalists, and religious leaders of very modernized churches. They were an elite, a select handful of top opinion leaders. They tended to fear the power the war gave to the great defense-contracting corporations and the military. They were less likely than most Americans to accept, unthinkingly, all criticisms of communism as equally worthwhile or to see the globe as divided neatly into the "free world" and the Communist world. But in these attitudes they did not get total support from former allies of theirs in domestic politics.

For one thing, there were the blacks. Black leaders became unhappy as white liberal funds and energy shifted from civil rights into antiwar protest in the mid-1960s. It seemed to many blacks that the quarrel over the war was a battle among whites and that blacks were better off concentrating on their own needs. Antiwar spokesmen tried to convince black communities that less money for Vietnam meant more money to upgrade black life. They succeeded in converting Martin Luther King to that position in 1967. But they could not entirely shake off a black feeling that the antiwar movement was white liberalism's new love.

Secondly, there was the working class. Its leaders and spokesmen, especially in the unions, remained loyally supportive of the war. One reason for this was that the working class was less touched than the upper middle classes by the changes in values that we saw stemming from technological revolutions in Chapter 25. For them patriotism was still a vital force. They did not want to turn their backs on their country when the road became rough. America had been good to them and their immigrant parents. Believing that the prosperity of the fifties was the result of living in "the best country in the world," they were not sympathetic to any criticism of the United States.

Workers, therefore, lined up on Vietnam, not with the urban liberals who had voted Democratic with them for years, but with the farmers and small business people of middle America, who also believed in all the values of the older America. These included respect for traditional religious faiths and for authority, commencing with parents and extending upward to teachers and officials. Liberals might be annoyed at politicians who dodged issues by praising God, mother, home, and the flag. But those were important items to a majority of Americans. They distrusted thinkers who questioned old patterns of child rearing, marriage, personal behavior, and race relations. A gap was opening between such spokesmen for social change and the mass of "square" Americans.

These attitudes were to become tremendously important in the elections of

1968 and 1972. They underlay the third-party campaign of George Wallace. They won two elections for Richard Nixon. They enabled Spiro Agnew, vice president from 1969 to 1973 (until he resigned under criminal charges), to win popularity by lashing out at "effete snobs" who opposed Nixon. They dissolved, at least temporarily and at the presidential election level, the old New Deal coalition. And they prevented antiwar sentiment from taking root in a place where it logically might have done so—amid those who suffered most from the war.

The odd thing was that draft regulations allowed college students to be deferred. Conscription fell most heavily on working-class and black youngsters. Yet black families raised no major protest. And blue-collar Americans, who bore the cruelest cost, stayed loyal to the flag. To an auto worker, a police officer, a nurse, a bookkeeper, to any middle American, man or woman, the war was often a deeply felt human burden. They were the ones who had sons in Vietnam. Yet even when they had doubts, they hesitated to join an antiwar movement that was mingled in their minds with support of long hair, marijuana, rock music, divorce, sexual promiscuity, abortion, and other evils.

The cultural forces tending to split the country were brought into prominence by the war. One thing both parties shared, however, was a feeling of helplessness to change things. This led to a spreading lack of faith in the political system. And there matters stood in February 1968. Then events in Indochina suddenly brought them toward a point of resolution.

## *Storm and Aftermath: 1968–1975*

### 1968: *the savage year*

The night of January 31, 1968, was the beginning of the Vietnamese lunar New Year, known as Tet. In predawn darkness VC commandos in every major city of South Vietnam suddenly rose from nowhere to strike at the Thieu government and the Americans. In Saigon they actually penetrated the American embassy before being driven off by paratroopers. Everywhere, it took weeks of bitter fighting to dislodge them.

By March 1 Saigon had regained control over most of its cities. The American command was claiming a great victory. But the American press and population was reading a different story. They had been told again and again that the enemy was all but beaten. Yet the Tet offensive had shown the VC and the North Vietnamese to be tough and very obviously able to move when and where they chose. Tet was not Dien Bien Phu. No American army was surrounded and captured. But it told the Americans in 1968 what it had told the French in 1954—they could not end the struggle among Vietnamese on their own terms.

The evidence was soon in. In the New Hampshire Democratic primary, early in March, Democratic Senator Eugene McCarthy, running on an antiwar platform against the incumbent president, received an astonishing 42 percent of the vote. The signal clearly was that the American people, both the longstanding supporters of the war known as "hawks" and their opponents, the "doves," wanted an end to it. Johnson understood the message. He refused a request of his military commanders for an additional 206,000 troops. Next he announced a halt in the bombing of North Vietnam. In return he got a North Vietnamese agreement to meet with Saigon, VC, and American representatives in Paris to work out a peace agreement. And, finally, in painful awareness of his own growing unpopularity, he announced that he would not be a candidate for his party's renomination.

Violence scarred the terrible spring and summer of 1968. Martin Luther King was shot early in April. Washington was torn by riots for nearly a week. In May students in one of America's great universities, Columbia, in New York, took over the main campus buildings. They were protesting, among other things, university participation in research projects related to the war. They were expelled after ten days by police. Property was destroyed, and heads were cracked. In June Robert F. Kennedy, running hard for the nomination on an antiwar platform, was shot in a Los Angeles hotel kitchen by a young pro-Arab extremist.

The Democratic convention met in Chicago in August. The hall was ringed by barbed wire and troops, allegedly to prevent antiwar demonstrators from disrupting the proceedings. A passionate floor debate broke out over whether the party platform should call for withdrawal from the war or support Johnson's past efforts. After stormy discussion the "hawks" won the platform fight and the nomination. The leaderless Kennedy delegates refused to join the McCarthy forces in significant numbers. Vice President Hubert Humphrey, an only slightly converted hawk, was chosen. On the night of his nomination, Chicago police, provoked beyond good sense and restraint by antiwar demonstrators, charged them with clubs and tear gas. Television cameras recorded the savage beatings they inflicted. It was the grimmest moment in American political life since 1860.

The Republicans nominated Nixon, who said that he would end the war by a plan that he could not reveal, for fear of undercutting the Americans negotiating in Paris. Humphrey trailed Nixon badly, at first, and even ran in some states behind the third-party candidate, Wallace. His problem was to win over both pro- and anti-war Democrats. A late campaign surge in the polls still left him behind Nixon, who won by a narrow popular-vote margin but by 301 to 191 in the electoral college. The race was so tight that it was not decided until the dawn hours of the day after election.

It could be said safely that both candidates were pledged, in one way or

MP
MP

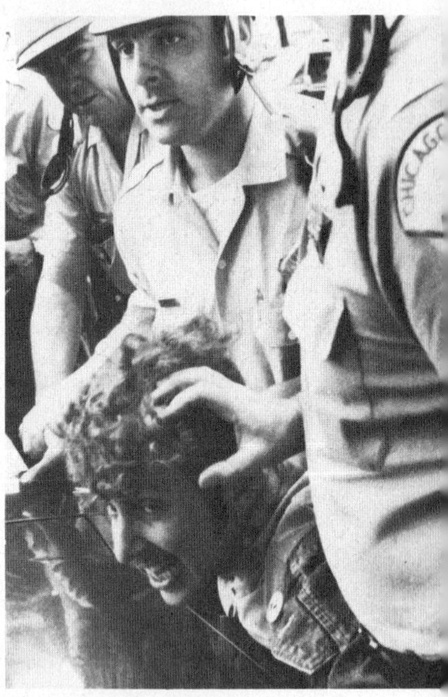

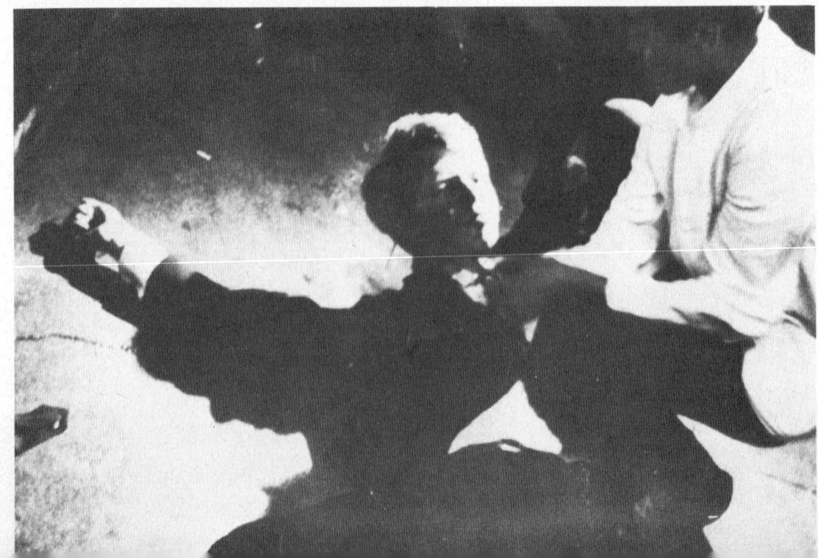

*In 1968, the violent feelings generated by the Vietnam war—or perhaps only brought to the surface by that bitterly debated adventure—seemed to spill over and taint other American institutions long accustomed to peaceful functioning.*

(Opposite page). *In January, the Viet Cong's Tet (or Lunar New Year) offensive briefly won control of South Vietnam's major cities, and suicide squads even penetrated the American embassy. Though it was finally subdued, the Tet disillusioned Americans still hopeful of "winning" in Vietnam, and it marked the beginning of the end of our involvement, and of the Saigon government.*

*In April, just after Lyndon B. Johnson announced that he would not run again for President, an assassin slew Martin Luther King, Jr., leading spokesman for nonviolent change in America's racial patterns. His coffin, on a mule-drawn cart, carried not only his body but many people's hopes of continued peaceful progress.*

*Street fighting between alleged radicals and the police broke out during the Democratic convention in Chicago. Within the convention hall, a bitterly divided group of delegates nominated Hubert Humphrey on a platform that was evasive about the war. He went down to defeat. The country seemed to be, in a phrase, "coming apart."*

*In June, an assassin's bullet changed the American political picture for the second time in five years, this time cutting down the frontrunning candidate for the Democratic nomination, Robert F. Kennedy, who had hoped to unite antiwar, pro-black, and traditional liberal and labor factions within the party.*

*In May* (above) *some students at Columbia University in New York, motivated by a variety of antiestablishment causes, seized and held campus buildings. Police fought their way into them and blood flowed in halls dedicated to the orderly discussion of ideas.*

another, to abandon the quest for victory in Vietnam. Reaction against the war had finally come to the voting booths.

*The Vietnam War under Nixon*

Nixon took office in January 1969. His plan for "ending" the war turned out to mean only ending the participation of American ground troops. He would gradually withdraw them but continue to furnish air and logistic support to Saigon, whose armies would take over the land fighting. This program was known as "Vietnamization." But Nixon warned Hanoi that any strong new offensive would bring heavy American counteraction.

Peace talks remained stalemated. The North Vietnamese insisted on nothing less than the complete withdrawal of the American "invaders." If the Americans would leave, prisoners of war (mostly shot-down air crews) whom Hanoi had captured would be returned. The Americans insisted on a part for the Thieu government in plans for new elections that would reunify the country.

Eventually, the war heated up again. In 1970 Nixon renewed the air attacks on North Vietnam and authorized American forces to invade neutral Cambodia for a limited period to destroy "Communist bases" there. It was later revealed that he had secretly ordered the bombing of that country as well. Americans also supported a South Vietnamese raid, for the same purpose, into Laos. These moves caused the last great waves of antiwar protest on the campuses. In one of them, at Kent State University in Ohio, students were fired on by National Guard troops called in to keep order. Four students died, casualties of the war, in their way, as much as the 50,000 or so Americans killed in Vietnam.

Gradually, however, the weekly totals of U.S. dead shrank from as many as 500 down to 5 or 10. South Vietnamese military and civilian casualties continued to mount. It was said that Vietnamization merely meant "changing the color of the corpses." But protest slackened as American deaths dropped, and Nixon could continue to claim that he was "winding down" the war.

Then, in 1972, the North Vietnamese brought matters to a head again. This time it was a spring offensive that badly mauled the South Vietnamese army, captured a provincial capital, and showed anew that any commitment to help South Vietnam "win" would have to be open-ended and indefinite. With an election coming on, Nixon could not advocate such a course. A war-weary Congress was now on the verge of passing resolutions absolutely demanding an end to the war. Nixon sent his national security affairs adviser, Henry Kissinger, to Paris and to Hanoi to work out a truce in a series of protracted negotiations. Shortly before election day, Kissinger announced that "peace was at hand" and that only the details remained to be worked out. A few days later, Nixon buried his "dove" opponent, George McGovern, who carried only one state, Massachusetts. Then the agreement broke down, and there was a renewed wave of American bombing of Hanoi. Finally, in January 1973, both sides returned to the table and signed a pact.

Its terms were that the Americans should withdraw all their forces. The North Vietnamese would return U.S. prisoners. The North Vietnamese would *not* withdraw their troops from South Vietnam. Teams from the VC, North Vietnam, *and* the Saigon government would meet to plan elections that would eventually reunify the country.

There was room for much argument over the meaning of the words. Nixon proudly proclaimed them to spell "peace with honor." And, indeed, the United States had compelled Hanoi to deal with General Thieu. But aside from that, as critics pointed out, the terms were essentially what the North Vietnamese had demanded: We left. They did not. And Thieu was supposed to negotiate with the VC, whom he had long refused to recognize. The situation was, in a sense, the same as it was in 1954, with both sides planning an election, fighting with each other, and being supplied by outside forces. There was no real peace for the Vietnamese. But the Americans, like the French, had gone. Behind them they left their empty camps, their stockpiles, their illegitimate children, their wreckage, and their memories.

America remained divided on the issues. Had it been a "famous victory"? Should "new priorities" be adopted? Should there be amnesty for those who had refused conscription or deserted because of objection to the war? Politicians still tried to read the signs that would give them a cue to the most popular answers to such questions. But the signs were obscure. They became no clearer when North Vietnam swept to a final victory two years later.

World War II had united America. The Vietnam War, as we have seen, left behind it wreckage and suffering in Vietnam and bitterness and confusion in America. Few American struggles ever offered such evidence of how all the developing problems of preceding decades were brough to a head by an unpopular conflict. America had eaten of the fruit of the tree of knowledge of good and evil—she had, in the words used by one of the fathers of the atomic bomb, "known sin." Her history from there on was bound to be different.

---

## *FOR FURTHER READING*

There are so many books on the Vietnam War that the basic problem is one of choosing a reasonable number that reflect divergent points of view. First of all, it is a good idea to have some sense of what was going on in Vietnam itself: Bernard B. Fall, *The Two Vietnams* (1967) is an excellent report by an objective journalist who was killed in the region; a French journalist, Jean LaCouture's *Ho Chi Minh: A Political Biography* (1968) is sympathetic but well documented; and a flat-out defense of all efforts to defeat communism in Vietnam is Sir Robert Thompson, *No Exit From Vietnam* (1969).

As for the story of American involvement, a basic source is Neil Sheehan, ed., *The Pentagon Papers* (1971). This is the inside story, from official documents "leaked" to the press, which the Nixon administration tried to suppress. A sharply critical study is David Halberstam, *The Best and the Brightest* (1972), outlining our gradual entrapment. A similar tack is taken in Frances FitzGerald, *Fire in the Lake* (1972), but with more emphasis on Vietnamese culture as it was affected by the American presence. Townsend Hoopes, *The Limits of Intervention* (1973) is the view of an insider who dropped out of the pro-war ranks eventually. Bernard Kalb's *Kissinger* (1974) is the biography of the secretary of state who remained a staunch defender of our Saigon allies to the end, though he negotiated a withdrawal of American troops in 1973. The effect of the Vietnam war on domestic politics in 1968 is touched on by Eric Goldman, *The Tragedy of Lyndon B. Johnson* (1969), a historian who served as an advisor to the President, and who believes that Johnson destroyed himself over Vietnam.

As for what the war itself was like, two works stand out: Seymour Hersh, *My Lai* (1970) and Jonathan Schell, *The Village of Ben Suc* (1967).

# *chapter 28*

# *America, the many-centered and perplexing*

*History is bunk.*
—Henry Ford

*Those who ignore history are condemned to repeat it.*
—George Santayana

These two statements clash head-on. One says that history is needless, for surely we have an oversupply of "bunk." The other warns us that we must accept its guidance, or else we are in danger.

Both are right, in a sense. Santayana meant that we cannot turn our backs on what we have been. We cannot leap, by pure acts of will, into brand-new identities, unmarked by our earlier experiences. And unless we know ourselves as we are, we may endlessly make the same mistakes. History is a necessary part of group self-knowledge.

But history is also an act of the imagination. What Ford meant was that it does not have the solid feel, the "touch-me-I-am-here" reality of a fender that can be thumped, a tire that can be kicked. In that sense, it *is* "bunk." It is a re-creation from scraps of evidence torn out of the infinite number of pages of the record of how it *might* have been. We reread Lincoln's first inaugural address; we imagine him standing there delivering it, but he is not with us, not actually *there.* And while we may all agree, on the basis of the evidence, to see him there in our minds, no two of us are likely to receive exactly the same meaning from his words.

So there is not one history but many histories. And we each need *a* history to give us a sense of orientation in time and place, much as we need a memory. When people collectively agree on *a* history, then the events that befall them make sense as part of a pattern of movement from past to present to future. The event of today is the seam where past, present, and future join. An agreed-on folk history or national history becomes part of a people's culture. But if the culture is swiftly changing, such agreement is difficult to reach.

What has this to do with a final chapter in a book of U.S. history? Simply this: It would be easy to select the events of recent years that seemed most important if there were general agreement today on the important themes of American history. (The word "theme" is used here to refer to a statement about the past that has meaning and emotional significance. A "development" is purely a descriptive term. To illustrate, "the broadening of freedom" is a statement of a theme; "urbanization" is a development.)

Until recently, most history books agreed on our key themes; they ended with a discussion of happenings that showed how those themes were carried out in recent years. That agreement among historians rested on the fact that American culture was unified and self-confident. It was essentially a Puritan culture, modified by eighteenth- and nineteenth-century faith in progress. That set the framework. "America" believed in one God and largely worshiped Him within the Protestant mold. She believed that the whole human race was watching the United States as a model of free government. She believed that all institutions—church, family, businesses, governments—were connected by some sort of moral purpose. All worked toward improvement. Everything held together.

This was the view of poets, professors, preachers, politicians. They were almost all white Anglo-Saxon Protestant males. They were not always and everywhere a majority. But they set the tone.

As the United States approaches the 200th birthday of the Declaration of Independence, however, that unified culture has begun to unravel. One has

---

*CHRONOLOGY*

1971 *Twenty-sixth Amendment gives vote to eighteen-year-olds*

1973 *Watergate scandals, connected with Nixon's* 1972 *presidential campaign, are revealed*

1974 *August 9, Richard Nixon resigns as president; Gerald Ford replaces him* only to listen to the voices of dissent or look at the exploded forms of modern art or hear the jangle of contemporary music to know that the old rules for everything from the sonata to the seminar are dissolving.

American culture may be coming apart. Or it may be developing many centers and subcultures. Each has its own style and uses its own lens to see the present and the past. Each, therefore, makes a separate judgment on where to fit every current event into the pattern of history.

That is why a neat final summary is difficult to achieve in the 1970s. The long-accepted themes of American history have been challenged by counterthemes. These are often stated or shouted by groups to whom the old American culture assigned minority roles: women, nonwhites, or the very poor. These counterthemes began to resound most loudly in the troubled, divisive 1960s. No one knows how long they will echo. Perhaps in our technological age, reeling from "future shock" (the dislocation caused by too much, too rapid change), whole new forms of belief are coming into being. They may mold a new kind of U.S. history that embodies neither the old themes nor the counterthemes of the sixties.

What can be done now is to illustrate how ideas affect the choice of historical subject matter by stating some of the traditional themes of American history along with the evidence used to support them. Then we will show how some events of the early 1970s could be fitted into those themes. Then, for contrast, we will list some challenging alternative views, or counterthemes, and suggest what outstanding moments of the present hour might confirm *those* views and who might be expressing them. Finally, you yourself may think of new ways to frame the past in the viewfinder and create a picture into which you can fit the current-events information pouring out at you daily. Some possible ways of doing this are offered to help you begin.

## *Theme I: America the Free*

From 1776 onward, liberty in the United States has gotten more elbowroom. We began with a system that restricted the vote to male, white taxpayers and property owners. By the 1820s, before the nation was a half-century old, the drive for universal manhood suffrage had reached a peak in the age of Jackson. Already by then, in the election for president, the electoral college was merely rubber-stamping the popular vote. Ninety-five years after the Declaration of Independence, in 1870, the right of voting was guaranteed to all men, regardless of race, color, or previous condition of servitude. Forty-three years after that, in 1912, the Seventeenth Amendment provided for the direct, popular election of senators. And six years later, in the Nineteenth, the polls were thrown open to women. By 1920 there was almost no adult American who could not, regardless of religion, economic status, opinions, sex, or color, step into the voting booth and choose among government officials. It was a privilege that much of the world still lacked.

The 1965 Voting Rights Act, offering federal protection to those illegally barred from the polls, especially in Southern states, fit into that tradition of ever-growing suffrage. So did one of the key pieces of lawmaking of the 1970s, the passage of the Twenty-sixth Amendment in 1971. It gave the ballot to eighteen year olds. At last the nation recognized that young men and women old enough to fight in America's wars, work in America's workshops, and start America's families deserved a say in America's future. Democracy, the principle of government only by consent of the governed, was still on the move.

*Countertheme: America the repressive and corrupt*

The mere idea of "giving" the vote that was rightfully theirs to blacks or to women shows the self-satisfaction of the ingroup that guarded the gates of American historical writing. The facts are that America has always been dominated by two tyrannies: one of majority opinion, the other of the dollar sign, which made political liberty meaningless. The " privilege" of voting, so grudgingly and belatedly given to the propertyless and to minorities, was a right to vote with the herd and to choose officials who would do the bidding of business. Witch hunts sear the American record. There were the Alien and Sedition Acts, the persecution of Mormons, the great "red scare" of 1919, the McCarthyist hysteria of the 1950s.

And what good did it do workingmen to get the vote in the 1820s, when they were plunged into the panic of 1837 by irresponsible speculators who brought on a crash? What value did the vote have for blacks in the 1870s? First, it was taken from them by violence, and then they sank into peonage. What good did the vote do coal miners and dirt farmers in the 1920s? What did most Americans care about freedom, in fact—especially freedom for people who desired to be different—as long as there was prosperity?

The best evidence of the real nature of American political life was the Watergate scandals, the most recent of a long line that ran back through the Harding and Grant administrations. Nixon was overwhelmingly reelected in 1972 by telling the American people that he stood for "law and order." But, early in 1973, ugly facts came to light. The president had received a gigantic campaign fund for his reelection, consisting largely of contributions from huge corporations. Much of it was given in secret and illegally, in expectation of favors. Nixon and his chief assistants used some of the money to finance a program of political espionage, wiretapping, and burglary to "get" political "enemies." One of these burglaries, at the headquarters of the Democratic National Committee, went awry. Nixon's agents then arranged for perjured testimony in the trial of the captured burglars and promised to pay them if they would plead guilty and pledge secrecy about their connections with the White

House. But the story leaked out because one of the burglars talked, because of vigorous investigative work done by some newspaperpeople, and finally because committees of the House and Senate dug into the facts. They received considerable help from the courts, which forced Nixon to turn over to a special prosecutor secret tape recordings of White House conversations in which the cover-up had been planned. On August 9, 1974, Nixon, facing certain impeachment and removal by Congress, resigned the office of president. It seemed as though the combination of the Constitution, a free press, and an independent judicial branch had turned back a bid to put the president above the law. The American system had worked.

Yet it could be argued that the crimes of Watergate were equally the logical outcome of "the system." The American people had long accepted the idea of heavy campaign financing by private interests. They accepted the president's right to conduct government behind closed doors. Finally, they supported a president who scrimped on social welfare budgets and doled out money to the military-industrial complex generously, as long as that president told them that the self-flattering platitudes of the past century were still true. Even if a spasm of reaction jerked Nixon out of office, the underlying truth of Watergate was the tainted pretense of freedom in American life.

*New framework*

Both sides could show evidence for their stances. It is hard to quarrel with the fact that civil liberties were seriously threatened after 1945. But it is equally hard to say that in the sixties the idea of freedom did not have its new followers. One after another, various minorities—blacks, Chicanos, Puerto Ricans, women, homosexuals, "ethnics"—demanded self-expression and new powers. Perhaps freedom is taking on new definitions. In the Depression it had become common to say that the freedom to vote meant little if a person was jobless and insecure. A regular pay or pension check was an absolute necessity to political freedom's having any meaning. So, it might be, men and women were now claiming new kinds of freedom not foreseen in the Constitution. The list would include freedom to advance new ideas, to demand openly freedom of sexual expression, to try different life-styles without handicaps, to break the restraints of sex roles. Could such freedoms exist *without* political freedom? Did they replace it? Or was freedom simply taking on new meanings? If that was the case, then the most important modern events that related to freedom might have little to do with traditional subjects like who voted.

## *Theme II: America, Creator of Abundance*

The New World loomed before the eyes of the first settlers as a land of milk and honey. Their grinding work and stubborn faith helped to make that vision real. In less than 300 years Americans, under a system that encouraged

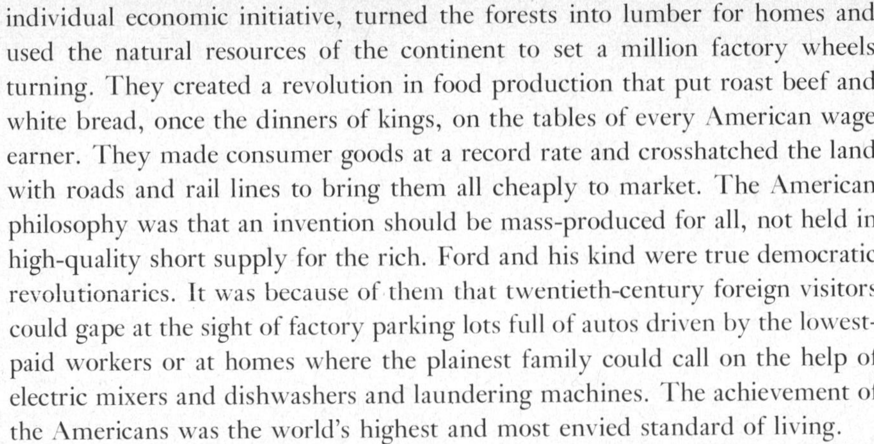

individual economic initiative, turned the forests into lumber for homes and used the natural resources of the continent to set a million factory wheels turning. They created a revolution in food production that put roast beef and white bread, once the dinners of kings, on the tables of every American wage earner. They made consumer goods at a record rate and crosshatched the land with roads and rail lines to bring them all cheaply to market. The American philosophy was that an invention should be mass-produced for all, not held in high-quality short supply for the rich. Ford and his kind were true democratic revolutionaries. It was because of them that twentieth-century foreign visitors could gape at the sight of factory parking lots full of autos driven by the lowest-paid workers or at homes where the plainest family could call on the help of electric mixers and dishwashers and laundering machines. The achievement of the Americans was the world's highest and most envied standard of living.

The great events of the 1960s and 1970s were not the protests and the marches, the bombs on Vietnam and the bombast of elections. They were rising production curves. They were the milestones on the road to a trillion-dollar gross national product sometime before 2000. Even temporary problems of inflation and recession could not dim the overall achievement.

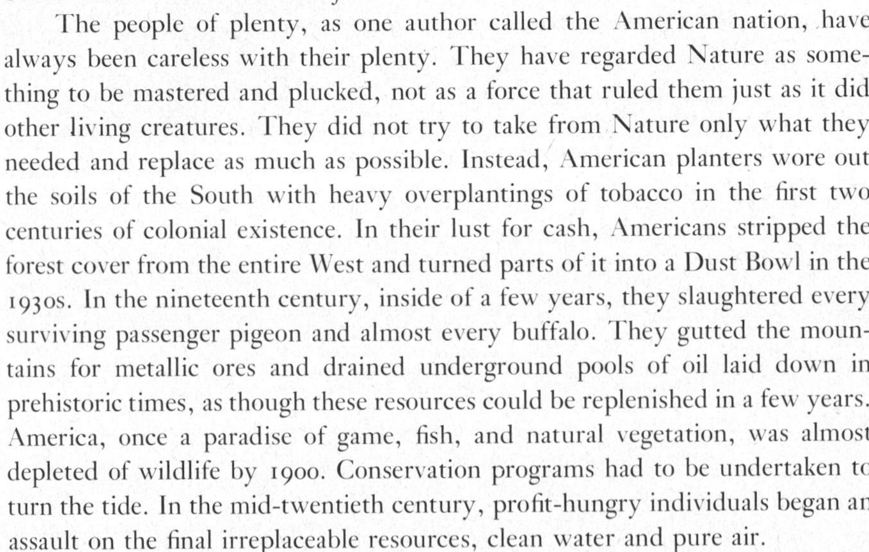

*Countertheme: America the wasteful*

The people of plenty, as one author called the American nation, have always been careless with their plenty. They have regarded Nature as something to be mastered and plucked, not as a force that ruled them just as it did other living creatures. They did not try to take from Nature only what they needed and replace as much as possible. Instead, American planters wore out the soils of the South with heavy overplantings of tobacco in the first two centuries of colonial existence. In their lust for cash, Americans stripped the forest cover from the entire West and turned parts of it into a Dust Bowl in the 1930s. In the nineteenth century, inside of a few years, they slaughtered every surviving passenger pigeon and almost every buffalo. They gutted the mountains for metallic ores and drained underground pools of oil laid down in prehistoric times, as though these resources could be replenished in a few years. America, once a paradise of game, fish, and natural vegetation, was almost depleted of wildlife by 1900. Conservation programs had to be undertaken to turn the tide. In the mid-twentieth century, profit-hungry individuals began an assault on the final irreplaceable resources, clean water and pure air.

And with all this riot of overconsumption, the key irony was that one-fourth to one-half of the population was still poor. Perhaps even the American poor lived better than the poor of other nations. But, nonetheless, the outpouring of consumer goods circulated only in the top segment of an economic pyramid, with a wide base of low-income families and a tiny peak of the powerful superrich.

The event of the seventies, revealing the true course and speed of American society, was the oil shortage that began in the last months of 1973. Whether it was temporary or permanent, the fault of Arabs or U.S. corporations or no one, it was a spotlight on how our society worked. We had become accustomed to the casual waste of energy. Petroleum was the base of the plastics that were critical components of thousands of items in daily private and industrial use. Oil-driven generators pumped out the electric power for trains and elevators, air conditioners and assembly lines, lights and business machines. Oil warmed our homes. Above all, oil was the lifeblood of the trucks and autos on which the whole economy depended. Nothing could have shown better than the panic of oil-hungry Americans how important a plentiful supply of low-cost energy had become to them.

*New framework*

The whole idea of progress in American life had been geared to abundance. Increased quantities of almost anything seemed a goal worth panting toward. Boosterism fattened on statistics of bigness and growth—this town was praised for producing more cottage cheese than ever before, that one for being the home of the longest assembly line, the deepest mine shaft, the biggest warehouse. A rising curve of production had done so much for jobs, for bigger bank balances, for more taxes to pay the costs of governing that it had become a symbol of power. It was worshiped almost as the Cross was by crusaders.

But perhaps it would be necessary after the 1970s to think in entirely new terms. Perhaps the energy crisis was a true turning point in American history. Perhaps the good life would have to come to mean not plenty of everything but of a few things of quality. Politics might become the art of democratically choosing which ones to concentrate upon. Perhaps Americans would now heed those who, in the nineteenth and twentieth centuries, had preached that happiness lay in simplicity and harmony with Nature.

Such a view would cause a recasting of our history, with many forgotten men and women "cranks" emerging as prophets. It was not entirely a viewpoint that everyone could easily adopt. It was much easier to retreat from overconsumption if one had grown up in the middle classes, taking full refrigerators and powerful cars for granted. To millions of Americans still poor and to others in the world still hungry and naked, ownership of a wasteful machine or the use of items that could be later thrown away (like soft-drink bottles or paper diapers) was a sign of having "made it." Waste was a good-conduct medal in the struggle to prove one's worth and power to command the terms of one's own life.

So if the energy crisis made Americans rethink the virtues of simplicity, it might divide classes more painfully than the old industrial revolutions had done and rouse political storms. Nevertheless, the shortages of the early seventies made one fact stand out. In the early twentieth century Gompers had been asked to state in general terms what workers wanted. He answered in a single word: "More." As America began her third century of independence, that simply might not be the correct answer any longer.

*Theme III: America the Asylum and Land of Equality*

We are one nation out of many, as the motto on the coinage proudly announces. Our first "immigrants" were the Spaniards looking for gold and eternal youth in Florida and South Carolina. From there on an unbroken line runs through the Pilgrim fathers, to the huddled masses pouring up from the steerages to stretch in New World air, to the Dominican doctor and Pakistani engineer landing at an American airport today. Between 40 and 50 million of the world's people came here. Most of those from Africa came by force. But with that exception, all of them were looking for new hopes and prospects.

And they found them here. They found a government that required no national origins test for holding office or voting. They found no established state church to tax their pockets and harass their minds. The found jobs waiting and a universal equalizer of status in the dollar. America took peasants and mill hands from every corner of the world and gave them and their children a chance. Millions took that chance to become what they desired. They climbed the heights to professions, homeownership, wealth. And those who decided to practice the arts of government found no doors that they could not force open. The Irish, the Italians, the Jews, and eventually the blacks came to have their own ward bosses and precinct leaders, then to name some of their own people to the mixed tickets. There was a climax of sorts in 1960 when white Protestant America elected Kennedy, the Catholic grandson of an Irish immigrant of the 1840s, to the White House. "Opportunity" was more than just a word.

What was the most meaningful event of the 1970s from this viewpoint? That would have been relatively easy to answer in 1973. In that year Henry Kissinger became U.S. secretary of state. In point of fact, he was America's president for foreign policy-making purposes, universally listened to and respected (if not always agreed with or admired) at home and abroad. But Kissinger had come with his family as a Jewish refugee from Germany only about thirty years earlier and still carried his German past visibly in a thick accent. It had been no handicap. Some had even talked of razing the last barrier in his way by amending the Constitution to wipe out the clause requiring the president to be born in the United States. Whether or not that happened, Kissinger, who probably would have been destroyed had he remained in Germany, had been clothed in honor and majesty in America. A later decline in his popularity did not change this basic fact.

*Countertheme: America the racist*

The "asylum" theory, or that of the "melting pot," can only bring mocking laughter to the lips of an American black. Africans were brought here in chains,

kept in bondage until 1865, and systematically humiliated and denied a man's or woman's chance thereafter. The record was not much better for other nonwhite groups. The Indians had been slaughtered and reduced to pitiful beggars, living on handouts on land they once owned. The Chinese had been beaten and expelled from western towns, then barred from entry as immigrants altogether from 1882 to 1945. And in 1942, 110,000 Japanese in California were forced, on short notice, to sell their homes and businesses built up over long struggling years and were herded into internment camps. It was something we did to no other group of Americans of foreign descent in any war—not even to the Japanese Americans of Hawaii, where wartime danger was closer. But, unlike California, Hawaii was not a state then with a long tradition of anti-Oriental feeling that could influence Washington.

And even a white skin was not enough for acceptance by the WASP elite, if it covered a Catholic or southern European body. Know-Nothing anti-Catholic riots in the 1840s sent monasteries up in flames. Our immigration laws from 1924 to 1965 deliberately cut the immigration of Poles, Slavs, Greeks, and Italians to a trickle. And "old-country" people who did not quickly give up their language, native costumes, food habits, traditions, and customs found the doors to employment and advancement closed in their faces. The "melting pot" melted people into imitation WASPs. It cut them off from their pasts and their ancestral roots and made them strangers to their more quickly assimilated children. And somehow, some way, the bulk of the poor and underprivileged in the United States, despite all talk of equality, turned out to be the nonwhites and so-called ethnics of Europe's Slavic and Mediterranean regions.

To this group the most important events of the years since 1969 could be the confrontation between Indians and whites at Wounded Knee, South Dakota, scene of an 1890 massacre of Sioux Indians by U.S. troopers. It was part of a series of continuing clashes that occurred as Indians became conscious both of their disadvantages and their tribal heritage. Or many militant blacks would have claimed that the Attica, New York, prison riot of 1971 was a revealing beacon. Prisoners there, demanding improved conditions, seized and held hostage a number of guards. New York state troopers and National Guardsmen, after some parleying, fought their way back into the prison. Forty-four prisoners were killed in indiscriminate gunfire. On the surface the issue did not appear racial. But many blacks argued that prison conditions were disgraceful (which they were) and remained disgraceful because a large part of the prison population had become black. They also insisted that the high proportion of jailed blacks was due to the fact that a white-dominated criminal justice system tended to stack the cards against black defendants, who were in court in the first place because a white-dominated economy had starved or goaded them into crime. Whatever the merits of the argument, it spelled out a new disillusionment with America's system of criminal justice.

*New framework*

To discuss the meaning of "black power" and "ethnic loyalty" poses special problems. In one sense, aroused Puerto Ricans, Chicanos, and blacks, as well as Italians and Poles, were looking for new ways of identifying themselves in a society that, as we saw, tended in a terrible way to reduce all people to statistics. Such rediscovery of special, different human styles could be a positive force. If it became a vogue, it might lead to a political reorientation in big cities, which gave different ethnic neighborhoods new independence.

But there were many potential trouble spots. White ethnics and nonwhites often contended for the same "turf" and for a share of the rebuilding and improvement funds provided by government. In Newark, New Jersey, Italians and blacks in 1973 fought over the construction of an apartment complex designed to be largely black inhabited. In New York, Jews and blacks in New York's school system battled in 1968 over questions such as whether black school supervisors were harassing Jewish teachers or permitting the teaching of anti-Semitic ideas in black studies classes. A new framework for governing cities, built on a recognition of pride of color, race, and national background, could upset political balances and might create stresses as bad as those it was supposed to help.

But if such a new framework of loyalty was developing, it would dictate a totally new look at immigration history. Being "Americanized" would no longer be regarded as the highest goal. Instead, the big developments would be those that helped differing race and nationality groups to realize their own importance, problems, and potential powers.

*Theme IV: America the Peaceful: At Home and Abroad*

Americans solved their social problems without the horrors of mass execution, class war, or tyranny. Not for us were the guillotine of the Reign of Terror in France, the crowds machine-gunned in the streets of Russia, the thump of boots on the cobblestones and the knock on the door by secret police in Nazi Germany. Not for us were the firing squads of "banana republics," but the ballot rather than the bullet. And what power has been less imperialistic abroad? Our War of 1812 was fought mostly on our own soil. Even if it is argued that we did attack Mexico, there was provocation and payment of a handsome sum for land taken. And we have since, in the Good Neighbor era, apologized many times over for the episode. After the war with Spain we annexed Puerto Rico and the Philippines. But by 1917 we had made Puerto Rico a commonwealth whose people enjoyed the status of U.S. citizens. And the Filipinos were promised independence in 1946 by an act of 1916, and the promise was kept. After World War I and World War II we did not annex a square foot of territory, except for protectorates over certain Pacific islands.

Moreover, our loans and aid rebuilt both our allies and enemies' lands. Whatever occasional stains may be on the American record, on the whole our claim that we seek only a just and peaceful world and have no territorial or power ambitions of our own is one that history sustains.

From this standpoint the most significant event of the early 1970s would be Nixon's historic visit to Peking in 1972. The door was opened to friendship and trade with China after twenty-three years. There could hardly be a more visible sign of Americans' desire for peaceful relations with any other power that was willing to go halfway.

*Countertheme: America the violent*

But the record on the other side is also formidable. When black activist Stokely Carmichael declared in the late 1960s, "Violence is as American as cherry pie," he was looking at the past through the lens of the black, underdog experience. And underdogs have a more jaundiced view of American "nonviolence" than historians sitting comfortably in university offices. The Tories who were tarred and feathered, driven from their flaming homes, or lynched by mobs would have a different tale to tell. So would the Southerners who survived the Civil War.

No revolution in America? The Civil War was one made by a section that failed. It cost 600,000 lives on both sides, out of a total white population of some 42 million—a colossal bloodletting. American violence not only rode with the hooded knights of the Ku Klux Klan but with the cavalrymen who cleared the plains of the Indians and with the marines who trundled in battle gear down gangplanks in Nicaragua, the Dominican Republic, Haiti, and China. America, for all her piety, is the only nation that ever *used* an atomic weapon in war. And she did so despite pleas from some of the scientists who worked on the bomb to try other ways of convincing the Japanese to surrender before unleashing the ultimate terror.

Finally, America since 1945 is the only nation that has not only claimed the right and duty to police the entire world against what she calls aggression but has also actually attempted to do it. The American fascination with violence shows in every kind of cultural evidence, from the taste for "shoot-em-up" gangster and western films to the popularity of the skillful but bruising game of professional football.

History seen from one of these citadels of "outsiders" would zero in on an event of 1970 as especially rich in overtones of meaning. In May of that year Americans launched an invasion of Cambodia, up to then neutral in the Indo-Chinese war. The official American excuse was that the North Vietnamese were using Cambodia as a refuge and communications route on their way southward to escape our bombs. (In actual fact, we had been secretly bombing them in Cambodia for a year.) But all through the Johnson administration, a North Vietnamese presence in Cambodia had been accepted as a necessary evil. Now, suddenly, Nixon widened the war at a time when he said he was "winding it down." He stirred up the Cambodian countryside, dragged the area deep into the heart of the war, and, though American ground troops withdrew after a time, Cambodia remained ravaged and bombed from then on, suffering thousands of casualties each month.

The violence of that May "incursion" soon brought tragedy to America's own shores. Protests on university campuses were immediate and widespread. One of them, as we saw earlier, was at Kent State University. National Guardsmen, called in to "maintain order," under circumstances by no means clear at this date, fired into a crowd, killing four students. That was the American answer to strong dissent—the domestic side of the coin of violence so freely spent abroad.

*New framework*

At this point, you yourself may try your hand, without guidance from the book, in creating a possible viewpoint that would put American violence in a new perspective. Is it something that was necessary in the frontier past and then was carried over into the present? Is it a necessary stage in reaching a certain peak of national power? Are Americans like ancient Romans or modern Russians? Is the American story simply a chapter in the rise of the whole Western world to global dominance? Experiment and decide what you would emphasize if you were telling the story of the past five years to an audience wanting to see the "big picture."

## *Theme V: America the Chosen*

There is a sense in which both the spokesmen of the old American history and the voices demanding a new, multicentered culture share a viewpoint. Both regard America as being somehow special. Those who have exalted our goodness, our steady progress toward democracy, our gifts to the world raise their voices in the tradition of the Puritan leader John Winthrop. He said that "we should be as a city on a hill. The eyes of all mankind are upon us." Another spokesman, George Washington, said that the destiny of liberty was "deeply, perhaps finally staked" on the American experiment in self-government. Lincoln declared that the Civil War in a nation "conceived in liberty and dedicated to the proposition that all men are created equal" was a test of whether *any* nation "so conceived and so dedicated can long endure."

It may seem strange to say that recent critics of American life and society stand on common ground with traditional "boosters." But they do. Their assault on America as being more corrupt and more violent than any other nation also seems to set the United States off as being "special," just as much as any Fourth of July praise. And their anger at the failure of America to fulfill her promises springs from disappointment.

The critics are not cynical. They believe that life here *can* and *should* be better than elsewhere—because we have said so and because people within our boundaries and the world over have believed so. The rage of the angry attackers on the failure of American commitments would be quieter if they accepted the limits of human goodness or the permanence of misery as a fact of human life. Instead, they have believed in the promises of the Declaration of Independence and think they have been betrayed.

In a curious way, this common sensing of the general nature of being an American is something that may disappear and be replaced by a broader outlook on the world family. This is a world of instant communication. In it, events in Africa and Asia are televised as instant reality to New York and Chicago. It is a world that has been photographed by humans 200,000 miles out in space and shown to be fragile, small, lonely, beautiful—and *one!* It may be that the new scale of distance imposed by these miracles will shift the focus of connection for people. Once, we began by feeling close to our family; then we grew to cherish our connections to city and state. Finally, there was devoted allegiance to our nation.

Today, however, "family" is no longer the strong social unit that it was, because of frequent migration and divorce. And people change their home cities and states often in their lives as they speed along the highways in quest of new jobs or different scenes. Only the nation has remained a strong symbol of community. It has given us definition and status. We have touched a base when each of us announces, "I am an American."

But perhaps this may change too. Perhaps in this shrunken world it will become more and more necessary to get a sense of ourselves from some other kind of "community."

The world cannot afford many more nationalistic confrontations. This point of view may become dominant in the next twenty years. Like the war on waste, it is something that will come easier to the haves than the have-nots. The nations that have already known the glory and the pain and cost of achieving greatness may be ready to soften national feelings. Those still small, weak, unformed, or only existent in the minds of some ethnic group may still sound the old battle cries and quite possibly pose grave problems in a small world struggling for peace.

One cannot see the future. If "Americanism" loses some of its meaning, the gains and losses will be hard to measure. One loss—that of optimism—would be especially sad. Our journey on the pathway to the present should have shown one thing: the tremendous faith in the future that every generation of

Americans displayed. America was promises. She was an encouragement to hope. In a sense, what America gave everyone in the country, regardless of national origin or class or sex or race, was a prospect that tomorrow might be better. Tomorrow was the gift.

And a better tomorrow may be an illusion. We may be chained more firmly than we think to our past mistakes. Or perhaps the pathway is circular and does not lead from the past below to the future ahead and on high but simply around and around. Perhaps the vision of a better tomorrow is part of an individual's or a nation's youth and disappears, with the years, into the realization that the more things change, the more they remain the same.

If all of us should come to believe it, that may be the greatest change that overtook America in two centuries. For the illusion of progress is a natural-born American citizen. Perhaps the last word should be left to F. Scott Fitzgerald in the brilliant conclusion of his novel *The Great Gatsby.* It is the story of Jay Gatsby, born Jimmy Gatz. He is a young midwesterner who falls in love with a beautiful girl during World War I. Returning from overseas duty, he finds her married to another man—rich, insensitive, and philandering. He vows to redeem his ideal, goes off to make a fortune in bootlegging under his new name, and returns to complete his quest.

He cannot see that his love, born in social position, will never accept him because of his lack of background. Nor does he realize that she is actually a weak and shallow woman and that the purity of his dream both purges his own shady activities and sets him forever apart from her. His idealism transforms him, yet it separates him from the reality of what she is.

In the end his dream destroys him. She kills a woman while carelessly driving his car. Gatsby, protecting her, is mistakenly shot in revenge by the dead woman's enraged husband. In the final paragraph, the narrator of the story, a friend of Gatsby's, looks at Gatsby's abandoned house on Long Island and muses about the country of the American, Jimmy Gatz's vision—his country and dream—and ours:

> . . . as the moon rose higher the inessential houses began to melt away until gradually I became aware of the old island here that flowered once for Dutch sailors' eyes—a fresh, green breast of the new world. Its vanished trees . . . had once pandered in whispers to the last and greatest of all human dreams. . . .
>
> . . . He had come a long way to this blue lawn, and his dream must have seemed so close that he could hardly fail to grasp it. He did not know that it was already behind him, somewhere back in that vast obscurity beyond the city, where the dark fields of the republic rolled on under the night.
>
> Gatsby believed in the green light, the orgiastic future that year by year recedes before us. It eluded us then, but that's no matter—tomorrow we will run faster, stretch out our arms further. . . . And one fine morning—
>
> So we beat on, boats against the current, borne back ceaselessly into the past.

## *FOR FURTHER READING*

It is a difficult task to name books that illustrate the diversity of American life in the mid-1970s and that are likely to have a lasting impact, but a few can be mentioned. Books on Watergate and Nixon will be coming out for a long time, but few can have the drama and impact of Bob Woodward and Carl Bernstein, *All The President's Men* (1974), by two *Washington Post* reporters who played an important role in "cracking" the story. An earlier and solid evaluation of Nixon is Gary Wills, *Nixon Agonistes* (1970).

What are the views of American radicals? A book written in the heat of the sixties and with sympathy for the dissidents is Jack Newfield, *A Prophetic Minority* (1971). A detached history of the protests of the decade is Irwin Unger, *The Movement: A History of the American New Left* (1974). Another view holds, however, that the left (new and old) never has had much influence with the great mass of the American people who are still faithful to traditional loyalties. This case is effectively related in Benjamin Wattenberg and Richard Scammon, *The Real Majority* (1970). And at the opposite extreme of the "prophetic minority" stand the arch conservatives described by Ronald Radosh in *Prophets on the Right* (1974).

In the end, the best you can do is to examine the facts as thoroughly and open-mindedly as you can, listen as hard as you can, strengthen your own values, and make your own decisions as to what prophecies to believe. To help understand the factual basis of all the theorizing, a book by E. J. Kahn, Jr., simply entitled *The American People* (1974), consists of a careful study of the 1970 census. This most recent "collective portrait" of the 200 million plus Americans is perhaps the best way to see where the pathways to the present have led.

# THOUGHT PROVOKERS

To survey the world of the 1970s and the American role in it is to plunge into a sea of uncertainty and doubt. Each day's headlines create a new problem and present a new situation. Historical perspective cannot supply an answer to the problems of securing peace, justice, an orderly distribution of the world's resources, and an even-handed sharing of the blessings of modern technology. What it can do, however, is to illustrate the complexities of international problems and show where their roots are sunk. At the very least, it can discourage undisciplined and emotional thought that leaps to easy answers for difficult questions.

Let us take, for example, the question of the world balance of power. How did the emergence of many new, small, formerly colonized nations change the pattern of decision making in international affairs? How did American foreign policy toward small nations change between the early 1900s and the 1960s? How much of the change had to do with the cold war? Why did the United States, which controlled Cuban policy from 1901 to about 1933, accept an anti-American pro-Communist Cuba in 1975? What are the rights of a small nation, like Saudi Arabia, that controls a vital resource, like oil, to withhold that resource from a large nation such as the United States, even when doing so causes a severe economic crisis in the large nation? How would Americans have answered that question in 1920? How would the U.S. government answer it now? Is there a difference, and why?

One mark of the struggle of "oppressed" peoples in the 1970s is a rise in terrorism—bombings, hijackings, and kidnappings. Why is this weapon of terrorism in particular use nowadays? Is there anything in the technological developments of the age (jet travel, for example) that makes nations more vulnerable to this kind of activity by small, determined groups? Does terrorism count on changes in the communications media to get its message across? Have there been shifts in the way in which human life is regarded that make the terrorist's task easier? From your study of modern technology and U.S. international relations, what forces would you say have increased the chances of peaceful settlement of disputes among peoples, and what forces have decreased them? Is nationalism any longer a useful political philosophy for large nations? For small ones?

The multinational corporation has made a deep impact on the American economy. What has it done to the world's economy? How does it make the economic interdependence of the various parts of the world more noticeable and important? Can *one country really afford for long to ignore both natural and manufactured problems—disease, famine, wars, revolutions, depressions—in another, when the other is "host" to a major corporation whose headquarters are in the first country? Are the multinationals the seeds of a new kind of international order?*

*At home how did the events of the fifties and sixties erode the power of Congress? The constitutional safeguards on privacy? Is international superpower status, as the United States knows it, compatible with democracy as the United States would have defined it* 100 *or* 200 *years ago? Is there any escape from such status for the United States?*

*And now let us look at the Vietnam War. How was the opposition at home to it different from the opposition to the War of* 1812 *and the Mexican War? Was it confined to a particular section? Or to a particular class? Did it have more lasting results? Were the opponents of those first two wars "justified" by later historians? Is the same fate likely to befall the draft resisters of the Vietnam War? What meanings did war and nationhood have throughout the nineteenth century that may have changed the twentieth? Is war any longer considered proof of a nation's health? Or virtue? If so, by whom? And if not, by whom? What are the points of difference between the two groups? And what arguments could each derive from the Vietnam story to back its case?*

*Was Vietnam a natural outgrowth of an American mentality that also led to the near extermination of Indians and the enslavement of blacks? Or was it an extension of the same ideals that led us into World War I? How did the divisions over Vietnam affect the veterans of the war? Why was there no veterans' legislation comparable to the post–World War II GI Bills of Rights? And, finally, what things do you think will have to happen before there is some final, national agreement to "bury" the issue of Vietnam and forgive all those who both fought in it and against it?*

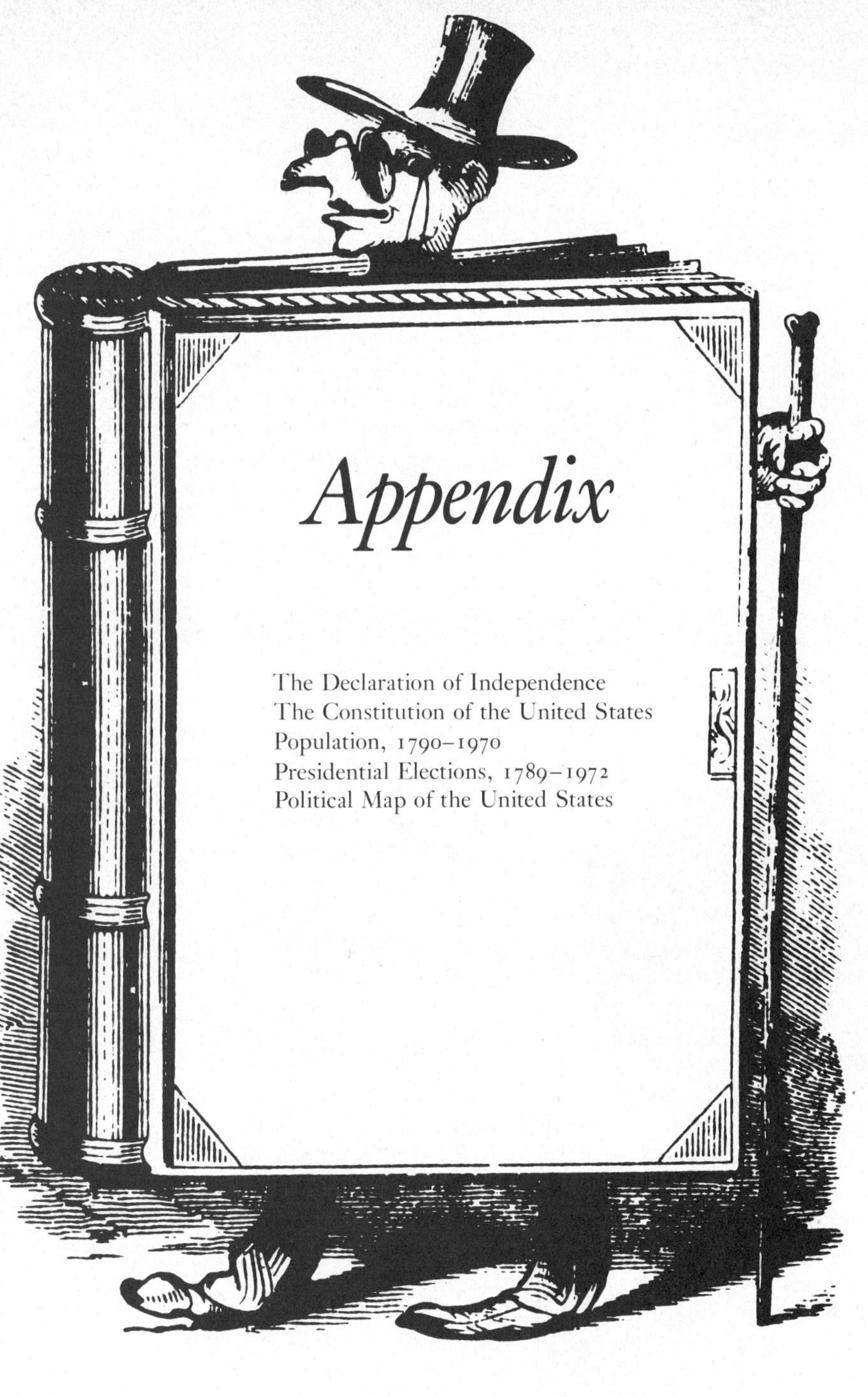

# Appendix

The Declaration of Independence
The Constitution of the United States
Population, 1790–1970
Presidential Elections, 1789–1972
Political Map of the United States

# *The Declaration of Independence*

When in the Course of human events, it becomes necessary for one people to dissolve the political bands which have connected them with another, and to assume among the Powers of the earth, the separate and equal station to which the Laws of Nature and of Nature's God entitle them, a decent respect to the opinions of mankind requires that they should declare the causes which impel them to the separation.

We hold these truths to be self-evident, that all men are created equal, that they are endowed by their Creator with certain unalienable Rights, that among these are Life, Liberty and the pursuit of Happiness. That to secure these rights, Governments are instituted among Men, deriving their just powers from the consent of the governed, That whenever any Form of Government becomes destructive of these ends, it is the Right of the People to alter or to abolish it, and to institute new Government, laying its foundation on such principles and organizing its powers in such form, as to them shall seem most likely to effect their Safety and Happiness. Prudence, indeed, will dictate that Governments long established should not be changed for light and transient causes; and accordingly all experience hath shown, that mankind are more disposed to suffer, while evils are sufferable, than to right themselves by abolishing the forms to which they are accustomed. But when a long train of abuses and usurpations, pursuing invariably the same Object evinces a design to reduce them under absolute Despotism, it is their right, it is their duty, to throw off such Government, and to provide new Guards for their future security.—Such has been the patient sufferance of these Colonies; and such is now the necessity which constrains them to alter their former Systems of Government. The history of the present King of Great Britain is a history of repeated injuries and usurpations, all having in direct object the establishment of an absolute Tyranny over these States. To prove this, let Facts be submitted to a candid world.

He has refused his Assent to Laws, the most wholesome and necessary for the public good.

He has forbidden his Governors to pass Laws of immediate and pressing importance, unless suspended in their operation till his Assent should be obtained; and when so suspended, he has utterly neglected to attend to them.

He has refused to pass other Laws for the accommodation of large districts of people, unless those people would relinquish the right of Representation in the Legislature, a right inestimable to them and formidable to tyrants only.

He has called together legislative bodies at places unusual, uncomfortable, and distant from the depository of their Public Records, for the sole purpose of fatiguing them into compliance with his measures.

He has dissolved Representative Houses repeatedly, for opposing with manly firmness his invasions on the rights of the people.

He has refused for a long time, after such dissolutions, to cause others to be elected; whereby the Legislative Powers, incapable of Annihilation, have returned to the People at large for their exercise; the State remaining in the mean time exposed to all the dangers of invasion from without, and convulsions within.

He has endeavoured to prevent the population of these States; for that purpose obstructing the Laws of Naturalization of Foreigners; refusing to pass others to encourage their migration hither, and raising the conditions of new Appropriations of Lands.

He has obstructed the Administration of Justice, by refusing his Assent to Laws for establishing Judiciary Powers.

He has made Judges dependent on his Will alone, for the tenure of their offices, and the amount and payment of their salaries.

He has erected a multitude of New Offices, and sent hither swarms of Officers to harass our People, and eat out their substance.

He has kept among us, in times of peace, Standing Armies without the Consent of our legislature.

He has affected to render the Military independent of and superior to the Civil Power.

He has combined with others to subject us to a jurisdiction foreign to our constitution, and unacknowledged by our laws; giving his Assent to their acts of pretended legislation:

For quartering large bodies of armed troops among us:

For protecting them, by a mock Trial, from Punishment for any Murders which they should commit on the Inhabitants of these States:

For cutting off our Trade with all parts of the world:

For imposing taxes on us without our Consent:

For depriving us in many cases, of the benefits of Trial by Jury:

For transporting us beyond Seas to be tried for pretended offences:

For abolishing the free System of English Laws in a neighbouring Province, establishing therein an Arbitrary government, and enlarging its Boundaries so as to render it at once an example and fit instrument for introducing the same absolute rule into these Colonies:

For taking away our Charters, abolishing our most valuable Laws, and altering fundamentally the Forms of our Governments:

For suspending our own Legislature, and declaring themselves invested with Power to legislate for us in all cases whatsoever.

He has abdicated Government here, by declaring us out of his Protection and waging War against us.

He has plundered our seas, ravaged our Coasts, burnt our towns, and destroyed the lives of our people.

He is at this time transporting large armies of foreign mercenaries to compleat the works of death, desolation and tyranny, already begun with circumstances of Cruelty & perfidy scarcely paralleled in the most barbarous ages, and totally unworthy the Head of a civilized nation.

He has constrained our fellow Citizens taken Captive on the high Seas to bear Arms against their Country, to become the executioners of their friends and Brethren, or to fall themselves by their Hands.

He has excited domestic insurrections amongst us, and has endeavoured to bring on the inhabitants of our frontiers, the merciless Indian Savages, whose known rule of warfare, is an undistinguished destruction of all ages, sexes and conditions.

In every stage of these Oppressions We have Petitioned for Redress in the most humble terms: Our repeated Petitions have been answered only by repeated injury. A Prince, whose character is thus marked by every act which may define a Tyrant, is unfit to be the ruler of a free People.

Nor have We been wanting in attention to our British brethren. We have warned them from time to time of attempts by their legislature to extend an unwarrantable jurisdiction over us. We have reminded them of the circumstances of our emigration and settlement here. We have appealed to their native justice and magnanimity, and we have conjured them by the ties of our common kindred to disavow these usurpations, which, would inevitably interrupt our connections and correspondence. They too have been deaf to the voice of justice and of consanguinity. We must, therefore, acquiesce in the necessity, which denounces our Separation, and hold them, as we hold the rest of mankind, Enemies in War, in Peace Friends.

We, therefore, the Representative of the United States of America, in General Congress, Assembled, appealing to the Supreme Judge of the world for the rectitude of our intentions, do, in the Name, and by Authority of the good People of these Colonies, solemnly publish and declare, That these United Colonies are, and of Right ought to be Free and Independent States; that they are Absolved from all Allegiance to the British Crown, and that all political connection between them and the State of Great Britain, is and ought to be totally dissolved; and that as Free and Independent States, they have full power to levy War, conclude Peace, contract Alliances, establish Commerce, and to do all other Acts and Things which Independent States may of right do. And for the support of this Declaration, with a firm reliance on the Protection of Divine Providence, we mutually pledge to each other our Lives, our Fortunes and our sacred Honor.

# *The Constitution of the United States*

We the people of the United States, in Order to form a more perfect Union, establish Justice, insure domestic Tranquility, provide for the common defence, promote the general Welfare, and secure the Blessings of Liberty to ourselves and our Posterity, do ordain and establish this CONSTITUTION for the United States of America.

*Article I*

*Section* 1. All legislative Powers herein granted shall be vested in a Congress of the United States, which shall consist of a Senate and House of Representatives.

*Section* 2. The House of Representatives shall be composed of Members chosen every second Year by the People of the several States, and the Electors in each State shall have the Qualifications requisite for Electors of the most numerous Branch of the State Legislature.

No Person shall be a Representative who shall not have attained to the Age of twenty-five Years, and been seven Years a Citizen of the United States, and who shall not, when elected, be an Inhabitant of that State in which he shall be chosen.

Representatives and direct Taxes shall be apportioned among the several States which may be included within this Union, according to their respective Numbers, which shall be determined by adding to the whole Number of free Persons, including those bound to Service for a Term of Years, and excluding Indians not taxed, three fifths of all other Persons. The actual Enumeration shall be made within three Years after the first Meeting of the Congress of the United States, and within every subsequent Term of ten Years, in such Manner as they shall by Law direct. The Number of Representatives shall not exceed one for every thirty Thousand, but each State shall have at Least one Representative; and until such enumeration shall be made, the State of New Hampshire shall be entitled to chũse three, Massachusetts eight, Rhode-Island and Providence Plantations one, Connecticut five, New-York six, New Jersey four, Pennsylvania eight, Delaware one, Maryland six, Virginia ten, North Carolina five, South Carolina five, and Georgia three.

When vacancies happen in the Representation from any State, the Executive Authority thereof shall issue Writs of Election to fill such Vacancies.

The House of Representatives shall chuse their Speaker and other Officers; and shall have the sole Power of Impeachment.

*Section* 3. The Senate of the United States shall be composed of two Senators from each State, chosen by the Legislature thereof, for six Years; and each Senator shall have one Vote.

Immediately after they shall be assembled in Consequence of the first Election, they shall be divided as equally as may be into three Classes. The Seats of the Senators of the first Class shall be vacated at the Expiration of the second Year, of the second Class at the Expiration of the fourth Year, and of the third Class at the Expiration of the sixth Year, so that one-third may be chosen every second Year; and if Vacancies happen by Resignation, or otherwise, during the Recess of the Legislature of any State, the Executive thereof may make temporary Appointments until the next Meeting of the Legislature, which shall then fill such Vacancies.

No Person shall be a Senator who shall not have attained to the Age of thirty Years, and been nine Years a Citizen of the United States, and who shall not, when elected, be an Inhabitant of that State in which he shall be chosen.

The Vice President of the United States shall be

President of the Senate, but shall have no vote, unless they be equally divided.

The Senate shall chuse their other Officers, and also a President pro tempore, in the absence of the Vice President, or when he shall exercise the Office of the President of the United States.

The Senate shall have the sole Power to try all Impeachments. When sitting for that purpose, they shall be on Oath or Affirmation. When the President of the United States is tried, the Chief Justice shall preside: And no person shall be convicted without the Concurrence of two thirds of the Members present.

Judgment in Cases of Impeachment shall not extend further than to removal from Office, and disqualification to hold and enjoy any Office of honor, Trust, or Profit under the United States: but the Party convicted shall nevertheless be liable and subject to Indictment, Trial, Judgment, and Punishment, according to Law.

*Section* 4. The Times, Places and Manner of holding Elections for Senators and Representatives, shall be prescribed in each state by the Legislature thereof; but the Congress may at any time by Law make or alter such Regulations, except as to the Places of Chusing Senators.

The Congress shall assemble at least once in every Year, and such Meeting shall be on the first Monday in December, unless they shall by Law appoint a different Day.

*Section* 5. Each House shall be the Judge of the Elections, Returns and Qualifications of its own Members, and a Majority of each shall constitute a Quorum to do Business; but a smaller number may adjourn from day to day, and may be authorized to compel the Attendance of absent Members, in such Manner, and under such Penalties, as each House may provide.

Each House may determine the Rules of its Proceedings, punish its Members for disorderly Behavior, and, with the Concurrence of two thirds, expel a Member.

Each House shall keep a Journal of its Proceedings, and from time to time publish the same, excepting such Parts as may in their Judgment require Secrecy; and the Yeas and Nays of the Members of either House on any question shall, at the Desire of one fifth of those Present, be entered on the Journal.

Neither House, during the Session of Congress, shall, without the Consent of the other, adjourn for more than three days, nor to any other Place than that in which the two Houses shall be sitting.

*Section* 6. The Senators and Representatives shall receive a Compensation for their Services, to be ascertained by Law, and paid out of the Treasury of the United States. They shall in all Cases, except Treason, Felony, and Breach of the Peace, be privileged from Arrest during their Attendance at the Session of their respective Houses, and in going to and returning from the same; and for any Speech or Debate in either House, they shall not be questioned in any other Place.

No Senator or Representative shall, during the Time for which he was elected, be appointed to any civil Office under the Authority of the Unites States, which shall have been created, or the Emoluments whereof shall have been increased, during such time; and no Person holding any Office under the United States shall be a Member of either House during his continuance in Office.

*Section* 7. All Bills for raising Revenue shall originate in the House of Representatives; but the Senate may propose or concur with Amendments as on other bills.

Every Bill which shall have passed the House of Representatives and the Senate, shall, before it become a Law, be presented to the President of the United States; If he approve he shall sign it, but if not he shall return it, with his Objections, to that House in which it shall have originated, who shall enter the Objections at large on their Journal, and proceed to reconsider it. If after such Reconsideration two thirds of that House shall agree to pass the bill, it shall be sent, together with the objections, to the other House, by which it shall likewise be reconsidered, and if approved by two thirds of that House, it shall become a Law. But in all such Cases the Votes of both Houses shall be determined by Yeas and Nays, and the Names of the Persons voting for and against the Bill shall be entered on the Journal of each House respectively. If any Bill shall not be returned by the President within ten Days (Sundays excepted) after it shall have been presented to him, the Same shall be a Law, in like Manner as if he had signed it, unless the Congress by their Adjournment prevent its Return, in which Case it shall not be a Law.

Every Order, Resolution, or Vote to which the Concurrence of the Senate and House of Representatives may be necessary (except on a question of Adjournment) shall be presented to the President of the United States; and before the Same shall take Effect, shall be approved by him, or being disapproved by him, shall be repassed by two thirds of the Senate and House of Representatives, according to the Rules and Limitations prescribed in the Case of a Bill.

*Section* 8. The Congress shall have Power To lay and collect Taxes, Duties, Imposts and Excises, to pay the Debts and provide for the common Defence and general Welfare of the United States; but all Duties, Imposts and Excises shall be uniform throughout the United States;

To borrow money on the credit of the United States;

To regulate Commerce with foreign Nations, and among the several States, and with the Indian Tribes;

To establish an uniform Rule of Naturalization, and uniform Laws on the subject of Bankruptcies throughout the United States;

To coin Money, regulate the Value thereof, and of foreign Coin, and fix the Standard of Weights and Measures;

To provide for the Punishment of counterfeiting the Securities and current Coin of the United States;

To establish Post Offices and post Roads;

To promote the Progress of Science and useful Arts, by securing for limited Times to Authors and Inventors the exclusive Right to their respective Writings and Discoveries;

To constitute Tribunals inferior to the Supreme Court;

To define and punish Piracies and Felonies committed on the high Seas, and Offences against the Law of Nations;

To declare War, grant Letters of Marque and Reprisal, and make Rules concerning Captures on Land and Water;

To raise and support Armies, but no Appropriation of Money to that Use shall be for a longer Term than two Years;

To provide and maintain a Navy;

To make Rules for the Government and Regulation of the land and naval forces;

To provide for calling forth the Militia to execute the Laws of the Union, suppress Insurrections and repel Invasions;

To provide for organizing, arming, and disciplining the Militia, and for governing such Part of them as may be employed in the Service of the United States, reserving to the States respectively, the Appointment of the Officers, and the Authority of training the Militia according to the discipline prescribed by Congress;

To exercise exclusive Legislation in all Cases whatsoever, over such District (not exceeding ten Miles square) as may, by Cession of particular States, and the acceptance of Congress, become the seat of Government of the United States, and to exercise like Authority over all Places purchased by the Consent of the Legislature of the State in which the Same shall be, for the Erection of Forts, Magazines, Arsenals, dock-Yards, and other needful Buildings;—And

To make all Laws which shall be necessary and proper for carrying into Execution the foregoing Powers, and all other Powers vested by this Constitution in the Government of the United States, or in any Department or Officer thereof.

*Section* 9. The Migration or Importation of such Persons as any of the States now existing shall think proper to admit, shall not be prohibited by the Congress prior to the Year one thousand eight hundred and eight, but a tax or duty may be imposed on such Importation, not exceeding ten dollars for each Person.

The privilege of the Writ of Habeas Corpus shall not be suspended, unless when in Cases of Rebellion or Invasion the public Safety may require it.

No Bill of Attainder or ex post facto Law shall be passed.

No capitation, or other direct, Tax shall be laid unless in Proportion to the Census or Enumeration herein before directed to be taken.

No Tax or Duty shall be laid on Articles exported from any State.

No Preference shall be given by any Regulation of Revenue to the Ports of one State over those of another: nor shall Vessels bound to, or from, one State, be obliged to enter, clear, or pay Duties in another.

No Money shall be drawn from the Treasury, but in Consequence of Appropriations made by Law; and a regular Statement and Account of the Receipts and Expenditures of all public Money shall be published from time to time.

No Title of Nobility shall be granted by the United States: And no Person holding any Office of Profit or Trust under them, shall, without the Consent of the Congress, accept of any present, Emolument, Office, or Title, of any kind whatever, from any King, Prince, or foreign State.

*Section* 10. No State shall enter into any Treaty, Alliance, or Confederation; grant Letters of Marque and Reprisal; coin Money; emit Bills of Credit; make any Thing but gold and silver Coin a Tender in payment of Debts; pass any Bill of Attainder, ex post facto Law, or Law impairing the Obligation of Contracts, or grant any Title of Nobility.

No State shall, without the Consent of the Congress, lay any Imposts or Duties on Imports or Exports, except what may be absolutely necessary for executing its inspection Laws: and the net Produce of all Duties and Imposts, laid by any State on imports or Exports, shall be for the Use of the Treasury of the United States; and all such Laws shall be subject to the Revision and Control of the Congress.

No State shall, without the Consent of Congress, lay any duty of Tonnage, keep Troops, or Ships of War in time of Peace, enter into any Agreement or Compact with another State, or with a foreign Power, or engage in War, unless actually invaded, or in such imminent Danger as will not admit of delay.

*Article II*

*Section* 1. The executive Power shall be vested in a President of the United States of America. He shall hold his Office during the Term of four years, and, together with the Vice President, chosen for the same Term, be elected, as follows:

Each State shall appoint, in such Manner as the Legislature thereof may direct, a Number of Electors, equal to the whole Number of Senators and Representatives to which the State may be entitled in the Congress; but no Senator or Representative, or Person holding an Office of Trust or Profit under the United States, shall be appointed an Elector.

The Electors shall meet in their respective States, and vote by Ballot for two persons, of whom one at least shall not be an Inhabitant of the same State with themselves. And they shall make a List of all the Persons voted for, and of the Number of Votes for each; which List they shall sign and certify, and transmit sealed to the Seat of the government of the United States, directed to the President of the Senate. The President of the Senate shall, in the Presence of the Senate and House of Representatives, open all the Certificates, and the Votes shall then be counted. The Person having the greatest Number of Votes shall be the President, if such Number be a Majority of the whole Number of Electors appointed; and if there be more than one who have such Majority, and have an equal Number of Votes, then the House of Representatives shall immediately chuse by Ballot one of them for President; and if no Person have a Majority, then from the five highest on the List the said House shall in like Manner chuse the President. But in chusing the President, the Votes shall be taken by States, the Representation from each State having one Vote; a quorum for this Purpose shall consist of a Member or Members from two-thirds of the States, and a Majority of all the States shall be necessary to a Choice. In every Case, after the Choice of the President, the Person having the greatest Number of Votes of the Electors shall be the Vice President. But if there should remain two or more who have equal votes, the Senate shall chuse from them by Ballot the Vice President.

The Congress may determine the Time of chusing the Electors, and the Day on which they shall give their Votes; which Day shall be the same throughout the United States.

No person except a natural-born Citizen, or a Citizen of the United States, at the time of the Adoption of this Constitution, shall be eligible to the Office of President; neither shall any Person be eligible to that Office who shall not have attained to the Age of thirty-five years, and been fourteen Years a Resident within the United States.

In Case of the Removal of the President from Office, or of his Death, Resignation, or Inability to discharge the Powers and Duties of the said Office, the same shall devolve on the Vice President, and the Congress may by Law provide for the Case of Removal, Death, Resignation, or Inability, both of the President and Vice President, and what Officer shall than act as President, and such Officer shall act accordingly, until the disability be removed, or a President shall be elected.

The President shall, at stated Times, receive for his Services a Compensation, which shall neither be increased nor diminished during the Period for which he shall have been elected, and he shall not receive within that Period any other Emolument from the United States, or any of them.

Before he enter on the execution of his Office, he shall take the following Oath or Affirmation:—"I do solemnly swear (or affirm) that I will faithfully execute the Office of President of the United States, and will, to the best of my Ability, preserve, protect, and defend the Constitution of the United States."

*Section* 2. The President shall be Commander in Chief of the Army and Navy of the United States, and of the Militia of the several States, when called into the actual Service of the United States; he may require the Opinion, in writing, of the principal Officer in each of the executive Departments, upon any subject relating to the Duties of their respective Offices, and he shall have Power to Grant Reprieves and Pardons for Offences against the United States, except in Cases of Impeachment.

He shall have Power, by and with the Advice and Consent of the Senate, to make Treaties, provided two thirds of the Senators present concur; and he shall nominate, and by and with the Advice and Consent of the Senate, shall appoint Ambassadors, other public Ministers and Consuls, Judges of the supreme Court, and all other Officers of the United States, whose Appointments are not herein otherwise provided for, and which shall be established by Law: but the Congress may by Law vest the Appointment of such inferior Officers, as they think proper, in the President alone, in the Courts of Law, or in the Heads of Departments.

The President shall have Power to fill up all Vacancies that may happen during the Recess of the Senate, by granting Commissions which shall expire at the End of their next Session.

*Section* 3. He shall from time to time give to the Congress Information of the State of the Union, and recommend to their Consideration such Measures as he shall judge necessary and expedient; he may, on extraordinary occasions, convene both Houses, or either of them, and in Case of Disagreement between them, with respect to the Time of Adjournment, he may adjourn them to such Time as he shall think proper; he shall receive Ambassadors and other public Ministers; he shall take Care that the Laws be faithfully executed, and shall Commission all the Officers of the United States.

*Section* 4. The President, Vice President and all civil Officers of the United States, shall be removed from Office on Impeachment for, and Conviction of, Treason, Bribery, or other high Crimes and Misdemeanors.

## *Article III*

*Section* 1. The judicial Power of the United States, shall be vested in one supreme Court, and in such inferior Courts as the Congress may from time to time ordain and establish. The Judges, both of the supreme and inferior Courts, shall hold their Offices during good Behaviour, and shall, at stated Times, receive for their Services, a Compensation, which shall not be diminished during their Continuance in Office.

*Section* 2. The judicial Power shall extend to all Cases, in Law and Equity, arising under this Constitution, the Laws of the United States, and treaties made, or which shall be made, under their Authority;—to all Cases affecting ambassadors, other public ministers and consuls;—to all cases of admiralty and maritime Jurisdiction;—to Controversies to which the United States shall be a Party;—to Controversies between two or more States;—between a State and Citizens of another State;—between Citizens of different States,—between Citizens of the same State claiming Lands under Grants of different States, and between a State, or the Citizens thereof, and foreign States, Citizens or Subjects.

In all Cases affecting Ambassadors, other public Ministers and Consuls, and those in which a State shall be Party, the supreme Court shall have original Jurisdiction. In all the other Cases before mentioned, the supreme Court shall have appellate Jurisdiction, both as to Law and Fact, with such Exceptions, and under such Regulations as the Congress shall make.

The trial of all Crimes, except in Cases of Impeachment, shall be by Jury; and such Trial shall be held in the State where the said Crimes shall have been committed; but when not committed within any State, the Trial shall be at such Place or Places as the Congress may by Law have directed.

*Section* 3. Treason against the United States, shall consist only in levying War against them, or in adhering to their Enemies, giving them Aid and Comfort. No Person shall be convicted of Treason unless on the Testimony of two Witnesses to the same overt Act, or on Confession in open Court.

The Congress shall have power to declare the Punishment of Treason, but no Attainder of Treason shall work Corruption of Blood, or Forfeiture except during the Life of the Person attainted.

*Article IV*

*Section* 1. Full Faith and Credit shall be given in each State to the public Acts, Records, and judicial Proceedings of every other State. And the Congress may by general Laws prescribe the Manner in which such Acts, Records and Proceedings shall be proved, and the Effect thereof.

*Section* 2. The Citizens of each State shall be entitled to all Privileges and Immunities of Citizens in the several States.

A Person charged in any State with Treason, Felony, or other Crime, who shall flee from Justice, and be found in another State, shall on demand of the executive Authority of the State from which he fled, be delivered up, to be removed to the State having Jurisdiction of the crime.

No Person held to Service or Labour in one State, under the Laws therof, escaping into another, shall, in Consequence of any Law or Regulation therein, be discharged from such Service or Labour, but shall be delivered up on Claim of the Party to whom such Service or Labour may be due.

*Section* 3. New States may be admitted by the Congress into this Union; but no new State shall be formed or erected within the Jurisdiction of any other State; nor any State be formed by the Junction of two or more States, or parts of States, without the Consent of the Legislatures of the States concerned as well as of the Congress.

The Congress shall have Power to dispose of and make all needful Rules and Regulations respecting the Territory or other Property belonging to the United States; and nothing in this Constitution shall be so construed as to Prejudice any Claims of the United States, or of any particular State.

*Section* 4. The United States shall guarantee to every State in this Union a Republican Form of Government, and shall protect each of them against Invasion; and on Application of the Legislature, or the Executive (when the Legislature cannot be convened) against domestic Violence.

*Article V*

The Congress, whenever two-thirds of both Houses shall deem it necessary, shall propose Amendments to this Constitution, or, on the Application of the Legislatures of two-thirds of the several States, shall call a Convention for proposing Amendments, which, in either Case, shall be valid to all Intents and Purposes, as part of this Constitution, when ratified by the Legislatures of three-fourths of the several States, or by Conventions in three-fourths thereof, as the one or the other Mode of Ratification may be proposed by the Congress; Provided that no Amendment which may be made prior to the Year One thousand eight hundred and eight shall in any Manner affect the first and fourth Clauses in the Ninth Section of the first Article; and that no State, without its Consent, shall be deprived of its equal Suffrage in the Senate.

*Article VI*

All Debts contracted and Engagements entered into, before the Adoption of this Constitution, shall be as valid against the United States under this Constitution, as under the Confederation.

This Constitution, and the Laws of the United States which shall be made in pursuance thereof; and all Treaties made, or which shall be made, under the Authority of the United States, shall be the supreme Law of the Land; and the Judges in every State shall be bound thereby, any Thing in the Constitution or Laws of any State to the Contrary notwithstanding.

The Senators and Representatives before mentioned, and the Members of the several State Legislatures, and all executive and judicial Officers, both of the United States and of the several States, shall be bound by Oath or Affirmation to support this Constitution; but no religious Test shall ever be required as a qualification to any Office or public Trust under the United States.

*Article VII*

The Ratification of the Conventions of nine States shall be sufficient for the Establishment of this Constitution between the States so ratifying the same.

Done in Convention by the Unanimous Consent of the States present the Seventeenth Day of September of the Year of our Lord one thousand seven hundred and Eighty seven, and of the

Independence of the United States of America the Twelfth. In Witness whereof We have hereunto subscribed our Names. *Articles in Addition to, and Amendment of, the Constitution of the United States of America, Proposed by Congress, and Ratified by the Legislatures of the Several States, Pursuant to the Fifth Article of the Original Constitution.*

*Amendment I* [1791]

Congress shall made no law respecting an establishment of religion, or prohibiting the free exercise thereof; or abridging the freedom of speech, or of the press; or the right of the people peaceably to assemble, and to petition the Government for a redress of grievances.

*Amendment II* [1791]

A well regulated Militia, being necessary to the security of a free State, the right of the people to keep and bear Arms shall not be infringed.

*Amendment III* [1791]

No Soldier shall, in time of peace, be quartered in any house, without the consent of the Owner, nor in time of war, but in a manner to be prescribed by law.

*Amendment IV* [1791]

The right of the people to be secure in their persons, houses, papers, and effects, against unreasonable searches and seizures, shall not be violated, and no Warrants shall issue, but upon probable cause, supported by Oath or affirmation, and particularly describing the place to be searched, and the persons or things to be seized.

*Amendment V* [1791]

No person shall be held to answer for a capital or otherwise infamous crime, unless on a presentment or indictment of a Grand Jury, except in cases arising in the land or naval forces, or in the Militia, when in actual service in time of War or public danger; nor shall any person be subject for the same offence to be twice put in jeopardy of life or limb; nor shall be compelled in any criminal case to be a witness against himself, nor be deprived of life, liberty, or property, without due process of law; nor shall private property be taken for public use, without just compensation.

*Amendment VI* [1791]

In all criminal prosecutions, the accused shall enjoy the right to a speedy and public trial, by an impartial jury of the State and district wherein the crime shall have been committed, which district shall have been previously ascertained by law, and to be informed of the nature and cause of the accusation; to be confronted with the witnesses against him; to have compulsory process for obtaining witnesses in his favor, and to have the Assistance of Counsel for his defence.

*Amendment VII* [1791]

In suits at common law, where the value in controversy shall exceed twenty dollars, the right of trial by jury shall be preserved, and no fact tried by a jury, shall be otherwise reexamined in any Court of the United States, than according to the rules of the common law.

*Amendment VIII* [1791]

Excessive bail shall not be required, nor excessive fines imposed, nor cruel and unusual punishments inflicted.

*Amendment IX* [1791]

The enumeration in the Constitution, of certain rights, shall not be construed to deny or disparage others retained by the people.

*Amendment X* [1791]

The powers not delegated to the United States by the Constitution, nor prohibited by it to the States, are reserved to the States respectively, or to the people

*Amendment XI* [1798]

The Judicial power of the United States shall not be construed to extend to any suit in law or equity, commenced or prosecuted against one of the United States by Citizens of another State, or by Citizens or Subjects of any Foreign State.

*Amendment XII* [1804]

The Electors shall meet in their respective States and vote by ballot for President and Vice President, one of whom, at least, shall not be an inhabitant of the same State with themselves; they shall name in their ballots the person voted for as President, and in distinct ballots the person voted for as Vice President, and they shall make distinct lists of all persons voted for as President, and of the number of votes for each, which lists they shall sign and certify, and transmit sealed to the seat of the government of the United States, directed to the President of the Senate;—The President of the Senate shall, in the presence of the Senate and House of Representatives, open all the certificates and the votes shall then be counted;—The person having the greatest number of votes for President, shall be the President, if such number be a majority of the whole number of Electors appointed; and if no person have such majority, then from the persons having the highest numbers not exceeding three on the list of those voted for as President, the House of Representatives shall choose immediately, by ballot, the President. But in choosing the President, the votes shall be taken by states, there presentation from each state having one vote; a quorum for this purpose shall consist of a member or members from two-thirds of the states, and a majority of all the states shall be necessary to a choice. And if the House of Representatives shall not choose a President whenever the right of choice shall devolve upon them, before the fourth day of March next following, then the Vice President shall act as President, as in the case of the death or other constitutional disability of the President.—The person having the greatest number of votes as Vice President, shall be the Vice President, if such number be a majority of the whole number of Electors appointed, and if no person have a majority, then from the two highest numbers on the list, the Senate shall choose the Vice President; a quorum for the purpose shall consist of two-thirds of the whole number of Senators, and a majority of the whole number shall be necessary to a choice. But no person constitutionally ineligible to the office of President shall be eligible to that of Vice President of the United States.

### *Amendment XIII* [1865]

*Section* 1. Neither slavery nor involuntary servitude, except as a punishment for crime whereof the party shall have been duly convicted, shall exist within the United States, or any place subject to their jurisdiction.

*Section* 2. Congress shall have power to enforce this article by appropriate legislation.

### *Amendment XIV* [1868]

*Section* 1. All persons born or naturalized in the United States, and subject to the jurisdiction thereof, are citizens of the United States and of the State wherein they reside. No State shall make or enforce any law which shall abridge the privileges or immunities of citizens of the United States; nor shall any State deprive any person of life, liberty, or property, without due process of law; nor deny to any person within its jurisdiction the equal protection of the laws.

*Section* 2. Representatives shall be apportioned among the several States according to their respective numbers, counting the whole number of persons in each State, excluding Indians not taxed. But when the right to vote at any election for the choice of electors for President and Vice President of the United States, Representatives in Congress, the Executive and Judicial officers of a State, or the members of the Legislature thereof, is denied to any of the male inhabitants of such State, being twenty-one years of age, and citizens of the United States, or in any way abridged, except for participation in rebellion, or other crime, the basis of representation therein shall be reduced in the proportion which the number of such male citizens shall bear to the whole number of male citizens twenty-one years of age in such State.

*Section* 3. No person shall be a Senator or Representative in Congress, or elector of President and Vice President, or hold any office, civil or military, under the United States, or under any State, who, having previously taken an oath, as a member of Congress, or as an officer of the United States, or as a member of any State legislature, or as an executive or judicial officer of any State, to support the Constitution of the United States, shall have engaged in insurrection or rebellion against the same, or given aid or comfort to the enemies thereof. But Congress may by a vote of two-thirds of each House, remove such disability.

*Section* 4. The validity of the public debt of the United States, authorized by law, including debts incurred for payment of pensions and bounties for services in suppressing insurrection or rebellion, shall not be questioned. But neither the United States nor any State shall assume or pay any debt or obligation incurred in aid of insurrection or rebellion against the United States, or any claim for the loss or emancipation of any slave; but all such debts, obligations, and claims shall be held illegal and void.

*Section* 5. The Congress shall have the power to enforce, by appropriate legislation, the provisions of this article.

*Amendment XV* [1870]

*Section* 1. The right of citizens of the United States to vote shall not be denied or abridged by the United States or by any State on account of race, color, or previous condition of servitude—

*Section* 2. The Congress shall have power to enforce this article by appropriate legislation.

*Amendment XVI* [1913]

The Congress shall have power to lay and collect taxes on incomes, from whatever source derived, without apportionment among the several States, and without regard to any census or enumeration.

*Amendment XVII* [1913]

The Senate of the United States shall be composed of two Senators from each State, elected by the people thereof, for six years, and each Senator shall have one vote. The electors in each State shall have the qualifications requisite for electors of the most numerous branch of the State legislatures.

When vacancies happen in the representation of any State in the Senate, the executive authority of such State shall issue writs of election to fill such vacancies: *Provided*, That the legislature of any State may empower the executive thereof to make temporary appointments until the people fill the vacancies by election as the legislature may direct.

This amendment shall not be so construed as to affect the election or term of any Senator chosen before it becomes valid as part of the Constitution.

*Amendment XVIII* [1919]

*Section* 1. After one year from the ratification of this article the manufacture, sale, or transportation of intoxicating liquors within, the importation thereof into, or the exportation thereof from the United States and all territory subject to the jurisdiction thereof for beverage purposes is hereby prohibited.

*Section* 2. The Congress and the several States shall have concurrent power to enforce this article by appropriate legislation.

*Section* 3. This article shall be inoperative unless it shall have been ratified as an amendment to the Constitution by the legislatures of the several States, as provided in the Constitution, within seven years from the date of the submission hereof to the States by the Congress.

*Amendment XIX* [1920]

The right of citizens of the United States to vote shall not be denied or abridged by the United States or by any State on account of sex.

Congress shall have power to enforce this article by appropriate legislation.

*Amendment XX* [1933]

*Section* 1. The terms of the President and Vice President shall end at noon on the 20th day of January, and the terms of Senators and Representatives at noon on the 3d day of January, of the years in which such terms would have ended if this article had not been ratified; and the terms of their successors shall then begin.

*Section* 2. The Congress shall assemble at least once in every year, and such meeting shall begin at noon on the 3d day of January, unless they shall by law appoint a different day.

*Section* 3. If, at the time fixed for the beginning of the term of the President, the President elect shall have died, the Vice President elect shall become President. If a President shall not have been chosen before the time fixed for the beginning of his term, or if the President elect shall have failed to qualify, the Vice-President elect shall act as President until a President shall have qualified; and the Congress may by law provide for the case wherein neither a President elect nor a Vice President elect shall have qualified, declaring who shall then act as President, or the manner in which one who is to act shall be selected, and such person shall act accordingly until a President or Vice President shall have qualified.

*Section* 4. The Congress may by law provide for the case of the death of any of the persons from whom the House of Representatives may choose a President whenever the right of choice shall have devolved upon them, and for the case of the death of any of the persons from whom the Senate may choose a Vice President whenever the right of choice shall have devolved upon them.

*Section* 5. Sections 1 and 2 shall take effect on the 15th day of October following the ratification of this article.

*Section* 6. This article shall be inoperative unless it shall have been ratified as an amendment to the Constitution by the legislatures of three-fourths of the several States within seven years from the date of its submission.

*Amendment XXI* [1933]

*Section* 1. The eighteenth article of amendment to the Constitution of the United States is hereby repealed.

*Section* 2. The transportation or importation into any State, Territory, or possession of the United States for delivery or use therein of intoxicating liquors, in violation of the laws thereof, is hereby prohibited.

*Section* 3. This article shall be inoperative unless it shall have been ratified as an amendment to the Constitution by conventions in the several States, as provided in the Constitution, within seven years from the date of the submission hereof to the States by the Congress.

*Amendment XXII* [1951]

No person shall be elected to the office of the President more than twice, and no person who has held the office of President, or acted as President, for more than two years of a term to which some other person was elected President shall be elected to the office of the President more than once.

But this Article shall not apply to any person holding the office of President when this Article was proposed by the Congress, and shall not prevent any person who may be holding the office of President, or acting as President, during the term within which this Article becomes operative from holding the office of President or acting as President during the remainder of such term.

*Amendment XXIII* [1961]

*Section* 1. The District constituting the seat of Government of the United States shall appoint in such manner as the Congress may direct:

A number of electors of President and Vice President equal to the whole number of Senators and Representatives in Congress to which the District would be entitled if it were a State, but in no event more than the least populous State; they shall be in addition to those appointed by the States, but they shall be considered, for the purposes of the election of President and Vice President, to be electors appointed by a State; and they shall meet in the District and perform such duties as provided by the twelfth article of amendment.

*Section* 2. The Congress shall have power to enforce this article by appropriate legislation.

*Amendment XXIV* [1964]

*Section* 1. The right of citizens of the United States to vote in any primary or other election for President or Vice President, for electors for President or Vice President, or for Senator or Representative in Congress, shall not be denied or abridged by the United States or any State by reason of failure to pay any poll tax or other tax.

*Section* 2. The Congress shall have the power to enforce this article by appropriate legislation.

*Amendment XXV* [1967]

*Section* 1. In case of the removal of the President from office or his death or resignation, the Vice President shall become President.

*Section* 2. Whenever there is a vacancy in the office of the Vice President, the President shall nominate a Vice President who shall take the office upon confirmation by a majority vote of both houses of Congress.

*Section* 3. Whenever the President transmits to the President pro tempore of the Senate and the Speaker of the House of Representatives his written declaration that he is unable to discharge the powers and duties of his office, and until he transmits to them a written declaration to the contrary, such powers and duties shall be discharged by the Vice President as Acting President.

*Section* 4. Whenever the Vice President and a majority of either the principal officers of the executive departments, or of such other body as Congress may by law provide, transmit to the President pro tempore of the Senate and the Speaker of the House of Representatives their written declaration that the President is unable to discharge the powers and duties of his office, the Vice President shall immediately assume the powers and duties of the office as Acting President.

Thereafter, when the President transmits to the President pro tempore of the Senate and the Speaker of the House of Representatives his written declaration that no inability exists, he shall resume the powers and duties of his office unless the Vice President and a majority of either the principal officers of the executive departments, or of such other body as Congress may by law provide, transmit within four days to the President pro tempore of the Senate and the Speaker of the House of Representatives their written declaration that the President is unable to discharge the powers and duties of his office. Thereupon Congress shall decide the issue, assembling within 48 hours for that purpose if not in session. If the Congress, within 21 days after receipt of the latter written declaration, or, if Congress is not in session, within 21 days after Congress is required to assemble, determines by two-thirds vote of both houses that the President is unable to discharge the powers and duties of his office, the Vice President shall continue to discharge the same as Acting President; otherwise, the President shall resume the powers and duties of his office.

*Amendment XXVI* [1971]

*Section* 1. The right of citizens of the United States who are eighteen years of age or older to vote shall not be denied or abridged by the United States or by any State on account of age.

*Section* 2. The Congress shall have power to enforce this article by appropriate legislation.

# *Population*, 1790–1970

| Year | Population | Year | Population | Year | Population |
|---|---|---|---|---|---|
| 1790 | 3,929,214 | 1860 | 31,443,321 | 1930 | 122,775,046 |
| 1800 | 5,308,483 | 1870 | 39,818,449 | 1940 | 131,669,275 |
| 1810 | 7,239,881 | 1880 | 50,155,783 | 1950 | 151,325,798 |
| 1820 | 9,638,453 | 1890 | 62,947,714 | 1960 | 179,323,175 |
| 1830 | 12,866,020 | 1900 | 75,994,575 | 1970 | 204,765,770 |
| 1840 | 17,069,453 | 1910 | 91,972,266 | | |
| 1850 | 23,191,876 | 1920 | 105,710,620 | | |

# *Presidential Elections*, 1789–1972

| *Year* | *Candidates* | *Party* | *Popular Vote (% of total)* | *Electoral Vote* |
|---|---|---|---|---|
| 1789 | GEORGE WASHINGTON | | | 69 |
| | John Adams | | | 34 |
| | Others | | | 35 |
| 1792 | GEORGE WASHINGTON | | | 132 |
| | John Adams | | | 77 |
| | George Clinton | | | 50 |
| | Others | | | 5 |
| 1796 | JOHN ADAMS | Federalist | | 71 |
| | Thomas Jefferson | Democratic-Republican | | 68 |
| | Thomas Pinckney | Federalist | | 59 |
| | Aaron Burr | Democratic-Republican | | 30 |
| | Others | | | 48 |
| 1800 | THOMAS JEFFERSON | Democratic-Republican | | 73 |
| | Aaron Burr | Democratic-Republican | | 73 |
| | John Adams | Federalist | | 65 |
| | Charles C. Pinckney | Federalist | | 64 |
| 1804 | THOMAS JEFFERSON | Democratic-Republican | | 162 |
| | Charles C. Pinckney | Federalist | | 14 |
| 1808 | JAMES MADISON | Democratic-Republican | | 122 |
| | Charles C. Pinckney | Federalist | | 47 |
| | George Clinton | Independent-Republican | | 6 |
| 1812 | JAMES MADISON | Democratic-Republican | | 128 |
| | DeWitt Clinton | Federalist | | 89 |
| 1816 | JAMES MONROE | Democratic-Republican | | 183 |
| | Rufus King | Federalist | | 34 |
| 1820 | JAMES MONROE | Democratic-Republican | | 231 |
| | John Quincy Adams | Independent-Republican | | 1 |
| 1824 | JOHN QUINCY ADAMS | Democratic-Republican | 108,740 (30.5%) | 84 |
| | Andrew Jackson | Democratic-Republican | 153,554 (43.1%) | 99 |
| | Henry Clay | Democratic-Republican | 47,136 (13.2%) | 37 |
| | William H. Crawford | Democratic-Republican | 46,618 (13.1%) | 41 |
| 1828 | ANDREW JACKSON | Democratic | 647,231 (56.0%) | 178 |
| | John Quincy Adams | National Republican | 509,097 (44.0%) | 83 |
| 1832 | ANDREW JACKSON | Democratic | 687,502 (55.0%) | 219 |
| | Henry Clay | National Republican | 530,189 (42.4%) | 49 |
| | William Wirt | Anti-Masonic | 33,108 (2.6%) | 7 |
| | John Floyd | National Republican | | 11 |
| 1836 | MARTIN VAN BUREN | Democratic | 761,549 (50.9%) | 170 |
| | William H. Harrison | Whig | 549,567 (36.7%) | 73 |
| | Hugh L. White | Whig | 145,396 (9.7%) | 26 |
| | Daniel Webster | Whig | 41,287 (2.7%) | 14 |

Because only the leading candidates are listed, popular vote percentages do not always total 100. The elections of 1800 and 1824, in which no candidate received an electoral-vote majority, were decided in the House of Representatives.

| Year | Candidates | Party | Popular Vote (% of total) | Electoral Vote |
|---|---|---|---|---|
| 1840 | WILLIAM H. HARRISON (JOHN TYLER, 1841) | Whig | 1,275,017 (53.1%) | 234 |
| | Martin Van Buren | Democratic | 1,128,702 (46.9%) | 60 |
| 1844 | JAMES K. POLK | Democratic | 1,337,243 (49.6%) | 170 |
| | Henry Clay | Whig | 1,299,068 (48.1%) | 105 |
| | James G. Birney | Liberty | 62,300 (2.3%) | |
| 1848 | ZACHARY TAYLOR (MILLARD FILLMORE, 1850) | Whig | 1,360,101 (47.4%) | 163 |
| | Lewis Cass | Democratic | 1,220,544 (42.5%) | 127 |
| | Martin Van Buren | Free Soil | 291,263 (10.1%) | |
| 1852 | FRANKLIN PIERCE | Democratic | 1,601,474 (50.9%) | 254 |
| | Winfield Scott | Whig | 1,386,578 (44.1%) | 42 |
| 1856 | JAMES BUCHANAN | Democratic | 1,838,169 (45.4%) | 174 |
| | John C. Frémont | Republican | 1,335,264 (33.0%) | 114 |
| | Millard Fillmore | American | 874,534 (21.6%) | 8 |
| 1860 | ABRAHAM LINCOLN | Republican | 1,865,593 (39.8%) | 180 |
| | Stephen A. Douglas | Democratic | 1,382,713 (29.5%) | 12 |
| | John C. Breckinridge | Democratic | 848,356 (18.1%) | 72 |
| | John Bell | Constitutional Union | 592,906 (12.6%) | 39 |
| 1864 | ABRAHAM LINCOLN (ANDREW JOHNSON, 1865) | Republican | 2,206,938 (55.0%) | 212 |
| | George B. McClellan | Democratic | 1,803,787 (45.0%) | 21 |
| 1868 | ULYSSES S. GRANT | Republican | 3,013,421 (52.7%) | 214 |
| | Horatio Seymour | Democratic | 2,706,829 (47.3%) | 80 |
| 1872 | ULYSSES S. GRANT | Republican | 3,596,745 (55.6%) | 286 |
| | Horace Greeley | Democratic | 2,843,446 (43.9%) | 66 |
| 1876 | RUTHERFORD B. HAYES | Republican | 4,036,572 (48.0%) | 185 |
| | Samuel J. Tilden | Democratic | 4,284,020 (51.0%) | 184 |
| 1880 | JAMES A. GARFIELD (CHESTER A. ARTHUR, 1881) | Republican | 4,449,053 (48.3%) | 214 |
| | Winfield S. Hancock | Democratic | 4,442,035 (48.2%) | 155 |
| | James B. Weaver | Greenback-Labor | 308,578 (3.4%) | |
| 1884 | GROVER CLEVELAND | Democratic | 4,874,986 (48.5%) | 219 |
| | James G. Blaine | Republican | 4,851,981 (48.2%) | 182 |
| | Benjamin F. Butler | Greenback-Labor | 175,370 (1.8%) | |
| 1888 | BENJAMIN HARRISON | Republican | 5,444,337 (47.8%) | 233 |
| | Grover Cleveland | Democratic | 5,540,050 (48.6%) | 168 |
| 1892 | GROVER CLEVELAND | Democratic | 5,554,414 (46.0%) | 277 |
| | Benjamin Harrison | Republican | 5,190,802 (43.0%) | 145 |
| | James B. Weaver | People's | 1,027,329 (8.5%) | 22 |
| 1896 | WILLIAM MCKINLEY | Republican | 7,035,638 (50.8%) | 271 |
| | William J. Bryan | Democratic; Populist | 6,467,946 (46.7%) | 176 |
| 1900 | WILLIAM MCKINLEY (THEODORE ROOSEVELT, 1901) | Republican | 7,219,530 (51.7%) | 292 |
| | William J. Bryan | Democratic; Populist | 6,356,734 (45.5%) | 155 |
| 1904 | THEODORE ROOSEVELT | Republican | 7,628,834 (56.4%) | 336 |
| | Alton B. Parker | Democratic | 5,084,401 (37.6%) | 140 |
| | Eugene V. Debs | Socialist | 402,460 (3.0%) | |
| 1908 | WILLIAM H. TAFT | Republican | 7,679,006 (51.6%) | 321 |
| | William J. Bryan | Democratic | 6,409,106 (43.1%) | 162 |
| | Eugene V. Debs | Socialist | 420,820 (2.8%) | |

| Year | Candidates | Party | Popular Vote (% of total) | Electoral Vote |
|---|---|---|---|---|
| 1912 | WOODROW WILSON | Democratic | 6,286,820 (41.8%) | 435 |
| | Theodore Roosevelt | Progressive | 4,126,020 (27.4%) | 88 |
| | William H. Taft | Republican | 3,483,922 (23.2%) | 8 |
| | Eugene V. Debs | Socialist | 897,011 (6.0%) | |
| 1916 | WOODROW WILSON | Democratic | 9,129,606 (49.3%) | 277 |
| | Charles E. Hughes | Republican | 8,538,221 (46.1%) | 254 |
| 1920 | WARREN G. HARDING (CALVIN COOLIDGE, 1923) | Republican | 16,152,200 (61.0%) | 404 |
| | James M. Cox | Democratic | 9,147,353 (34.6%) | 127 |
| | Eugene V. Debs | Socialist | 919,799 (3.5%) | |
| 1924 | CALVIN COOLIDGE | Republican | 15,725,016 (54.1%) | 382 |
| | John W. Davis | Democratic | 8,385,586 (28.8%) | 136 |
| | Robert M. La Follette | Progressive | 4,822,856 (16.6%) | 13 |
| 1928 | HERBERT C. HOOVER | Republican | 21,392,190 (58.2%) | 444 |
| | Alfred E. Smith | Democratic | 15,016,443 (40.8%) | 87 |
| 1932 | FRANKLIN D. ROOSEVELT | Democratic | 22,809,638 (57.3%) | 472 |
| | Herbert C. Hoover | Republican | 15,758,901 (39.6%) | 59 |
| | Norman Thomas | Socialist | 881,961 (2.2%) | |
| 1936 | FRANKLIN D. ROOSEVELT | Democratic | 27,751,612 (60.7%) | 523 |
| | Alfred M. Landon | Republican | 16,681,913 (36.4%) | 8 |
| | William Lemke | Union | 891,858 (1.9%) | |
| 1940 | FRANKLIN D. ROOSEVELT | Democratic | 27,243,466 (54.7%) | 449 |
| | Wendell L. Wilkie | Republican | 22,304,755 (44.8%) | 82 |
| 1944 | FRANKLIN D. ROOSEVELT (HARRY S TRUMAN, 1945) | Democratic | 25,602,505 (52.8%) | 432 |
| | Thomas E. Dewey | Republican | 22,006,278 (44.5%) | 99 |
| 1948 | HARRY S TRUMAN | Democratic | 24,105,812 (49.5%) | 303 |
| | Thomas E. Dewey | Republican | 21,970,065 (45.1%) | 189 |
| | J. Storm Thurmond | States' Rights | 1,169,063 (2.4%) | 39 |
| | Henry A. Wallace | Progressive | 1,157,172 (2.4%) | |
| 1952 | DWIGHT D. EISENHOWER | Republican | 33,936,234 (55.2%) | 442 |
| | Adlai E. Stevenson | Democratic | 27,314,992 (44.5%) | 89 |
| 1956 | DWIGHT D. EISENHOWER | Republican | 35,590,472 (57.4%) | 457 |
| | Adlai E. Stevenson | Democratic | 26,022,752 (42.0%) | 73 |
| 1960 | JOHN F. KENNEDY (LYNDON B. JOHNSON, 1963) | Democratic | 34,227,096 (49.9%) | 303 |
| | Richard M. Nixon | Republican | 34,108,546 (49.6%) | 219 |
| 1964 | LYNDON B. JOHNSON | Democratic | 43,126,233 (61.1%) | 486 |
| | Barry M. Goldwater | Republican | 27,174,989 (38.5%) | 52 |
| 1968 | RICHARD M. NIXON | Republican | 31,783,783 (43.4%) | 301 |
| | Hubert H. Humphrey | Democratic | 31,271,839 (42.7%) | 191 |
| | George C. Wallace | Amer. Independent | 9,899,557 (13.5%) | 46 |
| 1972 | RICHARD M. NIXON | Republican | 45,767,218 (60.6%) | 520 |
| | (GERALD R. FORD, 1974) | | Appointed on August 9, 1974 as President after the resignation of Richard M. Nixon. No election was held. | |
| | George S. McGovern | Democratic | 28,357,668 (37.5%) | 17 |

Seattle
Olympia
WASH.
Nov. 11,
1889
Portland
Salem
MONT.
Nov. 8, 1889
Helena
N. DAK.
Nov. 2, 1889
Bismarck
OREG.
Feb. 14, 1859
Boise
IDAHO
July 3, 1890
S. DAK.
Nov. 2, 1889
Pierre
WYO.
July 10, 1890
NEBR.
March 1, 1867
Cheyenne
NEV.
Oct. 31, 1864
Salt Lake City
Sacramento
Carson City
Lincoln
UTAH
Jan. 4, 1896
San Francisco
Denver
COLO.
Aug. 1, 1876
KANS.
Jan. 29, 1861
CALIF.
Sept. 9, 1850
ARIZ.
Feb. 14, 1912
Santa Fe
OKLA.
Nov. 16,
1907
Oklahoma
City
PACIFIC
OCEAN
Los Angeles
N. MEX.
Jan. 6, 1912
San Diego
Phoenix
TEX.
Dec. 29, 1845
Austin
ALASKA
Jan. 3, 1959
Honolulu
HAWAII
Aug. 21, 1959
Juneau
0 Miles 400
0 Miles 200

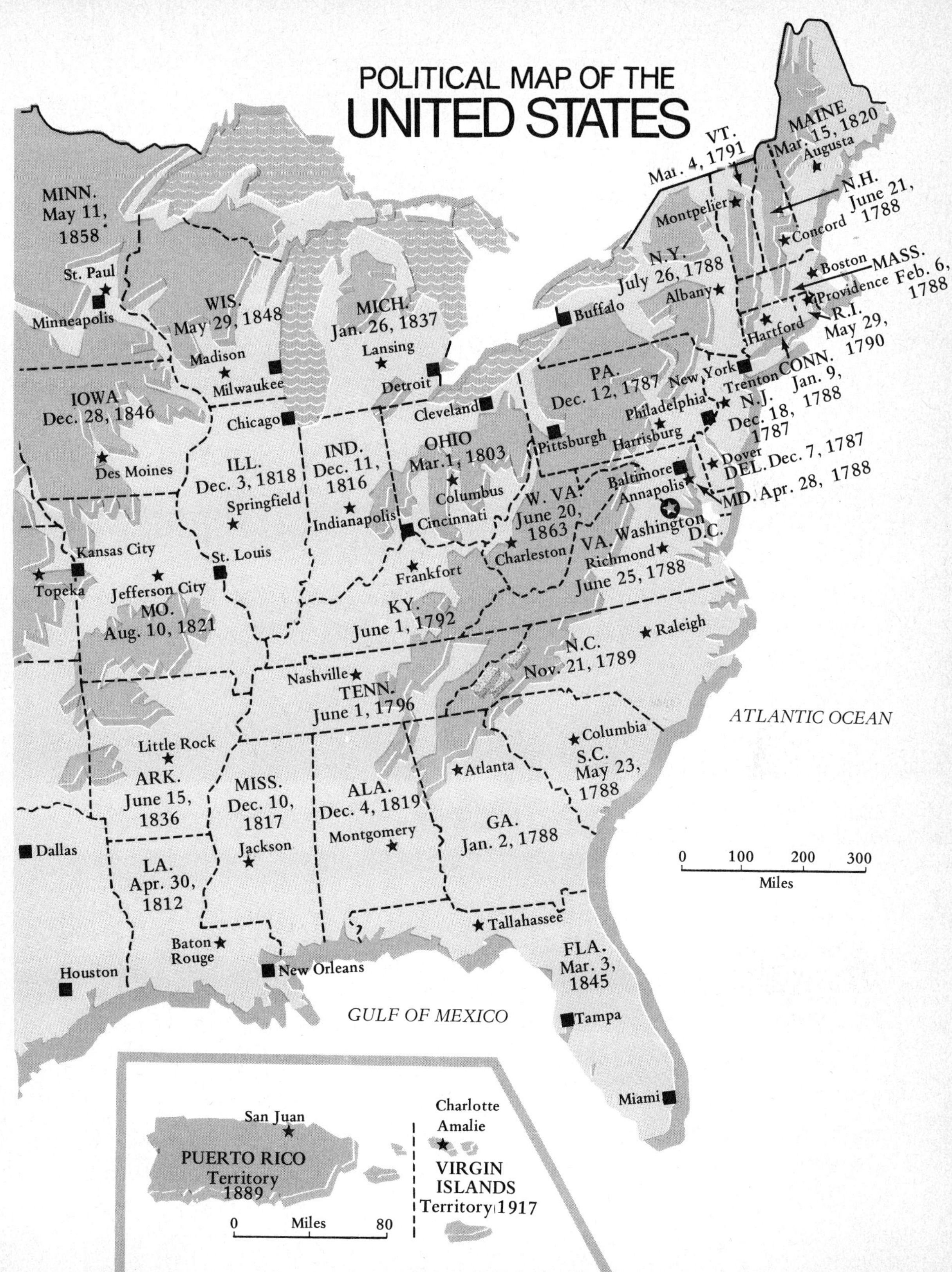
POLITICAL MAP OF THE
UNITED STATES
MAINE
Mar. 15, 1820
Augusta
VT.
Mar. 4, 1791
Montpelier
N.H.
June 21,
1788
Concord
N.Y.
July 26, 1788
Albany
Boston
MASS.
Feb. 6,
1788
Providence
R.I.
May 29,
1790
Hartford
CONN.
Jan. 9,
1788
MINN.
May 11,
1858
St. Paul
Minneapolis
WIS.
May 29, 1848
Madison
Milwaukee
MICH.
Jan. 26, 1837
Lansing
Detroit
Buffalo
New York
Trenton
N.J.
Dec. 18, 1788
1787
PA.
Dec. 12, 1787
Philadelphia
Harrisburg
Pittsburgh
Dover
DEL. Dec. 7, 1787
Baltimore
Annapolis
MD. Apr. 28, 1788
Washington
D.C.
IOWA
Dec. 28, 1846
Des Moines
Chicago
ILL.
Dec. 3, 1818
Springfield
IND.
Dec. 11,
1816
Indianapolis
Cleveland
OHIO
Mar. 1, 1803
Columbus
Cincinnati
W. VA.
June 20,
1863
Charleston
VA.
Richmond
June 25, 1788
Kansas City
Topeka
Jefferson City
St. Louis
MO.
Aug. 10, 1821
Frankfort
KY.
June 1, 1792
N.C.
Nov. 21, 1789
Raleigh
Nashville
TENN.
June 1, 1796
ATLANTIC OCEAN
Little Rock
ARK.
June 15,
1836
MISS.
Dec. 10,
1817
Jackson
ALA.
Dec. 4, 1819
Montgomery
Atlanta
GA.
Jan. 2, 1788
Columbia
S.C.
May 23,
1788
0 100 200 300
Miles
Dallas
LA.
Apr. 30,
1812
Baton Rouge
Tallahassee
FLA.
Mar. 3,
1845
Houston
New Orleans
GULF OF MEXICO
Tampa
Miami
San Juan
PUERTO RICO
Territory
1889
0 Miles 80
Charlotte
Amalie
VIRGIN
ISLANDS
Territory 1917

# *Index*

76 9 8 7 6 5 4 3 2 1